CLINICAL AND ORGANIZATIONAL APPLICATIONS OF APPLIED BEHAVIOR ANALYSIS

CLINICAL AND ORGANIZATIONAL APPLICATIONS OF APPLIED BEHAVIOR ANALYSIS

Edited by

HENRY S. ROANE

Upstate Medical University, Syracuse,
New York, USA

JOEL L. RINGDAHL

Rehabilitation Institute, Southern Illinois University,
Carbondale, Illinois, USA

TERRY S. FALCOMATA

Department of Special Education, The University of
Texas at Austin, Austin, Texas, USA

AMSTERDAM • BOSTON • HEIDELBERG • LONDON
NEW YORK • OXFORD • PARIS • SAN DIEGO
SAN FRANCISCO • SINGAPORE • SYDNEY • TOKYO
Academic Press is an imprint of Elsevier

Academic Press is an imprint of Elsevier
125 London Wall, London, EC2Y 5AS, UK
525 B Street, Suite 1800, San Diego, CA 92101-4495, USA
225 Wyman Street, Waltham, MA 02451, USA
The Boulevard, Langford Lane, Kidlington, Oxford OX5 1GB, UK

First published 2015

Notices
Knowledge and best practice in this field are constantly changing. As new research and
experience broaden our understanding, changes in research methods, professional
practices, or medical treatment may become necessary.

Practitioners and researchers must always rely on their own experience and knowledge
in evaluating and using any information, methods, compounds, or experiments described
herein. In using such information or methods they should be mindful of their own safety
and the safety of others, including parties for whom they have a professional responsibility.

To the fullest extent of the law, neither the Publisher nor the authors, contributors,
or editors, assume any liability for any injury and/or damage to persons or property as
a matter of products liability, negligence or otherwise, or from any use or operation
of any methods, products, instructions, or ideas contained in the material herein.

British Library Cataloguing in Publication Data
A catalogue record for this book is available from the British Library

Library of Congress Cataloging-in-Publication Data
A catalog record for this book is available from the Library of Congress

ISBN: 978-0-12-420249-8

For information on all Academic Press publications
visit our website at **store.elsevier.com**

Printed and bound in the United States

CONTENTS

CONTRIBUTORS

Keith D. Allen
Department of Psychology, Munroe-Meyer Institute for Genetics and Rehabilitation, University of Nebraska Medical Center, Omaha, Nebraska, USA

Scott P. Ardoin
Department of Educational Psychology and Instructional Technology, University of Georgia, Athens, Georgia, USA

Jonathan C. Baker
Rehabilitation Institute, Southern Illinois University, Carbondale, Illinois, USA

Yvonne Barnes-Holmes
Department of Psychology, National University of Ireland Maynooth, Co., Kildare, Ireland

Breanne J. Byiers
Department of Educational Psychology, University of Minnesota, Minneapolis, Minnesota, USA

Jacob H. Daar
Rehabilitation Institute, Southern Illinois University, Carbondale, Illinois, USA

Jesse Dallery
Department of Psychology, University of Florida, Gainesville, Florida, USA

Edward J. Daly III
Department of Educational Psychology, University of Nebraska Lincoln, Lincoln, Nebraska, USA

Erica Dashow
Rutgers, The State University of New Jersey, Douglass Developmental Disabilities Center, New Brunswick, New Jersey, USA

Anthony Defulio
Department of Psychiatry and Behavioral Sciences, Johns Hopkins University School of Medicine, Baltimore, Maryland, USA

Mark R. Dixon
Rehabilitation Institute, Southern Illinois University, Carbondale, Illinois, USA

Kathleen M. Fairchild
Rehabilitation Institute, Southern Illinois University, Carbondale, Illinois, USA

Terry S. Falcomata
Department of Special Education, The University of Texas at Austin, Austin, Texas, USA

Wayne W. Fisher
Center for Autism Spectrum Disorders, Munroe-Meyer Institute, The University of Nebraska Medical Center, Omaha, Nebraska, USA

Dana M. Gadaire
The Scott Center for Autism Treatment and Florida Institute of Technology, Melbourne, Florida, USA

Cindy Gevarter
Department of Special Education, The University of Texas at Austin, Austin, Texas, USA

Heather K. Gonzales
Department of Special Education, The University of Texas at Austin, Austin, Texas, USA

Nicole L. Hausman
Department of Behavioral Psychology, The Kennedy Krieger Institute, Baltimore, Maryland, USA

Jeffrey F. Hine
Department of Psychology, Munroe-Meyer Institute for Genetics and Rehabilitation, University of Nebraska Medical Center, Omaha, Nebraska, USA

David C. Houghton
Department of Psychology, Texas A&M University, College Station, Texas, USA

Robert W. Isenhower
Rutgers, The State University of New Jersey, Douglass Developmental Disabilities Center, New Brunswick, New Jersey, USA

SungWoo Kahng
Department of Health Psychology, University of Missouri, Columbia, Missouri, USA

Michael E. Kelley
The Scott Center for Autism Treatment and Florida Institute of Technology, Melbourne, Florida, USA

Michelle Kuhn
Department of Special Education, The University of Texas at Austin, Austin, Texas, USA

Giulio E. Lancioni
Department of Education, University of Bari, Bari, Italy

Russell Lang
Department of Curriculum and Instruction, Texas State University, San Marcos, Texas, USA

Robert H. LaRue
Rutgers, The State University of New Jersey, Douglass Developmental Disabilities Center, New Brunswick, New Jersey, USA

Linda A. LeBlanc
Trumpet Behavioral Health, Lakewood, Colorado, USA

Dorothea C. Lerman
Department of Clinical, Health, and Applied Sciences, University of Houston—Clear Lake, Houston, Texas, USA

Clare J. Liddon
The Scott Center for Autism Treatment and Florida Institute of Technology, Melbourne, Florida, USA

Timothy D. Ludwig
Department of Psychology, Appalachian State University, Boone, North Carolina, USA

James K. Luiselli
Clinical Solutions, Inc. and North East Educational and Developmental Support Center, Tewksbury, Massachusetts, USA

Brian K. Martens
Department of Psychology, Syracuse University, Syracuse, New York, USA

Monica M. Matthieu
School of Social Work, St Louis University, St Louis, Missouri, USA

Ciara McEnteggart
Department of Psychology, National University of Ireland Maynooth, Co., Kildare, Ireland

Heather M. McGee
Western Michigan University, Kalamazoo Michigan, USA

Steven E. Meredith
Department of Psychiatry and Behavioral Sciences, Johns Hopkins University School of Medicine, Baltimore, Maryland, USA

Suzanne M. Milnes
University of Nebraska Medical Center's Munroe-Meyer Institute, Omaha, Nebraska, USA

Raymond G. Miltenberger
Department of Child and Family Studies, University of South Florida, Tampa, Florida, USA

Matthew P. Normand
Department of Psychology, University of the Pacific, Stockton, California, USA

Triton Ong
Department of Psychology, University of the Pacific, Stockton, California, USA

Mark F. O'Reilly
Department of Special Education, The University of Texas at Austin, Austin, Texas, USA

Kerri P. Peters
Psychology Department, University of Florida, Gainesville, Florida, USA

Cathleen C. Piazza
University of Nebraska Medical Center's Munroe-Meyer Institute, Omaha, Nebraska, USA

Derek D. Reed
Department of Applied Behavioral Science, University of Kansas, Lawrence, Kansas, USA

Joe E. Reichle
Department of Educational Psychology, and Department of Speech-Language-Hearing Sciences, University of Minnesota, Minneapolis, Minnesota, USA

Aurelia Ribeiro
The Scott Center for Autism Treatment and Florida Institute of Technology, Melbourne, Florida, USA

Laura Rojeski
Department of Special Education, The University of Texas at Austin, Austin, Texas, USA

Patrick W. Romani
Munroe-Meyer Institute, University of Nebraska Medical Center, Omaha, Nebraska, USA

Nicolette Sammarco
Department of Special Education, The University of Texas at Austin, Austin, Texas, USA

Sindy Sanchez
Department of Child and Family Studies, University of South Florida, Tampa, Florida, USA

Kelly M. Schieltz
College of Education, University of Missouri, Columbia, Missouri, USA

Dawn A. Seefeldt
Rehabilitation Institute, Southern Illinois University, Carbondale, Illinois, USA

Rebecca A. Shalev
University of Nebraska Medical Center's Munroe-Meyer Institute, Omaha, Nebraska, USA

Jeff Sigafoos
Department of Special Education, Victoria University, Wellington, New Zealand

Sigurdur O. Sigurdsson
School of Behavior Analysis, Florida Institute of Technology, Melbourne, Florida, USA

Sarah K. Slocum
Psychology Department, University of Florida, Gainesville, Florida, USA

Kimberly N. Sloman
Rutgers, The State University of New Jersey, Douglass Developmental Disabilities Center, New Brunswick, New Jersey, USA

Diego A. Valbuena
Department of Child and Family Studies, University of South Florida, Tampa, Florida, USA

Amber L. Valentino
Trumpet Behavioral Health, Lakewood, Colorado, USA

Timothy R. Vollmer
Psychology Department, University of Florida, Gainesville, Florida, USA

David P. Wacker
Center for Disabilities and Development, The University of Iowa, Iowa City, Iowa, USA

Laci Watkins
Department of Special Education, The University of Texas at Austin, Austin, Texas, USA

David A. Wilder
School of Behavior Analysis, Florida Institute of Technology, Melbourne, Florida, USA

Alyssa N. Wilson
School of Social Work, St Louis University, St Louis, Missouri, USA

Douglas W. Woods
Department of Psychology, Texas A&M University, College Station, Texas, USA

Amanda N. Zangrillo
Center for Autism Spectrum Disorders, Munroe-Meyer Institute, The University of Nebraska Medical Center, Omaha, Nebraska, USA

PREFACE

The origin of this text arose from countless conversations with other professionals who generally reported, "I know about applied behavior analysis. I've seen it done before." Undoubtedly, many of those professionals had seen a version of applied behavior analysis (or "ABA" as it is often referred to) conducted with their child, student, or patient; however, it became clear that others held a relatively restricted notion of ABA. Without doubt, one of the most notable utilizations of ABA has been within the context of the interventions relating to skill deficits and behaviors of excess displayed by individuals with developmental disabilities, specifically autism. Although numerous procedures and approaches have been presented as potential treatments for the behavioral symptoms of autism, those based on the principles of ABA have received the most empirical support. As a result, in recent years, the term "applied behavior analysis" appears to be used quite often as a synonym for a very specific range of interventions for autism.

Many readers would note that ABA is but a subfield of the broader area of behavior analysis that also includes: (a) behaviorism, which focuses on the world view, theory, or philosophy of behavior analysis, and (b) the experimental analysis of behavior (EAB), which focuses on identifying and analyzing the basic principles, mechanisms, and processes that explain behavior. ABA is distinct from EAB in that it is considered a clinical discipline in which the general principles of learning and behavior are applied for the purpose of addressing socially relevant problems and issues. Thus, behavior analysts who work in ABA conduct research that assists in developing and evaluating evidence-based practices directed toward the remedy of problems associated with socially significant behavior. Applied behavior analysts then use the results of the applied research to create and implement effective evidence-based procedures in more natural settings such as schools, homes, and the community. Such work often focuses on behavioral problems that occur in particular settings, are associated with particular populations (e.g., individuals with autism or other developmental disabilities), and those that are present within larger social contexts (e.g., organizational behavior management).

In light of the efficacy of ABA-based procedures in addressing behaviors associated with autism, it is important to note that the principles underlying this therapeutic approach have been shown to be similarly effective when applied to other populations, settings, and behaviors. The current text provides a review of such clinical applications toward the purpose of expanding the reader's knowledge related to the breadth of ABA-based applications. Simply put, the goal is to illustrate the use of ABA beyond the realm of autism.

The content of this book was identified from an informal survey of ABA practitioners and researchers on their knowledge of current areas of clinical practice. In general, an attempt was made to limit the proposed content to clinical applications which have been divided into four broad areas: child applications, adult applications, broad-based health applications, and applications in the area of organizational behavior management. Undoubtedly, as the field continues to expand its breadth, there are some areas in which ABA methods are applied to novel areas of study that may have been omitted from inclusion.

The editors have drawn upon a range of subject-matter experts who have clinical and research experience in the application of ABA across multiple applications to serve as contributors to this volume. A great deal of thought was expended in determining whom we should contact for material on a given chapter. In many cases, the decision was difficult as there are a number of subject-matter experts who would have been appropriate. In the majority of cases, our initial approach to a potential contributor was met with an enthusiastic acceptance. Consequently, the resulting text includes contributions from individuals who have served as editors, associate editors, or editorial board members for prominent content-area journals such as the *Journal of Applied Behavior Analysis*, the *Journal of the Experimental Analysis of Behavior*, the *Journal of Organizational Behavior Management*, and the *Behavior Analyst*.

This book is best suited as a primary textbook for coursework in behavior analysis, psychology, or education. Also, while practitioners and students are the ultimate targets of this work, other professionals should find the content and language to be manageable. The hope is that this volume will be informative in demonstrating the range of application of ABA to various problems of social significance. We hope the reader finds this book as enjoyable as it was to edit.

Henry S. Roane

Joel E. Ringdahl

Terry S. Falcomata

CHAPTER 1

Defining Features of Applied Behavior Analysis

Terry S. Falcomata
Department of Special Education, The University of Texas at Austin, Austin, Texas, USA

INTRODUCTION

Individuals who work in applied behavior analysis (ABA) implement clinical interventions as well as conduct research to assist in the development of practices for addressing problems that occur with socially significant behavior. Applied behavior analysts often conduct applied research and use the results to create and implement effective, evidence-based procedures in more natural settings such as the home, schools, and the community. ABA-based research often focuses on behavioral issues that occur in specific settings, are associated with particular populations including children (e.g., obesity, autism or other developmental disabilities, traumatic brain injury, feeding disorders) and adults (e.g., caregiver training, sports performance, gambling), as well as those within other social contexts such as various workplace environments (e.g., performance management, workplace safety, systems analysis).

Although ABA has an extensive history of effectiveness in application and research across a diverse number of areas of focus, settings, and populations, perceptions exist in the media, various disciplines, and the public in general that ABA is synonymous with procedures for addressing issues related to autism spectrum disorder and other developmental disabilities (e.g., discrete-trial training and other procedures to promote skill acquisition; functional behavioral assessment and treatment of challenging behavior). In fact, the use of ABA-based methods and procedures to address issues relating to autism is just one of the many examples of the effective application of the ABA approach to addressing socially significant behavior. Said another way, although ABA has been demonstrated to be an effective approach to addressing issues with autism (e.g., Howard, Stanislaw, Green, Sparkman, & Cohen, 2014; MacDonald, Parry-Cruwys, Dupere, & Ahearn, 2014; Matson, Tureck, Turygin, Beighley, & Rieske, 2012), this aspect of ABA represents only one, relatively narrow application.

Clinical and Organizational Applications of Applied Behavior Analysis
http://dx.doi.org/10.1016/B978-0-12-420249-8.00001-0

This chapter provides an overview of the features of ABA within the framework provided by Baer, Wolf, and Risley (1968) and how those features characterize work conducted in various areas of focus, settings, and populations. Each of the dimensions is described and demonstrated using examples from various child, adult, and organizational ABA-based research.

DIMENSIONS OF ABA

Baer et al. (1968) provided what they contended were defining dimensions of ABA. As described by Baer et al., there are seven dimensions of ABA that must be present to ensure that effective practices are developed and implemented. According to Baer et al., ABA is (a) applied, (b) behavioral, (c) analytic, (d) technological, (e) conceptually systematic, (f) effective, and (g) generalizable. The remainder of this chapter will review the dimensions described by Baer et al. using applied studies across various populations and areas of focus as outlined in this text to illustrate how they characterize ABA.

Applied

The term *applied* indicates that a particular target behavior of interest is of social significance. Further, it is the emphasis on social significance that distinguishes ABA from laboratory analysis. Specifically, applied behavior analysts select behaviors that are socially meaningful and are currently of importance to the individual(s) whose behavior is being addressed. At various times, applied behavior analysts have opportunities to address numerous behaviors demonstrated by individuals, and it is considered vital that they prioritize those behaviors in terms of importance. Illustrations of the *applied* dimension of ABA are wide-ranging and can be observed in studies across numerous populations, settings, and areas.

Myriad child-focused studies have been conducted within ABA that exemplify the focus on social significance. These include (but are not limited to) studies evaluating treatments for feeding disorders (e.g., Kadey, Piazza, Rivas, & Zeleny, 2013; Kadey, Roane, Diaz, & Merrow, 2013; LaRue et al., 2011; Volkert, Vaz, Piazza, Frese, & Barnett, 2011), interventions for childhood obesity (e.g., Fogel, Miltenberger, Graves, & Koehler, 2010; Van Camp & Hayes, 2012), and issues relating to attention deficit hyperactivity disorder (ADHD; e.g., Northup, Fusilier, Swanson, Roane, & Borrero, 1997; Ridgway, Northup, Pellegrin, LaRue, & Hightsoe, 2003).

The ABA-based approach to the assessment and treatment of pediatric feeding disorders has included a wide variety of behaviors of significant social importance including food refusal (Borrero, Woods, Borrero, Masler, & Lesser, 2010), self-feeding (Vaz, Volkert, & Piazza, 2011), and swallowing (e.g., Kadey, Piazza, et al., 2013). For example, Kadey, Piazza, et al. (2013) addressed the food consumption of a 5-year-old girl who relied on a gastrostomy tube for her caloric needs. The authors conducted a texture assessment in which they evaluated various textures, across foods, to determine the one which the girl could successfully swallow. Through their systematic process of identifying a texture with which she could be successful with individual foods, the authors were able to increase the girl's consumption of those foods.

Child obesity is another socially significant area in which several ABA-based studies have been conducted. Fogel et al. (2010) evaluated the effects of video game-based exercise (i.e., exergaming) relative to traditional physical education (PE) with four physically inactive and overweight fifth grade students. The authors' purpose was to evaluate whether the physical activity of the children would increase through exposure to 10 exergames (e.g., Play Station; Nintendo Wii Boxing, Sports Baseball, Sports Tennis; iTech Fitness XrBoard). Through the use of the exergaming approach, the authors were able to substantially increase the physical activity of all four children above the levels observed during traditional PE.

A third socially significant, child-focused area of study deals with variables relating to ADHD. Northup et al. (1997) evaluated the effects of stimulant medication on five children with ADHD diagnoses. Specifically, the authors evaluated the children's preference for different reinforcers (quiet time, alone play, and social play) across the presence and absence of stimulant medications. Although the results of Northup et al. were idiosyncratic across children, the authors showed that stimulant medication can alter children's motivation for types of reinforcement.

Studies conducted in the areas of pediatric feeding disorders such as Kadey, Piazza, et al. (2013), childhood obesity such as Fogel et al. (2010), and ADHD such as LaRue et al. (2011) illustrate the emphasis of child-focused ABA on social significance. Each of the dependent variables, or target behaviors, in the above studies was meaningful and of practical importance to the children in the studies and to potential future consumers of the studies.

Similarly, a large number of adult-focused studies with high social significance have been conducted within ABA. These include (but are not limited to) studies evaluating assessment, treatment, and training practices in pathological gambling (e.g., Guercio, Johnson, & Dixon, 2012; Nastally, Dixon, & Jackson, 2010) as well as teacher and caregiver training (e.g., Lerman,

Tetreault, Hovanetz, Strobel, & Garro, 2008; Lerman, Vorndran, Addison, & Kuhn, 2004).

For example, the dimension of social significance is demonstrated in adult-focused, ABA-based studies pertaining to the assessment, treatment, and determination of the variables that contribute to pathological gambling. Guercio et al. (2012) studied a treatment intended to decrease urges to gamble and actual gambling behavior of three adults with acquired brain injury who were also indicated as pathological gamblers. The authors implemented a treatment program that consisted of one-on-one therapy that entailed providing instruction to the adults about motivating operations (MOs), antecedents, and consequences relating to gambling. Through the application of the treatment program, the authors demonstrated a reduction in urges to gamble (based on data collected via self-reports) and gambling behavior in each of the adults.

Another adult-focused area of study that illustrates the dimension of social significance in ABA is care provider training. Lerman et al. (2008) evaluated a training program intended to teach skills to teachers of children with autism relating to the implementation of preference assessment and teaching procedures. The training program consisted of a variety of teaching methods including lectures, discussion, and role-play procedures. The results showed that the training program resulted in the acquisition of the target skills by each of the teachers, and follow-up assessment suggested that those skills maintained over time following training. Similar to the child-based studies described above, each of the dependent variables evaluated in adult-based studies was meaningful and of obvious practical importance.

Many studies have also been conducted in the area of organizational behavior management (OBM) pertaining to safety (e.g., Ludwig & Geller, 1997) illustrating the applied nature of ABA. For example, Ludwig and Geller (1997) conducted a study in which they evaluated an intervention aimed at increasing safe driving behavior of pizza delivery drivers. Specifically, the authors implemented two interventions with two groups of drivers, respectively. One intervention consisted of goal setting in which the drivers participated in the setting of the goals. The second intervention consisted of goal setting but the drivers did not participate in the setting of goals. The results showed that both interventions were effective at increasing complete stops at intersections. Further, the results also showed that nontargeted safe driving behaviors (i.e., turn signal use, safety belt use) also increased during one of the interventions. The interventions, which were antecedent-based in nature, utilized by Ludwig and Geller (1997) demonstrated the effective use of an ABA-based approach to produce positive, socially significant changes with meaningful and practical target behaviors.

Behavioral

The term *behavioral* indicates that ABA concerns itself with the study of directly observable behavior. Specifically, applied behavior analysts emphasize the direct observation and manipulation of overt behavior. Indirect measures of behavior such as self-report, interviews, or checklists, although often used, are de-emphasized in ABA research in favor of direct methods of measurement and manipulation. In addition, applied behavior analysts do not attribute behavior as characteristics of, or based upon, nonbehavioral constructs or inner qualities (e.g., personality traits). Rather, ABA emphasizes the manipulation of environmental variables and the observation of relations between behaviors of interest and those variables for the purpose of demonstrating functional relations (i.e., functions of behavior). The behavioral dimension of ABA is vital because of the importance of precise measurements of behaviors of interest that, in turn, allow for valid evaluations and demonstrations of functional relations between interventions of interest and target behaviors of importance (see Section "Analytic"). Further, it allows for a systematic analysis of the extent to which applied behavior analysts are addressing the intended target behaviors and not approximations or nontarget behaviors (i.e., reliability of measurement).

The *behavioral* dimension of ABA can be illustrated in numerous child-based studies including those focusing on challenging behavior (e.g., Athens & Vollmer, 2010; Lustig et al., 2014) and academic skills (e.g., Martens, Werder, Hier, & Koenig, 2013). For example, Athens and Vollmer (2010) conducted a study in which they evaluated a treatment of challenging behavior exhibited by children with autism and ADHD. The authors focused exclusively on the direct observation of the target behaviors (i.e., aggression, disruption, compliance, communicative behaviors). To do so, the authors established a specific, operational definition of aggression for the participant (Henry) that consisted of "forcefully hitting and kicking others resulting in bruising his victims" (p. 573). This definition allowed for the direct observation and measurement of the presence and absence of the behavior. This approach can be contrasted with a nonbehavioral approach that might consist of anecdotal reports, or impressions provided by care providers regarding the behavior of the child.

Martens et al. (2013) focused on accuracy and fluency exhibited by children during oral reading. The authors specifically defined each of these target behaviors to allow for direct observation and measurement. Specifically, they established an operational definition of accuracy that consisted of the correct reading of a particular word, and they established an operational definition of fluency that consisted of the number of words correctly read per minute. Establishing these specific, observable operational definitions allowed the authors to evaluate variables (i.e., an intervention consisting of word training) impacting their occurrence, or lack thereof, in a systematic way. Without an emphasis on a behavioral approach, establishment of reliability of measurement would not be possible which would have precluded the authors from drawing conclusions about relations between their independent and dependent variables (i.e., conclusions about the effectiveness of their interventions would not be appropriate in the absence of demonstration of reliability of measurement made possible by the behavioral approach).

The *behavioral* dimension of ABA is also illustrated in numerous adult-based studies including those focusing on problem behaviors in gerontological populations (e.g., Baker, LeBlanc, Raetz, & Hilton, 2011) and acquired brain injury (e.g., Lancioni et al., 2012). For example, Baker et al. (2011) intervened with an individual with Alzheimer's-type severe dementia who was engaging in hoarding behaviors. The authors established a definition of hoarding that allowed for the direct observation and measurement of the behavior (i.e., putting items in her shirt or pants). This was opposed to a nonbehavioral approach that might have relied on the feelings of the staff that worked with her. Thus, by relying on directly observable behaviors, the authors minimized potential bias and accuracy issues that would likely impact nonbehavioral approaches (e.g., staff impressions). Subsequently, the authors were able to systematically evaluate the effectiveness of two interventions and demonstrate their effectiveness. In another adult-focused study, Lancioni et al. focused on text messaging skills with individuals with acquired brain injuries. To systematically evaluate the effectiveness of their intervention, the authors established operational definitions that allowed for the direct observation and measurement of target skills related to text messaging including number of messages sent, length of messages, the time needed to send and receive messages, and number of messages received and whether the individual read/listened to the message. Whereas this approach allowed for a systematic, empirical evaluation of the effects of the intervention, a nonbehavioral approach would not have allowed for a precise and accurate reflection of positive (or lack thereof) effects.

Many studies that illustrate the *behavioral* approach of ABA have also been conducted in the area of OBM pertaining to performance management (e.g., Fienup, Luiselli, Joy, Smyth, & Stein, 2013; Goomas, Smith, & Ludwig, 2011). For example, Fienup et al. (2013) evaluated an intervention intended to improve the performance of staff at a human services organization. Specifically, the authors intervened with the purpose of decreasing staff tardiness for supervision meetings. The authors measured latency from the scheduled beginning time for meetings until the actual time in which meetings began. This behavioral and observable measurement system minimized potential inaccurate inferences about the positive effects of the intervention they employed. Goomas et al. (2011) focused on the performance of employees at a retail distribution center. The authors directly measured the amount of time it took employees to complete specific tasks. By establishing direct measures of behavior, these authors were able to directly evaluate potential relations between their intervention and its effects on those targeted behaviors.

Analytic

The term *analytic* indicates that ABA emphasizes believable demonstrations of relations between behaviors of interest and environmental variables, interventions, and treatments under study. Systematic *analyses* of behavior are vital for the demonstration of experimental control with regard to the effects of independent variables (e.g., interventions and treatments) on dependent variables (e.g., socially relevant behaviors of interest). An emphasis is placed on the analytic nature of ABA because it is vital that applied behavior analysts base their practical recommendations on "believable demonstrations" (Baer et al., 1968, p. 93) that their interventions were responsible for positive changes in behaviors of interest. Thus, it is important that the inferences about causal relations between recommended interventions and positive outcomes should be based on systematic, empirical methods and demonstrations of experimental control.

Experimental control is achieved when an applied behavior analyst demonstrates a functional, or causal, relation between environmental variables of interest and behaviors of interest. In ABA, various single-subject experimental designs are utilized to demonstrate functional relations including (but not limited to) the reversal, multielement (and alternating treatments design), changing criterion, and multiple-baseline experimental designs. These basic designs share three common elements: (a) prediction—anticipated future levels of behavior, (b) verification—demonstration that the previously predicted levels of behavior would continue in the absence of a treatment, and (c) replication—repeating previous changes in behavior via the reintroduction and subsequent removal of the treatment across time, settings, and/or individuals.

The *analysis* dimension of ABA is illustrated in the child-based literature as reflected by emphasis on, and use of, various single-subject experimental designs to demonstrate functional relations between the independent variables (e.g., environmental variables, interventions, treatments) and socially relevant behaviors of interest. For example, in the study described above, Kadey, Piazza, et al. (2013) employed a reversal design to systematically demonstrate the relation between swallowing behavior (i.e., mouth cleans) demonstrated by a 5-year-old girl with feeding problems and specific texture levels. Using the reversal design, the authors first implemented a smooth texture level produced by a specific type of food processer (i.e., a Magic Bullet®) and documented the percentage of bite trials in which the child swallowed as reflected by mouth cleans. The authors conducted repeated sessions in this initial condition, and the child demonstrated high and relatively stable levels of swallowing behavior. The results of the first condition provided preliminary evidence of a relation between the child's swallowing behavior and the texture level of the food. However, without additional experimental manipulations, it would have been inappropriate to infer causality between food texture and swallowing. Therefore, the authors ended the condition and implemented a second condition in which pureed food was presented that was of a different texture than the food presented in the previous condition. The authors implemented repeated sessions in the second condition until they observed low and stable levels of swallowing. The results of the second condition provided additional evidence that the level of texture used in the first condition was responsible for the high levels of swallowing observed. However, the potential effects of extraneous variables on swallowing could not be ruled out (e.g., a variable outside of the evaluation may have coincided with the onset of the second condition and could have influenced the results). The authors reimplemented the initial condition and swallowing behavior increased back to levels observed during the initial condition. These results provided additional evidence that the high level swallowing resulted from the texture level rather than extraneous variables. The authors subsequently conducted an additional reversal (i.e., an additional puree condition and additional Magic Bullet® condition) and produced similar results. Thus, the co-occurrence of positive changes in the target behavior (i.e., swallowing) was demonstrated to occur only in the presence of the food texture produced by the Magic Bullet blender. Therefore, causality between positive effects observed with the swallowing behavior and the treatment could be reasonably inferred.

Normand (2008) provided an example of the use of a multiple-baseline (combined with an ABAB design), single-subject experimental design to demonstrate the functional relation between an intervention package and physical activity demonstrated by adults. Normand first introduced baseline conditions to each of four adult participants and measured the total number of steps taken by each participant. The treatment package (consisting of goal setting, self-monitoring, and feedback) was introduced with one of the participants after stable levels of steps taken were observed; while baseline continued to be implemented with the other three participants. Positive effects (i.e., increased levels of steps taken) were observed with the first participant while concurrently, levels of steps taken continued at consistent levels with the additional four participants. This result provided preliminary evidence that the treatment package was effective at increasing steps taken; however, extraneous variables could not be ruled out without replication of those effects across participants. Therefore, Normand introduced the intervention with the second participant while baseline conditions continued with the other three participants. Similar patterns of behavior were observed with the second participant as those observed with the first participant with an increase in steps taken. These results represented a replication of the positive effects observed with the first participant. Coupled with the continued consistent levels of steps taken with the other two participants during baseline conditions, evidence accrued suggesting a functional relation between the treatment package and an increase in steps taken. Normand went on to replicate the positive effects with the additional two participants, demonstrating three replications of the initial positive effects. Through this process, the author was able to rule out, to a reasonable degree, the possible effects of extraneous variables on the observed positive effects. Said another way, through the demonstration of functional relations, Normand could be confident that it was the treatment package that produced the positive results and not some other extra experimental variable(s).

Empirical methods that emphasize the demonstration of functional relations are also emphasized in the area of OBM. For example, Pampino, MacDonald, Mullin, and Wilder (2004) used a multiple-baseline, single-subject design to evaluate the effects of an intervention package consisting of task clarification, goal setting, positive reinforcement, and feedback on completion of maintenance tasks by workers in a framing and art store. The authors first collected baseline data prior to the implementation of the intervention package across two sets of duties. After stable levels of completion of duties were observed across both sets of duties, the authors implemented the intervention with one set of duties while continuing to collect baseline data with the second set of duties. Percentages of completion of the duties in the intervention condition immediately increased when the intervention was implemented, while levels of completion of the second set of duties (i.e., in baseline conditions) remained low. Next, the authors implemented the intervention with the second set of duties and an immediate increase in completion of those duties was observed; thus, the positive effects observed with the first set of duties were replicated with the second set of duties. The systematic methods used by the authors allowed them to infer causality between their intervention and the observed positive effects.

Technological

In addition to focusing on *analysis* and emphasizing functional relations through the use of appropriate experimental designs and the use of *behavioral* methods (e.g., precise measurements of target behaviors), ABA emphasizes thorough and accurate descriptions of procedures within the context of research and the application of behavioral interventions. Descriptions of procedures, operational definitions, and procedural integrity data are documented to allow other applied behavior analysts to replicate studies and evaluations in applied settings and research. A review of practically any study published in a peer-reviewed ABA journal (such as the *Journal of Applied Behavior Analysis*) will provide a demonstration of the technological aspect of ABA.

Conceptually Systematic

The practices utilized in ABA are applied in nature. However, there is a clear emphasis in ABA that these practices be *conceptually systematic*. Thus, basic behavioral principles empirically validated over many years by scientists and applied behavior analysts who conduct basic and applied research on the behavioral theories of experimental analysis of behavior underlie the practices of ABA. For example, intervention components that are based on conceptually systematic behavioral principles include (but are not limited to) reinforcement, extinction, punishment, stimulus control, discrimination, MOs, and schedules of reinforcement. Baer et al. (1968) asserted that by emphasizing behavioral principles along with precise descriptions of procedures, ABA would advance at a rate superior to an alternative approach that could be described as a "collection of tricks" (p. 96).

The emphasis on conceptual systems can be illustrated in the child-based behavioral literature pertaining to functional communication training (FCT;

Carr & Durand, 1985). FCT involves (a) evaluating and identifying the reinforcer maintaining challenging behavior via a functional assessment (e.g., functional analysis; Carr & Durand, 1985; Iwata, Dorsey, Slifer, Bauman, & Richman, 1982/1994); (b) training a new appropriate communicative behavior (e.g., card exchange, microswitch, sign language) and delivering the same reinforcer contingent on the response; (c) placing challenging behavior on extinction (i.e., reinforcement is withheld following occurrences of challenging behavior; Fisher et al., 1993; Hagopian, Fisher, Sullivan, Acquisto, & LeBlanc, 1998); and (d) in some cases, applying punishment contingent on challenging behavior (Hagopian et al., 1998; Wacker et al., 1990). Thus, the effectiveness of FCT is based on the behavioral mechanisms including reinforcement (positive and/or negative) and, in many cases, extinction and punishment, as well as training procedures such as the use of a time-delay prompt.

The approach of conceptualizing FCT using behavioral mechanisms and a conceptual system is distinct from a potential approach to the treatment that might focus on other aspects of the treatment. For example, a clinician focusing on FCT without considering the underlying conceptual system may favor conceptualizing the treatment as one that focuses on the utilization of technology (e.g., iPad technology, voice-output device) for communication and mistakenly assume that the effectiveness of the treatment is based on the provision of technology-based communicative techniques. Such an approach would be problematic for several reasons. First, without considering the antecedents and reinforcement contingencies associated with challenging behavior, while focusing solely on training communication using technology-based modalities, it is likely the treatment will fail to effectively treat the challenging behavior because the contingencies controlling the behavior will not have been addressed. Thus, to address the contingencies controlling the behavior, the effective applied behavior analyst considers the behavioral mechanisms responsible for the challenging behavior as well as the target-appropriate communicative behaviors (technology-based or otherwise). In addition, as Baer et al. (1968) asserted, without using a conceptual system when implementing the treatment, it is unlikely the clinician will generalize and apply the treatment effectively in other situations.

Guercio et al. (2012) provided an example of the application of a treatment based on a behavioral conceptual system for adult pathological gamblers in individuals with acquired brain injury. As described previously, the authors implemented a program that consisted of one-on-one treatment therapy sessions in which they focused on teaching the participants about the MOs, antecedents, and reinforcers associated with gambling behaviors.

Thus, the treatment was explicitly based on behavioral mechanisms conceptualized as controlling gambling behavior. An alternative conceptualization of the treatment might minimize or omit the behavioral components of the approach and instead focus on the format for therapy (e.g., one-on-one sessions, client-centered discussions). Similar to FCT, however, the focus and reliance on behavioral mechanisms is vital to the effectiveness of the treatment as well as the effective generalization and application of the procedures by future clinicians.

The use of a behavioral conceptual system is also emphasized in the area of OBM. For example, Cunningham and Austin (2007) utilized an intervention package consisting of goal setting, task clarification (via modeling), and feedback (description of performance, praise) via weekly meetings to improve the performance of hospital operating room employees pertaining to hands-free operating techniques. The authors conceptualized the behavioral mechanism of the feedback component of the intervention package as positive reinforcement of the target behavior. An alternative conceptualization that would not incorporate an underlying behavioral mechanism might focus not on the mechanism of reinforcement, but rather the implementation of weekly meetings to discuss the performance of staff. However, future attempted applications of the intervention that emphasize elements of the intervention that were not responsible for the observed positive behavior (rather than the behavioral mechanism responsible; i.e., positive reinforcement) would be much less likely to be effective. It should also be noted that although not explicitly stated in the study, the goal setting and modeling components could be conceptualized as antecedent-based and intended to increase discrimination and occasion the desired behaviors.

Effective

Effectiveness is a dimension that emphasizes the practical quality of ABA practices. That is, the *effectiveness* dimension of ABA focuses on whether the individual whose behavior was changed and the family and care providers of the individual view the behavior change to be practical and significant. Applied behavior analysts determine the *effectiveness* of their procedures by evaluating their data, often through visual inspection using valid single-subject experimental designs (as opposed to the use of statistical procedures to determine if behavior change is significant). Additionally, ABA emphasizes judgments of socially acceptable levels of improvement of target behaviors.

An example from the child-based ABA literature pertains to the assessment and treatment of pica. Pica (i.e., the insertion of inedible objects into the oral cavity or the ingestion of inedible objects; Piazza et al., 1998; Roane, Kelly, & Fisher, 2003) can be a life-threatening behavior displayed by children with autism and other developmental disabilities. Falcomata, Roane, and Pabico (2007) conducted a study that involved the assessment and treatment of pica in a 12-year-old boy with autism. During the study, the authors evaluated several treatment approaches by comparing their effects to each other as well as baseline conditions. The treatments included enriched environment (i.e., continuous access to highly preferred stimuli) and enriched environment plus a timeout procedure (i.e., visual screen timeout). The results showed that both treatments were effective at decreasing pica in comparison to baseline conditions. However, although the enriched environment treatment decreased pica relative to baseline (in which a mean rate of 6.7 occurrences per minute were observed), pica still occurred at a mean of 1.8 occurrences per minute. Thus, although it could be argued that the treatment produced an improvement, the dangerous nature of the behavior dictated that this was not a practical, or *effective*, level of improvement. An acceptable level of practical improvement (i.e., a demonstration of effectiveness) with a dangerous behavior such as pica is zero or near zero occurrences. The results of the study also showed, however, that the second treatment consisting of enriched environment plus timeout produced near zero levels of pica. Thus, this was considered a practical outcome, and the treatment could be deemed effective.

A study conducted by Normand and Osborne (2010) provides an example of the demonstration of effectiveness within an adult-focused application of ABA to healthier food choices demonstrated by college students. The authors first implemented a baseline condition in which they assessed college students' food choices via receipts and food checklists and tracked their daily calorie intake. Next, the authors implemented an intervention that involved providing feedback to the students by showing them graphs depicting daily calorie and fat intake. Additionally, the authors provided information to the students on recommended daily consumption for food groups as well as recommended levels of sugar and fat intake. Decreases in calorie and fat intake were demonstrated with three of the four participants. With each of the participants for whom clear effects of the intervention were demonstrated, their intake levels during the intervention condition occurred at or below United States Dairy Association (USDA) recommended daily guidelines. The clear demonstration of an experimental effect within the multiple-baseline, single-subject experimental design in Normand and Osborne did not, in and of itself, confirm the *effectiveness* of the intervention. However, the USDA recommended daily guidelines provided a benchmark with which to evaluate effectiveness; the favorable comparison to that benchmark provided clear evidence of the effectiveness of the intervention.

Lebbon, Sigurdsson, and Austin (2012) provided an example of the demonstration of effectiveness in OBM-based ABA research. The authors evaluated an intervention package consisting of training, peer observations, peer-directed feedback, and graphic feedback. To evaluate the intervention package, the authors collected data on several dependent variables including Occupational Safety Health Administration recordable incidents, lost workdays, and peer observations. The results suggested that the intervention package decreased the total number of incidents and lost days when compared to preintervention conditions. The authors provided a cost-effectiveness analysis by comparing the average direct cost of individual work-related disabling injuries and other injuries to the total cost of the intervention given the reduction in injuries during the course of the study. The results suggested that the intervention was clearly cost-effective, providing evidence of the *effectiveness* of the intervention.

Generality

The last dimension of ABA places an emphasis on the extent to which gains are *generalizable* to other settings, caregivers, or behaviors. *Generalization* is important because it is not beneficial to improve a client's behavior only in settings (e.g., clinics) outside of the natural environment, particularly if the client only spends a few hours of his/her week outside the natural environment. The behavioral intervention is only beneficial if it improves behavior across different settings and when it is implemented by different individuals (e.g., multiple caregivers).

Silber and Martens (2010) provided an example of the application of child-focused ABA in which the dimension of generality was evident. The authors evaluated a multiple exemplar approach to a program for generalized oral reading fluency demonstrated by children in the first and second grades. Specifically, the authors compared three conditions including a control, a reading intervention that consisted of teaching key words and sentence structures, and a typical reading intervention consisting of preview and repeated readings. Following the implementation of each condition, the authors conducted probes with nontrained reading passages to evaluate the extent to which the children's learned skills generalized. The results showed that both reading interventions were more effective at promoting generalization of reading skills as evidenced by significantly higher scores during the generalization probes with untrained readings. By showing the spread of the positive effects of the interventions to untrained reading passages, the authors demonstrated the generality of the interventions.

Stokes, Luiselli, Reed, and Fleming (2010) provided an example of the emphasis on generalization in the ABA-based sports management literature. During the study, the authors evaluated the utility of descriptive feedback alone; descriptive feedback in combination with video-based feedback; and a combination of descriptive feedback, video-based feedback, and an audio-based feedback procedure (i.e., teaching with acoustical guidance, TAG) to improve line pass-blocking skills in high school football players. After demonstrating the effectiveness of the intervention package consisting of descriptive feedback, video-based feedback, and TAG with improvements in blocking, the authors assessed improvements during game situations (with four of the five participants) in the absence of the intervention. The results showed that all four players demonstrated high levels of correct blocking techniques during game situations suggesting that generalization had occurred with the intervention.

The *generality* dimension of ABA is also illustrated in numerous OBM-based ABA studies. For example, as described earlier, Ludwig and Geller (1997) evaluated two approaches to improving intersection stopping by pizza delivery drivers as well as generalization to nontargeted safe driving behaviors (i.e., turn signal usage, safety belt usage). Both interventions were shown to improve intersection stopping. However, significant increases in nontargeted turn signal and safety belt usage were demonstrated with the drivers who participated in the goal-setting process. Thus, the results suggested a high level of *generality* of the intervention.

SUMMARY

Features of ABA include seven dimensions described by Baer et al. (1968) including applied, behavioral, analytic, technological, conceptually systematic, effective, and generalizable. Applied behavior analysts, through both applied work and research, have conducted practice characterized by these dimensions and features across populations and specific areas of focus for more than a half-century. In addition, assessment and intervention practices based on the principles of ABA have been implemented successfully in educational, clinical, sports, and business settings to address a wide range of behavioral issues.

This chapter highlighted the wide breadth and diversity of application of procedures and methodologies based on the discipline of ABA. Despite the impression that ABA is synonymous with specific assessment and treatment approaches to autism and developmental disabilities (e.g., Bowman & Baker, 2014), the wide range of studies described in this chapter in terms of populations, areas of focus, and settings illustrates the actual nature of the impact and discipline of ABA.

REFERENCES

Athens, E. S., & Vollmer, T. R. (2010). An investigation of differential reinforcement of alternative behavior without extinction. *Journal of Applied Behavior Analysis*, *43*, 569–589.

Baer, D. M., Wolf, M. M., & Risley, T. R. (1968). Some current dimensions of applied behavior analysis. *Journal of Applied Behavior Analysis*, *1*, 91–97.

Baker, J. C., LeBlanc, L. A., Raetz, P. B., & Hilton, L. C. (2011). Assessment and treatment of hoarding in an individual with dementia. *Behavior Therapy*, *42*, 135–142.

Borrero, C. S., Woods, J. N., Borrero, J. C., Masler, E. A., & Lesser, A. D. (2010). Descriptive analyses of pediatric food refusal and acceptance. *Journal of Applied Behavior Analysis*, *43*, 71–88.

Bowman, R. A., & Baker, J. P. (2014). Screams, slaps, and love: The strange birth of applied behavior analysis. *Pediatrics*, *133*(3), 364–366.

Carr, E. G., & Durand, V. M. (1985). Reducing behavior problems through functional communication training. *Journal of Applied Behavior Analysis*, *18*, 111–126.

Cunningham, T. R., & Austin, J. (2007). Using goal setting, task clarification, and feedback to increase the use of the hands-free technique by hospital operation room staff. *Journal of Applied Behavior Analysis*, *40*, 673–677.

Falcomata, T. S., Roane, H. S., & Pabico, R. R. (2007). Unintentional stimulus control during the treatment of pica displayed by a young man with autism. *Research in Autism Spectrum Disorders*, *1*, 350–359.

Fienup, D. M., Luiselli, J. K., Joy, M., Smyth, D., & Stein, R. (2013). Functional assessment and intervention for organizational behavior change: Improving the timeliness of staff meetings at a human services organization. *Journal of Organizational Behavior Management*, *33*, 252–264.

Fisher, W., Piazza, C., Cataldo, M., Harrell, R., Jefferson, G., & Conner, R. (1993). Functional communication training with and without extinction and punishment. *Journal of Applied Behavior Analysis*, *26*, 23–36.

Fogel, V. A., Miltenberger, R. G., Graves, R., & Koehler, S. (2010). The effects of exergaming on physical activity among inactive children in a physical education classroom. *Journal of Applied Behavior Analysis*, *43*, 591–600.

Goomas, D. T., Smith, S. M., & Ludwig, T. D. (2011). Business activity monitoring: Real-time group goals and feedback using an overhead scoreboard in a distribution center. *Journal of Organizational Behavior Management*, *31*, 196–209.

Guercio, J. M., Johnson, T., & Dixon, M. R. (2012). Behavioral treatment for pathological gambling in persons with acquired brain injury. *Journal of Applied Behavior Analysis*, *45*, 485–495.

Hagopian, L. P., Fisher, W. W., Sullivan, M. T., Acquisto, J., & LeBlanc, L. A. (1998). Effectiveness of functional communication training with and without extinction and punishment: A summary of 21 inpatient cases. *Journal of Applied Behavior Analysis*, *31*, 211–235.

Howard, J. S., Stanislaw, H., Green, G., Sparkman, C. R., & Cohen, H. G. (2014). Comparison of behavior analytic and eclectic early interventions for young children with autism after three years. *Research in Developmental Disabilities*, *35*, 3326–3344.

Iwata, B. A., Dorsey, M. F., Slifer, K. J., Bauman, K. E., & Richman, G. S. (1994). Toward a functional analysis of self-injury. *Journal of Applied Behavior Analysis, 27*, 197–209 [Reprinted from *Analysis and Intervention in Developmental Disabilities, 2*, 3–20, 1982].

Kadey, H., Piazza, C. C., Rivas, K. M., & Zeleny, J. (2013). An evaluation of texture manipulations to increase swallowing. *Journal of Applied Behavior Analysis, 46*, 539–543.

Kadey, H. J., Roane, H. S., Diaz, J. C., & Merrow, J. M. (2013). An evaluation of chewing and swallowing for a child diagnosed with autism. *Journal of Developmental and Physical Disabilities, 25*, 343–354.

Lancioni, G. E., O'Reilly, M. F., Singh, N. N., Green, V. A., Oliva, D., Buonocunto, F., et al. (2012). Special text messaging communication systems for persons with multiple disabilities. *Developmental Neurorehabilitation, 15*, 31–38.

LaRue, R. H., Stewart, V., Piazza, C. C., Volkert, V. M., Patel, M. R., & Zeleny, J. (2011). Escape as reinforcement and escape extinction in the treatment of feeding problems. *Journal of Applied Behavior Analysis, 44*, 719–735.

Lebbon, A., Sigurdsson, S. O., & Austin, J. (2012). Behavioral safety in the food services industry: Challenges and outcomes. *Journal of Organizational Behavior Management, 32*, 44–57.

Lerman, D. C., Tetreault, A., Hovanetz, A., Strobel, M., & Garro, J. (2008). Further evaluation of a brief, intensive teacher-training model. *Journal of Applied Behavior Analysis, 41*, 243–248.

Lerman, D. C., Vorndran, C. M., Addison, L., & Kuhn, S. C. (2004). Preparing teachers in evidence-based practices for young children with autism. *School Psychology Review, 33*, 510–525.

Ludwig, T. D., & Geller, E. S. (1997). Assigned versus participative goal setting and response generalization: Managing injury control among professional pizza deliverers. *Journal of Applied Psychology, 82*, 253–261.

Lustig, N. H., Ringdahl, J. E., Breznican, G., Romani, P., Scheib, M., & Vinquist, K. (2014). Evaluation and treatment of socially inappropriate stereotypy. *Journal of Developmental and Physical Disabilities, 26*, 225–235.

MacDonald, R., Parry-Cruwys, D., Dupere, S., & Ahearn, W. (2014). Assessing progress and outcome of early intensive behavioral intervention for toddlers with autism. *Research in Developmental Disabilities, 35*, 3632–3644.

Martens, B. K., Werder, C. S., Hier, B. O., & Koenig, E. A. (2013). Fluency training in phoneme blending: A preliminary study of generalized effects. *Journal of Behavioral Education, 22*, 16–36.

Matson, J. L., Tureck, K., Turygin, N., Beighley, J., & Rieske, R. (2012). Trends and topics in early intensive behavioral interventions for toddlers with autism. *Research in Autism Spectrum Disorders, 6*, 1412–1417.

Nastally, B. L., Dixon, M. R., & Jackson, J. W. (2010). Manipulating slot machine preference in problem gamblers through contextual control. *Journal of Applied Behavior Analysis, 43*, 125–129.

Normand, M. P. (2008). Increasing physical activity through self-monitoring, goal setting, and feedback. *Behavioral Interventions, 23*, 227–236.

Normand, M. P., & Osborne, M. R. (2010). Promoting healthier food choices in college students using individualized dietary feedback. *Behavioral Interventions, 25*, 183–190.

Northup, J., Fusilier, I., Swanson, V., Roane, H., & Borrero, J. (1997). An evaluation of methylphenidate as a potential establishing operation for some common classroom reinforcers. *Journal of Applied Behavior Analysis, 30*, 615–625.

Pampino, R. N., Jr., MacDonald, J. E., Mullin, J. E., & Wilder, D. A. (2004). Weekly feedback vs. daily feedback: An application in retail. *Journal of Organizational Behavior Management, 23*, 21–43.

Piazza, C. C., Fisher, W. W., Hanley, G. P., LeBlanc, L. A., Worsdell, A. S., Lindauer, S. E., et al. (1998). Treatment of pica through multiple analyses of its reinforcing functions. *Journal of Applied Behavior Analysis, 31*, 165–189.

Ridgway, A., Northup, J., Pellegrin, A., LaRue, R., & Hightsoe, A. (2003). Effects of recess on the classroom behavior of children with and without attention-deficit hyperactivity disorder. *School Psychology Quarterly, 18*, 253.

Roane, H. S., Kelly, M. L., & Fisher, W. W. (2003). The effects of noncontingent access to food on the rate of object mouthing across three settings. *Journal of Applied Behavior Analysis, 36*, 579–582.

Silber, J. M., & Martens, B. K. (2010). Programming for the generalization of oral reading fluency: Repeated readings of entire text versus multiple exemplars. *Journal of Behavioral Education, 19*, 30–46.

Stokes, J. V., Luiselli, J. K., Reed, D. D., & Fleming, R. K. (2010). Behavioral coaching to improve offensive line pass-blocking skills of high school football athletes. *Journal of Applied Behavior Analysis, 43*, 463–472.

Van Camp, C. M., & Hayes, L. B. (2012). Assessing and increasing physical activity. *Journal of Applied Behavior Analysis, 45*, 871–875.

Vaz, P., Volkert, V. M., & Piazza, C. C. (2011). Using negative reinforcement to increase self-feeding in a child with food selectivity. *Journal of Applied Behavior Analysis, 44*, 915–920.

Volkert, V. M., Vaz, P., Piazza, C. C., Frese, J., & Barnett, L. (2011). Using a flipped spoon to decrease packing in children with feeding disorders. *Journal of Applied Behavior Analysis, 44*, 617–621.

Wacker, D. P., McMahon, C., Steege, M., Berg, W., Sasso, G., & Melloy, K. (1990). Applications of a sequential alternating treatments design. *Journal of Applied Behavior Analysis, 23*, 333–339. http://dx.doi.org/10.1901/jaba.1990.23-333.

CHAPTER 2

Applied Behavior Analytic Assessment and Treatment of Autism Spectrum Disorder

Wayne W. Fisher, Amanda N. Zangrillo
Center for Autism Spectrum Disorders, Munroe-Meyer Institute, The University of Nebraska Medical Center, Omaha, Nebraska, USA

Type the word "autism" into any Internet search engine and the abundance of returned results is overwhelming. The prevalence of autism spectrum disorder (ASD) has steadily increased, nearly tripling over the last decade (i.e., increasing from 1 in 150 children to approximately 1 in 50 children; Blumberg et al., 2013; Centers for Disease Control and Prevention [CDC], 2014). Given this increase, it is not surprising that caregivers, clinicians, and the general public are generating considerable discussion about ASD. Eugen Bleuler provided an initial description of the symptoms of ASD in the early 1900s (Klinger, Dawson, & Renner, 2003). Over the past century, research has contributed significantly to the availability of information regarding diagnosis, assessment, and treatment of ASD. Unfortunately, not all research is created equal, and consumers are faced with the daunting task of differentiating empirical research and evidence-based practice from that which is invalid or pseudoscientific (National Autism Center, 2009). In this chapter, we provide (a) a review of the diagnostic criteria and hallmarks of ASD and recent changes to the diagnostic criteria; (b) a discussion of the impact of the disorder in terms of prevalence rates, etiology, and prognosis; (c) an overview of behavior analytic, evidence-based approaches to assessment and treatment; and (d) future directions and considerations for practitioners.

> A little learning is a dang'rous thing; Drink deep or taste not...
>
> *Alexander Pope*

THE IMPACT OF ASD ON AFFECTED CHILDREN AND THEIR FAMILIES

The impact of autism on affected children and their families is difficult to overstate. In the absence of effective intervention, long-term outcomes for children diagnosed with ASD have generally been poor. For example,

Clinical and Organizational Applications of Applied Behavior Analysis
http://dx.doi.org/10.1016/B978-0-12-420249-8.00002-2

19

in one long-term follow-up study of adults affected by autism, only 4% lived independently, only 13% worked independently (primarily in low paying occupations), and only 26% had one or more friends (Howlin, 2005; Howlin, Goode, Hutton, & Rutter, 2004). More recent studies on adolescent and adult outcomes for persons with ASD have produced somewhat more optimistic results; however, many of these studies have focused on outcomes for a small sample of relatively high-functioning individuals (see Levy & Perry, 2011 for a review). Finally, parents and siblings of individuals affected by ASD are at increased risk for developing stress-related mental disorders (Dumas, Wolf, Fisman, & Culligan, 1991; Feldman et al., 2007; Lofholm, 2008).

DEFINING FEATURES AND DIAGNOSIS

ASD is a neurodevelopmental disorder that is typically identified in early childhood, with symptoms often presenting at or before 18 months (Blumberg et al., 2013). Eugen Bleuler initially conceptualized autism as a form of childhood schizophrenia; however, ASD differs from schizophrenia on all of the factors that define a syndrome, including symptoms, age of onset, etiology, family history, and response to treatment. Based on the presentation of the unique symptoms associated with ASD, Leo Kanner and Hans Asperger later conceptualized autism and Asperger's syndrome, respectively, as separate disorders in the early 1940s (Klinger et al., 2003), and in 2013 the diagnostic label was changed to ASD. Although the specific naming conventions have changed over the years, the hallmarks of ASD established in the *Diagnostic and Statistical Manual of Mental Disorders* 5th ed. (DSM-5; American Psychiatric Association [APA], 2013a) have generally remained consistent and are deeply rooted in impairments in social-communication behaviors (e.g., social interaction, verbal and nonverbal communication) and restricted and repetitive interests and behaviors in a variety of contexts, and across many domains (APA, 2013a).

Clinicians use the DSM-5 as a guide to determine if the symptoms displayed by an individual meet the diagnostic criteria for ASD diagnosis. The DSM-5 outlines five key diagnostic criteria that are required for diagnosing ASD: (a) an individual must display persistent impairments or deficits in social communication and social interaction; (b) an individual must display restricted, repetitive patterns of behavior, interests, or activities; (c) the symptoms must be present in early childhood; (d) symptoms produce clinically significant impairments in current functioning in a variety of contexts (e.g., home, work, and school); and (e) the symptoms cannot be better explained by intellectual disability or global developmental delay. Each category is evaluated separately, and each criterion specified in the five areas listed above must be met to provide an individual with a diagnosis of ASD (APA, 2013a). What follows is a discussion of the observable and measureable symptoms that are described in the first two areas of the diagnostic criteria.

Social Communication and Social Interaction

The category of social communication and social interaction is divided into three distinct subdivisions. The first subcategory includes skills related to social-emotional reciprocity. An individual experiencing marked delays or deficits in this subcategory may (a) rarely initiate conversation with others, (b) fail to look at or acknowledge others when his or her name is called or when others enter the room, and (c) intrude on what is typically called another individual's "personal space."

The second subcategory describes deficits or impairments in social interactions involving nonverbal communicative behaviors (e.g., deficits in coordinated use of verbal and nonverbal communication, eye contact). The third subcategory includes deficits or impairments in developing, maintaining, and understanding relationships (e.g., adjusting behavior to fit social contexts, absence of interest in peers). An individual must present with impairments or deficits in *all* three subcategories in order to meet the criteria for a diagnosis of ASD.

Restricted, Repetitive Patterns of Behavior, Interests, or Activities

The category of restricted, repetitive patterns of behavior, interests, or activities is also divided into four distinct subdivisions. The first subcategory includes stereotyped or repetitive (a) motor movements (e.g., hand flapping, toe walking, spinning in circles), (b) use of objects (e.g., repeatedly dropping objects and watching them fall, lining up objects), and/or (c) speech (e.g., pedantic or overly formal speech, idiosyncratic words or phrases, echolalia). Behaviors that are included in this subcategory may vary depending on the cognitive level and vocal abilities of the individual. The second area includes insistence on sameness, inflexible adherence to routines, and/or ritualized patterns of verbal or nonverbal behavior (e.g., rigidly following rules, insisting on wearing the same shirt each day). The third area includes highly restricted, fixated interests that are abnormal in intensity or focus (e.g., only talking about one topic, significantly restricted food preferences, preoccupation with a limited range of toys or activities). The last area includes hyper- or hyporeactivity to sensory input or unusual interest in sensory aspects of the environment (e.g., extreme responses to specific sounds, textures, changes in the environment, indifference to exposure to pain or temperatures). An individual must display marked impairment in *at least two of the four* subcategories noted above to meet the diagnostic criteria for restricted, repetitive patterns of behavior, interests, or activities.

The defining features of ASD (previously discussed) exist along a continuum and may manifest differently in each individual. Specific characteristics may develop over time (i.e., as the child matures and social interactions become more complex), change form or topography, and/or increase or decrease in intensity or level of impairment of daily functioning (i.e., following exposure to environmental consequences or early intervention services; APA, 2013a). Individuals diagnosed with ASD may also present with a variety of features that are not included as hallmarks of the disorder, but are associated features. These associated features include disturbances in feeding and sleeping (see Kodak & Piazza, 2008), delayed toilet training (Kodak & Grow, 2011), genetic and medical conditions (e.g., intellectual disability, seizure disorders, fragile-X syndrome; Klinger et al., 2003; Kodak & Grow, 2011), severe self-injury, and/or other related behavior problems (e.g., aggression, pica, elopement, tantrums, etc.; Jones, Lerman, & Laechago, 2014).

MODIFICATIONS TO THE DSM

In 2013, the APA published the DSM-5, which included a number of revisions to the diagnostic criteria in the DSM-IV-Text Revision (TR; 2000) that have been somewhat controversial. The DSM-5 collapsed several of the DSM-IV-TR diagnoses (e.g., autistic disorder, Asperger syndrome) into a single disorder (i.e., ASD). In addition, Rett syndrome was considered a pervasive developmental disorder in DSM-IV-TR, but with DSM-5, a child with Rett syndrome would receive a diagnosis of ASD only if the new diagnostic criteria are met, in which case the diagnosis of Rett syndrome would be considered a "specifier" (e.g., ASD associated with the genetic condition called Rett syndrome; APA, 2013b). These changes have been controversial due to concerns that the new diagnostic criteria may be less sensitive than the prior version, which would result in fewer children being diagnosed with an ASD and receiving associated treatments (APA, 2013b). For example, a recent meta-analysis of studies comparing the

DSM-5 and DSM-IV-TR criteria found that the former reduced the number of diagnosed cases of ASD by an average of 31% (Kulage, Smaldone, & Cohn, 2014). However, other studies have applied diagnostic criteria specifically developed for the DSM-5 and found high levels of selectivity (percentage of "true" or actual cases of ASD identified) and specificity (percentage of noncases of ASD correctly identified as such; Carrington et al., 2014; Kent et al., 2013). Additional research will be needed before this controversy is satisfactorily resolved.

DIAGNOSTIC ASSESSMENT

A variety of etiological factors have been associated with increased risk of ASD (e.g., high paternal age: Kolevzon, Gross, & Reichenberg, 2007; fragile-X syndrome: Kaufmann et al., 2004), but none have shown a one-to-one correspondence with the behavioral syndrome; thus, clinicians must rely on indirect and direct observations of the measurable dimensions of an individual's behavior (as opposed to biological or genetic determinants) to render a diagnosis. Routine medical evaluations, such as well-child doctor visits, play a key role in early detection and access to treatment for many children and families. Examples of screening tools aimed specifically at identifying the hallmarks of ASD include the *Checklist for Autism in Toddlers* (CHAT; Baron-Cohen, Allen, & Gillberg, 1992), *Modified Checklist for Autism in Toddlers* (M-CHAT; Robins, Fein, Barton, & Green, 2001), and *Screening Tool for Autism in Toddlers* (Stone, Coonrod, & Ousley, 2000; see Taubman, Leaf, & McEachin, 2011 for a review). Pediatricians or caregivers may request additional referrals for assessment from clinicians with specialized training in diagnostic assessment with young children to determine if the current presentation meets the diagnostic criterion for ASD.

With regard to diagnostic assessment, the specific indirect and direct assessment methods used vary from clinic to clinic. It is important to note that no one assessment tool or method should be used alone to assess an individual. Many diagnostic evaluations use multimethod (e.g., indirect and direct methods) and multidisciplinary approaches during the diagnostic assessment process. For example, a clinician may use caregiver interviews and rating scales (such as the tools listed above), in combination with neuropsychological assessments, speech and language evaluations, assessments of adaptive functioning (e.g., *Vineland Adaptive Behavior Scale-Second Edition*; Sparrow, Cicchetti, & Balla, 2005), direct observation, and standardized assessments aimed at assessing the defining features of ASD. Tools that have been empirically validated for the diagnosis of ASD include *Autism Diagnostic Interview—Revised* (e.g., ADI-R; Rutter, Le Couteur, & Lord, 2003), *Childhood Autism Rating Scale-Second Edition* (CARS2; Schopler, Van Bourgondien, Wellman, & Love, 2010), *Gilliam Autism Rating Scale* (GARS; Gilliam, 2006), and *Autism Diagnostic Observation Schedule, Second Edition* (ADOS-2; Lord, Rutter, DiLavore, & Risi, 2001).

ESTIMATES OF THE PREVALENCE OF ASD

Estimates of the prevalence of ASD have varied widely over time and across studies. The latest reports from the CDC estimate the prevalence of ASD at 1 in 68 children (CDC, 2014), whereas the median estimate for prevalence studies worldwide since the 1960s is about 1 in 162 (Elsabbagh et al., 2012). In addition, Elsabbagh et al. found that the world-wide prevalence estimates have shown a statistically significant increase over time ($r = 0.4$; $p < 0.01$). Moreover, a small number of recent, well-designed studies (Baird et al., 2006; Kawamura, Takahashi, & Ishii, 2008; Kim et al., 2011) that have employed more vigorous case-ascertainment methods (i.e., using systematic, population-wide screening and diagnostic procedures rather than simply counting cases that have been identified and diagnosed clinically) reported prevalence estimates as high as 1 in 38 children (or 2.6% of the childhood population). Although some authors have argued that the increase in the reported prevalence rates of ASD over time represents a true increase in the number of affected children, the observed increase is probably due to (a) more inclusive diagnostic criteria, (b) increased recognition and diagnosis of the disorder, and (c) diagnostic substitution (i.e., children who may have received other diagnoses in the past are more likely to be diagnosed with ASD today; Elsabbagh et al., 2012). Finally, the results of the recent, well-designed studies that have used more aggressive case-ascertainment methods suggest that the observed prevalence of autism may continue to rise for some time going forward.

ETIOLOGICAL FACTORS IN ASD

Early accounts of the etiology of ASD varied between those that attributed the disorder to emotionally cold and distant parenting practices (the so-called refrigerator-mother hypothesis; Bettelheim, 1967; Kanner, 1943) to those that described it as primarily a biological condition (Rimland, 1964). Leo Kanner, who first applied the label of autism to this group of children, reportedly oscillated multiple times between the two views, calling it an "inborn" condition in his original paper (Kanner, 1943), attributing the disorder to parental inadequacies in a later publication (Kanner, 1954), and then vacillating between these two positions later on (see Rapin, 2011 and Sanua, 1990 for more detailed discussions). Today, ASD is viewed as having primarily a neurobiological basis due to (a) higher than expected concordance rates among monozygotic twins and among close family relatives (Folstein & Rutter, 1977); (b) frequent co-occurring clinical features associated with neurobiological conditions, such as seizures (Deykin & MacMahom, 1979) and genetic conditions (e.g., fragile-X syndrome: Harris et al., 2008); and (c) a wide variety of brain-imaging studies showing anomalies of brain structure (Stanfield et al., 2008), function (Pelphrey & Carter, 2008), and connectivity (Wass, 2011).

HISTORY OF BEHAVIORAL TREATMENT OF ASD

Jean-Marc-Gaspard Itard (1801), a French physician, treated a feral boy named Victor who lived on his own in the wild for 5 years or more until he was approximately 12 years old. Victor was described as having a number of symptoms of ASD, including a lack of communication and interest in social interaction and stereotypic motor responses. However, there has been considerable debate as to whether the symptoms resulted from his social isolation in the wild or whether his caretakers may have abandoned him due to a congenital behavior disorder, such as ASD (Frith, 1989; Lane, 1976). Itard's approach to treatment included (a) individualized instruction, (b) beginning with the child's current level of performance and then introducing increasingly more difficult material, (c) imitation training, and (d) delivering immediate rewards for correct and appropriate responses, procedures that remain highly relevant to the treatment of ASD today. After about 5 years of intervention, Victor could read and follow simple spoken or written sentences, request preferred items or activities using gestures or simple written phrases, and discriminate basic emotions expressed by others, but he never learned to emit spoken language. If Victor was on the autism spectrum, then Itard's description of his work with this boy represents the first detailed account of a child with ASD as well as the treatment of the symptoms of this disorder (Thompson, 2013). Little, if any progress was made in the treatment of ASD between Itard's time and the early 1960s.

EVIDENCE FOR THE EFFECTIVENESS OF EARLY INTENSIVE BEHAVIORAL INTERVENTION FOR ASD

Previous research has described various intervention approaches for addressing behavioral deficits and excesses associated with ASD. An exhaustive list of treatments is available to the general consumer; however, many treatments lack empirical support (e.g., steroid treatments, auditory integration training, immunotherapy, gluten avoidance; Green, 1996). By contrast, a substantial body of research has recognized behavioral approaches, specifically applied behavior analysis (ABA), as effective treatments for mitigating or ameliorating symptoms in children with ASD (Carr & Firth, 2005; Howard, Sparkman, Cohen, Green, & Stanislaw, 2005; Lovaas et al., 1981; Smith, 2001). Approaches based on the principles and procedures of ABA have been prevalent in the literature since the early 1960s (Carr & Firth, 2005) and have driven the development of comprehensive treatment programs aimed at early and intensive behavioral intervention (EIBI).

Lovaas (1987) reported the first group-design study on the effectiveness of an intensive form of ABA treatment for young children with autism called EIBI. Subjects were assigned to one of three groups: an intensive-treatment experimental group ($n = 19$) that received more than 40 h of one-to-one ABA treatment per week; a minimal-treatment control group ($n = 19$) that received 10 h or less of one-to-one ABA treatment per week; or a second control group ($n = 21$) that received treatment as usual in the community. Assignment to groups was not done at random, but the groups did not differ on key variables before treatment commenced. Mental age, summed pathology scores, abnormal speech, self-stimulatory behavior, appropriate toy play, and recognizable words were subjected to a multivariate analysis of variance (MANOVA). After completing 4 years of treatment, nine of the experimental-group children (47%) passed first grade in regular classrooms with no special services and obtained average or above average scores on IQ tests ($M = 107$, range $= 94$-120). Eight experimental-group participants (42%) passed first grade in language-disability classes and obtained mean IQ scores within the mildly disabled range of intellectual functioning ($M = 70$, range $= 56$-95). Two children (10%) were placed in classes for autistic/intellectually disabled children and had IQ scores below 30 post-treatment. Within the two comparison groups, one participant (2%) achieved normal functioning as evidenced by normal first-grade placement, 45% tested in the range of mild intellectual disability and were in language-delayed classes, and 21 (53%) were in classes for children with autism/severe intellectual disability (mean IQ $= 40$, range $= 20$-73).

A variety of systematic literature reviews and meta-analyses have evaluated the empirical evidence supporting the effectiveness of EIBI, including ones done by expert panels, such as the New York Department of Health (1999), the National Research Council (Lord & McGee, 2001a, 2001b), the National Autism Center (2009), and the Vanderbilt Evidence-based Practice Center (Warren et al., 2011). Others have been completed by one or a small group of authors, with most of these latter studies using meta-analysis methods (Eikeseth, 2009; Eldevik et al., 2009; Makrygianni & Reed, 2010; Howlin, Magiati, & Charman, 2009; Reichow & Wolery, 2009; Spreckley & Boyd, 2009; Virués-Ortega, 2010). Of the four reviews conducted by expert panels, three concluded that EIBI is an empirically supported treatment for young children with ASD, and the fourth (Warren et al., 2011) concluded that the evidence for its effectiveness was low. However, the government agency that commissioned the Vanderbilt group to conduct this review has since announced that their findings may be out of date and that an update of this study is in progress (Effective Health Care Program, 2014). In addition, the first three expert panels considered the results of research studies employing both single-subject and group-comparison designs, whereas the Warren et al. study only considered research using group-comparison methods and only ones that included a minimum of 10 participants.

Among the seven systematic reviews and meta-analyses published in 2009 and 2010, six of them found that EIBI was an effective intervention for young children with ASD; however, most found considerable individual variation in response to treatment, with some children benefiting greatly and others only marginally or not at all (Eikeseth, 2009; Eldevik et al., 2009; Howlin et al., 2009; Makrygianni & Reed, 2010; Reichow & Wolery, 2009; Spreckley & Boyd, 2009; Virués-Ortega, 2010). The meta-analysis by Spreckley and Boyd was the only one that concluded that there was insufficient empirical support for the effectiveness of EIBI, probably due to two major limitations of this study.

First, Spreckley and Boyd (2009) conducted their meta-analysis on a much smaller set of studies (relative to the other meta-analyses). They initially found 16 studies that met their descriptive inclusion criteria. However, they subsequently concluded that only four studies presented data in a format that their particular statistical package could analyze. They analyzed the data from these four studies using a specific statistical package (e.g., Review Manager, version 4.2 for Windows). After running reported mean scores from the four studies through the program, they concluded there was insufficient evidence of the effectiveness of early ABA treatment for young children with ASD.

In addition to excluding the vast majority of studies on EIBI, a second major limitation in the Spreckley and Boyd (2009) analysis was that they mischaracterized one of the four studies that they included in their analysis, the Sallows and Graupner (2005) randomized-clinical trial of EIBI. Both groups in that study received home-based EIBI individually delivered by staff from the same agency, one professionally directed and the other parent-managed with professional consultation. Spreckley and Boyd incorrectly designated the latter group as a no-treatment control group, which it clearly was not, as both groups received EIBI. By using a statistical package that excluded most relevant studies on ABA treatment of ASD and by misclassifying one of the groups in the Sallows and Graupner study, Spreckley and Boyd reduced the power of their meta-analysis to a point where it was nearly impossible to find significant treatment effects. The other meta-analyses that did not have these major limitations found that EIBI produced moderate to large effect sizes for IQ ($M = 0.95$, range 0.57-1.47) and adaptive behavior ($M = 0.84$, range 0.42-1.47).

Two recent group-comparison studies further extend the evidence supporting EIBI. Strain and Bovey (2011) completed a *clustered* randomized trial in which 56 preschool classrooms were randomly assigned to one of two conditions. In the test condition, classroom personnel received 2 years of training and coaching to fidelity in the Learning Experiences and Alternative Program for Preschoolers and Their Parents (LEAP) program. In the control condition, the classroom personnel received the LEAP manual but did not receive on-site training or coaching to fidelity. Results showed that the classrooms in the test condition (training and coaching to fidelity) showed significantly greater improvement than the control group (manual only) on all dependent measures, which included the Preschool Language Scale, the *Social Skills Rating System*, and all subtests of the *Mullen Scales of Early Learning*, the *Childhood Autism Rating Scale* (*CARS*); and the *Social Skills Rating System*, with Hedge's standardized difference scores in the moderate to large size ($M = 0.82$, range 0.59-1.2). Importantly, the study found large correlations between their measure of treatment fidelity and all of the outcome measures ($M = 0.73$, range 0.67-0.86), indicating that better outcomes were associated with more accurate treatment implementation.

Flanagan, Perry, and Freeman (2012) evaluated the effects of a large EIBI program for young children with ASD. The program was publicly funded and implemented across the entire province of Ontario, Canada. This study evaluated data collected in one of the nine service regions in Ontario (the Toronto area), thus representing the first trial of the effectiveness of EIBI when implemented at scale. Most of the data were retrieved via a file review. They compared children who received EIBI with those on the waitlist who were matched individually on age at intake and who were equivalent at the group level on the *CARS*, the composite, and all of the subscales of the *Vineland Adaptive Behavior Scale*. Results showed that children in the EIBI group showed significantly greater improvement than the waitlist control group on all dependent measures, which included the *CARS*, the composite, all of the subscales of the *Vineland Adaptive Behavior Scale*, and one of the three common standardized IQ measures, with most of the standardized difference scores in the moderate range ($M = 0.62$ for Cohen's d, range 0.49-0.83). Although these effect sizes are somewhat lower than the mean from the meta-analyses cited above, the results are impressive given that the program was implemented at scale. Taken together, the Strain and Bovey (2011) and Flanagan et al. (2012) studies strengthen the evidence supporting the effectiveness of EIBI.

COMPONENTS OF EIBI

Several studies published in the 1960s showed that appropriate behavior (e.g., imitation, social initiations, verbal behavior [VB]) could be increased and problem behavior (e.g., stereotypic behavior, tantrums, self-injurious behavior) could be decreased in some children with ASD (Hewett, 1965; Lovaas et al., 1966; Metz, 1965; Wolf, Risley, & Mees, 1964). Lovaas, Koegel, Simmons, and Long (1973) reported the results of a more comprehensive approach to the treatment of children with autism implemented with 20 children. This approach focused initially on suppressing stereotypic and self-destructive behavior and establishing compliance and instructional control followed by intensive language intervention. Roughly 80% of the instructional time focused on language training, and the remaining 20% was allocated toward building social and self-help skills. The first four children treated in this study were treated as inpatients (8 h per day for 12-14 months), and the children's parents were not involved in the intervention. Parent training was integrated into subsequent cohorts, and treatment was later moved to an outpatient model. Results showed decreases in self-stimulatory behavior and echolalia as well as increases in IQ and adaptive behavior and direct-observation measures of VB, social skills, and play skills. However, treatment gains tended to be specific to the environment in which treatment was implemented and many participants regressed when the intervention was terminated.

In a subsequent study, Lovaas (1987) attempted to produce more general and enduring changes in problem behavior and skill deficits displayed by children with ASD by (a) initiating treatment at a young age (before age 4), (b) delivering the treatment across all relevant individuals (e.g., parents, teachers) and environments (e.g., home, school, community), and (c) implementing treatment at a high intensity or dosage level (i.e., about 40 h per week over several years). Subsequent reviews of the EIBI have further refined and described the essential components of this intervention, including (a) an individualized comprehensive set of treatment targets; (b) use of a broad set of behavioral principles and procedures designed to reduce aberrant behavior and replace it with developmentally appropriate language, social, play, and adaptive skills; (c) treatment development, oversight, and supervision by a professional with advanced training in ABA; (d) parents are trained as therapists and involved in delivery of the intervention services; (e) treatment is initially delivered via one-on-one training and proceeds to group instruction as the individual's skills permit; (f) treatment usually is initiated in the individual's home or in a clinic setting and is subsequently carried out across relevant environments; (g) treatment is initiated early (preferably before age 4) and is carried out at a high intensity level (30 or more hours per week for two or more years); and (h) reliable, direct-observation measures are collected on an ongoing basis and these data are graphed and visually analyzed to monitor progress and determine whether adjustments to the treatment protocols are warranted (Green, Brennan, & Fein, 2002; Klintwall & Eikeseth, 2013).

Initial one-on-one treatment sessions based on the Lovaas model teach new skills using Discrete Trial Training (DTT). DTT is a procedure characterized by five distinct features presented in a specific order (Smith, 2001):

- The therapist provides a discriminative stimulus (S^D), or an initial instruction (e.g., "Touch red," with three different color cards in front of the child).
- The therapist provides a prompt that reliably occasions the correct response (e.g., modeling the correct response if the child reliably imitates a model).
- The learner makes a response (e.g., touches the red card).
- The therapist reinforces the child's correct response or withholds reinforcement for an incorrect response. If an incorrect response occurs, the therapist may represent the S^D, typically using a more intrusive prompt to evoke the correct response.

- Finally, the therapist initiates the beginning of the intertrial interval (ITI) and (if applicable) access to reinforcement. The therapist presents the next S^D to begin the next trial.

This trial format is generally repeated multiple times during a session (e.g., 10 trials per session), and sessions are repeated over time until the child achieves mastery performance (e.g., at least 90% correct for two consecutive sessions). New skills are often taught in this DTT format and then practiced under more naturalistic conditions as the child progresses. These methods have been used to teach a wide variety of skills across many domains (e.g., mands, tacts, intraverbals, mathematics, daily living skills; Sundberg, 2008; Sundberg & Partington, 1998).

CURRICULUM-BASED ASSESSMENT METHODS

Early learners present with skills across many domains and along a broad continuum. It is fitting that curriculum-based assessment methods are structured in a similar manner, sampling from various domains of skill development and arranging skills in a progressive fashion. A main focus when using curriculum-based assessment methods is to identify the skills that a child currently has in his or her repertoire and potential barriers to learning. Clinicians use this information to select skills to target for instruction. Curriculum-based assessment methods can also be used as a means to monitor ongoing progress. Two widely used assessment tools are the *Assessment of Basic Language and Learning Skills-Revised* (ABLLS-R; Sundberg & Partington, 1998) and the *Verbal Behavior Milestones Assessment and Placement Program* (VB-MAPP; Sundberg, 2008).

The ABLLS-R and VB-MAPP present similar formats for assessing learner skills and readiness. Both are criterion-referenced assessments aimed at measuring skill development in early developmental milestones. The ABLLS-R divides skill sets across 25 domains, and data are collected regarding an individual's skill level via indirect (e.g., caregiver or teacher interview) and direct (e.g., observation or specific testing scenarios) observation procedures.

The VB-MAPP is similar to the ABLLS-R in terms of function but differs somewhat in terms of organization. The VB-MAPP is also criterion-referenced and divides skill sets across three developmental levels or tiers (0-18, 18-30, and 30-48 months). The tiers cover a range of 16 skill areas and 170 language and learning milestones. The VB-MAPP is designed to provide a representative sample of a child's existing verbal and related skill repertoire across three developmental levels. In addition to language and learning milestones, the VB-MAPP includes a barriers assessment and a transition assessment, both of which are designed to evaluate potential barriers to learning and aid in setting goals for transition to less restrictive or more naturalistic environments.

VARIATIONS OF EIBI MODELS

Traditionally, the DTT approach to teaching language focused on the acquisition of receptive and expressive language skills, following a traditional view of language development (e.g., targeting receptive and expressive language skills; LeBlanc, Esch, Sidener, & Firth, 2006).

The instructional procedures evaluated by Lovaas have significantly impacted service delivery for children with ASD, and many of the EIBI models use and build upon the key features of Lovaas's methods (e.g., DTT, frequent and intensive intervention, use of reinforcement, sequential introduction of target stimuli; Carr & Firth, 2005; Sundberg & Michael, 2001). However, many variations to the methods described by Lovaas have developed, leading to advances in treatment and the development of treatment programming and procedures tailored to the individual needs of clients and caregivers.

Some of these variations to the DTT methodology include manipulations of ITI length (Koegel, Dunlap, & Dyer, 1980) and interspersal of mastered and non-mastered tasks (e.g., Neef, Iwata, & Page, 1980), prompting strategies and reinforcement contingencies (Charlop, Kurtz, & Milstein, 1992).

In addition to the DTT methodology and variations noted previously, the applied VB, or VB, approach has emerged as a technology for teaching children with ASD, specifically in the area of language development (Carr & Firth, 2005). The VB approach to teaching language shares many similarities with the method described by Lovaas (1987; e.g., uses a trial format; frequent, daily exposure to teaching environments; progressive curriculum; use of reinforcement; focus on teaching language). However, there are some distinct differences.

First, DTT and VB differ with regard to the composition of the learning environment. In DTT teaching procedures occur in structured, analog environments under tightly controlled stimulus and motivating conditions. After mastery occurs, generalization and maintenance are often assessed and trained under structured, tightly controlled stimulus conditions with programmed variations in S^Ds, exemplars, therapists, and settings. By contrast,

VB programs occur in a blend of discrete-trial and natural-teaching environments (also called natural environment teaching, NET). The focus of NET is to teach target skills in the presence of naturally occurring S^Ds so that these stimuli come to develop control over VB during and after treatment, thus facilitating generalization and maintenance (Carr & Firth, 2005).

This focus on the variables that control the VB of the learner leads to the second, and perhaps the most significant, difference between the two methods. While the traditional view focuses on receptive and expressive aspects of language, the VB approach uses the technical framework proposed by Skinner (1957) to account for the various S^Ds, motivating operations (MOs; Laraway, Snycerski, Michael, & Poling, 2003), and reinforcers that control VB (LeBlanc et al., 2006). Skinner's analysis of VB identified seven verbal operants (e.g., mand, tact, echoic, intraverbal, textual, transcriptive, and copying a text), each with its own functional relation within language and with controlling variables that are specific to the function of the operant. The VB approach incorporates Skinner's framework into curriculum development and assessment of skills (e.g., Sundberg & Partington, 1998).

Another approach to EIBI includes mand training, which focuses on the arrangement of MOs and teaches requests or mands in the presence of the MOs. This strategy is similar to, and is often embedded within, other EIBI models as an integral "first step" in language development (Drash, High, & Tudor, 1999).

ASSESSMENT AND TREATMENT OF RESTRICTED AND REPETITIVE BEHAVIOR

Repetitive and restrictive behaviors represent one of the most challenging characteristics that parents of children with ASD face. These behaviors often interfere with the learning and social engagement of the child with ASD and evoke family stress and negative parenting styles (Boyd, McDonough, & Bodfish, 2012).

Turner (1999) categorized repetitive and restrictive behavior into two broad categories, lower-order responses (e.g., repetitive motor movements, stereotypic use of objects) and higher-order responses (e.g., insistence on sameness, circumscribed interests). Most factor-analytic studies using the items from the ADI-R have generally found that either a two- or three-factor solution corresponding to Turner's conceptualization has provided a good fit to the data (Cucarro et al., 2003; Lam, Bodfish, & Piven, 2008; Mooney, Gray, Tonge, Sweeney, & Taffe, 2009; Richler, Bishop, Kleinke,

& Lord, 2007; Richler, Huerta, Bishop, & Lord, 2010). By contrast, factor-analytic studies using the Repetitive Behaviors Scale—Revised (Bodfish, Symons, Parker, & Lewis, 2000) have generally produced either a five- or six-factor model with self-injurious behavior, repetitive motor movements, restricted behaviors, compulsive behavior, and ritualistic/sameness behavior as the factors. Joseph and colleagues provide a framework showing how the results of various factor-analytic studies relate to Turner's conceptualization of these behaviors as being either higher-order or lower-order responses (see Figure 1 in Joseph, Thurm, Farmer, & Shumway, 2013). These various subtypes of repetitive and restrictive behaviors are particularly relevant to the treatment of ASD because the extant literature suggests that there are a variety of empirically supported interventions for responses categorized as lower-order behaviors (see Rapp & Vollmer, 2005 for a review), but only a small number of interventions have been developed and evaluated for responses categorized as higher-order behaviors (Boyd et al., 2012).

Most recent treatments for stereotypic (or lower-order) repetitive behaviors have been based on the results of a functional analysis (Rapp & Vollmer, 2005). Rapp and Vollmer identified five findings from the results of these studies that strongly supported the hypothesis that stereotypy is often maintained by automatic reinforcement. Numerous studies have shown that (a) stereotypy persists in the absence of social consequences (e.g., Piazza, Adelinis, Hanley, Goh, & Delia, 2000), (b) stereotypy decreases when matched or competing sources of stimulation are provided (e.g., Fisher, Lindauer, Alterson, & Thompson, 1998), (c) stereotypy decreases when its sensory consequence is identified and withdrawn (i.e., sensory extinction; e.g., Rincover, Cook, Peoples, & Packard, 1979), (d) contingent access to stereotypy can function as reinforcement for appropriate alternative behavior (e.g., Charlop, Kurtz, & Greenberg-Casey, 1990), and (e) restricting access to stereotypy (i.e., deprivation) results in subsequent increases in the response, whereas free access to stereotypy (i.e., satiation) typically results in subsequent decreases in the response (e.g., Rapp, Vollmer, Dozier, St. Peter, & Cotnoir, 2004).

As previously mentioned, Boyd et al. (2012) noted that only a small number of studies have employed functional-analysis procedures to identify the operant function of higher-order repetitive behavior. However, additional function-analysis studies of higher-order repetitive behaviors have been conducted more recently. For example, Rodriguez and colleagues conducted functional analyses of compulsive-like behavior (e.g., ordering and arranging furniture and other objects in the environment) in three teenagers diagnosed with ASD (Rodriguez, Thompson, Schlichenmeyer, & Stocco, 2012). The results of the functional analyses were consistent with the hypothesis that these behaviors were maintained by automatic reinforcement. In addition, a second analysis was done with one of the participants (Christie) in which the establishing operation for the hypothesized reinforcer was systematically manipulated in an ABAB (i.e., the establishing operation was absent in the "A" phase, present in the "B" phase, and these procedures were systematically replicated) reversal design. Results showed near-zero levels of ordering and arranging when the establishing operation was absent (i.e., when the items were already in the participant's preferred arrangement) and high levels of ordering and arranging when the establishing operation was present (i.e., when the items were not in the participant's preferred arrangement). Finally, implementation of a function-based treatment consisting of matched items prompts to interact with the matched items, and response blocking for ordering and arranging reduced these problematic behaviors and replaced them with appropriate alternative responses.

In another recent study, Fisher, Rodriguez, and Owen (2013) conducted a functional analysis of "restricted interests" consisting of perseverative speech about a small number of topics such as comic-book characters (e.g., "Batman") or violent activities (e.g., shooting) in a youth with Asperger syndrome. Results indicated that the young man's restricted interests were reinforced by contingent attention. Two function-based treatments were subsequently developed and evaluated in which attention was used to differentially reinforce (a) the absence of perseverative speech (differential reinforcement [DR] of nonperseverative speech) and (b) appropriately talking about a topic selected by the therapist (DR-on topic). These treatments were evaluated in the context of a multiple schedule in which discriminative stimuli were used to signal when it was the participant's turn to select the conversation topic and when it was the therapist's turn. Both treatments reduced perseverative speech to near-zero levels during the therapist's turn, but appropriate, on-topic speech increased only when it was specifically reinforced during the DR-on topic condition.

Finally, Peterson, Piazza, and Volkert (submitted for publication) treated six children with ASD who displayed severe food selectivity (a unique form of resistance to change). They compared function-based treatments involving escape extinction (e.g., nonremoval of the spoon for bite acceptance; redistribution of the food for packing) with a sensory integrative approach called the Sequential-Oral-Sensory (SOS) approach. Participants were randomly assigned to the two treatments in pairs. The two treatments were then evaluated using a multiple-baseline-across-foods design. In addition, if a participant did not show clinically significant improvements from the treatment to which they were initially assigned, then that participant subsequently received the alternative treatment. None of the three children assigned to SOS showed clinically significant improvements, whereas all six children showed dramatic improvement to the ABA intervention (i.e., escape extinction). One minor limitation of the Peterson et al. study was that they did not conduct functional analyses of food selectivity with these participants prior to initiating treatment. Nevertheless, results of prior research using functional-analysis methods suggest that negative reinforcement is almost always at least partially responsible for the maintenance of food refusal and food selectivity (Piazza et al., 2003). In addition, the fact that food selectivity was effectively treated with escape extinction in all six children strongly suggests that this response was maintained by negative reinforcement.

The Fisher et al. (2013) and Peterson et al. (submitted for publication) investigations are noteworthy in that they illustrate how higher-order responses that could be characterized as "restricted interests" and "resistance to change," respectively, may have different operant functions than lower-order repetitive behaviors, which are primarily maintained by automatic reinforcement (Rapp & Vollmer, 2005). These preliminary studies also suggest that considerably more functional-analysis research is needed on higher-order restricted and repetitive behavior in children with ASD.

TREATMENT APPROACHES FOR SOCIAL SKILLS DEFICITS

Individuals with ASD are deeply impacted by impairments in social communication and social interaction. Social behaviors exist along a broad continuum and range from seemingly simple actions (e.g., orienting toward a speaker, requesting a preferred item, eye contact) to more difficult exchanges (e.g., turn taking, using body gestures, and navigating romantic relationships; Dooley, Wilczenski, & Torem, 2001; Hénault, 2006; Tullis & Zangrillo, 2013). Delays or deficits in social behaviors may become more pronounced in individuals with ASD as the nature of these interactions become more complex (i.e., in adolescence and adulthood; Eaves & Ho, 1996; Stokes & Kaur, 2005) or when combined with other psychiatric conditions (e.g., anxiety disorders; White et al., 2013). The nuances involved in communicative and social interactions on the part of the listener and the speaker increase the difficulty of assessment and intervention for clinicians and caregivers, specifically when it comes to operationally defining and collecting data on these interactions and exchanges. Researchers and clinicians have developed a number of tools aimed at screening for delays or deficits in social or communication skills or to aid in diagnosis of ASD (see Freeman, 2011 for a review).

Similar to the EIBI assessment and curriculum development discussed above, screening or diagnostic tools may also provide a foundation for further assessment and intervention. These tools can be used to describe and develop a baseline of skills specifically related to social and communicative behaviors that the individual already has in his or her repertoire. In addition, these tools, in combination with other indirect, direct, and experimental-assessment methods (e.g., functional analysis), may aid in identifying areas where impairments or deficits are observed and guide the development of goals related specifically to skill development. Other formalized assessments (e.g., speech and language evaluations, psychological testing) also provide valuable information regarding the oral-motor skills necessary for developing fluent vocal behavior.

In recent years, there has been a substantial increase in research focused on both assessment and intervention surrounding social communication and social interaction (Matson, Matson, & Rivet, 2007; Reichow & Volkmar, 2010). Given the significant role that development of social skills and social interactions play in the treatment focus for children with ASD, it is expected that research will continue to grow in this area. Reichow and Volkmar (2010) evaluated 66 studies employing social skills intervention for individuals with ASD. A total of 513 participants were included and covered a range of preschool-aged children (53%), school-aged children (42%), and adolescents and adults (5%). Overwhelmingly, ABA interventions were the most commonly used interventions across all age groups, with the highest percentage of ABA interventions occurring in the preschool-aged group. In addition, ABA interventions were the most commonly used treatment component included to supplement and support other intervention strategies. Other strategies used to teach social skills for children, adolescents, and adults with ASD include cognitive behavior therapy, social stories, social scripts, video modeling, and other packaged curricula and social skills groups, with video modeling and social skills groups containing empirical support as evidence-based practice. Other packaged curricula are gaining support and have promising results as evidence-based practice (e.g., PEERS® Program; Laugeson, Ellingsen, Sanderson, Tucci, & Bates, 2014; see Reichow & Volkmar, 2010 for a full review).

What is also evident from the research review conducted by Reichow and Volkmar (2010) is the limited empirical support for interventions involving adolescents and adults with ASD (i.e., 5% of studies included adolescents and adults), particularly for individuals with lower levels of cognitive functioning. More research is warranted in this area to develop evidence-based interventions across a broad range of ages, cognitive levels, and formats (e.g., group versus individual, adult implemented versus peer).

FUTURE DIRECTIONS AND CONSIDERATIONS FOR PRACTITIONERS

The field of ABA and its approaches to the assessment and treatment of ASDs continues to evolve and rapidly change. Recent and upcoming changes that practitioners will have to grapple with include (a) understanding how the changes in the DSM diagnostic criteria may affect referrals for ABA services (e.g., fewer children with high-functioning autism and those with milder symptoms); (b) increases in the number of states requiring a license to practice ABA (see http://bacb.com/index.php?page=100170 for updated information on relevant state laws); (c) changing from the currently used billing codes to the new Adaptive Behavior Codes developed and published by the American Medical Association (see http://www.abainternational.org/constituents/practitioners/practice-resources/cptcodes.aspx for information on these new billing codes); and (d) changes in the requirements for supervisors for students and others seeking to become a board certified behavior analyst (see http://www.bacb.com/index.php?page=100872 for specific information).

Keeping up with the recent and upcoming changes listed above is important for practitioners. However, it is equally, if not more, important for practitioners to keep abreast of recent research findings relevant to the assessment and treatment of ASD using ABA procedures. One way of keeping up to date on the relevant research literature is by reading literature reviews and/or recent chapters, such as the current one. However, no single article or chapter can comprehensively describe the current body of ABA research relevant to the assessment and treatment of autism. Therefore, it is also important to directly read ABA research findings in journals, such as the *Journal of Applied Behavior Analysis*, the flagship journal for the field of ABA. Why is it important for practitioners to read the relevant research studies? Well, consider an analogous situation in which you or a member of your family requires surgery for breast or prostate cancer. You have a choice between two surgeons, one that subscribes to, and routinely reads the latest research in the *American Journal of Surgery* and *Clinical Cancer Research* and the other surgeon who relies solely on his or her clinical experience since completing residency training 15 years ago. Who would you choose? The answer is obvious. Consumers of ABA services will increasingly be faced with similar choices between practitioners who do and do not keep abreast of the latest research findings. As such, a subscription to *JABA* represents a low cost, high return investment in a practitioner's professional future. The future is bright for practitioners who deliver ABA services to children and families affected by autism, especially those who continually hone their skills by maintaining contact with the most recent research findings.

REFERENCES

American Medical Association. (2014). *Adaptive behavior codes.* Retrieved from: http://www. abainternational.org/constituents/practitioners/practice-resources/cptcodes.aspx.
American Psychiatric Association. (2000). *Diagnostic and statistical manual of mental disorders, a text revision* (4th). Washington, DC: American Psychiatric Association.
American Psychiatric Association. (2013a). *Diagnostic and statistical manual of mental disorders* (5th). Washington, DC: American Psychiatric Publishing.
American Psychiatric Association. (2013b). *Highlights of changes from DSM-IV to DSM-5.* Retrieved from: http://www.dsm5.org/Documents/changes%20from%20dsm-iv-tr% 20to%20dsm-5.pdf.
Baird, G., Simonoff, E., Pickles, A., Chandler, S., Loucas, T., Meldrum, D., et al. (2006). Prevalence of disorders of the autism spectrum in a population cohort of children in South Thames: The Special Needs and Autism Project (SNAP). *Lancet, 368*(9531), 210–215.
Baron-Cohen, S., Allen, J., & Gillberg, C. (1992). Can autism be detected at 18 months? The needle in the haystack and the CHAT. *British Journal of Psychiatry, 161*, 839–843.
Bettelheim, B. (1967). *The empty fortress: Infantile autism and the birth of the self.* New York, NY: The Free Press.
Blumberg, S. J., Bramlett, M. D., Kogan, M. D., Schieve, L. A., Jones, J. R., & Lu, M. C. (2013). Changes in prevalence of parent-reported autism spectrum disorder in school-aged U.S. children: 2007 to 2011–2012. *National Health Statistics Reports, 65*, 1–11, Retrieved from: http://www.cdc.gov/nchs/data/nhsr/nhsr065.pdf.
Bodfish, J. W., Symons, F. J., Parker, D. E., & Lewis, M. H. (2000). Varieties of repetitive behavior in autism: Comparisons to mental retardation. *Journal of Autism and Developmental Disorders, 30*(3), 237–243.
Boyd, B. A., McDonough, S. G., & Bodfish, J. W. (2012). Evidence-based behavioral interventions for repetitive behaviors in autism. *Journal of Autism and Developmental Disorders, 42*(6), 1236–1248. http://dx.doi.org/10.1007/s10803-011-1284-z.
Carr, J. E., & Firth, A. M. (2005). The verbal approach to early and intensive behavioral intervention for autism: A call for additional empirical support. *Journal of Early and Intensive Behavior Intervention, 2*, 8–27.
Carrington, S. J., Kent, R. G., Maljaars, J., Le Couteur, A., Gould, J., Wing, L., et al. (2014). DSM-5 autism spectrum disorder: In search of essential behaviors for diagnosis. *Research in Autism Spectrum Disorders, 8*(6), 701–715. http://dx.doi.org/10.1016/j. rasd.2014.03.017.
Centers for Disease Control and Prevention. (2014, April 28). *Autism spectrum disorder (ASD).* Retrieved from: http://www.cdc.gov/ncbddd/autism/index.html.

Charlop, M. H., Kurtz, P. F., & Greenberg-Casey, F. (1990). Using aberrant behaviors as reinforcers for autistic children. *Journal of Applied Behavior Analysis, 23*(2), 163–181. http://dx.doi.org/10.1901/jaba.1990.23-163.

Charlop, M. H., Kurtz, P. F., & Milstein, J. P. (1992). Too much reinforcement, too little behavior: Assessing task interspersal procedures in conjunction with different reinforcement schedules with autistic children. *Journal of Applied Behavior Analysis, 25*(4), 795–808. http://dx.doi.org/10.1901/jaba.1992.25-795.

Cucarro, M. L., Shao, Y., Grubber, J., Slifer, M., Wolpert, C. M., Donnelly, S. L., et al. (2003). Factor analysis of restricted and repetitive behaviors in autism using the Autism Diagnostic Interview-R. *Child Psychiatry and Human Development, 34*(1), 3–16.

Deykin, E. Y., & MacMahom, B. (1979). The incidence of seizures among children with autistic symptoms. *The American Journal of Psychiatry, 136*(10), 1310–1312.

Dooley, P., Wilczenski, F., & Torem, C. (2001). Using an activity schedule to smooth school transitions. *Journal of Positive Behavior Interventions, 3,* 57–61.

Drash, P. W., High, R. L., & Tudor, R. M. (1999). Using mand training to establish an echoic repertoire in young children with autism. *Analysis of Verbal Behavior, 16,* 29–44.

Dumas, J. E., Wolf, L. C., Fisman, S. N., & Culligan, A. (1991). Parenting stress, child behavior problems, and dysphoria in parents of children with autism, down syndrome, behavior disorders, and normal development. *Exceptionality: A Special Education Journal, 2*(2), 97–110. http://dx.doi.org/10.1080/09362839109524770.

Eaves, L. C., & Ho, H. H. (1996). Stability and change in cognitive and behavioral characteristics of autism through childhood. *Journal of Autism and Developmental Disabilities, 26,* 557–569.

Effective Health Care Program. (2014). Retrieved from: http://www.ahrq.gov/professionals/clinicians-providers/ehclibrary/index.html.

Eikeseth, S. (2009). Outcome of comprehensive psycho-educational interventions for young children with autism. *Research in Developmental Disabilities, 30*(1), 158–178. http://dx.doi.org/10.1016/j.ridd.2008.02.003.

Eldevik, S., Hastings, R. P., Hughes, J. C., Jahr, E., Eikeseth, S., & Cross, S. (2009). Meta-analysis of early intensive behavioral intervention for children with autism. *Journal of Clinical Child & Adolescent Psychology, 38*(3), 439–450. http://dx.doi.org/10.1080/15374410902851739.

Elsabbagh, M., Divan, G., Koh, Y., Kim, Y. S., Kauchali, S., Marcín, C., et al. (2012). Global prevalence of autism and other pervasive developmental disorders. *Autism Research, 5*(3), 160–173. http://dx.doi.org/10.1002/aur.239.

Feldman, M., McDonald, L., Serbin, L., Stack, D., Secco, M. L., & Yu, C. T. (2007). Predictors of depressive symptoms in primary caregivers of young children with or at risk for developmental delay. *Journal of Developmental Disability Research, 51*(8), 606–619.

Fisher, W. W., Lindauer, S. E., Alterson, C. J., & Thompson, R. H. (1998). Assessment and treatment of destructive behavior maintained by stereotypic object manipulation. *Journal of Applied Behavior Analysis, 31*(4), 315–527. http://dx.doi.org/10.1901/jaba.1998.31-513.

Fisher, W. W., Rodriguez, N. M., & Owen, T. M. (2013). Functional assessment and treatment of perseverative speech about restricted topics in an adolescent with Asperger syndrome. *Journal of Applied Behavior Analysis, 46*(1), 307–311. http://dx.doi.org/10.1002/jaba.19.

Flanagan, H. E., Perry, A., & Freeman, N. L. (2012). Effectiveness of large-scale community-based intensive behavioral intervention: A waitlist comparison study exploring outcomes and predictors. *Research in Autism Spectrum Disorders, 6*(2), 673–682. http://dx.doi.org/10.1016/j.rasd.2011.09.011.

Folstein, S., & Rutter, M. (1977). Infantile autism: A genetic study of 21 twin pairs. *Journal of Child Psychology and Psychiatry, 18*(4), 297–321. http://dx.doi.org/10.1111/j.1469-7610.1977.tb00443.x.

Freeman, B. J. (2011). Assessment of social skills in ASD: A user's guide. In M. Taubman, R. Leaf, & J. McEachin (Eds.), *Crafting connections: Contemporary applied behavior analysis for enriching the social lives of persons with autism spectrum disorder* (pp. 59–70). New York, NY: DRL Books Inc.

Frith, U. (1989). Explaining the enigma. *British Journal of Developmental Psychology, 21*(3), 465–468. http://dx.doi.org/10.1348/026151003322277801.

Gilliam, J. E. (2006). *Gilliam Autism Rating Scale*. Austin, TX: Pro-Ed.

Green, G. (1996). Early behavioral intervention for autism: What does research tell us? In C. Maurice, G. Green, & S. Luce (Eds.), *Behavioral intervention for young children with autism* (pp. 29–44). Austin, TX: PRO-ED.

Green, G., Brennan, L. C., & Fein, D. (2002). Intensive behavioral treatment for a toddler at high risk for autism. *Behavior Modification, 26*(1), 69–102. http://dx.doi.org/10.1177/0145445502026001005.

Harris, S. W., Hessl, D., Goodlin-Jones, B., Ferranti, J., Bacalman, S., Barbato, I., et al. (2008). Autism profiles of males with Fragile-X syndrome. *American Journal on Mental Retardation, 113*(6), 427–438.

Hénault, I. (2006). *Asperger's syndrome and sexuality: From adolescence through early adulthood.* Philadelphia, PA: Jessica Kingsley Publishers.

Hewett, F. M. (1965). Teaching speech to an autistic child through operant conditioning. *American Journal of Orthopsychiatry, 35*, 927–936.

Howard, J. S., Sparkman, C. R., Cohen, H. G., Green, G., & Stanislaw, H. (2005). A comparison of intensive behavior analytic and eclectic treatments for young children with autism. *Research in Developmental Disabilities, 26*, 359–383.

Howlin, P. (2005). Outcomes in autism spectrum disorders. In E. Volkmar, R. Paul, A. Klin, & D. Cohen (Eds.), *Diagnosis, development, neurobiology, and behavior: Vol. 1. Handbook of autism and pervasive developmental disorders* (3rd ed., pp. 201–220). Hoboken, NJ: John Wiley & Sons.

Howlin, P., Goode, S., Hutton, J., & Rutter, M. (2004). Adult outcomes for children with autism. *Journal of Child Psychology and Psychiatry, 45*(2), 212–229.

Howlin, P., Magiati, I., & Charman, T. (2009). Systematic review of early intensive behavioral interventions for children with autism. *American Journal on Intellectual and Developmental Disabilities, 114*(1), 23–41.

Jones, J., Lerman, D. C., & Laechago, S. (2014). Assessing stimulus control and promoting generalization via video modeling when teaching social responses to children with autism. *Journal of Applied Behavior Analysis, 47*, 37–50. http://dx.doi.org/10.1002/jaba.81.

Joseph, L., Thurm, A., Farmer, C., & Shumway, S. (2013). Repetitive behavior and restricted interests in young children with autism: Comparisons with controls and stability over two years. *Autism Research, 6*(6), 584–595. http://dx.doi.org/10.1002/aur.1316.

Kanner, L. (1943). Autistic disturbances in affective contact. *Nervous Child, 2*, 217–250.

Kanner, L. (1954). Discussion of Robinson and Vitale's paper on "Children with circumscribed interests" *American Journal of Orthopsychiatry, 24*, 764–766.

Kaufmann, W. E., Cortell, R., Kau, A. S. M., Bukelis, I., Tierney, E., Gray, R. M., et al. (2004). Autism spectrum disorder in fragile X syndrome: Communication, social interaction, and specific behaviors. *American Journal of American Genetics, 129A*(3), 225–234.

Kawamura, Y., Takahashi, O., & Ishii, T. (2008). Reevaluating the incidence of pervasive developmental disorders: Impact of elevated rates of detection through implementation of an integrated system of screening in Toyota, Japan. *Psychiatry and Clinical Neurosciences, 62*(2), 152–159. http://dx.doi.org/10.1111/j.1440-1819.2008.01748.x.

Kent, R. G., Carrington, S. J., Le Couteur, A., Gould, J., Wing, L., Maljaars, J., et al. (2013). Diagnosing autism spectrum disorder: Who will get a DSM-5 diagnosis? *Journal of Child Psychology and Psychiatry, 54*(11), 1242–1250. http://dx.doi.org/10.1111/jcpp.12085.

Kim, Y. S., Leventhal, B. L., Koh, Y. J., Fombonne, E., Laska, E., & Grinker, R. R. (2011). Prevalence of autism spectrum disorders in a total population sample. *American Journal of Psychiatry*, *168*, 904–912. http://dx.doi.org/10.1176/appi.ajp.2011.10101532.

Klinger, L. G., Dawson, G., & Renner, P. (2003). Autistic disorder. In E. J. Mash, & R. A. Barkley (Eds.), *Child psychopathology* (pp. 409–454). New York, NY: Guilford Press.

Klintwall, L., & Eikeseth, S. (2013). Early and intensive behavioral intervention (EIBI) in autism. In V. Patel, V. Preedy, & C. Martin (Eds.), *The comprehensive guide to autism* (pp. 117–137). New York: Springer-Science.

Kodak, T., & Grow, L. L. (2011). Behavioral treatment of autism. In W. W. Fisher, C. C. Piazza, & H. S. Roane (Eds.), *Handbook of applied behavior analysis* (pp. 402–416). New York, NY: Guilford Press.

Kodak, T., & Piazza, C. C. (2008). Assessment and behavioral treatment of feeding and sleeping disorders in children with autism spectrum disorders. *Child and Adolescent Psychiatric Clinics of North America*, *17*, 887–905.

Koegel, R. L., Dunlap, G., & Dyer, K. (1980). Intertrial interval duration and learning in autistic children. *Journal of Applied Behavior Analysis*, *13*, 91–99.

Kolevzon, A., Gross, R., & Reichenberg, A. (2007). Prenatal and perinatal risk factors for autism: A review and integration of findings. *Archives of Pediatrics and Adolescent Medicine*, *161*(4), 326–333. http://dx.doi.org/10.1001/archpedi.161.4.326.

Kulage, K. M., Smaldone, A. M., & Cohn, E. G. (2014). How will DSM-5 affect autism diagnosis? A systematic literature review and meta-analysis. *Journal of Autism and Developmental Disorders*. http://dx.doi.org/10.1007/s10803-01402065-2.

Lam, K. S. L., Bodfish, J. W., & Piven, J. (2008). Evidence for the three subtypes of repetitive behavior in autism that differ in familiarity and association with other symptoms. *Journal of Child Psychology and Psychiatry*, *49*(11), 1193–1200. http://dx.doi.org/10.1111/j.1469-7610.2008.01944.x.

Lane, H. (1976). *The wild boy of Aveyron*. Cambridge: Harvard University Press.

Laraway, S., Snycerski, S., Michael, J., & Poling, A. (2003). Motivating operations and terms to describe them: Some further refinements. *Journal of Applied Behavior Analysis*, *36*(3), 407–414.

Laugeson, E. A., Ellingsen, R., Sanderson, J., Tucci, L., & Bates, S. (2014). The ABC's of teaching social skills to adolescents with autism spectrum disorder in the classroom: The UCLA PEERS® Program. *Journal of Autism and Developmental Disorders*. http://dx.doi.org/10.1007/s10803-014-2108-8.

LeBlanc, L., Esch, J., Sidener, T. M., & Firth, A. M. (2006). Behavioral language interventions for children with autism: Comparing applied verbal behavior and naturalistic teaching approaches. *Analysis of Verbal Behavior*, *22*(1), 49–60.

Levy, A., & Perry, A. (2011). Outcomes in adolescents and adults with autism: A review of the literature. *Research in Autism Spectrum Disorders*, *5*(4), 1271–1282. http://dx.doi.org/10.1016/j.rasd.2011.01.023.

Lofholm, N. (2008, December 2). Autism's terrible toll: Parents risk hitting "a breaking point". *Denver Post*. Retrieved from: http://www.denverpost.com/search/ci_11116100.

Lord, C., & McGee, J. P. (Eds.), (2001a). *Educating children with autism*. Washington, DC: National Academy Press, Committee on Educational Interventions for Children with Autism, Division of Behavioral and Social Sciences and Education, National Research Council.

Lord, C., & McGee, J. P. (2001b). *Educating children with autism*. Washington, DC: National Academy Press.

Lord, C., Rutter, M., DiLavore, P. C., & Risi, S. (2001). *Autism diagnostic observation schedule*. Los Angeles: Western Psychological Services.

Lovaas, O. I. (1987). Behavioral treatment and normative educational and intellectual functioning in young autistic children. *Journal of Consulting and Clinical Psychology*, *55*, 3–9.

Lovaas, O. I., Ackerman, A., Alexander, D., Firestone, P., Perkins, M., & Newsome, C. (1981). *Teaching developmentally disabled children: The ME book.* Austin, TX: PRO-ED.

Lovaas, O. I., Freitag, G., Kinder, M. I., Rubenstein, B. D., Schaeffer, B., & Simmons, J. Q. (1966). Establishment of social reinforcers in two schizophrenic children on the basis of food. *Journal of Experimental Child Psychology, 4,* 109–125.

Lovaas, O. I., Koegel, R., Simmons, J. Q., & Long, J. S. (1973). Some generalization and follow-up measures on autistic children in behavior therapy. *Journal of Applied Behavior Analysis, 6*(1), 131–165. http://dx.doi.org/10.1901/jaba.1973.6-131.

Makrygianni, M. K., & Reed, P. (2010). A meta-analytic review of the effectiveness of behavioural early intervention programs for children with Autistic Spectrum Disorders. *Research in Autism Spectrum Disorders, 4*(1), 577–593. http://dx.doi.org/10.1016/j.rasd.2010.01.014.

Matson, J. L., Matson, M. L., & Rivet, T. T. (2007). Social-skills treatments for children with autism spectrum disorders. *Behavior Modification, 31,* 682–707.

Metz, J. R. (1965). Conditioning generalized imitation in autistic children. *Journal of Experimental Child Psychology, 2,* 389–399.

Mooney, E. L., Gray, K. M., Tonge, B. J., Sweeney, D. J., & Taffe, J. R. (2009). Factor analytic study of repetitive behaviours in young children with pervasive developmental disorders. *Journal of Autism and Developmental Disorders, 39,* 765–774. http://dx.doi.org/10.1007/s10803-008-0680-5.

National Autism Center. (2009). National Standards Report: The national standards project—addressing the need for evidence-based practice guidelines for autism spectrum disorders. Retrieved from: http://www.nationalautismcenter.org/pdf/NAC%20Standards%20Report.pdf.

Neef, N. A., Iwata, B. A., & Page, T. J. (1980). The effects of interspersal training versus high-density reinforcement on spelling acquisition and retention. *Journal of Applied Behavior Analysis, 13,* 153–158.

New York State Department of Health. (1999). *Clinical practice guideline: Report of the recommendations. Autism/pervasive developmental disorders, assessment and intervention for young children (age 0–3 years).* Publication No. 4215. Retrieved from: https://www.health.ny.gov/community/infants_children/early_intervention/disorders/autism/.

Pelphrey, K. A., & Carter, E. J. (2008). Brain mechanisms for social perception. *Annals of the New York Academy of Sciences, 1145,* 283–299. http://dx.doi.org/10.1196/annals.1416.007.

Peterson, K. M., Piazza, C. C., & Volkert, V. M. (submitted for publication). A comparison of the sequential-oral-sensory approach to an applied behavior analytic approach in the treatment of food selectivity in children with autism. *Journal of Applied Behavior Analysis.*

Piazza, C. C., Adelinis, J. D., Hanley, G. P., Goh, H., & Delia, M. D. (2000). An evaluation of the effects of matched stimuli on behaviors maintained by automatic reinforcement. *Journal of Applied Behavior Analysis, 33*(1), 13–27. http://dx.doi.org/10.1901/jaba.2000.33-13.

Piazza, C. C., Fisher, W. W., Brown, K. A., Shore, B. A., Patel, M. R., Katz, R. M., et al. (2003). Functional analysis of inappropriate mealtime behaviors. *Journal of Applied Behavior Analysis, 36*(2), 187–204. http://dx.doi.org/10.1901/jaba.2003.36-187.

Rapin, I. (2011). Autism turns 65: A neurologist's bird's eye view. In D. G. Amaral, G. Dawson, & D. H. Geschwind (Eds.), *Autism spectrum disorders.* New York, NY: Oxford.

Rapp, J. T., & Vollmer, T. R. (2005). Stereotypy I: A review of behavioral assessment and treatment. *Research in Developmental Disabilities, 26*(6), 527–547. http://dx.doi.org/10.1016/j.ridd.2004.11.005.

Rapp, J. T., Vollmer, T. V., Dozier, C. L., St. Peter, C., & Cotnoir, N. (2004). Analysis of response allocation in individuals with multiple forms of stereotyped behavior. *Journal of Applied Behavior Analysis, 37,* 481–501.

Reichow, B., & Volkmar, F. R. (2010). Social skills interventions for individuals with autism: Evaluation for evidence-based practices within a best evidence synthesis framework. *Journal of Autism and Developmental Disorders*, *40*(2), 149–166. http://dx.doi.org/10.1007/s10803-009-0842-0.

Reichow, B., & Wolery, M. (2009). Comprehensive synthesis of early intensive behavioral interventions for young children with autism based on the UCLA young autism project model. *Journal of Autism and Developmental Disorders*, *39*, 23–41. http://dx.doi.org/10.1007/s10803-008-0596-0.

Richler, J., Bishop, S. L., Kleinke, J. R., & Lord, C. (2007). Restricted and repetitive behaviors in young children with autism spectrum disorders. *Journal of Autism and Developmental Disorders*, *37*, 73–85. http://dx.doi.org/10.1007/s10803-006-0332.

Richler, J., Huerta, M., Bishop, S. L., & Lord, C. (2010). Developmental trajectories of restricted and repetitive behaviors and interests in children with autism spectrum disorders. *Development and Psychopathology*, *22*(1), 55–69. http://dx.doi.org/10.1017/S0954579409990265.

Rimland, B. (1964). *Infantile autism: The syndrome and its implications for a neural theory of behavior*. East Norwalk, CT: Appleton-Century-Crofts.

Rincover, A., Cook, R., Peoples, A., & Packard, D. (1979). Sensory extinction and sensory reinforcement principles for programming multiple adaptive behavior change. *Journal of Applied Behavior Analysis*, *12*(2), 221–233. http://dx.doi.org/10.1901/jaba.1979.12-221.

Robins, D. L., Fein, D., Barton, M. L., & Green, J. A. (2001). The modified checklist for autism in toddlers: An initial study investigating the early detection of autism and pervasive developmental disorders. *Journal of Autism and Developmental Disorders*, *31*, 131–144.

Rodriguez, N. M., Thompson, R. H., Schlichenmeyer, K., & Stocco, C. S. (2012). Functional analysis and treatment of arranging and ordering by individuals with an autism spectrum disorder. *Journal of Applied Behavior Analysis*, *45*(1), 1–22. http://dx.doi.org/10.1901/jaba.2012.45-1.

Rutter, M., Le Couteur, A., & Lord, C. (2003). *Autism Diagnostic Interview-Revised (ADI-R)*. Los Angeles, CA: Western Psychological Services.

Sallows, G. O., & Graupner, T. D. (2005). Intensive behavioral treatment for children with autism: Four-year outcome and predictors. *American Journal on Mental Retardation*, *110*(6), 417–438.

Sanua, V. D. (1990). Leo Kanner (1894–1981): The man and the scientist. *Child Psychiatry and Human Development*, *21*(1), 3–23.

Schopler, E., Van Bourgondien, M. E., Wellman, G. J., & Love, S. R. (2010). *The Childhood Autism Rating Scale (2nd ed.) (CARS2)* (2nd). Los Angeles, CA: Western Psychological Services.

Skinner, B. F. (1957). *Verbal behavior*. New York: Appleton Century Crofts.

Smith, T. (2001). Discrete trial training in the treatment of autism. *Focus on Autism and Other Developmental Disabilities*, *16*, 86–92.

Sparrow, S., Cicchetti, D., & Balla, D. (2005). *Vineland adaptive behavior scales* (2nd). Circle Pines, MI: AGS.

Spreckley, M., & Boyd, R. (2009). Efficacy of applied behavioral intervention in preschool children with autism for improving cognitive, language, and adaptive behavior: A systematic review and meta-analysis. *Journal of Pediatrics*, *154*(3), 338–344. http://dx.doi.org/10.1016/j.jpeds.2008.09.012.

Stanfield, A. C., McIntosh, A. M., Spencer, M. D., Philip, R., Gaurb, S., & Lawrie, S. M. (2008). Towards a neuroanatomy of autism: A systematic review and meta-analysis of structural magnetic resonance imaging studies. *European Psychiatry*, *23*(4), 289–299. http://dx.doi.org/10.1016/j.eurpsy.2007.05.006.

Stokes, M. A., & Kaur, A. (2005). High-functioning autism and sexuality: A parental perspective. *Autism*, *9*, 266–289.

Stone, W. L., Coonrod, E. E., & Ousley, O. Y. (2000). Brief report: Screening tool for autism in two-year-olds (STAT). Development and Preliminary Data. *Journal of Autism and Developmental Disorders*, *30*, 607–612.

Strain, P. S., & Bovey, E. H. (2011). Randomized, controlled trial of the LEAP Model of early intervention for young children with autism spectrum disorders. *Topics in Early Childhood Special Education*, *31*(3), 133–154. http://dx.doi.org/10.1177/0271121411408740.

Sundberg, M. L. (2008). *The Verbal Behavior Milestones Assessment and Placement Program: The VB-MAPP*. Concord, CA: AVP Press.

Sundberg, M. L., & Michael, J. (2001). The benefits of Skinner's analysis of verbal behavior for children with autism. *Behavior Modification*, *25*, 698–724.

Sundberg, M. L., & Partington, J. W. (1998). *The Assessment of Basic Language and Learning Skills (the ABLLS): An assessment, curriculum guide, and skills tracking system for children with autism or other developmental disabilities*. Pleasant Hill, CA: Behavior Analysts, Inc.

Taubman, M., Leaf, R., & McEachin, J. (2011). *Crafting connections: Contemporary applied behavior analysis for enriching the social lives of persons with autism spectrum disorder*. New York, NY: DRL Books Inc.

Thompson, T. (2013). Autism research and services for young children: History, progress, and challenges. *Journal of Applied Research in Intellectual Disabilities*, *26*(2), 81–107. http://dx.doi.org/10.1111/jar.12021.

Tullis, C. A., & Zangrillo, A. N. (2013). Sexuality education for adolescents and adults with autism spectrum disorders. *Psychology in the Schools*, *50*, 866–875.

Turner, M. (1999). Annotation: Repetitive behavior in autism: A review of psychological research. *Journal of Child Psychology and Psychiatry*, *40*(6), 839–849. http://dx.doi.org/10.1111/1469-7610.00502.

Virués-Ortega, J. (2010). Applied behavior analytic intervention for autism in early childhood: Meta-analysis, meta-regression, and dose–response meta-analysis of multiple outcomes. *Clinical Psychology Review*, *30*(4), 387–399. http://dx.doi.org/10.1016/j.cpr.2010.01.008.

Warren, Z., McPheeters, M. L., Sathe, N., Foss-Feig, J. H., Glasser, A., & Veenstra-VanderWeele, J. (2011). A systematic review of early intensive intervention for autism spectrum disorders. *Pediatrics*, *127*(5), 1303–1311. http://dx.doi.org/10.1542/peds.2011-0426.

Wass, S. (2011). Distortions and disconnections: Disrupted brain connectivity in autism. *Brain and Cognition*, *75*(10), 18–28.

White, S. W., Ollendick, T., Albano, A. M., Oswald, D., Johnson, C., & Scahill, L. (2013). Randomized controlled trial: Multimodal anxiety and social skill intervention for adolescents with autism spectrum disorder. *Journal of Autism and Developmental Disorders*, *43*(2), 382–394.

Wolf, M., Risley, T., & Mees, H. (1964). Application of operant conditioning procedures to the behavior problems of an autistic child. *Behaviour Research and Therapy*, *1*, 305–312.

CHAPTER 3

Treatment of Severe Behavior Disorders

Timothy R. Vollmer, Kerri P. Peters, Sarah K. Slocum
Psychology Department, University of Florida, Gainesville, Florida, USA

OVERVIEW: BEHAVIOR DISORDERS AS OPERANT BEHAVIOR

One overall aim of this book is to demonstrate that applied behavior analysis is an effective approach in a wide range of socially relevant domains. An argument could be made that the field has had its greatest influence in the assessment and treatment of behavior disorders displayed by individuals with autism spectrum disorder and intellectual disabilities. Indeed, behavior-analytic research and the principles derived from such research have influenced public policy (e.g., IDEA, 2004; NIH, 1989), scientific best practices (e.g., Odom et al., 2003), and educational standards (Sugai et al., 2000) in relation to the treatment of individuals who display severe behavior disorders.

For educators, care providers, family members, and the individuals themselves, severe behavior disorders can be, at a minimum, life inhibiting and, at the extremes, life threatening. Some general categories of behavior disorders include self-injurious behavior (SIB), aggression, property destruction, pica (eating inedible items), rumination (regurgitation and reswallowing previously consumed food), tantrums, and extreme stereotypy (highly repetitive and inflexible behavior), among others. Clearly, behavior that causes harm to one's self or others, or causes damage to property, is of great concern. A major breakthrough in understanding behavior disorders occurred in 1982 when Iwata, Dorsey, Slifer, Bauman, and Richman published a paper demonstrating an experimental approach to the assessment of SIB.

Iwata, Dorsey, Slifer, Bauman, and Richman's (1982/1994) study synthesized prior research suggesting that SIB and related disorders might be learned, operant forms of behavior. In a series of 15-min sessions, Iwata et al. tested possible sources of reinforcement for SIB including adult attention in the form of social reprimands (i.e., positive reinforcement), escape from instructional demands (i.e., negative reinforcement), and reinforcement produced by the behavior itself without social mediation (i.e., automatic positive or negative

Clinical and Organizational Applications of Applied Behavior Analysis
http://dx.doi.org/10.1016/B978-0-12-420249-8.00003-4

reinforcement). In Iwata et al. and hundreds of subsequent studies, such assessments, known as *functional analyses*, have shown that severe behavior disorders are sensitive to one or more of the aforementioned consequences as reinforcement (Hanley, Iwata, & McCord, 2003).

The experimental approach to behavioral assessment is important for at least three general reasons. (1) It has laid the groundwork for a vast literature base, clarifying through parsimonious logic why such seemingly counterintuitive behavior would persist. In short, the behavior continues to occur because it produces favorable consequences, at least in the short term, for the individual engaging in the behavior. (2) It has provided a screening method by which to identify appropriate subjects to address specific research questions. For example, it was previously not possible to investigate interventions for behavior maintained by negative reinforcement because, without a functional analysis, the operant function of behavior was unknown. To date, hundreds of studies have used particular functional-analysis outcomes as inclusion criteria to address specific research questions. (3) It has provided a method of clinical assessment that directly prescribes a treatment for the behavior disorder. For example, if a functional analysis shows that SIB is reinforced by adult attention, SIB could be placed on extinction (i.e., it would no longer produce attention) and some alternative behavior could be taught or strengthened via reinforcement in the form of attention.

This chapter, then, is based on the premise, supported by decades of research, that behavior disorders are learned forms of operant behavior. Many other chapters and reviews have covered the most basic forms of intervention derived from a functional analysis of behavior, including extinction, differential reinforcement, and noncontingent reinforcement (NCR). We will cover those treatments in this chapter as well, but we will also focus on some particularly challenging issues surrounding behavioral treatments in contemporary research and clinical application. For example, it is widely known that behavioral treatments work best when they include an extinction component (Fisher et al., 1993; Hagopian, Fisher, Sullivan, Acquisto, & LeBlanc, 1998; Patel, Piazza, Martinez, Volkert, & Christine, 2002; Shirley, Iwata, Kahng, Mazaleski, & Lerman, 1997). But, what if extinction is not possible for practical, legal, or ethical reasons (e.g., when blocking is required for attention–maintained behavior)? As another example, it is widely known that behavioral treatments involving reinforcement of alternative behavior using the reinforcer maintaining problem behavior will be effective in the long-term if the treatment is conducted with reasonable integrity (Vollmer & Iwata, 1992; Vollmer, Roane, Ringdahl, & Marcus,

1999). But, what if the behavior is so severe that it must be stopped immediately? What if the reinforcer for problem behavior is itself undesirable from
the teacher's or caregiver's perspective, such as leaving school for the day or
leaving classwork to watch videos on a computer? As a final example, it is
widely known that behavioral treatments based on a functional analysis are
highly effective for behavior maintained by socially mediated reinforcement.
But, what if the behavior produces its own source of reinforcement (i.e.,
automatic reinforcement)? Behavioral treatments are known to have some
influence on behavior maintained by automatic reinforcement, but there is
also evidence that such behavior remains a major challenge in intervention
research and practice (Rapp & Vollmer, 2005). In the process of describing
commonly used behavioral treatments for severe behavior disorders, we will
highlight several of these unique predicaments that emerge in the prescription of treatments based on a functional analysis.

TREATMENT OF SOCIALLY REINFORCED BEHAVIOR DISORDERS

Generally speaking, problem behavior maintained by social reinforcement is
relatively easier to treat compared to problem behavior maintained by automatic reinforcement. The reason for this is that, once identified via a functional analysis, the socially mediated reinforcer(s) can be withheld, delivered
contingent upon some alternative or other behavior, delivered independent
of the problem behavior, or some combination.

Extinction

As treatment for problem behavior, extinction involves withholding the
reinforcer that previously maintained problem behavior. For example, if
problem behavior is maintained by attention, extinction would involve
withholding any sort of attention following instances of problem behavior
(Iwata, Pace, Cowdery, & Miltenberger, 1994). If problem behavior is
maintained by other sorts of socially mediated positive reinforcement,
extinction would involve withholding the specific item(s) maintaining the
problem behavior. For example, if a child engages in severe tantrums
because in the past such tantrums have produced access to preferred toys,
extinction would involve withholding those toys when tantrums occur.
Extinction of problem behavior maintained by socially mediated negative
reinforcement takes a different form. If problem behavior is reinforced by
escape from an instructional activity, extinction involves continuation of
the instructional activity following instances of problem behavior (Iwata,

Pace, Kalsher, Cowdery, & Cataldo, 1990). This typically involves physical hand-over-hand guidance to complete an instruction.

At times, extinction presented in isolation (i.e., without an accompanying reinforcement procedure) can produce negative side effects. Although there is evidence that negative side effects are not as pervasive as once believed (Lerman, Iwata, & Wallace, 1999), they can include: (a) response bursting (i.e., behavior increasing in intensity, rate, or both before improving), (b) emotional behavior such as crying, (c) response variation that might include the emergence of other forms of problem behavior, and (d) spontaneous recovery (i.e., after a period away from extinction trials, the behavior resurfaces in a similar context), among others.

In addition to potential side effects, it is sometimes difficult or even impossible to implement extinction with high integrity. Some reasons for difficult implementation include (but are not limited to) the following: (a) large or fast individuals might be able to escape or avoid an instructional activity despite the best efforts of a parent, teacher, or therapist. (b) Some severe SIB and aggression cannot be allowed to occur for safety reasons, so it is impossible to "ignore" the behavior, and response blocking might serve as a source of reinforcement in the form of physical contact. (c) Well-trained individuals will occasionally make integrity errors. Even if someone implements extinction correctly on average 95% of the time (but accidently reinforces the behavior 5% of the time), this integrity lapse represents a variable ratio (VR) schedule of reinforcement which tends to make behavior exceptionally resistant to extinction (Ferster & Skinner, 1957).

As a result of the potential side effects, and as a result of some implementation problems associated with extinction, extinction is not usually recommended as a stand-alone treatment. Rather, it is more often a component of a larger treatment approach. One good example of that larger treatment approach is known as differential reinforcement.

Differential Reinforcement of Alternative Behavior

Differential reinforcement of alternative (DRA) behavior involves providing reinforcement for some specific response while minimizing (ideally, eliminating) reinforcement for problem behavior (Vollmer & Iwata, 1992). This means DRA is often implemented along with extinction as described above. One common example of DRA is functional communication training (FCT; Carr & Durand, 1985). In FCT, the specific alternative response is some type of verbal behavior (i.e., communication), often taking the form of vocalizations, augmentative devices, picture cards, sign language, or some combination.

Usually, the reinforcer in a DRA procedure is the reinforcer previously shown via a functional analysis to maintain problem behavior. For example, a person who exhibits attention-maintained problem behavior would receive attention when the alternative response occurs but not when the problem behavior occurs. At times, this arrangement yields a very high rate of the alternative response, which in itself can become problematic. For example, a child might begin to ask for attention more frequently than a parent or teacher is willing or able to give attention. Similarly, a student might ask for a break before any work has been completed (Marcus & Vollmer, 1995). One way to address this problem is to provide signals to indicate when the reinforcer is or is not available (Hanley, Iwata, & Thompson, 2001).

Because it might not be feasible or desired for the teacher or caregiver to provide a reinforcer immediately and following every response, it is advisable to thin the schedule of reinforcement to a more practical goal (Hanley et al., 2001). In addition, the appropriate alternative response might not only occur at an undesirable frequency, but also occur at inappropriate times. For example, a student could begin to repeatedly recruit attention during quiet reading time or while the teacher is attending to another student. Responding during periods in which reinforcement is not readily available might weaken the contingency and possibly would result in extinction or weakening of the newly acquired response. In some cases, a teacher or caregiver might intermittently reinforce the alternative responses during these periods; this outcome could result in strengthening that response during undesirable times.

Several methods for thinning a DRA schedule of reinforcement have been evaluated and include increasing the delay to reinforcement (Hagopian, Contrucci-Kuhn, Long, & Rush, 2005) and delivering reinforcers on an initially dense and progressively leaner fixed-interval schedule of reinforcement (Hanley et al., 2001). Both methods of thinning can result in undesirable responding during periods in which reinforcement is not available and might result in inadvertently weakening the alternative response. Hanley et al. presented a solution with adults with developmental disabilities that involved alternating between signaled periods of continuous reinforcement and extinction for the appropriate alternative response, specifically mands (requests) for attention. This specific schedule of reinforcement is known as a multiple schedule. In a multiple schedule, there are two alternating schedules of reinforcement (in the case of Hanley et al., the alternating schedules were reinforcement and extinction), and each schedule is associated with a specific stimulus. A multiple schedule provides a means of maintaining the newly acquired appropriate response while also implementing periods in which the reinforcer is unavailable, thus making the DRA procedure more practical (Hanley et al., 2001; Tiger & Hanley, 2004).

When implementing a multiple schedule, the delivery of rules describing the schedule-specific stimuli, at the beginning of each session, results in more discriminated responding compared to a multiple schedule without rules (Tiger & Hanley, 2004). Multiple schedules have been demonstrated to be effective at a class-wide level as well (Cammilleri, Tiger, & Hanley, 2008). Cammilleri et al. evaluated the effectiveness of multiple schedules in the classroom and were able to maintain approaches for teacher attention during desirable periods and minimize approaches during undesirable periods even with somewhat low levels of treatment integrity during the reinforcement conditions (i.e., classroom treatment integrity averaged between 51% and 61%). In addition, Tiger and Hanley (2006) found that children preferred conditions with signaled availability and unavailability of reinforcement in comparison to conditions in which the signals were absent or unclear, and Luczynski and Hanley (2009) found that children preferred a multiple schedule of reinforcement to a briefly signaled delay to reinforcement, such as "wait please."

Because DRA ideally involves an extinction component, some of the practical issues surrounding the implementation of extinction surface when using DRA. For example, it is possible that the therapist is not strong or fast enough to physically guide compliance as treatment for escape behavior. It is also possible that attention-maintained problem behavior requires physical attention to protect the individual or others in the environment. In these cases, though not ideal, DRA can be arranged such that the reinforcer(s) for appropriate behavior outweigh the reinforcer(s) for problem behavior along one or more dimensions, with no true extinction component in place (Athens & Vollmer, 2010). For example, even if an attention-maintained problem behavior must be blocked (i.e., attended to), the appropriate alternative could be reinforced more frequently, with a shorter delay, with higher-quality attention (e.g., verbal and physical attention), with a greater duration of attention, or some combination. DRA involves providing the reinforcer contingent on some specific alternative response while minimizing reinforcement for an undesired response. This is one variation of the larger treatment approach of differential reinforcement, a second variation is known as differential reinforcement of other behaviors (DRO).

Differential Reinforcement of Other Behaviors

DRO involves the delivery of reinforcers contingent on the omission of the target behavior. Typically, the reinforcer maintaining problem behavior (as identified via a functional analysis) is the reinforcer presented contingent on the nonoccurrence of problem behavior for some specified interval of time. Further, as with the DRA procedure discussed previously, extinction is often embedded into this procedure such that while appropriate behavior results in the functional reinforcer, problem behavior does not. There are numerous variations of DRO that have been discussed elsewhere (e.g., Vollmer & Iwata, 1992). In short, these variations include but are not limited to a resetting DRO, a whole-interval DRO, and a momentary DRO (mDRO).

In a resetting DRO, a reinforcer is delivered after a period of time during which no target behavior has occurred, and any occurrence of the target behavior resets the interval. For example, in a 5-min resetting DRO, if the target behavior occurs 3 min into the interval, the interval would reset, and the individual would need to refrain from engaging in the target behavior for 5 new minutes to obtain the reinforcer (e.g., Repp & Deitz, 1974).

In a whole-interval DRO, a reinforcer is delivered after a period of time in which no target behavior has occurred, and any occurrence of the target behavior results in a loss of opportunity to obtain a reinforcer for that specific interval of time. For example, in a 5-min whole-interval DRO, if a target behavior occurs 3 min into the interval, the interval continues to time out at 5 min, but no reinforcer is delivered at the end of that 5-min interval. It would not be until the end of the next scheduled 5-min interval that a reinforcer becomes available (pending nonoccurrence of the target behavior throughout that ensuing 5-min interval; Repp, Barton, & Brulle, 1983).

In a mDRO, a reinforcer is delivered if the target behavior does not occur at the very "moment" of a scheduled reinforcer delivery. In a 5-min mDRO, early instances of the target behavior have no effect on reinforcer delivery. If the target behavior is not occurring at the end of the interval (i.e., at the 5-min mark), the reinforcer is delivered. If the target behavior is occurring at the end of the interval (i.e., at the 5-min mark), the reinforcer is not delivered. In some variations of mDRO, the timer resets to some relatively small value such as 10 or 15 s to ensure that the behavior and reinforcer are not contiguous (e.g., Britton, Carr, Kellum, Dozier, & Weil, 2000; Hagopian, Crockett, van Stone, DeLeon, & Bowman, 2000). In other variations of mDRO, the reinforcer does not become available again until the next scheduled delivery (so, in a 5-min mDRO, it would be 5 min later).

In recent years, DRA applications tend to be more prevalent than DRO applications. There are several possible reasons for this. (1) DRA teaches a specific alternative response, whereas DRO does not. (2) DRA is relatively insensitive to integrity failures (St. Peter Pipkin, Vollmer, & Sloman, 2010). Yet, any error of commission in DRO (i.e., delivering the reinforcer when the behavior has, in fact, occurred) changes the schedule from DRO to a VR schedule of reinforcement for the target behavior. (3) If schedules based on time intervals are preferred over DRA for some reason, time-based schedules such as NCR seem to be easier to implement than DRO (Vollmer, Iwata, Zarcone, Smith, & Mazaleski, 1993), have similar effects as DRO, and can be used readily in conjunction with DRA (Goh, Iwata, & DeLeon, 2000; Marcus & Vollmer, 1996). The selection of NCR over DRO further reduces the relative usage of DRO in comparison to DRA.

Noncontingent Reinforcement

NCR-based treatments involve the delivery of reinforcers on a time-based schedule such as a fixed-time or variable-time schedule, independent of the occurrence of target behavior (Vollmer & Sloman, 2005). Typically, the reinforcer maintaining problem behavior (as identified via a functional analysis) is the reinforcer presented in NCR. This arrangement is designed to reduce motivation to engage in problem behavior (i.e., the reinforcer is made available freely and frequently) and also to disrupt the contingency between problem behavior and the functional reinforcer (i.e., the problem behavior no longer results in contingent reinforcement). Dozens of studies have shown the efficacy of NCR as treatment for behavior maintained by positive reinforcement (e.g., Hagopian, Fisher, & Legacy, 1994; Vollmer et al., 1993) and by negative reinforcement (e.g., Vollmer, Marcus, & Ringdahl, 1995).

One concern with NCR is that, because the reinforcer delivery is strictly time-based, it is possible that the delivery of the reinforcer will occur in close proximity with the occurrence of the target behavior, and hence, the target behavior will be accidentally reinforced. However, this effect has been reported rarely in the literature (but see Vollmer, Ringdahl, Roane, & Marcus, 1997, for an exception) and, if accidental reinforcement occurs, a fairly simple solution is to add an omission contingency using mDRO as described previously. That is, the reinforcer would be delivered on some schedule independent of problem behavior with the exception that if problem behavior is occurring at the exact time a scheduled reinforcer is to be delivered, the reinforcer is withheld until the next scheduled reinforcer. A second concern related to NCR-based treatment is that NCR by itself does not strengthen specific alternative skills. However, most behavior analysts would agree that NCR should not be used in isolation. Rather, it should be "superimposed" on an individual's daily schedule in which all sorts of appropriate skills and alternative behaviors produce reinforcement.

Punishment

As discussed above, behavior maintained by social reinforcers is typically treated with reinforcement-based procedures, such as DRA, DRO, and NCR. That being said, these procedures do not always produce clinically acceptable reductions in problem behavior (Grace, Kahng, & Fisher, 1994; Hagopian et al., 1998; Wacker et al., 1990) or do not reduce behavior rapidly enough (Dura, 1991; see also Iwata et al., 1990; Vollmer & Iwata, 1993). Another method to treat socially reinforced behavior disorders is through the use of punishment procedures. Similar to reinforcement procedures, punishment procedures of this sort should be functionally based. Without knowledge of the behavioral function, procedures intended to punish behavior can be ineffective or, worse, counter-therapeutic.

Consider common punishment procedures such as timeout, contingent demands (sometimes called contingent effort or overcorrection), and response cost. Problem behavior maintained by negative reinforcement probably will not decrease if timeout is the selected punishment procedure. If, contingent on problem behavior, the individual is removed from the current environment, one might actually see a reinforcement effect. Instead, a more effective punishment procedure might be contingent demands (Fischer & Nehs, 1978; Fisher et al., 1993) or overcorrection (Foxx & Azrin, 1972). In these procedures, contingent on problem behavior, an individual would be required to complete demands. For an individual who finds the presentation of demands aversive, these procedures should result in a decreased likelihood of problem behavior in the future.

Now, consider behavior maintained by social-positive reinforcement in the form of attention. Providing contingent demands when problem behavior occurs might be counter-therapeutic. The presentation of those demands might serve as a reinforcer (i.e., presenting demands coincides with the presentation of attention). The result would be an increase in problem behavior. Instead, timeout from positive reinforcement or attention might be effective at reducing the problem behavior (Hagopian et al., 1998; Kazdin, 1980).

Finally, for behavior maintained by positive reinforcement in the form of tangible items, one might select response cost as a punishment procedure (Pietras, Brandt, & Searcy, 2010). In this procedure, a preferred item is removed for some period of time contingent on problem behavior. If that item is preferred and access to that item is the functional reinforcer, this punishment procedure should be effective at reducing the likelihood of problem behavior in the future.

EMERGENCY TREATMENTS FOR SOCIALLY REINFORCED BEHAVIOR

There are cases in which problem behavior is so severe that it cannot be allowed to occur at all, or at least its occurrence must be minimized as quickly as possible. In decades past, such severe behavior was likely treated with some type of arbitrary punishment procedure to obtain a rapid cessation of the behavior. More recently, knowledge of behavioral function can suggest the use of particular treatments to immediately reduce the occurrence of behavior without the necessity of relying on punishment procedures.

Elimination of the Establishing Operation

In the case of an emergency, it is possible to completely eliminate the establishing operation(s) related to the problem behavior to produce an immediate suppression of the behavior. For example, if problem behavior is maintained by attention, the individual could receive free attention throughout the day. The eventual goal would be to thin the schedule of attention. However, to deal with the behavioral emergency, it is possible that the initial schedule of attention could be continuous. Evidence for this approach can be seen in NCR studies in which behavior is suppressed immediately and substantially when the initial schedule is rich or continuous (e.g., Vollmer et al., 1993, 1998). An argument against this approach might relate to resources (e.g., not enough personnel to provide continuous attention); however, the assumption of this emergency approach is that the target behavior requires continuous or nearly continuous attention to block the behavior or to protect others in the environment, and possibly from more than one adult, so there may be no net increased time expenditure.

Analogously, if the problem behavior is reinforced by access to tangible items, the individual could be given continuous access to the item(s) to immediately suppress dangerous behavior. A clear case of this approach was demonstrated in Vollmer et al. (1997). When a girl who was referred for the treatment of severe aggression was given continuous access to magazines (which she would hold, clutch, and sometimes leaf through), she displayed zero instances of aggression.

Similarly, if behavior is reinforced by escape from an instructional activity, all instructional activities can be stopped. Evidence for this approach can be seen at the beginning of interventions using continuous noncontingent escape (e.g., Vollmer et al., 1995) or instructional fading (e.g., Zarcone et al., 1993). Of course, this approach might be contested in educational settings because instructional activity is initially terminated. However, the disruption to educational activities must be balanced against the need to stop extremely dangerous behavior immediately. Educational or other normal activities can then gradually be reinstituted.

Instructional Fading

Behavior maintained by negative reinforcement occurs in the presence of an aversive stimulus. As implied above, the emergency procedure for this type of behavior would be to stop presenting that aversive stimulus. If the aversive stimulus is an instructional activity, no instructional demands would be given initially. Contingent on low levels of problem behavior, demands would be slowly and systematically introduced (Pace, Iwata, Cowdery, Andree, & McIntyre, 1993; Zarcone et al., 1993). This procedure is known commonly as instructional or demand fading. Instructional demands can be introduced along the dimension of frequency (e.g., Pace et al., 1993), difficulty (Mace et al., 1988), or duration of instructional sessions (Smith, Iwata, Goh, & Shore, 1995).

DRA with Socially Unacceptable Sources of Reinforcement

At times, behavior occurs because it is intermittently reinforced by access to reinforcers that normally would be considered unacceptable to provide to the individual. For example, a student might engage in severe behavior because he or she is sent home from school (i.e., escape from school and access to whatever preferred items or people might be found in the home environment). Using the logic of DRA, it might seem counterintuitive to provide such reinforcers contingent on appropriate requests. For example, most school personnel would likely balk at a suggestion to honor a student's request (using a communication board, for instance) to "go home now." However, the administrative choice actually reduces to the following: the student could either go home by asking calmly or go home by engaging in extremely dangerous behavior. In emergency cases, it might be recommended to teach and honor the appropriate request, and subsequently use stimulus–control procedures such as those described previously using multiple schedules to gradually increase intervals of time in which the individual is in school. Similar procedures could be used when an alternative behavior occurs frequently to gain access to food or other items that would not be appropriate to deliver throughout the day.

An interesting finding in the behavioral treatment literature is that at times escape behavior can be suppressed by using food reinforcers during instructional activity (e.g., Lalli et al., 1999; Lomas, Fisher, & Kelley, 2010; Piazza et al., 1997). Evidence supporting this approach as an emergency procedure can be seen at the beginning of these treatment studies where response rates are typically very low. Again, many educators are likely to balk at the idea of using food reinforcers throughout the day. However, food reinforcers should be considered a viable option in the case of emergencies wherein behavioral suppression is needed immediately. Again, schedules of food reinforcement can be thinned via use of ratio or interval schedules (Lalli et al., 1999), with an aim toward a more natural academic experience.

TREATMENT OF AUTOMATICALLY REINFORCED BEHAVIOR DISORDERS

The prognosis for the treatment of behavior maintained by automatic reinforcement is usually not as favorable as the treatment for behavior maintained by social reinforcement. It is often difficult to identify the specific reinforcers maintaining this type of behavior, and, even when the reinforcers are identified, it is difficult to withhold them or present them contingent on some alternative behavior. In this section we will revisit some of the previously discussed treatments while incorporating a discussion of why these approaches might be limited as interventions for behavior maintained by automatic reinforcement.

Extinction

In cases in which behavior is maintained by social reinforcement, extinction of that behavior would consist of withholding access to the socially mediated reinforcer. For problem behavior maintained by adult attention, for example, adults are taught to withhold attention when the behavior occurs. In the case of behavior maintained by automatic reinforcement, extinction can be more difficult because the behavior produces its own reinforcement. The so-called "sensory extinction" approach involves eliminating access to the putative reinforcer by eliminating the stimulation produced by the behavior (Rincover, 1978; Rincover, Cook, Peoples, & Packard, 1979). With sensory extinction, the individual is still able to engage in the target behavior, but the stimulation produced by the problem behavior is discontinued. For example, auditory sensation can be discontinued with headphones, and the sensory stimulation produced by head hitting can be discontinued with the use of a helmet. Sensory extinction is presumed to be effective in reducing problem behavior by breaking the contingency between the behavior and the putative reinforcer (Rapp & Vollmer, 2005; Vollmer, 1994). However, it is also possible that the procedures are effective due to punishment (Mazaleski, Iwata, Rodgers, Vollmer, & Zarcone, 1994). For example, the stimulation produced by hitting a helmet might be painful or otherwise aversive. Thus, not only is the reinforcer discontinued, but the aversive stimulation now functions as a punishing stimulus. Response blocking is another method to treat behavior maintained by automatic reinforcement (Lerman & Iwata, 1996; Smith, Russo, & Le, 1999). Response blocking involves physically interrupting the behavior and preventing it from occurring, thus preventing the stimulation associated with that behavior. Like protective equipment, blocking can function in some cases as extinction (Smith et al., 1999) or punishment (Lerman & Iwata, 1996).

Differential Reinforcement

Differential reinforcement as treatment for behavior maintained by automatic reinforcement involves reinforcing either some explicit alternative response (such as toy play) in a DRA arrangement or reinforcing periods of time without the target response in a DRO arrangement. Although an extinction component is sometimes difficult to include for socially reinforced behavior, extinction is especially difficult to include for behavior maintained by automatic reinforcement. This difficulty arises when the specific reinforcer has not been identified or when eliminating the reinforcer is difficult because the behavior itself produces the reinforcement.

Thus, differential-reinforcement procedures for behavior maintained by automatic reinforcement often rely on the reinforcers used in treatment to "override" the reinforcers maintaining problem behavior. It becomes especially important, then, to conduct stimulus preference assessments (e.g., DeLeon & Iwata, 1996; Fisher et al., 1992; Roane, Vollmer, Ringdahl, & Marcus, 1998) and to attempt some form of extinction. In addition, the use of varied reinforcers can be useful to avoid satiation (e.g., Vollmer, Marcus, & LeBlanc, 1994).

Environmental Enrichment

There is a great deal of research suggesting that environmental enrichment (EE), or noncontingent access to preferred stimuli, can be effective in reducing problem behavior maintained by automatic reinforcement. EE might be effective because a continuous competing source of reinforcement is provided (Horner, 1980). The research on EE related to automatic reinforcement has evaluated the effects of highly preferred versus less-preferred stimuli (Vollmer et al., 1994) as well as stimuli with sensory consequences matched to that of the consequences hypothesized to maintain the problem behavior versus stimuli with unmatched sensory consequences (Favell, McGimsey, & Schell, 1982; Piazza, Adelinis, Hanley, Goh, & Delia, 2000). Assessing the preference of the alternative stimuli prior to implementing the EE procedure and providing access to items identified as highly preferred likely will produce greater treatment effects compared to less-preferred items (Ahearn, Clark, DeBar, & Florentine, 2005).

EMERGENCY TREATMENTS FOR AUTOMATICALLY REINFORCED BEHAVIOR

When a functional analysis shows that problem behavior is automatically reinforced and the behavior is particularly dangerous, behavior analysts find themselves in one of the most difficult situations. At the least, socially reinforced behavior can often be reduced by manipulating the establishing operation(s). It is possible that dangerous behavior maintained by automatic reinforcement is not receptive to standard treatments. When that happens, there is little choice but to: (a) seek medical consultation to rule out physical problems contributing to the behavior, (b) block or prevent the behavior or dangerous outcomes of the behavior to the greatest extent possible, (c) further increase resources to ensure EE, or (d) implement punishment procedures. These approaches are discussed briefly here.

Medical Consultation

In most cases, before beginning a functional analysis, a behavior analyst would attempt to rule out medical variables. A concern about possible medical variables becomes even more salient when a functional analysis shows that problem behavior is maintained by automatic reinforcement. If the behavior is maintained by automatic negative reinforcement, it is possible that there is some physical irritant (e.g., skin allergy associated with skin scratching) or pain (e.g., ear infection) that is momentarily attenuated by the behavior (Cataldo & Harris, 1982). Thus, one emergency procedure is to request a full physical examination when dangerous behavior persists, particularly SIB maintained by automatic reinforcement.

Blocking or Preventing

As mentioned previously, it is possible that all instances of dangerous behavior must be blocked or prevented through some sort of mechanical or physical restraint. Blocking requires a great deal of resources because someone needs to be available at all times. Restraint requires extensive training, monitoring, and approvals (Vollmer et al., 2011). Despite these limitations, in an emergency situation, prevention of the behavior sometimes must occur and in each situation one must measure the ethical considerations of restraint against those that arise from the ongoing occurrence of dangerous behavior.

Continuous EE

The same general emergency approach described under "treatment of socially reinforced problem behavior" applies to behavior maintained by automatic reinforcement. In short, the notion is to provide as many alternative sources of reinforcement as possible to compete with the problem behavior. Any time the individual spends interacting with items is presumably time they are not engaging in the problem behavior.

Punishment

When a functional analysis has shown that behavior is not socially reinforced, and the behavior has persisted in the face of NCR, differential reinforcement, attempted extinction, medical intervention, and continuous EE, there might be a need for emergency procedures involving punishment. Punishment can take forms that are relatively innocuous. For example, the previously discussed use of protective equipment and response blocking might function as punishment (e.g., Mazaleski et al., 1994). Other procedures that have been used include overcorrection (Peters & Thompson, 2013) and body holds (Favell, McGimsey, & Jones, 1978). Some procedures that have been used in the past, including noxious taste (Sajwag, Libet, & Agras, 1974), noxious odor (Singh, Dawson, & Gregory, 1980), contingent shock (e.g., Linscheid, Iwata, Ricketts, Williams, & Griffin, 1990), and water misting (Dorsey, Iwata, Ong, & McSween, 1980), are considered controversial and usually would require extensive peer review, consent, and institutional approvals. In fact, to be safe, behavior analysts should solicit formal or informal peer review for any use of punishment procedures (Bailey & Burch, 2011). It is important to recognize that the behavior is being punished, in a technical sense. The individual is not being "punished" for engaging in the behavior. Although the technical and lay terms are the same, their meaning and implications are disparate.

CONCLUSIONS

Understanding the notion that severe behavior disorders are learned, operant forms of behavior provides a framework for decision-making in the development of behavioral interventions. The prognosis for effective treatment is generally good when the behavior is socially reinforced. In such cases, the reinforcer(s) maintaining problem behavior can be withheld contingent on problem behavior and presented contingent on some alternative, adaptive behavior. Interventions become a bit more complex when there is a need to immediately stop the behavior. In this chapter, we have referred to interventions designed to immediately stop the behavior as "emergency" procedures. By understanding the operant mechanisms supporting the behavior, it is possible to stop socially reinforced behavior without the use of punishment. This represents a significant advance in the field over the past several decades.

The complexity of intervention is often increased when the functional analysis shows that behavior is maintained by automatic reinforcement. In these cases, the therapist does not have direct control over the delivery of the reinforcer(s). In fact, at times, the specific form of the reinforcer is difficult to ascertain. The principles of extinction and differential reinforcement still apply in the case of automatic reinforcement, but they are more difficult to implement effectively. Behavior maintained by automatic reinforcement becomes an even greater challenge when the behavior is so dangerous it must be stopped immediately. In such cases, medical evaluations, response blocking, and protective equipment might enter into consideration as treatment components. The use of arbitrary aversive stimuli as punishers was posed as a last resort that should only be used under the umbrella of the standard ethical guidelines for behavior analysts.

ACKNOWLEDGMENT

A portion of this work was conducted with support from the Autism Speaks' Dennis Weatherstone Predoctoral Fellowship, #9166, PI: Sarah Slocum.

REFERENCES

Ahearn, W. H., Clark, K. M., DeBar, R., & Florentine, C. (2005). On the role of preference in response competition. *Journal of Applied Behavior Analysis, 38,* 247–250. http://dx.doi.org/10.1091.jaba/2005.36-04.

Athens, E. S., & Vollmer, T. R. (2010). An investigation of differential reinforcement of alternative behavior without extinction. *Journal of Applied Behavior Analysis, 43,* 569–589. http://dx.doi.org/10.901/jaba.2010.43-569.

Bailey, J., & Burch, M. (2011). *Ethics for behavior analysts: 2nd expanded edition.* New York, NY: Routledge.

Britton, L. N., Carr, J. E., Kellum, K. K., Dozier, C. L., & Weil, T. M. (2000). A variation of noncontingent reinforcement in the treatment of aberrant behavior. *Research in Developmental Disabilities, 21,* 425–435. http://dx.doi.org/10.1016/S0891-4222(00)00056-1.

Cammilleri, A. P., Tiger, J. H., & Hanley, G. P. (2008). Developing stimulus control of young children's requests to teachers: Classwide applications of multiple schedules. *Journal of Applied Behavior Analysis, 41,* 299–303. http://dx.doi.org/10.1901/jaba.2008.41-299.

Carr, E. G., & Durand, V. M. (1985). Reducing behavior problems through functional communication training. *Journal of Applied Behavior Analysis, 18,* 111–126. http://dx.doi.org/10.1901/jaba.1985.18-111.

Cataldo, M. F., & Harris, J. (1982). The biological basis for self-injury in the mentally retarded. *Analysis and Intervention in Developmental Disabilities, 2,* 21–39. http://dx.doi.org/10.1016/0270-4684(82)90004-0.

DeLeon, I. G., & Iwata, B. A. (1996). Evaluation of a multiple-stimulus presentation format for assessing reinforcer preferences. *Journal of Applied Behavior Analysis, 29,* 519–533. http://dx.doi.org/10.1901/jaba.1996.29-519.

Dorsey, M. F., Iwata, B. A., Ong, P., & McSween, T. E. (1980). Treatment of self-injurious behavior using a water mist: Initial response suppression and generalization. *Journal of Applied Behavior Analysis, 13,* 343–353. http://dx.doi.org/10.1901/jaba.1980.13-343.

Dura, J. R. (1991). Controlling extremely dangerous aggressive outbursts when functional analysis fails. *Psychological Reports, 69,* 451–459. http://dx.doi.org/10.2466/pr0.1991.69.2.451.

Favell, J. E., McGimsey, J. F., & Jones, M. L. (1978). The use of physical restraint in the treatment of self-injury and as positive reinforcement. *Journal of Applied Behavior Analysis, 11,* 225–241. http://dx.doi.org/10.1901/jaba.1978.11-225.

Favell, J. E., McGimsey, J. F., & Schell, R. M. (1982). Treatment of self-injury by providing alternate sensory activities. *Analysis and Intervention in Developmental Disabilities, 2,* 83–104. http://dx.doi.org/10.1016/0270-4684(82)90007-6.

Ferster, C. B., & Skinner, B. F. (1957). *Schedules of reinforcement.* New York: Appleton-Century-Crofts.

Fischer, J., & Nehs, R. (1978). Use of a commonly available chore as contingent punishment to reduce a boy's rate of swearing. *Journal of Behavior Therapy and Experimental Psychiatry, 9,* 81–83. http://dx.doi.org/10.1016/0005-7916(78)90096-4.

Fisher, W., Piazza, C. C., Bowman, L. G., Hagopian, L. P., Owens, J. C., & Sleven, I. (1992). A comparison of two approaches for identifying reinforcers for persons with severe and profound disabilities. *Journal of Applied Behavior Analysis, 25,* 491–498. http://dx.doi.org/10.1901/jaba.1992.25-491.

Fisher, W., Piazza, C., Cataldo, M., Harrell, R., Jefferson, G., & Conner, R. (1993). Functional communication training with and without extinction and punishment. *Journal of Applied Behavior Analysis, 26,* 23–36. http://dx.doi.org/10.1901/jaba.1993.26.26-23.

Foxx, R. M., & Azrin, N. H. (1972). Restitution: A method of eliminating aggressive-disruptive behavior of retarded and brain damaged patients. *Behaviour Research and Therapy, 10,* 15–27. http://dx.doi.org/10.1016/0005-7967(72)90003-4.

Goh, H. L., Iwata, B. A., & DeLeon, I. G. (2000). Competition between noncontingent and contingent reinforcement schedules during response acquisition. *Journal of Applied Behavior Analysis, 33,* 195–205. http://dx.doi.org/10.1901/jaba.2000.33-195.

Grace, N. C., Kahng, S. W., & Fisher, W. W. (1994). Balancing social acceptability with treatment effectiveness of an intrusive procedure: A case report. *Journal of Applied Behavior Analysis, 27*, 171–172. http://dx.doi.org/10.1901/jaba.1994.27-171.

Hagopian, L. P., Contrucci-Kuhn, S. A., Long, E. S., & Rush, K. S. (2005). Schedule thinning following communication training: Using competing stimuli to enhance tolerance to decrements in reinforcer density. *Journal of Applied Behavior Analysis, 38*, 177–193. http://dx.doi.org/10.1901/jaba.2005.43-04.

Hagopian, L. P., Crockett, J. L., van Stone, M., DeLeon, I. G., & Bowman, L. G. (2000). Effects of noncontingent reinforcement on problem behavior and stimulus engagement: The role of satiation, extinction, and alternative reinforcement. *Journal of Applied Behavior Analysis, 33*, 433–449. http://dx.doi.org/10.1901/jaba.2000.33-433.

Hagopian, L. P., Fisher, W. W., & Legacy, S. M. (1994). Schedule effects of noncontingent reinforcement on attention-maintained destructive behavior in identical quadruplets. *Journal of Applied Behavior Analysis, 27*, 317–325. http://dx.doi.org/10.1901/jaba.1994.27-317.

Hagopian, L. P., Fisher, W. W., Sullivan, M. T., Acquisto, J., & LeBlanc, L. A. (1998). Effectiveness of functional communication training with and without extinction and punishment: A summary of 21 inpatient cases. *Journal of Applied Behavior Analysis, 31*, 211–235. http://dx.doi.org/10.1901/jaba.1998.31-211.

Hanley, G. P., Iwata, B. A., & McCord, B. E. (2003). Functional analysis of problem behavior: A review. *Journal of Applied Behavior Analysis, 36*, 147–185. http://dx.doi.org/10.1901/jaba.2003.36-147.

Hanley, G. P., Iwata, B. A., & Thompson, R. H. (2001). Reinforcement schedule thinning following treatment with functional communication training. *Journal of Applied Behavior Analysis, 34*, 17–38. http://dx.doi.org/10.1901/jaba.2001.34-17.

Horner, R. D. (1980). The effects of an environmental "enrichment" program on the behavior of institutionalized profoundly retarded children. *Journal of Applied Behavior Analysis, 13*, 473–491. http://dx.doi.org/10.1901/jaba.1980.13-473.

Individuals with Disabilities Education Act. (2004). 20 U.S.C. § 1400.

Iwata, B. A., Dorsey, M. F., Slifer, K. J., Bauman, K. E., & Richman, G. S. (1982/1994). Toward a functional analysis of self injury. *Journal of Applied Behavior Analysis, 27*, 197–209. http://dx.doi.org/10.1901/jaba.1994.27-197.

Iwata, B. A., Pace, G. M., Cowdery, E., & Miltenberger, R. G. (1994). What makes extinction work: An analysis of procedural form and function. *Journal of Applied Behavior Analysis, 27*, 131–144. http://dx.doi.org/10.1901/jaba.1994.27-131.

Iwata, B. A., Pace, G. M., Kalsher, M. J., Cowdery, G. E., & Cataldo, M. F. (1990). Experimental analysis of extinction and self-injurious escape behavior. *Journal of Applied Behavior Analysis, 23*, 11–27. http://dx.doi.org/10.1901/jaba.1990.23-11.

Kazdin, A. E. (1980). Acceptability of time out from reinforcement procedures for disruptive child behavior. *Behavior Therapy, 11*, 329–344. http://dx.doi.org/10.1016/S0005-7894(80)80050-5.

Lalli, J. S., Vollmer, T. R., Progar, P. R., Wright, C., Borrero, J., Daniel, D., et al. (1999). Competition between positive and negative reinforcement in the treatment of escape behavior. *Journal of Applied Behavior Analysis, 32*, 285–295. http://dx.doi.org/10.1901/jaba.1999.32-285.

Lerman, D. C., & Iwata, B. A. (1996). Developing a technology for the use of operant extinction in clinical settings: An examination of basic and applied research. *Journal of Applied Behavior Analysis, 29*, 345–382. http://dx.doi.org/10.1901/jaba.1996.29-345.

Lerman, D. C., Iwata, B. A., & Wallace, M. D. (1999). Side effects of extinction: Prevalence of bursting and aggression during the treatment of self-injurious behavior. *Journal of Applied Behavior Analysis, 32*, 1–8. http://dx.doi.org/10.1901/jaba.1999.32-1.

Linscheid, T. R., Iwata, B. A., Ricketts, R. W., Williams, D. E., & Griffin, J. C. (1990). Clinical evaluations of the self-injurious behavior inhibiting system (SIBIS). *Journal of Applied Behavior Analysis, 23*, 53–78. http://dx.doi.org/10.1901/jaba.1990.23-53.

Lomas, J. E., Fisher, W. W., & Kelley, M. E. (2010). The effects of variable-time delivery of food item and praise on problem behavior reinforced by escape. *Journal of Applied Behavior Analysis, 43*, 425–435. http://dx.doi.org/10.1901/jaba.2010.43-425.

Luczynski, K. C., & Hanley, G. P. (2009). Do young children prefer contingencies? An evaluation of preschooler's preference for contingent versus noncontingent social reinforcement. *Journal of Applied Behavior Analysis, 42*, 511–525. http://dx.doi.org/10.1901/jaba.2009.42-511.

Mace, F. C., Hock, M. L., Lalli, J. S., West, B. J., Belfiore, P., Pinter, E., et al. (1988). Behavioral momentum in the treatment of noncompliance. *Journal of Applied Behavior Analysis, 21*, 123–141. http://dx.doi.org/10.1901/jaba.1988.21-123.

Marcus, B. A., & Vollmer, T. R. (1995). Effects of differential negative reinforcement on disruption and compliance. *Journal of Applied Behavior Analysis, 28*, 229–230. http://dx.doi.org/10.1901/jaba.1995.28-229.

Marcus, B. A., & Vollmer, T. R. (1996). Combining noncontingent reinforcement (NCR) and differential reinforcement schedules as treatment for aberrant behavior. *Journal of Applied Behavior Analysis, 29*, 43–51. http://dx.doi.org/10.1901/jaba.1996.29-43.

Mazaleski, J. L., Iwata, B. A., Rodgers, T. A., Vollmer, T. R., & Zarcone, J. R. (1994). Protective equipment as treatment for stereotypic hand mouthing: Sensory extinction or punishment effects? *Journal of Applied Behavior Analysis, 27*, 345–355. http://dx.doi.org/10.1901/jaba.1994.27-345.

National Institutes of Health. (1989). *NIH consensus development conference on the treatment of destructive behaviors in persons with developmental disabilities*. Bethesda, MD: Author.

Odom, S. L., Brown, W. H., Frey, T., Karasu, N., Smith-Canter, L. L., & Strain, P. S. (2003). Evidence based practice for young children with autism: Contributions for single-subject design research. *Focus on Autism and Other Developmental Disabilities, 18*, 166–175. http://dx.doi.org/10.1177/10883576030180030401.

Pace, G. M., Iwata, B. A., Cowdery, G. E., Andree, P. J., & McIntyre, T. (1993). Stimulus (instructional) fading during extinction of self-injurious escape behavior. *Journal of Applied Behavior Analysis, 26*, 205–212. http://dx.doi.org/10.1901/jaba.1993.26-205.

Patel, M. R., Piazza, C. C., Martinez, C. J., Volkert, V. M., & Christine, M. S. (2002). An evaluation of two differential reinforcement procedures with escape extinction to treat food refusal. *Journal of Applied Behavior Analysis, 35*, 363–374. http://dx.doi.org/10.1901/jaba.2002.35-363.

Peters, L. C., & Thompson, R. H. (2013). Some indirect effects of positive practice overcorrection. *Journal of Applied Behavior Analysis, 46*, 613–625. http://dx.doi.org/10.1002/jaba.63.

Piazza, C. C., Adelinis, J. D., Hanley, G. P., Goh, H., & Delia, M. D. (2000). An evaluation of the effects of matched stimuli on behaviors maintained by automatic reinforcement. *Journal of Applied Behavior Analysis, 33*, 13–27. http://dx.doi.org/10/1901/jaba.2000.33-13.

Piazza, C. C., Fisher, W. W., Hanley, G. P., Remick, M. L., Contrucci, S. A., & Aitken, T. L. (1997). The use of positive and negative reinforcement in the treatment of escapemaintained destructive behavior. *Journal of Applied Behavior Analysis, 30*, 279–298. http://dx.doi.org/10.1901/jaba.1997.30-279.

Pietras, C. J., Brandt, A. E., & Searcy, G. D. (2010). Human responding on random-interval schedules of response-cost punishment: The role of reduced reinforcement density. *Journal of the Experimental Analysis of Behavior, 93*, 5–26. http://dx.doi.org/10.1901/jeab.2010.93-5.

Rapp, J. T., & Vollmer, T. R. (2005). Stereotypy: I. A review of behavioral assessment and treatment. *Research in Developmental Disabilities*, *26*, 527–547. http://dx.doi.org/10.1016/j.ridd.2004.11.005.

Repp, A. C., Barton, L. E., & Brulle, A. R. (1983). A comparison of two procedures for programming the differential reinforcement of other behaviors. *Journal of Applied Behavior Analysis*, *16*, 435–445. http://dx.doi.org/10.1901/jaba.1983.16-435.

Repp, A. C., & Deitz, S. M. (1974). Reducing aggressive and self-injurious behavior of institutionalized retarded children through reinforcement of other behaviors. *Journal of Applied Behavior Analysis*, *7*, 313–325. http://dx.doi.org/10.1901/jaba.1974.7-313.

Rincover, A. (1978). Sensory extinction: A procedure for eliminating self-stimulatory behavior in developmentally disabled children. *Journal of Abnormal Child Psychology*, *6*, 299–310. http://dx.doi.org/10.1007/BF00924733.

Rincover, A., Cook, R., Peoples, A., & Packard, D. (1979). Sensory extinction and sensory reinforcement principles for programming multiple adaptive behavior change. *Journal of Applied Behavior Analysis*, *12*, 221–233. http://dx.doi.org/10.1901/jaba.1979.12-221.

Roane, H. S., Vollmer, T. R., Ringdahl, J. E., & Marcus, B. A. (1998). Evaluation of a brief stimulus preference assessment. *Journal of Applied Behavior Analysis*, *31*, 605–620. http://dx.doi.org/10.1901/jaba.1998.31-605.

Sajwag, T., Libet, J., & Agras, S. (1974). Lemon-juice therapy: The control of life-threatening rumination in a six-month old infant. *Journal of Applied Behavior Analysis*, *7*, 557–563. http://dx.doi.org/10.1901/jaba.1974.7-557.

Shirley, M. J., Iwata, B. A., Kahng, S., Mazaleski, J. L., & Lerman, D. C. (1997). Does functional communication training compete with ongoing contingencies of reinforcement? An analysis during response acquisition and maintenance. *Journal of Applied Behavior Analysis*, *30*, 93–104. http://dx.doi.org/10.1901/jaba.1997.30-93.

Singh, N. D., Dawson, M. J., & Gregory, P. R. (1980). Self-injury in the profoundly retarded: Clinically significant versus therapeutic control. *Journal of Mental Deficiency Research*, *24*, 87–97.

Smith, R. G., Iwata, B. A., Goh, H. -L., & Shore, B. A. (1995). Analysis of establishing operations for self-injury maintained by escape. *Journal of Applied Behavior Analysis*, *28*, 515–535. http://dx.doi.org/10.1901/jaba.28-515.

Smith, R. G., Russo, L., & Le, D. D. (1999). Distinguishing between extinction and punishment effects of response blocking: A replication. *Journal of Applied Behavior Analysis*, *32*, 367–370. http://dx.doi.org/10.1901/jaba.1999.32-367.

St. Peter Pipkin, C., Vollmer, T. R., & Sloman, K. N. (2010). Effects of treatment integrity failures during differential reinforcement of alternative behavior: A translational model. *Journal of Applied Behavior Analysis*, *43*, 47–70. http://dx.doi.org/10.1901/jaba.2010.43-47.

Sugai, G., Horner, R. H., Dunlap, G., Hieneman, M., Nelson, C. M., Scott, T., et al. (2000). Applying positive behavior support and functional behavioral assessment in schools. *Journal of Positive Behavior Interventions*, *2*, 131–143. http://dx.doi.org/10.1177/109830070000200302.

Tiger, J. H., & Hanley, G. P. (2004). Developing stimulus control of preschooler mands: An analysis of schedule-correlated and contingency-specifying stimuli. *Journal of Applied Behavior Analysis*, *37*, 517–521. http://dx.doi.org/10.1901/jaba.2004.37-517.

Tiger, J. H., & Hanley, G. P. (2006). Using reinforcer pairing and fading to increase the milk consumption of a preschool child. *Journal of Applied Behavior Analysis*, *39*, 399–403. http://dx.doi.org/10.1901.jaba.2006.6-06.

Vollmer, T. R. (1994). The concept of automatic reinforcement: Implications for behavioral research in developmental disabilities. *Research in Developmental Disabilities*, *15*, 187–207. http://dx.doi.org/10.1016/0891-4222(94)90011-6.

Vollmer, T. R., Hagopian, L. P., Bailey, J. S., Dorsey, M. F., Hanley, G. P., Lennox, D., et al. (2011). The association for behavior analysis international position statement on restraint and seclusion. *The Behavior Analyst, 34*, 103–110.

Vollmer, T. R., & Iwata, B. A. (1992). Differential reinforcement as treatment for behavior disorders: Procedural and functional variations. *Research in Developmental Disabilities, 13*, 393–417. http://dx.doi.org/10.1016/0891-4222(92)90013-V.

Vollmer, T. R., & Iwata, B. A. (1993). Implications of a functional analysis technology for the use of restricted behavioral interventions. *Child and Adolescent Mental Health Care, 3*, 95–113.

Vollmer, T. R., Iwata, B. A., Zarcone, J. R., Smith, R. G., & Mazaleski, J. L. (1993). The role of attention in the treatment of attention-maintained self-injurious behavior: Non-contingent reinforcement and differential reinforcement of other behavior. *Journal of Applied Behavior Analysis, 26*, 9–21. http://dx.doi.org/10.1901/jaba.1993.26-9.

Vollmer, T. R., Marcus, B. A., & LeBlanc, L. (1994). Treatment of self injury and hand-mouthing following inconclusive functional analyses. *Journal of Applied Behavior Analysis, 27*, 331–344. http://dx.doi.org/10.1901/jaba.1994.27-331.

Vollmer, T. R., Marcus, B. A., & Ringdahl, J. E. (1995). Noncontingent escape as treatment for self-injury maintained by negative reinforcement. *Journal of Applied Behavior Analysis, 28*, 15–26. http://dx.doi.org/10.1901/jaba.1995.28-15.

Vollmer, T. R., Progar, P. R., Lalli, J. S., Van Camp, C. M., Sierp, B. J., Wright, C. S., et al. (1998). Fixed-time schedules attenuate extinction-induced phenomena in the treatment of severe aberrant behavior. *Journal of Applied Behavior Analysis, 31*, 529–542. http://dx. doi.org/10.1901/jaba.1998.31-529.

Vollmer, T. R., Ringdahl, J. E., Roane, H. S., & Marcus, B. A. (1997). Negative side effects of noncontingent reinforcement. *Journal of Applied Behavior Analysis, 30*, 161–164. http://dx.doi.org/10.1901/jaba.1997.30-161.

Vollmer, T. R., Roane, H. S., Ringdahl, J. E., & Marcus, B. A. (1999). Evaluating treatment challenges with differential reinforcement of alternative behavior. *Journal of Applied Behavior Analysis, 32*, 9–23. http://dx.doi.org/10.1901/jaba.1999.32-9.

Vollmer, T. R., & Sloman, K. N. (2005). The historical context of noncontingent reinforcement as a behavioral treatment. *European Journal of Behavior Analysis, 5*, 9–19.

Wacker, D. P., Steege, M. W., Northup, J., Sasso, G., Berg, W., Reimers, T., et al. (1990). A component analysis of functional communication training across three topographies of severe behavior problems. *Journal of Applied Behavior Analysis, 23*, 417–429. http://dx. doi.org/10.1901/jaba.1990.23-417.

Zarcone, J. R., Iwata, B. A., Vollmer, T. R., Jagtiani, S., Smith, R. G., & Mazaleski, J. L. (1993). Extinction of self-injurious escape behavior with and without instructional fading. *Journal of Applied Behavior Analysis, 26*, 353–360. http://dx.doi.org/10.1901/jaba.1993.26-353.

CHAPTER 4

A Behavior-Analytic Approach to the Assessment and Treatment of Pediatric Feeding Disorders

Cathleen C. Piazza, Suzanne M. Milnes, Rebecca A. Shalev
University of Nebraska Medical Center's Munroe-Meyer Institute, Omaha, Nebraska, USA

Caregivers are tasked with the ultimate challenge, maintaining the safety and lives of children. What happens when caregivers are confronted with a child who cannot or will not eat or drink enough to grow and remain healthy? Undoubtedly, out of fear for the child's health, they seek advice from friends, family, and healthcare treatment providers (e.g., pediatricians, psychologists, behavior analysts). It is the treatment provider's responsibility to recognize a feeding disorder and refer the child to a specialist or intervene if qualified. This chapter is designed to help the treatment provider recognize a feeding disorder, to describe the environmental variables implicated in the etiology and maintenance of feeding disorders, and to provide a behavior-analytic approach to the assessment and treatment of various feeding difficulties.

RECOGNIZING A PEDIATRIC FEEDING DISORDER

Feeding and mealtime difficulties (e.g., picky eating) are fairly common during childhood (Jacobi, Schmitz, & Agras, 2008; Mascola, Bryson, & Agras, 2010). The prevalence of feeding difficulties in the pediatric population can make it difficult to identify when normative feeding difficulties become a feeding disorder warranting intervention (Milnes & Piazza, 2013a). One approach to evaluating the severity of a feeding problem is to compare the child's feeding behavior with typical developmental feeding patterns (see Table 4.1; Piazza, 2008).

The longer a child refuses to consume a sufficient quantity or variety of solids or liquids to maintain proper nutrition, the greater the likelihood that growth rates will fall below average (Schwarz, 2003). Thus, the most

Clinical and Organizational Applications of Applied Behavior Analysis
http://dx.doi.org/10.1016/B978-0-12-420249-8.00004-6

Table 4.1 Typical and atypical feeding

Age	Typical feeding	Atypical feeding
Infant	Successfully feeds from breast or bottle from birth Exhibits tongue-thrust pattern (in-and-out tongue movement) and successfully coordinates suck-swallow-breathe response, which assists with feedings	Consistently refuses breast or bottle Poorly coordinates suck-swallow-breathe response
6 months	Starts accepting baby food May expel baby food early on Eventually exhibits tongue lateralization (i.e., side-to-side and up-and-down movement)	Exhibits persistent tongue thrust resulting in continued mismanagement and expulsion of the bolus resulting in lengthy meals or low oral intake
12 months	Begins eating mashed table food As teeth develop, successfully manages small bites of table food	Poorly manages or persistently refuses increased textures (e.g., baby food, mashed food, table food)
1–5 years	Displays pickiness by having strong food preferences for a few foods while rejecting many others May consume varying amounts of calories from day to day	Displays selective eating and variable caloric intake, resulting in poor growth and severe nutrient deficits
All ages	Eats and drinks enough to sustain adequate growth and hydration May experience poor appetite and weight loss during times of illness, but quickly recovers Displays transient fussiness	Fails to eat and drink enough to sustain adequate growth (may necessitate a feeding tube) Requires frequent trips to the hospital for dehydration or malnutrition Displays persistent and overly challenging mealtime behavior

obvious and worrisome measure that a feeding difficulty has become a severe feeding disorder is prolonged periods of poor growth (Piazza, 2008). A child who is failing to grow may not have enough energy to eat (Cohen, Piazza, & Navathe, 2006), creating a situation where the consequence of the feeding disorder (i.e., growth failure) becomes one of the possible contributing factors to the maintenance and severity of the problem.

ETIOLOGICAL AND MAINTAINING FACTORS

Case Vignette: Betsy is a 2-year-old child with food and liquid refusal and nasogastric-tube dependence. Early in life, Betsy cried, spit up, and arched her back during and following breast and bottle feedings. After trying multiple formulas, her pediatrician diagnosed Betsy with gastroesophageal reflux and placed her on a hypoallergenic infant formula and medication. At 6 months of age, Betsy's caregivers introduced baby food. Soon after, Betsy began crying, turning her head away from the spoon, and batting at the feeder's hands during meals. Both caregivers responded to Betsy's behavior by coaxing Betsy to take bites and ending the meal when Betsy's behavior became "too intense." They explained that removing the food from the room was the only thing that would "resume the peace." Betsy's growth suffered. A gastroenterologist conducted a full medical work-up and diagnosed Betsy with an inflammatory condition of the esophagus resulting from various food allergies. The doctor placed Betsy on medications to manage inflammation and prevent further allergic reaction and started nasogastric-tube feedings (i.e., Betsy received her formula through a tube that was inserted into the nasal canal down the esophagus and into the stomach). Betsy's caregivers rid all allergens from Betsy's diet and attempted feeding Betsy again. After a few months without improvement in Betsy's oral intake, the physician is considering surgery to place a permanent feeding tube into Betsy's stomach. Betsy's caregivers are confused and frustrated; they do not understand why Betsy continues to refuse to eat.

The development of Betsy's feeding disorder was complex, not unlike the development of most feeding disorders. A number of anatomical, neurodevelopmental, medical, oral-motor, and environmental factors may interact with each other to produce and maintain a feeding disorder (Rommel, De Meyer, Feenstra, & Veereman-Wauters, 2003). In the case of Betsy, a medical condition (i.e., reflux and food allergies) likely caused recurrent discomfort during or immediately after eating. Betsy responded with inappropriate mealtime behavior and a decline in oral intake. Betsy's subsequent refusal to eat resulted in insufficient opportunity and energy to practice the skills of eating, making the task of eating difficult in addition to painful. Caregiver responses to Betsy's refusal to eat and drink may have inadvertently made the problem worse. Specifically, caregiver attention and termination of the meal may have functioned as reinforcement for inappropriate mealtime behavior, thereby increasing the probability of the inappropriate mealtime behavior occurring in the future (Bachmeyer et al., 2009; Piazza, Fisher, et al., 2003). Piazza, Fisher, et al. conducted functional analyses to examine the extent to which escape from bites, access to attention, and delivery of tangible items functioned as reinforcement for the inappropriate mealtime behavior of 15 children with feeding disorders. They identified negative reinforcement (i.e., escape from bites) as the most common maintaining variable followed closely by positive reinforcement in the form of attention.

In summary, Betsy learned early in life that eating is a painful experience and she can avoid eating by behaving inappropriately. Although Betsy received medical treatment to alleviate and prevent pain, her negatively-reinforced inappropriate mealtime behavior prevents her from obtaining new, less painful experiences with eating. Consequently, the feeding difficulties continue.

ASSESSMENT

Given the complexity of feeding disorders, assessment and treatment will need to address multiple etiological and maintaining factors (Cohen et al., 2006; Milnes & Piazza, 2013b; Piazza, 2008) to ensure the child's safety and success with oral feeding. Speech specialists assess the child's oral-motor status and swallow safety and identify appropriate food textures and bolus sizes. Dietitians monitor growth, estimate the child's caloric needs, and identify nutritional deficits. Medical specialists identify and treat relevant medical conditions and may use tube feedings to provide the child with calories and nutrients. Unfortunately, medical intervention or consultation with speech and dietetics may not be enough to treat the feeding disorder and increase oral consumption successfully. Luckily, physicians can refer children like Betsy to a feeding specialist or pediatric feeding disorder program that uses applied behavior analysis (ABA) to treat feeding difficulties.

Assessment and treatment procedures based on the principles of ABA have the most empirical support for treating feeding difficulties effectively (for recent reviews see Sharp, Jaquess, Morton, & Herzinger, 2010; Volkert & Piazza, 2012). Treatment programs using a behavior-analytic approach are successful at increasing oral intake, weaning children off tube feedings, and preventing tube placement altogether (Cohen et al., 2006; Laud, Girolami, Boscoe, & Gulotta, 2009; Williams, Riegel, Gibbons, & Field, 2007). The primary characteristic of a behavior-analytic approach to the treatment of feeding difficulties is a goal-directed, data-based approach that allows for objective assessment of feeding behavior, development and systematic evaluation of individualized treatment plans, and objective evaluation of outcomes.

OBJECTIVE ASSESSMENT OF FEEDING BEHAVIOR

An initial evaluation often includes a caregiver interview inquiring about the feeding history of the child and direct observations of the caregiver and child during meals under unstructured and structured baseline conditions. The baseline assessments are designed to gather data regarding the child's current feeding skills and identify possible environmental events that may maintain appropriate and inappropriate mealtime behaviors. Ideally, two individuals (i.e., a feeder and an observer) conduct assessment and treatment sessions to allow for appropriate data collection. If an observer is unavailable, treatment providers videotape all sessions for data collection purposes. Treatment providers operationally define target behaviors so observers can record child and caregiver responses objectively (Table 4.2 lists examples of common target behaviors and corresponding operational definitions).

Table 4.2 Common target mealtime behaviors and corresponding operational definitions

Target behavior	Operational definition
Presentation (nonself-feeding)	The feeder touches the utensil (e.g., cup, spoon) to the child's lips
Acceptance (nonself-feeding)	The child leans toward the utensil or opens his or her mouth and the feeder deposits the entire bolus of food or liquid into the child's mouth within 5 seconds of presentation
Inappropriate mealtime behavior (nonself-feeding)	The child turns his or her head 45° or more away from the utensil or bats at the utensil or the feeder's hand
Mouth clean	The child has an empty mouth (except for an amount pea-size or smaller) 30 s after the feeder deposited the entire bolus into the child's mouth, not due to expulsion
Pack	The child has food or drink greater than the size of a pea in his or her mouth 30 s after the feeder deposited the bite or drink into the child's mouth
Expulsion	Food or liquid larger than the size of a pea is present outside the child's mouth at any point after the feeder deposited the bite or drink into the child's mouth
Chews	The child's teeth and/or jaw complete one up-and-down motion with the teeth parted at least 1.3 cm while food is visible anywhere in the mouth except the center of the tongue or between the front teeth

Food Record

Prior to the baseline assessments, the child's caregivers and pediatrician or dietitian identify several food items to target during intervention. To facilitate this process, caregivers record all foods and liquids the child consumes orally or via tube over the course of 3–5 days. Treatment providers use the food record to help identify nutritional gaps and caloric deficits in the child's current diet and identify foods and liquids to target during intervention.

Home Baseline

This unstructured assessment simulates a meal in the home with caregivers feeding the child as they typically would. Caregivers feed foods and liquids the child readily accepts and foods and liquids the child often refuses, using the child's usual feeding utensils and mealtime items (e.g., toys). During this assessment, treatment providers obtain information regarding: (a) what foods, liquids, food textures, bolus sizes, and mealtime items caregivers use during the meal; (b) whether the caregivers feed the child (i.e., nonself-feeding) or the child feeds him- or herself (i.e., self-feeding); (c) which food items and textures the child accepts; (d) whether the child expels, packs, or has a mouth clean following acceptance of bites; (e) what consequences caregivers provide in response to inappropriate mealtime behavior; and (f) the child's fine and gross motor control (e.g., does child maintain good postural control?).

Structured Baseline

During this assessment, caregivers behave as they naturally would during meals; however, the treatment provider structures the meal. Specifically, the treatment provider identifies the bolus size and texture (often in collaboration with an ancillary service treatment provider such as a speech therapist or dietician), and whether the caregiver should feed the child or prompt the child to feed him- or herself. Caregivers present the same foods and drinks that will be targeted during intervention. Bolus sizes for the bites and drinks are small and designed to be easily managed by the child (e.g., level baby spoon, 2 ml of formula). The treatment provider instructs the caregivers to provide a new bite or drink to the child on a fixed-time schedule (e.g., every 30 s) and determines how many bites or drinks will comprise a feeding session (e.g., five bites will comprise one session). The treatment provider may conduct several sessions of each of the following assessments: self-feeding pureed food, self-feeding table-texture food, nonself-feeding pureed food, self-feeding liquids, and nonself-feeding liquids. The imposed structure and standardization of this assessment allow the treatment provider to set measurable goals for improvement (e.g., increase acceptance of drinks from 0% to 80%), compare the child's behavior at the time of the evaluation with the child's behavior at various points during the treatment process, evaluate the child's oral-motor skill, and evaluate the child's mealtime behavior when the feeder varies the response effort associated with eating.

When the treatment provider has collected all relevant data on child and caregiver mealtime behavior, he or she graphically depicts the data and answers the following questions: (a) does the child accept any bites or drinks and if so, under what conditions (e.g., is the child more likely to accept bites during nonself-feeding sessions relative to self-feeding sessions?); (b) does the child expel, pack, or swallow any food or drink; (c) under what conditions is the child most likely to engage in inappropriate mealtime behavior; and (d) does the child adequately and consistently chew table-texture bites or fatigue over time (e.g., as evidenced by a decreasing trend in the number of chews per bite across sessions) or swallow bites without chewing?

A comprehensive medical and feeding history along with the previous assessments will help treatment providers identify what the child can and will do, pinpointing a starting point for treatment or providing information about what assessments may still be necessary. For instance, if a child is refusing to self- and nonself-feed most pureed and table-texture foods, treatment providers should begin targeting the area that requires the lowest response effort for the child (i.e., nonself-feeding with pureed food). Alternatively, if a child is accepting all bites and drinks during the previous assessments, treatment providers may want to conduct similar assessments that require greater effort from the child (e.g., present larger boluses or present small portions of food rather than individual bites and drinks) to examine what the child can and will do more closely.

Food and Food-Texture Preference Assessments

If the child displays high levels of inappropriate mealtime behavior in the presence of specific foods or specific textures of food, the treatment provider can conduct a food-preference (Munk & Repp, 1994) or food-texture preference assessment (Adelinis, Piazza, Fisher, & Hanley, 1997; Munk & Repp, 1994; Patel, Piazza, Layer, Coleman, & Swartzwelder, 2005; Patel, Piazza, Santana, & Volkert, 2002). During the food-preference assessment, the treatment provider presents all target foods in pairs so that each food is paired with every other food once. During the food-texture preference assessment, the treatment provider presents all target foods at different textures in pairs so that each food and texture is paired with every other food and texture. Upon presentation of the pair in both assessments, the feeder prompts the child to "pick one." Treatment providers use the resulting data on the child's choices and consumption of chosen food items to identify a hierarchy of food and/or texture preferences for the child. The resulting data for each preference assessment can be depicted using a bar graph (see Figure 4.1 for an example).

Preference Assessment

It is common for treatment providers to conduct preference assessments to identify preferred items that may serve as potential reinforcers. Treatment providers can begin the information gathering by interviewing caregivers using the Reinforcer Assessment for Individuals with Disabilities (RAISD; Fisher, Piazza, Bowman, & Amari, 1996). The RAISD prompts caregivers to produce a list of preferred items across a variety of domains, including visual, auditory, olfactory, edible, tactile, and social. After the caregiver selects a sufficient number of preferred items (e.g., 12–16), treatment providers conduct a paired-choice preference assessment (e.g., Fisher et al., 1992). During this assessment, the treatment provider simultaneously presents two items to the child, with each item randomly presented with all other items in the set and prompts the child to "pick one." The treatment provider uses the data on the child's choices to rank-order items in regard to preference and uses the most preferred items in future assessments (e.g., functional analysis) and treatment planning.

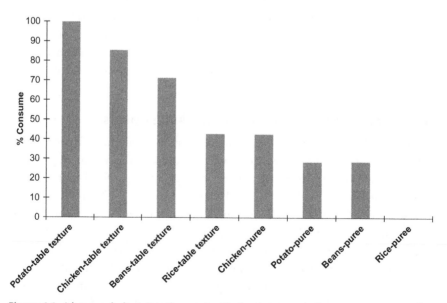

Figure 4.1 A bar graph depicting the results of a food-texture preference assessment. This particular child consumed table-texture potato and chicken more than any other foods.

Functional Analysis

As discussed earlier, caregivers use a variety of consequences (e.g., escape, attention, toys) to motivate children to eat (e.g., Borrero, Woods, Borrero, Masler, & Lesser, 2010), and these consequences may worsen feeding problems if they function as reinforcement (e.g., Piazza, Fisher, et al., 2003). Accordingly, if the child has high rates of inappropriate mealtime behavior, the treatment provider can conduct a functional analysis to determine how specific environmental events affect each child's behavior (Piazza, Fisher, et al., 2003). The hallmark of a functional analysis is the observation of behavior under well-defined test and control conditions. Table 4.3 provides example procedures for a functional analysis of inappropriate mealtime behavior. The test conditions allow the treatment provider to observe the

Table 4.3 Example functional analysis procedures

Condition	Procedure
All conditions	Present a new bite by touching the spoon or cup to the child's lips approximately every 30 s Present five bites per session Score occurrences of inappropriate mealtime behavior Convert inappropriate mealtime behavior to a rate by dividing the number of occurrences in the session by the total duration of time that the bite was within arms' reach of the child
Escape	Following inappropriate mealtime behavior, remove the spoon and provide the child with a 30-s break
Attention	Following inappropriate mealtime behavior, keep the bite where you initially presented it in space and provide 30 s of attention, matching the type and quality of attention caregivers provided contingent on inappropriate mealtime behavior during the baseline assessments
Tangible	Following inappropriate mealtime behavior, keep the bite where you initially presented it in space and provide access to a preferred item (preferably the same item(s) that the caregivers provided in the baseline assessments) for 30 s
Control	Prior to beginning the session, place the child's three highest preferred items in front of the child and prompt, "Pick one" Keep the bite where you initially presented it in space and provide free access to the preferred item and high quality attention

child's inappropriate behavior when it results in brief escape from bite or drink presentations, adult attention, or access to a tangible item. The purpose of the control condition is to serve as a comparison for the test condition and to observe the rate of inappropriate behavior when the child has free access to feeder attention and preferred items (Piazza, Fisher, et al., 2003).

Figure 4.2 shows the rate of inappropriate mealtime behavior per session during a functional analysis for Frank (LaRue et al., 2011). A pairwise design compared the differential effects of each test condition (i.e., escape, attention, and tangible) with the control condition on the rate of Frank's inappropriate mealtime behavior. Visual inspection shows elevated responding in the escape condition relative to the control condition suggesting that Frank's inappropriate mealtime behavior was maintained by negative reinforcement. Alternatively, the attention and tangible condition data paths are undifferentiated from the control condition, failing to establish positive reinforcement as a maintaining factor in Frank's inappropriate mealtime behavior. The results of this functional analysis helped lead Frank's treatment team to develop an individualized and effective intervention that addressed the function of Frank's inappropriate mealtime behavior (LaRue et al., 2011).

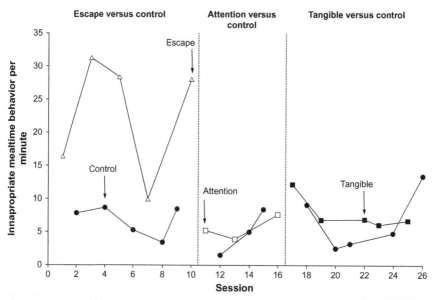

Figure 4.2 Rate of inappropriate mealtime behavior during a functional analysis for a child with escape-maintained inappropriate mealtime behavior. *(Adapted from LaRue et al. (2011). Copyright 2011 by the Society for the Experimental Analysis of Behavior, Inc.).*

TREATMENT

Increasing Acceptance and Decreasing Inappropriate Mealtime Behavior

Following a comprehensive assessment, treatment providers develop an individualized treatment plan that is informed by the current research literature and based on the results from the above assessments. The following section will outline treatment procedures with the most empirical support for treating common feeding problems (acceptance, inappropriate mealtime behavior, expulsion, and packing) and provide case examples of the evaluative techniques feeding clinicians and researchers commonly employ.

Escape Extinction

Given the role that negative reinforcement plays in the maintenance of inappropriate mealtime behavior, it is not surprising that the most widely applied and empirically supported intervention for feeding disorders is escape extinction (i.e., the elimination of escape following inappropriate mealtime behavior; Ahearn, 2002; Ahearn, Kerwin, Eicher, Shantz, & Swearingin, 1996; Borrero, Schlereth, Rubio, & Taylor, 2013; Cooper et al., 1995; Hoch, Babbitt, Coe, Krell, & Hackbert, 1994; Kerwin, 1999; LaRue et al., 2011; Patel, Piazza, Martinez, Volkert, & Santana, 2002; Piazza, Patel, Gulotta, Sevin, & Layer, 2003; Reed et al., 2004; Volkert & Piazza, 2012). The most commonly reported escape extinction procedure is nonremoval of the spoon (Hoch et al., 1994) followed by physical guidance (Ahearn, 2002). Nonremoval of the spoon consists of the feeder placing the utensil to the child's lips and keeping it at the lips until the feeder can deposit the bite into the child's mouth. During physical guidance, the feeder applies gentle pressure to the temporomandibular joint of the child's jaw until the child's mouth opens and the feeder can deposit the bite.

Although these procedures are well described in the literature, implementation can prove to be difficult and harmful if done incorrectly. For a small portion of children, inappropriate mealtime behavior may increase before it gets better, making it difficult for an untrained feeder to implement the procedure with good integrity and maintain the safety of the child. If escape extinction procedures are done improperly or terminated too early, the child's feeding behavior may worsen. Moreover, once a novice feeder is successful at depositing drinks and bites into the child's mouth, he or she may miss signs indicating a safety risk, including increased coughing, tongue or facial swelling, changes in facial color, gasping, wet vocal sounds, or skin rashes (e.g., hives). Continued feeding of a child exhibiting one or more of the above signs could harm the child (e.g., result in aspiration). Consequently, treatment providers with little to no experience treating feeding difficulties will require training and supervision in the provision of escape extinction procedures.

Although the escape extinction procedures described previously are well supported in the literature, they are not a panacea for all feeding difficulties. Milder feeding difficulties, although not the focus of the present chapter, may warrant less intensive intervention. Additionally, not all children with severe feeding disorders will obtain clinically meaningful changes in feeding behavior following implementation of escape extinction. Consequently, the effectiveness of escape extinction should be evaluated for each individual child. One commonly reported evaluative procedure is the use of a reversal design. See Figure 4.3 for a graphical depiction of an ABAB design evaluating the effectiveness of escape extinction for Ira. Specifically, an ABAB design is a single-case experimental design in which an initial baseline phase (A) is followed by an intervention phase (B), a return to baseline (A), and then another intervention phase (B) to determine whether behavior changes systematically with the introduction and withdrawal of treatment. Each data point represents the percentage of 5-s acceptance (top panel) or inappropriate mealtime behavior per minute (bottom panel) for a five-bite session (the feeder presented a new bite approximately every 30 s). In Phase A, the initial baseline, the feeder conducted an escape baseline, which looked identical to the escape condition in the functional analysis. Specifically, if Ira engaged in inappropriate mealtime behavior the feeder immediately removed the spoon for 30 s. During the initial baseline for Ira, her percentage of 5-s acceptance was stable at zero, and her rate of inappropriate mealtime behavior was high and increasing. Conducting a baseline prior to implementing the treatment procedure provided the clinician with information on Ira's existing levels of behavior. In Phase B, the feeder implemented escape extinction (i.e., non-removal of the spoon) and observed an immediate, but modest jump in percentage of 5-s acceptance, eventually increasing to and stabilizing at clinically meaningful levels (80% or greater). The feeder also observed an immediate downward level shift in inappropriate mealtime behavior, eventually decreasing to and stabilizing at low levels. A replication of the previous phases resulted in similar responding. Specifically, withdrawal of escape extinction resulted in similar levels of inappropriate mealtime behavior and 5-s acceptance as observed in the initial baseline phase. And, finally, reintroduction of escape extinction in the final phase reproduced the clinically meaningful levels of inappropriate mealtime behavior and 5-s acceptance as observed in the initial treatment phase. Because Ira's behavior changed in the therapeutically desired direction when escape extinction

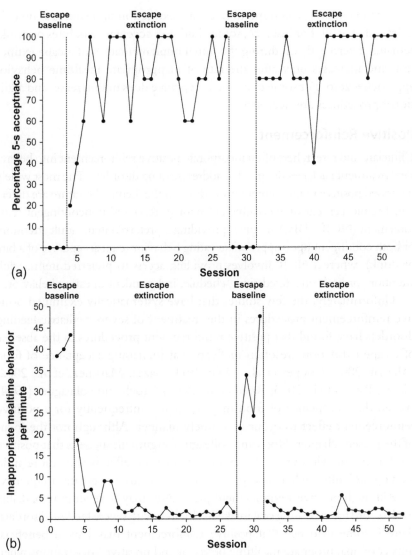

Figure 4.3 Ira's percentage of 5-s acceptance (a) and inappropriate mealtime behavior per minute (b) during a treatment evaluation of escape extinction using an ABAB reversal design.

was introduced, reverted back to baseline levels when withdrawn, and improved again when the feeder reinstated treatment, the treatment provider can make a strong argument that the intervention was responsible for the change rather than an extraneous uncontrolled variable. The data from Ira's treatment evaluation are clear: escape extinction worked quickly, predictably, and reliably.

Not all children will respond to escape extinction procedures as quickly as Ira did or at all. For instance, some children's acceptance of bites or drinks remains at zero early on during the initial implementation of escape extinction and increases only after the rate of inappropriate mealtime behavior approaches zero. For some children, acceptance does not increase, and additional procedures are necessary.

Positive Reinforcement

Clinicians and researchers often incorporate positive reinforcement into behavioral treatment packages designed to address feeding disorders. The most widely described positive reinforcement procedures in the feeding literature are differential reinforcement of alternative behavior (DRA) and noncontingent reinforcement (NCR). DRA involves providing a preferred item, adult attention, or both contingent upon appropriate eating behavior (e.g., acceptance of a bite or drink), whereas NCR involves providing access to preferred items, adult attention, or both on a fixed-time schedule, independent of eating behavior.

Unfortunately, the few studies that have systematically examined positive reinforcement procedures in the treatment of severe pediatric feeding disorders have found that positive reinforcement procedures in the absence of escape extinction are often ineffective at increasing acceptance of food (Ahearn, 2002; Cooper et al., 1995; Patel, Piazza, Martinez, et al., 2002; Piazza, Patel, et al., 2003; Reed et al., 2004). Hoch and colleagues (1994) argued that acceptance of food may occur too infrequently for a positive reinforcement effect to occur in a timely manner. Although not the focus of the present chapter, Hoch and colleagues' argument suggests that positive reinforcement without escape extinction may be effective for more mild feeding difficulties where acceptance of food occurs at a greater frequency.

Although positive-reinforcement procedures may have an unremarkable track record for increasing oral intake in children with severe feeding disorders, there is some evidence that positive reinforcement may have a beneficial impact on inappropriate mealtime behavior and negative vocalizations when combined with escape extinction for some children (Piazza, Patel, et al., 2003; Reed et al., 2004). Additional research is necessary to identify the characteristics that predict for whom NCR or DRA will be beneficial.

Treatment providers can evaluate the relative effects of different positive reinforcement procedures on target mealtime behaviors using any number of experimental designs. For example, the treatment provider may choose to directly compare two or more procedures (e.g., DRA, NCR, no reinforcement) using a multielement design, where the feeder conducts each condition in alternating succession, independent of the child's response to determine which procedure, if any, is most effective at increasing or decreasing target mealtime behaviors. See Figure 4.4 for an alternating treatments design evaluating NCR, DRA, and no reinforcement on percentage negative vocalizations. Alternatively, the treatment provider may choose to evaluate reinforcement procedures concurrently with escape extinction procedures using an alternating treatments design embedded in a reversal design (see Piazza, Patel, et al., 2003; Reed et al., 2004 for an example). We will provide an illustration of this design later.

High-Probability Instructional Sequence

Some evidence exists for the effectiveness of a high-probability (high-p) instructional sequence alone (Meier, Fryling, & Wallace, 2012; Patel et al., 2007) or in combination with escape extinction (Patel et al., 2006) on increasing acceptance of food in children with feeding disorders. The instructional sequence involves delivering a series of instructions with which the child is very likely to comply (e.g., "take a bite" of preferred food) followed by an instruction for which a child with a feeding disorder is unlikely to comply (e.g., "take a bite" of nonpreferred food).

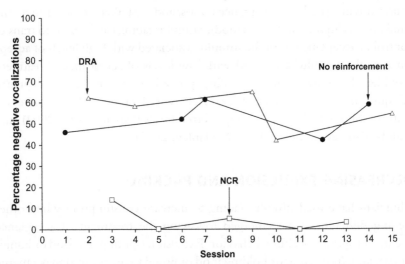

Figure 4.4 Example evaluation of the effect of NCR, DRA, and no reinforcement on percentage-negative vocalizations. The NCR condition resulted in low levels of negative vocalizations; whereas the DRA and no reinforcement conditions resulted in overlapping and higher levels of negative vocalizations than NCR.

Simultaneous Presentation

Simultaneous presentation of preferred (or readily accepted) and nonpreferred (or frequently refused) food or liquid also shows some promise as an alternative or additional procedure to escape extinction (e.g., Ahearn, 2003; Kern & Marder, 1996; Mueller, Piazza, Patel, Kelley, & Pruett, 2004; Patel, Piazza, Kelly, Ochsner, & Santana, 2001; Piazza et al., 2002; Shore, Babbitt, Williams, Coe, & Snyder, 1998). This particular procedure is appropriate when the child has demonstrated that he or she will consistently eat some foods or liquids but not others. The treatment provider conducts a food preference assessment to determine the child's most preferred food(s) and presents the preferred food with (i.e., next to or blended into) the target or nonpreferred food. The presence of the preferred food or liquid may reduce the aversive quality of the nonpreferred food or liquid, potentially altering the effectiveness of escape as reinforcement (Piazza et al., 2002). Once the child is accepting bites with the above procedure, treatment providers can add a fading component by systematically decreasing the ratio of preferred to nonpreferred food over time (for an example, see Mueller et al., 2004).

Stimulus Fading

During stimulus fading treatment providers begin by evaluating the stimulus conditions under which acceptance is most and least likely to occur (e.g., the child accepts liquids but refuses food). Stimulus fading can be used to transfer control of acceptance from the stimulus associated with high levels of acceptance to the stimulus associated with low levels of acceptance. Treatment providers have used stimulus-fading procedures to increase acceptance of liquids from a cup (Groff, Piazza, Zeleny, & Dempsey, 2011), increased textures (Shore et al., 1998), nonpreferred foods (Mueller et al., 2004), and liquids (Patel et al., 2001; Tiger & Hanley, 2005).

DECREASING EXPULSION AND PACKING

Clinicians have used stimulus fading to increase consumption when other feeding difficulties have emerged following the treatment of acceptance and inappropriate mealtime behavior. Expulsion (spitting out food or liquid) and packing (pocketing or holding food or liquid in the mouth) may emerge as alternative topographies of food refusal, result from oral–motor deficits, or both (Sharp, Odom, & Jaquess, 2012; Vaz et al., 2012; Volkert, Vaz, Piazza, Frese, & Barnett, 2011). Bachmeyer, Gulotta, and Piazza (2013) successfully used liquid-to-solids stimulus fading to treat expulsion and increase mouth clean with two children who consistently expelled baby food, but swallowed liquids, following a treatment of escape extinction and differential reinforcement of mouth clean. See Figure 4.5 for the evaluation of liquid to solids fading on the percentage mouth clean for one of their participants, Kenny. A multielement design comparing Kenny's mouth clean when the feeder presented liquid relative to baby food demonstrated that Kenny was significantly more likely to have mouth cleans during liquid sessions. Bachmeyer et al. then used a brief experimental design with mini-reversals, a variant of an ABAB design, to evaluate the effects of a multistep stimulus fading procedure that involved gradually adding baby food to the liquid. The initial A phase consisted of the baby food condition of the multielement comparison. The liquid to baby food fading comprised each B phase. The investigators then repeated mini-reversals back to the 100% baby food baseline after every two fading steps. For Kenny, percentage of bites with mouth clean were within clinically acceptable levels during each phase of the fading treatment, but the magnitude of responding immediately changed to countertherapeutic levels during each mini-reversal to 100% baby food. These immediate changes in the magnitude of responses between the fading intervention and the mini-reversals to 100% baby food demonstrate both the treatment effects of the fading intervention as well as the need to continue the fading process. The investigators conducted brief reversals only periodically to minimize the likelihood that Kenny would discriminate the changes being made during the fading process. After 11 fading steps, Kenny was having mouth cleans on 100% of bites consisting of 100% baby food.

Re-presentation

Re-presentation is a consequence-based procedure that is often used in conjunction with the previously described escape extinction procedures. Re-presentation entails scooping up expelled food or liquid and immediately depositing it back into the child's mouth. Conceptually, re-presentation may be understood as a form of escape extinction because it minimizes escape from eating. Alternatively, re-presentation's success may result from the child's increased opportunity to practice the skill of managing and retaining the bolus in the mouth. Sevin, Gulotta, Sierp, Rosica, and Miller (2002) evaluated re-presentation in conjunction with escape extinction when expulsion emerged following the treatment of acceptance and inappropriate mealtime behavior for a 34-month-old girl with a feeding disorder. An evaluation utilizing an ABAB reversal design where the A phase was escape extinction and the B phase was escape extinction plus re-presentation suggested introduction

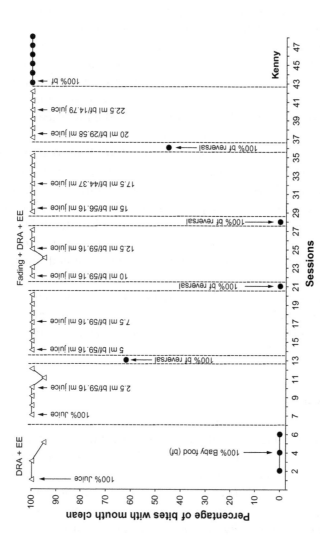

Figure 4.5 Example functional analysis procedures. (Adapted from Bachmeyer et al. (2013). Copyright 2013 by John Wiley & Sons, Ltd.).

of re-presentation resulted in decreased expulsion. Unfortunately, expulsion for some children may persist despite implementation of re-presentation.

Chin Prompt

One study provided evidence that the addition of a chin prompt during presentation and re-presentation reduced liquid expulsion to clinically acceptable levels in children who demonstrated an open-mouth posture following acceptance (Wilkins, Piazza, Groff, & Vaz, 2011). During the chin-prompt procedure, the feeder placed his or her thumb under the child's lower lip and his or her forefinger under the child's chin while depositing the drink. After depositing the drink, the feeder applied gentle upward pressure on the child's lower lip and chin for 5 s while counting audibly. The chin prompt was designed to prompt mouth closure, thereby assisting with the swallow, increasing the response effort associated with expulsion, and decreasing the likelihood that liquid could passively run out of the child's mouth.

Presentation Manipulations

Some clinicians have treated expulsion by modifying how bites are placed in the child's mouth during presentation (Girolami, Boscoe, & Roscoe, 2007; Rivas, Piazza, Kadey, Volkert, & Stewart, 2011; Sharp, Harker, & Jaquess, 2010; Sharp et al., 2012) and re-presentation (Girolami et al., 2007; Sharp et al., 2012). Specifically, clinicians have used a flipped spoon or a NUK Brush® (i.e., soft, bristled massaging toothbrush) to deposit food into the mouth. During the flipped-spoon deposit, the feeder places a spoon in the child's mouth, flips the spoon 180°, and deposits the food onto the middle or back center of the child's tongue by applying gentle downward pressure and sliding the spoon out of the mouth (Sharp, Harker, et al., 2010). During NUK-Brush® presentations, the feeder places bites onto a brush and wipes the food onto the middle or back center of the child's tongue. For some children, both presenting and re-presenting expelled food using a NUK Brush® (Girolami et al., 2007) or a flipped spoon (e.g., Rivas et al., 2011; Sharp et al., 2012) may be necessary to achieve clinically acceptable levels of mouth clean and expulsion. The placement of the bolus directly onto the tongue during the flip spoon and the NUK-Brush® deposit increases the response effort associated with expulsion and may compensate for oral-motor skill deficits by assisting with bolus formation and propulsion. Adding the flipped-spoon or NUK-Brush® deposit contingent on re-presentation might also serve as punishment for expulsion.

A presentation manipulation alone may be insufficient to increase mouth clean in children with treatment resistant expulsion (Dempsey, Piazza, Groff, & Kozisek, 2011). Dempsey et al. evaluated the effects on mouth clean of a flipped spoon versus an upright spoon presentation using a multielement comparison and evaluated the additive effects of a chin prompt using a BAB design (see Figure 4.6). Specifically, the investigators introduced a treatment procedure in Phase B, withdrew the treatment procedure in Phase A, and reintroduced the treatment procedure in Phase B. The B phases incorporated the chin prompt into both the upright-spoon and flipped-spoon conditions. The A phase examined the upright versus flipped spoon comparison alone. Across all three phases, the flipped-spoon condition resulted in increased levels of mouth clean. However, only when the chin prompt was incorporated in the two B phases did mouth clean reach clinically acceptable levels.

Texture Reduction

Investigators have evaluated reducing the texture of foods as a treatment for expulsion (Patel, Piazza, Santana, et al., 2002) and packing (Kadey, Piazza, Rivas, & Zeleny, 2013; Patel et al., 2005). For instance, Patel et al. (2005) evaluated the effects of texture (e.g., pureed, wet ground, chopped) on packing and caloric intake for three children with food refusal and oral-motor skill deficits. Specifically, the authors used a reversal design to show that

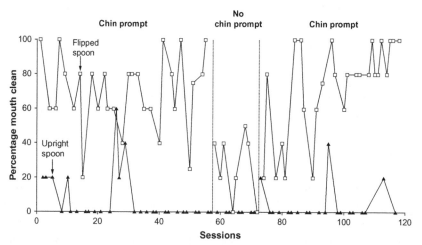

Figure 4.6 Percentage of mouth clean during flipped spoon with chin prompt, upright spoon with chin prompt, flipped spoon without chin prompt, and upright spoon without chin prompt. *(Adapted from Dempsey et al. (2011). Copyright 2011 by the Society for the Experimental Analysis of Behavior, Inc.).*

packing rates decreased and thus caloric consumption increased, when participants were presented lower-texture food. Lowering the texture of foods may result in decreased expulsion or packing because swallowing lower textures is easier than swallowing higher textures. Alternatively, the reduced texture may eliminate the aversive quality of the foods (e.g., coarse texture) and therefore decrease the child's motivation to expel or pack food.

Redistribution

Sevin et al. (2002) and Gulotta, Piazza, Patel, and Layer (2005) used redistribution, a consequence-based procedure, to successfully treat packing. The redistribution procedure consisted of collecting packed food and redepositing it in the middle of the child's tongue using a NUK Brush®. Volkert et al. (2011) tested redistribution in combination with swallow facilitation. During swallow facilitation, the feeder used the feeding utensil (i.e., NUK Brush® or spoon) to apply gentle, downward pressure on the posterior portion of the tongue (Hoch, Babbitt, Coe, Ducan, & Trusty, 1995) while redistributing the bite. Rather than use a NUK Brush® as employed by past investigators (e.g., Gulotta et al., 2005; Hoch et al., 1995; Sevin et al., 2002), Volkert et al. implemented redistribution with a flipped spoon. The flipped-spoon procedure may be more appealing to clinicians and families because children with typical eating behaviors use spoons rather than NUK Brushes® (Volkert et al., 2011). Furthermore, the addition of swallow facilitation may better support children with oral-motor deficits.

Despite the effectiveness of redistribution, little is understood about the operant mechanism that underlies its effects (Volkert et al., 2011). Several authors have hypothesized that redistribution functions as negative reinforcement for packing (Gulotta et al., 2005; Volkert et al., 2011). When packing is a refusal behavior and the redistribution procedure is more aversive than swallowing, children may swallow independently to avoid redistribution (Gulotta et al., 2005; Volkert et al., 2011). Alternatively, placing the bite on the back of the tongue may increase the response effort required to pack the bite (e.g., children swallow because it is easier than packing). Although these theories hold for children who engage in packing to escape food consumption, they do not fit for children who lack the oral-motor skills necessary to swallow (Gulotta et al., 2005; Patel et al., 2005; Volkert et al., 2011). Rather, redistribution may help children with poor oral-motor skills manipulate the food (e.g., bolus formation). Along these lines, swallow facilitation may be particularly helpful in assisting bolus propulsion, which is necessary for swallowing (Volkert et al., 2011).

Chaser

Vaz et al. (2012) used a chaser to decrease packing of solid foods in three children with feeding disorders. Specifically, the feeder delivered a small bolus of preferred food or liquid following acceptance of a target bite. For two participants, the authors examined the effects of a liquid chaser on packing using an ABAB reversal design (phase A was baseline and phase B was presentation of the chaser). For the third participant, they evaluated packing in the presence and absence of a solid chaser using a multielement design. Across all participants, packing decreased to low levels when the feeder presented a chaser to the participant following acceptance of the target food.

The results of Vaz et al. (2012) are particularly meaningful because the treatment involves a strategy used by typically eating children (e.g., children often use chasers to swallow difficult to swallow food). Despite these benefits, the chaser may only be effective for children who readily accept and swallow certain liquids or solid food (Vaz et al., 2012).

CAREGIVER TRAINING

Following the development and evaluation of the treatment protocol, treatment providers train caregivers on the procedures. Like the approach to treating problematic feeding behavior, empirical caregiver training methods are based on the principles of applied behavior analysis (McCartney, Anderson, & English, 2005; Mueller et al., 2003; Najdowski, Wallace, Doney, & Ghezzi, 2003; Paul, Williams, Riegal, & Gibbons, 2007). The work of Mueller et al. suggests that successful caregiver training (e.g., caregivers deliver treatments with high levels of integrity) can be achieved with the implementation of a multicomponent training package which consists of written instructions and at least one of the following components: (a) verbal instructions, (b) modeling, or (c) rehearsal (i.e., having the caregiver role play the treatment procedures with the treatment provider serving as the child). To ensure understanding, therapists provided feedback to parents regarding errors in implementation during role-plays.

Although caregiver training may initially occur in the clinic setting, it should also take place in natural settings (e.g., the child's home, daycare, or school; Milnes & Piazza, 2013b; Mueller et al., 2003). Eventually, caregivers will conduct all of the child's meals outside the clinic, and therefore, it is essential to understand the extent to which training generalizes to real-world settings (Mueller et al., 2003). Comprehensive caregiver training is central to producing positive long-term outcomes for children with feeding disorders. Additional research that clarifies the processes which facilitate successful caregiver training of feeding procedures in routine clinical practice will further enhance our ability to produce durable treatments.

CONCLUSION

The goal of this chapter has been to provide clinicians and researchers a brief overview of the identification and development of feeding disorders, review the current treatment literature, and provide a behavior-analytic approach to the assessment and treatment of various feeding difficulties. Assessment and treatment procedures based on the applied behavior analysis have received a great deal of empirical support in the feeding literature over the last couple of decades. Nonetheless, there is work to be done. Specifically, clinical researchers should identify additional treatment procedures, replicate existing findings, evaluate the mechanism of change for existing procedures, and identify for whom specific procedures are most and least likely to work.

REFERENCES

Adelinis, J. D., Piazza, C. C., Fisher, W. W., & Hanley, G. P. (1997). The establishing effects of client location on self-injurious behavior. *Research in Developmental Disabilities, 18,* 383–391.

Ahearn, W. H. (2002). Effect of two methods of introducing foods during feeding treatment on acceptance of previously rejected items. *Behavioral Interventions, 17,* 111–127.

Ahearn, W. H. (2003). Using simultaneous presentation to increase vegetable consumption in a mildly selective child with autism. *Journal of Applied Behavior Analysis, 36*(3), 361–365.

Ahearn, W. H., Kerwin, M. E., Eicher, P. S., Shantz, J., & Swearingin, W. (1996). An alternating treatments comparison of two intensive interventions for food refusal. *Journal of Applied Behavior Analysis, 29,* 321–332.

Bachmeyer, M. H., Gulotta, C. S., & Piazza, C. C. (2013). Liquid to baby food fading in the treatment of food refusal. *Behavioral Interventions, 28*(4), 281–298.

Bachmeyer, M. H., Piazza, C. C., Fredrick, L. D., Reed, G. K., Rivas, K. D., & Kadey, H. J. (2009). Functional analysis and treatment of multiply controlled inappropriate mealtime behavior. *Journal of Applied Behavior Analysis, 42,* 641–658.

Borrero, C. S., Schlereth, G. J., Rubio, E. K., & Taylor, T. (2013). A comparison of two physical guidance procedures in the treatment of pediatric food refusal. *Behavioral Interventions, 28*(4), 261–280.

Borrero, C. S., Woods, J. N., Borrero, J. C., Masler, E. A., & Lesser, A. D. (2010). Descriptive analyses of pediatric food refusal and acceptance. *Journal of Applied Behavior Analysis, 43,* 71–88.

Cohen, S. A., Piazza, C. C., & Navathe, A. (2006). Feeding and nutrition. In I. L. Rubin, & A. C. Crocker (Eds.), *Medical care for children and adults with developmental disabilities* (pp. 295–307). Baltimore: Paul H. Brooks Publishing Co.

Cooper, L. J., Wacker, D. P., McComas, J. J., Peck, S. M., Richman, D., Drew, J., et al. (1995). Use of component analyses to identify active variables in treatment packages for children with feeding disorders. *Journal of Applied Behavior Analysis, 28*, 139–154.

Dempsey, J., Piazza, C. C., Groff, R. A., & Kozisek, J. M. (2011). A flipped spoon and chin prompt to increase mouth clean. *Journal of Applied Behavior Analysis, 44*(4), 961–965.

Fisher, W., Piazza, C. C., Bowman, L. G., & Amari, A. (1996). Integrating caregiver report with a systematic choice assessment to enhance reinforcer identification. *American Journal on Mental Retardation, 101*, 15–25.

Fisher, W., Piazza, C. C., Bowman, L. G., Hagopian, L. P., Owens, J. C., & Slevin, I. (1992). A comparison of two approaches for identifying reinforcers for person with severe and profound disabilities. *Journal of Applied Behavior Analysis, 25*, 491–498.

Girolami, P. A., Boscoe, J. H., & Roscoe, N. (2007). Decreasing expulsions by a child with a feeding disorder: Using a brush to present and re-present food. *Journal of Applied Behavior Analysis, 40*(4), 749–753.

Groff, R. A., Piazza, C. C., Zeleny, J. R., & Dempsey, J. R. (2011). Spoon-to-cup fading as treatment for cup drinking in a child with intestinal failure. *Journal of Applied Behavior Analysis, 44*, 949–954.

Gulotta, C. S., Piazza, C. C., Patel, M. R., & Layer, S. A. (2005). Using food redistribution to reduce packing in children with severe food refusal. *Journal of Applied Behavior Analysis, 38*, 39–50.

Hoch, T. A., Babbitt, R. L., Coe, D. A., Ducan, A., & Trusty, E. M. (1995). A swallow induction avoidance procedure to establish eating. *Journal of Behavior Therapy and Experimental Psychiatry, 26*, 41–50.

Hoch, T. A., Babbitt, R. L., Coe, D. A., Krell, D. M., & Hackbert, L. (1994). Contingency contacting: Combining positive reinforcement and escape extinction procedures to treat persistent food refusal. *Behavior Modification, 18*, 106–128.

Jacobi, C., Schmitz, G., & Agras, W. (2008). Is picky eating an eating disorder? *International Journal of Eating Disorders, 41*(7), 626–634.

Kadey, H., Piazza, C. C., Rivas, K. M., & Zeleny, J. (2013). An evaluation of texture manipulations to increase swallowing. *Journal of Applied Behavior Analysis, 46*, 539–543.

Kern, L., & Marder, T. J. (1996). A comparison of simultaneous and delayed reinforcement as treatments for food selectivity. *Journal of Applied Behavior Analysis, 29*, 243–246.

Kerwin, M. E. (1999). Empirically supported treatments in pediatric psychology: Severe feeding problems. *Journal of Pediatric Psychology, 24*, 193–214.

LaRue, R. H., Stewart, V., Piazza, C. C., Volkert, V. M., Patel, M. R., & Zeleny, J. (2011). Escape as reinforcement and escape extinction in the treatment of feeding problems. *Journal of Applied Behavior Analysis, 44*, 719–735.

Laud, R. B., Girolami, P. A., Boscoe, J. H., & Gulotta, C. S. (2009). Treatment outcomes for severe feeding problems in children with autism spectrum disorder. *Behavior Modification, 33*, 520–536.

Mascola, A. J., Bryson, S. W., & Agras, W. (2010). Picky eating during childhood: A longitudinal study to age 11 years. *Eating Behaviors, 11*(4), 253–257.

McCartney, E. J., Anderson, C. M., & English, C. L. (2005). Effect of brief clinic-based training on the ability of caregivers to implement escape extinction. *Journal of Positive Behavior Interventions, 7*(1), 18–32.

Meier, A., Fryling, M. J., & Wallace, M. (2012). Using an enhanced high-probability instructional sequence to increase the variety of foods consumed by a young child with autism. *Journal of Applied Behavior Analysis, 45*, 149–153.

Milnes, S. M., & Piazza, C. C. (2013a). Feeding disorders. In R. Hastings & J. Rojahn (Eds.), *International review of research in developmental disabilities* (pp. 143–166). San Diego, CA: Academic Press.

Milnes, S. M., & Piazza, C. C. (2013b). Intensive treatment of pediatric feeding disorders. In D. D. Reed, F. D. Digennaro Reed, & J. K. Luiselli (Eds.), *Handbook of crisis intervention and developmental disabilities* (pp. 393–408). New York: Springer.

Mueller, M. M., Piazza, C. C., Moore, J. W., Kelley, M. E., Bethke, S. A., Pruett, A. E., et al. (2003). Training parents to implement pediatric feeding protocols. *Journal of Applied Behavior Analysis, 36*(4), 545–562.

Mueller, M. M., Piazza, C. C., Patel, M. R., Kelley, M. E., & Pruett, A. (2004). Increasing variety of foods consumed by blending nonpreferred foods into preferred foods. *Journal of Applied Behavior Analysis, 37*(2), 159–170.

Munk, D. D., & Repp, A. C. (1994). Behavioral assessment of feeding problems of individuals with severe disabilities. *Journal of Applied Behavior Analysis, 27*, 241–250.

Najdowski, A. C., Wallace, M. D., Doney, J. K., & Ghezzi, P. M. (2003). Parental assessment and treatment of food selectivity in natural settings. *Journal of Applied Behavior Analysis, 36*(3), 383–386.

Patel, M. R., Piazza, C. C., Kelly, M. L., Ochsner, C. A., & Santana, C. M. (2001). Using a fading procedure to increase fluid consumption in a child with feeding problems. *Journal of Applied Behavior Analysis, 34*, 357–360.

Patel, M. R., Piazza, C. C., Layer, S. A., Coleman, R., & Swartzwelder, D. M. (2005). A systematic evaluation of food textures to decrease packing and increase oral intake in children with pediatric feeding disorders. *Journal of Applied Behavior Analysis, 38*, 89–100.

Patel, M. R., Piazza, C. C., Martinez, C. J., Volkert, V. M., & Santana, C. M. (2002). An evaluation of two differential reinforcement procedures with escape extinction to treat food refusal. *Journal of Applied Behavior Analysis, 35*, 363–374.

Patel, M. R., Piazza, C. C., Santana, C. M., & Volkert, V. M. (2002). An evaluation of food type and texture in the treatment of a feeding problem. *Journal of Applied Behavior Analysis, 35*, 183–186.

Patel, M. R., Reed, G. K., Piazza, C. C., Bachmeyer, M. H., Layer, S. A., & Pabico, R. S. (2006). An evaluation of a high-probability instructional sequence to increase acceptance of food and decrease inappropriate behavior in children with pediatric feeding disorders. *Research in Developmental Disabilities, 27*, 430–442.

Patel, M. R., Reed, G. K., Piazza, C. C., Mueller, M., Bachmeyer, M. H., & Layer, S. A. (2007). Use of a high-probability instructional sequence to increase compliance to feeding demands in the absence of escape extinction. *Behavioral Interventions, 22*(4), 305–310.

Paul, C., Williams, K. E., Riegal, K., & Gibbons, B. (2007). Combining repeated taste exposure and escape prevention: An intervention for the treatment of extreme food selectivity. *Appetite, 49*, 708–711.

Piazza, C. C. (2008). Feeding disorders and behavior: What have we learned? *Developmental Disabilities Research Reviews, 14*, 174–181.

Piazza, C. C., Fisher, W. W., Brown, K. A., Shore, B. A., Patel, M. R., Katz, R. M., et al. (2003). Functional analysis of inappropriate mealtime behaviors. *Journal of Applied Behavior Analysis, 36*(2), 187–204.

Piazza, C. C., Patel, M. R., Gulotta, C. S., Sevin, B. M., & Layer, S. A. (2003). On the relative contributions of positive reinforcement and escape extinction in the treatment of food refusal. *Journal of Applied Behavior Analysis, 36*(3), 309–324.

Piazza, C. C., Patel, M. R., Santana, C. M., Goh, H., Delia, M. D., & Lancaster, B. M. (2002). An evaluation of simultaneous and sequential presentation of preferred food and nonpreferred food to treat food selectivity. *Journal of Applied Behavior Analysis, 35* (3), 259–270.

Reed, G. K., Piazza, C. C., Patel, M. R., Layer, S. A., Bachmeyer, M. H., Bethke, S. D., et al. (2004). On the relative contributions of noncontingent reinforcement and escape extinction in the treatment of food refusal. *Journal of Applied Behavior Analysis, 37*(1), 24–42.

Rivas, K. D., Piazza, C. C., Kadey, H. J., Volkert, V. M., & Stewart, V. (2011). Sequential treatment of a feeding problem using a pacifier and flipped spoon. *Journal of Applied Behavior Analysis, 44*(2), 387–391.

Rommel, N., De Meyer, A. M., Feenstra, L., & Veereman-Wauters, G. (2003). The complexity of feeding problems in 700 infants and young children presenting to a tertiary care institution. *Journal of Pediatric Gastroenterology and Nutrition, 37*, 75–84.

Schwarz, S. M. (2003). Feeding disorders in children with developmental disabilities. *Infants and Young Children, 16*, 317–330.

Sevin, B. M., Gulotta, C. S., Sierp, B. J., Rosica, L. A., & Miller, L. J. (2002). Analysis of response covariation among multiple topographies of food refusal. *Journal of Applied Behavior Analysis, 35*(1), 65–68.

Sharp, W. G., Harker, S., & Jaquess, D. L. (2010). Comparison of bite-presentation methods in the treatment of food refusal. *Journal of Applied Behavior Analysis, 43*(4), 739–743.

Sharp, W. G., Jaquess, D. L., Morton, J. F., & Herzinger, C. V. (2010). Pediatric feeding disorders: A quantitative synthesis of treatment outcomes. *Clinical Child and Family Psychology Review, 13*(4), 348–365.

Sharp, W. G., Odom, A., & Jaquess, D. L. (2012). Comparison of upright and flipped spoon presentations to guide treatment of food refusal. *Journal of Applied Behavior Analysis, 45*(1), 83–96.

Shore, B. A., Babbitt, R. L., Williams, K. E., Coe, D. A., & Snyder, A. (1998). Use of texture fading in the treatment of food selectivity. *Journal of Applied Behavior Analysis, 31*(4), 621–633.

Tiger, J. H., & Hanley, G. P. (2005). An example of discovery research involving the transfer of stimulus control. *Journal of Applied Behavior Analysis, 38*, 499–509.

Vaz, P. M., Piazza, C. C., Stewart, V., Volkert, V. M., Groff, R. A., & Patel, M. R. (2012). Using a chaser to decrease packing in children with feeding disorders. *Journal of Applied Behavior Analysis, 45*(1), 97–105.

Volkert, V. M., & Piazza, C. C. (2012). Pediatric feeding disorders. In P. Sturmey & M. Hersen (Eds.), *The handbook of evidence based practice in clinical psychology* (Vol 1, Hoboken, NJ: John Wiley & Sons, Ltd.

Volkert, V. M., Vaz, P. M., Piazza, C. C., Frese, J., & Barnett, L. (2011). Using a flipped spoon to decrease packing in children with feeding disorders. *Journal of Applied Behavior Analysis, 44*(3), 617–621.

Wilkins, J. W., Piazza, C. C., Groff, R. A., & Vaz, P. M. (2011). Chin prompt plus re-presentation as treatment for expulsion in children with feeding disorders. *Journal of Applied Behavior Analysis, 44*(3), 513–522.

Williams, K. E., Riegel, K., Gibbons, B., & Field, D. G. (2007). Intensive behavioral treatment for severe feeding problems: A cost-effective alternative to tube feeding? *Journal of Developmental and Physical Disabilities, 19*(3), 227–235.

CHAPTER 5

ABA Applications in the Prevention and Treatment of Medical Problems

Keith D. Allen, Jeffrey F. Hine
Department of Psychology, Munroe-Meyer Institute for Genetics and Rehabilitation, University of Nebraska Medical Center, Omaha, Nebraska, USA

INTRODUCTION

In applied behavior analysis (ABA), the subject matter of interest has long been identified as that which matters to people and society (Baer, Wolf, & Risley, 1968). There is little that matters more to people than their physical health. Indeed, physical health is so important that there are both public and private institutes (e.g., National Institutes of Health, Centers for Disease Control and Prevention, Institute of Medicine) devoted entirely to its study and care. Moreover, chronic health conditions affect as many as 50% of the population over 18 (Ward & Schiller, 2013), and both the incidence and costs associated with those conditions are rising (Paez, Zhao, & Hwang, 2009).

Perhaps surprising to many in the field, applied behavior analysts have not ignored this need. While developmental disabilities have certainly garnered the lion's share of attention, applied behavior analysts have been actively trying to prevent and treat health-related problems for decades. As early as the 1970s, applied behavior analysts were tackling chronic health conditions such as high blood pressure (Elder, Ruiz, Deabler, & Dillenkoffer, 1973), Hirschsprung's disease (Kohlenberg, 1973), and asthma (Alexander, Cropp, & Chai, 1979; da Costa, Rapoff, Lemanek, & Goldstein, 1997; Renne & Creer, 1976). Indeed, the range of physical health conditions that have been addressed by applied behavior analysts since that time is extensive and includes cystic fibrosis (Bernard, Cohen, & Moffett, 2009; Hagopian & Thompson, 1999; Stark et al., 1993; Stark, Miller, Plienes, & Drabman, 1987), arthritis (Pieper, Rapoff, Purviance, & Lindsley, 1989; Rapoff, Purviance, & Lindsley, 1988), diabetes (Epstein et al., 1981;

Clinical and Organizational Applications of Applied Behavior Analysis
http://dx.doi.org/10.1016/B978-0-12-420249-8.00005-8

Raiff & Dallery, 2010; Wysocki et al., 2000), and burns (Kelley, Jarvie, Middlebrook, McNeer, & Drabman, 1984; Tarnowski, Rasnake, Linscheid, & Mulick, 1989), as well as efforts to prevent health problems via adherence to universal precautions (DeVries, Burnette, & Redmon, 1991; Finney, Miller, & Adler, 1993; Luke & Alavosius, 2011) and preparation for medical and dental procedures (Slifer, Cataldo, Cataldo, Llorente, & Gerson, 1993; Slifer, Koontz, & Cataldo, 2002; Stark et al., 1989).

In some of these investigations, the resulting publication represents a single foray by applied behavior analysts into the treatment of the presenting medical problem. Thus, there is no subsequent line of programmatic research addressing the same condition, or, alternatively, it is very difficult to find evidence of systematic replications or follow-up studies targeting the same physical health condition by the same author(s). Nevertheless, these types of "one-and-done" publications are often the logical end-product of a thorough assessment and analysis of a solution to a socially significant problem encountered in clinical practice. As such, these publications are, as a group, models for how to conduct ABA in clinical practice across a broad range of presenting conditions outside of autism and developmental disabilities.

There are, however, some investigations reported by applied behavior analysts that represent a line of programmatic research by an individual or group of researchers. However, finding such research can often be difficult when that series of studies is published across one or more journals both inside and outside of the field of ABA. Indeed, deciding where to publish studies addressing physical health conditions can pose a significant challenge for applied behavior analysts. To publish in the *Journal of Applied Behavior Analysis (JABA)*, which values the methodological and conceptual systems of behavior analysis but is not widely read by the medical community, is to risk being ignored by the very audience most interested in the problems being studied. Conversely, to publish in journals valued and read by the medical community risks losing contact with one's professional home and community of support. In addition, many in the medical community and many funding agencies place high value on randomized, controlled group studies as well as more cognitively centered conceptual systems. This often forces applied behavior analysts who study and treat physical health conditions to make career decisions about the sort of questions they will ask and the type of research they will conduct. So, it is not surprising to see applied behavior analysts who at one time were publishing in *JABA, Behavior Modification,* or *Behavior Therapy* eventually publish their research almost exclusively in journals such as *Pediatric Pulmonology, American Journal of Health Promotion, Archives of Physical Medicine and Rehabilitation,* or *Pediatrics.*

The good news is that applied behavior analysts have been, and still are, working directly to address the prevention and treatment of problems of physical health, many of which are relatively common and have the potential to increase both the visibility and acceptance of ABA. The bad news is that we have yet to find a way to create a home for these researchers within our profession and our journals. As a result, the evidence of our reach into these domains can be hard to find. Our purpose in this chapter is to show three programs of research in ABA that have addressed prevention and treatment of chronic medical problems in pediatric neurology (recurrent headaches), pediatric dentistry (distress during invasive dental procedures), and otolaryngology (voice dysphonias). The hope is that each program of research will provide guidance in the treatment of these specific medical problems and also serve as one type of model for how applied behavior analysts might conduct programs of research with medical problems. Each section will define and describe the prevalence and social significance of the medical problem, outline the methods of behavioral assessment to guide data-based decision-making, and describe the systematic analysis of interventions that has led to viable treatment protocols for use in practice.

PEDIATRIC NEUROLOGY—RECURRENT HEADACHES
Prevalence and Significance

Recurrent headaches in children and youth are characterized by repeated painful episodes experienced across several months that often occur in the absence of a well-defined medical cause. These recurrent headaches typically include infrequent but intense, pulsing migraine headaches and more frequent dull, aching tension headaches. Both types are commonly viewed as representing different points on a continuum of severity (e.g., Turkdogan et al., 2006). Recurrent headaches appear in about 10% of all preadolescent children and up to 17% of all adolescents (Hershey, 2005; Lateef et al., 2009). In addition, the prevalence of recurrent headaches increases with age (Abu-Arafeh, Razak, Sivaraman, & Graham, 2010) with the highest prevalence observed in girls aged 16-18 years (Lateef et al., 2009). Headaches are among the most common clinical problems encountered in schools (Haraldstad, Sorum, Eide, Natvig, & Helseth, 2010) and can result in prolonged absences (Kernick & Campbell, 2009; Lateef et al., 2009). Recurrent headaches can also result in increased health care utilization (Lateef et al., 2009; Stovner et al., 2007). Finally, children and adolescents with recurrent headaches have been found to experience impairment in school and social functioning compared to other children with significant chronic diseases (e.g., Petersen,

Hagglof, & Bergstrom, 2009). As a result, recurrent headaches represent a clinically significant health problem for many children and youth.

Etiology

There is now considerable evidence that both environment and genetics play an important interactive role in the etiology of many recurrent headaches. Individuals with recurrent headaches are thought to have a genetic predisposition for autonomic dysregulation (Lewis, 2004; Maher & Griffiths, 2011). In this model, the genetically predisposed individual experiences an increased number of unconditioned stimuli which elicit a cascade of autonomic reactivity (e.g., Borsook, Maleki, Becerra, & McEwen, 2012). The sustained autonomic reactivity is what is thought to lead to the pain. Common stimuli that can elicit reactivity and subsequent headache pain can include typical stress inducers such as academic demands, family or peer conflict, and performance situations (Larsson & Zaluha, 2003); however, eliciting stimuli might also include events commonly considered to be neutral or even positive, such as going to an amusement park, attending a birthday party, or playing actively outside. In this model, recurrent headaches are not evidence of psychopathology or malingering. Instead, headaches result from an interaction between a genetic predisposition for autonomic reactivity and the unconditioned stimuli in the environment that elicits them (Nash & Thebarge, 2006).

In addition to these respondent components, learned responses to pain can play an important role in understanding how it is maintained (Fordyce, 1976; Rachlin, 1985). When children experience recurrent headaches, they engage in a wide range of behaviors designed to reduce the intensity or duration of pain, behaviors that often include withdrawal from activities and isolation from eliciting stimuli. Pain behaviors are also learned through imitation of adults with recurrent pain symptoms (Goubert, Vlaeyen, Crombez, & Craig, 2011) and can be further strengthened through increased attention from parents, peers, and medical personnel (Peterson & Palermo, 2004) or through the absence of reinforcement for well-behavior (Allen & Mathews, 1998). In addition, children may learn that some pain behaviors allow them to escape unpleasant social, academic, or family demands.

Behavioral Interventions

Given the combined roles of both respondent and operant components in the etiology and maintenance of recurrent headaches, behavioral treatments have typically involved a combination of efforts to either control the autonomic reactivity elicited by the environment, manage the contingencies related to pain behavior, or both. Interestingly, the idea that individuals might be able to control autonomic reactivity would have been considered impossible in the mid-twentieth century, because most physiological behaviors were considered involuntary. But by the 1970s, applied behavior analysts had become some of the first to provide empirical demonstrations that individuals can, in fact, gain volitional control over numerous autonomic nervous system functions (e.g., blood pressure, stomach acid secretion, muscle tension) via operant conditioning (Budzynski & Stoyva, 1969; Elder et al., 1973; Whitehead, Renault, & Goldiamond, 1975). This eventually became known as biofeedback. Currently, one of the most common means of producing autonomic stability via biofeedback is to teach individuals to increase peripheral blood flow. In this approach to treatment, individuals have a temperature sensor attached to their hands and subsequently learn (typically across 8–12 sessions) to increase peripheral blood flow (i.e., hand temperature) by observing moment-to-moment changes in temperature as depicted on a display screen. By the late 1980s, investigations had repeatedly demonstrated that this "thermal biofeedback" could be an effective component of treatment for recurrent headaches (Duckro & Cantwell-Simmons, 1989; Hermann, Kim, & Blanchard, 1995).

Response Measurement and Clinical Decision-Making

Prior to treatment, a functional assessment typically involves efforts to identify environmental stimuli that may elicit autonomic arousal and also environmental contingencies that support existing pain behavior. To this end, children and youth are asked to self-monitor daily changes in pain parameters using the pain record depicted in Figure 5.1. This typically involves recording pain intensity on four separate occasions throughout the day. The result is that the provider can see, at a glance, pain intensity, duration, and frequency as well as observe patterns within and across days. Pain frequency is particularly important to assess as low baseline rates (i.e., less than one episode/month) tend to predict poorer adherence to treatment. The form also allows one to monitor changes in pain parameters during treatment with "clinically significant" reductions defined as a change of 50% or greater in one or more pain parameters (Blanchard, 1992). Finally, the monitoring form allows the client to track aspects of functional impairment (e.g., classes and activities missed) as well as use of medication. The pain records are typically reviewed with the client and eliciting events

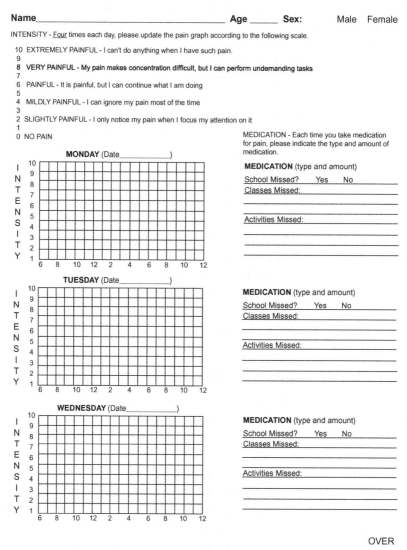

Figure 5.1 Weekly pain record.

and patterns are discussed and incorporated into treatment planning. As a part of the functional assessment, parents are also asked to report on the manner in which they respond to their children when they are in pain and when they are not.

Autonomic responding can be monitored with any of a variety of physiological monitoring (biofeedback) devices. We have typically used the ProComp Infiniti Encoder hardware combined with Biograph Infiniti software (Thought Technology®) which allows comprehensive assessment, monitoring, and feedback across multiple response measures such as skin conductance, peripheral blood flow (hand temperature), electromyography (EMG) (muscle tension), heart rate, blood volume pulse, and respiration. However, we have also used a portable Autogenics AT42® which monitors and provides feedback for hand temperature only. Temperature is typically monitored from the volar surface of an index or middle finger of the non-dominant hand. Clients typically observe a visual display of moment-to-moment changes in hand temperature via a digital readout and a moving colored bar that indicates goal attainment with color changes in the moving bar. For home practice and maintenance of skills learned in the clinic, we have used relatively inexpensive indoor/outdoor temperature monitors available in local electronics and discount stores (e.g., Aube Technology TE503®) and have asked clients to self-monitor home-based practices using biofeedback logs that show frequency and duration of practices as well as amount of behavior (temperature) change.

Intervention Analysis

In the early 1990s, we began our own program of research to answer a number of questions about the combined "biobehavioral" treatment that included both biofeedback management of autonomic dysregulation and operant contingency management of pain-related behavior. The research questions generally addressed were: (a) whether the treatment could be streamlined, relying more on home-based than clinic-based management, (b) the extent to which contingency management of pain behavior was important to the success of treatment, and (c) whether treatment could be effective with tension headache sufferers as well as migraine sufferers.

Our initial investigation examined the efficacy of shifting from a clinic-based treatment format to a home-based treatment (Allen & McKeen, 1991). The treatment required participants to learn thermal biofeedback in the clinic but were asked to practice daily in the home (about 10 min/practice) using small portable inexpensive temperature trainers. These "noncontingent" practices were considered important for acquiring general autonomic stability and generally were scheduled to occur during pain-free periods of the day. However, participants were also asked to use biofeedback when pain was first noticed (i.e., contingent practices). Reviewing pain

records from baseline reports helped identify when to schedule daily practices and helped increase client awareness about when pain episodes typically
began and when contingent practices would most likely be needed.

The treatment also required parents to (a) provide social praise to their
child or adolescent for observed practice/use of the self-regulation skills
while (b) discouraging more typical responses (e.g., withdrawal, isolation,
avoidance) that interfered with adaptive functioning. The specific types
of behaviors parents were asked to engage in are identified in Table 5.1.

The combined treatment program was introduced in a multiple-baseline
design across three groups of children ages 7-12 years, and the results were
published in *Headache: The Journal of Head and Face Pain* (Allen & McKeen,
1991). Participants reported marked reductions in self-reported pain with
the introduction of treatment, accompanied by corresponding reductions
in medication utilization and school absences. Equally important, the results
showed that treatment integrity was critical; that is, those who did not
adhere to both autonomic regulation and the operant contingency management components showed markedly poorer response to treatment.

5.1 Pain behavior management guidelines for parents

1. Encourage independent pain management: Praise and publically acknowledge
   practice of self-regulation (i.e., biofeedback or relaxation) skills during pain-free
   episodes. If pain is reported by child, issue a single prompt to practice/use self-
   regulation skills. Look for opportunities to praise and reward normal activity
   when report of pain has been made
2. Encourage normal activity during pain episodes: Insist upon attendance at
   school, maintenance of daily chores and responsibilities, as well as participation
   in regular activities (e.g., lessons, rehearsals, clubs, etc.)
3. Eliminate status checks: Parents are to ask no questions about whether there is
   pain or how much it hurts
4. Reduce response to pain behavior: No effort should be made to assist the child in
   coping. Do not offer suggestions for coping. Do not offer pain medication
5. Reduce pharmacological dependence: If medication is requested, deliver only as
   prescribed and only on recommended time table
6. Recruit others to follow the same guidelines: School personnel should follow
   same guidelines and not send child home in response to pain; child should be
   encouraged and permitted to practice self-regulation skills in the classroom;
   workload should not be modified
7. Treat pain requiring a reduction in activity as illness: If school, activities, chores,
   or responsibilities are missed, the child should be treated as ill and remain in bed
   for the remainder of the day, even if pain is resolved. Do not permit playing
   games, watching TV, or special treatment

Two follow-up studies were conducted to address questions about each component of the biobehavioral treatment package. In the first follow-up study, we asked whether specific aspects of the visual feedback during bio-feedback training impacted treatment outcome. Using a multiple-baseline design across six individuals ages 9-13, results (published in *Headache*) demonstrated that the magnitude and frequency of feedback during biofeedback training impacted treatment outcomes, but there were marked individual differences in whether magnitude or frequency of feedback had a greater impact (Allen & Shriver, 1997). That is, for some individuals, increasing the magnitude of feedback had little impact, but increasing the frequency of feedback did, suggesting (not surprisingly) that there are clinical benefits to providing everyone with increased magnitude and frequency of feedback from the outset of biofeedback training.

The second component study centered on an attempt to isolate the relative impact of the operant pain behavior management guidelines found in Table 5.1 (Allen & Shriver, 1998). In a randomized clinical trial, 27 children ages 7-18 were assigned to either a thermal biofeedback only group (i.e., no guidelines provided to parents) or a group that included biofeedback for the children *and* provided contingency management guidelines for the parents. The biofeedback training and home practice requirements were the same as in our original study in 1991, and the parent guidelines were those depicted in Table 5.1. In an effort to reach a broader audience than just those who read *Headache*, the results were published in *Behavior Therapy*. Results showed that all participants learned to increase peripheral blood flow, and all participants practiced biofeedback frequently at home. However, there were nearly four times more children who experienced clinically significant reductions in pain and improvements in adaptive functioning in the combined treatment group. In addition, over a third of those in the combined group were headache-free at 3 months follow up, while none of those in the biofeedback-alone group were headache-free. These results suggested that teaching children and adolescents' skills for self-regulation of autonomic reactivity might likely have little long-term benefit if there are not efforts to arrange an environment to differentially reinforce incompatible behaviors.

In each of these early studies, the focus of treatment was on migraine headaches, with either pain frequency as the primary outcome measure or a pain "index" that combined frequency, intensity, and duration. Our subsequent study (Arndorfer & Allen, 2001), designed to evaluate the effectiveness of the biobehavioral treatment package with tension headache sufferers, tracked the three pain parameters independently. In a multiple-baseline design across five children ages 8–14, results showed that when the treatment package was sequentially introduced, there were corresponding reductions in pain; however, visual analysis showed that the benefits were not equal across all three pain parameters. When visual analysis focused solely on pain frequency (see Figure 5.2), Adam, Cindy, and Jane

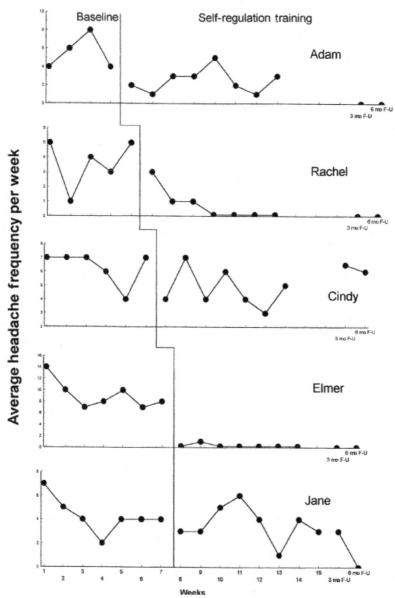

Figure 5.2 Headache frequency per week.

appeared unresponsive to treatment compared to Rachel and Elmer. However, Adam, Cindy, and Jane all demonstrated clinically meaningful reductions in pain intensity (not shown) and duration (Figure 5.3). Thus, the results suggested the importance of monitoring and evaluating pain frequency, intensity, and duration independently when determining treatment outcomes.

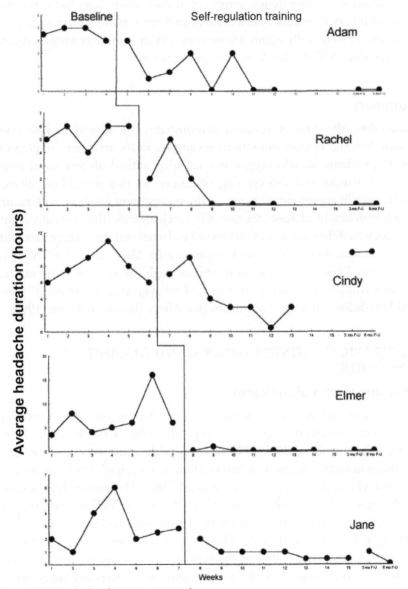

Figure 5.3 Headache duration per week.

The final study in this line of research explored extending the reach of ABA from the controlled clinic environment into a primary care setting (Allen, Elliott, & Arndorfer, 2002). Our interest was in whether the benefits of the treatment would be compromised when delivered by less experienced applied behavior analysts in a loud, sometimes unpredictable, primary care environment, using rooms designed for medical evaluation and treatment. In a multiple-baseline design across seven individuals, ages 8-15, referred from a primary care clinic, the treatment package was implemented successfully and with clinically significant outcomes by practitioners without extensive training in biofeedback or pain management.

Summary

Altogether, this line of research demonstrates the important role both respondent and operant conditioning can play in the treatment of physical health problems. Results suggest that teaching individuals to control autonomic reactivity and also creating contingencies that strengthen reliance on these skills are important parts of pain management for those with recurrent headaches. In addition, the line of research indicates the generality of this approach to different types of recurrent headaches and the relative ease with which practitioners with basic competence in ABA can deliver effective treatment. These types of demonstrations might be seen by those outside of ABA as important evidence that applied behavior analysts can bring "powerful medicine" into the mainstream (see Allen, Barone, & Kuhn, 1993).

PEDIATRIC DENTISTRY—MANAGING DISRUPTIVE BEHAVIOR
Prevalence and Significance

While most children are cooperative at the dentist, one in five exhibits marked distress and subsequently disrupts the delivery of care (Brill, 2000; Klingberg & Broberg, 2007). The intensity of the distress is even more pronounced in young children (Allen, Hutfless, & Larzelere, 2003) and is exacerbated when invasive procedures are used (Brill). Unfortunately, as a result of the increased probability of disruptive behavior in children, many dentists will refuse to treat children in general (Casamassimo, Seale, & Ruehs, 2004), thereby reducing access to care. This reduced access to care is a socially significant problem, especially in light of evidence that tooth decay is one of the most common diseases worldwide, with prevalence rates five times that of asthma and related complications that include respiratory disease, cardiovascular disease, and diabetes (National Research Council, 2011).

Etiology

Observations and subsequent functional assessments of disruptive behavior in the dental clinic have suggested that much of the disruptive responding observed in children undergoing restorative treatment and even minor screening procedures is maintained by escape from and avoidance of treatment, even if that escape and avoidance is only temporary (Allen & Stokes, 1989). Although the discomforts experienced at the dentist today are a far cry from what patients encountered 50 years ago, the oral cavity has some of the most tightly bundled, sensitive nerve endings in the body (Fried, Sessle, & Devor, 2011) and the painless injection has yet to be achieved. When these painful experiences are combined with other uncomfortable sensations (e.g., pulling, pushing, and pressure), unusual sights (e.g., masked provider), and unfamiliar sounds (e.g., hissing, grinding), it is not surprising that escape and avoidance are reinforcing for children (Allen & Wallace, 2013). Dentists typically try to manage disruptive behavior using a variety of profession-recommended behavior management procedures such as warnings, reprimands, restraint, and sedation (American Academy of Pediatric Dentistry, 2011) but implementation of these procedures typically results in brief termination of treatment as well.

Behavioral Interventions

Applied behavior analysts have been interested in helping meet the oral health needs of individuals for nearly 40 years. Initial efforts focused on trying to improve access to quality oral health care (Greene & Neistat, 1983; Iwata & Becksfort, 1981; Reiss & Bailey, 1982; Reiss, Piotrowski, & Bailey, 1976) but also involved efforts to reduce the distress of those undergoing restorative dental treatment (e.g., procedures involving injections, drilling, and tooth repair; Stokes & Kennedy, 1980; Williams, Hurst, & Stokes, 1983). These investigations typically targeted neurotypical populations; however, some of the research targeted populations with developmental disabilities as well (e.g., Conyers et al., 2004).

Since the late 1980s, we have conducted several lines of research related to managing child behavior during restorative dental treatment. The first line of research focused on efforts at creating painless injections (i.e., altering motivating operations related to escape) through computerized and modified oral injection strategies (Gibson, Allen, Hutfless, & Beiraghi, 2000; Roeber, Wallace, Rothe, Salama, & Allen, 2011). The second line of research included efforts to "distract" children from the immediate environment by introducing more salient visual and auditory competing stimuli (e.g., Filcheck et al., 2004; Hoge, Howard, Wallace, & Allen, 2012; Stark et al., 1989). The third line of research, and the focus of the rest of this section, has centered on evaluating interventions designed to take advantage of a child's motivation to escape dental treatment.

Response Measurement and Clinical Decision-Making

Prior to intervention, a functional assessment is important to help determine the intensity of the disruptiveness as well as which dental procedures are evoking the most disruptive behavior. Disruptive behavior is operationalized as either vocal disruptions (i.e., gagging, crying, or complaining about dental procedures) or physical disruptions (i.e., head and body movements of either small repetitive motions [without interruption of 1 s or more] or one continuous motion by any part of the body totaling movement of 15 cm or more). Intensity is coded separately as any vocal or physical disruption that results in the temporary termination of dental procedures. Standard restorative dental procedures typically include those with varying "invasiveness," and not surprisingly, escape behavior is observed to vary as a function of that invasiveness. These procedures include, from most-to-least invasive: injections, drilling, water to rinse, and suction to remove excess water, as well as tooth repair involving placement of fillings or crowns. Typically, the most invasive procedures tend to be at the beginning of the treatment visit. As a result, a typical pattern of disruptive behavior can be seen across a 20- to 30-min visit in which the most intense and frequent disruptive behaviors occur within the first 2-5 min of the visit. An observation revealing this common pattern of responding would suggest a need for more intensive programming early in the visit (e.g., denser schedule of reinforcement), while a child who shows more scattered levels of disruptiveness might require a more consistent schedule of reinforcement throughout the entire visit.

Observations of the intensity and frequency of child disruptions as well as patterns of disruptiveness in relation to dental procedures are best conducted by an independent observer. While we do have data to suggest that subjective behavior ratings, completed by a dentist using a common dental behavior rating scale (Frankl, Shiere, & Fogels, 1962), can provide valid estimates of disruptive intensity (Allen et al., 2003), these ratings do not provide measures of frequency or duration and do not provide information on procedure-related variability. Thus, throughout our research we most often rely on direct observations by an independent observer who codes the occurrence of any physical or vocal disruptive behaviors and codes the specific dental procedures in use with a 15-s partial-interval recording system.

Intervention Analysis

Participants in most of the investigations in this line of research were referred for "behavioral consultation" because they were too disruptive to access oral health care without requiring either passive restraint (i.e., a medical stabilization board with Velcro straps) or general anesthesia in an operating room. This included children less than 3 years of age, even though many dentists consider these children to be "precooperative" or unable to be cooperative without sedation or restraint (e.g., Nathan, 1995). The referred children typically required multiple visits for restorative treatment, thus allowing for repeated measurements within and across visits to the dentist.

The original intervention (Allen & Stokes, 1987) was designed to teach children functionally equivalent alternative responses during dental procedures, responses that included remaining quiet and lying very still with hands folded. Gradually longer periods of calm and quiet behaviors were reinforced with repeated but brief (10-15 s) access to periods of escape from ongoing dental treatment. Alternatively, if the child was disruptive, escape was postponed until cooperation was regained. Thus, the treatment involved differential (negative) reinforcement of incompatible behaviors with escape extinction. Researchers delivered the intervention during mock dental treatment in which the children were exposed to many of the sights and sounds of dental treatment, but without actual injections or drilling. Baseline and treatment observations, however, were conducted *in situ* during actual restorative treatment visits conducted by the dentist, including injections and drilling. In a multiple-baseline across subjects design, five children ages 3-6 with highly disruptive behavior in baseline, including gagging and vomiting, showed marked reductions in disruptive behavior and distress when, and only when, the contingent escape and escape extinction were used. The study was replicated with a similar population and small-*n* design resulting in comparable outcomes and, in an effort to reach a broader audience, the findings were published in *Journal of Dentistry for Children* (Allen, Stark, Rigney, Nash, & Stokes, 1988).

Subsequent to these original studies, the referring dentists expressed concern that the delivery of the intervention during analog dental treatment procedures was too time-consuming and impractical for dissemination. Thus, a follow-up study was designed to evaluate the extent to which a dentist could deliver the intervention *in situ* (Allen, Loiben, Allen, & Stanley, 1992). In addition, the participating dentists expressed concern that the escape extinction component would have poor social acceptability with parents and also potentially expose the dentist to increased liability risks; thus, the escape extinction component was removed. A participating dentist was then trained to deliver escape contingently when the dentist observed the patient lying still and quiet for anywhere from 5 to 15 s. The dentist was trained to notice and deliver escape during at least 80% of these opportunities during treatment.

In a multiple-baseline design across four participants ages 3-7, we found that the contingent escape alone, without the escape extinction component, was effective in reducing child disruptive behavior in a relatively short amount of time (see Figure 5.4). The results also showed a strong correspondence between treatment fidelity and response to treatment. In Beth's second treatment visit (fourth visit overall), the dentist did not meet the criterion for treatment fidelity and disruptive behavior increased to near baseline levels, serving as an unintentional treatment reversal. In addition, Ray's second visit was intended to be a treatment visit; however, the dentist delivered the contingent escape procedure only 25% of the time. This resulted in continued high rates of disruptive behavior, thus confirming the importance of measuring treatment fidelity. Finally, we found that on average the dentist did not spend any more time using behavior management during implementation of the contingent escape procedure than during baseline sessions. This was considered critical for dissemination and broader adoption by general practitioners.

Although the contingent escape procedure was effective, the participating dentist expressed concern that maintaining treatment fidelity required a high response effort related to noticing cooperative behavior, thereby distracting him from attending to the delivery of quality dental treatment. Thus, we began discussions about how to modify the procedure to accommodate the needs of the dentist to attend more fully to dental treatment. The discussions centered on the possibility of making access to escape noncontingent and based on time rather than behavior. The result would be a fixed-time (FT) schedule of negative reinforcement (see Carr, Severtson, & Lepper, 2009).

The noncontingent reinforcement (NCR) procedure required the dentist to wear an electronic prompter (MotivAider®) that signaled to the dentist the FT schedule under which he was to deliver access to 10 s of escape from treatment. The dentist initially began by following an FT 15-s

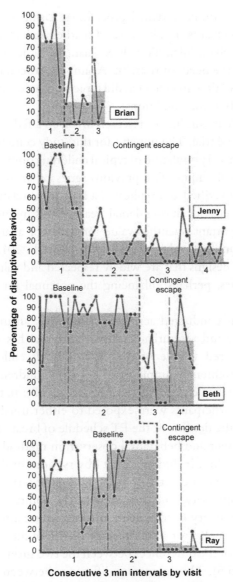

Figure 5.4 Percentage of 15 s intervals with disruptive behavior. Asterisks by visit number indicate treatment integrity below criterion.

schedule. Then, over time, the dentist lengthened the time between rein-forcement deliveries based on fewer occurrences of disruptive behavior. The treatment was delivered sequentially across five highly disruptive young children, four of whom required physical restraint to prevent injury to self and others and to complete dental procedures. Using a multiple-baseline design across participants, results showed marked reductions in disruptive behavior (O'Callaghan, Allen, Powell, & Salama, 2006). The procedure also nearly eliminated the need for restraint. Again, the procedure took virtually the same amount of time to deliver as did typical behavior management used by the dentist in baseline conditions.

The final study in this line of research involved a federally funded, randomized, controlled trial. The impetus for this study centered on extending the research to a broad population of typical children commonly seen in general pediatric dental clinics. The previous series of small-n experimental-design studies had verified and replicated a functional relationship between escape and child behavior during dental treatment. Randomized controlled trials can add important scientific value for behavior analysts by showing external validity and generality of procedures (Smith, 2013), and they are also experimental designs that are widely respected and valued in nonbehavioral communities, perhaps enhancing the potential for acceptance and dissemination.

The study was conducted across two locations: an urban university-based dental clinic and a suburban children's hospital-based clinic. Rather than using a referred sample of the most difficult children, this study focused on a convenience sample of 151 typical children, ages 2-9 years who were visiting the dentist (Allen & Wallace, 2013). In the randomized, controlled trial, participants were exposed to either usual behavior management used by the dentists or the FT schedule of breaks from treatment. The dental treatment and behavioral observation methods matched those of the previous studies, including direct observations of distress behavior, observer training, and measures of reliability, close scrutiny of treatment implementation integrity, and treatment acceptability. Results showed that the routine delivery of scheduled breaks from treatment significantly reduced disruptive behavior. A cumulative record of the rate of disruptive behavior shows that the differences between the two groups increased over time (see Figure 5.5). This increasing difference between the two groups makes sense if one views access to noncontingent escape as a process that takes some time to exert its influence; either by reducing the effectiveness of escape as a reinforcer or by disrupting the contingency that maintained disruptive behavior in the first place. Finally, consistent with all previous studies, results showed that the children exposed to the NCR procedure required significantly less restraint to manage their behavior and that the NCR procedure did not significantly increase the time spent on behavior management by dentists.

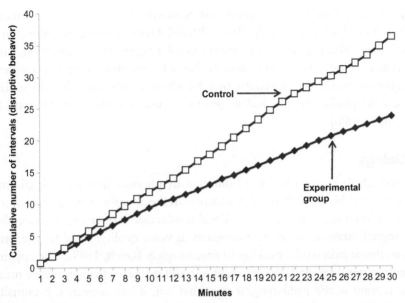

Figure 5.5 Cumulative intervals of disruptive behavior across minutes within each dental visit.

Summary

This line of research in behavioral dentistry demonstrates a logical progression of research within ABA, from small-*n* studies showing clear functional relations and strong efficacy with the most demanding children, to a large randomized controlled study showing good generality and practical utility with the most common children. Overall, the procedure of using brief breaks from ongoing dental treatment has good efficacy, acceptability, and generality and may have the potential to make an important contribution to public health by reducing the distress associated with oral health care. Ultimately, children and parents may be more likely to seek services that are not as distressing, and dentists may be more likely to provide those services if they have management tools that allow them to feel more comfortable providing oral health care. Whether this type of approach to behavior management gains widespread acceptance among dentists remains to be seen.

OTOLARYNGOLOGY—VOICE DYSPHONIAS
Prevalence and Significance

Dysphonias are a broad group of voice disorders characterized by hoarseness, weakness, or loss of voice that occur in about 1% of the population and have significant public health impacts and economic costs to society (Cohen, Kim, Roy, Asche, & Courey, 2012a, 2012b). Dysphonias can result in laryngeal pain, pharyngolaryngeal reflux, vocal fatigue, throat irritation, and throat clearing. Dysphonias directly impact communication effectiveness on the job and in the classroom, thereby adversely affecting physical, social, and work performance as well as general quality of life (Cohen, Dupont, & Courey, 2006).

Etiology

Although there are a variety of different dysphonias, functional dysphonia involves problems with vocal production in the absence of structural lesions (e.g., House & Andrews, 1988). Vocal production is often characterized by strangled, strained, or severe hoarseness in voice quality, vocal fatigue, and even throat pain while speaking (Redenbaugh & Reich, 1989). The impairment in vocal production is thought to result primarily from excessive muscle tension in the paralaryngeal areas that can, if left untreated, eventually result in structural abnormalities such as mucosal changes and fleshy vocal nodules (i.e., callouses) and polyps (i.e., blisters) on the vocal cords (Morrison, Nichol, & Rammage, 1986). Left untreated or if unresponsive to traditional interventions, they can result in the need for invasive surgical interventions.

Behavioral Interventions

Treatments for functional dysphonias are typically directed by speech therapist/vocal coaches who conduct voice therapy. Voice therapy commonly centers on the use of modeling and feedback to teach individuals a wide variety of vocal techniques that are designed to improve voice quality. Voice therapy includes such strategies as reducing excessive demands on the voice, adjusting pitch and volume, using diaphragmatic breathing, coordinating phonation with breathing, and developing optimal resonance (Carding, Horsley, & Docherty, 1999). While treatment outcomes can be good for many of those that participate in vocal therapy, more than half continue to experience dysfunction after treatment (Van Lierde, Claeys, De Bodt, & van Cauwenberge, 2007).

When traditional voice therapy is not sufficient, one treatment alternative for functional dysphonia involves directly targeting changes in laryngeal muscle tension via EMG biofeedback. In EMG biofeedback, a recording of electrical activity from a muscle or group of muscles (typically reported in microvolts, μV) is provided to the individual in visual or auditory form. The signal is obtained from electrodes applied to the skin surface above the targeted muscles around the vocal cords, and the information is used by the individual to learn to control muscle activity. Success with learning to control targeted muscles depends upon the specificity of the information that the signal provides, which itself depends upon the placement and arrangement of the electrodes (Fogel, 1995; Sherman, 2003). Fortunately, progress in biofeedback research has led to significant advancements in instrumentation (Peek, 1995), resulting in noninvasive and sophisticated technology for using surface recordings to measure muscle activity near the vocal cords. Thus, it is possible to accurately and reliably monitor, amplify, and transform that activity around the vocal cords into audio and/or visual signals that are easily understandable and observable.

Response Measurement and Clinical Decision-Making

Direct measurement of the laryngeal muscle tension can be achieved with a wide variety of sophisticated electronic systems for measuring EMG including the ProComp Infiniti Encoder hardware combined with Biograph Infiniti software (Thought Technology®; described above). However, at the time of the studies that comprise the current review, EMG activity was measured using an older J & J Clinical Series M57 monitor and BioTrack software (Epanded Technologies, Inc.). To measure laryngeal muscle tension, surface EMG electrodes are best placed vertically, in parallel alignment along one side of the voice box, over the thyrohyoid membrane with a ground electrode placed on the wrist. The raw EMG signal is recorded in microvolts (μV) and presented on the monitor as a vertical bar moving up and down; down corresponding to decreases in tension and up corresponding to increases in tension. Regardless of the specific hardware and software used, the electrode placements for EMG monitoring of laryngeal tension would likely remain the same. Assistance in interpreting the levels observed can be gained from normative studies showing typical levels of EMG tension in nonvoice-disordered individuals (Stemple, Weiler, Whitehead, & Komray, 1980).

Additional baseline measures of dysphonias also can include estimated measures of subglottal pressure from oral air pressure via a pneumotachograph and direct visual examination of the vocal cords via fiber optic endoscopy. However, these procedures are typically performed by otolaryngeal specialists. The social significance of both impairments and treatment-related changes can be determined by having a speech therapist provide independent perceptual assessment using a rating scale such as the Quick Screen for Voice (Lee, Stemple, Glaze, & Kelchner, 2004).

Intervention Analysis

In 1991, we applied EMG biofeedback technology to treat a 9-year-old boy with functional dysphonia and vocal nodules, referred after traditional voice therapy had proven ineffective (Allen, Bernstein, & Chait, 1991). The analysis of EMG biofeedback as a treatment for the dysphonia was considered important for averting planned "last resort" surgical intervention. In the EMG biofeedback treatment, the primary dependent measure was laryngeal muscle tension. During baseline recording, the client could not observe the feedback displays. After stable baseline measures were observed during both quiet and speaking conditions, the subject participated in EMG biofeedback. During the sessions, the client was instructed to watch the visual display and attempt to relax the vocal muscles. Success criterion was visually displayed for the client as a vertical line superimposed over the vertical moving bar such that lowering the moving bar below the criterion line was considered "success." The client received continuous visual biofeedback during biweekly, 30-min sessions. In a combined multiple-baseline with changing-criterion design, EMG biofeedback was introduced sequentially, first during the resting condition to help establish success during a less vocally demanding activity. Once improvements were observed in the resting condition, feedback was introduced during the speaking condition. Separate criteria were established for each condition and then lowered each time the participant met the established criterion for three consecutive sessions. Results showed marked reductions in muscle tension that corresponded with the introduction of biofeedback and with each subsequent change in criteria. In addition, five speech pathologists who listened to before and after voice samples provided independent ratings of voice quality that confirmed the social validity of the observed changes in muscle tension. Equally important, posttreatment medical examinations showed that the vocal nodules were eliminated and surgery was unnecessary.

In a follow-up study (Watson, Allen, & Allen, 1993), we treated ventricular fold dysphonia, which is a rare type of functional dysphonia in which muscular tension in the throat forces ventricular folds to adduct over the true vocal cords during phonation while the true vocal folds remain open. These false vocal folds are then used to produce speech, resulting in a raspy, hoarse, or strangulated voice. EMG treatment focused on teaching the individual to reduce laryngeal muscle tension under three different sets of conditions:

quiet, counting out loud, and conversation. After stable baseline responding was observed, EMG biofeedback treatment was introduced sequentially in a multiple-baseline design with changing criteria across the three response conditions during biweekly, 30-min sessions. Changing criteria were set at 5 μV below the mean of the last three baseline measurements. Subsequent criteria were set at 5 μV below the previously established criterion. Figure 5.6 shows that with the introduction of EMG biofeedback training there were stepwise reductions in the average level of muscle tension that corresponded with the changing-criterion levels. In addition, speech experts independently evaluated the changes as clinically significant.

Finally, we applied the same methodology again to treat a 16-year-old girl with a third type of functional dysphonia called paradoxical vocal fold motion (PVCM; Warnes & Allen, 2005). In PVCM, excessive laryngeal muscle tension causes the vocal folds to close over the airway when breathing, restricting the airway opening resulting in labored breathing and feelings of being choked (Mathers-Schmidt, 2001). The symptoms are frequently misdiagnosed and treated as asthma. This particular client had a 2-year history of misdiagnosis and treatment and was missing extended amounts of school. During treatment, success criteria were initially set at 2 μV below baseline levels and new criteria (i.e., 2 μV lower) were set when the patient achieved three consecutive sessions at or below the current criterion. Two 10-min EMG biofeedback sessions were conducted once per week over the course of 10 weeks. In a changing-criterion design, EMG biofeedback produced stepwise reductions in laryngeal muscle activity and disorder-related school absences were eliminated.

Summary

Together, this sample of small-n design studies provides repeated demonstrations that with EMG biofeedback, patients were able to achieve good control over disordered muscle activity that was creating functional impairments and marked health complications. These EMG studies served as important reminders that operant learning combined with sophisticated electronic technology can be both a powerful teaching tool and a therapeutic agent. By amplifying and reinforcing small, gradual changes in muscle tension near the vocal cords, each participant achieved selective control of these covert behaviors, improved voice quality, and in some cases avoided more invasive surgical interventions. Thus, EMG biofeedback is clearly an applied behavioral technology that can make important contributions to the treatment of chronic health conditions.

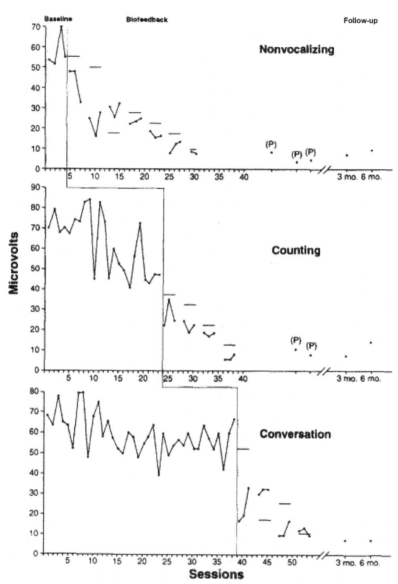

Figure 5.6 Mean EMG levels per session across three conditions.

CONCLUSIONS

Applied behavior analysts have a long-standing tradition of addressing myriad physical health problems of importance to society. Evidence of the breadth of these efforts in *JABA* alone is impressive. However, finding sustained programs of research addressing physical health problems can be more challenging, largely because that evidence is often dispersed broadly across a wide range of medical and behavioral journals. Our intent in the present review has been to provide an overview of three such programs of research by applied behavior analysts in clinical practice. The three programs take on a diverse array of acute (dentistry), recurrent (neurology), and chronic (otolaryngology) medical conditions, but all demonstrate, to varying degrees, the application of behavioral principles to solve significant health-related problems. The programs of research also include small-n and group experimental designs to demonstrate both internal and external validity. Individually, these programs of research should help applied behavior analysts in managing these challenging health conditions. Together, we hope they will provide an increased appreciation for the scope of ABA in addressing issues of social significance and perhaps encourage others to seek opportunities to extend the reach of ABA into the mainstream of physical health care.

REFERENCES

Abu-Arafeh, I., Razak, S., Sivaraman, B., & Graham, C. (2010). Prevalence of headache and migraine in children and adolescents: A systematic review of population-based studies. *Developmental Medicine and Child Neurology, 52*(12), 1088–1097.

Alexander, A. B., Cropp, G. J., & Chai, H. (1979). Effects of relaxation training on pulmonary mechanics in children with asthma. *Journal of Applied Behavior Analysis, 12*(1), 27–35.

Allen, K. D., Barone, V. J., & Kuhn, B. R. (1993). A behavioral prescription for promoting applied behavior analysis within pediatrics. *Journal of Applied Behavior Analysis, 26*(4), 493–502.

Allen, K. D., Bernstein, B., & Chait, D. H. (1991). EMG biofeedback treatment of pediatric hyperfunctional dysphonia. *Journal of Behavior Therapy and Experimental Psychiatry, 22*(2), 97–101.

Allen, K. D., Elliott, A. E., & Arndorfer, R. (2002). Behavioral pain management for pediatric headache in primary care. *Children's Health Care, 31*(3), 175–189.

Allen, K. D., Hutfless, S., & Larzelere, R. (2003). Evaluation of two predictors of child disruptive behavior during restorative dental treatment. *Journal of Dentistry for Children (Chicago, Ill), 70*(3), 221–225.

Allen, K. D., Loiben, T., Allen, S. J., & Stanley, R. T. (1992). Dentist-implemented contingent escape for management of disruptive child behavior. *Journal of Applied Behavior Analysis, 25*(3), 629–636.

Allen, K. D., & Mathews, J. R. (1998). Behavior management of recurrent pain in children. In T. S. Watson & F. Gresham (Eds.), *Handbook of child behavior therapy: Ecological considerations in assessment, treatment, and evaluation* (pp. 263–285). New York, NY: Plenum Press.

Allen, K. D., & McKeen, L. R. (1991). Home-based multicomponent treatment of pediatric migraine. *Headache, 31*(7), 467–472.

Allen, K. D., & Shriver, M. D. (1997). Enhanced performance feedback to strengthen biofeedback treatment outcome with childhood migraine. *Headache, 37*(3), 169–173.

Allen, K. D., & Shriver, M. D. (1998). Role of parent-mediated pain behavior management strategies in biofeedback treatment of childhood migraine headaches. *Behavior Therapy*, *29*, 477–490.

Allen, K. D., Stark, L. J., Rigney, B. A., Nash, D. A., & Stokes, T. F. (1988). Reinforced practice of children's cooperative behavior during restorative dental treatment. *ASDC Journal of Dentistry for Children*, *55*(4), 273–277.

Allen, K. D., & Stokes, T. F. (1987). Use of escape and reward in the management of young children during dental treatment. *Journal of Applied Behavior Analysis*, *20*(4), 381–390.

Allen, K. D., & Stokes, T. F. (1989). Pediatric behavioral dentistry. In M. Hersen, R. Eisler, & P. Miller (Eds.), *Progress in behavior modification* (pp. 60–90). Newbury Park, CA: Sage Publications, Inc.

Allen, K. D., & Wallace, D. P. (2013). Effectiveness of using noncontingent escape for general behavior management in a pediatric dental clinic. *Journal of Applied Behavior Analysis*, *46*(4), 723–737.

American Academy of Pediatric Dentistry. (2011). Guideline on behavior guidance for the pediatric dental patient. *Pediatric Dentistry*, *33*, 161–173 (Reference Manual 2011/2012).

Arndorfer, R. E., & Allen, K. D. (2001). Extending the efficacy of a thermal biofeedback treatment package to the management of tension-type headaches in children. *Headache*, *41*, 183–192.

Baer, D. M., Wolf, M. M., & Risley, T. R. (1968). Some current dimensions of applied behavior analysis. *Journal of Applied Behavior Analysis*, *1*(1), 91–97.

Bernard, R. S., Cohen, L. L., & Moffett, K. (2009). A token economy for exercise adherence in pediatric cystic fibrosis: A single-subject analysis. *Journal of Pediatric Psychology*, *34*(4), 354–365.

Blanchard, E. B. (1992). Psychological treatment of benign headache disorders. *Journal of Consulting and Clinical Psychology*, *60*(4), 537–551.

Borsook, D., Maleki, N., Becerra, L., & McEwen, B. (2012). Understanding migraine through the lens of maladaptive stress responses: A model disease of allostatic load. *Neuron*, *73*(2), 219–234.

Brill, W. A. (2000). Child behavior in a private pediatric dental practice associated with types of visits, age and socio-economic factors. *The Journal of Clinical Pediatric Dentistry*, *25*(1), 1–7.

Budzynski, T. H., & Stoyva, J. M. (1969). An instrument for producing deep muscle relaxation by means of analog information feedback. *Journal of Applied Behavior Analysis*, *2*(4), 231–237.

Carding, P. N., Horsley, I. A., & Docherty, G. (1999). A study of the effectiveness of voice therapy in the treatment of 45 patients with nonorganic dysphonia. *Journal of Voice*, *13*(1), 72–104.

Carr, J. E., Severtson, J. M., & Lepper, T. L. (2009). Noncontingent reinforcement is an empirically supported treatment for problem behavior exhibited by individuals with developmental disabilities. *Research in Developmental Disabilities*, *30*(1), 44–57.

Casamassimo, P. S., Seale, N. S., & Ruehs, K. (2004). General dentists' perceptions of educational and treatment issues affecting access to care for children with special health care needs. *Journal of Dental Education*, *68*(1), 23–28.

Cohen, S. M., Dupont, W. D., & Courey, M. S. (2006). Quality-of-life impact of non-neoplastic voice disorders: A meta-analysis. *The Annals of Otology, Rhinology, and Laryngology*, *115*(2), 128–134.

Cohen, S. M., Kim, J., Roy, N., Asche, C., & Courey, M. (2012a). Direct health care costs of laryngeal diseases and disorders. *Laryngoscope*, *122*(7), 1582–1588.

Cohen, S. M., Kim, J., Roy, N., Asche, C., & Courey, M. (2012b). Prevalence and causes of dysphonia in a large treatment-seeking population. *Laryngoscope*, *122*(7), 343–348.

Conyers, C., Miltenberger, R. G., Peterson, B., Gubin, A., Jurgens, M., Selders, A., et al. (2004). An evaluation of in vivo desensitization and video modeling to increase compliance with dental procedures in persons with mental retardation. *Journal of Applied Behavior Analysis, 37*(2), 233–238.

da Costa, I. G., Rapoff, M. A., Lemanek, K., & Goldstein, G. L. (1997). Improving adherence to medication regimens for children with asthma and its effect on clinical outcome. *Journal of Applied Behavior Analysis, 30*(4), 687–691.

DeVries, J. E., Burnette, M. M., & Redmon, W. K. (1991). AIDS prevention: Improving nurses' compliance with glove wearing through performance feedback. *Journal of Applied Behavior Analysis, 24*(4), 705–711.

Duckro, P. N., & Cantwell-Simmons, E. (1989). A review of studies evaluating biofeedback and relaxation training in the management of pediatric headache. *Headache, 29*(7), 428–433.

Elder, S. T., Ruiz, Z. R., Deabler, H. L., & Dillenkoffer, R. L. (1973). Instrumental conditioning of diastolic blood pressure in essential hypertensive patients. *Journal of Applied Behavior Analysis, 6*(3), 377–382.

Epstein, L. H., Beck, S., Figueroa, J., Farkas, G., Kazdin, A. E., Daneman, D., et al. (1981). The effects of targeting improvements in urine glucose on metabolic control in children with insulin dependent diabetes. *Journal of Applied Behavior Analysis, 14*(4), 365–375.

Filcheck, H., Allen, K. D., Ogren, H., Darby, B., Holstein, B., & Hupp, S. (2004). The use of choice-based distraction to decrease the distress of children at the dentist. *Child and Family Behavior Therapy, 26*(4), 59–68.

Finney, J. W., Miller, K. M., & Adler, S. P. (1993). Changing protective and risky behaviors to prevent child-to-parent transmission of cytomegalovirus. *Journal of Applied Behavior Analysis, 26*(4), 471–472.

Fogel, E. R. (1995). Biofeedback assisted musculoskeletal therapy and neuromuscular re-education. In M. S. Schwartz (Ed.), *Biofeedback: A practitioner's guide* (2nd, pp. 560–593). New York, NY: Guilford Press.

Fordyce, W. E. (1976). *Behavioral methods for chronic pain and illness.* Saint Louis, MO: Mosby.

Frankl, S., Shiere, F., & Fogels, H. (1962). Should the parent remain with the child in the dental operatory? *Journal of Dentistry for Children, 29*, 150–163.

Fried, K., Sessle, B. J., & Devor, M. (2011). The paradox of pain from tooth pulp: Low-threshold "algoneurons"? *Pain, 152*(12), 2685–2689.

Gibson, R. S., Allen, K., Hutfless, S., & Beiraghi, S. (2000). The wand vs. traditional injection: A comparison of pain related behaviors. *Pediatric Dentistry, 22*(6), 458–462.

Goubert, L., Vlaeyen, J. W., Crombez, G., & Craig, K. D. (2011). Learning about pain from others: An observational learning account. *The Journal of Pain: Official Journal of the American Pain Society, 12*(2), 167–174.

Greene, B. F., & Neistat, M. D. (1983). Behavior analysis in consumer affairs: Encouraging dental professionals to provide consumers with shielding from unnecessary X-ray exposure. *Journal of Applied Behavior Analysis, 16*(1), 13–27.

Hagopian, L. P., & Thompson, R. H. (1999). Reinforcement of compliance with respiratory treatment in a child with cystic fibrosis. *Journal of Applied Behavior Analysis, 32*(2), 233–236.

Haraldstad, K., Sorum, R., Eide, H., Natvig, G. K., & Helseth, S. (2010). Pain in children and adolescents: Prevalence, impact on daily life, and parents' perception, a school survey. *Scandinavian Journal of Caring Sciences, 25*, 27–36.

Hermann, C., Kim, M., & Blanchard, E. B. (1995). Behavioral and prophylactic pharmacological intervention studies of pediatric migraine: An exploratory meta-analysis. *Pain, 60* (3), 239–255.

Hershey, A. D. (2005). Pediatric headache. *Pediatric Annals, 34*(6), 426–429.

Hoge, M. A., Howard, M. R., Wallace, D. P., & Allen, K. D. (2012). Use of video eyewear to manage distress in children during restorative dental treatment. *Pediatric Dentistry, 34* (5), 378–382.

House, A. O., & Andrews, H. B. (1988). Life events and difficulties preceding the onset of functional dysphonia. *Journal of Psychosomatic Research, 32*(3), 311–319.

Iwata, B. A., & Becksfort, C. M. (1981). Behavioral research in preventive dentistry: Educational and contingency management approaches to the problem of patient compliance. *Journal of Applied Behavior Analysis, 14*(2), 111–120.

Kelley, M. L., Jarvie, G. J., Middlebrook, J. L., McNeer, M. F., & Drabman, R. S. (1984). Decreasing burned children's pain behavior: Impacting the trauma of hydrotherapy. *Journal of Applied Behavior Analysis, 17*(2), 147–158.

Kernick, D., & Campbell, J. (2009). Measuring the impact of headache in children: A critical review of the literature. *Cephalalgia: An International Journal of Headache, 29*(1), 3–16.

Klingberg, G., & Broberg, A. G. (2007). Dental fear/anxiety and dental behaviour management problems in children and adolescents: A review of prevalence and concomitant psychological factors. *International Journal of Paediatric Dentistry / The British Paedodontic Society [and] the International Association of Dentistry for Children, 17*(6), 391–406.

Kohlenberg, R. J. (1973). Operant conditioning of human anal sphincter pressure. *Journal of Applied Behavior Analysis, 6*(2), 201–208.

Larsson, B., & Zaluha, M. (2003). Swedish school nurses' view of school health care utilization, causes and management of recurrent headaches among school children. *Scandinavian Journal of Caring Sciences, 17*(3), 232–238.

Lateef, T. M., Merikangas, K. R., He, J., Kalaydjian, A., Khoromi, S., Knight, E., et al. (2009). Headache in a national sample of American children: Prevalence and comorbidity. *Journal of Child Neurology, 24*(5), 536–543.

Lee, L., Stemple, J. C., Glaze, L., & Kelchner, L. N. (2004). Quick screen for voice and supplementary documents for identifying pediatric voice disorders. *Language, Speech, and Hearing Services in Schools, 35*(4), 308–319.

Lewis, D. W. (2004). Toward a definition of childhood migraine. *Current Opinion in Pediatrics, 16*, 628–636.

Luke, M. M., & Alavosius, M. (2011). Adherence with universal precautions after immediate, personalized performance feedback. *Journal of Applied Behavior Analysis, 44*(4), 967–971.

Maher, B. H., & Griffiths, L. R. (2011). Identification of molecular genetic factors that influence migraine. *Molecular Genetics and Genomics, 285*(6), 433–446.

Mathers-Schmidt, B. A. (2001). Paradoxical vocal fold motion: A tutorial on a complex disorder and the speech-language pathologist's role. *American Journal of Speech-Language Pathology, 10*, 111–125.

Morrison, M. D., Nichol, H., & Rammage, L. A. (1986). Diagnostic criteria in functional dysphonia. *The Laryngoscope, 96*(1), 1–8.

Nash, J. M., & Thebarge, R. W. (2006). Understanding psychological stress, its biological processes, and impact on primary headache. *Headache, 46*(9), 1377–1386.

Nathan, J. E. (1995). Managing behavior of precooperative children. *Dental Clinics of North America, 39*(4), 789–816.

National Research Council. (2011). *Advancing oral health in America.* Washington, DC: The National Academies Press.

O'Callaghan, P. M., Allen, K. D., Powell, S., & Salama, F. (2006). The efficacy of noncontingent escape for decreasing children's disruptive behavior during restorative dental treatment. *Journal of Applied Behavior Analysis, 39*(2), 161–171.

Paez, K. A., Zhao, L., & Hwang, W. (2009). Rising out-of-pocket spending for chronic conditions: A ten-year trend. *Health Affairs (Project Hope), 28*(1), 15–25.

Peek, C. J. (1995). A primer of biofeedback instrumentation. In M. S. Schwartz (Ed.), *Biofeedback: A practitioner's guide* (2nd, pp. 45–95). New York: Guilford Press.

Petersen, S., Hagglof, B. L., & Bergstrom, E. I. (2009). Impaired health-related quality of life in children with recurrent pain. *Pediatrics, 124*(4), 759–767.

Peterson, C. C., & Palermo, T. M. (2004). Parental reinforcement of recurrent pain: The moderating impact of child depression and anxiety on functional disability. *Journal of Pediatric Psychology, 29*(5), 331–341.

Pieper, K. B., Rapoff, M. A., Purviance, M. R., & Lindsley, C. B. (1989). Improving compliance with prednisone therapy in pediatric patients with rheumatic disease. *Arthritis Care and Research: The Official Journal of the Arthritis Health Professions Association, 2*(4), 132–135.

Rachlin, H. (1985). Pain and behavior. *The Behavioral and Brain Sciences, 8*(1), 43–83.

Raiff, B. R., & Dallery, J. (2010). Internet-based contingency management to improve adherence with blood glucose testing recommendations for teens with type 1 diabetes. *Journal of Applied Behavior Analysis, 43*(3), 487–491.

Rapoff, M. A., Purviance, M. R., & Lindsley, C. B. (1988). Educational and behavioral strategies for improving medication compliance in juvenile rheumatoid arthritis. *Archives of Physical Medicine and Rehabilitation, 69*(6), 439–441.

Redenbaugh, M. A., & Reich, A. R. (1989). Surface EMG and related measures in normal and vocally hyperfunctional speakers. *The Journal of Speech and Hearing Disorders, 54*(1), 68–73.

Reiss, M. L., & Bailey, J. S. (1982). Visiting the dentist: A behavioral community analysis of participation in a dental health screening and referral program. *Journal of Applied Behavior Analysis, 15*(3), 353–362.

Reiss, M. L., Piotrowski, W. D., & Bailey, J. S. (1976). Behavioral community psychology: Encouraging low-income parents to seek dental care for their children. *Journal of Applied Behavior Analysis, 9*(4), 387–397.

Renne, C. M., & Creer, T. L. (1976). Training children with asthma to use inhalation therapy equipment. *Journal of Applied Behavior Analysis, 9*(1), 1–11.

Roeber, B., Wallace, D. P., Rothe, V., Salama, F., & Allen, K. D. (2011). Evaluation of the effects of the VibraJect attachment on pain in children receiving local anesthesia. *Pediatric Dentistry, 33*(1), 46–50.

Sherman, R. A. (2003). Instrumentation methodology for recording and feeding-back surface electromyographic (SEMG) signals. *Applied Psychophysiology and Biofeedback, 28*(2), 107–119.

Slifer, K. J., Cataldo, M. F., Cataldo, M. D., Llorente, A. M., & Gerson, A. C. (1993). Behavior analysis of motion control for pediatric neuroimaging. *Journal of Applied Behavior Analysis, 26*(4), 469–470.

Slifer, K. J., Koontz, K. L., & Cataldo, M. F. (2002). Operant-contingency-based preparation of children for functional magnetic resonance imaging. *Journal of Applied Behavior Analysis, 35*(2), 191–194.

Smith, T. (2013). What is evidence-based behavior analysis? *Behavior Analyst, 36*, 7–33.

Stark, L. J., Allen, K. D., Hurst, M., Nash, D. A., Rigney, B., & Stokes, T. F. (1989). Distraction: Its utilization and efficacy with children undergoing dental treatment. *Journal of Applied Behavior Analysis, 22*(3), 297–307.

Stark, L. J., Knapp, L. G., Bowen, A. M., Powers, S. W., Jelalian, E., Evans, S., et al. (1993). Increasing calorie consumption in children with cystic fibrosis: Replication with 2-year follow-up. *Journal of Applied Behavior Analysis, 26*(4), 435–450.

Stark, L. J., Miller, S. T., Plienes, A. J., & Drabman, R. S. (1987). Behavioral contracting to increase chest physiotherapy. A study of a young cystic fibrosis patient. *Behavior Modification, 11*(1), 75–86.

Stemple, J. C., Weiler, E., Whitehead, W., & Komray, R. (1980). Electromyographic biofeedback training with patients exhibiting a hyperfunctional voice disorder. *Laryngoscope, 90*(3), 471–476.

Stokes, T. F., & Kennedy, S. H. (1980). Reducing child uncooperative behavior during dental treatment through modeling and reinforcement. *Journal of Applied Behavior Analysis, 13*(1), 41–49.

Stovner, L., Hagen, K., Jensen, R., Katsarava, Z., Lipton, R., Scher, A., et al. (2007). The global burden of headache: A documentation of headache prevalence and disability worldwide. *Cephalalgia: An International Journal of Headache, 27*(3), 193–210.

Tarnowski, K. J., Rasnake, L. K., Linscheid, T. R., & Mulick, J. A. (1989). Ecobehavioral characteristics of a pediatric burn injury unit. *Journal of Applied Behavior Analysis*, *22*(1), 101–109.

Turkdogan, D., Cagirici, H., Soylemez, D., Haydar, H., Bilge, C., & Turk, U. (2006). Characteristics and overlapping features of migraine and tension-type headache. *The Journal of
Head and Face Pain*, *46*(3), 461–468.

Van Lierde, K. M., Claeys, S., De Bodt, M., & van Cauwenberge, P. (2007). Long-term
outcome of hyperfunctional voice disorders based on a multiparameter approach. *Journal
of Voice*, *21*(2), 179–188.

Ward, B. W., & Schiller, J. S. (2013). Prevalence of multiple chronic conditions among US
adults: Estimates from the national health interview survey, 2010. *Preventing Chronic Disease*, *10*, E65.

Warnes, E., & Allen, K. D. (2005). Biofeedback treatment of paradoxical vocal fold motion
and respiratory distress in an adolescent girl. *Journal of Applied Behavior Analysis*, *38*(4),
529–532.

Watson, T. S., Allen, S. J., & Allen, K. D. (1993). Ventricular fold dysphonia: Application of
biofeedback technology to a rare voice disorder. *Behavior Therapy*, *24*, 439–446.

Whitehead, W. E., Renault, P. F., & Goldiamond, I. (1975). Modification of human gastric
acid secretion with operant-conditioning procedures. *Journal of Applied Behavior Analysis*,
8(2), 147–156.

Williams, J. A., Hurst, M. K., & Stokes, T. F. (1983). Peer observation in decreasing uncooperative behavior in young dental patients. *Behavior Modification*, *7*(2), 225–242.

Wysocki, T., Harris, M. A., Greco, P., Bubb, J., Danda, C. E., Harvey, L. M., et al. (2000).
Randomized, controlled trial of behavior therapy for families of adolescents with insulin-
dependent diabetes mellitus. *Journal of Pediatric Psychology*, *25*(1), 23–33.

CHAPTER 6

Applications of Applied Behavior Analysis to School-Based Instructional Intervention

Brian K. Martens[1], Edward J. Daly III[2], Scott P. Ardoin[3]
[1]Department of Psychology, Syracuse University, Syracuse, New York, USA
[2]Department of Educational Psychology, University of Nebraska Lincoln, Lincoln, Nebraska, USA
[3]Department of Educational Psychology and Instructional Technology, University of Georgia, Athens, Georgia, USA

INTRODUCTION

Most individuals regard applied behavior analysis (ABA) as a set of practices for evaluating the aberrant behavior of individuals with disabilities, replacing inappropriate with appropriate behavior, and/or training functional living and communication skills. However, those familiar with ABA know that the strategies and tactics used to assess severe problem behavior (e.g., self-injury) can also be applied to identify the functions of more common behavior problems. For example, a functional assessment might be conducted to determine why a child has a tantrum when denied a candy bar at the store. Likewise, behavioral strategies used to teach functional living skills to individuals with autism (e.g., video modeling) can be employed to enhance typically developing children's gymnastic skills (Ayres, Maguire, & McClimon, 2009; Boyer, Miltenberger, Batsche, & Fogel, 2009). The same ABA principles that explain how students learn to read, write, and successfully complete math problems can be used when assessing students' academic needs and developing instructional interventions. Employing ABA principles in the assessment and development of instructional interventions, however, requires consulting teams to use strategies that vary from those typically used in school settings.

This chapter describes how ABA principles and strategies can be used in the assessment of children's academic problems and as bases for designing effective school-based interventions. We begin with a discussion of academic responding as the target of instruction; the relationship of component skills to more complex, composite repertoires; and how to assess academic responding in ways that inform intervention. The chapter then focuses on

Clinical and Organizational Applications of Applied Behavior Analysis
http://dx.doi.org/10.1016/B978-0-12-420249-8.00006-X

the importance of developing stimulus control over academic responding as a fundamental goal of instruction. In so doing, we describe instructional interventions shown to be effective at establishing stimulus control through the basic processes of differential reinforcement (DR), modeling, prompting, and error correction. The chapter concludes with a discussion of stimulus generalization as the ultimate goal of instruction, describing strategies for promoting generalized academic responding.

ASSESSMENT OF CHILDREN'S ACADEMIC RESPONDING

School-Based Assessments

Teachers often complain that testing takes away from instructional time (Nelson, 2013). This complaint seems at odds with an ABA framework, as proponents of ABA view assessment as an essential activity that informs instruction. Unfortunately, high-stakes tests, which are central to teacher complaints, are generally *not* developed to inform instruction (William, 2010). Rather, the assessments that teachers often spend considerable time preparing their students to take and from which the quality of their instruction is often judged are developed from a traditional psychometric framework (Broatch & Lohr, 2012). Such tests are evaluated based on their reliability and validity as opposed to the extent to which results inform instruction. The results provide schools with information regarding how students perform relative to their peers and the probability with which students will succeed academically. Although this information is critical for some types of decisions (e.g., screening), knowing that a struggling student is performing worse than peers and is unlikely to succeed without intervention has little treatment utility. In short, information regarding a student's relative standing does not guide the development of functionally relevant interventions (Hosp & Ardoin, 2008).

Several factors limit the treatment utility of standardized, norm-referenced test results. In particular, norm-referenced tests must (a) be reliable across short periods of time, (b) be predictive of student performance on similar measures, and (c) differentiate skills within and between groups of struggling, average, and above-average students. As a result of these needs, norm-referenced tests cannot be composed of multiple items assessing a single skill, or even multiple items assessing a narrow range of skills. To do so would decrease the reliability of the measures, as with quality instruction students' scores might change across short time frames. Instead, the items on norm-referenced tests generally measure a wide range of skills, allowing for greater test-retest reliability and the differentiation of student performance (Ardoin, Wagner, & Bangs, in press).

Although teacher-developed or end-of-chapter tests may be more popular among teachers than norm-referenced tests, they also are of limited utility for developing functionally relevant instructional interventions. Analyses of the items on teacher-developed or end-of-chapter tests can potentially yield information regarding a teacher's expectations for a student. However, the results of these tests are unlikely to provide information regarding the component skills a student does and does not have to accomplish composite goal-level tasks. To develop an effective intervention, assessments must adequately evaluate the individual skills that comprise the complex tasks required of the student (Reeves, Umbreit, Ferro, & Liaupsin, 2013; Shapiro, 2011; Zheng, Flynn, & Swanson, 2013).

Academic skills are not unlike any other repertoire of composite skills that individuals learn during childhood and perform on a daily basis. Just as with other complex skill sets, academic skill sets require students to respond correctly to a series of discriminative stimuli (S^Ds). When responding is met with reinforcement (i.e., teacher praise, production of correct work), the association between stimulus and response is strengthened and the behavior is more likely to occur again in the presence of the S^D. For instance, fluent oral reading requires students to respond with accuracy and fluency to the letters that make up words and to recognize punctuation signifying when to pause and/or change their tone of voice (Ardoin, Morena, Binder, & Foster, 2013). Adults shape these reading behaviors by modeling appropriate responses, initially reinforcing production of the sounds that the stimuli represent, later reinforcing only accurate blending of the letter sounds which make up words, providing error correction when mistakes are made, and eventually reinforcing only rapid reading with appropriate pauses and fluctuations in tone. Considering the sheer number of potential S^Ds that are expected to control academic responding, it is not possible to teach every one; thus, instruction must promote generalized responding (Daly, Martens, Barnett, Witt, & Olson, 2007).

The number of reinforced responses to S^Ds needed by, and provided to, students for them to become proficient in a skill varies. To meet curriculum demands, teachers often must transition to teaching the next skill(s) in the curriculum before some students have mastered the current skill(s). It is these students who are typically identified as needing instructional intervention. To assess their needs, composite academic repertoires (e.g., reading) must be task-analyzed into their component skills (e.g., sight word vocabulary, phoneme blending, spelling) and taught explicitly. Assessment must be conducted to determine student accuracy and fluency in each of these component skills, and explicit instruction must be provided to remediate deficits (Reeves et al., 2013; Shapiro, 2011; Zheng et al., 2013).

Curriculum-Based Measurement

The Individuals with Disabilities Education Improvement Act of 2004 (IDEA, 2004) facilitated the identification of students with instructional needs by allowing for a Response to Intervention (RtI) model. ABA serves as a theoretical foundation for RtI models (Martens & Ardoin, 2010). Under an RtI model, students identified as needing special education are those who require the greatest number of training trials to develop accuracy and fluency in composite skill sets. In order to identify such students, most school districts employing an RtI model use curriculum-based measurement (CBM) probes for both identifying students potentially at risk for needing special education and for evaluating how these students respond to intervention (Mellard, McKnight, & Woods, 2009). According to Deno, Fuchs, Marston, & Shin (2001), CBM combines traditional and behavioral assessment practices, allowing for both normative comparisons with peers and ongoing formative evaluation through the use of time-series graphs.

The most widely used of the CBM measures is CBM in reading (CBM-R). This assessment procedure requires students to read a text for 1 min while an examiner records reading errors and provides words for hesitations of more than 3 s. Performance is recorded as the number of words read correctly per minute (WCPM), a fluency measure that combines accuracy and rate. Extensive research exists to support the use of WCPM on CBM-R probes as a measure of reading comprehension as well as a measure of global reading achievement (Deno et al., 2001). Although some suggest that CBM-R procedures simply measure students' responding to the words presented in a text, researchers have provided abundant evidence that WCPM is heavily impacted by readers' comprehension of the text as text comprehension aids word reading rate (Ardoin, Eckert et al., 2013).

In what are referred to as universal screening procedures, school personnel administer CBM-R probes to students three to four times per year (e.g., fall, winter, spring) and identify those students whose WCPM is discrepant from that of their same-grade peers or falls below a criterion score indicating need for intervention. CBM-R probes are generally administered to the first- through the fifth-grade students. For younger students who have yet to develop the skills to read connected text, alternative CBM probe types are administered. Typically, these probes measure specific component skills as opposed to composite or global skills, measured by CBM-R probes. For instance, there are CBM probes available that measure students' accuracy and fluency in (a) providing letter names/sounds, (b) blending a sequence of letter sounds that make up words and nonwords, and (c) producing sounds that correspond with words whose letter combinations do not follow typical patterns (i.e., nondecodable sight words; Good & Kaminski, 2011).

Once students are identified as needing intervention, schools often administer interventions in the form of a standardized treatment protocol that may or may not target a student's specific instructional needs (Daly et al., 2007). From an ABA perspective, it would be beneficial to know exactly which instructional stimuli evoke accurate and fluent responding and which stimuli fail to evoke appropriate responding. Although most publishers of CBM probes provide normative rates of fluency believed to be predictive of future academic success (Howe & Shinn, 2002), data are not available regarding the levels of accuracy and fluency on the basic skills necessary to succeed on goal level or general outcome measures. These data could easily be collected through administration of basic skill level probes to students who perform adequately on general outcome measures (composite skills).

In addition to using students' performance on CBM probes to identify which students need intervention, students' performance across time on CBM probes are used widely to evaluate the impact of intervention on academic growth (Mellard et al., 2009). Typically, this process involves assessing student performance on a weekly basis for 7-10 weeks using CBM probes, estimating student growth based upon the data collected, and comparing the estimate of growth to a pre-established goal level (Ardoin, Christ, Morena, Cormier, & Klingbeil, 2013). Although we support the use of data-based decision making in schools, evaluating growth rates across time as opposed to the effects of intervention on the skills targeted may unnecessarily delay decisions regarding intervention effectiveness. Whereas the effects of intervention on the complex academic skills measured by most CBM probes may be small and thus require an extended period of time to be observed (Christ, Zopluoglu, Monaghen, & Van Norman, 2013), the effects of intervention on the skills directly targeted by intervention should occur quickly. Furthermore, if intervention does not positively impact students' responding to the stimuli on which intervention is applied, it is unlikely to result in improvements on the complex sequence of stimuli that comprise goal-level academic tasks (Ardoin, 2006).

The Importance of Developing Stimulus Control over Academic Responding

Academic tasks constitute S^Ds designed to evoke a response of some type. The desired response is ultimately to be brought under stimulus control of the academic task itself alone without other forms of assistance (e.g., hinting at the correct response or pointing out clues that increase the salience of some of the stimuli; Vargas, 1984). The response class in question can be defined with varying degrees of specificity, depending on one's purpose. To establish the generality of the principles governing behavior in this case, one might refer broadly to the response class as "academic responding," understanding that it encompasses a wide variety of topographies (e.g., reading a word on a page, answering a math problem) that do, however, retain a common distinctiveness relative to other response classes (e.g., disruptive classroom behavior). This perspective is helpful to understanding at a strategic level that the stimulus relations that should control responding for everything from reading a letter on a page to correctly performing a chemistry experiment (and all things in between) are grounded in this single basic behavioral process of stimulus control. A narrower definition of the response class in question (e.g., oral reading fluency, completing math computation problems) is more helpful when a specific problem has been identified and the basic behavioral processes have to be operationalized at a tactical level for a given student. For example, the topography of prompting methods used to increase oral reading fluency will look different from those used to increase correctly written responses on a math worksheet. Yet, each form of prompting when used appropriately works effectively for the same functional reason.

Two distinctive features of academic responding have implications for designing instructional interventions. First, responding is at low (or even zero) levels when the teacher begins instruction. Such low response levels may also occur when a consulting team is called upon to help a teacher develop an intervention for a student who is not progressing adequately following instruction. The key issue is that the teacher is dealing with a behavioral *deficit*, which means functionally that there are no controlling variables at the present time. By contrast, for a behavioral excess like self-injury the problem is the very existence of controlling variables that maintain the problem through evocative and reinforcing events. It is possible to conduct a functional analysis with self-injury as the target behavior because the controlling variables are discoverable. For an academic performance problem, there are no maintaining contingencies to investigate. Indeed, the problem to resolve is the lack of maintaining contingencies. Thus, the fundamental goal of instructional intervention is to *establish* stimulus control which is developed through DR (Cooper, Heron, & Heward, 2007).

Another distinctive feature of academic responding is that it includes a myriad of interrelated behavioral repertoires. These repertoires are specified in advance by an educational curriculum the objective of which is to prepare students to be successful in the "real world" where reinforcement schedules and other relevant variables are not tidily packaged. Helping prepare students for what comes after the educational curriculum (e.g., a job, college) is obviously a long process, given the complexity of the skills that these environments require. The curriculum specifies a continuum of behavioral repertoires that begin with the most basic skills and progress toward closer and closer approximations to real-world activities meant to prepare the student for when he or she encounters similar situations beyond school. As the student ascends through the curriculum and instructional tasks become increasingly more difficult, he or she must be able to coordinate multiple behavioral repertoires smoothly and in a timely fashion to be successful, which amounts to getting the right answer "on demand." Teachers jump into a spot along this continuum by isolating and targeting specific subordinate or component response classes for instruction (e.g., teaching to segment phonemes versus teaching to improve oral reading fluency). This feature makes establishing both the validity and sequencing of component response classes absolutely critical. Targeting a wrong or unnecessary behavioral repertoire or incorrectly sequencing how they are targeted may slow down or stall the efficiency with which stimulus control develops while potentially having a negative cumulative effect on the terminal goal of real-world preparation. The idea of isolating a particular component response class for instruction is akin to taking a "slice" along the continuum of response repertoires, the purpose of which is to strengthen it in such a way that learning at later points in the curriculum is easier and more efficient for the student.

Achieving a level of responding that makes it possible for the student to integrate the newly learned skill with other skills and as a part of more complex tasks with minimal instruction is an indication of stimulus control. The problem is that the student has been referred for a lack of progress following instruction with the current skill, which is often an indication that prerequisite skills have not been sufficiently developed (Howell & Nolet, 2000).

Continuing instruction at the current level may create cumulative skill deficits that attenuate future instructional effects and make school tasks progressively harder (Binder, 1996; Johnson & Layng, 1992). Wolery, Bailey, and Sugai (1988) recommend either "slicing back" to an easier version of the skill (e.g., teaching addition problems with sums to 10 rather than with sums to 18) or "stepping back" to a prerequisite skill (e.g., teaching a student to blend and segment phonemes before giving phonics instruction). The reader is referred to Carnine, Silbert, Kame'enui, and Tarver (2010), Stein, Kinder, Silbert, and Carnine (2005), and Howell and Nolet (2000) for well-established sequences of basic academic skills.

DIFFERENTIAL REINFORCEMENT AND HOW TO DRESS IT UP

Because DR is the treatment of choice for a stimulus control problem, this seems like the most appropriate place to start. However, reinforcement is unlikely to have much of an effect for academic responding if it is not under any form of stimulus control at the point at which intervention begins. In many cases, more intervention strategies will need to be added to DR to evoke behavior so that reinforcement can produce its intended effect. How then does one determine whether DR is sufficient alone or whether more strategies need to be added? Of course, the student's response is the most telling indicator of whether an intervention is appropriate or not. The surest way to know whether DR is sufficient, therefore, is to test it out directly with programmed reinforcement through a performance-deficit analysis (PDA, otherwise referred to as a "Can't do/Won't do" analysis; Daly, Witt, Martens, & Dool, 1997; VanDerheyden, in press). The analysis should start with identifying potentially effective reinforcers using a strong preference-assessment method that is appropriate for use in the schools (Daly et al., 2009). The results can be used for the PDA. The PDA was developed, operationalized, and popularized by Joe Witt on the basis of a distinction made by Lentz (1988) between a skill deficit and a performance deficit. For a skill deficit, low academic performance reflects a lack of discriminative control and no amount of programmed contingencies can improve behavior; for a performance deficit, low academic performance reflects a lack of motivational control that can be remedied through stronger reinforcement contingencies. Briefly, high-preference items or activities are offered contingent on improved performance in previously failed assignments. A PDA can be used at the individual (Daly et al., 1997), classwide

(Duhon et al., 2004), and even school level as a part of a multitiered RtI model (VanDerHeyden, Witt, & Gilbertson, 2007; VanDerHeyden, Witt, & Naquin, 2003). If the results demonstrate that the student improves with reinforcement only, then DR is the preferred treatment. If the student does not improve, other strategies need to be added to DR to evoke responding so that reinforcement can be applied.

In reality, instruction rarely, if ever, relies on a single procedure. Instead, instruction is "packaged" with a variety of strategies. Due to competing constraints of limited resource availability over and against an urgent need to remediate skill deficits, achieving the optimum balance of efficiency (no more strategies than are necessary) and effectiveness (obtaining desired outcomes) is the essence of instructional intervention. So, how does one determine which strategies to apply? Again, the student's response is the vital factor in guiding treatment selection. Although the occurrence or nonoccurrence of a response when an instructional demand is presented can be seen as a binary event, the strength of academic responding is more a matter of degree than an all-or-nothing occurrence. Over the years, researchers have developed and relied on a common useful heuristic for conceptualizing how strength of responding changes over time as a student gains proficiency. Haring and Eaton's (1978) instructional hierarchy has achieved incredible staying power in fueling the work of multiple generations of academic intervention researchers (Ardoin & Daly, 2007). Wolery et al. (1988) organized their ABA textbook using a similar conceptualization of response strengthening, and for many years precision teachers have preached a message of the critical importance of going beyond acquisition-level training to strengthen both fluency and generalization (Binder, 1996; Johnson & Layng, 1992). According to this common conceptualization, academic responding proceeds from no response in the presence of an instructional task to accuracy to fluency and then to generalization: responding initially is slow and marked by frequent errors (accuracy), but improves in rate with a concurrent reduction in errors as fluency develops, and finally occurs across a broad variety of stimulus situations, most notably contexts in which instruction has not occurred. The remainder of this section addresses strategies for improving accuracy and fluency.

Imagine the scenario that led to the teacher referring a student for an academic intervention in the first place. Instructions for the task were given, a reward may have been promised for meeting some criterion level of performance, the task was presented, the teacher eagerly awaited a response . . . and . . . nothing happened, or a wrong response was given. Something more needs to be added to the natural stimulus conditions to make the response occur so that a consequence can be applied. The "something more" is a *prompt* that effectively evokes the correct response. Touchette and Howard (1984) described it elegantly when they stated, "Prompting is the substitution of an effective but inappropriate stimulus for an ineffective but appropriate one" (p. 175). In other words, the response is occurring for the wrong reason when a prompt is delivered, but it serves a useful purpose: responding can now be reinforced in the presence of the natural antecedent, which contributes to stimulus control. The use of prompting is common in instructional interventions, having been shown to improve reading (Browder, Wakeman, Spooner, Ahlgrim-Delzell, & Algozzine, 2006), writing (Pennington, Stenhoff, Gibson, & Ballou, 2012), and math (Everett & Edwards, 2007) performance. A common prompting method used at the beginning of instruction is modeling, in which the instructor gives the correct response in the presence of the natural stimulus and then prompts the student to respond. Listening passage preview (LPP) is an example of a modeling prompt for improving oral reading fluency. The instructor reads the passage to the student before prompting him or her to then read the passage aloud. LPP has been shown to be more effective than student previewing (the student reads the passage without modeling) and even modeling isolated word reading, presumably because modeling occurs in the natural stimulus context of connected text (Chard, Vaughn, & Tyler, 2002; Daly & Martens, 1994; Rose & Beattie, 1986; Skinner, Cooper, & Cole, 1997).

Another example of a strategy that contains a strong modeling component is Cover-Copy-Compare (CCC; Skinner, Turco, Beatty, & Rasavage, 1989). In CCC, two versions of an instructional exercise (e.g., a math worksheet) are given to the student: a copy with the correct answers and a copy with blanks for student responses. The student is instructed to look at the version of the problem with the correct answer, cover the answer, write a response on the student copy, and then compare his or her response to the correct one. CCC has been shown to improve spelling (Jaspers et al., 2012), mathematics (Skinner et al., 1989), and geography (Skinner, Belfiore, & Pierce, 1992). CCC contains more than just modeling and its positive effects are surely due to a combination of factors. But, it is the modeling component that makes it most appropriate for use when a student is just learning a new skill.

Instruction is not complete until stimulus control is transferred from the prompt to the natural stimulus (Touchette & Howard, 1984). If transfer of stimulus control does not happen naturally, an effective way to accomplish it is to introduce a time delay before the modeling prompt is given following one or more trials with modeling. The time delay can be either constant (i.e., the same from one trial to the next; Schuster, Gast, Wolery, & Guiltinan, 1988) or progressive (i.e., increasing over trials; Reichow & Wolery, 2011). Over time, as responding is strengthened, the learner will emit more and more responses before the modeling prompt is given. Kupzyk, Daly, and Andersen (2011) added two prompting methods—a combined modeling procedure (delivered first) and a subsequent constant time-delay prompting procedure—to incremental rehearsal (IR), a well-supported flashcard intervention that provides a strong dosage of repeated practice. Kupzyk et al. showed that their procedure (strategic incremental rehearsal, SIR) produced a greater number of words learned and maintained than IR. It appears that SIR's additional antecedent prompting strategies relative to IR make it a more efficient and efficacious instructional strategy.

We noted earlier that one of the characteristics of responding in the initial stages of learning is a high error rate. Prompting methods can be expected to reduce errors to some degree. However, some errors probably will still occur. Errors are tragic: each and every error means that the wrong response has occurred in the presence of the natural antecedent, which increases the probability that responding will come under faulty stimulus control. Therefore, an error correction strategy that overrides the effects of the incorrect response is an essential element of any instructional intervention. For instance, in Direct Instruction, when an error is made, the teacher models the correct response, prompts the student to give the correct response, and then reviews the correct response (Carnine et al., 2010). There are two things that can be manipulated, however, to strengthen error correction further: the number of correct response repetitions and the context in which the student is made to practice correct responses. Worsdell et al. (2005) showed that having learners repeat the correct reading of error words was more effective than having them read corrected error words only once for improving sight-word reading. O'Shea, Munson, and O'Shea (1984) conducted a comparative study of three types of error correction that examined both response repetitions and the context in which responding was prompted. In the word-supply condition, the experimenter modeled correct reading of an error word. In the word-drill condition, the experimenter had the learner repeatedly read the error word correctly. In the phrase-drill (PD) condition, the experimenter had the learner repeatedly read the entire phrase containing the error word. They found that word drill and PD were superior to word supply for improving subsequent word reading. They also found that PD was superior for improving subsequent reading of the error word in text. This finding is not surprising in light of the fact that PD constituted training in the natural stimulus conditions (connected text), a stronger generalization strategy than teaching words in isolation (word supply and word drill). Therefore, it appears that the best strategy is to prompt the learner to respond repeatedly following an error and, if at all possible, to do so under the most natural stimulus conditions (e.g., in connected text for reading).

The antecedent- (i.e., prompting) and consequence-based (i.e., DR and error correction) strategies discussed up to this point form the basis of the learning trial (another term for the three-term contingency), which, according to Heward (1994), should be seen as the basic unit of instruction. All instruction should be geared primarily toward maximizing the number of observable responses to instructional antecedents, which is easier to accomplish when one has a solid grasp of the student's proficiency with the skill being taught. In a separate review of the literature, Skinner, Fletcher, and Henington (1996) showed that learning improved most when student response rates were increased through complete learning trials. The combination of antecedent and consequence components used influences the number of trials that can be delivered in an instructional session.

The emphasis up to this point has been on improving accuracy. However, an indispensable method for building fluency is repeated practice (Binder, 1996; Daly, Lentz, & Boyer, 1996). For example, for improving oral reading fluency, the method of repeated readings (RR) is superior to any other treatment component (Chard et al., 2002), and its routine use is strongly recommended by the National Reading Panel (2000). Therefore, as soon as error rates drop and accurate responses become more consistent, instruction should change to provide increased opportunities for repeated practice. The use of repeated practice also creates the opportunity to shift reinforcement contingencies from targeting accuracy to targeting fluency (e.g., obtaining a higher fluency score), which can be expected to also strengthen responding (Daly et al., 1996). The bottom line is that instructional time should be planned in such a way that it produces the maximum number of responses per time unit through strategic selection of antecedent strategies and programmed consequences.

Two other approaches that relate to motivational factors may give an additional boost to intervention effects. Giving performance feedback on some aspect of responding (e.g., accuracy of assignment completion, reading fluency, latency to compliance) has been shown to improve reading (Eckert, Dunn, & Ardoin, 2006), math (Codding, Lewandowski, & Eckert, 2005), writing (Scriven & Glynn, 1983), and spelling (Bourque, Dupuis, & Van Houten, 1986). Performance feedback is easily tied to repeated practice and reinforcement contingencies and may even add motivational value, as the student might eventually try to "beat" his or her last score. Finally, motivating operations can be arranged in a number of different ways, including identifying the aversive features of instructional situations and modifying them (McComas, Hoch, Paone, & El-Roy, 2000), embedding novel tasks into routine or repetitive tasks (Dunlap, Kern-Dunlap, Clarke, & Robbins, 1991), decreasing task difficulty level (Daly, Martens, Kilmer, & Massie, 1996), and offering choice of instructional assignments (Cosden, Gannon, & Haring, 1995).

PROMOTING GENERALIZED ACADEMIC RESPONDING
Why Stimulus Control Is Not Enough

Although stimulus control is essential to learning from an ABA perspective, it is insufficient for preparing learners to use skills beyond the classroom as the stimuli presented in training necessarily constitute only a small sample of all possible stimulus variations students will encounter. Without additional training that employs stimulus variations, responding is unlikely to maintain over time or transfer to situations that differ from training. For skills to be transferrable, the focus of instruction must shift from establishing stimulus control to promoting *stimulus generalization*, or the DR of accurate and rapid responding to variations of key stimuli or the presentation of these stimuli in different contexts (Codding & Poncy, 2010).

When instruction in a skill or set of skills occurs over a long period of time (e.g., months or years), learners are exposed to a wide variety of academic tasks and curricular materials presented in slightly different contexts and formats and even by different teachers. Under these conditions, responding to both programmed (e.g., increasingly more difficult passages, different types of math problems) and naturally occurring stimulus variations (e.g., different settings and distractions) makes stimulus generalization a natural consequence of prolonged instruction (Martens, Daly, Begeny, & VanDerHeyden, 2011). In their seminal review of generalization programming strategies used in behavior analytic research, Stokes and Baer (1977) reported that the most frequently used method for addressing generalization was to "Train and Hope." That is, following effective instruction in the training environment, generalization was assessed but not actively programmed. Although active programming strategies existed in the literature, the majority of "Train and Hope" studies (90%) reported some form of generalized responding.

Whereas children typically receive years of instruction in basic academic skills (e.g., reading, math) or specific content areas (e.g., history, social studies), school-based interventions for academic problems are evaluated over much shorter time periods. For example, in a typical RtI model, intervention trials may consist of implementation two to three times per week over a 7-10 week period, and even briefer analyses involving one or two sessions have been used (Jones et al., 2009; McComas et al., 2009).

The relatively small number of intervention episodes during an intervention trial combined with the use of CBM-R general outcome measures to index growth creates both an assessment problem and an instructional design problem for school-based intervention teams. With respect to the former, interventions are deemed effective if the child's growth rate on randomly selected global outcome measures exceeds that of comparison peers under typical instructional conditions. Note that the use of global outcome measures to probe for generalized gains on untrained CBM-R passages constitutes a form of "Train and Hope" in that generalization is assessed but not programmed. However, a problem arises when expected growth rates are *not* observed as these may result from an ineffective intervention or an effective intervention that failed to promote generalized responding. The answer to this question requires assessment of intervention effects along a continuum of training-related stimuli (i.e., a *generalization gradient*; Reynolds, 1975). In reading, this continuum might range from passages that were just trained to passages that are similar to those trained based on the word overlap to passages that are dissimilar from those trained (i.e., CBM-R global outcome measures; Daly, Bonfiglio, Mattson, Persampieri, & Foreman-Yates, 2006; Daly, Martens, Dool, & Hintze, 1998; McComas et al., 2009).

Some would argue that the goal of instructional intervention is always to promote generalized responding, and this has merit. The instructional design problem is created when generalized effects (beyond whatever point on the assessment continuum) are not observed and therefore must be actively programmed. As described by Stokes and Baer (1977), programming for generalization requires that instructional materials be altered to include common or representative stimulus variations from the natural environment. Given the limited time over which most instructional interventions are implemented, incorporating these variations into task materials must be both *efficient* from a training perspective and *functional* from a generalization perspective.

Generalization Strategies for Instructional Interventions

Beyond the "Train and Hope" approach, Stokes and Baer (1977) grouped various methods for actively programming generalization under eight categories. Strategies that have been reported in the literature for promoting generalized academic responding fit nicely under several of these categories, so we use the Stokes and Baer taxonomy as a framework for this section. Because the majority of academic referrals involve reading, the examples in this section focus on generalization strategies applied to school-based reading interventions.

Train loosely: With this strategy, "teaching is conducted with relatively little control over the stimuli presented. . ., so as to maximize sampling of relevant dimensions for transfer to other situations" (Stokes & Baer, 1977, p. 357). This approach is perhaps the most commonly used generalization strategy by intervention teams whereby children are exposed to task materials in whatever sequence is dictated by the curriculum and practice opportunities are arranged to bring responding under control of each set of stimuli. When applied to oral reading fluency, the "train loosely" method involves selecting a graded series of passages that the child can practice (i.e., a basal reading curriculum), identifying the child's "instructional" reading level in the series based on the normative placement standards (e.g., passages the child can read orally with at least 70 WCPM in grades 3-5; Shapiro, 2004), starting training with passages at this difficulty level, and moving to the next passage in the sequence.

This approach represents a "train loosely" method of generalization programming because both the difficulty and sequence of passages is left to curriculum developers. For published reading series like Scott Foresman Reading Street (2008), passage difficulty is calibrated using one or more readability formulas which weigh variables such as the average number of words per sentence and the percentage of low-frequency words in a passage (e.g., Spache, 1953). Research has shown, however, that published reading series indeed constitute a "train loosely" approach given that series differ in overall passage difficulty and number of phonetically regular words, that the difficulty of passages varies considerably at each grade level, and that readability estimates are relatively poor predictors of WCPM (Ardoin, Suldo, Witt, Aldrich, & McDonald, 2005; Fuchs & Deno, 1992; Martens, Steele, Massie, & Diskin, 1995).

When combined with other instructional procedures (e.g., LPP, PD, and rate-contingent reinforcement), RR has been shown to double students' WCPM on trained passages (e.g., Daly et al., 1998; Daly, Martens, Hamler, Dool, & Eckert, 1999; Eckert, Ardoin, Daly, & Martens, 2002). More importantly, RR has also been shown to produce moderate generalized increases on untrained or global outcome measures (Chard et al., 2002; Jones et al., 2009). As a "train loosely" approach, generalized gains in oral reading fluency that result from the application of RR to multiple passages are likely due to common high-frequency words at each grade level, the development of strong stimulus control over both high- and low-frequency words through modeling and repeated practice, or both (Ardoin, Binder, Zawoyski, Foster, & Blevins, 2013; Ardoin, McCall, & Klubnik, 2007).

Train to functional fluency aims: Fluency refers to the continuous performance of skills with both speed and accuracy and is widely recognized as being critical for the maintenance and generalization of basic academic skills like oral reading, math computation, and writing (Chard et al., 2002; Johnson & Layng, 1996; LaBerge & Samuels, 1974; Olinghouse, 2008). Although school-based intervention teams establish fluency aims based on the *normative* standards and growth models (Nese et al., 2013), training basic or component skills to *functional* fluency aims can make it easier to combine them into more complex composite skills and promote their application to different contexts. Functional fluency aims refer to levels of fluent skill performance that result in retention over time, endurance during longer performance runs, stability in the face of distraction, application of component skills into composite repertoires, and adduction of untrained skills (Daly et al., 2007; Martens et al., 2011).

With respect to oral reading, there is some evidence to suggest that reading connected text at a rate of at least 100 WCPM may represent a functional fluency aim that promotes generalization to untrained passages (Bonfiglio, Daly, Martens, Lan-Hsiang, & Corsaut, 2004; Martens et al., 2007). For example, Martens et al. evaluated the direct and generalized effects of an after-school reading program that included training to a functional fluency aim. Specifically, after finding each student's instructional level in a graded series of passages, oral reading of each passage was trained to a retention criterion of 100 WCPM 2 days later in the absence of practice. The training package itself consisted of LPP, RR, and PD along with rate-contingent reinforcement and performance charting. Students who regularly met the retention criterion required fewer trainings to master subsequent passages and often read the next more difficult passage in the sequence above criterion without training (i.e., showed generalized fluency gains). Generalized fluency gains were also found on five of the six untrained global outcome probes for the treatment group but on only one of six probes for the control group.

Train using common stimuli: As noted by Ardoin, Binder, et al. (2013), a lack of word overlap between trained and global outcome passages will mask intervention effects, and the sensitivity of such measures for indexing growth is also influenced by passage readability as well as if and how passages were equated for difficulty (Christ & Silberglitt, 2007). One way to increase the similarity between trained and generalization passages on all of these variables and therefore promote generalization is to create high word overlap (HWO) versions of the same passage. Because HWO passages contain 80% or more of the same words (e.g., Daly et al., 1998), they represent a common stimuli approach to generalization programming. When HWO passages are used for training and as generalization probes, generalized gains in levels of oral reading fluency approximate those on trained passages (Daly et al., 1998) and generalized gains in slope of improvement exceed those for global outcome measures (Daly et al., 1998; McComas et al., 2009).

In an application of the common stimuli approach to word list reading, Mesmer et al. (2010) used a common extra stimulus prompt to promote the generalization of student's reading from trained to untrained words. During training, the common rime of each word in a family was highlighted in color on flashcards (e.g., *en* in t*en*), and 11 of 35 total words were trained using modeling by the experimenter and practice by the student with corrective feedback. Immediately after training, students were assessed on both trained and untrained words without the color cue. All four students increased their accurate reading of trained words, and three of the four students showed some generalized increases on untrained words. When the color cues were added (i.e., the common stimulus), all four students showed additional increases in their accurate reading of untrained words.

Train multiple or sufficient stimulus exemplars: When generalization fails to occur after training to a narrow range of stimuli and there is insufficient time to train loosely, another strategy for introducing stimulus variation is to train using multiple stimulus exemplars (Stokes & Osnes, 1989). This strategy involves specifying a class of stimuli to which the learner is expected to respond, identifying one or more dimensions along which stimuli in the class vary, and then including representative samples of these stimulus variations in training. Because only representative variations are trained, the multiple exemplar approach can be both an effective and efficient way to promote generalized responding (Silber & Martens, 2010). As a variation of multiple exemplar training, training *sufficient* exemplars involves the sequential application of instruction to different stimulus materials and assessing for generalization at each step.

Using a multiple exemplars approach, Ardoin et al. (2007) assembled passages in sets of three with all three passages in a set sharing between 64% and 76% of words (i.e., HWO passages). Using a RR intervention, children read either one passage four times or two passages two times and then were assessed on a generalization passage. Given the HWO between passages, reading two passages two times constituted a ME condition because children were exposed to and practiced additional words that overlapped with those in the generalization probe. Although all six children showed generalized increases in WCPM on the third untrained passage in each set regardless of condition (RR or ME), the RR condition was actually superior for three of the six participants. More recently, Ardoin, Binder, et al. (2013) found that gains in oral reading fluency following either RR or ME training were not equivalent for all words in a passage. Rather, repeated practice of a passage primarily increased the rate at which children read low-frequency (i.e., more difficult) words.

Silber and Martens (2010) evaluated a different strategy for configuring ME to promote generalized oral reading fluency. Specifically, they created a 16-sentence passage that featured one of four keywords in each of four different sentence types (e.g., "Do you see the big *rabbit*?", "The *mouse* ran away!") as well as a HWO version containing the same keywords and types of sentences. After random assignment to groups, children received one exposure to an LPP/RR intervention applied to all 16 sentences, only the four representative sentences (i.e., the ME condition), or no training (i.e., control). Both intervention groups made gains in WCPM on the first version of the passage that were significantly greater than those of the control group. Although both treatment groups also made gains on the second HWO version of the passage, only the performance of students in the ME condition differed significantly from controls. In addition to being as, or more, effective at producing generalized reading gains than practice with the entire passage, the ME condition was also more than twice as efficient based on the number of words gained per minute of practice time.

Train broadly applicable skills: In addition to oral reading fluency, phonemic awareness is widely recognized as an important prerequisite skill for proficient reading and involves the ability to identify and manipulate units of spoken language (i.e., phonemes) to form syllables and words (Ehri et al., 2001; Snow, Burns, & Griffin, 1998). The National Reading Panel (2000) concluded that, "fluent and automatic application of phonics skills to text is another critical skill that must be taught and learned to maximize oral reading and reading comprehension" (p. 11). Along these lines, Daly, Chafouleas, Persampieri, Bonfiglio, and LaFleur (2004) argued that teaching students to form words by blending letter sounds constitutes a *minimal textual repertoire* that is readily generalized to oral reading of novel or untrained words. In support of this argument, two first-grade students were taught lists of nonsense words using either a phoneme blending and segmenting strategy or a sight-word strategy. In the phoneme blending and segmenting condition, students were prompted to read each phoneme in a nonsense word individually and then blend the sounds to make the whole word with modeling and corrective feedback. Generalized effects of both training conditions were assessed by having the children read real words that were similar to the trained nonsense words. Results showed that both students were able to correctly read a larger number of real (generalization) words in the phoneme blending condition presumably because this condition trained skills that could be broadly applied across stimuli.

Martens, Werder, Hier, and Koenig (2013) taught three second-grade children to blend phonemes of words containing three target vowel teams (*au, aw, oi*) and evaluated generalized effects to untrained words in lists and both trained and untrained words in passages. Results showed generalized increases in oral reading accuracy for target words (trained and untrained) presented in both lists and passages for all three students on two vowel teams. Generalized increases in oral reading fluency in both lists and passages were also found for all students on the vowel team that was trained to a fluency criterion.

CONCLUSION

In a conversation with Dr. Owen White (personal communication, September 29, 2011), an expert in precision teaching, he asked how one should establish the level of fluency to which a skill should be trained and answered his own question by stating, "It depends." For some tasks, he suggested there is a criterion above which you do not want people to exceed. For instance, early infantry men were trained to shoot a gun to the level of fluency (speed) just prior to that which would cause the barrel to begin melting and then bend, resulting in poor shooting accuracy. Other tasks, he suggested, must be taught to the level of fluency at which the user chooses to use that skill over other skills that might lead to the same outcome. He then provided the example of an elementary teacher who would determine whether he had sufficiently taught his students math facts by assessing whether or not they chose to use a calculator when completing math problems. Students' choice not to use a calculator suggested they had developed sufficient fluency in the skill so that it was less effortful for them to employ their math skills than to use a calculator. Once such a level is achieved, Dr. White believed the elementary students would naturally practice the skill on their own resulting in further development of fluency and application of the skill in novel settings.

This conversation nicely captures the essence of ABA principles applied to instructional interventions—as with any other behavioral repertoire, basic academic skills must be trained in such a way that they become instrumental for the child, less effortful than competing behaviors, reinforcing to perform, and readily combined to address complex problems. Since the passage of IDEA (2004), consulting teams have been tasked with relying on evidence-based practices to determine children's eligibility for special education in an RtI model. As we attempted to show in this chapter, ABA represents a particularly comprehensive set of principles and strategies upon which such evidence-based practices can be based and therefore should be of great value to school-based consulting teams in their efforts to design, implement, and evaluate effective interventions for children's learning problems.

REFERENCES

Ardoin, S. P. (2006). The response in response to intervention: Evaluating the utility of assessing maintenance of intervention effects. *Psychology in the Schools, 43*, 713–725.

Ardoin, S. P., Binder, K. S., Zawoyski, A. M., Foster, T. E., & Blevins, L. A. (2013). Using eye-tracking procedures to evaluate generalization effects: Practicing target words during repeated readings within versus across texts. *School Psychology Review, 42*, 477–495.

Ardoin, S. P., Christ, T. J., Morena, L. S., Cormier, D. C., & Klingbeil, D. A. (2013). A systematic review and summarization of the recommendations and research surrounding curriculum-based measurement of oral reading fluency (CBM-R) decision rules. *Journal of School Psychology, 51*, 1–18.

Ardoin, S. P., & Daly, E. J., III, (2007). Introduction to the special series: Close encounters of the instructional kind—How the instructional hierarchy is shaping instructional research 30 years later. *Journal of Behavioral Education, 16*, 1–6.

Ardoin, S. P., Eckert, T. L., Christ, T. J., White, M. J., Morena, L. S., January, S. A., et al. (2013). Examining variance in reading comprehension among developing readers: Words in context (CBM-R) versus words out of context (Word Lists). *School Psychology Review, 42*, 243–261.

Ardoin, S. P., McCall, M., & Klubnik, C. (2007). Promoting generalization of oral reading fluency: Providing drill versus practice opportunities. *Journal of Behavioral Education, 16*, 54–69.

Ardoin, S. P., Morena, L. S., Binder, K. S., & Foster, T. E. (2013). Examining the impact of feedback and repeated readings on oral reading fluency: Let's not forget prosody. *School Psychology Quarterly, 28*, 391–404.

Ardoin, S. P., Suldo, S., Witt, J., Aldrich, S., & McDonald, E. (2005). Accuracy of readability estimates' predictions of CBM performance. *School Psychology Quarterly, 20*, 1–22.

Ardoin, S. P., Wagner, L., & Bangs, K. E. (in press). Applied behavior analysis: A foundation for RtI. In S. R. Jimerson, M. K. Burns, & A. M. VanDerHeyden (Eds.), *Handbook of response to intervention: The science and practice of multi-tiered systems of support* (2nd). New York: Springer.

Ayres, K. M., Maguire, A., & McClimon, D. (2009). Acquisition and generalization of chained tasks taught with computer based video instruction to children with autism. *Education and Training in Developmental Disabilities, 44*, 493–508.

Binder, C. (1996). Behavioral fluency: Evolution of a new paradigm. *The Behavior Analyst, 19*, 163–197.

Bonfiglio, C. M., Daly, E. J., III, Martens, B. K., Lan-Hsiang, R. L., & Corsaut, S. (2004). An experimental analysis of reading interventions: Generalization across instructional strategies, time, and passages. *Journal of Applied Behavior Analysis, 37*, 111–114.

Bourque, P., Dupuis, N., & Van Houten, R. (1986). Public posting in the classroom: Comparison of posting names and coded numbers of individual students. *Psychological Reports, 59*, 295–298.

Boyer, E., Miltenberger, R. G., Batsche, C., & Fogel, V. (2009). Video modeling by experts by experts with video feedback to enhance gymnastics skills. *Journal of Applied Behavior Analysis, 42*, 855–860. http://dx.doi.org/10.1901/jaba. 2009.42-855.

Broatch, J., & Lohr, S. (2012). Multidimensional assessment of value added by teachers to real-world outcomes. *Journal of Educational and Behavioral Statistics, 37*, 256–277. http://dx.doi.org/10.3102/1076998610396900.

Browder, D. H., Wakeman, S. Y., Spooner, F., Ahlgrim-Delzell, L., & Algozzine, B. (2006). Research on reading instruction for individuals with significant cognitive disabilities. *Exceptional Children, 72*, 392–408.

Carnine, D. W., Silbert, J., Kame'enui, E., & Tarver, S. G. (2010). *Direct instruction reading* (5th). New York: Merrill.

Chard, D. J., Vaughn, S., & Tyler, B. J. (2002). A synthesis of research on effective interventions for building reading fluency with elementary students with learning disabilities. *Journal of Learning Disabilities, 35*, 386–406. http://dx.doi.org/10.1177/00222194020350050101.

Christ, T. J., & Silberglitt, B. (2007). Estimates of the standard error of measurement for curriculum-based measures of oral reading fluency. *School Psychology Review, 36*, 130–146.

Christ, T. J., Zopluoglu, C., Monaghen, B. D., & Van Norman, E. R. (2013). Curriculum-based measurement of oral reading: Multi-study evaluation of schedule, duration, and dataset quality on progress monitoring outcomes. *Journal of School Psychology, 51*, 19–57. http://dx.doi.org/10.1016/j.jsp.2012.11.001.

Codding, R. S., Lewandowski, L., & Eckert, T. (2005). Examining the efficacy of performance feedback and goal-setting interventions in children with ADHD: A comparison of two methods. *Journal of Evidence-Based Practices for Schools, 6*, 42–58.

Codding, R. S., & Poncy, B. C. (2010). Introduction to the special issue: Toward an explicit technology for generalizing academic behavior. *Journal of Behavioral Education, 19*, 1–6.

Cooper, J. O., Heron, T. E., & Heward, W. L. (2007). *Applied behavior analysis* (2nd). New York, NY: Macmillan.

Cosden, M., Gannon, C., & Haring, I. G. (1995). Teacher-control versus student-control over choice of task and reinforcement for students with severe behavior problems. *Journal of Behavioral Education, 5,* 11–27. http://dx.doi.org/10.1007/BF02110212.

Daly, E. J., III, Bonfiglio, C. M., Mattson, T., Persampieri, M., & Foreman-Yates, K. (2006). Refining the experimental analysis of academic skills deficits: Part II. Use of brief experimental analysis to evaluate reading fluency treatments. *Journal of Applied Behavior Analysis, 39,* 323–331.

Daly, E. J., III, Chafouleas, S. M., Persampieri, M., Bonfiglio, C. M., & LaFleur, K. (2004). Teaching phoneme segmenting and blending as critical early literacy skills: An experimental analysis of minimal textual repertoires. *Journal of Behavioral Education, 13,* 165–178.

Daly, E. J., III, Lentz, F. E., & Boyer, J. (1996). The instructional hierarchy: A conceptual model for understanding the effective components of reading interventions. *School Psychology Quarterly, 11,* 369–386.

Daly, E. J., III, & Martens, B. K. (1994). A comparison of three interventions for increasing oral reading performance: Application of the instructional hierarchy. *Journal of Applied Behavior Analysis, 27,* 459–469.

Daly, E. J., III, Martens, B. K., Barnett, D., Witt, J. C., & Olson, S. C. (2007). Varying intervention delivery in response to intervention: Confronting and resolving challenges with measurement, instruction and intensity. *School Psychology Review, 36,* 562–581.

Daly, E. J., III, Martens, B. K., Dool, E. J., & Hintze, J. M. (1998). Using brief functional analysis to select interventions for oral reading. *Journal of Behavioral Education, 8,* 203–218.

Daly, E. J., III, Martens, B. K., Hamler, K. R., Dool, E. J., & Eckert, T. L. (1999). A brief experimental analysis for identifying instructional components needed to improve oral reading fluency. *Journal of Applied Behavior Analysis, 32,* 83–94.

Daly, E. J., III, Martens, B. K., Kilmer, A., & Massie, D. (1996). The effects of instructional match and content overlap on generalized reading performance. *Journal of Applied Behavior Analysis, 29,* 507–518.

Daly, E. J., III, Wells, J. N., Swanger-Gagne, M., Carr, J. E., Kunz, G. M., & Taylor, A. M. (2009). Evaluation of the multiple-stimulus without replacement stimulus preference assessment method using activities as stimulus events. *Journal of Applied Behavior Analysis, 42,* 563–574.

Daly, E. J., III, Witt, J. C., Martens, B. K., & Dool, E. J. (1997). A model for conducting a functional analysis of academic performance problems. *School Psychology Review, 26,* 554–574.

Deno, S. L., Fuchs, L. S., Marston, D., & Shin, J. (2001). Using curriculum-based measurement to establish growth standards for students with learning disabilities. *School Psychology Review, 30,* 507–524.

Duhon, G. J., Noell, G. H., Witt, J. C., Freeland, J. T., Dufrene, B. A., & Gilbertson, D. N. (2004). Identifying academic skills and performance deficits: The experimental analysis of brief assessments of academic skills. *School Psychology Review, 33,* 429–443.

Dunlap, G., Kern-Dunlap, L., Clarke, S., & Robbins, F. R. (1991). Functional assessment, curricular revision, and severe behavior problems. *Journal of Applied Behavior Analysis, 24,* 387–397.

Eckert, T. L., Ardoin, S. P., Daly, E. J., III, & Martens, B. K. (2002). Improving oral reading fluency: A brief experimental analysis of combining an antecedent intervention with consequences. *Journal of Applied Behavior Analysis, 35,* 271–281.

Eckert, T. L., Dunn, E. K., & Ardoin, S. P. (2006). The effects of alternate forms of performance feedback on elementary-aged students' oral reading fluency. *Journal of Behavioral Education, 15,* 149–162.

Ehri, L. C., Nunes, S. R., Willows, D. M., Schuster, B. V., Yaghoub-Zadeh, Z., & Shanahan, T. (2001). Phonemic awareness instruction helps children learn to read: Evidence from the National Reading Panel's meta-analysis. *Reading Research Quarterly, 36,* 250–287.

Everett, G. E., & Edwards, R. P. (2007). Targeting subtraction inversion errors through within-stimulus prompting: A case study. *Psychology Journal, 4,* 128–139.

Scott Foresman Reading Street (2008). Pearson Education, Inc. http://www.pearsonschool.com/index.cfm?locator=PSZ4Z4&PMDbProgramID=30321 Retrieved 31 March 2014.

Fuchs, L. S., & Deno, S. L. (1992). Effects of curriculum within curriculum-based measurement. *Exceptional Children, 58,* 232–242.

Good, R. H., & Kaminski, R. A. (2011). *DIBELS next technical manual.* Eugene, OR: Dynamic Measurement Group. Retrieved from: https://dibels.org/next/index.php.

Haring, N. G., & Eaton, M. D. (1978). Systematic instructional procedures: An instructional hierarchy. In N. G. Haring, T. C. Lovitt, M. D. Eaton, & C. L. Hansen (Eds.), *The fourth R: Research in the classroom* (pp. 23–40). Columbus, OH: Merrill.

Heward, W. L. (1994). Three "low-tech" strategies for increasing the frequency of active student response during group instruction. In R. Gardner III,, D. M. Sainato, J. O. Cooper, T. E. Heron, W. L. Heward, J. W. Eshleman, & T. A. Grossi (Eds.), *Behavior analysis in education: Focus on measurably superior instruction* (pp. 283–320). Pacific Grove, CA: Brooks/Cole Publishing.

Hosp, J. L., & Ardoin, S. P. (2008). Assessment for instructional planning. *Assessment for Effective Intervention, 33*(2), 69–77.

Howe, K., & Shinn, M. M. (2002). *Standard reading assessment passages (RAPs) for use in general outcome measurement: A manual describing development and technical features.* 6/29/04, http://www.aimsweb.com/uploads/pdfs/passagestechnicalmanual.pdf.

Howell, K. W., & Nolet, V. (2000). *Curriculum-based evaluation: Teaching and decision making* (3rd). Belmont, CA: Wadsworth.

Individuals with Disabilities Education Improvement Act. (2004). PL 108-446, 20 U.S.C § 1400 et seq.

Jaspers, K. E., Williams, R. L., Skinner, C. H., Cihak, D., McCallum, R. S., & Ciancio, D. J. (2012). How and to what extent do cover, copy, and compare spelling interventions contribute to spelling, word recognition, and vocabulary development? *Journal of Behavioral Education, 21,* 80–98.

Johnson, K. R., & Layng, T. V. J. (1992). Breaking the structuralist barrier: Literacy and numeracy with fluency. *American Psychologist, 47,* 1475–1490.

Johnson, K. R., & Layng, T. V. J. (1996). On terms and procedures: Fluency. *The Behavior Analyst, 19,* 281–288.

Jones, K. M., Wickstrom, K. F., Noltemeyer, A. L., Brown, S. M., Schuka, J. R., & Therrien, W. J. (2009). An experimental analysis of reading fluency. *Journal of Behavioral Education, 18,* 35–55.

Kupzyk, S., Daly, E. J., III, & Andersen, M. N. (2011). A comparison of two flashcard methods for improving sight-word reading. *Journal of Applied Behavior Analysis, 44,* 781–792.

LaBerge, D., & Samuels, S. J. (1974). Toward a theory of automatic information processing in reading. *Cognitive Psychology, 6,* 293–323.

Lentz, F. E. (1988). Effective reading interventions in the regular classroom. In J. L. Graden, J. Zins, & M. J. Curtis (Eds.), *Alternative educational delivery systems: Enhancing instructional options for all students* (pp. 351–370). Washington, DC: The National Association of School Psychologists.

Martens, B. K., & Ardoin, S. P. (2010). Assessing disruptive behavior within a problem-solving model. In G. G. Peacock, R. A. Ervin, E. J. Daly, III, & K. W. Merrell (Eds.), *Practical handbook in school psychology: Effective practices for the 21st century* (pp. 157–174). New York: Guilford.

Martens, B. K., Daly, E. J., III, Begeny, J. C., & VanDerHeyden, A. (2011). Behavioral approaches to education. In W. Fisher, C. Piazza, & H. Roane (Eds.), *Handbook of applied behavior analysis* (pp. 385–401). New York: Guilford.

Martens, B. K., Eckert, T. L., Begeny, J. C., Lewandowski, L. J., DiGennaro, F., Montarello, S., et al. (2007). Effects of a fluency-building program on the reading performance of low-achieving second and third grade students. *Journal of Behavioral Education, 16*, 39–54.

Martens, B. K., Steele, E. S., Massie, D. R., & Diskin, M. T. (1995). Curriculum bias in standardized tests of reading decoding. *Journal of School Psychology, 33*, 287–296.

Martens, B. K., Werder, C. S., Hier, B. O., & Koenig, E. A. (2013). Fluency training in phoneme blending: A preliminary study of generalized effects. *Journal of Behavioral Education, 22*, 16–36.

McComas, J. J., Hoch, H., Paone, D., & El-Roy, D. (2000). Escape during academic tasks: A preliminary analysis of idiosyncratic establishing operations. *Journal of Applied Behavior Analysis, 33*, 479–494.

McComas, J. J., Wagner, D., Chaffin, M. D., Holton, E., McDonnell, M., & Monn, E. (2009). Prescriptive analysis: Further individualization of hypothesis testing in brief experimental analysis of reading fluency. *Journal of Behavioral Education, 18*, 56–70.

Mellard, D. F., McKnight, M., & Woods, K. (2009). Response to intervention screening and progress-monitoring practices in 41 local schools. *Learning Disabilities Research & Practice, 24*, 186–195. http://dx.doi.org/10.1111/j.1540-5826.2009.00292.x.

Mesmer, E. M., Duhon, G. J., Hogan, K., Newry, B., Hommema, S., Fletcher, C., et al. (2010). Generalization of sight word accuracy using a common stimulus procedure: A preliminary investigation. *Journal of Behavioral Education, 19*, 47–61.

National Reading Panel. (2000). *Teaching children to read: An evidence-based assessment of the scientific research literature on reading and its implications for reading instruction.* Available on-line, http://www.nationalreadingpanel.org/.

Nelson, H. (2013). *Testing more, teaching less: What America's obsession with student testing costs in money and lost instructional time.* Washington, DC: American Federation of Teachers.

Nese, J. F. T., Biancarosa, G., Cummings, K., Kennedy, P., Alonzo, J., & Tindal, G. (2013). In search of average growth: Describing within-year oral reading fluency growth across grades 1-8. *Journal of School Psychology, 51*, 625–642.

O'Shea, L. J., Munson, S. M., & O'Shea, D. J. (1984). Error correction in oral reading: Evaluating the effectiveness of three procedures. *Education and Treatment of Children, 7*, 203–214.

Olinghouse, N. G. (2008). Student- and instruction-level predictors of narrative writing in third-grade students. *Reading and Writing, 21*, 3–26.

Pennington, R. C., Stenhoff, D. M., Gibson, J., & Ballou, K. (2012). Using simultaneous prompting to teach computer-based story writing to a student with autism. *Education & Treatment of Children, 35*, 389–406.

Reeves, L. M., Umbreit, J., Ferro, J. B., & Liaupsin, C. J. (2013). Function-based intervention to support the inclusion of students with autism. *Education and Training in Autism and Developmental Disabilities, 48*(3), 379–391.

Reichow, B., & Wolery, M. (2011). Comparison of progressive prompt delay with and without instructive feedback. *Journal of Applied Behavior Analysis, 44*, 327–340.

Reynolds, G. S. (1975). *A primer of operant conditioning.* Glenview, IL: Scott, Foresman and Co.

Rose, T. L., & Beattie, J. R. (1986). Relative effects of teacher-directed and taped previewing on oral reading. *Learning Disability Quarterly, 9*, 193–199. http://dx.doi.org/10.2307/1510464.

Schuster, J. W., Gast, D. L., Wolery, M., & Guiltinan, S. (1988). The effectiveness of a constant time-delay procedure to teach chained responses to adolescents with mental retardation. *Journal of Applied Behavior Analysis*, *21*, 169–178. http://dx.doi.org/10.1901/jaba. 1988.21-169.

Scriven, J., & Glynn, T. (1983). Performance feedback on written tasks for low-achieving secondary students. *New Zealand Journal of Educational Studies*, *18*, 134–145.

Shapiro, E. S. (2004). *Academic skills problems: Direct assessment and intervention*. New York: Guilford Press.

Shapiro, E. S. (2011). *Academic skills problems: Direct assessment and intervention* (4th). New York: Guilford Press.

Silber, J. M., & Martens, B. K. (2010). Programming for the generalization of oral reading fluency: Repeated readings of entire text versus multiple exemplars. *Journal of Behavior Education*, *19*, 30–46.

Skinner, C. H., Belfiore, P. J., & Pierce, N. L. (1992). Cover, copy, and compare: Increasing geography accuracy in students with behavior disorders. *School Psychology Review*, *21*, 73–81.

Skinner, C. H., Cooper, L., & Cole, C. L. (1997). The effects of oral presentation previewing rates on reading performance. *Journal of Applied Behavior Analysis*, *30*, 331–333. http://dx.doi.org/10.1901/jaba.1997.30-331.

Skinner, C. H., Fletcher, P. A., & Henington, C. (1996). Increasing learning rates by increasing student response rates: A summary of research. *School Psychology Quarterly*, *11*, 313–325.

Skinner, C. H., Turco, T. L., Beatty, K. L., & Rasavage, C. (1989). Cover, copy, and compare: A method for increasing multiplication performance. *School Psychology Review*, *18*, 412–420.

Snow, C. E., Burns, S. M., & Griffin, P. (Eds.). (1998). *Preventing reading difficulties in young children*. Washington, DC: National Academy Press.

Spache, G. (1953). A new readability for primary grade materials. *Elementary English*, *53*, 410–413.

Stein, M., Kinder, D., Silbert, J., & Carnine, D. W. (2005). *Designing effective mathematics instruction: A direct instruction approach* (4th). New Jersey: Prentice Hall.

Stokes, T. F., & Baer, D. M. (1977). An implicit technology of generalization. *Journal of Applied Behavior Analysis*, *10*, 349–367.

Stokes, T. F., & Osnes, P. G. (1989). An operant pursuit of generalization. *Behavior Therapy*, *20*, 335–357.

Touchette, P. E., & Howard, J. S. (1984). Errorless learning: Reinforcement contingencies and stimulus control transfer in delayed prompting. *Journal of Applied Behavior Analysis*, *17*, 175–188.

VanDerheyden, A. M. (in press). Best practices in can't do/won't do academic assessment. In A. Thomas & P. Harrison (Eds.), *Best practices in school psychology VI*. Washington, DC: The National Association of School Psychologists.

VanDerHeyden, A. M., Witt, J. C., & Gilbertson, D. A. (2007). Multi-year evaluation of the effects of a response to intervention (RTI) model on identification of children for special education. *Journal of School Psychology*, *45*, 225–256. http://dx.doi.org/10.1016/j.jsp.2006.11.004.

VanDerHeyden, A. M., Witt, J. C., & Naquin, G. (2003). Development and validation of a process for screening referrals to special education. *School Psychology Review*, *32*, 204–227.

Vargas, J. S. (1984). What are your exercises teaching? An analysis of stimulus control in instructional materials. In W. L. Heward, T. E. Heron, D. S. Hill, & J. Trap-Porter (Eds.), *Focus on behavior analysis in education* (pp. 126–141). Columbus, OH: Merrill.

William, D. (2010). Standardized testing and school accountability. *Educational Psychologist*, *45*(2), 107–122. http://dx.doi.org/10.1080/00461521003703060.

Wolery, M., Bailey, D. B., Jr., & Sugai, G. M. (1988). *Effective teaching: Principles and procedures of applied behavior analysis with exceptional children*. Boston, MA: Allyn & Bacon, Inc.

Worsdell, A. S., Iwata, B. A., Dozier, C. L., Johnson, A. D., Neidert, P. L., & Thomason, J. L. (2005). Analysis of response repetition as an error-correction strategy during sight-word reading. *Journal of Applied Behavior Analysis, 38,* 511–527.

Zheng, X., Flynn, L. J., & Swanson, H. L. (2013). Experimental intervention studies on word problem solving and math disabilities: A selective analysis of the literature. *Learning Disability Quarterly, 36,* 97–111.

CHAPTER 7

Brief Experimental Analyses of Problem Behavior in a Pediatric Outpatient Clinic

David P. Wacker[1], Kelly M. Schieltz[2], Patrick W. Romani[3]
[1]Center for Disabilities and Development, The University of Iowa, Iowa City, Iowa, USA
[2]College of Education, University of Missouri, Columbia, Missouri, USA
[3]Munroe-Meyer Institute, University of Nebraska Medical Center, Omaha, Nebraska, USA

In this chapter, we describe an outpatient behavioral assessment model based on the brief experimental analysis procedures that has evolved within our Behavioral Pediatrics Clinic (BPC) with children who have a combination of learning and behavioral concerns. We first describe the history of the clinic and the subgroup of children who are commonly evaluated in the clinic. Within this section, we describe the challenges posed by children with a combination of behavioral and learning problems and our goals for these evaluations. We then provide multiple case examples that show the response–consequence and antecedent–response analyses we often conduct for children who have combinations of learning and behavioral problems.

BRIEF HISTORY OF THE BEHAVIORAL PEDIATRICS CLINIC

In 1990, Cooper, Wacker, Sasso, Reimers, and Donn described a brief version of the experimental analysis procedures developed by Carr and Durand (1985) and Iwata, Dorsey, Slifer, Bauman, and Richman (1982/1994). Two aspects made the assessment procedures described in the article notable. First, this was the initial application of experimental analysis procedures to an outpatient clinic. The results, which have been replicated (e.g., Boelter et al., 2007; Call, Wacker, Ringdahl, Cooper-Brown, & Boelter, 2004; Gardner, Wacker, & Boelter, 2009), showed that, even under the severe time restrictions of a single 2-h outpatient assessment, the variables evoking and maintaining problem behavior could be identified within a brief multielement design (Wacker, Berg, Harding, & Cooper-Brown, 2004) and treatment initiated (Wacker, Berg, Schieltz, Romani, & Padilla Dalmau, 2013).

Clinical and Organizational Applications of Applied Behavior Analysis
http://dx.doi.org/10.1016/B978-0-12-420249-8.00007-1

Although these brief multielement analyses often lack the internal validity of more extended analyses (Wacker et al., 2004) and can lead to false negatives (Derby et al., 1992), they can provide important data about stimulus-response and/or response–reinforcer relationships that can, in turn, lead to treatment.

The second notable aspect of the Cooper, Wacker, Sasso, Reimers, and Donn (1990) study was that the brief experimental analyses were conducted on behavior exhibited by typically developing children. Although concerns continue to be expressed regarding the applicability of experimental analysis procedures to outpatient clinics and to typically developing children (Anderson & St. Peter, 2013; Hanley, 2012), our outpatient clinicians have conducted these assessments routinely across all subgroups of children. Beginning with Cooper et al. (1990), multiple authors (e.g., Boelter et al., 2007; Call et al., 2004; Cooper et al., 1992; Gardner et al., 2009; Harding et al., 1999; Millard et al., 1993; Reimers et al., 1993; Richman, Wacker, Cooper-Brown, Kayser, & Crosland, 2001; Stephens, Wacker, Cooper, Richman, & Kayser, 2003) have published the results of brief experimental analyses with children who were typically developing but displayed problem behavior. A systematic review of these studies provided preliminary evidence that the brief analyses meet criteria for being empirically supported procedures with typically developing children (Gardner, Spencer, Boelter, DuBard, & Jennett, 2012). Although most of these evaluations were focused on severe problem behavior and the consequences that maintained those behaviors, the antecedents that evoked problem behavior (e.g., Richman et al., 2001) or that occasioned appropriate behavior (e.g., McComas, Wacker, & Cooper, 1996) also were commonly assessed.

DESCRIPTION OF THE CLINIC

Population

The BPC is a part of the pediatric specialty clinics at the University of Iowa Children's Hospital. The most common patient referrals to the BPC are young children between the ages of 2 and 10 years. The children referred to BPC are most often typically developing and display problem behaviors at home, at school, or in the community. A majority of referrals are male (Seyfer et al., 2011), and most families have Medicaid insurance. Primary behavior concerns for patients referred to BPC are noncompliant and aggressive problem behaviors. Other behavioral concerns include property destruction, self-injurious behavior, tantrums, and pica. A moderate percentage of patients referred to BPC are currently prescribed psychotropic medications (Seyfer et al., 2011). Thus, the modal patient is young, typically developing, and from a low-income family. These children often have multiple problems such as learning problems in addition to their behavior problems.

Referrals to BPC are initiated by the patient's primary care physician, medical staff at the University of Iowa Hospitals and Clinics, school teams, or the patient's caregivers. Information regarding the target behavior and the referral question is requested several weeks prior to the patient's clinic appointment. Although patients are often scheduled several months in advance, approximately 25% of patients "no show" to the clinic and an additional 14% cancel their appointment prior to their evaluation date. The "no show"/cancelation rate is perhaps the biggest challenge confronting our clinic, and this challenge is increasing despite our efforts (e.g., pre clinic phone calls) to curb this challenge. There are likely many reasons for this challenge, but two of the major factors are the wait time (often over 3 months) and distance to the clinic (90 miles one way for a 2-h appointment). Few behavioral clinics in Iowa evaluate typically developing children who display behavior problems and are insured by Medicaid, and this creates the wait time and distance problems mentioned above. Given both the wait time and the distance problems that families encounter, we attempt to complete a behavioral evaluation that is as comprehensive as possible.

Staff

The BPC offers interdisciplinary evaluations of problem behavior. The clinic consists of a behavioral psychologist, medical staff (i.e., a behavioral pediatrician and pediatric nurse practitioner), and a speech and language pathologist. Total time for clinic appointments are generally 3 h with the behavioral psychologists conducting their evaluations within 90-120 min, and medicine and speech and language pathology each having 30 min. Four to six children are evaluated per day. As discussed by Richman et al. (2001), children with behavior problems often also have concerns or delays in their language skills. We routinely screen for language problems, and over half of the children we evaluate have either diagnosed or undiagnosed language problems and even more have learning disabilities.

The general procedures conducted by the behavioral psychology team consist of: (a) an antecedent-behavior-consequence (ABC) interview by phone (if possible) or in the clinic, (b) a brief experimental analysis to directly assess the variables identified via the interview, (c) a demonstration of the treatment if possible, and (d) follow-up via email, phone, or Skype™ 2 weeks to 1 month following the clinic appointment. Very few families return to clinic but return visits can be scheduled as desired by the families.

The ABC interview is conducted to develop hypotheses regarding response-environment relations, and specifically about antecedent-response and response-consequence relations. The behavioral psychologist asks the family to indicate the target behavior (e.g., noncompliance at home). We then ask the family to describe the three most recent occasions when the behavior has occurred, and we focus on the antecedents and consequences surrounding the behavior. This information is then used to develop functional hypotheses regarding the environmental variables that evoke or maintain the response (e.g., noncompliance is the target behavior and likely serves an escape or negative reinforcement function). The results from the speech and language pathologist might offer a further explanation. For example, if the child is only noncompliant with homework, or is most often noncompliant with multistep directions, we may find that there is a correlation with his or her language skills. Similarly, if the child has good and bad days relative to complying to the same demands, we may find there is a correlation with sleep issues or other biologic events (e.g., constipation).

The results of these descriptive and indirect assessments are then used to develop hypotheses that are tested either in the clinic or at home via follow-up. In the majority of cases, we conduct a brief experimental analysis in the clinic.

PURPOSES OF BRIEF EXPERIMENTAL ANALYSES

The primary goal of the BPC is to conduct assessments that lead directly to treating the target behavior. This broad goal encompasses several ethical guidelines set forth by the Behavior Analyst Certification Board (2010), which state that "the behavior analyst conducts a functional assessment to provide the necessary data to develop an effective behavior change program" (3.02) and "the behavior analyst recommends reinforcement rather than punishment whenever possible" (4.05). The broad goal of our clinic and these ethical guidelines are important because one cornerstone of applied behavior analysis has been matching behavioral interventions to the function of problem behavior. For over 30 years, and especially since the development of functional analysis procedures (Iwata et al., 1982/1994), researchers and practitioners have demonstrated the positive effects of behavioral interventions, and primarily those based on reinforcement, on target problem behaviors following the identification of the response-reinforcer relation of problem behavior (Beavers, Iwata, & Lerman, 2013). These last 30 years are a contrast to behavioral intervention programs that were largely punishment based or selected via trial and error (Pelios, Morren, Tesch, & Axelrod, 1999). As described by Wacker et al. (2004, 2014), the primary purpose of brief experimental analyses conducted in the BPC has remained the same: to identify the function of problem behavior. In the next section, we provide three case examples showing how these analyses can be conducted across different functions of behaviors. These evaluations also represent the most common brief experimental analyses conducted in the BPC (see also Gardner et al., 2012, for a description of procedures).

Brief Functional Analysis
Case Example 1
Caleb was a 6-year-old boy who had a diagnosis of attention–deficit hyper activity disorder (ADHD). He was referred to the BPC for behavioral management strategies to address noncompliance, tantrums, and aggression that occurred both at home and at school. During the ABC interview, Caleb's parents reported that problem behaviors occurred primarily when he was instructed to complete a task such as picking up his toys. In response to these problem behaviors, his parents either placed him in time out or directed him to a different activity. Given this information, it was hypothesized that Caleb's problem behaviors occurred to escape tasks. A brief functional analysis was conducted to test this hypothesis.

Brief functional analysis conditions conducted with Caleb were free play, escape, and attention. During the free play condition, Caleb had access to toys and his parents' attention, and demands were not placed on him. During the escape condition, he was instructed to complete an academic task. Caleb received a brief break from the task contingent on problem behavior. Noncompliance was ignored by the adults but functionally served as a break from the task because he was not forced to continue working. During the attention condition, Caleb had access to toys alone. During this condition, his parents talked to each other at a nearby table. Caleb received brief access to attention contingent on the occurrence of problem behavior. The escape and attention conditions were conducted to determine if Caleb's problem behaviors were maintained by negative reinforcement (escape from tasks), positive reinforcement (access to attention), or both. For most of our evaluations, data on target behavior are recorded with a 6-s or 10-s partial interval recording system.

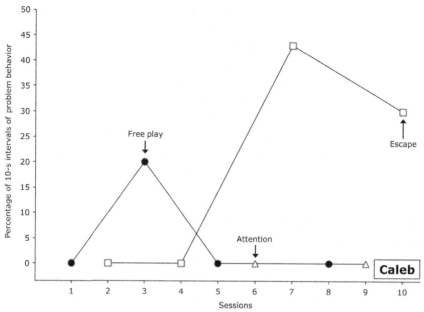

Figure 7.1 Percentage of 10-s intervals of problem behavior during the brief functional analysis for Caleb.

Figure 7.1 displays the results from Caleb's brief functional analysis. During the first five sessions, free play sessions were alternated with escape sessions to test our initial hypothesis, but the results showed that problem behavior (e.g., aggression, property destruction) occurred only briefly during one of the free play sessions. We continued the assessment by including attention sessions. The overall results of this analysis showed that problem behavior most commonly occurred during the escape sessions. Given these results, recommendations for home and school focused on increasing Caleb's compliance with task demands while eliminating time out. The results also highlight two aspects of our current procedures for conducting brief functional analyses. First, although we originally often conducted only one session of a test condition (Northup et al., 1991), we currently always conduct at least two sessions for test conditions hypothesized to be related to problem behavior. We often find that two or three sessions are needed before the response-reinforcer relation is identified. Second, we most often begin the functional analysis with the hypothesized test condition alternated with free play (Iwata, Duncan, Zarcone, Lerman, & Shore, 1994). We conduct the analysis beginning with the hypothesized test condition to increase the efficiency of the analysis. If target behavior occurs during the test condition, but not during free play, we discontinue the assessment component after about five total sessions and focus on treatment. If the results are not consistent with our hypothesis, we extend the analysis as shown in Figure 7.1. Even with these types of extensions, total assessment time is still brief (50 min for the assessment depicted in Figure 7.1). Thus, a brief functional analysis does not necessarily mean that only one session is conducted. To us, a brief functional analysis means it was completed within a short amount of time and was not replicated across days. As discussed by Gardner et al. (2012), it also means that most often parents conducted the evaluation with coaching provided by highly trained applied behavior analysts.

Case Example 2

Chase was a 3-year-old boy who was referred to the BPC for behavioral management strategies to address noncompliance, tantrums, and aggression that occurred at home. During the ABC interview, Chase's mother indicated that problem behaviors occurred when adult attention was diverted from him such as when she was talking on the phone and when he was asked to complete a task such as picking up his toys. In response to his problem behaviors, his mother implemented a variety of strategies including placing him in time out, engaging him in a discussion, spanking, and taking things away. Given this information, it was hypothesized that Chase's problem behaviors occurred to gain access to attention and to escape tasks.

A brief functional analysis was conducted to test these hypotheses. Conditions conducted with Chase were free play, attention, and escape. All conditions were conducted in the same manner as described above for Caleb. Figure 7.2 displays the results from the brief functional analysis (left panel) for Chase. Problem behavior occurred most often in the attention condition suggesting that Chase's problem behavior was maintained by positive reinforcement (access to attention). Although problem behavior occurred during one escape session, it was noted that problem behavior occurred briefly at the beginning of the session, and Chase complied with all demands. In contrast, during the attention condition problem behavior escalated as each session continued. These results confirmed one of the two hypotheses that were made prior to the brief functional analysis being conducted.

Given the results suggesting that access to attention was a maintaining variable for problem behavior, recommendations focused on increasing the amount of time Caleb appropriately played alone. This recommendation was practiced in the clinic with key components being to start him playing on a preferred task before removing adult attention, signaling with a timer when attention was available, ignoring problem behavior, and gradually increasing the amount of time he was required to wait before receiving

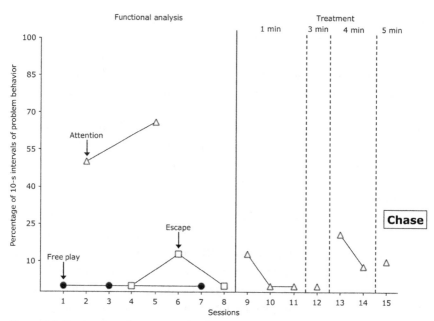

Figure 7.2 Percentage of 10-s intervals of problem behavior during the brief functional analysis and treatment evaluation for Chase.

attention. Overall, results showed (right panel) that problem behavior decreased and remained at relatively low levels as the wait time increased from 1 to 5 min. In comparison to the amount of problem behavior that occurred during the brief functional analysis during the attention condition, the average percent reduction during the treatment condition at wait times of 4–5 min was 33%. Thus, in approximately 20 min, Chase's problem behavior decreased by 33% with the implementation of behavioral strategies that were matched to the attention function.

This example shows how we match treatment to the results of the functional analysis in the clinic. When we can quickly identify the function (in Chase's case it took 40 min), we are able to allocate time to demonstrating treatment to parents and coaching them on how to implement the treatment with their child.

Escape from demands is by far the most common function we identify in the clinic, with various positive reinforcement functions (attention from adults or siblings, tangible items, preferred activities, preferred foods, etc.) occurring a distant second. However, we also often identify multiple social functions as shown in the next case example.

Case Example 3

Blake was a 4-year-old boy who was referred to the BPC for behavior management strategies to address aggression, noncompliance, and tantrums that occurred at home and school. During an ABC interview, Blake's parents reported that his problem behaviors occurred when adult attention was diverted and when he was asked to complete a task. For example, problem behaviors frequently occurred when Blake's mother was talking on the telephone and when she asked him to pick up his toys. In response to his problem behaviors, a variety of strategies were used including placing him in time out, engaging him in a discussion, spanking, ignoring him, and taking things away. Specific to the examples provided, strategies often included ending the telephone conversation early and completing the task for Blake. Given this information, we hypothesized that Blake's problem behaviors occurred to gain access to attention and to escape requests.

A brief functional analysis was conducted to test these hypotheses. Conditions included free play, attention, and escape. All conditions were conducted in the same manner as described above. Results of Blake's brief functional analysis are provided in Figure 7.3. Problem behavior occurred during both the attention and escape conditions suggesting that Blake's

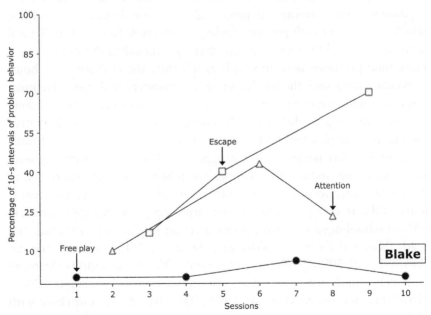

Figure 7.3 Percentage of 10-s intervals of problem behavior during the brief functional analysis for Blake.

problem behavior was multiply maintained by positive and negative rein-forcements. Given these results, recommendations focused on increasing Blake's compliance with task demands by requiring him to complete a task before giving him access to toys and attention. During the brief functional analysis, Blake's problem behavior increased with each subsequent escape session, which is why we focused first on increasing compliance as a recommendation.

CHALLENGES TO THE CLINIC AND EXTENSIONS OF THE BRIEF FUNCTIONAL ANALYSIS PROCEDURES

In 1992, Derby et al. reviewed the results obtained in our behavioral clinic and showed that 63% of participants engaged in the target problem behavior dur-ing the 90 min evaluation, leaving 37% who did not engage in problem behavior. We estimate that over the years, approximately 50% of children evaluated in the BPC displayed target behavior in the clinic. Children who do not exhibit problem behavior during a clinic visit pose a significant chal-lenge to the behavioral psychologist when attempting to develop behavioral interventions that address the response-reinforcer and/or stimulus-response relationships. The ABC interviews conducted prior to or during a clinic appointment only correlate with functional analyses on about 50% of the cases, which is consistent with previous findings (Lerman & Iwata, 1993). Several strategies are used to overcome this challenge, including the evaluation of more mild precursor behaviors such as whining, the evaluation of choice responding to identify the relative value of reinforcers, and alternative mea-sures of desired, adaptive behavior such as task accuracy or rate of responding.

One subgroup of children with whom we often use these alternative assessment strategies are children who, although they do not have formal learning disability diagnoses, are struggling to keep up academically with same-aged peers and are displaying problem behaviors when instructed to complete academic-related tasks both at school and at home. The preva-lence of this referral population is not surprising given that approximately 63% of school-aged children are not meeting proficiency in reading and math (National Center for Education Statistics, 2013), and research has shown that 10-50% of children will present with a combination of learning and behavioral concerns (American Psychiatric Association, 2000; Glassberg, Hooper, & Mattison, 1999). The challenge to our clinic with children who display this combination of learning and behavioral concerns is to discriminate between the variables that are associated with motivation (e.g., escape-maintained problem behavior related to the child's preferences) versus variables that are associated with skill issues (e.g., even when motivated to comply, accuracy of task completion is a problem). This is especially difficult with this subgroup because they often do not display significant problem behavior in the clinic.

When presented with these cases in BPC, our goal remains the same: identify behavioral interventions to address target behavior based on the results of our assessments. We seek to identify behavioral interventions that not only decrease the occurrence of problem behavior but also improve the child's academic performance. Our focus in the clinic is to identify variables that improve or increase task completion. If we can identify those variables, we are able to implement treatment and evaluate whether it decreases problem behavior. To achieve this goal, different types of behavioral assessments are conducted to identify the variables associated with both problem behaviors and academic performance. In Figure 7.4, we provide an example of a decision chart we often use in the clinic to guide our assessment. Using this

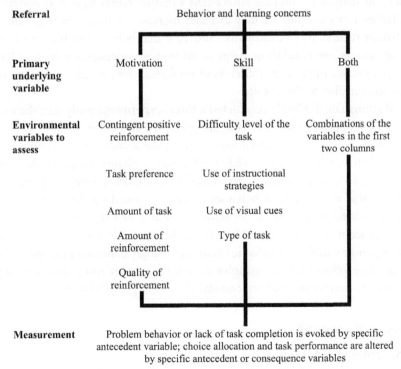

Figure 7.4 Decision chart to guide an assessment of behavioral and learning concerns.

chart, we attempt to isolate combinations of motivational variables (e.g., contingent positive reinforcement, amount of the task, preference for the task) and skill variables (e.g., difficulty level of the task, availability of instructional strategies) that may affect compliance and accuracy. If possible (if problem behavior is occurring), we obtain a measure of both problem behavior and accuracy or amount of task completed, as different variables may affect problem behavior versus task performance (Richman et al., 2001). For these evaluations, the hypotheses generated from the ABC interview are used to determine both the variables to manipulate and the method to analyze those variables. For example, if problem behavior is occurring primarily with academic tasks, the hypothesis might be that noncompliance is related to task preference (motivation) and that can be shown by requiring the child to complete different types of tasks (to show differential compliance across tasks) or that increased contingent positive reinforcement will be sufficient to maintain task completion. Either or both of these analyses can be conducted within a brief experimental analysis.

If our hypothesis is based on the skills of the child, we almost always conduct the analysis by altering antecedent variables rather than consequence variables. For example, we may evaluate increases or decreases in problem behavior relative to task difficulty. Showing that behavior improves under some antecedent conditions helps us to better understand why problem behavior is occurring (e.g., difficulty or preference for the task) and to match a treatment plan to the results.

Richman et al. (2001) conducted a three-experiment study that showed the relation between the way tasks are presented and either accurate or non compliant behavior. In Experiments 1 and 2, the authors showed that accuracy of behavior was strongly related to the way academic and play tasks were presented to young children. For one of these children, a third experiment showed that noncompliant behavior could be evoked quickly if the directives provided did not guide accurate responding and if praise was contingent on accurate responding. Identifying the interaction of antecedent and consequence variables of behavior is an increasingly common purpose of the clinic. The following case examples show how we alter antecedent variables to identify conditions that are correlated with target behavior.

CASE EXAMPLES

Antecedent Analysis

Antecedent variables, such as complexity of demands (Richman et al., 2001) or specific instructional strategies (McComas et al., 1996), can help identify the conditions under which problem behavior or task accuracy will occur. In one example, McComas and colleagues (1996) evaluated the use of two instructional strategies to increase accurate responding to more or less difficult demands for children with learning difficulties. Results showed that accurate responding occurred only when specific instructional strategies were in place. As discussed, many children referred to the BPC have underlying language delays or learning problems. Thus, a common focus of the clinic evaluation is separating motivation versus skill issues. Antecedent evaluation of instructional strategies can help answer this question for some children.

Case Example 1

Jared was a 7-year-old first-grade student diagnosed with disruptive behavior disorder, ADHD, mixed receptive/expressive language disorder, cognitive disorder, and specific learning disabilities for reading, math, and writing. Jared was referred to the BPC to evaluate behavior management strategies to address noncompliance occurring at home and school.

Given Jared's history of learning concerns, we focused the assessment on evaluating problem behavior and task completion (i.e., number of individual problems completed) when he was presented with more and less difficult demands. One treatment recommendation focused on the identification of instructional strategies to decrease Jared's motivation to escape demands if problem behavior occurred most reliably when more difficult demands were presented. Within a multielement design, an antecedent analysis of problem behavior and task completion when he was presented with grade-level math tasks (more difficult demands) and kindergarten-level math tasks (less difficult demands) occurred. Conditions conducted with Jared were free play, more difficult demands, and less difficult demands. During the demands conditions, Jared was directed to a table and presented with either a more or less difficult demand. There were no programmed consequences for problem behavior.

As shown in Figure 7.5, problem behavior occurred at higher levels during the more difficult demands sessions ($M = 38\%$) relative to the less difficult demands sessions ($M = 15\%$). No problem behavior occurred during free play. Task completion was also higher in the less difficult demand sessions. Jared completed an average of 4.4 problems per minute for less difficult demands and an average of 0.2 problems per minute for the more difficult demands. In summary, Jared's problem behavior seemed related to the difficulty of the demands. He was more compliant and completed more tasks during the less difficult demand sessions, and it appeared that at least some of his problem behaviors were related to learning and not just to motivation.

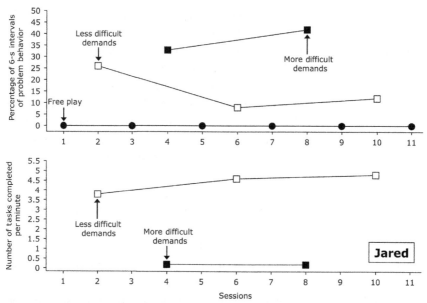

Figure 7.5 The top panel represents the percentage of 6-s intervals of problem behavior during the antecedent analysis for Jared. The bottom panel represents the number of tasks completed per minute.

Case Example 2

Renee was a 7-year-old girl who was referred to the BPC for behavior management strategies to address noncompliance and aggression that occurred at both home and school. During an ABC interview, Renee's mother reported that problem behaviors occurred more often when (a) tasks were instructed vocally, (b) Renee was required to provide a vocal response, and (c) the task materials required the use of paper and pencil. In contrast, Renee was more likely to complete tasks that were instructed with the support of visual cues, the response requirement was tactile such as pointing, and the task materials required the use of an iPad.

An antecedent analysis was conducted to identify the conditions that occasioned Renee's problem behaviors and task completion. Conditions during this analysis focused on manipulating various dimensions of academic tasks that included the materials used and the response requirement and were free play, paper/pencil task, vocal response requirement, and tactile response requirement conducted within a multielement design. During the paper/pencil task, Renee was instructed to trace dotted letters of the alphabet and dotted letters of her name using a pencil on paper. During the vocal

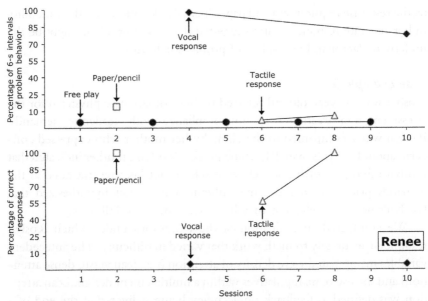

Figure 7.6 The top panel represents the percentage of 6-s intervals of problem behavior during the antecedent analysis for Renee. The bottom panel represents the percentage of correct responses.

response requirement condition, Renee was instructed to vocally identify the letter displayed on a flash card or iPad screen. During the tactile response requirement condition, Renee was instructed to match letters of the alphabet using flash cards or an iPad. During all of the task conditions, problem behavior was ignored and Renee was redirected to the task. She was provided with encouragement to continue completing the task and praise when she completed a portion of the task.

As shown in Figure 7.6, the highest levels of problem behavior (top panel) and inaccurate performance (bottom panel) for Renee occurred during the vocal response requirement condition, suggesting that vocal tasks were difficult and were related to the occurrence of problem behavior. The lowest levels of problem behavior occurred during both the tactile response requirement and the paper/pencil task conditions. During these versions of the task, Renee's accurate performance varied. During the tactile response requirement condition, she completed 50-100% of the task. This variability may have been due to the number of distraction items in the array (nine for flash cards versus three for iPad). During the paper/pencil task, she completed 100% of the task accurately, but she was only required to trace dotted letters. Taken together, although Renee was compliant with the tactile response requirement and paper/pencil task conditions, the variability in her accurate responding also suggested that a skill problem might be the underlying factor in her displays of problem behavior.

Case Example 3

Roslyn was a 6-year-old girl referred by her primary care physician for the assessment and treatment of noncompliance with academic demands. Roslyn was accompanied to the clinic by her mother who expressed concerns about Roslyn's overall learning profile. Roslyn's mother indicated that Roslyn often put forth good effort at school but became frustrated as the demands placed on her became difficult. Clinic staff hypothesized that Roslyn's problem behaviors may have been mostly a skill issue.

We conducted an evaluation of the conditions under which Roslyn responded accurately to math work that varied in difficulty. The antecedent variables manipulated were density of attention (i.e., lean versus dense attention) and the use of manipulatives within a multielement design. Lean attention was defined as feedback on accuracy being delivered at the end of a work task. Dense attention was defined as feedback on accuracy being delivered following each problem completed. Manipulatives were small plastic bears that Roslyn could use to help count. Contingent reinforcement, in the form of play with toys and attention, was delivered after Roslyn completed an academic task and was delivered independent of accuracy.

The results for Roslyn are displayed in Figure 7.7. Roslyn displayed a discrepancy in accurate responding when she was presented with less and more difficult demands. She responded to the less difficult demands with 100% accuracy (open squares) but did not complete any of the more difficult demands accurately (closed diamond). Density of attention did not affect accuracy (closed triangles). The addition of contingent reinforcement increased accuracy slightly (closed circle; 17%) but was still low compared to accuracy for the less difficult demands. These data showed that a skill issue may have been affecting Roslyn's academic performance. The addition of the manipulatives increased accurate responding on the more difficult academic demands from 0% to 83% (open diamonds). Accurate responding on the more difficult demands was low (0% and 17%) when manipulatives and contingent reinforcement were not included.

These results showed an example of the type of interaction that can occur between antecedent and consequence variables. These interactions can become very complex, and we need hypotheses about these interactions to guide the design of the assessment.

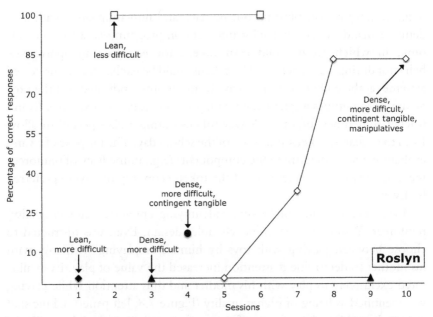

Figure 7.7 Percentage of correct responses during the antecedent analysis for Roslyn.

Choice Analyses

In some cases, the children referred to the clinic have behavioral treatment plans at school or home that on the surface appear to be a good match for the functions of their behavior. For example, the child may have a compliance treatment at school based on the results of a functional analysis that identified negative reinforcement, but the child continues to engage in noncompliance. One way we address these concerns is to evaluate the child's preferences (e.g., Hanley, Piazza, Fisher, & Maglieri, 2005) for the various components of the treatment package or variations in how the components are delivered (e.g., more immediate versus delayed reinforcement). We determine preference based on the child's choices, and our goal is to identify the conditions under which the child chooses to work on the target task. These evaluations are conducted within multielement or concurrent schedules designs, as shown in the following case examples.

Case Example 1

Evan was a 7-year-old boy diagnosed with ADHD and was referred by his mother for an evaluation of the behavior intervention program being implemented with Evan at his school. Primary behavior concerns were aggression (e.g., pushing peers), blurting out in class, and noncompliance with academic demands. Evan's behavior intervention program was a token economy, in which Evan could earn tokens for engaging in appropriate behavior during a class period. The tokens could be exchanged for preferred activities at the end of the school day. Evan's mother indicated that the program was sometimes implemented with poor integrity. For example, Evan's teacher sometimes forgot to deliver tokens during a class period or allow Evan to exchange tokens at the end of the school day. The purpose of Evan's evaluation was to determine the components (e.g., immediacy of reinforcement, quality of reinforcement) of the token economy that were preferred by Evan.

Evan's clinic evaluation began by identifying a preferred (higher quality) reinforcer. Within a concurrent schedules design, Evan was instructed to choose between playing with toys by himself or playing with toys with his mother to determine if attention increased the value of play. Evan allocated exclusively to play with his mother and thus attention while playing was identified as being of higher quality (Figure 7.8, left panel). Clinic staff next evaluated Evan's preference for rate of token delivery and the quality of

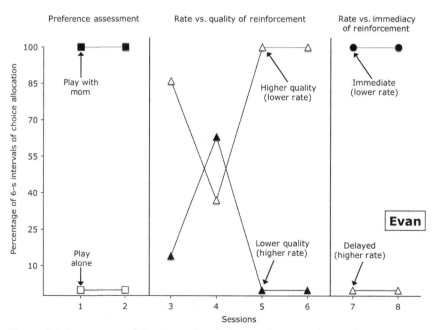

Figure 7.8 Percentage of 6-s intervals of choice allocation during the concurrent operants assessment for Evan.

reinforcement earned contingent on acquiring a predetermined number of tokens (middle panel). Evan was given the choice to work (complete academic tasks) for orange tokens or yellow tokens. Orange tokens were delivered on a fixed-interval (FI) 15-s schedule of reinforcement and resulted in access to a lower quality reinforcer (play alone) after five tokens had been earned. Yellow tokens were delivered at a lower rate (FI 60-s schedule of reinforcement) and resulted in access to a higher quality reinforcer (play with mother) after five tokens had been earned. Evan's preference was for the higher quality reinforcer; he allocated exclusively to the higher quality reinforcer for the last two sessions.

We next evaluated Evan's preference for rate of token delivery versus the immediacy of reinforcement (right panel). Evan continued to work for orange or yellow tokens. Orange tokens were delivered on an FI 15-s schedule of reinforcement and could be exchanged 1 min after Evan earned five tokens for play with his mother. Yellow tokens were delivered on an FI 60-s schedule of reinforcement and could be exchanged immediately after he earned five tokens for play with his mother. Results showed that Evan allocated exclusively to the choice of immediate reinforcement.

The results of Evan's evaluation suggested that the quality of reinforcement he obtained for the exchange of the tokens and the immediacy with which tokens could be exchanged were two preferred dimensions of reinforcement. We told his mother to make sure that at least one of these components was always in place in his token program at school. For Evan, the entire evaluation focused on consequences or motivation variables. We observed that Evan completed his work accurately but he did not always complete the work. In other cases, the choice analysis involves the skills of the child and focuses on antecedent variables.

Case Example 2

Henry was a 10-year-old boy who had diagnoses of dysgraphia, reading disorder, and disorder of written expression. In addition, he had fine motor difficulties. He was referred to our outpatient behavioral clinic for behavior management strategies to address noncompliance that occurred both at home and at school when he was instructed to complete difficult tasks such as writing and reading. He was not receiving special education services within the school setting. Previous evaluations recommended the implementation of accommodations to assist with the reduction of Henry's frustration and noncompliance demonstrated during difficult tasks. Suggested accommodations included alternative formats for writing, such as dictation, use of lined paper, and use of a word bank to decrease his frustration with the physical act of writing.

A choice analysis was conducted to determine Henry's preferences for these alterations for writing tasks. Four writing strategies were evaluated: dictation, writing on lined paper (paper/pencil), writing on lined paper with the use of a word bank, and typing. For all sessions, two writing strategies were presented to Henry, and he was instructed to choose the strategy he wanted to use for a subsequent writing task (based on the forced choice preference assessment described by Fisher et al., 1992). After choosing a writing strategy, a story starter topic sentence was read to him, he was asked to think about what he was going to write for 1 min, and then he was instructed to write his story using the chosen strategy for 3 min. At any point in the session, if Henry did not want to complete the writing task, he could choose to sit alone and not complete the task.

Figure 7.9 displays the results for Henry. During all sessions, Henry always engaged in the writing task, meaning that he never chose to sit alone to escape the task. Henry chose dictation (top panel) during each session it was available as a writing strategy, suggesting that he preferred to complete the writing task with that strategy. His second most preferred form of writing

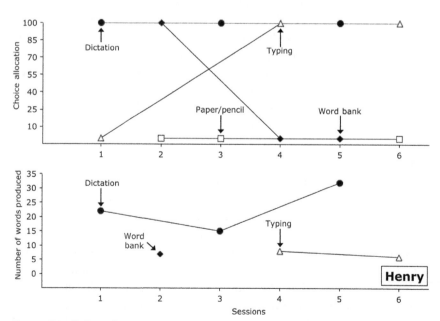

Figure 7.9 Choice allocation (top panel) and number of words produced (bottom panel) during the concurrent operants assessment for Henry.

was typing, followed by the use of a word bank. He never chose to complete the writing task with the use of paper and pencil. Task completion (bottom panel) was the highest when Henry completed the task using dictation. During the sessions in which Henry chose dictation, he was observed to elaborate more on his stories and to make corrections to his sentences, suggesting that he had the skills to complete the writing task with appropriate strategies in place.

Another type of choice assessment we conduct relates to the potency of a reinforcer, defined as how much work a child is willing to complete given other variables such as the amount of reinforcement that is provided. In these cases, we often base our evaluations on behavioral economic theory (Madden, Bickel, & Jacobs, 2000). Behavioral economics permits evaluation of the conditions under which various sources of reinforcement are obtained or consumed (Reed, Niileksela, & Kaplan, 2013). In a treatment context, multiple sources of reinforcement (i.e., attention, tangible, and escape) are often concurrently available, and the response effort needed to obtain the reinforcement may vary. A child might find a reward to be reinforcing when the response demands are low but not when they are high. For example, Roane, Lerman, and Vorndran (2001) showed that tangible reinforcers were differentially preferred as the response requirement to access each reinforcer increased. Thus, it is important to consider the relative effort to complete a demand as the value of a reinforcer may decrease as effort increases.

School teams working with children referred to the BPC often have concerns regarding reinforcer identification. The school team is sometimes able to assess function and implement function-based strategies to decrease problem behavior but continues to encounter problems that may be related to variables such as the potency of reinforcement. The next case provides an example of this type of analysis conducted within a concurrent schedules design.

Case Example 3

Kyle was an 8-year-old boy referred by his primary care physician for the assessment and treatment of problem behaviors occurring at home and school. Primary behavioral concerns were aggression (e.g., hitting, kicking), property destruction (e.g., throwing items), and noncompliance with demands. A functional analysis conducted by Kyle's school team suggested that his problem behaviors were maintained by escape from demands. Despite the introduction of function-based treatment strategies, his school continued to struggle to identify reinforcers that would maintain task completion when demands became difficult.

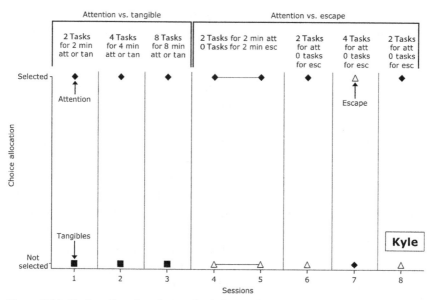

Figure 7.10 Choice allocation during the behavioral economic analysis for Kyle.

The purpose of the first phase of Kyle's evaluation (Figure 7.10) was to identify reinforcers that maintained responding at lower or higher response requirements. Access to attention or tangibles was made available following completion of a predetermined number of tasks. Kyle first needed to complete two work tasks (second-grade math) to earn access to 2 min of attention (with no tangibles) or 2 min of tangibles (with no attention). The effort to access both attention and tangibles increased to four work tasks for 4 min of time with attention or tangibles, and again to eight work tasks for 8 min of time with attention or tangibles. Kyle allocated exclusively to attention during this evaluation showing that attention was a potent reinforcer. Given this finding and the results of the previous functional analysis, we next evaluated the potency of attention when escape from the task was also a choice. We conducted this assessment by requiring progressively more work to obtain attention, while escaping the task altogether was also a choice. Thus, he could complete work to receive attention or to sit alone and not work. Kyle allocated to attention when he needed to complete two work tasks for 2 min of time with attention. Kyle allocated to escape when he needed to complete four work tasks for 2 min of attention. These results showed that compliance for attention would occur, but only at certain demand levels. Recommendations for Kyle's school and parents focused on delivering positive attention contingent on relatively small amounts of task completion. In Kyle's case, we showed that he could complete the work and would complete a certain amount of work for adult attention. Thus, his problem behaviors appear to be primarily motivational. In the next case example, we show how a similar analysis can occur with an antecedent variable related to a possible skill problem.

Case Example 4

Jake was a 14–year-old boy who had diagnoses of Smith-Lemli-Opitz syndrome and autism spectrum disorder. The majority of his instruction was in a special education classroom and consisted of instruction in reading and math at the kindergarten level as well as life skills instruction. His communication consisted of sign language, gestures, and the use of an augmentative communication device. Behaviors of concern included noncompliance and sloppy work.

Choice analyses were conducted to determine Jake's preferences between the amount of task he was willing to complete, use of an instructional strategy to complete the task, and the type of task requested (Figure 7.11). The first phase of this analysis evaluated the effects of work

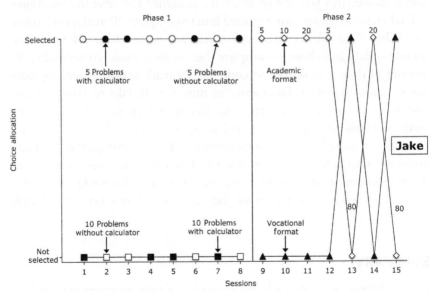

Figure 7.11 Choice allocation during the behavioral economic analysis for Jake. Numbers above the open diamonds represent the required number of math problems in the academic format. In the vocational format (closed triangles), the requirement was always five sets of photocopies.

and use of an instructional strategy. Jake was instructed to complete a specific amount of a single-digit subtraction math task with or without the use of a calculator. During each session, two choices were presented to Jake, and he was instructed to choose one. After choosing one of the available options, he was instructed to complete the task. Figure 7.11 (left panel) displays the results of Phase 1 for Jake. Jake always chose to complete the option that included the least amount of math problems regardless of the presence of the calculator, showing that the amount of task influenced his choice responding.

During Phase 2 of this analysis, the amount and type of the task were manipulated. Type of task consisted of completing a specific amount of a single-digit subtraction math task or making a specific amount of photocopies. With the photocopying task, Jake was required to complete a similar single-digit subtraction problem to determine how many copies were needed for the page being requested. The photocopying task was assessed to determine if Jake had a preference for vocational tasks (that contained an academic component) over academic tasks. Similar to the first phase, Jake was provided with two choices and instructed to choose one. Following his choice, he was instructed to complete the task. Results of this analysis (right panel) showed that Jake always chose the academic task over the vocational task when the academic task required him to complete 20 math problems or less. When the academic task requirement was 80 problems, Jake switched his responding and chose to complete the vocational task. Anecdotally, the amount of time it took Jake to complete 20 math problems was approximately 6 min, whereas the amount of time it took Jake to complete five photocopying sets was approximately 16 min. Given this information, 80 math problems should have taken Jake approximately 24 min. Thus, his choosing to complete five photocopying tasks over completing 80 math problems was the lesser amount of work. Therefore, these results suggested that response effort, in the form of amount of work, influenced Jake's choice responding across both phases of this analysis and was not related only to skill.

SUMMARY

In this chapter, we provided case examples of brief experimental analyses conducted in a BPC. The case examples showed how the analyses can be conducted with antecedent and consequent variables to identify the function of problem behavior, the variables that evoke problem behavior or accurate task completion, and the preferences children have for various treatment components. We use the results of these types of evaluations to develop behavioral treatment plans and to clarify what components of a treatment plan may be important. Each analysis is conducted within brief versions of single-case designs to increase the internal validity of the procedures. Brief versions of multielement and concurrent schedule designs make it possible to evaluate highly complex issues (e.g., skill versus motivational variables) within a limited amount of time, and especially if the evaluation is based on the hypotheses generated via ABC interviews.

REFERENCES

American Psychiatric Association. (2000). *Diagnostic and statistical manual of mental disorders* (4th, text rev.). Washington, DC: American Psychiatric Association.

Anderson, C. M., & St. Peter, C. C. (2013). Functional analysis with typically developing children: Best practice or too early to tell? In response to Hanley (2012). *Behavior Analysis in Practice, 6*(2), 62–76.

Beavers, G. A., Iwata, B. A., & Lerman, D. C. (2013). Thirty years of research on the functional analysis of problem behavior. *Journal of Applied Behavior Analysis, 46*, 1–21. http://dx.doi.org/10.1002/jaba.30.

Behavior Analyst Certification Board (2010). *BACB guidelines for responsible conduct for behavior analysts.* Retrieved from: http://www.bacb.com/index.php?page=57.

Boelter, E. W., Wacker, D. P., Call, N. A., Ringdahl, J. E., Kopelman, T., & Gardner, A. W. (2007). Effects of antecedent variables on disruptive behavior and accurate responding in young children in outpatient clinics. *Journal of Applied Behavior Analysis, 40*, 321–326. http://dx.doi.org/10.1901/jaba.2007.51-06.

Call, N. A., Wacker, D. P., Ringdahl, J. E., Cooper-Brown, L. J., & Boelter, E. W. (2004). An assessment of antecedent events influencing noncompliance in an outpatient clinic. *Journal of Applied Behavior Analysis, 37*, 145–157. http://dx.doi.org/10.1901/jaba.2004.37-145.

Carr, E. G., & Durand, V. M. (1985). Reducing behavior problems through functional communication training. *Journal of Applied Behavior Analysis, 18*, 111–126. http://dx.doi.org/10.1901/jaba.1985.18-111.

Cooper, L. J., Wacker, D. P., Sasso, G. M., Reimers, T. M., & Donn, L. K. (1990). Using parents as therapists to evaluate appropriate behavior of their children: Application to a tertiary diagnostic clinic. *Journal of Applied Behavior Analysis, 23*, 285–296. http://dx.doi.org/10.1901/jaba.1990.23-285.

Cooper, L. J., Wacker, D. P., Thursby, D., Plamann, L. A., Harding, J., Millard, T., et al. (1992). Analysis of the effects of task preferences, task demands, and adult attention on child behavior in outpatient and classroom settings. *Journal of Applied Behavior Analysis, 25*, 823–840. http://dx.doi.org/10.1901/jaba.1992.25-823.

Derby, K. M., Wacker, D. P., Sasso, G., Steege, M., Northup, J., Cigrand, K., et al. (1992). Brief functional assessment techniques to evaluate aberrant behavior in an outpatient setting: A summary of 79 cases. *Journal of Applied Behavior Analysis, 25*, 713–721.

Fisher, W., Piazza, C. C., Bowman, L. G., Hagopiain, L. P., Owens, J. C., & Slevin, I. (1992). A comparison of two approaches for identifying reinforcers for persons with severe and profound disabilities. *Journal of Applied Behavior Analysis, 25*, 491–498.

Gardner, A. W., Spencer, T. D., Boelter, E. W., DuBard, M., & Jennett, H. K. (2012). A systematic review of brief functional analysis methodology with typically developing children. *Education and Treatment of Children*, *35*(2), 313–332. http://dx.doi.org/10.1353/etc.2012.0014.

Gardner, A. W., Wacker, D. P., & Boelter, E. W. (2009). An evaluation of the interaction between quality of attention and negative reinforcement with children who display escape-maintained problem behavior. *Journal of Applied Behavior Analysis*, *42*, 343–348. http://dx.doi.org/10.1901/jaba.2007.51-06.

Glassberg, L. A., Hooper, S. R., & Mattison, R. E. (1999). Prevalence of learning disabilities at enrollment in special education students with behavioral disorders. *Behavioral Disorders*, *25*, 9–21.

Hanley, G. P. (2012). Functional assessment of problem behavior: Dispelling myths, overcoming implementation obstacles, and developing new lore. *Behavior Analysis in Practice*, *5*(1), 54–72.

Hanley, G. P., Piazza, C. C., Fisher, W. W., & Maglieri, K. A. (2005). On the effectiveness of and preference for punishment and extinction components of function-based interventions. *Journal of Applied Behavior Analysis*, *38*(1), 51–65. http://dx.doi.org/10.1901/jaba.2005.6-04.

Harding, J., Wacker, D. P., Cooper, L. J., Asmus, J., Jensen-Kovalan, P., & Grisolano, L. A. (1999). Combining descriptive and experimental analyses of young children with behavior problems in preschool settings. *Behavior Modification*, *23*(2), 316–333. http://dx.doi.org/10.1177/0145445599232008.

Iwata, B. A., Dorsey, M. F., Slifer, K. J., Bauman, K. E., & Richman, G. S. (1982/1994). Toward a functional analysis of self-injury. *Journal of Applied Behavior Analysis*, *27*, 197–209. http://dx.doi.org/10.1901/jaba.1994.27-197 [Reprinted from *Analysis and Intervention in Developmental Disabilities*, *2*, 3–20, 1982].

Iwata, B. A., Duncan, B. A., Zarcone, J. R., Lerman, D. C., & Shore, B. A. (1994). A sequential, test-control methodology for conducting functional analyses of self-injurious behavior. *Behavior Modification*, *18*(3), 289–306. http://dx.doi.org/10.1177/01454455940183003.

Lerman, D. C., & Iwata, B. A. (1993). Descriptive and experimental analyses of variables maintaining self-injurious behavior. *Journal of Applied Behavior Analysis*, *26*, 193–319. http://dx.doi.org/10.1901/jaba.1993.26-293.

Madden, G. J., Bickel, W. K., & Jacobs, E. A. (2000). Three predictions of the economic concept of unit price in a choice context. *Journal of the Experimental Analysis of Behavior*, *73*, 45–64. http://dx.doi.org/10.1901/jeab.2000.73-45.

McComas, J. J., Wacker, D. P., & Cooper, L. J. (1996). Experimental analysis of academic performance in a classroom setting. *Journal of Behavioral Education*, *6*(2), 191–201. http://dx.doi.org/10.1007/BF02110232.

Millard, T., Wacker, D. P., Cooper, L. J., Harding, J., Drew, J., Plagmann, L. A., et al. (1993). A brief component analysis of potential treatment packages in an outpatient clinic setting with young children. *Journal of Applied Behavior Analysis*, *26*, 475–476. http://dx.doi.org/10.1901/jaba.1993.26-475.

National Center for Education Statistics (2013). *The nation's report card: 2013 mathematics and reading*. Retrieved from: http://nationsreportcard.gov/reading_math_2013/#/.

Northup, J., Wacker, D., Sasso, G., Steege, M., Cigrand, K., Cook, J., et al. (1991). A brief functional analysis of aggressive and alternative behavior in an outclinic setting. *Journal of Applied Behavior Analysis*, *24*, 509–522. http://dx.doi.org/10.1901/jaba.1991.24-509.

Pelios, L., Morren, J., Tesch, D., & Axelrod, S. (1999). The impact of functional analysis methodology on treatment choice for self-injurious and aggressive behavior. *Journal of Applied Behavior Analysis*, *32*, 185–195. http://dx.doi.org/10.1901/jaba.1999.32-1985.

Reed, D. D., Niileksela, C. R., & Kaplan, B. A. (2013). Behavioral economics: A tutorial for behavior analysis in practice. *Behavior Analysis in Practice, 6*(1), 34–54.

Reimers, T. M., Wacker, D. P., Cooper, L. J., Sasso, G. M., Berg, W. K., & Steege, M. W. (1993). Assessing the functional properties of noncompliant behavior in an outpatient setting. *Child & Family Behavior Therapy, 15*(3), 1–15. http://dx.doi.org/10.1300/J019v15n03_01.

Richman, D. M., Wacker, D. P., Cooper-Brown, L. J., Kayser, K., & Crosland, K. (2001). Stimulus characteristics within directives: Effects on accuracy of task completion. *Journal of Applied Behavior Analysis, 34*, 289–312. http://dx.doi.org/10.1901/jaba.2001.34-289.

Roane, H. S., Lerman, D. C., & Vorndran, C. M. (2001). Assessing reinforcers under progressive schedule requirements. *Journal of Applied Behavior Analysis, 34*, 145–167. http://dx.doi.org/10.1901/jaba.2001.34-145.

Seyfer, D. L., Van Dyke, D. C., Wacker, D. P., McConkey, S. A., Cooper-Brown, L., Bachmeyer, M. H., et al. (2011). Observations in psychotropic medication usage in patients with behavior disorders presenting to a specialty clinic. *Clinical Pediatrics, 50*, 44–49. http://dx.doi.org/10.1177/0009922810379500.

Stephens, T. J., Wacker, D. P., Cooper, L., Richman, D., & Kayser, K. (2003). Brief experimental analysis of antecedent variables related to noncompliance in young children in an outpatient clinic. *Child & Family Behavior Therapy, 25*(4), 1–18. http://dx.doi.org/10.1300/J019v25n04_01.

Wacker, D. P., Berg, W. K., Bassingthwaite, B. J., Kopelman, T. G., Schieltz, K. M., Padilla Dalmau, Y. C., et al. (2014). Conducting functional analyses of behavior. In R. L. DePry, F. Brown, & J. Anderson (Eds.), *Individual positive behavior supports: A standards-based guide to practices in school and community-based settings* (pp. 295–313). Baltimore, MD: Paul H. Brookes.

Wacker, D. P., Berg, W., Harding, J., & Cooper-Brown, L. (2004). Use of brief experimental analyses in outpatient clinic and home settings. *Journal of Behavioral Education, 13*(4), 213–226. http://dx.doi.org/10.1023/B:JOBE.0000044732.42711.f5.

Wacker, D. P., Berg, W. K., Schieltz, K. M., Romani, P. W., & Padilla Dalmau, Y. C. (2013). Outpatient units. In D. D. Reed, F. D. Reed, & J. L. Luiselli (Eds.), *Handbook of crisis intervention for individuals with developmental disabilities* (pp. 409–422). New York, NY: Springer.

CHAPTER 8

Inborn and Acquired Brain and Physical Disabilities

Mark F. O'Reilly[1], Nicolette Sammarco[1], Michelle Kuhn[1], Cindy Gevarter[1], Laci Watkins[1], Heather K. Gonzales[1], Laura Rojeski[1], Jeff Sigafoos[2], Giulio E. Lancioni[3], Russell Lang[4]

[1]Department of Special Education, The University of Texas at Austin, Austin, Texas, USA
[2]Department of Special Education, Victoria University, Wellington, New Zealand
[3]Department of Education, University of Bari, Bari, Italy
[4]Department of Curriculum and Instruction, Texas State University, San Marcos, Texas, USA

INTRODUCTION

In this chapter, we describe the application of interventions, based on the principles of applied behavior analysis (ABA), to individuals with a variety of intellectual and physical disabilities. ABA has an extensive and successful record in terms of developing evidence-based effective interventions for individuals with a variety of disabilities. In fact, the application of ABA with these populations is so diverse it would warrant several volumes to describe it in adequate detail. Within the confines of this chapter we have elected to give just a flavor of the wide variety of applied issues addressed with this broad population. The chapter is divided into four sections to reflect four broad categories of disability—inborn brain disorders, acquired brain disabilities, inborn physical disabilities, and, finally, acquired physical disabilities. Each of the four sections begins with a definition of the disability and then describes three or four empirically evaluated applied behavioral interventions.

INBORN BRAIN DISORDERS

This section of the chapter will describe a selection of applied behavioral interventions that have been used to treat various deficits and excesses that arise from inborn brain disorders. Inborn brain disorders are characterized as neurological conditions that are caused by genetic variations or mutations, brain malformations, or prenatal trauma to the brain. Inborn brain disorders

Clinical and Organizational Applications of Applied Behavior Analysis
http://dx.doi.org/10.1016/B978-0-12-420249-8.00008-3

may impact multiple aspects of development, including but not limited to, intellectual ability, physical movement, and metabolic processing. However, each specific disorder impacts distinctive characteristics of development at variable rates. This section will specifically focus on four inborn brain disorders—Cerebral Palsy, Prader-Willi syndrome, Angelman syndrome, and Lesch-Nyhan syndrome—and the use of a variety of behavioral strategies to address common challenges encountered by each condition.

Cerebral Palsy (CP) is a neurological disorder that is caused by abnormalities in the brain, is most often acquired before birth, and affects body movement and muscle coordination. Although CP can be acquired after birth, for the purposes of this chapter we describe a study that included a participant who acquired CP before birth. Tongue thrusting is a common problem associated with CP and has been addressed in past research through surgical procedures, restraints, speech therapy, and oral myofunctional therapy (Thompson, Iwata, & Poynter, 1979). For example, Thompson et al. (1979) used an operant approach of differential reinforcement and a punishment procedure to decrease tongue thrusts and food expulsion exhibited by a child with CP.

The participant in the Thompson et al. (1979) study was a 10-year-old boy with severe intellectual disability and spastic CP with general motor dysfunction. He lived in a private nursing home for individuals with disabilities and attended school 5 h a day. Treatment was conducted during lunchtime and lasted between 10 and 30 min. Researchers assessed changes in tongue thrust, food expulsion, chewing, and pushback. The participant had been receiving daily myofunctional therapy unsuccessfully for 2 years prior to baseline, and this prefeeding program remained in effect throughout the study.

During baseline, the participant was fed approximately 5 g of pureed food regardless of tongue position until 300 g of food had been consumed. Treatment conditions remained the same as baseline with two exceptions. First, food was only presented when the participant's tongue was in his mouth (differential reinforcement) and second, each time the tongue moved past the middle lower lip it would be gently pushed back into the mouth with the spoon (punishment). Results indicated that the behavioral strategies of differential reinforcement and punishment were successful in substantially reducing tongue thrusts and food expulsion exhibited by this child.

Prader-Willi syndrome is a rare genetic disorder that causes low muscle tone, low levels of sex hormones, and a constant feeling of hunger. These feelings of hunger accompany an insatiable appetite, resulting in overeating and food stealing as common characteristics of Prader-Willi syndrome.

To address these problems, Maglieri, DeLeon, Rodriguez-Catter, and Sevin (2000) used behavioral strategies, including positive punishment and stimulus control, to decrease food stealing in a 14-year-old girl (Libby) with Prader-Willi syndrome and moderate intellectual disability. When left unsupervised, Libby would steal food from appropriate sources (counter top, refrigerator, etc.), and past interventions, including reinforcement-based procedures, had been unsuccessful.

All sessions reported by Maglieri et al. (2000) occurred in a clinic setting and lasted 10 min. Prohibited packaged foods were left in a room where the participant was directed to play with a leisure activity while the therapist worked in another room. The therapist instructed the participant not to eat the food. During baseline, food consumption did not result in any additional programmed consequences. The within-session reprimand treatment condition was identical to baseline, except that attempted food stealing would result in the therapist immediately entering the room and verbally reprimanding the participant. If the participant did not put the food down, the food was taken from the room. The second baseline occurred in a novel setting, a bedroom, with procedures similar to the first baseline. Because there was not a one-way mirror available to observe behavior in this setting, food was weighed after each session ended. During the postsession reprimand treatment phase, if food had been consumed, the participant received the reprimand immediately after the food was weighed. Both within-session and postsession reprimands resulted in a decrease in consumption of the prohibited foods.

Following the implementation of the reprimand-based intervention, the authors evaluated a stimulus control procedure using orange stickers to indicate prohibited foods. Once the participant was taught and able to identify containers of prohibited and nonprohibited food, sessions were conducted in a kitchen with conditions identical to baseline. During the first treatment condition, one of two containers had an orange sticker, and this prohibited food was weighed at the end of the session. A reprimand was given if the prohibited food was consumed, and no reprimand was given if the prohibited food was not consumed. The second treatment condition had both containers labeled with a sticker, and the participant was reprimanded after the session if the weight of either container varied from the original weight. The participant consumed only foods from the unlabeled containers, and the effects of the stimulus control procedure were generalized to novel foods. Results indicate that an intervention using stimulus control and punishment reduced food stealing in a child with Prader-Willi syndrome.

While often discussed with Prader-Willi syndrome, Angelman syndrome (AS) is its own distinct disability that also has had behavioral interventions shown to be effective for treating core symptoms. Sleep challenges are a characteristic typical to individuals with AS. Allen, Kuhn, DeHaai, and Wallace (2013) used a behavioral treatment package to reduce sleep disturbance exhibited by five children with AS. The intervention addressed the sleep environment, sleep-wake schedule, and parent-child interactions during sleep times. The participants were five children between the ages of 2 and 11 years diagnosed with AS. Each had at least 4 weeks of sleep disturbances, defined by resistance to bedtime, delayed sleep onset, and awakening throughout the night. All participants were taking antiseizure medication, and dosage was kept constant throughout the intervention. Parents completed a sleep-wake diary recording sleep latency, total sleep time, frequency and duration of nighttime awakenings, and sleep efficiency (i.e., total sleep time divided by total time in bed). Parents also recorded number of disruptive behaviors during bedtime routine, after "lights out," and throughout the night. Additionally, the participants wore a MicroMini Motionlogger actigraph, which monitors motor movements, around their ankle to further monitor sleep-wake activity.

During baseline, parents completed the sleep activity using the diary and the actigraph under typical nightly conditions. The behavioral treatment package components included creating a quality sleep-compatible environment, regulating the participant's sleep-wake schedule, and reinforcing appropriate parent-child interactions. During treatment, parents were asked to create a sleep-compatible environment by reducing light and noise and adjusting the temperature in the sleep environment. Parents were asked to maintain a consistent sleep-wake schedule by putting the participant to bed and waking them up at the same time each day. If the child was slow to fall asleep, parents were initially asked to postpone bedtime transition to encourage falling asleep quicker. For the third component, parent-child interactions were targeted by requesting that parents not respond to the child's disruptive behaviors or if necessary, only respond to the participant when behaviors are appropriate. Results showed that the introduction of the behavioral treatment package improved participants' ability to fall asleep independently and reduced disruptive behaviors in young children with AS.

Another behavioral treatment package with varied components has been shown effective for treating the compulsive self-injury exhibited by an individual with Lesch-Nyhan syndrome (Grace, Cowart, & Matson, 1988). Grace et al. (1988) used self-monitoring, positive reinforcement, and brief time-outs from attention to reduce severe self-injurious behavior (SIB) exhibited by a 14-year-old boy with LNS. The participant had been living in a residential facility since he was 5 years old and was restrained to a metal crib with his front teeth removed to limit his compulsive self-biting and SIB including significant loss of lip tissue, spasticity, and involuntary movements. He was diagnosed with moderate ID and severe impairments in verbal expression and motor control.

A 1-min interval recording system was used to record self-biting attempts during baseline. During the self-assessment procedure, the participant was trained to indicate whether he had engaged in SIB by nodding or pointing to a picture of a happy or sad face. A trainer modeled SIB and non-SIB and demonstrated self-assessment by pointing to the correct picture that corresponded with each picture. During training, the participant was reinforced with hugs for correct self-assessment and a 30-s time out from attention for incorrect self-assessment. When the participant demonstrated an understanding of self-assessment, the intervention phase began. A care worker told the participant to not engage in SIB, set a kitchen timer for a designated amount of time, and left the room. Upon return, the care worker directed the participant to self-assess his SIB engagement. Verbal reprimands were given for SIB attempts and positive statements were given for no attempts at SIB. Results showed that the initiation of the behavioral treatment package drastically reduced the SIB attempts across settings and maintained at a 19-week follow-up.

These four studies demonstrate the use of behavioral interventions to address characteristics of inborn brain disorders. A variety of behavioral strategies including reinforcement, punishment, and self-monitoring were used to produce positive effects and were selected for each intervention and desired outcome.

ACQUIRED BRAIN DISABILITIES

Acquired brain disabilities are a broad category of disabilities, and there may be some level of overlap between acquired and inborn brain disorders (e.g., epilepsy may be an acquired or inborn brain disability). In general, acquired brain disabilities describe anomalies in brain function that are not attributed to genetic, inherited, or congenital influences. The most prevalent type of acquired brain disability results from some form of acquired or traumatic brain injury (TBI). Acquired brain injury refers to an injury that occurs after birth and is not a result of external trauma to the brain. Examples of acquired brain injury would include stroke, neurotoxins, infection, tumor, hypoxia, and anoxia. We would also argue that some forms of degenerative disease, such as Alzheimer's, might be considered an acquired brain disability. The most prevalent form of acquired brain disability is TBI. TBI describes an alteration in brain function caused by an external force such as a car accident and fall. In this section, we describe applied behavioral interventions to treat maladaptive behavioral patterns resulting from acquired brain disabilities due to TBI, Alzheimer's disease, and encephalitis (infection of the brain).

O'Reilly, Green, and Braunling-McMorrow (1990) taught four individuals who had suffered from TBI how to identify and remediate potential hazards in the home. All four participants had suffered TBIs in bike and automobile accidents and were receiving services in a private rehabilitation facility for adults with brain injuries. All participants had sufficient motor control to perform the targeted skills and were at a reading level of at least third grade. As a part of their rehabilitation plan, these participants were targeted for independent or semi-independent living. One of the skill sets addressed as a part of their rehabilitation plan was that they can be able to identify and remediate potential in-home hazards.

A list of common and preventable household accidents was compiled from expert sources such as the National Safety Council. A set of hazardous situations was then identified, and task analyzes for preventing such hazards were developed by observing nonhandicapped individuals to remediate these potential hazards. Some of the common hazards identified included: flammable items close to space heaters or stove, poison close to food, and items placed precariously on the floor.

Participants were trained to remediate these potential hazards using written checklists in combination with positive and/or corrective feedback from a therapist. If participants could not remediate a potential hazard using a checklist then the specific steps to complete the task (i.e., remediate the hazard) were added to the checklist and coupled with therapist feedback. Written checklists combined with therapist feedback were evaluated using individual participant multiple baseline designs across settings (kitchen, living room, bathroom, bedroom). The results demonstrated that all participants learned to remediate the potential hazards and that the skills remained intact at follow up probes of 1 month.

Lancioni et al. (2012) evaluated the use of assistive technology combined with pictorial and verbal instructions to teach basic daily living skills to three individuals with Alzheimer's disease. Alzheimer's disease is an irreversible neurodegenerative condition characterized by a progressive decline in

memory and higher cognitive functions and gradual loss in the ability to perform daily living activities. Interventions designed to help persons to recover
some of these daily living skills is of obvious applied significance. In fact, such
skill-based interventions may reduce the oft-noted apathy and negative
mood of this population.

Three individuals (age 73–79 years) participated in this study and were all
diagnosed with moderate levels of Alzheimer's disease. Two participants
were also diagnosed with depression. All three participants attended a day
care facility in which various forms of supervised activity occurred such
as mild physical exercise and supervised self-help and occupational activities.
All three participants possessed the motor abilities to perform physical tasks
and the cognitive ability to understand simple pictorial and oral directions.

Participants were taught to perform several routine daily living skills
(preparing vegetables and fruit, arranging and serving such food, cleaning
utensils). Each of these skills was broken down into a series of discrete steps.
Participants were given instruction on each step of the task using a combination of pictorial and verbal prompts. The prompts were delivered automatically via a variety of technologies such as MP3 players and optic
sensors. For example, if a participant moved a bowl to a designated area
an optic sensor was triggered that produced an instruction (via MP3) on
the next step of the task. Participants could therefore complete the tasks
independent of prompts from others such as direct care staff. The study
employed individual participant alternating treatments designs in which
instruction was delivered via technology in the form of pictorial, oral, or
a combination of oral and pictorial prompts. Results of the study demonstrated that all forms of instruction were effective in teaching these skills
to the three participants.

Wong, Seroka, and Ogisi (2000) evaluated the effects of an antecedent
checklist to enhance accurate self-assessment of blood glucose levels by a
woman with diabetes mellitus who suffered from brain injury due to
encephalitis. Encephalitis is a rare condition produced by viral infection that
results in swelling of the brain tissue and subsequent brain damage. Many
viruses can cause encephalitis including measles, mumps, polio, and rubella.
Such viruses can be contracted from breathing respiratory droplets from an
infected person, contaminated food or drink, insect bites, or skin contact.
The very young and old present with the more severe cases of encephalitis.
The participant in this study was a 56-year-old woman who had contracted
encephalitis 1 year prior to the study. At the time of the study she continued
to show severe impairment of verbal and visual memory and orientation in

space and time. The participant had a long history of diabetes mellitus that had been managed through diet and insulin injection.

A core skill of managing diabetes mellitus is continuous monitoring of blood glucose levels. This task is a complicated multistep one that, if not followed, may produce complications such as worsening of the condition or secondary infections. The procedure involves accessing necessary equipment, preparing the puncture site, pricking the finger, placing the blood sample on the glucometer, reading and logging the reading correctly, and cleaning and restoring the environment.

The Wong et al. (2000) study involved an individual participant and employed an alternating treatments design that included baseline and intervention conditions (simulated and actual). During baseline the participant independently performed the assessment. If an error was about to occur or there was a long delay between steps the therapist completed the step and set the participant up for the next step in the chain of responses. The participant was then trained to use a written checklist of the essential steps in the process through therapist feedback. This training involved a simulated training process with a blunted needle and bogus glucometer readings. Following training the participant independently implemented the procedure using the checklist without therapist feedback (in both simulated and actual tests). Results indicated that the participant was capable of independently and successfully implementing the glucose test procedure using the checklist. This contrasted to baseline assessment (without the checklist) where she was unable to complete the test successfully.

These four studies demonstrate the use of behavioral interventions to address characteristics of acquired brain injuries. A variety of behavioral strategies including task analysis, feedback, antecedent-based interventions, and mand training were used to produce positive effects and were selected for each intervention and desired outcome.

INBORN PHYSICAL DISABILITIES

This section will describe a variety of applied behavioral interventions that have been used to address functional and academic challenges that are characteristic of certain inborn physical disabilities. Physical disabilities are impairments that significantly impact physical performance and daily life activities with inborn being classified as hereditary, congenital, or induced by birth trauma. Examples of such inborn physical disabilities include, but are not limited to, Crohn's disease, Tourette's syndrome, visual and hearing impairments, cystic fibrosis (CF), and spina bifida (SB). Although visual and hearing impairments may be acquired after birth, for the purpose of this chapter we describe studies that included participants who acquired visual and hearing impairments prior to birth. In the following section, we will outline examples of interventions specifically designed around the needs of participants with inborn physical disabilities.

To address functional needs of children with visual impairments, Hanney and Tiger (2012) utilized an instructional package that taught participants to use tactile cues to receptively and expressively identify coin names and values. Participants included a 6-year-old female with visual impairment and typically developing cognitive abilities, and an 8-year-old male with mild developmental delays in addition to visual impairment.

During baseline assessments, participants did not reliably identify coin names or values in either receptive or expressive formats. Using a combination of time delay, physical prompting, contingent reinforcement, and systematic stimulus prompt fading, participants were first taught to receptively identify coins. More specifically, receptive discrimination training began by presenting a coin in a field of one (asking participants to "find the [name of the coin]"; i.e., trainer instructed participant to give her the penny, and the penny was the only coin available). After a 5-s delay, physical prompting was used to guide participants to drag their finger along the outer edge of a coin, and then hand it to the teacher. Independent responses were reinforced with praise and a tangible reward while prompted responses were rewarded with praise alone. When participants mastered the task in a field of one, additional coins were gradually introduced and participants were also taught to stack coins to compare sizes (using similar physical prompting procedures for assessing ridge differences). Participants were eventually expected to find the correct coin from a field of four (penny, nickel, dime, quarter).

After participants mastered receptive labeling tasks, identical prompt and prompt-fading procedures were used to introduce labeling coins by value (e.g., find the 1 cent coin). Untrained skills (e.g., expressively labeling coin names and values) were then assessed. Results indicated that the intervention was effective for teaching receptive identification of coin names and values, and training generalized to additional expressive tasks.

While Hanney and Tiger (2012) utilized tactile cueing to address deficits associated with visual impairments, Heward and Eachus (1979) incorporated a visual feedback system to teach individuals with hearing impairments to expand written expressive language. The intervention package incorporated a visual support technology system that enabled a teacher to project written sentence models, view and visually correct students' writing samples in real time, and provide immediate visual reinforcement. Contingent reinforcement and correction were used to systematically teach participants to add new sentence components. The study demonstrated that the procedures were effective at increasing the use of various written expression elements including complete sentences, sentences with adjectives, sentences with adverbs, and sentences with adjectives and adverbs.

In contrast to teaching functional and/or academic skills, Stark, Miller, Plienes, and Drabman (1987) taught a young girl with CF to comply with a medical treatment procedure associated with her disability. CF is a hereditary disease of the secretory glands, which produce mucous and sweat. Mucous can build up in the lungs of individuals with CF and potentially block airways, as well as lead to infection and serious lung damage.

During baseline assessments, the 11-year-old participant showed low compliance with chest physiotherapy (CPT), a procedure designed to help clear mucous from the lungs of individuals with CF. CPT requires individuals with CF to assume a variety of physical positions while a person delivering treatment claps on the patient's lungs. The procedure can last between 20 and 30 min. CPT was prescribed to be delivered three times a day for the participant. After baseline, the participant and her mother created and signed a behavioral contract dictating specific reinforcement that the participant would receive contingent on compliance with each CPT treatment.

Upon introduction of the contract and reinforcement, the participant immediately increased CPT compliance, steadily achieving 100% compliance with CPT delivery. The reinforcement schedule outlined in the behavioral contract was then gradually reduced (reinforcement every three treatments, reinforcement every week, no contingent reinforcement), and the participant's compliance remained high. While the effects of the intervention appeared to be strong, it is important to note that only a pre–post-test design was used, so it is possible that other factors (e.g., maturation) could have affected results.

Similar to Stark et al. (1987), White, Mathews, and Fawcett (1989) designed an intervention to decrease a medical risk that may affect individuals with SB. SB is a neural tube defect (caused by incomplete fetal spinal closure) that can lead to spine and nerve damage including varying degrees of paralysis in the lower limbs. Due to limb paralysis, individuals with SB may require the use of assistive devices such as wheelchairs. Individuals who utilize wheelchairs may be at risk for developing pressure sores associated with prolonged sitting (White et al., 1989). Wheelchair pushups (briefly lifting oneself up off the seat) are a simple exercise that may reduce the risk of pressure sores (White et al.).

In the study by White et al. (1989), two 11-year-old children did not have pressure sores during initial assessments, but infrequently practiced wheelchair pushups. Using a combination of antecedent and mildly aversive procedures, the focus of intervention was to increase the rate of wheelchair push-ups. The study demonstrated that the combined use of an audio-reminder (antecedent component) and alarm noise that went off when participants did not practice push-ups (punishment component) was effective at increasing push-up rates. The use of the audio-reminder alone was also more effective than baseline, but not as effective as combining the antecedent and punishment procedures. While participants noted that they would recommend the procedures to others, they rated the use of the audio-reminder as very acceptable, and the use of the alarm as moderately unacceptable.

Together, these studies demonstrate the breadth of behavioral interventions that can be used with individuals with inborn physical abilities. Interventions can be tailored to meet the specific needs (including academic, functional, and medical needs) of individuals with these disabilities. More specifically, individualized behavioral components (e.g., reinforcement, antecedent stimuli, systematic discrimination training) can be selected based upon such needs.

ACQUIRED PHYSICAL DISABILITIES

Acquired physical disabilities include those conditions that are acquired or developed after birth and are not hereditary, congenital, degenerative, or induced by birth trauma. These disabilities substantially impair physical performance and can limit one or more major life activities. Acquired disabilities can include conditions such as arthritis, asthma, deafness, blindness, diabetes, multiple sclerosis, paralysis, CP, epilepsy, and kidney disease. Behaviorally based interventions have been used to treat individuals with acquired physical disabilities who have specific behavioral needs related to their conditions. In the following section, we outline examples of these interventions designed to treat the specific needs of individuals with acquired physical disabilities.

Shabani and Fisher (2006) used stimulus fading and differential reinforcement of other behavior (DRO) to successfully treat an 18-year-old with autism and Type 2 diabetes whose needle phobia had prevented medical professionals from drawing blood to monitor his glucose levels for over

2 years. The intervention proved successful both in reducing the participant's fear as well as facilitating his medical treatment.

The participant attended an outpatient clinic 4 days a week for treatment of noncompliance with diabetes-related medical procedures. Prior to the behavioral intervention, attempts by medical professionals to draw blood resulted in the participant's distress and avoidance, with behaviors including whimpering, crying, screaming, elopement, self-injury, and aggression toward medical staff. The participant consistently pulled his hand and arm away every time an attempt was made to draw blood with a lancet.

Before beginning the intervention, a preference assessment was conducted to determine potential food reinforcers, followed by the implementation of an intervention consisting of a stimulus fading plus DRO condition. In this condition, if the participant did not move his hand and arm from an outlined space on a posterboard during a 10-s interval while the lancet was positioned above his index finger at varying levels, he received access to the preferred food item. If he moved his arm more than 3 cm from the outline, the trial was terminated, materials were removed, and the experimenter turned away for 10 s. Progressive fading steps were implemented following 100% success for two or three consecutive sessions.

By Session 31, the participant was able to keep his hand and arm still to allow a successful blood draw attempt, and all following attempts to draw blood were successful. In addition, the positive effects of the treatment generalized to an additional setting and trials conducted at a 2-month follow-up indicated that blood draws postintervention was successful. Stimulus fading and differential reinforcement successfully treated the participant's needle phobia and resulted in compliance with daily blood draws that allowed medical professionals to monitor his glucose levels.

Differential reinforcement was similarly used in conjunction with a behavioral contract to successfully treat noncompliance in adolescents with spinal cord injuries (Gorski, Slifer, Townsend, Kelly-Suttka, & Amari, 2005). After receiving acute medical care for their spinal cord injuries at other hospitals, three teenagers (ages 14–16 years) were admitted to an inpatient hospital unit specializing in neurorehabilitation treatment for children and adolescents. All were noncompliant with aspects of their rehabilitation regimen. These noncompliant behaviors included difficult wheelchair and bed transfers, verbal refusal to cooperate during therapy sessions, and yelling, cursing, and spitting at hospital staff.

In collaboration with the participants, therapists, and physicians, the hospital psychologist developed and implemented a behavioral contract designed to increase the participants' compliance with prescribed therapies. The contracts clearly outlined all expectations regarding daily activities and rehabilitation therapies. Staff and nurses recorded compliance for each item if the participants cooperated with each task. The percentage of compliance with rehabilitation demands was reviewed with the participants each week. Reinforcement was provided (e.g., CDs, posters, make-up, gift certificates) if the participants completed an average of 80% of their rehabilitation tasks. If the participants achieved less than 80% of their rehabilitation tasks, reinforcement was withheld.

The behavioral contract, in combination with delayed differential reinforcement, resulted in an increase in compliance in the rehabilitation regimens for all participants. The authors of the study suggested this treatment package increased the participants' motivation to cope with the anxiety or discomfort of rehabilitation demands, as well as the staff's ability to reinforce appropriate behaviors.

Carton and Schweitzer (1996) used a token economy system to decrease the noncompliant behavior of a 10-year-old hemodialysis patient with renal failure. Prior to treatment, his noncompliance during lengthy 4-h hemodialysis sessions resulted in reduced staff availability for other patients. The behaviors exhibited by the participant included screaming at nurses, kicking or hitting the nurses, and movements to hinder the implementation of a medical procedure. Previous attempts to increase compliance had been unsuccessful.

Upon implementation of a token economy, the participant was able to earn one token for every 30-min interval with zero noncompliant behaviors within the entire 4-h hemodialysis session. A total of eight tokens could be awarded during one session, with the primary nurse responsible for recording the number of tokens earned on a chart. At the end of the week, tokens could be exchanged for prizes (e.g., baseball cards, comic books, or small toys), with the value of the prizes being determined by having the participant rank them in order of preference.

The token economy was successful in reducing noncompliant behaviors. After the token economy was faded and the intervention terminated, noncompliant behavior remained at similar levels. The token economy proved so successful at increasing compliance that the nursing staff and physicians requested the behavioral intervention for other hemodialysis patients.

Similarly, a token economy was effective in improving adherence to medication regimens for both an 8-year-old and a 10-year-old with asthma (Da Costa, Rapoff, Lemanek, & Goldstein, 1997). An allergist recommended the behavioral intervention to both participants for poor adherence to their medical regimens. A token system economy was implemented in which the participants earned points for taking their medication. Points were awarded based on the adherence as recorded by the participants' parents, and the accuracy of the recording was measured by comparing the parents' points with the asthma inhalers' electronic recording of activations by the participants. The awarded points could then be exchanged for privileges, with a loss of privileges for 1 day when participants failed to take their medication. Results indicate that the token economy was successful in increasing adherence to asthma medication for both participants.

The examples provided in these studies demonstrate the scope and utility of behavioral interventions to treat individuals with acquired physical disabilities. Behavioral interventions, including differential reinforcement, contingency contracting, and token economies can be used to treat the needs of these individuals and tailored to specifically address their unique concerns.

SUMMARY

In this chapter, we provided a selective overview of applied behavior analytic interventions across four broad disability types—inborn brain disorders, acquired brain disabilities, inborn physical disabilities, and acquired physical disabilities. One of the primary objectives of the chapter was to provide the reader with a flavor of the robust applicability of the applied behavioral technologies across these disabilities. And the range of application is impressive—from treating feeding problems in children with Prader-Willi syndrome and teaching skills to children with hearing and visual impairments, to enhancing compliance to medical regimens with individuals with spinal cord injuries, and teaching home safety skills to persons with brain injuries. The range of behavioral strategies used as clinical interventions is also quite diverse, including a variety of antecedent and consequence-based strategies. Intervention strategies included augmentative technologies to enhance the probability of correct responding (e.g., optic sensors, checklists). Often these technologies were combined with corrective and positive feedback from therapists to enhance performance. Consequence strategies involving reinforcement contingencies were also evident in many of these interventions. Additionally, all of the clinical examples reported in this chapter incorporated controlled experimental analyzes (objective identification and verification of the dependent measures, rigorous research designs, and in some cases measures of generalization, maintenance, and social validity of treatment effects). In essence, ABA incorporates a range of evidence-based clinical and educational strategies that can be used across a broad spectrum of disability conditions.

REFERENCES

Allen, K. D., Kuhn, B. R., DeHaai, K. A., & Wallace, D. P. (2013). Evaluation of a behavioral treatment package to reduce sleep problems in children with angelman syndrome. *Research in Developmental Disabilities, 34*(1), 676–686.

Carton, J., & Schweitzer, J. (1996). Use of a token economy to increase compliance during hemodialysis. *Journal of Applied Behavior Analysis, 29*, 111–113.

Da Costa, I., Rapoff, M., Lemanek, K., & Goldstein, G. (1997). Improving adherence to medication regimens for children with asthma and its effect on clinical outcome. *Journal of Applied Behavior Analysis, 30*, 687–691.

Gorski, J., Slifer, K., Townsend, V., Kelly-Suttka, J., & Amari, A. (2005). Behavioural treatment of non-compliance in adolescents with newly acquired spinal cord injuries. *Pediatric Rehabilitation, 8*(3), 187–198.

Grace, N., Cowart, C., & Matson, J. L. (1988). Reinforcement and self-control for treating a chronic case of self-injury in Lesch–Nyhan syndrome. *Journal of the Multihandicapped Person, 1*(1), 53–59.

Hanney, N. M., & Tiger, J. H. (2012). Teaching coin discrimination to children with visual impairments. *Journal of Applied Behavior Analysis, 45*(1), 167–172.

Heward, W. L., & Eachus, H. T. (1979). Acquisition of adjectives and adverbs in sentences written by hearing impaired and aphasic children. *Journal of Applied Behavior Analysis, 12* (3), 391–400.

Lancioni, G., Perilli, V., Singh, N., O'Reilly, M., Sigafoos, J., Cassano, G., et al. (2012). Technology-aided pictorial cues to support the performance of daily activities by persons with moderate Alzheimer's disease. *Research in Developmental Disabilities, 33*, 265–273.

Maglieri, K. A., DeLeon, I. G., Rodriguez-Catter, V., & Sevin, B. M. (2000). Treatment of covert food stealing in an individual with Prader–Willi syndrome. *Journal of Applied Behavior Analysis, 33*(4), 615–618.

O'Reilly, M. F., Green, G., & Braunling-McMorrow, D. (1990). Self-administered written prompts to teach home accident prevention skills to adults with brain injuries. *Journal of Applied Behavior Analysis, 23*, 431–446.

Shabani, D., & Fisher, W. (2006). Stimulus fading and differential reinforcement for the treatment of needle phobia in a youth with autism. *Journal of Applied Behavior Analysis, 39*, 449–452.

Stark, L. J., Miller, S. T., Plienes, A. J., & Drabman, R. S. (1987). Behavioral contracting to increase chest physiotherapy. A study of a young cystic fibrosis patient. *Behavior Modification, 11*(1), 75–86.

Thompson, G. A., Iwata, B. A., & Poynter, H. (1979). Operant control of pathological tongue thrust in spastic cerebral palsy. *Journal of Applied Behavior Analysis, 12*(3), 325–333.

White, G. W., Mathews, R. M., & Fawcett, S. B. (1989). Reducing risk of pressure sores: Effects of watch prompts and alarm avoidance on wheelchair push-ups. *Journal of Applied Behavior Analysis, 22*(3), 287–295.

Wong, S., Seroka, P., & Ogisi, J. (2000). Effects of a checklist on self-assessment of blood glucose level by a memory-impaired woman with diabetes mellitus. *Journal of Applied Behavior Analysis, 33*, 251–254.

CHAPTER 9

Behavior Therapy for Childhood Tic Disorders

Douglas W. Woods, David C. Houghton
Department of Psychology, Texas A&M University, College Station, Texas, USA

INTRODUCTION

As has been demonstrated with autism spectrum disorders, applied behavior analysis can successfully alter unwanted behavioral repertoires commonly labeled as psychiatric or neurodevelopmental conditions. One area of successful implementation involves tic disorders (including Tourette syndrome, TS), which have been managed via behavioral methods for more than four decades (Azrin & Nunn, 1973). Empirical support for behavior analytic approaches to tic treatment originates from studies using small-*n*, single-subject designs as well as randomized controlled trials. Additionally, a growing body of literature from both neuroscience and behavioral psychology supports a neurobehavioral conceptualization of tics.

This chapter will review the basic characteristics of tic disorders followed by a description of the neurobehavioral model. Effective behavioral treatment packages will be discussed, providing a basic overview of treatment methods along with corresponding empirical support. Recent scientific developments and future directions are also noted.

History and Diagnosis

Tic disorders have been studied since the late nineteenth century, when a French physician, Gilles de la Tourette, provided the first extensive account of the condition. A student of Jean-Martin Charcot and colleague of Sigmund Freud, Tourette was one of the early experts on psychotherapy and neurology (Rickards & Cavanna, 2009). In his original paper, Tourette observed nine patients with uncontrollable motor movements that seemed to conform to a distinct pathology. The condition was labeled "maladie des tics" (Tourette, 1885).

Currently, the diagnostic category of "Neurodevelopmental Disorders" (American Psychiatric Association, 2013) includes a number of tic-related

Clinical and Organizational Applications of Applied Behavior Analysis
http://dx.doi.org/10.1016/B978-0-12-420249-8.00009-5
195

conditions, including Tourette disorder/syndrome, persistent (chronic) motor or vocal tic disorder (CTD), and provisional tic disorder. Diagnosis of a tic disorder is based on the presence of either motor or vocal tics and duration of illness. Onset must occur before age 18. Both TS and CTD require tics for more than 12 months, but TS requires the presence of both motor and vocal tics whereas a diagnosis of CTD designates either motor or vocal tics (but not both). A diagnosis of provisional tic disorder is appropriate for situations in which tics are present (motor and/or vocal) for less than 1 year. This chapter will hereafter refer to any form of tic disorder as the same entity, as there appears to be no important functional difference between these designations (Tourette Syndrome Classification Study Group, 1993).

Differential diagnosis of tic disorders can be challenging and may require the aid of a qualified neurologist. Motor tics can be confused with the symptoms of Sydenham's chorea (Aron, Freeman, & Carter, 1965), and there have been documented cases of tic-like symptoms in individuals who suffer from conversion disorder (Hinson & Haren, 2006). Furthermore, clinicians might also mistake stereotypies for tics (APA, 2013). If there is any ambiguity in tic symptoms, the clinician should refer the client for assessment by a neurologist.

Tics themselves are defined as sudden, rapid motor movements and vocalizations that are repeated in a similar manner (Leckman, Bloch, Sukhodolsky, Scahill, & King, 2013). Any conceivable array of motor or vocal actions could potentially become a tic, and tics can range from the ordinary to the bizarre. Tics can sometimes be disruptive or socially inappropriate, making it seem as though the child is "acting out." Moreover, tics can mimic normal movements or sounds (e.g., a sniff or cough), contributing to the incorrect assumption that tics are voluntary behaviors. Tics are frequently sudden and unexpected, and children with tic disorders report little to no control over these movements or vocalizations.

Diagnoses of tic disorders are based on the visible expression of tics, and the severity of the disorder is based primarily on observable behavioral dimensions, including the tic's location, frequency, duration, intensity, and complexity. Common tic topographies are presented in Table 9.1. Frequency refers to how often a tic occurs per hour, day, week, or even month. Some tics can happen multiple times per minute, while others are far less frequent. Duration refers to the length of time it takes for a tic to occur. "Simple" tics are sudden, brief, seemingly meaningless movements that are typically no longer than 1 s in duration (e.g., eye blinking, abdominal

Table 9.1 Examples of common tics

| Simple tics | | Complex tics | |
Motor	Vocal	Motor	Vocal
Eye blinking	Sniffing	Eye, mouth, and facial movements	Syllables
Eye movements	Grunting		Words
Nose movements	Whistling	Head gestures or movements	Coprolalia
Mouth movements	Throat clearing		Echolalia
Facial grimace		Shoulder movements	Palilalia
Head jerks		Arm movements	Blocking
Shoulder shrugs		Hand movements	Disinhibited speech
Arm movements		Writing tics	
Hand movements		Abnormal postures	
Abdominal tensing		Bending or gyrating	
Leg, foot, or toe movements		Rotating	
		Leg, foot, or toe movements	
		Tic-related compulsive behaviors (touching, tapping, grooming, evening-up)	
		Copropraxia (obscene gestures)	
		Self-abusive behavior	

tensing, grunting), whereas "complex" tics can be much longer. Intensity describes the "forcefulness" or "noticeability" of a tic, and intensity can range from barely noticeable (e.g., slight grimacing or eye darting) to quite obvious (e.g., screeching or arm waving). Finally, the complexity of a tic can range from those that are extremely brief and discreet to those involving longer and seemingly purposeful behaviors. "Complex" tics are more diverse and difficult to catalog and may include such actions as repeating a sentence, stiffening of the entire body, or jerking the head back and forth.

Onset of tics usually happens before age 10, with most beginning between 5 and 7 years of age (Freeman et al., 2000; Khalifa & von Knorring, 2003). Most often, the first observable sign of the disorders is motor tics localized in the head (Shapiro, Shapiro, Young, & Feinberg, 1988), which generally progress in a rostral-caudal direction. Tics of the extremities and torso, if they appear, show up later in the progression of the disorder (Jagger et al., 1982). Vocal tics usually begin 1-2 years after the onset of motor symptoms and are typically simple in nature (Jagger et al., 1982;

Shapiro et al., 1988). Some children will experience a gradual increase in frequency, intensity, and complexity of tics, and for those whose tics persist, a peak in tic severity is reached during late childhood or early adolescence (11-14 years old; Leckman et al., 1998). Following this peak, most adolescents will show a gradual reduction in tics that persists into adulthood (Bloch et al., 2006; Torup, 1962).

Although tics are classified and assessed based on their observable characteristics, various private events (i.e., sensory and mental phenomena) are commonly experienced and are central to the behavior analytic understanding of tic disorders. Many individuals with tic disorders report experiencing somatosensory phenomena that precede tics. These phenomena (sometimes described as "tense feelings," "energy surges," "itchy feelings," and "cramps") are frequently experienced as aversive, build up before the tic or while attempting to suppress tics, and are temporarily relieved after the occurrence of a tic (Leckman, Walker, & Cohen, 1993). Referred to as "premonitory urges," these sensations can be more distressing than the tics themselves (Kane, 1994). Early accounts of the urge phenomenon hypothesized a functional relationship between premonitory urges and tics. Kane (1994) described this relationship by stating, "these sensations are not mere precursors to tics … they precipitate tics more than providing a signal of imminence, the pre-tic sensation acts as the aversive stimulus toward which tics are directed" (p. 806). The first two formal investigations of premonitory urges confirmed their presence in a majority of individuals with TS (Cohen & Leckman, 1992; Leckman et al., 1993), and validation of the Premonitory Urges for Tics Scale (PUTS) found that 98% of surveyed youth reported premonitory urges (Woods, Piacentini, Himle, & Chang, 2005). More recently, several studies have used the PUTS to examine urges in an older adolescent and adult sample (Reese et al., 2014), a Hebrew-speaking youth sample (Steinberg et al., 2010), and a British adult sample (Crossley, Seri, Stern, Robertson, & Cavanna, 2014). Later, this chapter will discuss recent findings relating to premonitory urges and their hypothesized function in tic disorders.

Contextual Factors in Tic Expression

Tics are highly sensitive to contextual variation, are well understood to wax and wane, and fluctuate in frequency over hours, days, weeks, and months (Peterson & Leckman, 1998). There is no widely accepted explanation for this variability, but contextual and environmental factors may be implicated. Conelea and Woods (2008a) reviewed research supporting the influential role environmental factors have on tic expression, citing literature from case studies, small-*n* functional analytic studies, and prospective longitudinal studies. The review clearly demonstrated that psychosocial stressors (e.g., positive and negative emotion, changes in routine, desire for caregiver attention) are associated with short-term changes in tic frequency. Furthermore, talking about tics can increase tic frequency, suggesting that tics can have an automatically reinforced echoic function (O'Connor, Brisebois, Brault, Robillard, & Loiselle, 2003; Silva, Munoz, Barickman, & Friedhoff, 1995; Woods, Watson, Wolfe, Twohig, & Friman, 2001). Some tics are reflexive in nature in that they respond to specific environmental cues (Commander, Corbett, Prendergast, & Ridley, 1991). An example of a reflexive tic might be doing a highly noticeable vocal tic every time the teacher quiets the class. Such tics can be especially impairing when they violate social standards or safety rules. For instance, one might have the urge to pull fire alarms or stick his or her hand in boiling water.

Some individuals appear to be capable of volitionally suppressing or controlling their tics for brief periods of time, though the contingencies underlying such suppression are not fully understood. External contingencies, such as monetary rewards for tic suppression, have been shown to influence tic expression, suggesting that environmental contingencies play an important role. For example, Woods and Himle (2004) showed that reinforced suppression was more effective at reducing tics than simply providing instructions to suppress tics, and Himle, Woods, Conelea, Bauer, and Rice (2007) and Himle, Woods, and Bunaciu (2008) showed that contingent reinforcement of tic suppression resulted in fewer tics than noncontingent reinforcement. More recently, research has shown that differential reinforcement of tic suppression in the presence of specific stimuli can result in the development of stimulus control over tics. Woods, Walther, Bauer, Kemp, and Conelea (2009) differentially reinforced tic suppression in children and adolescents while in the presence of a purple light and found that tics indeed reduced in frequency. Interestingly, in later trials the participants reduced the occurrence of tics in the presence of the purple light, despite the fact that they were no longer reinforced for suppressing tics.

Treatments for Tic Disorders

There are several methods for treating tic disorders, with some being more widely used than others. Effective techniques include pharmacological treatment (Shapiro & Shapiro, 1984), transcranial magnetic stimulation (Ziemann, Paulus, & Rothenberger, 1997), neurosurgery (Rauch, Baer, Cosgrove, & Jenike, 1995), and behavioral treatments (Azrin & Nunn, 1973).

The most common treatment is some type of pharmacological approach (Pauls, 2003; Robertson & Stern, 2000). Despite the fact that pharmacological treatments are effective at reducing tics (Scahill et al., 2006), these methods carry significant limitations, such as unwanted side effects (Scahill et al., 2006), poor treatment adherence (Peterson & Azrin, 1992), varying degrees of treatment response (Scahill et al., 2006), and the lack of attention toward a repertoire-building approach (Cook & Blacher, 2007). Therefore, individuals that are either resistant to, or do not obtain desirable results from, pharmacological treatment might consider alternative or adjunct forms of therapy. Below, we describe a neurobehavioral model of tics and behavioral treatments derived from that conceptualization.

BEHAVIORAL TREATMENT FOR TICS

Neurobehavioral Model of Tics

Tic disorders are a set of neurological conditions with a relatively clear biological etiology (Mink, 2003). However, a strictly biological perspective does not explain the role of the contextually bound variation described earlier. Behavioral conceptualizations of these conditions add to our etiologic understanding by offering an account for contextual influences. Although behavioral treatment for tics is based on learning principles, it should be understood that this model does not imply that tics are learned. Rather, research supporting the contextual influences on the disorder indicates that tics are manipulated (i.e., shaped, strengthened, and maintained) by environmental contingencies. Within a framework composed of operant and respondent learning principles, the neurobehavioral model argues that tics can be systematically altered through manipulation of environmental factors (Capriotti & Woods, 2013).

Tics are often influenced by stimuli that precede them. These antecedents can be either internal or external, meaning that they occur outside the person's body or inside the person. Common external factors that exacerbate tics include holidays, birthdays, and returning to school; whereas studying, physical exercise, and socialization tend to attenuate tics (Conelea & Woods, 2008a). Similarly, internal factors such as stress, anxiety, and fatigue tend to make tics worse, while relaxation and concentration tend to improve tics. It is important to note that antecedents have idiosyncratic effects on tics. For instance, Silva et al. (1995) found that 45% of patients reported tic exacerbation in social gatherings, while 42% reported tic attenuation in the same situations.

Consequences also influence tic expression. As with antecedents, consequences can be external or internal and can either exacerbate or attenuate tics. Common consequences include social reactions (e.g., teasing, staring, comforting) and phenomenological changes within the individual (e.g., shame, embarrassment, fear). A well-documented consequence is tic-contingent caregiver-delivered contingencies (i.e., affection, comfort), which are known to increase the future likelihood of tics (Carr, Bailey, Carr, & Coggin, 1996; Packer, 2005; Scotti, Schulman, & Honjacki, 1994; Watson & Sterling, 1998). Conversely, providing monetary awards for suppressing tics results in short-term reductions (Conelea & Woods, 2008b; Himle & Woods, 2005; Woods & Himle, 2004), suggesting that other socially mediated reinforcers for tic suppression (i.e., lack of aversive peer attention) can also effectively reduce tics.

The aforementioned phenomenon of premonitory urges is also functionally related to tics. As previously noted, most individuals with tic disorders experience premonitory urges, which are experienced as aversive and temporarily fade after the emission of a tic. Behaviorally, we would consider the urge a reflexive establishing operation (Michael, 1993), and the relationship between the tic and urge represents negative reinforcement. In other words, the tic produces relief from the urge.

The neurobehavioral model argues that tic genesis is rooted in neurological dysfunction, but maladaptive functional relations eventually emerge between tics and the environment. Tics are not completely the result of random motor impulses, but rather are shaped and expressed through the individual's interaction with internal and external contingencies. As with all conditioning, it is important to understand that such functional relations occur outside of conscious awareness. Persons with TS do not tic purposefully to receive attention or be excused from aversive tasks. Based on the model, various behavioral procedures have been developed for the treatment of tics.

Evolution of Behavioral Techniques for Tic Management

Beginning in the 1950s, psychologists began translating learning-based behavioral principles discovered in laboratories into treatments for various conditions, including tic disorders. The most prominent of these techniques was self-monitoring, massed negative practice, contingency management, and relaxation training. Most were developed before a contemporary behavioral understanding of tic disorders was established, but a few procedures (e.g., self-monitoring, relaxation training, and habit reversal training

(HRT)) have been incorporated into modern treatment packages. In the following paragraphs, we describe these procedures.

Self-monitoring usually involves the use of an overt monitoring system, such as a diary, that is used to note the occurrence of each tic. Little evidence suggests that self-monitoring is effective as a standalone therapy for tics (Woods, Miltenberger, & Lumley, 1996). Generally, it is seen as an adjunct to larger therapeutic packages (Ollendick, 1981; Varni, Boyd, & Cataldo, 1978). Similarly, relaxation strategies have been suggested for tic patients to use in stressful situations to prevent harmful bouts of tics (Turpin & Powell, 1984), but evidence shows that relaxation is not effective as a standalone treatment (Bergin, Waranch, Brown, Carson, & Singer, 1998; Peterson & Azrin, 1992). Like self-monitoring, relaxation training is often useful as a component of larger therapeutic packages (Woods, Piacentini, et al., 2008).

Massed negative practice involves having the patient intentionally perform their tics throughout the day. It was believed that such practice would increase what theorists called "reactive inhibition," a process that would reduce the frequency of the actual tic (Tophoff, 1973). Despite early case studies arguing for the use of this technique, massed negative practice was found to have a negligible impact on tics (Azrin, Nunn, & Frantz, 1980) and is not recommended in current clinical practice (Cook & Blacher, 2007).

Contingency management involves actively reinforcing tic suppression and/or punishing tic performance. As a treatment, this technique usually involves providing small reinforcers (e.g., tokens or small amounts of money) in exchange for progressively longer periods of successful tic suppression. Support for reinforcing tic suppression has been found in case studies (Doleys & Kurtz, 1974) and controlled single-subject design experiments (Wagaman, Miltenberger, & Williams, 1995) but has not been evaluated in a large, randomized controlled trial. Punishing tics (i.e., by providing small degrees of electric shock or equivalent aversive stimuli) has not been extensively investigated, but existing evidence suggests it is not well tolerated (Alexander et al., 1973), and it is not recommended (Capriotti & Woods, 2013). Similar to self-monitoring and relaxation training, Woods, Piacentini, et al. (2008) suggested that contingency management might not be appropriate as a standalone treatment but rather as an adjunctive element of larger behavioral treatment packages.

Habit Reversal Training

Behavioral treatment packages often consist of several techniques, including those just discussed, but the core of nearly all of the behavioral interventions for tics is HRT. Azrin and Nunn (1973) developed HRT for repetitive movements, such as tics, chronic hair pulling, and stuttering. HRT has changed little over the past several decades, but it has recently been enhanced by incorporating additional psychosocial techniques. The components of HRT are described here, followed by a review of the empirical literature examining its effectiveness. Finally, contemporary versions of HRT-based treatment packages are discussed, along with future directions.

HRT is a treatment designed to manage (not cure) tics. The goal of HRT is significant reduction in bothersome tics and subsequent improvements in quality of life. Treatment addresses tics one at a time, beginning with the most bothersome and interfering tic. Each session is typically devoted to a single tic, but this varies depending on how readily the client implements the techniques and how successfully he or she achieves tic management. HRT begins with awareness training, which is followed by competing response (CR) training and social support.

If tic management is to be effective, the client needs to be able to recognize and preferably anticipate the targeted tic. Awareness training teaches the client to notice the target tic as it occurs in real time. In some cases, particularly young children or those with attention problems, clients are not aware of every single tic occurrence. Awareness training starts by gathering a detailed description of the tic. In this "response description" phase, the clinician asks the client to describe exactly what occurs during tic performance. From somatic factors relating to the urge (i.e., location and characteristics of the premonitory urge) to the muscles involved in the emission of a tic, a highly detailed description is obtained. The clinician asks the client to describe his or her urge and where it originates, getting as detailed a description as possible. The act of engaging in a tic is then broken down into a chain of behaviors. Even the most simple of tics can usually be deconstructed into individual motor movements, which the clinician then connects into a string of components that make up the full expression of the tic. For instance, head-jerking tics generally begin with flexing of the neck and shoulders. The tic might then progress with the head tilting to one direction, and one or both of the shoulders might rise and meet the chin. Furthermore, the facial muscles might grimace and the position might be held for a few seconds. Obtaining this level of detail is imperative both for identifying tic occurrences and selecting a CR.

After a thorough description of the tic has been developed, the "response detection" phase begins. The client and therapist engage in conversation about an innocuous topic unrelated to tics, and during this time the client is asked to indicate when the tic occurs by raising a finger. This practice is done for two reasons. First, the client should learn to detect tics while his or her attention is focused on another topic. Second, this practice helps therapeutic skills generalize beyond the treatment environment and into the client's normal activities. When the client successfully acknowledges a tic, the therapist provides praise by saying, "good job." When the client misses a tic, the clinician gently reminds him or her by saying something like, "Did you catch that one? Remember to show me you caught it." This exercise continues until the client is able to identify at least 80% (4 out of 5) of tic occurrences. After the client has displayed competency in identifying occurrences of the actual tic, he or she is asked to repeat the aforementioned exercise, but this time identifying urges to tic, and not just the overt tics. Ideally, the client should raise his or her finger just before a tic occurs. Successful awareness training should result in the client learning to anticipate the targeted tic nearly every time. After awareness of the tic has been established, CR training can begin.

CR training teaches the client an incompatible behavior to combat tics. Depending on the exact manifestation of each tic, the client and therapist collaboratively decide on a behavior that can be performed in place of the targeted tic. Ideally, a CR should satisfy three criteria (Woods, Piacentini, et al., 2008). First, it must be physically incompatible with the tic, meaning that one cannot perform both behaviors simultaneously. Second, the CR must be capable of being performed in any physical location for a sustained period of time. Third, the CR must be less noticeable and bothersome than the tic itself. An example of a good CR for a head-jerking tic is gently tensing the shoulder and neck muscles. Breathing in and out through the mouth slowly and purposefully could be used to combat a sniffing tic. Formulating the CR typically begins by describing ideal examples and then asking the client to generate suggestions. Each suggestion is compared against the three criteria until an acceptable and agreeable behavior is identified. After the CR is selected, the client is encouraged to use it whenever he or she feels the urge to tic or actually engages in the behavior. When the tic or urge to tic occurs, the CR should be held for 1 min or until the urge dissipates (whichever is longer). Similar to awareness training, the client is asked to practice the CR in session whenever the targeted tic occurs in real time. While practicing use of the CR, the client and therapist should engage in conversation about topics unrelated to tics. Successful uses of the CR are praised, while tics not followed by a CR are addressed by gently prompting the client to remember to "use the exercise." Ideally, use of the CR should result in habituation to the premonitory urge. Clients might report that it is difficult to resist engaging in a tic at first, but after several successful attempts at using the CR, the urge to tic should decrease significantly. Between sessions, the client is instructed to perform the prescribed CR whenever the tic occurs or is about to occur. Over time, the CR should become less effortful and the tic less frequent.

To reinforce the use of the CR, HRT requires that a support person or persons praise the patient for using HRT skills in the home environment and prompt the patient to use the CR when a targeted tic occurs but a CR is not utilized. Some, particularly younger children, can benefit from the development of a concrete reward system for using CRs and other HRT skills. It is important to note that social support is not about praising tic suppression, but rather about reinforcing child engagement in treatment exercises outside of therapy.

Empirical evidence supporting HRT for tics has burgeoned over the past decade. Two reviews (Cook & Blacher, 2007; Himle, Woods, Piacentini, & Walkup, 2006) collectively identified 35 studies in which HRT resulted in clinically significant reductions in tics. These studies consisted of both randomized controlled trials and methodologically rigorous single-subject analyses. In a recent meta-analysis, Bate, Malouff, Thorsteinsson, and Bhullar (2011) found that HRT produces a large effect size ($d = 0.8$).

The effects of HRT have also shown to be independent of confounding variables, such as natural fluctuations in tics and nonspecific therapeutic factors. Studies on the mechanism of HRT's efficacy have ruled out tic disclosure (Deckersbach, Rauch, Buhlmann, & Wilhelm, 2006), increased knowledge and validation gained from psychoeducation (Piacentini et al., 2010), or treatment expectancy (Wilhelm et al., 2003) as explanatory variables. HRT also outperforms relaxation training (Peterson & Azrin, 1992) and massed negative practice (Azrin et al., 1980), providing further support for the overall efficacy of the HRT package.

HRT is an empirically supported treatment for managing tics as they occur, but researchers have suggested that the standard HRT package may neglect key elements of the behavioral model. In particular, HRT does not systematically address other behavioral factors that influence tics (e.g., systems that reinforce tics). Because of this, it was believed that adding additional therapeutic strategies to HRT might result in better tic and quality of life outcomes. In the following section, we detail the successful efforts to enhance HRT with additional components.

Comprehensive Behavioral Intervention for Tics

As mentioned earlier, several contextual factors influence tic expression. To address this, comprehensive behavioral intervention for tics (CBIT) added to HRT the well-established behavioral practice of functional analyses/ assessment and function-based intervention. In conducting the functional assessment, the therapist asks the client about stimuli (both internal and external) that tend to worsen tics (e.g., school, homework, video games). When a tic-exacerbating situation is identified, the therapist queries as to the consequences of tics during these situations (e.g., verbal comfort from the teacher or parent, allowing special treatment during bouts of tics). With antecedents and consequences identified, the therapist strategizes with the client and support persons to develop a behavioral treatment plan to be implemented during these "high-risk" situations. Strategies are designed to either minimize engagement in stimuli that exacerbate tics or help the client to better cope during these situations (whichever is more practical and feasible). An important requirement of functional interventions is that parents or support persons learn to identify and stop actions that might be inadvertently reinforcing tics. By reducing these maladaptive, tic-dependent reinforcers, the home should ideally become a "tic-neutral environment." Tics are neither reinforced nor punished. In fact, the parents or support persons should be instructed to pay no attention to tics, except when engaged in activities surrounding the development of therapeutic skills. For many children with tics, simply altering problematic contextual and environmental variables can have a substantial impact (Watson & Sterling, 1998).

CBIT also contains relaxation training and psychoeducation. Tics are not directly targeted through relaxation, but rather the technique is used for stress management, as stress has often been found to worsen tics or make tics more difficult to control (Conelea & Woods, 2008a; Conelea, Woods, & Brandt, 2011; Lin et al., 2007). Psychoeducation has a positive effect for children and families dealing with tics (Leckman & Cohen, 1999), as well as various other mental disorders (e.g., Kendall, Hudson, Gosch, Flannery-Schroeder, & Suveg, 2008; Miklowitz, George, Richards, Simoneau, & Suddath, 2003). Psychoeducation is also a good way to detect and correct any problematic or unscientific ideas about tics, such as "bad parenting causes tics" or "medication is the only viable treatment option."

The existing empirical evidence for CBIT in children (and adults) is strong. One methodologically rigorous study has evaluated the efficacy of CBIT in children, and a parallel study has been performed on adults (Wilhelm et al., 2012). Piacentini et al. (2010) conducted a multisite, randomized controlled trial of CBIT in children ages 9-17, providing eight weekly sessions followed by booster sessions. Treatment was based on a published manual (Woods, Piacentini, et al., 2008), and an active psycho-supportive therapy (PST) was used as a control condition. Blinded independent examiners using a well-validated measure of tic severity were used to assess outcome. Results showed that CBIT significantly reduced tics to a greater degree than PST, and 52.5% of children receiving CBIT were considered clinical responders at the end of 10 weeks of treatment as compared to 18.5% who received PST. Furthermore, tic reduction with CBIT was equivalent to that found in studies evaluating commonly used psychopharmacological medications for TS (Sallee et al., 2000; Scahill, Leckman, Schultz, Katsovich, & Peterson, 2003). CBIT also produced no adverse side effects and attrition was low (8%), demonstrating the tolerability and efficacy of the intervention in children. Secondary benefits of treatment included durable results at 6-month follow-up (i.e., 87% still responding) as well as improvements in overall psychosocial functioning (i.e., decreases in disruptive behavior, anxiety, obsessive-compulsive disorder symptoms, and family strain; Woods et al., 2011). Results in the adult study were comparatively positive, with 38.1% of those receiving CBIT responding to treatment as compared to 6.8% of control participants (Wilhelm et al., 2012).

Recent Advances in Translational Science

Behavior therapy for tic disorders is effective and has considerable empirical support. However, the body of research supporting the purported mechanisms of change in HRT and the functional relationships between contextual factors and tic expression is still small. Next, we will summarize these recent findings and suggest several future directions in the field.

Azrin and Nunn (1973) originally believed that tics were the result of tension in previously injured muscles. They proposed that CRs in HRT functioned to strengthen muscles that opposed tics (Azrin & Nunn, 1973). This explanation is no longer widely accepted. Modern conceptualizations of HRT are based on the premise that CRs are effective through their ability to break the negative reinforcement cycle believed to maintain tic occurrence. Tics are reinforced via their reduction of premonitory urges. The CR allows habituation of the urge to take place, thus reducing the reinforcer available for tics. Experimental research has supported this hypothesis. For instance, studies have shown that CRs must be contingent on the tic or the urge to be effective (Miltenberger & Fuqua, 1985) and that use of the CR results in short-term increases in urges but long-term decreases (Woods, Himle, et al., 2008). However, there is another plausible explanation for the effectiveness of HRT. It is possible that CRs strengthen generalized response inhibition abilities, which might explain why some have found that adults with TS demonstrate improved motor dexterity and electroencephalogram signatures during response inhibition tasks (Lavoie, Imbriglio, Stip, & O'Connor, 2011).

One of the most interesting domains of current tic research focuses on the development of the premonitory urges. Research has shown that premonitory urges frequently develop several years after tic onset (Leckman et al., 1993), and younger children (<10 years of age) are less likely to report urges than older children (Woods et al., 2005). Some have speculated on reasons for this gap, offering that young children do not yet possess the generalized capacity to verbally describe interoceptive sensations (Banaschewski, Woerner, & Rothenberger, 2003; Leckman et al., 1993). Recent studies have put forth a behavioral model of premonitory urge appearance that accounts for both developmental and neurological factors. This model posits that environmental events, specifically aversive social reactions to tics, are responsible for urge development (Himle et al., 2006; Woods et al., 2005). In this framework, the neurological dysfunction underlying urges might be present during tic onset, but at this stage urges are either not recognized or experienced as aversive. As tics continue and the child ages, negative physical (e.g., pain) and/or social (e.g., teasing, bullying, being told to stop) consequences often emerge as a result of tics (Conelea & Woods, 2008a). Due to these consequences, the child then becomes more vigilant to sensations that precede tics, and as with any stimulus that signals an impending aversive event, the urges acquire an aversive valence (Woods et al., 2005). Stated another way, urges originate as benign interoceptive experiences and become aversive through interactions with the environment.

Empirical evidence supporting the behavioral model of premonitory urge development cuts across multiple methodologies. For instance, Wang et al. (2011) found that urges were associated with activation of neural structures involved in negative affect and punishment-based learning. Woods et al. (2005) showed that urge severity correlated positively with obsessive-compulsive symptoms, anxiety/mood, withdrawal, social impairment, and aggression, and that these associations were only present in children above 11 years of age. These older children also showed positive correlations between urge severity and tic number, complexity, and interference. Peer victimization (e.g., being bullied or teased) has also been linked to premonitory urge severity (Zinner, Conelea, Glew, Woods, & Budman, 2012). Finally, a recent cross-sectional study found that tic and urge severity were positively correlated with each other and with tic-related impact, and that the relationship between urge severity and tic-related impact was present even after controlling for comorbid psychiatric diagnoses and tic severity (Capriotti, Espil, Conelea, & Woods, 2013).

Here we suggest several lines of potential research directions that stem from the neurobehavioral conceptualization of tic disorders. First, investigators should develop novel behavioral and physiological measures for premonitory urges, because we are clearly limited by the sole use of verbal rating systems. Such behavioral measures might shed light on habituation processes that occur on both behavioral and biological levels, thereby enhancing treatment development and early intervention. Second, methods of external reinforcement for tic suppression should be further investigated. For instance, what are the behavioral effects of suppression with and without contingent reinforcement and are specific magnitudes and schedules of reinforcement more effective at reducing tics than others? Third, does exposure to aversive consequences to tics (i.e., punishment) subsequently provide negative reinforcement for tic suppression? While punishing tics might be unethical in certain human-subjects research paradigms, children who have tics often experience real world consequences for their tics (e.g., bullying, embarrassment). Research should examine the effects of both social and nonsocial factors that affect tic expression, as such information could lead to more effective treatments.

Another direction for future efforts involves the dissemination of behavioral therapies. Behavior therapy is an effective nonpharmacological alternative treatment, but it is not widely available (Marcks, Woods, Teng, & Twohig, 2004; Woods, Conelea, & Walther, 2007). Steps have been taken to improve knowledge about the treatments, such as through the educational efforts of the Tourette Syndrome Association (www.tsa-usa.org) and published reports of the pediatric CBIT trial in the popular media (e.g., Harding, 2010; Holohan, 2011). Additionally, Canadian, European, and US clinical guidelines recommend the use of behavior therapy for tic disorders (Murphy, Lewin, Storch, Shook, & AACAP CQI, 2013; Steeves et al., 2012; Verdellen, van de Griendt, Hartmann, & Murphy, 2011). Despite this high demand, patients rarely know how to access it, and few practitioners actually offer HRT and/or CBIT, particularly in rural areas (Woods et al., 2007). Given this lack of accessibility, some experts have suggested that access could be improved through telehealth solutions. Technological advances in videoconferencing and improved access to high-speed internet have led to dramatic increases in telehealth therapies for neurobehavioral disorders (Postel, de Haan, & De Jong, 2008). As such, Himle, Olufs, Himle, Tucker, and Woods (2010) and Himle et al. (2012) tested the efficacy of CBIT delivered via teleconference and found that it significantly reduces tics as well as face-to-face delivery. These recent advances could combat arguments that behavior therapy is not widely available due to the lack of trained therapists (e.g., Jankovic & Kurlan, 2011).

CONCLUSIONS

Tic disorders are influenced by contextual and environmental factors. As such, a modern understanding of their etiology, phenomenology, assessment, and effective treatment has been greatly influenced through applications of applied behavior analytic methods. As is true with other childhood psychiatric disorders (e.g., autism spectrum, attention deficit/hyperactivity disorder), parallel lines of research in neuroscience and behavioral psychology continue to offer complementary viewpoints. In line with the current understanding of dimensional and functional classifications of mental disorders, as well as demands of NIMH funding initiatives (i.e., Research Domain Criteria), behavior analytic conceptualizations are more important now than ever before.

REFERENCES

Alexander, A. B., Chai, H., Creer, T. L., Miklich, D. R., Renne, C. M., De, A., et al. (1973). The elimination of chronic cough by response suppression shaping. *Journal of Behavior Therapy and Experimental Psychiatry, 4*, 75–80.

American Psychiatric Association. (2013). *Diagnostic and statistical manual of mental disorders* (5th). Arlington, VA: Author.

Aron, A. M., Freeman, J. M., & Carter, S. (1965). The natural history of Sydenham's chorea: Review of the literature and long-term evaluation with emphasis on cardiac sequelae. *American Journal of Medicine, 38*, 83–95.

Azrin, N. H., & Nunn, R. G. (1973). Habit reversal: A method of eliminating nervous habits and tics. *Behaviour Research and Therapy, 11*, 619–628.

Azrin, N. H., Nunn, R. G., & Frantz, S. E. (1980). Habit reversal vs. negative practice treatment of nervous tics. *Behaviour Therapy, 11*, 169–178.

Banaschewski, T., Woerner, W., & Rothenberger, A. (2003). Premonitory sensory phenomena and suppressibility of tics in Tourette syndrome: Developmental aspects in children and adolescents. *Developmental Medicine and Child Neurology, 45*, 700–703.

Bate, K. S., Malouff, J. M., Thorsteinsson, E. T., & Bhullar, N. (2011). The efficacy of habit reversal therapy for tics, habit disorders, and stuttering: A meta-analytic review. *Clinical Psychology Review, 31*, 865–871.

Bergin, A., Waranch, H. R., Brown, J., Carson, K., & Singer, H. S. (1998). Relaxation therapy in Tourette syndrome: A pilot study. *Pediatric Neurology, 18*, 136–142.

Bloch, M. H., Peterson, B. S., Scahill, L., Otka, J., Katsovich, L., & Leckman, J. F. (2006). Clinical predictors of future tic and OCD severity in children with Tourette syndrome. *Archives of Pediatric and Adolescent Medicine, 160*, 65–69.

Capriotti, M. R., Espil, F. M., Conelea, C. A., & Woods, D. W. (2013). Environmental factors as potential determinants of premonitory urge severity in youth with Tourette syndrome. *Journal of Obsessive-Compulsive and Related Disorders, 2*, 37–42.

Capriotti, M. R., & Woods, D. W. (2013). Cognitive-behavioral treatment for tics. In D. Martino, & J. F. Leckman (Eds.), *Tourette syndrome*. New York, NY: Oxford University Press, p. 503.

Carr, J. E., Bailey, J. S., Carr, C. A., & Coggin, A. M. (1996). The role of independent variable integrity in the behavioral management of Tourette syndrome. *Behavioral Interventions, 11*, 35–45.

Cohen, D. J., & Leckman, J. F. (1992). Sensory phenomena associated with Gilles de la Tourette's syndrome. *Journal of Clinical Psychiatry, 53*, 319–323.

Commander, M., Corbett, J., Prendergast, M., & Ridley, C. (1991). Reflex tics in two patients with Gilles de la Tourette syndrome. *British Journal of Psychiatry, 159*, 877–879.

Conelea, C. A., & Woods, D. W. (2008a). The influence of contextual factors on tic expression in Tourette's syndrome: A review. *Journal of Psychosomatic Research, 65*, 487–496.

Conelea, C. A., & Woods, D. W. (2008b). Examining the impact of distraction of tic suppression in children and adolescents with Tourette syndrome. *Behaviour Research and Therapy, 46*, 1193–1200.

Conelea, C. A., Woods, D. W., & Brandt, B. C. (2011). The impact of a stress induction task on tic frequencies in youth with Tourette syndrome. *Behaviour Research and Therapy, 49*, 492–497.

Cook, C. R., & Blacher, J. (2007). Evidence-based psychosocial treatments for tic disorders. *Clinical Psychology: Science and Practice, 14*, 252–267.

Crossley, E., Seri, S., Stern, J. S., Robertson, M. M., & Cavanna, A. E. (2014). Premonitory urges for tics in adult patients with Tourette syndrome. *Brain and Development, 36*, 45–50.

Deckersbach, T., Rauch, S., Buhlmann, U., & Wilhelm, S. (2006). Habit reversal versus supportive psychotherapy in Tourette's disorder: A randomized controlled trial and predictors of treatment response. *Behaviour Research and Therapy, 44*, 1079–1090.

Doleys, D. M., & Kurtz, P. S. (1974). A behavioral treatment program for the Gilles de la Tourette syndrome. *Psychological Reports, 35*, 43–48.

Freeman, R. D., Fast, D. K., Burd, L., Kerbeshian, J., Robertson, M. M., & Sandor, P. (2000). An international perspective on Tourette syndrome: Selected findings from 3500 individuals in 22 countries. *Developmental Medicine and Child Neurology, 42*, 436–447.

Harding, A. (2010). Behavior therapy matches drugs for calming tics. *Reuters*, Retrieved from: http://www.reuters.com/article/2010/05/18/us-calming-tics-idUSTRE64H3P220100518.

Himle, M. B., Freitag, M., Walther, M., Franklin, S. A., Ely, L., & Woods, D. W. (2012). A randomized pilot trial comparing videoconference versus face-to-face delivery of behavior therapy for childhood tic disorders. *Behaviour Research and Therapy, 50*, 565–570.

Himle, M. B., Olufs, E., Himle, J., Tucker, B. T., & Woods, D. W. (2010). Behavior therapy for tics via videoconference delivery: An initial pilot test in children. *Cognitive and Behavioral Practice, 17*, 329–337.

Himle, M. B., & Woods, D. W. (2005). An experimental evaluation of tic suppression and the tic rebound effect. *Behaviour Research and Therapy, 43*, 1443–1451.

Himle, M. B., Woods, D. W., & Bunaciu, L. (2008). Evaluating the role of contingency in differentially reinforced tic suppression. *Journal of Applied Behavior Analysis, 41*, 285–289.

Himle, M. B., Woods, D. W., Conelea, C. A., Bauer, C. C., & Rice, K. A. (2007). Investigating the effects of tic suppression on premonitory urge ratings in children and adolescents with Tourette's syndrome. *Behaviour Research and Therapy, 45*, 2964–2976.

Himle, M. B., Woods, D. W., Piacentini, J. C., & Walkup, J. T. (2006). Brief review of habit reversal training for Tourette syndrome. *Journal of Child Neurology, 21*, 719–725.

Hinson, V. K., & Haren, W. B. (2006). Psychogenic movement disorders. *The Lancet Neurology, 5*, 695–700.

Holohan, E. (2011). Behavior therapy may reduce Tourette tics, symptoms. *HealthDay*. Retrieved from: http://consumer.healthday.com/mental-health-information-25/behavior-health-news-56/behavioral-therapy-may-reduce-tourette-tics-symptoms-652115.html.

Jagger, J., Prusoff, B. A., Cohen, D. J., Kidd, K. K., Carbonari, C. M., & John, K. (1982). The epidemiology of Tourette's syndrome: A pilot study. *Schizophrenia Bulletin, 8*(2), 267–278.

Jankovic, J., & Kurlan, R. (2011). Tourette syndrome: Evolving concepts. *Movement Disorders, 26*, 1149–1156.

Kane, M. J. (1994). Premonitory urges as "attentional tics" in Tourette's syndrome. *Journal of the American Academy of Child and Adolescent Psychiatry, 33*, 805–808.

Kendall, P. C., Hudson, J. L., Gosch, E., Flannery-Schroeder, E., & Suveg, C. (2008). Cognitive-behavioral therapy for anxiety disordered youth: A randomized clinical trial evaluating child and family modalities. *Journal of Consulting and Clinical Psychology, 76*, 282–297.

Khalifa, N., & von Knorring, A. L. (2003). Prevalence of tic disorders and Tourette syndrome in a Swedish school population. *Developmental Medicine and Child Neurology, 45*, 1346–1353.

Lavoie, M. E., Imbriglio, T. V., Stip, E., & O'Connor, K. P. (2011). Neurocognitive changes following cognitive-behavioral treatment in Tourette syndrome and chronic tic disorder. *International Journal of Cognitive Therapy, 4*, 34–50.

Leckman, J. F., Bloch, M. H., Sukhodolsky, D. G., Scahill, L., & King, R. A. (2013). Phenomenology of tics and sensory urges: The self under siege. In D. Martino, & J. F. Leckman (Eds.), *Tourette syndrome*. New York, NY: Oxford University Press. p. 4.

Leckman, J. F., & Cohen, D. J. (1999). Evolving models of pathogenesis. In J. F. Leckman, & D. J. Cohen (Eds.), *Tourette's syndrome—Tics, obsessions, compulsions: Developmental psychopathology and clinical care* (pp. 155–176). New York: Wiley.

Leckman, J. F., Walker, D. E., & Cohen, D. J. (1993). Premonitory urges in Tourette's syndrome. *American Journal of Psychiatry, 150*, 98–102.

Leckman, J. F., Zhang, H., Vitale, A., Lahnin, F., Lynch, K., Bondi, C., et al. (1998). Course of tic severity in Tourette syndrome: The first two decades. *Pediatrics, 102*, 157–166.

Lin, H., Katsovich, L., Ghebremichael, M., Findley, D. B., Grantz, H., Lombroso, P. J., et al. (2007). Psychosocial stress predicts future symptom severities in children and adolescents with Tourette syndrome and/or obsessive-compulsive disorder. *Journal of Child Psychology and Psychiatry, 48*, 157–166.

Marcks, B. A., Woods, D. W., Teng, E. J., & Twohig, M. P. (2004). What do those who know, know? Investigating providers' knowledge about Tourette's syndrome and its treatment. *Cognitive and Behavioral Practice, 11*, 298–305.

Michael, J. (1993). Establishing operations. *The Behavior Analyst, 16*, 191–206.

Miklowitz, D. J., George, E. L., Richards, J. A., Simoneau, T. L., & Suddath, R. L. (2003). A randomized study of family-focused psychoeducation and pharmacotherapy in the outpatient management of bipolar disorder. *Archives of General Psychiatry, 60*, 904–912.

Miltenberger, R. G., & Fuqua, R. W. (1985). A comparison of contingent vs. non-contingent competing response practice in the treatment of nervous habits. *Journal of Behavior Therapy and Experimental Psychiatry, 16*, 195–200.

Mink, J. W. (2003). The basal ganglia and involuntary movements: Impaired inhibition of competing motor patterns. *Archives of Neurology, 60*, 1365–1368.

Murphy, T. K., Lewin, A. B., Storch, E. A., Shook, S., & the American Academy of Clinical Child and Adolescent Psychiatry (AACAP) Committee on Quality Issues (CQI). (2013). Practice parameter for the assessment and treatment of children and adolescents with chronic tic disorders. *Journal of the American Academy of Clinical Child and Adolescent Psychiatry, 52*(12), 1341–1359.

O'Connor, K. P., Brisebois, H., Brault, M., Robillard, S., & Loiselle, J. (2003). Behavioral activity associated with onset in chronic tic and habit disorder. *Behaviour Research and Therapy*, *41*, 241–249.

Ollendick, T. H. (1981). Self-monitoring and self-administered overcorrection: The modification of nervous tics in children. *Behavior Modification*, *5*, 75–84.

Packer, L. E. (2005). Tic-related school problems: Impact on functioning, accommodations, and interventions. *Behavior Modification*, *29*, 876–899.

Pauls, D. L. (2003). An update on the genetics of Gilles de la Tourette syndrome. *Journal of Psychosomatic Research*, *55*, 7–12.

Peterson, A. L., & Azrin, N. H. (1992). An evaluation of behavioral treatments for Tourette syndrome. *Behaviour Research and Therapy*, *30*, 167–174.

Peterson, B. S., & Leckman, J. F. (1998). The temporal dynamics of tics in Gilles de la Tourette syndrome. *Biological Psychiatry*, *44*, 1337–1348.

Piacentini, J., Woods, D. W., Scahill, L., Wilhelm, S., Peterson, A. L., Chang, S., et al. (2010). Behavior therapy for children with Tourette disorder: A randomized controlled trial. *JAMA*, *303*, 1929–1937.

Postel, M. G., de Haan, H. A., & De Jong, C. A. J. (2008). E-therapy for mental health problems: A systematic review. *Telemedicine and e-Health*, *14*(7), 707–714.

Rauch, S. L., Baer, L., Cosgrove, G. R., & Jenike, M. A. (1995). Neurosurgical treatment of Tourette's syndrome: A critical review. *Comprehensive Psychiatry*, *36*, 141–156.

Reese, H. E., Scahill, L., Peterson, A. L., Crowe, K., Woods, D. W., Piacentini, J., et al. (2014). The premonitory urge to tic: Measurement, characteristics, and correlates in older adolescents and adults. *Behavior Therapy*, *45*, 177–186.

Rickards, H., & Cavanna, A. E. (2009). Gilles de la Tourette: The man behind the syndrome. *Journal of Psychosomatic Research*, *67*, 469–474.

Robertson, M. M., & Stern, J. S. (2000). Gilles de la Tourette syndrome: Symptomatic treatment based on evidence. *European Child & Adolescent Psychiatry*, *9*, 160–175.

Sallee, F. R., Kurlan, R., Goetz, C. G., Singer, H., Scahill, L., Law, G., et al. (2000). Ziprasidone treatment of children and adolescents with Tourette's syndrome: A pilot study. *Journal of the American Academy of Child and Adolescent Psychiatry*, *39*, 292–299.

Scahill, L., Erenberg, G., Berlin, C. M., Budman, C., Coffey, B. J., Jankovic, J., et al. (2006). Contemporary assessment and pharmacotherapy of Tourette syndrome. *NeuroRx: The Journal of the American Society for Experiential NeuroTherapeutics*, *3*, 192–206.

Scahill, L., Leckman, J., Schultz, R., Katsovich, L., & Peterson, B. (2003). A placebo-controlled trial of risperidone in Tourette syndrome. *Neurology*, *60*, 1130–1135.

Scotti, J. R., Schulman, D. E., & Honjacki, R. M. (1994). Functional analysis and unsuccessful treatment of Tourette's syndrome in a man with profound mental retardation. *Behavior Therapy*, *25*, 721–738.

Shapiro, A. K., & Shapiro, E. S. (1984). Controlled study of pimozide vs. placebo in Tourette syndrome. *Journal of the American Academy of Child and Adolescent Psychiatry*, *23*, 161–173.

Shapiro, A. K., Shapiro, E. S., Young, J. G., & Feinberg, T. E. (1988). *Gilles de la Tourette syndrome* (2nd). New York: Raven Press.

Silva, R. R., Munoz, D. M., Barickman, J., & Friedhoff, A. J. (1995). Environmental factors and related fluctuation of symptoms in children and adolescents with Tourette's disorder. *Journal of Child Psychology and Psychiatry*, *36*, 305–312.

Steeves, T., McKinlay, B. D., Gorman, D., Billinghurst, L., Day, L., Carroll, A., et al. (2012). Canadian guidelines for the evidence-based treatment of tic disorders: Behavioural therapy, deep brain stimulation, and transcranial magnetic stimulation. *Canadian Journal of Psychiatry*, *57*, 144–151.

Steinberg, T., Baruch, S. S., Harush, A., Dar, R., Woods, D. W., Piacentini, J., et al. (2010). Tic disorders and the premonitory urge. *Journal of Neural Transmission*, *117*, 277–284.

Tophoff, M. (1973). Masses practice, relaxation, and assertion training in the treatment of Gilles de la Tourette syndrome. *Journal of Behavior Therapy and Experimental Psychiatry*, 4, 71–73.

Torup, E. (1962). A follow-up study of children with tics. *Acta Paediatrica*, 51, 261–268.

Tourette, G. D. L. (1885). Etude sur une affection nerveuse caracterisee par de l'incoordination motrice accompagnee d'echolalie et de comprolalie. *Archives of Neurology*, 9, 19–42.

Tourette Syndrome Classification Study Group. (1993). Definitions and classification of tic disorders. *Archives of Neurology*, 50, 1013.

Turpin, G., & Powell, G. E. (1984). Effects of massed practice and cue-controlled relaxation on tic frequency in Gilles de la Tourette's syndrome. *Behaviour Research and Therapy*, 22, 165–178.

Varni, J. W., Boyd, E. F., & Cataldo, M. F. (1978). Self-monitoring, external reinforcement, and timeout procedures in the control of high rate tic behaviors in a hyperactive child. *Journal of Behavior Therapy and Experimental Psychiatry*, 9, 353–358.

Verdellen, C. W., van de Griendt, J., Hartmann, A., & Murphy, T. (2011). European clinical guidelines for Tourette syndrome and other tic disorders. Part III: Behavioural and psychosocial interventions. *European Child & Adolescent Psychiatry*, 20, 197–207.

Wagaman, J. R., Miltenberger, R. G., & Williams, D. E. (1995). Treatment of a vocal tic by differential reinforcement. *Journal of Behavior Therapy and Experimental Psychiatry*, 26, 35–39.

Wang, Z., Maia, T., Marsh, R., Colibazzi, T., Gerber, A., & Peterson, B. S. (2011). The neural circuits that generate tics in Tourette's syndrome. *The American Journal of Psychiatry*, 168, 1326–1337.

Watson, T. S., & Sterling, H. E. (1998). Brief functional analysis and treatment of a vocal tic. *Journal of Applied Behavior Analysis*, 31, 471–474.

Wilhelm, S., Deckersbach, T., Coffey, B. J., Bohne, A., Peterson, A. L., & Baer, L. (2003). Habit reversal versus supportive psychotherapy for Tourette's disorder: A randomized controlled trial. *American Journal of Psychiatry*, 160, 1175–1177.

Wilhelm, S., Peterson, A. L., Piacentini, J., Woods, D. W., Deckersbach, T., Sukhodolsky, D. G., et al. (2012). Randomized trial of behavior therapy for adults with Tourette syndrome. *Archives of General Psychiatry*, 69, 795–803.

Woods, D. W., Conelea, C. A., & Walther, M. R. (2007). Barriers to dissemination: Exploring the criticisms of behavior therapy for tics. *Clinical Psychology: Science and Practice*, 14, 279–282.

Woods, D. W., & Himle, M. B. (2004). Creating tic suppression: Comparing the effects of verbal instruction to differential reinforcement. *Journal of Applied Behavior Analysis*, 37, 417–420.

Woods, D. W., Himle, M. B., Miltenberger, R. G., Carr, J. E., Osmon, D. C., Karsten, A. M., et al. (2008). Durability, negative impact, and neuropsychological predictors of tic suppression in children with chronic tic disorder. *Journal of Abnormal Child Psychology*, 36, 237–245.

Woods, D. W., Miltenberger, R. G., & Lumley, V. A. (1996). Sequential application of major habit-reversal components to treat motor tics in children. *Journal of Applied Behavior Analysis*, 29, 483–493.

Woods, D. W., Piacentini, J., Chang, S., Deckersbach, T., Ginsburg, G., Peterson, A., et al. (2008). *Managing Tourette syndrome: A behavioral intervention for children and adults (therapists guide)*. New York: Oxford University Press.

Woods, D. W., Piacentini, J., Himle, M. B., & Chang, S. (2005). Premonitory Urge for Tics Scale (PUTS): Initial psychometric results and examination of the premonitory urge phenomenon in youths with tic disorders. *Journal of Developmental and Behavioral Pediatrics*, 26, 397–403.

Woods, D. W., Piacentini, J., Scahill, L., Peterson, A., Wilhelm, S., Chang, S., et al. (2011). Behavior therapy for tics in children: Acute and long-term effects on psychiatric and psychosocial functioning. *Journal of Child Neurology, 26,* 858–865.

Woods, D. W., Walther, M. R., Bauer, C. C., Kemp, J. J., & Conelea, C. A. (2009). The development of stimulus control over tics: A potential explanation for contextually-based variability in the symptoms of Tourette syndrome. *Behaviour Research and Therapy, 47,* 41–47.

Woods, D. W., Watson, T. S., Wolfe, E., Twohig, M. P., & Friman, P. C. (2001). Analyzing the influence of tic-related talk on vocal and motor tics in children with Tourette's syndrome. *Journal of Applied Behavior Analysis, 34,* 353–356.

Ziemann, U., Paulus, W., & Rothenberger, A. (1997). Decreased motor inhibition in Tourette's disorder: Evidence from tanscranial magnetic stimulation. *American Journal of Psychiatry, 154,* 1277–1284.

Zinner, S. H., Conelea, C. A., Glew, G. M., Woods, D. W., & Budman, C. L. (2012). Peer victimization in youth with Tourette syndrome and other chronic tic disorders. *Child Psychiatry and Human Development, 43,* 124–136.

CHAPTER 10

Assessment and Intervention for Individuals with Attention-Deficit Hyperactivity Disorder

Robert H. LaRue, Kimberly N. Sloman, Erica Dashow, Robert W. Isenhower
Rutgers, The State University of New Jersey, Douglass Developmental Disabilities Center, New Brunswick, New Jersey, USA

Attention-deficit hyperactivity disorder (ADHD) is one of the most commonly diagnosed childhood psychiatric disorders (Pliszka, 2007), affecting approximately 5.9-7.1% of children (Willcutt, 2012). Common characteristics of the disorder include difficulty remaining on task and a lack of attending skills, such as sitting still and focusing on instructions. Additionally, individuals with ADHD frequently exhibit impulsive behavior (e.g., choosing a smaller, more immediate consequence over a larger, more delayed consequence; Rachlin & Green, 1972). These patterns of behavior may be present across multiple settings, such as at school and home, and may reduce individuals' performance in the educational, social, and work environments.

DIAGNOSIS/ASSESSMENT RATING SCALES

ADHD is characterized by persistent inattention and/or hyperactivity and impulsivity that interfere with functioning or development. In order for a diagnosis to be made, a child must show a persistent pattern of inattention, displaying at least six of the following symptoms for at least 6 months: making careless mistakes or showing a lack of attention to details, difficulty sustaining attention, seeming not to listen when directly spoken to, not following through on instructions or failing to finish tasks, difficulty organizing tasks and activities, avoiding or disliking tasks that require sustained effort, often losing objects, being easily distracted, and being often forgetful (American Psychiatric Association, 2013).

Similarly, the child must show at least six of the following symptoms of hyperactivity and impulsivity frequently for a period of at least 6 months: fidgeting in seat, leaving seat when sitting is expected, running or climbing in inappropriate situations, inability to play quietly, often "on the go," talking excessively, blurting out an answer before a question has been fully asked, difficulty waiting his or her turn, and interrupting or intruding on others. In addition, several of these symptoms must be present in two or more settings, occur before age 12, and interfere with or reduce the quality of social, academic, or occupational functioning. In adults, at least five symptoms from each category must be present in order for a diagnosis to be made (American Psychiatric Association, 2013).

ADHD can be assessed using the above criteria or through the use of several diagnostic rating scales including the Connors Third Edition (Conners 3; Conners, 2008), the Child Behavior Checklist (CBCL/6-18; Achenbach & Edelbrock, 1991), the Vanderbilt ADHD Diagnostic Parent and Teacher Scales (Wolraich, Lambert, Baumgaertel, et al., 2003; Wolraich, Lambert, Doffing, et al., 2003), and the ADHD Rating Scale-IV (ADHD-IV; DuPaul, Power, Anastopoulos, & Reid, 1998). The rating scales are typically available in both parent and teacher forms and can be completed in 10-20 min. Rating scales focus on assessing areas such as inattention, hyperactivity/impulsivity, social and academic skill deficits, and inappropriate behavior and are designed for school-aged children (ages 6-18 years).

PREVALENCE AND ETIOLOGY OF ADHD

The prevalence of ADHD is estimated to be approximately 2.5% in children and 4.4% in adults, and studies have suggested that the disorder tends to persist into adulthood (American Psychiatric Association, 2013; Kessler et al., 2006; Martel, von Eye, & Nigg, 2012).

There is no known cause of ADHD; however, the disorder is thought to be caused by the interaction of biological and environmental factors. ADHD tends to run in families, and heritability is estimated to be approximately 76% (Faraone et al., 2005). In children, twice as many males are diagnosed than females; while in adults, males with ADHD outnumber females six to one (American Psychiatric Association, 2013). Genes related to the dopamine transmission and cortical serotonin pathways have been found to be associated with ADHD (Levy, McStephen, & Hay, 2001). There are a number of risk factors associated with ADHD, including maternal smoking during pregnancy (Langley, Rice, & van den Bree, 2005), low birth weight (Bhutta, Cleves, & Casey, 2002), pregnancy and delivery complications (Banerjee, Middleton, & Faraone, 2007), and home environment (e.g., presence of abuse, neglect, inconsistent parenting practices; Carlson, Jacob-vitz, & Sroufe, 1995; Colvert et al., 2008; Kreppner, O'Connor, & Rutter, 2001). Overall, it is thought that environmental factors can interact with a genetic susceptibility to affect brain development, which in turn has negative effects on behavior (Howe, 2010).

IMPACT OF ADHD

The presentation of ADHD changes over the course of the lifespan. During the preschool years, hyperactivity is prominent, and delayed development, oppositional behavior, and poor social skills may be present (DuPaul, McGoey, Eckert, & VanBrakle, 2001; Harpin, 2005). Functioning becomes more impaired in school-aged children, where inattention becomes more prominent (American Psychiatric Association, 2013). Children with ADHD may also experience difficulties in school, peer rejection, low levels of self-esteem, and difficulties at home.

During adolescence, hyperactivity typically decreases, but inattentive-ness, restlessness, and impulsivity may still cause impairments in functioning. During this period, individuals with ADHD may also show an increase in aggressive and antisocial behavior. Additionally, adolescents with ADHD are at an increased risk of criminal behavior, teenage pregnancy, academic fail-ure, or dropping out of school (Harpin, 2005). Although only a portion of children with ADHD meet strictly defined diagnostic criteria in adulthood, approximately 65% continue to experience impaired functioning (Martel et al., 2012). Adults with ADHD experience difficulties in both employment and social aspects of their lives. Problems such as interpersonal difficulties, lateness, excessive errors, inability to keep up with workloads, and absentee-ism contribute towards increased rates of employment dismissal. These indi-viduals are also much more likely to experience difficulties in relationships and abuse substances (Biederman, Wilens, Mick, Faraone, & Spencer, 1998).

ADHD affects not only the diagnosed individual, but also his or her fam-ily members. During the preschool years, parental stress increases and parents have less time for themselves, as high levels of supervision are necessary. Having a child with ADHD was found to be associated with increased like-lihood of strained family relationships, marital problems, financial and social difficulties, reduced parenting efficacy, and increased levels of parental stress (Johnston & Mash, 2001). Siblings of children with ADHD have been found to have an increased risk of developing conduct and emotional disorders (Harpin, 2005).

BEST PRACTICES IN THE TREATMENT OF ADHD

The most effective treatment for ADHD includes a multimodal approach that combines both stimulant medication and behavioral intervention (Jensen et al., 2001; MTA Cooperative Group, 1999). The focus of this section will be on behavioral assessment and treatment. The effectiveness of medication plus behavioral interventions will be reviewed later in the chapter.

Behavioral Treatment of ADHD

Behavior analytic approaches to the assessment and treatment of ADHD have involved operationalizing the core behavioral features of the disorder (i.e., impulsivity, hyperactivity, and inattentiveness), identifying environmental causes of the behavior (antecedents and consequences), and developing function-based treatments. The following section will review the literature on the assessment and treatment of impulsivity and off-task/disruptive behavior in individuals with ADHD.

Behavioral Analysis of Impulsivity

Behavior analytic theory defines impulsivity as selecting a smaller more immediate consequence over a larger more delayed consequence (Ainslie, 1974; Rachlin & Green, 1972). In contrast, self-control is defined as selection of a larger delayed consequence over a smaller more immediate consequence (Ainslie, 1974; Rachlin & Green, 1972). Research has shown that students with ADHD engage in more impulsive behavior than typically developing peers (e.g., Hoerger & Mace, 2006; Neef, Bicard, & Endo, 2001; Neef et al., 2005; Sonuga-Barke, Taylor, Sembi, & Smith, 1992). For example, a student with ADHD may engage in calling out in class to receive immediate, but brief, teacher attention rather than raise his/her hand, which would be reinforced with delayed attention of a longer duration. Neef et al. (2005) evaluated impulsivity and self-control in students with ADHD and typically developing peers via computerized math tasks. Participants had the choice of engaging in two math tasks that differed by rate of reinforcement (e.g., task completion would be reinforced approximately once every minute vs. once every 30 s), quality of reinforcement (i.e., task completion was reinforced with high quality items vs. low quality items), immediacy of reinforcement (i.e., reinforcers were presented at the end of the session vs. the beginning of the subsequent session), and response effort (i.e., participants completed mastered tasks vs. acquisition tasks). Results from the study showed that the choices of participants with ADHD were most sensitive to immediacy of reinforcement. That is, ADHD participants consistently selected tasks, which resulted in a shorter delay to reinforcement, even when the alternate task provided a greater rate or higher quality of reinforcement or easier task. These results differed from non-ADHD participants whose responding was most affected by quality of reinforcement.

The predilection of individuals with ADHD to engage in impulsive behavior can have detrimental long-term consequences. Research has shown that individuals with ADHD may be more likely to engage in risky behavior such as substance abuse and dangerous driving (Barkley, Fisher, Edelbrock, & Smallish, 1990; Molina & Pelham, 2003). Given the potential social significance of impulsive behavior, numerous interventions have been evaluated to develop self-control by decreasing an individual's sensitivity to delay to reinforcement and increasing the sensitivity to the other parameters of reinforcement (e.g., amount, quality). Several studies have evaluated the effects of variations of instructions and modeling to increase sensitivity to the rate of reinforcement (e.g., Bicard & Neef, 2002; Neef et al., 2005). For example, Neef et al. (2005) found that both individuals with ADHD and typically developing individuals' responses were not sensitive to differences in rate of reinforcement across two academic tasks. When participants were told or shown how to maximize reinforcement on experimental tasks, their behavior became more sensitive to the experimental contingencies. In general, this line of research on the effects of instructions on responding have shown that the behavior of individuals with ADHD can be changed by providing instructions and that their behavior can become more sensitive to specific environmental contingencies (e.g., rate of reinforcement).

Other studies have evaluated treatments involving delay fading (e.g., Neef et al., 2001; Schweitzer & Sulzer-Azaroff, 1988), intervening activities (e.g., Mischel, Ebbesen, & Zeiss, 1972), or a combination of both (e.g., Binder, Dixon, & Ghezzi, 2000; Dixon et al., 1998) to decrease impulsive behavior. During delay fading, initially both the small and large amounts of reinforcers are available to the participant immediately. As the participant consistently selects the larger reinforcer, the delay to access that reinforcer is gradually increased. Research has also shown that providing access to intervening activities (e.g., vocational tasks) may increase tolerance of delays to reinforcers (e.g., Dixon et al., 1998; Dixon & Tibbetts, 2009).

In summary, research on the assessment of impulsivity in individuals with ADHD has shown that although impulsive behavior is more prevalent in this population, it can be remediated by providing instructions and self-control training (e.g., delay fading). However, additional research is needed on the generalization of effects to clinical settings as well as long-term effectiveness of these interventions.

Behavioral Assessment of Inappropriate Behavior

Individuals with ADHD are likely to be referred for functional assessment and behavioral intervention due to numerous forms of inappropriate behavior including disruption (e.g., calling out, property destruction), elopement, and aggression (e.g., hitting or kicking others). However, the function of inappropriate behavior cannot be assumed topographically or based on the ADHD diagnosis alone. Individuals with ADHD may engage in inappropriate behavior for a number of reasons including to access adult or peer attention, escape demands, or access-preferred items. The purpose of a functional assessment is to identify functional relations between the behavior of interest and relevant environmental events. Information gathered from functional assessment informs the development of behavioral treatment. Functional assessment is an important starting point for behavioral intervention because different treatments are required based on the function of the behavior and certain treatments may be contraindicated. For example, if data from the functional assessment indicate that target behavior is maintained by access to caregiver attention, a treatment could be developed in which the individual is taught alternative ways to access attention or reprimands following target behavior would be inappropriate based on this function. Functional assessments can include interviews with caregivers; direct observation of the behavior, including collecting descriptive data on antecedents and consequences surrounding the behavior; and experimental (functional analyses) methods. Functional analyses are considered to be best practice to identify the antecedents that occasion target behaviors and the consequences that maintain them.

Much of the research on functional assessment procedures has been conducted with individuals with developmental disabilities (Beavers, Iwata, & Lerman, 2013). However, functional assessment procedures have also been adapted for individuals with ADHD. Several studies have conducted descriptive or antecedent assessments of inappropriate behavior for students with ADHD (e.g., Anderson, English, & Hedrick, 2006; Ervin, DuPaul, Kern, & Friman, 1998; Ervin et al., 2000; Flood & Wilder, 2002; Hawkins & Axelrod, 2008). For example, Ervin and colleagues collected descriptive data on the problem behavior of three individuals with ADHD. Results showed that problem behavior was correlated with specific classes (e.g., science) and instructional techniques (e.g., group vs. individual instruction).

Flood and Wilder conducted an antecedent assessment of off-task behavior in an individual with ADHD. The researchers evaluated four conditions (easy tasks/high attention, easy tasks/low attention, difficult tasks/high attention, difficult tasks/low attention) and there were no programmed consequences for off-task behavior. Results from the antecedent assessment showed that task difficulty was correlated with off-task behavior, regardless of the level of attention provided. Overall, these few studies on descriptive assessment effectively identified environmental correlates to problem behavior and from these assessments developed effective treatments. However, a limitation of descriptive or antecedent assessments is that they identify environmental correlations, which may not be functionally related to target behavior.

During functional analyses, test conditions are arranged to evoke and reinforce problem behavior. Responding in test conditions is compared to a control condition to identify the function of target behavior. Typical procedures used in functional analyses were first described by Iwata, Dorsey, Slifer, Bauman, and Richman (1982/1994) and include conditions to test if target behavior is reinforced by access to attention, escape from demands, or automatic (nonsocial) reinforcement. Functional analyses have been successfully used across a wide variety of settings, participants, and target behaviors. Numerous studies have conducted functional analyses of inappropriate behavior in individuals with ADHD (e.g., Athens & Vollmer, 2010; Boyajian, DuPaul, Handler, Eckert, & McGoey, 2001; Broussard & Northup, 1995, 1997; Kodak, Grow, & Northup, 2004; Northup et al., 1995; Umbreit, 1995). In some cases, the procedures were adapted so that the analysis could be conducted in the setting that the target behavior was occurring (i.e., classroom environment). Additional variables such as the effects of peer attention on target behavior were also evaluated. For example, Broussard and Northup (1995) first conducted descriptive assessments of disruptive behavior in a classroom setting for three individuals with ADHD. During the classroom observation, data were collected on the events that followed disruptive behavior (i.e., peer attention, teacher attention, escape from demands). The effects of the most prevalent consequence for the disruptive behavior were then evaluated in an experimental analysis. Results showed different functions of disruptive behavior for each participant, highlighting the importance of an individualized assessment and treatment approach. In a subsequent study, Broussard and Northup (1997) conducted functional analyses of disruptive behavior for four individuals with ADHD. Results of this study showed that disruptive behavior was more sensitive to attention from peers than teachers. Therefore, peer attention is an important variable to consider during functional assessments.

When sound functional assessment procedures are used to identify the causes of inappropriate behavior, function-based treatments can be implemented. Function-based interventions have been shown to be highly effective at decreasing inappropriate behavior in individuals with ADHD. These interventions may involve antecedent strategies such as providing the maintaining reinforcer noncontingently to decrease motivation to engage in behavior (e.g., Broussard & Northup, 1995; Jones, Drew, & Weber, 2000; Kodak et al., 2004). For example, Jones et al. (2000) conducted functional analyses of disruptive behavior for an individual with ADHD and found that disruption was maintained by access to peer attention. The treatment involved providing noncontingent (scheduled) access to attention every 90 s. Several studies have evaluated differential reinforcement of appropriate behavior as a treatment for inappropriate behavior in individuals with ADHD (e.g., Flood, Wilder, Flood, & Masuda, 2002; Grauvogel-MacAleese & Wallace, 2010; Hagopian, Contrucci-Kuhn, Long, & Rush, 2005; Stahr, Cushing, Lane, & Fox, 2006; Vollmer, Borrero, Lalli, & Daniel, 1999). For example, Hagopian et al. taught individuals with ADHD ways to appropriately request reinforcers (e.g., attention, tangible items) rather than engage in problem behavior. Results showed that when appropriate requests were reinforced and inappropriate behavior was placed on extinction, inappropriate behavior decreased, and appropriate behavior increased. The study also showed that access to alternative activities facilitated the thinning of the reinforcement schedule for appropriate requests. Grauvogel-MacAleese and Wallace (2010) conducted functional analyses of inappropriate behavior for three participants with ADHD and found that inappropriate behavior was maintained by access to peer attention. A treatment was implemented in which peer attention was delivered for on-task behavior rather than inappropriate behavior. Results showed decreases in inappropriate behavior and increases on on-task behavior.

When reinforcement of appropriate alternative behavior and extinction for inappropriate behavior are not sufficient, punishment procedures may be used (e.g., time out from reinforcement, removal of preferred items). Some studies have evaluated the effects of time out on inappropriate behavior for individuals with ADHD (e.g., Fabiano et al., 2004; Northup et al., 1999). For example, Northup et al. (1999) evaluated a 30-s time out from reinforcement for four participants with ADHD. Results showed that time out was effective at decreasing inappropriate behavior for three out of four participants. However, it is imperative to identify the function of behavior prior to the implementation of punishment procedures as some consequences (e.g., time out during demands) may result in increases in inappropriate behavior.

Treatments to Increase Appropriate Academic Behavior

Both antecedent interventions (e.g., choice-making, environmental and curricular adaptations) and consequent interventions (e.g., direct reinforcement on compliance and on-task behavior, token economies, time out or response cost) have been implemented to decrease off-task behavior and increase appropriate academic behavior individuals with ADHD.

Numerous studies have shown the positive effects of choice-making on academic behavior (e.g., Dunlap et al., 1994; Kern, Mantegna, Vorndran, Bailin, & Hilt, 2001; Powell & Nelson, 1997). For example, Powell and Nelson evaluated the effects of choice of academic task on inappropriate behavior (noncompliance, disruption, off-task behavior) for a student with ADHD. In the baseline condition, the participant followed the regular classroom curriculum. In the treatment phase, the participant was given a choice between three tasks. Results showed that inappropriate behavior was decreased in the choice condition. However, task choice may be more effective for individuals whose behavior is sensitive to escape from demands rather than other variables (e.g., Romaniuk et al., 2002).

Several studies have found beneficial effects of the presentation of white noise on on-task behavior (e.g., Cook, Bradley-Johnson, & Johnson, 2014; Soderlund, Sikstrom, & Smart, 2007). For example, Cook et al. evaluated the effects of white noise presented via headphones on performance on academic tasks in a classroom environment with students with ADHD. Results showed that off-task behavior decreased for the three participants relative to a no white noise (headphones only) condition. However, no effect was observed on accuracy of responding. It is possible that the presentation of white noise reduces the impact of other environmental stimuli that might occasion off-task behavior (e.g., the student is less distracted by classroom noise).

Reinforcement systems have also been successfully used to increase on-task behavior for individuals with ADHD. These interventions identify items or activities that function as reinforcers for individuals and provide them contingent upon appropriate academic behavior. Reinforcement is provided based on the student's current level of responding and may be used to increase duration and complexity of academic skills. For example, Azrin, Ehle, and Beaumont (2006) used contingent access to the playground to shape increasingly longer durations of on-task behavior in a preschool student with ADHD. Results showed that the shaping procedure increased on-task behavior relative to descriptive praise only and noncontingent access to the playground.

Token systems are another commonly recommended reinforcement system for individuals with ADHD (DuPaul & Stoner, 1994). These reinforcement systems involve delivering tokens contingent upon appropriate behavior, which are then exchanged for backup reinforcers. Both individual and group-based token economies have been shown effective with individuals with ADHD (e.g., Reitman, Murphy, Hupp, & O'Callaghan, 2004). However, several factors may influence the effectiveness of token economies including whether tokens are established as conditioned reinforcers, the schedule of token delivery and exchange, and the availability of effective backup reinforcers.

As noted previously, self-management procedures have been used to remediate behavioral correlates of ADHD, including on-task behavior (e.g., Freeman & Dexter-Mazza, 2004; Gureasko-Moore, Dupaul, & White, 2006; Posavac, Sheridan, & Posavac, 1999). Self-management programs may be effective because they may make the participant more aware of his or her behavior via self-monitoring. They also allow the participant to select goals and deliver reinforcers for meeting specific criteria.

Summary

A behavior analytic approach to the assessment and treatment of ADHD involves the identification and manipulation of environmental variables affecting behavior. Numerous studies have shown that the core symptoms of ADHD can be ameliorated using procedures to strengthen appropriate alternative responses (e.g., engaging in on-task behavior, tolerating delays in access to preferred activities) and minimizing reinforcement of off-task or other inappropriate behavior. The most effective behavioral interventions use an individualized approach to identify environmental correlates of the target behaviors as well as effective reinforcers for these individuals.

Medication Use for the Treatment of ADHD

Medications are the most commonly used intervention strategies for ADHD (Purdie, Hattie, & Carroll, 2002). Several studies have described the efficacy of medication for the treatment of ADHD. For several decades, stimulant medications have been the most commonly prescribed treatment option (Barkley, 1998; Purdie et al., 2002); however, in recent years, new nonstimulant medications have been approved for use in the treatment of ADHD.

Stimulant Medications

Stimulant medications have been used to treat what is now referred to as ADHD since the 1930s (Bradley, 1937). Stimulants are considered to be the first-line agents in the treatment of ADHD (Pelham, 1993; Subcommittee on Attention-Deficit/Hyperactivity Disorder, Steering Committee on Quality Improvement and Management, 2011). This class of medication exerts its effects by increasing the amount of dopamine in certain areas of the brain (e.g., by increasing dopamine levels and/or blocking dopamine reuptake).

The most commonly used stimulants are methylphenidate and amphetamine compounds (and their derivatives). Methylphenidate comes in a number of different forms, including short-acting compounds (e.g., Ritalin®, Methylin®, and Metadate®) and long-acting preparations (e.g., Ritalin-LA® and Concerta®). Common forms of amphetamine include dextroamphetamine (e.g., Dexedrine®) and mixed amphetamine salts (e.g., Adderall®). Amphetamine compounds also have long-acting preparations (e.g., Adderall XR®).

A fairly robust literature has emerged demonstrating the efficacy of stimulant medications for the treatment of ADHD. Stimulants are generally well tolerated and have been shown to be effective for reducing disruptive behavior and hyperactivity (for a review, see Swanson et al., 1993). Previous studies have also shown that stimulants can be effective for increasing focus and on-task behavior in individuals with ADHD (Prasad et al., 2013; Swanson et al., 1993). In a study by Kelley, Fisher, Lomas, and Sanders (2006), the authors found that Adderall (amphetamine), shifted responding from disruptive behavior to appropriate responding even when both responses were reinforced.

While generally well-tolerated, stimulants do have notable side effects. Common side effects include decreased appetite, sleep disturbances, and nervousness (Klorman, Brumaghim, Fitzpatrick, & Borgstedt, 1990). In rare cases, psychosis or mania may be observed (Mosholder, Gelperin, Hammad, Phelan, & Johann-Liang, 2009). In addition, some studies have suggested that social behavior may be adversely affected by stimulant medication in high doses for some individuals (LaRue et al., 2008).

It is interesting to note that there is a relative paucity of literature to suggest that stimulants produce long-term benefits for individuals with ADHD (Hazell, 2011). These findings may not be surprising given that stimulant medications alone are not associated with improvements in academic or social skills (Pelham, Wheeler, & Chronis, 1998). In fact, some researchers have suggested that stimulants may be used as a "crutch" when implemented in the short term, which results in postponing nonpharmacological interventions that may more effectively address social and academic deficits (Purdie et al., 2002).

Nonstimulant Medications

In recent decades, nonstimulant compounds have emerged for the treatment of ADHD (Wigal, 2009). Approved classes of nonstimulant medications for ADHD include norepinephrine reuptake inhibitors (atomoxetine) and alpha-2 adrenergic agonists (e.g., clonidine, guanfacine).

Atomoxetine is a nonstimulant medication commonly used for treatment ADHD. Atomoxetine exerts its effects by increasing norepinephrine in the brain by blocking its reuptake. Research has shown that atomoxetine is effective for reducing the core symptoms for ADHD (Garnock-Jones & Keating, 2009; Newcorn, Sutton, Weiss, & Sumner, 2009). As with stimulants, atomoxetine is generally well tolerated, but may produce a range of side effects including headaches, drowsiness, gastrointestinal discomfort, and decreased appetite.

Alpha-2 adrenergic agonists are another nonstimulant option for treating ADHD. These medications have traditionally been used to treat hypertension. However, both clonidine (e.g., Catapres, Kapvay) and guanfacine (e.g., Tenex, Intuniv) have some evidence suggesting that they may be effective for treating the core symptoms of ADHD (Sallee, Kollins, & Wigal, 2012; Scahill, 2009). Common side effects for alpha-2 adrenergic agonists include headaches, sleepiness, and sedation.

In summary, medication is the most commonly utilized intervention for the treatment of ADHD. Historically, stimulant medications have been the most commonly used and most effective class of drugs for ADHD treatment; however, in recent years viable nonstimulant medications have also been shown to be effective at reducing ADHD symptoms.

TREATMENT EVALUATION

Any time a treatment for ADHD is implemented, whether behavioral or pharmacological in nature, the results of the intervention should be critically evaluated to determine their effectiveness. By evaluating the interventions, practitioners can determine what works and what does not, which can enhance effectiveness and ultimately lead to less complicated interventions.

While such evaluative procedures are fairly common with behavioral interventions, ongoing systematic evaluation is somewhat less common for medical interventions. In practice, the evaluation of behavioral treatments tends to be somewhat simpler (e.g., you can ask staff to start or stop implementing a behavior plan). However, the evaluation of pharmacological treatments may require coordination with staff and medical professionals, thereby making systematic monitoring more difficult. As a result, pharmacological treatments are often not systematically evaluated. The end result is that pharmacological treatments are evaluated using indirect measures (e.g., asking a parent or teacher how well a medication is working). While this information can be useful for identifying treatment effects (or noneffects), these reports are often unreliable and subject to bias (Fisher, Piazza, Bowman, & Amari, 1996; Northup, 2000; Northup, George, Jones, Broussard, & Vollmer, 1996; Umbreit, 1996). This state of affairs highlights the importance of objective treatment evaluation procedures for nonbehavioral treatments.

Treatment Evaluation Procedures

When evaluating treatment effects, direct measures can provide objective information about the occurrence of a target behavior. Observational procedures can be of particular use given that they limit bias when evaluating the effectiveness of treatments. Some particularly useful direct observation strategies include: observation/data collection, reinforcer assessments, and functional analyses.

Direct observation/data collection. Direct observation is a particularly useful tool for evaluating the effectiveness of interventions. Observation is generally superior to indirect measures in that it limits bias in the evaluation of treatment effects. When planning a direct observation, the first step is to identify the most relevant variables to be measured (Cooper, Heron, & Heward, 2007). This step will likely require a discussion with both parents and medical professionals to prioritize treatment goals. Direct observation should target at least three general areas: core/associated features, adaptive behavior, and side effects.

(1) Core symptoms and associated features: Primary observation targets for ADHD should include measures of the core symptoms. Measures of impulsivity or hyperactivity might include out-of-seat behavior, calling out, or disruptive/maladaptive behavior (e.g., verbal or physical aggression). Measures of inattentiveness may include off-task behavior (not oriented to tasks), a lack of persistence (only capable of working

for brief periods of time), or being disorganized. Associated features for ADHD may include social deficits or academic problems. Practitioners may choose to include measures of academic performance (e.g., scores on math worksheets, performance during fluency sprints) or measurement of social behavior during unstructured periods (e.g., lunch or recess) to help evaluate the effectiveness of intervention strategies.

(2)   Adaptive behavior: Parents and practitioners should also monitor adaptive behavior during direct observation. These behaviors include those that the individual *should be doing* as an alternative to the core symptoms (e.g., raising their hand instead of calling out, remaining in their seat during class, appropriate social interactions, number of minutes playing appropriately at recess). When treatment is evaluated, the goal should be to increase (or at least not decrease) adaptive responding.

(3)   Side effects: Side effects should also be measured during any intervention evaluation. Side effects are likely to vary depending on a number of factors, such as the kind of intervention used (e.g., stimulants vs. nonstimulants). Systematic evaluation of side effects can provide valuable information to parents and prescribing physicians and can inform dosage titration.

Arranging the Observation

After determining the variables to measure, practitioners should establish procedures for conducting behavioral observations. In some cases, it may be beneficial to arrange controlled observations, in which the behavior is monitored in the same setting repeatedly, to reduce variability resulting from different activities at different points during the observation. For example, Gulley and Northup (1997) used brief academic probes (e.g., math worksheets) for observation activities to ensure each observation session was directly comparable to another. When evaluating medication effects, practitioners may want to test at a specific time of the day (or at a specific time in relation to medication dose). By controlling the time of observation, practitioners can reduce variability produced by varying concentrations of the medication in the blood stream.

Practitioners can then conduct observations at different dosages/stages of treatment. For example, data could be collected while the student is off the medication (baseline) and when they are on the medication (treatment). It is important to note that any changes to the independent variable (i.e., medication dose) should be done under the supervision of medical professionals.

If possible, it is ideal to evaluate medication effective via the use of a double-blind placebo controlled evaluation, where neither the student/individual nor the data collector knows the medication condition. At a minimum, data collectors should not know what the dose condition is. Such procedures reduce the risk of observer bias and reactivity during data collection.

AB Designs

AB designs are a useful strategy for evaluating treatment effects. The "A" condition usually refers to the baseline (prior to intervention), and the "B" condition usually refers to the treatment. In using an AB design, practitioners can compare the treatment effects to a period of time before the treatment was started. Under ideal circumstances, the baseline data (prior to treatment) are stable.

Figure 10.1 depicts a *positive clinical effect* using an AB design. During baseline, the rates of maladaptive behavior (e.g., calling out) remain high. When treatment is implemented, rates of disruptive behavior decrease while appropriate behavior remains high. This type of effect is desirable because the maladaptive behavior decreases while adaptive responding is relatively unaffected.

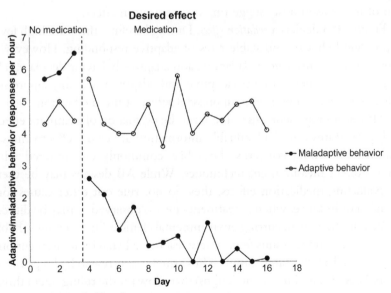

Figure 10.1 Desired effect for treatment.

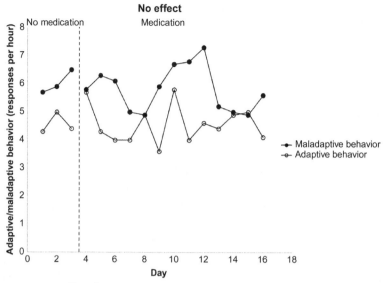

Figure 10.2 No effect for treatment.

Figure 10.2 depicts a *noneffect* for an intervention. During baseline, rates of disruptive behavior and adaptive behavior are fairly stable. With the implementation of treatment (medication), the rates do not change as a function of medication dose, suggesting no medication effect.

Figure 10.3 depicts a *sedation effect*. During baseline, there are high levels of problem behavior and stable rates of adaptive responding. However, as intervention begins, *both* maladaptive and adaptive behavior decrease. This suggests that all behavior (maladaptive and adaptive) is being suppressed, indicating a general behavior suppressant effect of the medication.

AB designs represent a useful tool for the evaluation of treatment effects. Such procedures can yield valuable information about the effectiveness of treatment, lessening concerns about bias commonly encountered when using indirect measurement techniques. While AB designs may be useful for evaluating medication effects, they do not rule out other causes for a change. For instance, when a treatment effect is observed, it may be difficult to rule out other co-occurring environmental changes/intervening variables that may explain the results (e.g., a new teacher, a behavioral intervention is implemented at the same time). Thus, single case research designs (e.g., reversal designs, multielement designs) that allow for the ruling out of threats to internal validity are preferred over AB design.

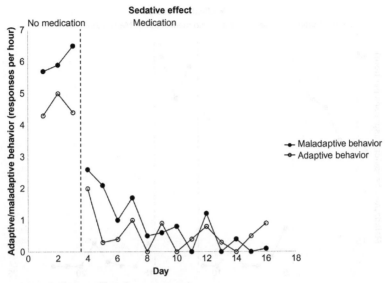

Figure 10.3 Sedative effect for treatment.

Reversal Designs

Reversal designs are particularly useful for the evaluation of medication effects because they provide additional information about the effectiveness of treatment. Reversal designs share the same advantages as AB designs but also include a withdrawal of treatment to verify treatment effects and a re-implementation of the treatment to replicate the treatment results (an ABAB reversal design; Kazdin, 2011), thus controlling for extraneous variables that might impact the results (i.e., threats to internal validity). In Figure 10.4, an example reversal design is shown. Rates of maladaptive behavior are high during baseline (no medication) and decrease when medication begins. High rates of maladaptive behavior return when the treatment is briefly withdrawn. The low rates are then replicated when treatment is reimplemented.

Reversal designs are valuable tools for practitioners because they provide a greater degree of control than that of AB designs. The degree of control provided by reversal designs allows for more confidence that observed treatment effects are the result of the treatment and not some other extraneous variables.

Multielement Designs

Multielement designs involve the rapid alternation of conditions to quickly determine the presence of treatment effects (Kazdin, 2011). Multielement

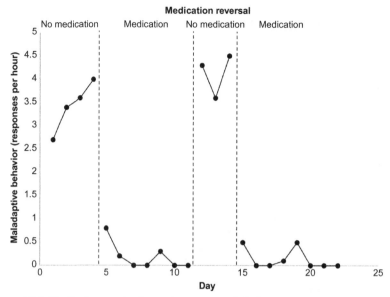

Figure 10.4 Medication evaluation using a reversal design.

designs may be particularly useful for the evaluation of fast-acting medications (as many stimulant medications are). When evaluating fast-acting medications, dose level could change day-to-day to allow for rapid treatment evaluation. Figures 10.5 and 10.6 show an evaluation of medication effects using a multielement design. In Figure 10.5, the rates of disruptive behavior are displayed. Both the low and high doses decrease the rate of disruptive behavior relative to the placebo dose.

In Figure 10.6, the levels of social interaction are depicted. The graph shows that social interaction remains fairly high in the placebo and low dose conditions. However, social interaction is considerably lower in the high dose condition, suggesting a general suppressant/sedative effect. The results from this graph suggest that the low dose of medication may be the most appropriate.

Multielement designs are another useful strategy for evaluating treatment effects. As with reversal designs, they control for extraneous factors that may contribute to treatment effects. However, the utility of multielement designs is largely limited to the class of medication used. These designs are only useful for fast acting medications, such as stimulants like methylphenidate, that can be eliminated from the body within a short period of time to prevent carryover effects from one condition to the next.

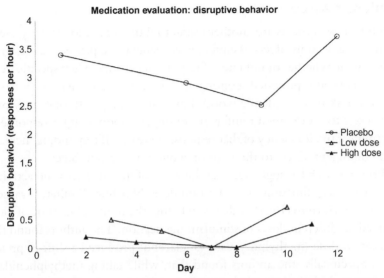

Figure 10.5 Medication evaluation of disruptive behavior using a multielement design.

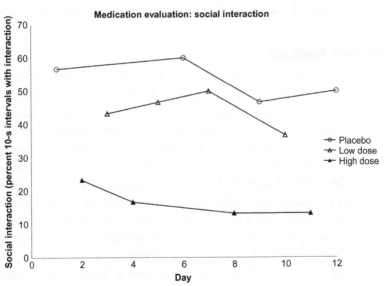

Figure 10.6 Medication evaluation of adaptive behavior using a multielement design.

Reinforcer Assessments

Reinforcer assessments are another useful tool that practitioners may use to evaluate medication effects. Reinforcer assessments are procedures designed to determine whether or not rates of responding change when specific items or activities are provided contingent upon the completion of some response/task (e.g., academic work). For example, a practitioner may provide access to a presumed reinforcer contingent upon a target response to determine if the frequency of that response increases. If responding increases with contingent access to the item or activity, it is a reinforcer.

Prior research has suggested that the value of specific items and activities may change as a function of medication dose. Northup, Fusilier, Swanson, Roane, and Borrero (1997) evaluated whether the reinforcing value of items changed on different doses of stimulant medication. The authors found that medication dose (methylphenidate vs. placebo) produced a shift in preferences. Specifically, the authors found that, while taking methylphenidate, preferences shifted from edible reinforcers (e.g., candy) to activity-based reinforcers (e.g., using a computer) for several students.

LaRue et al. (2008) conducted a similar study comparing preference for social and nonsocial reinforcers while on varying doses of stimulant medication. The authors found that student preference for social activities varied as a function of medication dose. One student, in particular, displayed a decrease in the value of social reinforcers while on a high dose of stimulant medication.

Functional Analyses

To gain a better understanding of how medications affect motivation, practitioners have used functional analyses to evaluate medication effects. Functional analyses are assessment techniques that involve the manipulation of environmental antecedents and consequences to determine the causal factors for maladaptive behavior (Iwata et al., 1994). Several studies have suggested that specific environmental variables may be influenced by medication dose (Dicesare, McAdam, Toner, & Varrell, 2005; Northup, Jones, et al., 1997).

Northup, Jones, et al. (1997) evaluated drug–behavior interaction effects in an 8-year-old with ADHD. In the investigation, the authors conducted a functional analysis of teacher attention, peer attention, and time out (i.e., escape) on and off methylphenidate. The results indicated that the target behavior was maintained by peer attention during the placebo condition; however, the target behavior was suppressed during functional analysis conditions in which the student was taking methylphenidate.

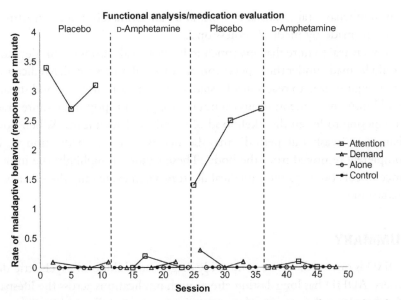

Figure 10.7 Medication evaluation of maladaptive behavior using a functional analysis.

In a similar study, Dicesare et al. (2005) conducted a functional analysis for an 18-year-old male with ADHD and moderate mental cognitive delay while on and off methylphenidate. Consistent with previous findings, the authors found that disruptive behavior only occurred while the individual was taking the placebo dose. The target behavior did not occur while taking methylphenidate, suggesting a value-altering effect for social attention.

An example functional analysis used to evaluate medication effects is shown in Figure 10.7. In the first 12 sessions of the functional analysis, the individual was receiving a placebo (no medication). The attention condition was clearly differentiated from control during this phase. In the second phase, functional analysis conditions were conducted while the individual was taking D-amphetamine. Very little problem behavior was observed in this phase. The attention function was verified in the next phase (placebo). In the final phase with D-amphetamine, very little problem behavior was observed. These findings suggest that D-amphetamine may decrease the value of social attention as a reinforcer for problem behavior.

Understanding the manner in which nonbehavioral treatments impact environmental contingencies represents a useful strategy for practitioners when evaluating interventions. Such strategies may provide insight into how nonbehavioral treatments work and can ultimately inform treatment decisions made by medical professionals.

It is critical to note that any time medication evaluations occur, decisions should be made under the supervision of a medical professional. Medications often require time to reach steady-state concentrations in the blood stream. In addition, many medications cannot be stopped abruptly and require gradual tapering to lessen the likelihood of withdrawal symptoms. When doses change, a "wash out period" may be necessary for a medication to be completely removed from the body. These factors all highlight the importance of collaborating with medical doctors when evaluating the efficacy of medication.

SUMMARY

ADHD is one of the most commonly diagnosed childhood psychiatric disorders. ADHD has long-lasting effects with implications across the lifespan. The disorder is characterized by inattentiveness (e.g., difficulty remaining on task, a lack of attending skills, disorganization) and hyperactivity (e.g., an inability to sit still, impulsive behavior). Literature has shown that ADHD is a complex disorder that may result from a number of different factors.

As practitioners have gained a better understanding of ADHD, the diagnostic process has evolved. Several diagnostic instruments have been developed to accurately diagnose the disorder. Some of the most commonly used assessment instruments include the Conners 3, the CBCL, the Vanderbilt ADHD Diagnostic Parent and Teacher Scales, and the ADHD Rating Scale-IV.

A substantial literature has developed related to the treatment ADHD. These intervention approaches have primarily included behavioral interventions and pharmacological interventions. Behavior analytic approaches to the assessment and treatment of ADHD have involved operationalizing the core behavioral features of the disorder (i.e., impulsivity, hyperactivity, and inattentiveness), identifying environmental causes of the behavior (antecedents and consequences), and developing function-based treatments. A substantial literature exists supporting this approach to intervention.

Medications are often the first-line intervention used for the treatment of ADHD. Stimulant medications, such as methylphenidate and amphetamine are, by far, the most commonly used drugs to treat ADHD, and a voluminous literature exists validating their effectiveness for the suppression of problem behavior (e.g., Brown et al., 2005; Swanson et al., 1993). In recent years, some nonstimulant medications (e.g., atomoxetine, guanfacine, and clonidine) have emerged as treatment for ADHD symptoms.

As with any intervention, treatment effects should be evaluated systematically and objectively. To the extent that it is possible, measures should be taken to ensure that behavioral or medical interventions are having the desired effects. Direct observation may be the easiest strategy to determine if an intervention is having its desired effect. The use of AB, reversal, and multielement designs can provide valuable information about treatment effects. Reinforcer assessments and functional analyses are also tools that have been shown to be sensitive to medication effects that can yield useful clinical information.

To effectively treat ADHD, parents and practitioners are faced with a number of challenges. The literature is clear that behavioral intervention can be effective for the treatment of ADHD and should be the logical starting point prior to moving to more intrusive interventions. However, effectiveness can be compromised by the response effort required to implement behavioral interventions with adequate integrity. These interventions can be labor intensive and require a considerable amount of resources.

These factors often lead to the treatment of ADHD with medication. The empirical literature has shown that, in some cases, the use of medication may be required to see significant clinical benefits (MTA Cooperative Group, 1999). However, while the literature regarding the short-term effectiveness is robust, the long-term benefits are less clear (e.g., Hazell, 2011). While this observation is somewhat disturbing, it is the logical outcome of flawed reasoning regarding the nature of ADHD. Medications are extremely useful for suppressing problem behavior. Medications do not provide individuals with skills not previously possessed. Medications do not teach important academic skills or provide social skills to individuals with ADHD. If medication is used as a "crutch" in the absence of behavioral interventions, it is likely that the deficits that existed prior to medication would still exist after medication has stopped.

This highlights the importance of a combined approach when using medication. Several studies have investigated the combined use of medication and behavioral intervention (e.g., Blum, Mauk, McComas, & Mace, 1996; Gulley et al., 2003; Kayser et al., 1997). By using treatment evaluation strategies like the ones described above, valuable information can be conveyed to medical professionals. In fact, the combination of behavioral intervention and medication may allow for lower doses of medication and/or stopping medication entirely.

As practitioners generally attempt to use the least restrictive intervention that is effective, they may consider starting with nonintrusive behavioral interventions implemented in home and school settings. In the event that behavioral interventions alone are not successful, medication may be added to the treatment regimen. When medication is added to a treatment package, it should not occur at the exclusion of behavioral intervention. Medications can suppress problem behavior to allow important behavioral interventions to be implemented (e.g., teaching students important functional academics, social skills training). The combination of both behavioral and medical interventions can lead to the best possible outcomes for this clinical population. With the systematic evaluation of behavioral and medical interventions, parents and professionals can make informed decisions about treatment and ultimately improve outcomes for individuals with ADHD.

REFERENCES

Achenbach, T. M., & Edelbrock, C. (1991). *The child behavior checklist.* Burlington, VT: University Associates in Psychiatry.

Ainslie, G. W. (1974). Impulse control in pigeons. *Journal of the Experimental Analysis of Behavior, 21*(3), 485–489.

American Psychiatric Association. (2013). *Diagnostic and statistical manual of mental disorders* (5th). Arlington, VA: American Psychiatric Publishing.

Anderson, C. M., English, C. L., & Hedrick, T. M. (2006). Use of the structured descriptive assessment with typically developing children. *Behavior Modification, 30,* 352–378.

Athens, E. S., & Vollmer, T. R. (2010). An investigation of differential reinforcement of alternative behavior without extinction. *Journal of Applied Behavior Analysis, 43,* 569–589.

Azrin, N. H., Ehle, C. T., & Beaumont, A. L. (2006). Physical exercise as a reinforcer to promote calmness of an ADHD child. *Behavior Modification, 30,* 564–570.

Banerjee, T. D., Middleton, F., & Faraone, S. V. (2007). Environmental risk factors for attention-deficit hyperactivity disorder. *Acta Paediatrica, 96*(9), 1269–1274.

Barkley, R. A. (1998). *Attention-deficit hyperactivity disorder: A handbook for diagnosis and treatment* (2nd). New York: Guilford Press.

Barkley, R. A., Fisher, R., Edelbrock, C. S., & Smallish, L. (1990). The adolescent outcome of hyperactive children diagnosed by research criteria: 1. An 8-year prospective follow-up study. *Journal of the American Academy of Child and Adolescent Psychiatry, 29,* 546–557.

Beavers, G. A., Iwata, B. A., & Lerman, D. C. (2013). Thirty years of research on the functional analysis of problem behavior. *Journal of Applied Behavior Analysis, 46*(1), 1–21.

Bhutta, A. T., Cleves, M. A., & Casey, P. H. (2002). Cognitive and behavioral outcomes of school-aged children who were born pre-term: A meta-analysis. *Journal of the American Medical Association, 288,* 728–737.

Bicard, D. F., & Neef, N. A. (2002). Effects of strategic versus tactical instructions on adaptation to changing contingencies in children with ADHD. *Journal of Applied Behavior Analysis, 35,* 375–389.

Biederman, J., Wilens, T. E., Mick, E., Faraone, S. V., & Spencer, T. (1998). Does attention-deficit hyperactivity disorder impact the developmental course of drug and alcohol abuse and dependence? *Biological Psychiatry, 44*(4), 269–273.

Binder, L. M., Dixon, M. R., & Ghezzi, P. M. (2000). A procedure to teach self-control to children with attention deficit hyperactivity disorder. *Journal of Applied Behavior Analysis, 33,* 233–237.

Blum, N. J., Mauk, J. E., McComas, J. J., & Mace, F. C. (1996). Separate and combined effects of methylphenidate and a behavioral intervention on disruptive behavior in children with mental retardation. *Journal of Applied Behavior Analysis, 29*(3), 305–319.

Boyajian, A. E., DuPaul, G. J., Handler, M. W., Eckert, T. L., & McGoey, K. E. (2001). The use of classroom-based brief functional analyses with preschoolers at-risk for attention deficit hyperactivity disorder. *School Psychology Review, 30,* 278–291.

Bradley, C. (1937). The behaviour of children receiving benzedrine. *American Journal of Psychiatry, 94,* 577–585.

Broussard, C. D., & Northup, J. (1995). An approach to functional assessment and analysis of disruptive behavior in regular education classrooms. *School Psychology Quarterly, 10,* 151–164.

Broussard, C. D., & Northup, J. (1997). The use of functional analysis to develop peer interventions for disruptive classroom behavior. *School Psychology Quarterly, 12,* 65–76.

Brown, R. T., Amler, R. W., Freeman, W. S., Perrin, J. M., Stein, M. T., Feldman, H. M., et al. (2005). Treatment of attention-deficit/hyperactivity disorder: Overview of the evidence. *Pediatrics, 115,* e749–e757.

Carlson, E. A., Jacobvitz, D., & Sroufe, L. A. (1995). A developmental investigation of inattentiveness and hyperactivity. *Child Development, 66*(1), 37–54.

Colvert, E., Rutter, M., Kreppner, J., Beckett, C., Castle, J., Groothues, C., et al. (2008). Do theory of mind and executive function deficits underlie the adverse outcomes associated with profound early deprivation?: Findings from the English and Romanian adoptees study. *Journal of Abnormal Child Psychology, 36*(7), 1057–1068.

Conners, C. K. (2008). *The Conners 3rd edition (Conners 3).* North Tonawanda, NJ: Multi-Health System.

Cook, A., Bradley-Johnson, S., & Johnson, C. M. (2014). Effects of white noise on off-task behavior and academic responding for children with ADHD. *Journal of Applied Behavior Analysis, 47,* 160–164.

Cooper, J. O., Heron, T. E., & Heward, W. L. (2007). *Applied behavior analysis* (2nd). Upper Saddle River, NJ: Pearson.

Dicesare, A., McAdam, D. B., Toner, A., & Varrell, J. (2005). The effects of methylphenidate on a functional analysis of disruptive behavior: A replication and extension. *Journal of Applied Behavior Analysis, 38*(1), 125–128.

Dixon, M. R., Hayes, L. J., Binder, L. M., Manthey, S., Sigman, C., & Zdanowski, D. M. (1998). Using a self-control training procedure to increase appropriate behavior. *Journal of Applied Behavior Analysis, 31,* 203–210.

Dixon, M. R., & Tibbetts, P. A. (2009). The effects of choice on self-control. *Journal of Applied Behavior Analysis, 42,* 243–252.

Dunlap, G., dePerczel, M., Clarke, S., Wilson, D., Wright, S., White, R., et al. (1994). Choice making to promote adaptive behavior for students with emotional and behavioral challenges. *Journal of Applied Behavior Analysis, 27,* 505–518.

DuPaul, G. J., McGoey, K. E., Eckert, T. L., & VanBrakle, J. (2001). Preschool children with attention-deficit/hyperactivity disorder: Impairments in behavioral, social, and school functioning. *Journal of the American Academy of Child and Adolescent Psychiatry, 40*(5), 508–515.

DuPaul, G. J., Power, T. J., Anastopoulos, A. D., & Reid, R. (1998). *ADHD Rating Scale-IV: Checklists, norms, and clinical interpretation.* New York: Guilford Press.

DuPaul, G. J., & Stoner, G. (1994). *ADHD in the schools: Assessment and intervention strategies.* New York: Guilford Press.

Ervin, R. A., DuPaul, G. J., Kern, L., & Friman, P. C. (1998). Classroom-based functional and adjunctive assessments: Proactive approaches to intervention selection for adolescents with attention deficit hyperactivity disorder. *Journal of Applied Behavior Analysis*, *31*, 65–78.

Ervin, R. A., Kern, L., Clarke, S., DuPaul, G. J., Dunlap, G., & Friman, P. C. (2000). Evaluating assessment-based intervention strategies for students with ADHD and comorbid disorders within the natural classroom context. *Behavioral Disorders*, *25*, 344–358.

Fabiano, G. A., Pelham, W. E., Jr., Manos, M. J., Gnagy, E. M., Chronis, A. M., Onyango, A. N., et al. (2004). An evaluation of three time-out procedures for children with attention-deficit/hyperactivity disorder. *Behavior Therapy*, *35*, 449–469.

Faraone, S. V., Perlis, R. H., Doyle, A. E., Smoller, J. W., Goralnick, J. J., Holmgren, M. A., et al. (2005). Molecular genetics of attention-deficit/hyperactivity disorder. *Biological Psychiatry*, *57*(11), 1313–1323.

Fisher, W. W., Piazza, C. C., Bowman, L. G., & Amari, A. (1996). Integrating caregiver report with systematic choice assessment to enhance reinforcer identification. *American Journal of Mental Retardation*, *101*(1), 15–25.

Flood, W. A., & Wilder, D. A. (2002). Antecedent assessment and assessment-based treatment of off-task behavior in a child diagnosed with attention deficit-hyperactivity disorder (ADHD). *Education and Treatment of Children*, *25*, 331–338.

Flood, W. A., Wilder, D. A., Flood, A. L., & Masuda, A. (2002). Peer mediated reinforcement plus prompting as treatment for off-task behavior in children with attention deficit hyperactivity disorder. *Journal of Applied Behavior Analysis*, *35*, 199–204.

Freeman, K. A., & Dexter-Mazza, E. T. (2004). Using self-monitoring with an adolescent with disruptive classroom behavior: Preliminary analysis of the role of adult feedback. *Behavior Modification*, *28*, 402–419.

Garnock-Jones, K. P., & Keating, G. M. (2009). Atomoxetine: A review of its use in attention-deficit hyperactivity disorder in children and adolescents. *Pediatric Drugs*, *11*(3), 203–226.

Grauvogel-MacAleese, A. N., & Wallace, M. D. (2010). Use of peer-mediated intervention in children with attention deficit hyperactivity disorder. *Journal of Applied Behavior Analysis*, *43*, 547–551.

Gulley, V., & Northup, J. (1997). Comprehensive school-based assessment of the effects of methylphenidate. *Journal of Applied Behavior Analysis*, *30*, 627–638.

Gulley, V., Northup, J., Hupp, S., Spera, S., Levelle, J., & Ridgway, A. (2003). Sequential evaluation of behavioral treatments and methylphenidate dosage for children with attention deficit hyperactivity disorder. *Journal of Applied Behavior Analysis*, *36*, 375–378.

Gureasko-Moore, S., Dupaul, G. J., & White, G. P. (2006). The effects of self-management in general education classrooms on the organizational skills of adolescents with ADHD. *Behavior Modification*, *30*, 159–183.

Hagopian, L. P., Contrucci-Kuhn, S. A., Long, E. S., & Rush, K. S. (2005). Schedule thinning following communication training: Using competing stimuli to enhance tolerance to decrements in reinforcer density. *Journal of Applied Behavior Analysis*, *38*, 177–193.

Harpin, V. A. (2005). The effect of ADHD on the life of an individual, their family, and community from preschool to adult life. *Archives of Disease in Childhood*, *90*(Suppl. 1), i2–i7.

Hawkins, R. O., & Axelrod, M. I. (2008). Increasing the on-task homework behavior of youth with behavior disorders using functional behavioral assessment. *Behavior Modification*, *32*, 840–859.

Hazell, P. (2011). The challenges to demonstrating long-term effects of psychostimulant treatment for attention-deficit/hyperactivity disorder. *Current Opinion in Psychiatry*, *24*(4), 286–290.

Hoerger, M. L., & Mace, F. C. (2006). A computerized test of self-control predicts classroom behavior. *Journal of Applied Behavior Analysis, 39*, 147–159.

Howe, D. (2010). ADHD and its comorbidity: An example of gene–environment interaction and its implications for child and family social work. *Child and Family Social Work, 15*(3), 265–275.

Iwata, B. A., Dorsey, M. F., Slifer, K. J., Bauman, K. E., & Richman, G. S. (1994). Toward a functional analysis of self-injury. *Journal of Applied Behavior Analysis, 27*, 197–209.

Jensen, P. S., Hinshaw, S. P., Swanson, J. M., Greenhill, L. L., Conners, C. K., Arnold, L. E., et al. (2001). Findings from the NIMH Multimodal Treatment Study of ADHD (MTA): Implications and applications for primary care providers. *Journal of Developmental and Behavioral Pediatrics, 22*(1), 60–73.

Johnston, C., & Mash, E. J. (2001). Families of children with attention–deficit/hyperactivity disorder: Review and recommendations for future research. *Clinical Child and Family Psychology Review, 4*(3), 183–207.

Jones, K. M., Drew, H. A., & Weber, N. L. (2000). Noncontingent peer attention as treatment for disruptive classroom behavior. *Journal of Applied Behavior Analysis, 33*, 343–346.

Kayser, K. H., Wacker, D. P., Derby, K. M., Andelman, M. S., Golonka, Z., & Stoner, E. A. (1997). A rapid method for evaluating the necessity for both a behavioral intervention and methylphenidate. *Journal of Applied Behavior Analysis, 30*, 177–180.

Kazdin, A. E. (2011). *Single-case research designs: Methods for clinical and applied settings.* New York, NY/Boston, MA: Oxford University Press/Allyn & Bacon.

Kelley, M. E., Fisher, W. W., Lomas, J. E., & Sanders, R. Q. (2006). Some effects of stimulant medication on response allocation: A double-blind analysis. *Journal of Applied Behavior Analysis, 39*, 243–247.

Kern, L., Mantegna, M. E., Vorndran, C. M., Bailin, D., & Hilt, A. (2001). Choice of task sequence to reduce problem behaviors. *Journal of Positive Behavior Interventions, 3*, 3–10.

Kessler, R., Adler, L., Barkley, R., Biederman, J., Conners, C., Demler, O., et al. (2006). The prevalence and correlates of adult ADHD in the United States: Results from the National Comorbidity Survey Replication. *American Journal of Psychiatry, 163*(4), 716–723.

Klorman, R., Brumaghim, J. T., Fitzpatrick, P. A., & Borgstedt, A. D. (1990). Clinical effects of controlled trial of methylphenidate on adolescents with attention deficit disorder. *Journal of the American Academy of Child and Adolescent Psychiatry, 29*, 702–709.

Kodak, T., Grow, L., & Northup, J. (2004). Functional analysis and treatment of elopement for a child with attention deficit hyperactivity disorder. *Journal of Applied Behavior Analysis, 37*, 229–232.

Kreppner, J. M., O'Connor, T. G., & Rutter, M. (2001). Can inattention/overactivity be an institutional deprivation syndrome? *Journal of Abnormal Child Psychology, 29*(6), 513–528.

Langley, K., Rice, F., & van den Bree, M. B. (2005). Maternal smoking during pregnancy as an environmental risk factor for attention deficit hyperactivity disorder behaviour: A review. *Minerva Pediatrica, 57*, 359–371.

LaRue, R. H., Northup, J., Baumeister, A. A., Hawkins, M. F., Williams, T., & Seale, L. (2008). An evaluation of the effects of stimulant medication on the reinforcing efficacy of play. *Journal of Applied Behavior Analysis, 41*, 143–147.

Levy, F., McStephen, M., & Hay, D. A. (2001). The diagnostic genetics of ADHD symptoms and subtypes. In F. Levy, & D. A. Hay (Eds.), *Attention, genes, and ADHD* (pp. 35–57). Philadelphia, PA: Taylor and Francis.

Martel, M. M., von Eye, A., & Nigg, J. (2012). Developmental differences in structure of attention–deficit/hyperactivity disorder (ADHD) between childhood and adulthood. *International Journal of Behavioral Development, 36*(4), 279–292.

Mischel, H. N., Ebbesen, E. B., & Zeiss, A. R. (1972). Cognitive and attentional mechanisms in delay of gratification. *Journal of Personality and Social Psychology, 16*, 204–218.

Molina, B. S. G., & Pelham, W. E. (2003). Childhood predictors of adolescent substance use in a longitudinal study of children with ADHD. *Journal of Abnormal Psychology, 112*, 497–507.

Mosholder, A. D., Gelperin, K., Hammad, T. A., Phelan, K., & Johann-Liang, R. (2009). Hallucinations and other psychotic symptoms associated with the use of attention-deficit/hyperactivity disorder drugs in children. *Pediatrics, 123*(2), 611–616.

MTA Cooperative Group. (1999). 14 month randomized clinical trial of treatment strategies for children with attention deficit hyperactivity disorder. *Archives of General Psychiatry, 56*, 1073–1086.

Neef, N. A., Bicard, D. F., & Endo, S. (2001). Assessment of impulsivity and the development of self-control in students with attention deficit hyperactivity disorder. *Journal of Applied Behavior Analysis, 34*, 397–408.

Neef, N. A., Marckel, J., Ferreri, S. J., Bicard, D. F., Endo, S., Aman, M. G., et al. (2005). Behavioral assessment of impulsivity: A comparison of children with and without attention deficit hyperactivity disorder. *Journal of Applied Behavior Analysis, 38*, 23–37.

Newcorn, J. H., Sutton, V. K., Weiss, M. D., & Sumner, C. R. (2009). Clinical responses to atomoxetine in attention-deficit/hyperactivity disorder: The Integrated Data Exploratory Analysis (IDEA) study. *Journal of the American Academy of Child and Adolescent Psychiatry, 48*(5), 511–518.

Northup, J. (2000). Further evaluation of the accuracy of reinforcer surveys: A systematic replication. *Journal of Applied Behavior Analysis, 33*, 335–338.

Northup, J., Broussard, C., Jones, K., George, T., Vollmer, T. R., & Herring, M. (1995). The differential effects of teacher and peer attention on the disruptive classroom behavior of three children with a diagnosis of attention deficit hyperactivity disorder. *Journal of Applied Behavior Analysis, 28*, 227–228.

Northup, J., Fusilier, I., Swanson, V., Huete, J., Bruce, T., Freeland, J., et al. (1999). Further analysis of the separate and interactive effects of methylphenidate and common classroom contingencies. *Journal of Applied Behavior Analysis, 32*, 35–50.

Northup, J., Fusilier, I., Swanson, V., Roane, H., & Borrero, J. (1997). An evaluation of methylphenidate as a potential establishing operation for some common classroom reinforcers. *Journal of Applied Behavior Analysis, 30*(4), 615–625.

Northup, J., George, T., Jones, K., Broussard, C., & Vollmer, T. (1996). A comparison of reinforcer assessment methods: The utility of verbal and pictorial choice procedures. *Journal of Applied Behavior Analysis, 29*, 201–212.

Northup, J., Jones, K., Broussard, C., DiGiovanni, G., Herring, M., Fusilier, I., et al. (1997). A preliminary analysis of interactive effects between common classroom contingencies and methylphenidate. *Journal of Applied Behavior Analysis, 30*, 121–125.

Pelham, W. (1993). Pharmacotherapy for children with attention deficit hyperactivity disorder. *School Psychology Review, 22*, 199–227.

Pelham, W. E., Wheeler, T., & Chronis, A. (1998). Empirically supported psycho-social treatments for attention deficit hyperactivity disorder. *Journal of Clinical Child Psychology, 27*, 190–205.

Pliszka, S. (2007). Practice parameter for the assessment and treatment of children and adolescents with attention-deficit/hyperactivity disorder. *Journal of the American Academy of Child and Adolescent Psychiatry, 46*(7), 894–921.

Posavac, H. D., Sheridan, S. M., & Posavac, S. S. (1999). A cueing procedure to control impulsivity in children with attention deficit hyperactivity disorder. *Behavior Modification, 23*, 234–253.

Powell, S., & Nelson, B. (1997). Effects of choosing academic assignments on a student with attention deficit hyperactivity disorder. *Journal of Applied Behavior Analysis, 30*, 181–183.

Prasad, V., Brogan, E., Mulvaney, C., Grainge, M., Stanton, W., & Sayal, K. (2013). How effective are drug treatments for children with ADHD at improving on-task behaviour and academic achievement in the school classroom? A systematic review and meta-analysis. *European Child & Adolescent Psychiatry, 22*(4), 203–216.

Purdie, N., Hattie, J., & Carroll, A. (2002). A review of the research on interventions for attention deficit hyperactivity disorder: What works best? *Review of Educational Research, 72*, 61–99.

Rachlin, H., & Green, L. (1972). Commitment, choice, and self-control. *Journal of the Experimental Analysis of Behavior, 17*, 15–22.

Reitman, D., Murphy, M. A., Hupp, S. D., & O'Callaghan, P. M. (2004). Behavior change and perceptions of change: Evaluating the effectiveness of a token economy. *Child and Family Behavior Therapy, 26*, 17–36.

Romaniuk, C., Miltenberger, R., Conyers, C., Jenner, N., Jurgens, M., & Ringenberg, C. (2002). The influence of activity choice on problem behaviors maintained by escape versus attention. *Journal of Applied Behavior Analysis, 35*, 349–362.

Sallee, F. R., Kollins, S. H., & Wigal, T. L. (2012). Efficacy of guanfacine extended release in the treatment of combined and inattentive only subtypes of attention-deficit/hyperactivity disorder. *Journal of Child and Adolescent Psychopharmacology, 22*(3), 206–214.

Scahill, L. (2009). Alpha-2 adrenergic agonists in children with inattention, hyperactivity and impulsiveness. *CNS Drugs, 23*(Suppl. 1), 43–49.

Schweitzer, J. B., & Sulzer-Azaroff, B. (1988). Self-control: Teaching tolerance for delay in impulsive children. *Journal of the Experimental Analysis of Behavior, 50*, 173–186.

Soderlund, G., Sikstrom, S., & Smart, A. (2007). Listen to the noise: Noise is beneficial for cognitive performance in ADHD. *Journal of Child Psychology and Psychiatry, 48*, 840–847.

Sonuga-Barke, E. J. S., Taylor, E., Sembi, S., & Smith, J. (1992). Hyperactivity and delay aversion: I. The effects of delay on choice. *Journal of Child Psychology and Psychiatry, 33*, 387–398.

Stahr, B., Cushing, D., Lane, K., & Fox, J. (2006). Efficacy of a function-based intervention in decreasing off-task behavior exhibited by a student with ADHD. *Journal of Positive Behavior Interventions, 8*, 201–211.

Subcommittee on Attention-Deficit/Hyperactivity Disorder, Steering Committee on Quality Improvement and Management. (2011). ADHD: Clinical practice guideline for the diagnosis, evaluation, and treatment of attention-deficit/hyperactivity disorder in children and adolescents. *Pediatrics, 128*, 1007–1022.

Swanson, J. M., McBurnett, K., Wigal, T., Pfiffner, L. J., Lerner, M. A., Williams, L., et al. (1993). Effect of stimulant medication on children with attention deficit disorder: A "Review of Reviews". *Exceptional Children, 60*, 154–162.

Umbreit, J. (1995). Functional assessment and intervention in a regular classroom setting for the disruptive behavior of a student with attention deficit hyperactivity disorder. *Behavioral Disorders, 20*, 267–278.

Umbreit, J. (1996). Functional analysis of disruptive behavior in an inclusive classroom. *Journal of Early Intervention, 20*(1), 18–29.

Vollmer, T. R., Borrero, J. C., Lalli, J. S., & Daniel, D. (1999). Evaluating self-control and impulsivity in children with severe behavior disorders. *Journal of Applied Behavior Analysis, 32*, 451–466.

Wigal, S. B. (2009). Efficacy and safety limitations of attention-deficit hyperactivity disorder pharmacotherapy in children and adults. *CNS Drugs, 23*(Suppl. 1), 21–31.

Willcutt, E. G. (2012). The prevalence of DSM-IV attention-deficit/hyperactivity disorder: A meta-analytic review. *Neurotherapeutics*, *9*, 490–499.

Wolraich, M. L., Lambert, E. W., Baumgaertel, A., Garcia-Tornel, S., Feurer, I. D., Bickman, L., et al. (2003). Teachers' screening for attention deficit/hyperactivity disorder: Comparing multinational samples on teacher ratings of ADHD. *Journal of Abnormal Child Psychology*, *31*(4), 445–455.

Wolraich, M. L., Lambert, W., Doffing, M. A., Bickman, L., Simmons, T., & Worley, K. (2003). Psychometric properties of the Vanderbilt ADHD diagnostic parent rating scale in a referred population. *Journal of Pediatric Psychology*, *28*(8), 559–568.

CHAPTER 11

Sleep, Elimination, and Noncompliance in Children

Aurelia Ribeiro, Clare J. Liddon, Dana M. Gadaire, Michael E. Kelley
The Scott Center for Autism Treatment and Florida Institute of Technology, Melbourne, Florida, USA

SLEEP

Problem Identification

Between 25% and 35% of typically developing children (Mindell & Owens, 2003) and up to 80% of children with developmental disabilities (Patzold, Richdale, & Tonge, 1998; Richdale & Prior, 1995) experience some form of sleep disturbance. These children often demonstrate symptoms including inattention, irritability, hyperactivity, impulsivity, academic underachievement, mood disorders, and increases in aggression and self-injurious behavior (Beebe, 2011; Dewald, Meijer, Oort, Kerkhof, & Bogels, 2010; Gregory & Sadeh, 2012). Altogether, these symptoms often resemble symptoms of other common childhood disorders such as attention-deficit hyperactivity disorder and autism, leading practitioners to overlook the need for intervention to improve sleep habits. For example, when Owens (2001) asked primary care physicians to report on their screening practices, nearly half of respondents reported that they did not routinely screen for sleep disturbances beyond the toddler years. This finding is surprising given that more than 90% of these same physicians rated the impact of sleep problems on academic performance as being either "important" or "very important." Owens also found that the majority of physicians reported limited confidence in their ability to screen for and treat sleep disturbance, especially in older children. Thus, primary care physicians admittedly do not screen for or treat sleep disturbance at a level commensurate with the value they ascribe to sleep (c.f. Owens). Research by Meltzer, Courtney, Crosette, Ramos, and Mindell (2010) also revealed discrepancies in the screening and diagnostic practices of primary care professionals related to sleep. These researchers conducted electronic reviews of primary care records indicating that, contrary to epidemiological studies, only 3.7% of patients received formal ICD-9 diagnoses related to sleep.

Clinical and Organizational Applications of Applied Behavior Analysis
http://dx.doi.org/10.1016/B978-0-12-420249-8.00011-3

The authors concluded that these data indicated that sleep disorders are under-diagnosed, especially in school-age children and adolescents.

Given the incidence and impact of disturbed and inadequate sleep in children's development, assessment and treatment of such a problem may be of great value. For instance, Gruber, Cassoff, Frenette, Wiebe, and Carrier (2012) randomly assigned participants (ages 7–11 years) to conditions of sleep extension (one added hour of sleep per night) or sleep restriction (one fewer hour of sleep per night). The primary dependent variable was the *teacher-rated daytime functioning of participants* on the Conners' Global Index-Teachers (CGI-T, 3rd ed.; Conners, 1997), which is a tool to score behavior in school. The teacher, unaware of the participants' sleep status (i.e., sleep extension or sleep restriction), completed the CGI-T at the end of both baseline and experimental conditions. Based on the CGI-T scores, children in the extended sleep condition exhibited statistically significant improvements in emotional and behavioral performances as well as decreased sleepiness, whereas the opposite effects were observed for children in the sleep restriction condition.

Assessment of Common Problems Associated with Sleep

Several screening methods exist for sleep disturbance. One commonly used and efficacious method of screening for sleep disturbance in primary care settings involves the use of the "BEARS" Screening Tool (Owens & Witmans, 2004). "BEARS" is an acronym that covers five major sleep domains: **B**edtime problems, **E**xcessive daytime sleepiness, **A**wakening during the night, **R**egularity and duration of sleep, and **S**noring. According to the medical record reviews conducted by Owens and Datzell (2005), simple inquiry regarding these five areas may result in two- to fourfold increases in the number of sleep issues discussed as well as references to sleep issues in treatment plans.

In addition to brief screening regarding a child's sleep patterns, practitioners may ask caregivers to complete a sleep log (see Figure 11.1) to gather observational data regarding a child's nightly sleep patterns. Sleep logs can be adapted based on the prior screening to assess areas that are believed to be potential targets for intervention (e.g., naps, bedtime), whether the child falls asleep independently or requires an adult presence, frequency of night waking, total sleep time, location of sleep (i.e., in own bed or in parents' bed), and ratio of time in bed to time asleep. For example, according to the sleep log depicted in Figure 11.1, the child slept for around 2 h before getting out of bed

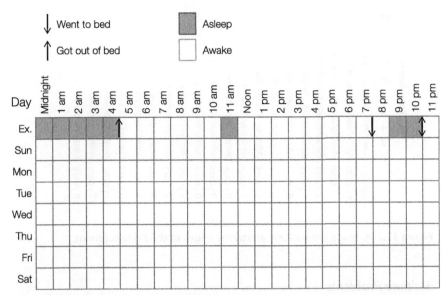

Figure 11.1 Sample sleep log. The sleep log above includes arrows (↓, ↑), respectively, indicating when the child was put to bed and when he or she arose. Shaded boxes indicate the times in which the child was observed or believed to be sleeping.

(at 11 pm) and immediately being escorted back to bed. Then, he remained awake for another hour. The child was then reported to fall asleep at approximately midnight and remained asleep until 5 am. The log also indicates a nap was taken (in a location other than his own bed given the absence of arrows) between 11 am and 12 pm. The sleep log can also be useful in determining whether a child's total sleep time is commensurate with developmentally appropriate sleep needs, as depicted in Figure 11.2.

Treatment of Common Sleep Disturbances

Based on the results of screening questions and parent-completed sleep logs, clinicians may identify sleep disturbances that fall into one or more of the categories described earlier, such as bedtime problems (i.e., sleep onset disorders), poor regularity of sleep or insufficient duration of sleep (i.e., sleep schedule disorders), frequent nighttime arousals (i.e., nightmares, night terrors, difficulty returning to sleep upon waking), and physiological concerns (e.g., snoring associated with sleep apnea), which may all contribute to excessive daytime sleepiness.

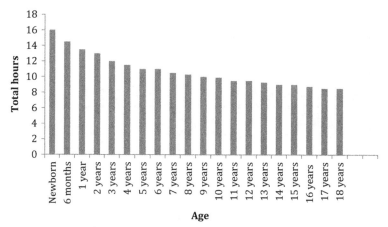

Figure 11.2 Average sleep needs at various stages in child development.

Bedtime Problems

Bedtime problems are at the core of various behavioral sleep disturbances, which is why many interventions focus on increasing sleep-compatible behavior at onset of the bedtime routine. Attending to physiological factors associated with sleep can mitigate many bedtime problems. Specifically, children, like any other mammal, are more likely to feel tired and fall asleep in reasonably dark, quiet surroundings (Figueiro, Bierman, Plitnick, & Rea, 2009). Furthermore, restricting afternoon naps, caffeinated beverages, sugar, and electronics prior to bedtime can also increase physiological preparedness for sleep. Ensuring that children receive adequate exercise during the day can also facilitate increased tiredness, provided the sleep schedule is consistent and children are not highly active in the hours immediately prior to bedtime (Durand, 1998). Finally, bedtime-fading procedures involve delaying bedtime (while keeping wake-up time constant) to increase the likelihood that the child will fall asleep more readily. Typically, the initial bedtime is based on the average time at which the child tends to fall asleep naturally and fading is based on the latency to sleep onset for the previous night (Piazza & Fisher, 1991).

Bedtime problems may also arise due to skill and/or motivational deficits that require additional behavioral supports. Specifically, *Behavioral Insomnia—Sleep Onset Association Type* (American Academy of Sleep Medicine, 2005) is often associated with faulty stimulus control over sleep-compatible behaviors. In other words, the bedtime environment contains insufficient cues signaling the availability of automatic reinforcement for sleep-compatible behavior and the withdrawal of reinforcement for behaviors incompatible with sleep. To improve stimulus control, consistent bedtime routines should be established in which caregivers participate in the early components of a behavioral chain (e.g., bath time, reading books, singing songs) after which children are expected to complete the final component (falling asleep) independently. Although parents are often advised to establish independent sleep onset at an early age (i.e., leaving their children in bed drowsy but still awake), many parents develop the habit of helping their babies to fall asleep at bedtime by rocking, feeding, holding, or having their baby on their own bed (Mindell & Owens, 2010). This approach may be further reinforced (in the short run) if children fall asleep faster in the presence of their caregivers.

When the child's dependence on his or her caregivers becomes problematic, parental attempts to disrupt firmly established patterns may lead to significant behavioral resistance. In such cases, extinction-based procedures may be necessary to train independent sleep onset by disrupting the contingency between a child's distress signals and adult attention and/or escape. Such procedures can be implemented aggressively (e.g., complete withdrawal of parental attention once the child is placed in bed) or modified to reduce child distress (e.g., graduated extinction, "excuse-me drill"). Because extinction may result in a temporary increase in negative behaviors, clinicians should educate parents about this possible effect and provide support during implementation of such an intervention (Vriend, Corkum, Moon, & Smith, 2011). In addition, clinicians should educate parents regarding sleep and sleep associations (i.e., stimulus control), the functions of bedtime resistance behaviors (e.g., attention, escape), and the establishment of consistent bedtime routines with contingencies that favor compliant behavior.

When implementing unmodified extinction, parents are instructed to ignore all attempts to access adult attention and/or escape from the designated sleep environment. If the child attempts to leave his or her bedroom, he or she should be gently guided back to bed with no additional communication or physical attention provided. Although this procedure is often highly effective, it may be associated with significant escalations in problem behavior (Rickert & Johnson, 1988). Thus, modifications might include parental checks on the child at standard (i.e., time-based) intervals. Parents may also choose to gradually increase the interval of time between these checks and/or gradually decrease the length of time spent in the room upon returning (see Ferber, 2006; Reid, Walter, & O'Leary, 1999). These modifications may decrease child resistance and increase treatment integrity. However, the possibility remains that bedtime resistance will inadvertently be strengthened if the child consistently receives parental attention contiguous with increasingly intense resistance behaviors. To address this concern, Kuhn (2007) developed the "excuse-me drill" whereby high rates of noncontingent parental attention are gradually faded to minimize child resistance. This intervention requires the caregiver to determine an interval of time whereby the child will tolerate the caregiver's absence without signaling distress. In some cases, this interval may be a matter of seconds whereby the caregiver places the child in his or her crib and then immediately retrieves the child before he or she begins to cry. For older children, caregivers may say something like "*Excuse me, I need to go . . . [insert reason]. . . but I will be right back to check on you.*" The key is to reduce opportunities for child resistance by providing high rates of attention on a noncontingent basis. Thus, it is critical that the caregiver's departure be carefully planned prior to implementation to insure that the parent will be able to return before the child has the opportunity to engage in resistance behaviors. Once an interval is determined whereby the caregiver can leave the child briefly in the absence of problem behavior, this interval can gradually be increased until the caregiver is spending longer periods outside the child's bedroom, and the child is likely to fall asleep independently. Of course, it is imperative that parents remain vigilant in returning to the child's room at specified intervals rather than attempting to thin the schedule of attention too rapidly and re-establishing contingency between the child's distress signals and the parent's return.

In addition to overt distress signals, older children may learn to "stall" or postpone bedtime by engaging in disruptive behaviors, refusing to go to, or stay in, bed, repeatedly seeking adult assistance and/or tangible items (e.g., hugs, songs, drinks). *Behavioral Insomnia—Parent Limit Setting Type* (American Academy of Sleep Medicine, 2005) describes sleep disturbances in which children are capable of falling asleep independently (and may do so under certain conditions), but frequently engage in sleep-incompatible behaviors associated with gaining access to environmental reinforcers. In order to disrupt the relation between sleep-incompatible behaviors and access to functional reinforcers, Friman et al. (1999) combined escape extinction with differential reinforcement of alternative behavior in a procedure known as the "bedtime pass." Children were given the opportunity to exchange a "bedtime pass" for a brief trip out of the bedroom (e.g., to give an extra hug, use the bathroom, obtain a drink). Once this pass was surrendered, all subsequent attempts to leave the room or access parental attention were ignored. Friman et al. found this intervention to be associated with significant decreases in bedtime resistance and, interestingly, high levels of "self-control" whereby children saved the pass to exchange in the morning for access to a tangible reinforcer.

More recently, Moore, Friman, Fruzzetti, and MacAleese (2007) employed a group design to assess the long-term effects of the bedtime pass. Children who received the bedtime pass intervention called and cried out significantly less (than in baseline and compared to children in the control condition), and extinction bursts were avoided in all participants who received the treatment. Further, these researchers reported that fewer than 10% of children in the treatment group continued to leave their rooms at 3-month follow up compared to 56% of children who did not receive the treatment.

Excessive Daytime Sleepiness
Excessive daytime sleepiness may be indicated if the child continues to nap past the pre-school years, frequently falls asleep in the car or locations other than the bed, and/or displays general symptoms of fatigue including irritability, sluggishness, hyperactivity, and forgetfulness (Heussler, 2005). Excessive sleepiness may be associated with insufficient time in bed (e.g., late or inconsistent bedtimes, limited naps). Daytime sleepiness also takes into account that some children need more sleep than others or may be obtaining poor quality sleep. Thus, even in the absence of nighttime behavioral concerns, excessive daytime sleepiness may be indicative of physiological sleep disruptions (e.g., sleep apnea) that may warrant medical evaluation (Mindell & Owens, 2010).

Awakening During the Night
Awakening during the night is a normal part of the sleep cycle, and all children (and adults) experience multiple partial arousals every night (Mindell & Owens, 2010). As mentioned previously, children who learn positive sleep associations will typically transition back to sleep independently. For example, children who are taught to fall asleep when they are tired, in a dimly lit room, holding a special stuffed animal, will re-experience these same conditions upon arousal and have little difficulty falling back to sleep. However, nighttime arousals that lead to extended periods of wakefulness and/or require parental presence may indicate that these associations are not well established. For example, a child who sleeps in the same playpen where

he/she actively engages with toys during the day will have difficulty discriminating whether it is time to play or sleep in that setting. Alternatively, children who have learned to fall asleep only when being rocked or lying alongside a caregiver will have difficulty re-establishing sleep in the caregiver's absence (Meltzer, 2010). Thus, frequent nighttime awakenings are typically addressed by fostering independent sleep onset (see Bedtime Problems listed earlier). Also, the extinction-based procedures described above for addressing bedtime problems may also be used throughout the night to address nighttime awakenings.

Regularity and Duration of Sleep

Understanding the regularity and duration of sleep can also help to elucidate how inconsistent sleep routines may be contributing to sleep difficulties. Physiologically, our bodies are programmed to respond to light signals (circadian rhythms) and to become drowsy when we have been awake for extended periods of time (homeostatic sleep drive; Kong et al., 2002). When sleep schedules are inconsistent, children may experience a mismatch between environmental and biological cues. In other words, variable daytime demands interfere with the body's ability to establish a regular sleep-wake cycle. In such cases, environmental demands may need to be adjusted (e.g., reducing extracurricular activities) to accommodate a more consistent and developmentally appropriate sleep schedule.

Children may also benefit from strategies to increase biological preparedness for sleep such as restricting daytime sleep, maintaining consistent (early) wake times (especially on weekends), and bedtime fading procedures. Such procedures can be combined with a response cost component (Piazza & Fisher, 1991) in which children who do not fall asleep within 15 min of their already delayed bedtime are taken out of bed and restricted from returning to bed for 1 h. The inclusion of such a response cost component is hypothesized to strengthen the association between the sleep setting and rapid sleep onset as well as punishing sleep-incompatible behavior (especially as it contributes to an increased biological drive to go to sleep).

Finally, in relation to sleep schedule disorders in older children, it is important to identify daytime stressors that may contribute to sleep resistance (Ferber, 2006). For example, children who are experiencing difficulties at school may stay up late to functionally postpone their return to that aversive environment. In this case, intervention strategies may include reassurance, calming bedtime routines, and cognitive-behavioral therapy (Ferber, 2006). Alternatively, children may stay up late in order to access extra time watching television. Indeed, Owens et al. (1999) found that television-viewing habits such as bedtime television viewing and amount of television viewing daily may be associated with at least one sleep disturbance in children 4- to 10-years old. In this sense, parental monitoring may be critical to addressing motivational issues behind disruptive sleep schedules.

Snoring

Finally, screening for snoring is imperative given its association with physiological concerns such as sleep apnea, a condition whereby respiration is interrupted for anywhere from 10 s to several minutes. Risk factors for sleep apnea include enlarged tonsils, adenoids, or other anatomical obstructions (commonly seen in children with Down syndrome) as well as childhood obesity (Marcus et al., 2012; Schroeder & Gordon, 2002). If children exhibit these risk factors in combination with excessive daytime sleepiness, mouth breathing, and/or morning headaches/vomiting, referral should be made to a medical professional for further evaluation.

Other signs that may indicate a medical condition include: sudden, complete or partial loss of control of muscles; vivid, dreamlike experiences while falling asleep (hallucinations); frequent, repetitive leg or foot movements (i.e., extending the big toe, and flexing the ankle, knee, or hip); and feelings of unpleasant "creeping or crawling" sensations in the legs. Certain parasomnias including night terrors and nightmares are also more common at certain stages in child development and may remit on their own or respond to increased total sleep time (Mindell & Owens, 2010).

Practical Considerations

Parents often report extreme distress on account of their children's nighttime difficulties, and treatment integrity failures are typically the greatest obstacle to addressing these difficulties (Chu & Richdale, 2009; Mindell, Kuhn, Lewin, Meltzer, & Sadeh, 2006). First, caregivers who are sleep deprived are less likely to follow through on effortful treatment recommendations (Durand, 1998). Also, parents may be hesitant to follow through on recommendation that appear to exacerbate their child's nighttime distress because they fear that allowing their children to "cry-it-out" even in a controlled manner will result in lasting psychological trauma (Mindell, 1999).

To investigate this hypothesis, Price, Wake, Ukoumunne, and Hiscock (2012) followed parent-child dyads that received either extinction-based behavioral interventions or no programmed intervention. These researchers found no main differences in terms of parent- or child-reported emotional well-being, behavior problems, or parent-child attachment at 5 year follow-up. In response to similar sleep interventions, Mindell and Owens (2010) found significant positive outcomes related to parents' and children's emotional well-being.

The only adverse outcome that has been demonstrated involves the inconsistent application of extinction-based treatments (Higley & Dozier, 2009), which may be more likely to occur when parents are not adequately trained or prepared to implement behavioral protocols with reasonable fidelity. Research by Moore et al. (2007) suggests a strong association between the severity of extinction bursts exhibited by children and parental treatment integrity failures. Thus, parents should be informed that, despite the likelihood of initial escalation of problem behavior as a result of extinction, this procedure has been empirically demonstrated as one of the most effective when consistently implemented (Morgenthaler et al., 2006). Alternatively, some modifications may be incorporated into treatment to increase parents' acceptance, such as parental presence in the child's room at bedtime during extinction and graduated extinction (Morgenthaler et al., 2006), to the extent that such modifications are empirically supported. Finally, guidance should also be provided as to appropriate time lines by which they should expect improvement. Further, it is advisable that parents carefully select a night to begin treatment in which they are rested and have the social and emotional support necessary to ensure proper follow-through. In order to support parents through this process, practitioners should always be cognizant of potential barriers to effective treatment implementation and individualize treatment programs accordingly.

ELIMINATION

Elimination is the behavior of interest during toilet training. Toilet training can be a challenging task for caregivers, independent of the functioning level and age of the child. When individuals lack independent toileting skills, they may be at risk for quality of life impairments. In this section, we review common problems associated with toilet training, and some procedures to help treat such issues.

Common Behavior Problems Associated with Elimination

The two major problems associated with elimination in children include enuresis and encopresis (American Psychiatric Association, 2013). Enuresis is defined as the repeated release of urine outside of the toilet (incontinence), such as into bedding and clothing (Paredes, 2004). Enuresis may be common among children under 5 years of age due to insufficient production of hormones responsible for decreasing urine production. However, with each year of maturity, this problem is expected to decrease (Thiedke, 2003). Indeed, approximately 15% of cases of nocturnal enuresis remit spontaneously every year beyond the age of five (Tu & Baskin, 2014). According to the Diagnostic and Statistical Manual of Mental Disorders, 5th ed. (DSM-5), the incidence of enuresis among 5-year-old children is 5-10%.

The other major elimination problem in children over 4 years of age, encopresis, is defined by the repeated release of feces into inappropriate places (American Psychiatric Association, 2013). This problem is estimated to affect approximately 1% of 5-year-old children. Some of the complications associated with urinary and bowel incontinences include constipation and urinary tract infection. In addition, elimination problems may affect the child's interaction with others and may result in problem behavior such as aggression, property disruption, and noncompliance. For instance, the child may avoid interaction with other children due to fear of having their problem discovered and, as a result, being teased (Butler, 2004).

Given the negative impact produced by both enuresis and encopresis, treatments aimed at developing independent toileting are of primary importance. Various published studies state that children need to master two major goals to independently toilet: recognize the sensation signaling, a need for elimination and mastery of the entire behavior chain involved in toileting (e.g., removing clothing, elimination in toilet, cleaning oneself, redressing, flushing, and hand washing; Lott & Kroeger, 2004; Taras & Matese, 1990). Research suggests that there are multiple avenues for practitioners to take to address these prerequisites. In the following section, we will present the common treatments to attain these goals.

Common Treatments for Successful Elimination

Effective treatments for elimination problems may be more likely if caregivers are better informed about developmental and motivational issues that might be involved and how to address the problem. Unfortunately, many caregivers seem to lack this information. For example, between one-third and one-fourth of parents respond to their child's bedwetting with the use of punishment, which may adversely affect the child's mental health as well as the parent-child relationship (Shelov et al., 1981). On the contrary, physicians may lean on medication as a first line treatment for nighttime enuresis despite significant side effect profiles and high relapse rates when the medications are discontinued (Thiedke, 2003).

Thus, before selecting a treatment to address elimination problems, caregivers should take into consideration the child's age. For instance, for children below 5 years of age, treatment may consist of simply providing parents psychoeducation to ensure parental expectations are in line with the child's developmental status and instructions on how to respond to inappropriate elimination (Pachter & Dowrkin, 1997).

Besides maturational factors, caregivers may need to evaluate whether the child's elimination problem is the result of another biological problem. For example, urinary infection may result in the child avoiding using the toilet, which may, in turn, result in involuntary voiding. As another example, encopresis may be the result of the so-called "functional" megacolon, which leads to rectal insensitivity. In such cases, the child is unable to feel when bowel movements occur, which puts her at risk for encopresis (Issenman, Filmer, & Gorski, 1999). Thus, when considering treatments for elimination problems in these cases, caregivers may start by addressing those biological setting events.

Though listed separately below, it is common for elimination treatments to be used in conjunction with one another, rather than independently. The combination of treatment strategies is demonstrated in the classic Azrin and Foxx (1989) "Toilet Training in a Day" and many successfully published protocols that followed it (see Averink, Melein, & Duker, 2005; Cicero & Pfadt, 2002; Duker, Averink, & Melein, 2001; LeBlanc, Carr, Crossett, Bennett, & Detweiler, 2005; Taras & Matese, 1990 for examples).

Graduated Guidance

Graduated guidance is a procedure typically used to teach skills that involve several responses sequentially arranged to form a more complex skill (e.g., brushing teeth, toileting). This procedure involves the use of the least intrusive, yet effective, prompt needed to produce each response in the chain (e.g., undressing, voiding, redressing, flushing, washing hands). The prompting hierarchies are graduated in the level of required assistance and may include verbal, gestural, model, and physical prompts (Kroeger & Sorensen-Burnworth, 2009). According to Neitzel and Wolery (2009), successful implementation of graduated guidance requires efficient decisions about when to apply and fade the prompts.

An example of graduated guidance to teach independent toileting may be found in the seminal toilet training article by Azrin and Foxx (1971). In this study, a rapid toilet training (RTT) method was implemented with nine adults with profound intellectual disability and included reinforcement for appropriate elimination, reprimands and time-out from positive reinforcement contingent on inappropriate elimination, and graduated guidance for dressing (i.e., pulling pants down, then pulling pants up) and flushing the toilet bowl after elimination. In addition, edibles and praise were provided for the completion of each step in the dressing sequence until consistent performance was observed, at which point reinforcers were provided exclusively for elimination in the bowl. Results of this study demonstrated decreases in incontinence to near-zero levels.

Reinforcement-Based Treatments

Both positive and negative reinforcements have been cited in the literature as useful components of successful toilet training. Positive reinforcement may be used to reinforce eliminating on the toilet by presenting a preferred stimulus immediately following appropriate elimination. Response restriction (Averink et al., 2005) has been used as a form of negative reinforcement to encourage successful elimination. During this procedure, the child is restricted to a very small area around the toilet, limiting all competing actions (e.g., standing up, stereotypic movements, falling to the ground). Only after successful elimination, or a predetermined amount of time has passed, he or she is allowed to move away from the restricted area.

Scheduled Toilet Sits and Elimination Schedules

Scheduled toilet sits include sitting the child on the toilet for a set amount of time at predetermined intervals (Boles, Roberts, & Vernberg, 2008). Most often, if a void occurs during a scheduled sit, a combination of positive and negative reinforcement is used to reinforce elimination (e.g., the child is given a preferred edible and is allowed to leave the toileting area). The predetermined intervals at which the child sits on the toilet may be chosen arbitrarily, or using elimination schedules. Elimination schedules involve the identification of a child's pattern of voiding. This includes identifying how often and at what times of the day the child eliminates. When scheduled sits are based on the elimination schedules, the child may have the benefit of a more individualized treatment, with a focus on the most effective times to intervene.

In the case of nocturnal enuresis, the child is awakened at scheduled intervals, based on his or her pattern of nighttime voiding. For example, caregivers may schedule awakenings to occur 30 min to an hour before the child is likely to experience incontinence, thus avoiding multiple awakenings at night. Caregivers may rely on cues such as the child awakening and requesting parental assistance to identify patterns in the child's nighttime incontinence. If the child is wearing pull-ups or other protective undergarments that wick moisture away from the body, he or she may not notice and/or alert parents to episodes of incontinence. Thus, the first step to identifying patterns in nighttime wetting is often to transition from diapers/pull-ups to cotton underpants (that result in increased discomfort and leakage). This transition typically increases the frequency with which the child awakens and alerts parents of the episode. Of course, caregivers are often resistant to making this transition (i.e., committing to greater sleep disruption) prior to their child achieving consistent overnight continence. However, therapists can emphasize the monetary savings of cotton underpants as well as the temporary nature of the nighttime disruption. That is, when caregivers can consistently predict when their child will experience incontinence, they can intervene to prevent such occurrences.

Hydration

Hydration involves providing unlimited access to high preference liquids to children during elimination training to increase the number of available opportunities for urinary elimination. When safely monitored, hydration is effective for increasing urinary opportunities. However, there are risks associated with excessive liquid intake. When given in inappropriate quantities, liquids can cause an imbalance in electrolytes. Therefore, liquids given should never exceed the appropriate body weight proportion. Additionally, hydration should not be used for any child with a medical condition resulting in urinary retention (National Kidney & Urologic Diseases Information Clearinghouse, 2014).

Punishment

Punishment involves the presentation or the removal of a stimulus following a response, resulting in a decrease in the future frequency of the response (Skinner, 1953). Though used less often in current training models, there are common punishment procedures used during elimination training. Verbal reprimands often are used as corrective feedback following an inappropriate elimination (e.g., "*No more wet pants. Pee-pee goes in the potty*"). Overcorrection (Foxx & Azrin, 1973) is most frequently used in two forms: positive practice and restitution. During positive practice, the child may be walked from the spot of the inappropriate elimination to the toilet a specific number of times, in order to "practice" appropriate toileting. During restitution, the child must restore the environment back to its original, or an improved state, following an accident. Responses may include cleaning themselves and any soiled objects.

Urine Alarm

Urine alarms are devices used to alert children that elimination has occurred. The alarm is connected to a small clip-on sensor that is strategically placed in the child's undergarments. When the sensor detects moisture, an alarm sounds. Evidence suggests that the efficacy of the urine alarm is a result of negative reinforcement, and eventually avoidance behavior (Mellon, Scott, Haynes, Schmidt, & Houts, 1997; Thiedke, 2003). That is, the child learns to attend to aversive sensory signals (the sound emitted by the urine alarm) such that avoidance responses (e.g., bladder contraction) are evoked. Once the child is capable of contracting in response to the alarm (until he or she can successfully finish voiding in the toilet), parents can begin fading the urine alarm by lowering the volume and/or disconnecting the sensor altogether.

Urine alarms can be used similarly to address daytime and nighttime enuresis. However, parents are often concerned about using alarms that emit loud, jarring noises to signal wetness in the middle of the night. Fortunately, many companies have begun making alarms that emit lower volume voice signals (e.g., "time to go potty") that may be less startling for sleeping children. In addition to training children to awaken independently, Taneli et al. (2004) found that overnight urine alarm usage increased bladder storage capacity, through pre-post measures.

Manipulation of Stimulus Control

Though the above treatments have been shown in the literature to be successful, some children still may be resistant to appropriate elimination. When this occurs, practitioners should look to other avenues of elimination training. One such avenue is through the manipulation of stimulus control. This technique includes manipulating the discriminative stimuli involved in the child's current, inappropriate elimination routine, and transferring stimulus control to the appropriate stimuli and contexts. For example, Luiselli (1996, 1997) demonstrated a manipulation of stimulus control for a child who engaged in elimination exclusively in a diaper. In this study, experimenters gradually moved the diaper towards the toilet, eventually fading the diaper out completely.

Regardless of the treatment approach, caregivers should be advised to increase their child's motivation to maintain continence through the use of effective contingencies (Issenman et al., 1999). For example, caregivers may provide access to preferred tangibles, leisure activities (playing a special game with a parent) in the morning based on the child meeting specific criteria (e.g., voiding in the toilet bowl in the middle of the night). Caregivers may also be advised to incorporate-related behaviors (e.g., bedtime behavior) into existing token economy systems to encourage compliance. However, it is critical that caregivers appreciate that continence may be affected by both maturational and motivational factors. Thus, caregivers should be advised to base reinforcement on specific behaviors (e.g., going to the bathroom in the middle of the night, wearing urine alarm, rather than for maintaining continence throughout the night). In this way, children are more likely to receive access to reinforcing consequences, and caregivers are encouraged to focus on the child's effort as opposed to restricting privileges or punishing failures.

NONCOMPLIANCE

In general, noncompliance, or disobedience, is defined by failure to obey laws, rules, or demands. The term noncompliance may not be appropriate from a behavioral perspective, as it does not specify a behavior, but rather the absence of it. Nonetheless, the term noncompliance is frequently used in behavior analysis to describe the behavior of an individual who consistently fails to comply with instructions from caregivers, teachers, or other authority figures within a specified period of time (Kalb & Loeber, 2003). When considering children, the exact definition of noncompliance may vary to reflect the child's skill level, the type of task involved, and how long after the instruction the child is expected to engage in the response and complete the task. For instance, younger children may take longer to complete a two-step instruction (e.g., "pick up the book and put it on the bookshelf") compared to older children.

Noncompliance is a frequent problem among both children and adolescents, and it has been the focus of a large number of behavioral interventions (Miles & Wilder, 2009). Indeed, according to Kalb and Loeber (2003), noncompliance is observed in 65-92% of children referred to pediatric, psychiatric, and psychological services and in 10-57% of nonreferred children.

In addition to being a prevalent problem, noncompliance may have a significant impact in the child's life. For instance, noncompliance may make interactions with adults more difficult and stressful and may impact interactions with other children who are more compliant. In addition, because noncompliance entails failure to follow instructions and rules, it may also impact the child's academic progress and put the child at risk for physical injury (Kalb & Loeber, 2003).

Besides its direct effects on the child's life, persistent noncompliance may also influence behavior later in life. According to Watson and Gresham (1998), noncompliance may be among early signs observed in those who are later identified as exhibiting antisocial behavior. Antisocial behavior generally entails a recurrent failure to abide to socially acceptable behaviors, and it may be expressed as aggression, failure to follow rules, defiance of adult authority, and other terms (Watson & Gresham, 1998). Given the prevalence and potential negative impact in the individual's life, noncompliance may be considered a problem of extreme social significance and therefore should receive special attention from caregivers, researchers, and practitioners.

Noncompliance Assessment

The first step in the assessment of noncompliance is evaluating the individual's listener repertoire and ability to perform the expected action. This assessment may guide the treatment approach to decrease noncompliance and/or increase compliance (Wilder & Majdalany, 2014). For instance, if the individual's failure to comply with instructions is due to their poor listener repertoire or inadequate receptive language skills, treatment may focus on improving those skills. On the other hand, if noncompliance is due to a motivational issue, treatment may then focus on the behavioral function that noncompliance plays in the individual's life.

Assessing the behavioral function of noncompliance involves systematic manipulation of environmental variables with the purpose of identifying functional relations between these variables and noncompliance. Because noncompliance is usually observed when children are asked to terminate a preferred activity (e.g., turn off a preferred video) or initiate a nonpreferred activity such as brush their teeth (Wilder, Zonneveld, Harris, Marcus, & Reagan, 2007), functional analyses most frequently include test conditions for both positive reinforcement in the form of access to preferred stimuli and negative reinforcement in the form of escape from, or avoidance of, nonpreferred stimuli. A number of studies have included a functional analysis to assess the behavioral function for noncompliance prior to implementing an intervention (e.g., McKerchar & Abby, 2012; Wilder, Harris, Reagan, & Rasey, 2007; Wilder, Zonneveld, et al., 2007).

In one of the first studies on functional analysis of noncompliance, Wilder, Harris, et al. (2007) both identified the behavioral function of noncompliance in two typically developing children in a short period of time and successfully implemented a function-based treatment to increase compliance. Participants were exposed to two test conditions and one control condition in an alternate fashion. Each condition was presented as a trial, which consisted of a 2-min preinstruction period, the presentation of instruction, and a 3-min postinstruction period. In each session, participants were exposed to three trials, one for each condition. In the preferred activity condition, participants were instructed to turn off the high-preferred video they were watching and noncompliance resulted in continued access to the video. This condition was intended to test for maintenance by positive reinforcement. In the nonpreferred activity condition, participants were instructed to pick up papers from the floor (i.e., nonpreferred activity), and there were no programmed consequences for noncompliance. This condition was designed to test for maintenance by negative reinforcement. In the control condition, participants had access to low-preference items during the preinstruction period. Then, they were instructed to turn on the video, but there were no programmed consequences for noncompliance. The authors hypothesized noncompliance to be unlikely in this condition, as a noncompliance would result in continued access to the low-preferred items and no access to the preferred activity. For both participants, the highest levels of noncompliance were associated with the preferred activity condition compared to the other conditions, which indicated that noncompliance was maintained by continued access to preferred items.

Based on the functional analysis results, Wilder, Harris, et al. (2007) implemented a treatment that consisted of differentially reinforcing compliance with a coupon that could be exchanged for 3 min of uninterrupted access to the preferred video (e.g., three coupons would result in 9 min of access to the video). Similar to the preferred activity condition of the functional analysis, there were no programmed consequences for noncompliance (i.e., participants continued to have access to the video for the remainder of the 3-min postinstruction period). The authors found that the intervention resulted in an immediate and sustained increase in compliance to levels above 80%. This study demonstrates the feasibility and benefit of assessing the behavioral function of noncompliance.

Treatment

According to Wilder et al. (2012), interventions to increase compliance may be classified as antecedent- or consequence-based. Antecedent-based interventions include the manipulation of environmental variables that are present before the opportunity to comply. This type of intervention may include interruption of child's play before presenting the instruction, teacher's distance from the child, advance notice or warning (i.e., a warning given to the child that anticipates what she will be instructed to do within a given period of time), rationales (i.e., reasons why the child should comply with the instruction), high-probability instructional sequence (i.e., presentation of instructions with a high probability of compliance before presenting the target instruction).

Antecedent-based interventions have not been consistently effective at increasing compliance. In many cases, additional consequence components are necessary (e.g., Wilder, Nicholson, & Allison, 2010; Wilder, Zonneveld, et al., 2007). For instance, Wilder, Zonneveld, et al., (2007) first attempted to increase compliance by systematically implementing noncontingent reinforcement, a warning, and a high-probability sequence. The results suggested that for all three participants, noncontingent reinforcement and the use of the warning were each ineffective at increasing compliance. Furthermore, the high-probability sequence was effective for only one participant. For the other two participants, the authors implemented extinction, resulting in compliance.

While antecedent-based interventions have not been reliably successful in the treatment of noncompliance, consequence-based interventions have been demonstrated as an effective alternative for treatment. In this type of intervention, compliance (or noncompliance) is followed by the delivery or removal of a stimulus (Wilder et al., 2012). For example, Wilder, Allison, Nicholson, Abellon, and Saulnier (2010) increased levels of compliance by providing access to preferred edible items contingent on compliance. Other examples of consequence-based interventions include time-out from positive reinforcement (i.e., removing access to positive reinforcement for a brief period of time contingent on noncompliance) and escape extinction (i.e., contingent on noncompliance, physical guidance is provided to assist the child in completing the task).

Although most interventions for noncompliance clearly fall into one of the two previously described categories, some interventions may include aspects of both. One example of such an intervention is guided compliance, which was first described by Horner and Keilitz (1975). Typically, this procedure starts with a vocal prompt to perform an action (e.g., "Clean up your toys"). In the absence of a response (i.e., noncompliance), the caregiver models the correct response while repeating the vocal prompt. If the child does not comply with the model prompt, the caregiver repeats the vocal prompt while physically guiding the child to perform the required action. Usually, compliance is scored if the participant performs the required action after the first or second prompt (i.e., vocal and model, respectively). According to Wilder and Atwell (2006), decreased levels of noncompliance that result from guided compliance may be related to behavioral mechanisms such as escape extinction (i.e., noncompliance does not result in removal of the request, but rather the presentation of prompts until the child ultimately engages in the response) and punishment (e.g., the physical guidance may be aversive for some children). Alternatively, it is possible that the vocal and modal prompts evoke compliance because they either signal the availability of reinforcement for compliance or allows the child to avoid punishment (i.e., compliance to the vocal or model prompt avoids the physical prompt).

In a recent study on guided compliance, Wilder et al. (2012) implemented two modified versions of the procedure with four typically developing children after implementing the three-step-guided compliance. In the first modification, the two-step-guided compliance, the authors eliminated the model prompt (i.e., noncompliance to the vocal prompt within 10 s was followed by physical prompt). The authors argued that keeping the model prompt would simply prolong the time between the first vocal prompt and compliance, with consequent prolonged access to the reinforcing stimulation for noncompliance. Furthermore, the model prompt might be unnecessary for children with appropriate listener repertoires. In the second modification of the three-step guidance, besides the elimination of the model prompt, the authors reduced the time required for compliance from 10 to 5 s. This modification resulted in further reduction of the interval between the first vocal prompt and compliance. The authors found that for all four participants, the three-step-guided compliance produced elevated but variable levels of compliance. However, each modification of this procedure was effective for one participant. For the remaining two participants, differential reinforcement was necessary to increase compliance. Thus, this study demonstrated that, for some children, three-step-guided compliance might be modified to enhance treatment effects.

Because noncompliance levels vary across different ages, the goal of treatments intended to increase compliance should take into consideration compliance levels of similar-age peers. For instance, increasing compliance to 100% may not be a reasonable treatment goal. Using a standardized assessment, Stephenson and Hanley (2010) were able to measure noncompliance of 15 preschoolers in comparison to same-age peers and identify those who consistently demonstrated lower compliance levels compared to their peers. Following assessment, the authors selected for treatment four children who displayed low levels of compliance. Two of these children were exposed to two conditions in a reversal design. During baseline sessions, the teacher stood at least 1 m away from the child, did not make eye contact or interact with the child except to deliver the instruction. Then, the teacher stated the child's name, delivered the instruction (i.e., one-step instruction), and waited 6 s for a response. Compliance resulted in praise from the teacher, however, there were no programmed consequences for either noncompliance or incorrect response. The intervention consisted of sequentially adding six antecedent variables (i.e., one variable was added in each session). The antecedent variables were added in the following order: the teacher was within 0.3 m of the child; the teacher crouched next to the child; the teacher gently touched the child's shoulder; the teacher delivered 5 s of vocal attention in the form of comments; teacher attempted to make eye contact with the child; and the teacher interrupted the child's play prior to and while delivering the instruction. For both participants, manipulation of antecedent variables resulted in increased levels of compliance, especially when six elements were in place.

The remaining two participants selected for the second phase during Stephenson and Hanley (2010) were initially exposed to the same conditions previously described (i.e., baseline and additive antecedent intervention or AAI). However, because antecedent manipulation did not result in increased compliance, the authors implemented noncompliance intervention, which consisted of a three-step prompting to promote compliance to instructions. Correct responses at any prompt level were followed by descriptive praise and incorrect responses were ignored. This intervention resulted in increased compliance levels for one participant but had no effect on the other. The authors then exposed these participants to the full antecedent plus noncompliance intervention, in which both antecedent variables and consequences were in place (i.e., this condition was a combination of the two previous conditions). This package resulted in increased levels of compliance for both participants. This study demonstrated the effectiveness of antecedent-based interventions for two of the four participants. In addition, for the other two participants, the most effective intervention consisted of a combination of antecedent variables and consequences for noncompliance.

In summary, noncompliance is a problem of great impact and needs to be addressed early. Usually, treatments are designed to increase compliance and may be more effective if they are based on assessment of the functional relation between environmental variables and noncompliance. Treatment outcomes may vary according to a child's age, the difficulty level of the tasks, and other variables. However, in general, guided compliance and consequence-based interventions have been more effective in the treatment of noncompliance. These interventions may be combined to further enhance treatment outcomes.

CONCLUSION

Pediatric problems such as sleep, elimination, and noncompliance are of great concern for caregivers and physicians. In this chapter, we included a description of each of these problems and provided a variety of empirically supported interventions. Specifically, behavior analytic interventions, which focus on promoting the development of critical skills, are the most effective interventions when motivational issues are involved. However, the evaluation, treatment, and treatment outcomes may consider the interaction between biologic and behavioral factors. Thus, the collaborative work of caregivers, physicians, and behavioral health professionals may contribute to treatment success.

REFERENCES

American Academy of Sleep Medicine. (2005). *International classification of sleep disorders: Diagnostic and coding manual* (2nd). Westchester: American Academy of Sleep Medicine.

American Psychiatric Association. (2013). *Diagnostic and statistical manual of mental disorders* (5th). Arlington, VA: American Psychiatric Publishing.

Averink, K., Melein, L., & Duker, P. C. (2005). Establishing diurnal bladder control with the response restriction method: Extended study on its effectiveness. *Research in Developmental Disabilities, 26*, 143–151.

Azrin, N. H., & Foxx, R. M. (1971). A rapid method of toilet training the institutionalized retarded. *Journal of Applied Behavior Analysis, 4*, 89–99.

Azrin, N. H., & Foxx, R. M. (1989). *Toilet training in less than a day: A tested method for teaching your child quickly and happily!*. New York: Pocket Books.

Beebe, D. W. (2011). Cognitive, behavioral, and functional consequences of inadequate sleep in children and adolescents. *Pediatric Clinics of North America, 58*(3), 649–665.

Blum, N. J., & Friman, P. C. (2000). Behavioral pediatrics: The confluence of applied behavior analysis and pediatric medicine. In J. Austin, & J. E. Carr (Eds.), *Handbook of applied behavior analysis* (pp. 161–185). Oakland, CA: Context Press.

Boles, R. E., Roberts, M. C., & Vernberg, E. M. (2008). Treating non-retentive encopresis with rewarded scheduled toilet visits. *Behavior Analysis in Practice, 1*(2), 68–72.

Butler, R. J. (2004). Childhood nocturnal enuresis: Developing a conceptual framework. *Clinical Psychology Review, 24*, 909–931.

Center for American Progress. (2010). Retrieved from: http://www.americanprogress.org/press/view/2010/03/.

Chu, J., & Richdale, A. L. (2009). Sleep quality and psychological wellbeing in mothers of children with developmental disabilities. *Research in Developmental Disabilities, 30*(6), 1512–1522. http://dx.doi.org/10.1016/j.ridd.2009.07.007.

Cicero, F., & Pfadt, A. (2002). Investigation of a reinforcement-based toilet training procedure for children with autism. *Research in Developmental Disabilities, 23*(5), 319–331.

Conners, C. (1997). *Conners' rating scales-revised: Technical manual.* North Tonawanda, NY: Multi-Health Systems, Inc.

Cooper, J. O., Heron, T. E., & Heward, W. L. (2007). *Applied behavior analysis* (2nd). New Jersey: Prentice Hall.

Dewald, J. F., Meijer, A. M., Oort, F. J., Kerkhof, G. A., & Bogels, S. M. (2010). The influence of sleep quality, sleep duration and sleepiness on school performance in children and adolescents: A meta-analytic review. *Sleep Medicine Reviews, 14*(3), 179–189.

Duker, O. C., Averink, M., & Melein, L. (2001). Response restriction as a method to establish diurnal bladder control. *American Journal of Mental Deficiency, 106*, 209–215.

Durand, V. M. (1998). *Sleep better! A guide to improving sleep for children with special needs.* Baltimore, MD: Paul H. Brookes Publishing.

Ferber, R. (2006). Solving your child's sleep problems: New, revised, and expanded edition. New York: Fireside. See more at: http://www.parentingscience.com/Ferber-method. html#sthash.zm4Xh6uv.dpuf.

Figueiro, M. G., Bierman, A., Plitnick, B., & Rea, M. S. (2009). Preliminary evidence that both blue and red light can induce alertness at night. *BMC Neuroscience, 10*(1), 105.

Foxx, R. M., & Azrin, N. H. (1973). *Toilet training the retarded: A rapid program for day and nighttime independent toileting.* Champaign, IL: Research Press Company.

Friman, P. C. (2010). Come on in, the water is Fine: Achieving mainstream relevance through integration with primary medical care. *Behavior Analyst, 33*(1), 19–36.

Friman, P. C., Hoff, K. E., Schnoes, C., Freeman, K. A., Woods, D. W., & Blum, N. (1999). The bedtime pass: An approach to bedtime crying and leaving the room. *Archives of Pediatrics and Adolescent Medicine, 153*, 1027–1029.

Gregory, A. M., & Sadeh, A. (2012). Sleep, emotional and behavioral difficulties in children and adolescents. *Sleep Medicine Reviews, 16*(2), 129–136.

Gruber, R., Cassoff, J., Frenette, S., Wiebe, S., & Carrier, J. (2012). Impact of sleep extension and restriction on children's emotional lability and impulsivity. *Pediatrics, 130*(5), e1155–e1161.

Heussler, H. S. (2005). Common causes of sleep disruption and daytime sleepiness: Childhood sleep disorders II. *The Medical Journal of Australia, 182*(9), 484–489.

Higley, E., & Dozier, M. (2009). Nighttime maternal responsiveness and infant attachment at one year. *Attachment & Human Development, 11*(4), 347–363.

Horner, R. D., & Keilitz, I. (1975). Training mentally retarded adolescents to brush their teeth. *Journal of Applied Behavior Analysis, 8*, 301–309.

Issenman, R. M., Filmer, R. B., & Gorski, P. A. (1999). A review of bowel and bladder control development in children: How gastrointestinal and urologic conditions relate to problems in toilet training. *Pediatrics, 103*, 1346–1352.

Kalb, L. M., & Loeber, R. (2003). Child disobedience and noncompliance: A review. *Pediatrics, 111*, 641–652.

Kong, J., Shepel, P. N., Holden, C. P., Mackiewicz, M., Pack, A. I., & Geiger, J. D. (2002). Brain glycogen decreases with increased periods of wakefulness: Implications for homeostatic drive to sleep. *Journal of Neuroscience, 22*(13), 5581–5587.

Kroeger, K. A., & Sorensen-Burnworth, R. (2009). Toilet training individuals with autism and other developmental disabilities: A critical review. *Research in Autism Spectrum Disorders, 3*, 607–618.

Kuhn, B. R. (2007). Sleep disorders. In M. Hersen & J. C. Thomas (Eds.), *Handbook of clinical interviewing with children* (pp. 420–447). New York: Sage Publications.

Lavigne, J. V., Gibbons, R. D., Arend, R., Rosenbaum, D., Binns, H. J., & Christoffel, K. K. (1999). Rational service planning in pediatric primary care: Continuity and change in psychopathology among children enrolled in pediatric practices. *Journal of Pediatric Psychology*, *24*(5), 393–403.

LeBlanc, L. A., Carr, J. E., Crossett, S. E., Bennett, C. M., & Detweiler, D. D. (2005). Intensive outpatient behavioral treatment of primary urinary incontinence of children with autism. *Focus on Autism and Other Developmental Disabilities*, *2*, 98–105.

Lott, J. D., & Kroeger, K. A. (2004). Self-help skills in persons with mental retardation. In J. L. Matson, R. B. Laud, & M. L. Matson (Eds.), *Behavior modification for persons with developmental disabilities* (Vol. 2). New York: NADD Press.

Luiselli, J. K. (1996). A transfer of stimulus control procedure applicable to toilet training programs for children with developmental disabilities. *Child and Family Behavior Therapy*, *18*, 29–34.

Luiselli, J. K. (1997). Teaching toilet skills in a public school setting to a child with pervasive developmental disorder. *Journal of Behavior Therapy and Experimental Psychiatry*, *28*, 163–168.

Marcus, C. L., Brooks, L. J., Davidson, W., Draper, K. A., Gozal, D., Halbower, A. C., et al. (2012). Diagnosis and management of childhood obstructive sleep apnea syndrome. *Pediatrics*, *130*, 714–755.

McKerchar, P. M., & Abby, L. (2012). Systematic evaluation of variables that contribute to noncompliance: A replication and extension. *Journal of Applied Behavior Analysis*, *45*, 607–611.

Mellon, M. W., Scott, M. A., Haynes, K. B., Schmidt, D. F., & Houts, A. C. (1997). EMG recording of pelvic floor conditioning in nocturnal enuresis during urine alarm treatment: A preliminary study. In *Paper presentation at the sixth Florida conference on child health psychology*. Gainsville, FL: University of Florida.

Meltzer, L. J. (2010). Clinical management of behavioral insomnia of childhood: Treatment of bedtime problems and night wakings in young children. *Behavioral Sleep Medicine*, *8*(3), 172–189.

Meltzer, L. J., Courtney, J., Crosette, J., Ramos, M., & Mindell, J. A. (2010). Prevalence of diagnosed sleep disorders in pediatric primary care practices. *Pediatrics*, *125*(6), 1410–1418.

Miles, N. I., & Wilder, D. A. (2009). The effects of behavioral skills training on caregiver implementation of guided compliance. *Journal of Applied Behavior Analysis*, *42*, 405–410.

Mindell, J. A. (1999). Empirically supported treatments in pediatric psychology: Bedtime refusal and night wakings in young children. *Journal of Pediatric Psychology*, *24*(6), 465–481.

Mindell, J. A., Kuhn, B., Lewin, D. S., Meltzer, L. J., & Sadeh, A. (2006). Behavioral treatment of bedtime problems and night wakings in infants and young children. *Sleep*, *29*(10), 1263–1276.

Mindell, J. A., & Owens, J. A. (2003). Sleep problems in pediatric practice: Clinical issues for the pediatric nurse practitioner. *Journal of Pediatric Health Care*, *17*(6), 324–331.

Mindell, J. A., & Owens, J. A. (2010). *A clinical guide to pediatric sleep: Diagnosis and management of sleep problems* (2nd, pp. 63–64). Philadelphia, PA: Lippincott, Williams & Wilkins.

Moore, B. A., Friman, P. C., Fruzzetti, A. E., & MacAleese, K. (2007). Brief report: Evaluating the bedtime pass program for child resistance to bedtime—A randomized, controlled trial. *Journal of Pediatric Psychology*, *32*(3), 283–287.

Morgenthaler, T. I., Owens, J., Alessi, C., Boehlecke, B., Brown, T. M., Coleman, J., et al. (2006). Practice parameters for behavioral treatment of bedtime problems and night wakings in infants and young children. *Sleep*, *29*(10), 1277–1281.

National Kidney and Urologic Diseases Information Clearinghouse. (2014). Retrieved from: http://kidney.niddk.nih.gov.

Neitzel, J., & Wolery, M. (2009). *Steps for implementation: Graduated guidance*. Chapel Hill, NC: The National Professional Development Center on Autism Spectrum Disorders, FPG

Child Development Institute, The University of North Caroline. Retrieved from: *http://autismpdc.fpg.unc.edu/sites/autismpdc.fpg.unc.edu/files/Prompting_Steps-Graduated.pdf.*

Owens, J. A. (2001). The practice of sleep medicine: Results of a Community Survey. *Pediatrics, 108*(3), E51. Retrieved from: www.pediatrics.org/cgi/content/full/108/3/e51.

Owens, J. A., & Datzell, V. (2005). Use of the 'BEARS' sleep screening tool in a pediatric residents' continuity clinic: A pilot study. *Sleep Medicine, 6*(1), 63–69.

Owens, J., Maxim, R., McGuinn, M., Nobile, C., Msall, M., & Alario, A. (1999). Television-viewing habits and sleep disturbance in school children. *Pediatrics, 104*(3), e27.

Owens, J. A., & Witmans, M. (2004). Sleep problems. *Current Problems in Pediatric and Adolescents Health Care, 34*, 154–179.

Pachter, L. M., & Dowrkin, P. H. (1997). Maternal expectations about normal child development in cultural groups. *Archives of Pediatrics and Adolescent Medicine, 151*, 1144–1150.

Paredes, P. R. (2004). Enuresis. In *Case based pediatrics for medical students and residents* (pp. 466–467). Department of Pediatrics, University of Hawaii John A. Burns School of Medicine. Retrieved from: *http://www.hawaii.edu/medicine/pediatrics/pedtext/pedtext5.pdf.*

Patzold, L. M., Richdale, A. L., & Tonge, B. J. (1998). An investigation into sleep characteristics of children with autism and Asperger's Disorder. *Journal of Pediatrics & Child Health, 34*, 528–533.

Piazza, C. C., & Fisher, W. (1991). A faded bedtime with response cost protocol for treatment of multiple sleep problems in children. *Journal of Applied Behavior Analysis, 24*, 129–140.

Price, A. M., Wake, M., Ukoumunne, O. C., & Hiscock, H. (2012). Five-year follow-up of harms and benefits of behavioral infant sleep intervention: Randomized trial. *Pediatrics, 130*, 643–651.

Reid, M. J., Walter, A. L., & O'Leary, S. G. (1999). Treatment of young children's bedtime refusal and nighttime wakings: A comparison of 'standard' and graduated ignoring procedures. *Journal of Abnormal Child Psychology, 27*(1), 5–16.

Richdale, A., & Prior, M. R. (1995). The sleep-wake rhythm in children with autism. *European Child & Adolescent Psychiatry, 4*, 175–186.

Rickert, V. I., & Johnson, C. M. (1988). Reducing nocturnal awakening and crying episodes in infants and young children: A comparison between scheduled awakenings and systematic ignoring. *Pediatrics, 81*(2), 203–212.

Schroeder, C. S., & Gordon, B. N. (2002). *Assessment and treatment of childhood problems: A clinician's guide* (2nd). New York: The Guilford Press.

Shelov, S. P., Gundy, J., Weiss, J. C., McIntire, M. S., Olness, K., Staub, H. P., et al. (1981). Enuresis: A contrast of attitudes of parents and physicians. *Pediatrics, 67*, 707–710.

Skinner, B. F. (1953). *Science and human behavior.* New York: Macmillan.

Stephenson, K. M., & Hanley, G. P. (2010). Preschoolers' compliance with simple instructions: A descriptive and experimental evaluation. *Journal of Applied Behavior Analysis, 43*, 229–247.

Taneli, C., Ertan, P., Taneli, F., Genç, A., Günsar, C., Sencan, A., et al. (2004). Effect of alarm treatment on bladder storage capacities in monosymptomatic nocturnal enuresis. *Scandinavian Journal of Urology and Nephrology, 38*, 207–210.

Taras, M. E., & Matese, M. (1990). Acquisition of self-help skills. In J. L. Matson (Ed.), *Handbook of behavior modification with the mentally retarded* (pp. 255–271). New York: Plenum Press.

Thiedke, C. C. (2003). Nocturnal enuresis. *American Family Physician, 67*(7), 1499–1506.

Tu, N. D., & Baskin, L. S. (2014). *Nocturnal enuresis in children: Management.* Retrieved from: http://www.uptodate.com/contents/nocturnal-enuresis-in-children-management.

Vriend, J. L., Corkum, P. V., Moon, E. C., & Smith, I. M. (2011). Behavioral interventions for sleep problems in children with autism spectrum disorders: Current findings and future directions. *Journal of Pediatric Psychology, 36*(9), 1017–1029.

Watson, T. S., & Gresham, F. M. (1998). *Handbook of child behavior therapy*. New York, NY: Plenum Press.

Wilder, D. A., Allison, J., Nicholson, K., Abellon, O. E., & Saulnier, R. (2010). Further evaluation of antecedent interventions on compliance: The effects of rationales to increase compliance among preschoolers. *Journal of Applied Behavior Analysis, 43*, 601–613.

Wilder, D. A., & Atwell, J. (2006). Evaluation of a guided compliance procedure to reduce noncompliance among preschool children. *Behavioral Interventions, 21*, 265–272.

Wilder, D. A., Harris, C., Reagan, R., & Rasey, A. (2007). Functional analysis and treatment of noncompliance by preschool children. *Journal of Applied Behavior Analysis, 40*, 173–177.

Wilder, D., & Majdalany, L. (2015). Increasing compliance in children with autism spectrum disorders. *International Journal of Behavior Analysis and Autism Spectrum Disorders, 1*, 84–96.

Wilder, D. A., Myers, K., Fischetti, A., Leon, Y., Nicholson, K., & Allison, J. (2012). An analysis of modifications to the three-step guided compliance procedure necessary to achieve compliance among preschool children. *Journal of Applied Behavior Analysis, 45*, 121–130.

Wilder, D. A., Nicholson, K., & Allison, J. (2010). An evaluation of advance notice to increase compliance among preschoolers. *Journal of Applied Behavior Analysis, 43*, 751–755.

Wilder, D. A., Zonneveld, K., Harris, C., Marcus, A., & Reagan, R. (2007). Further analysis of antecedent interventions on preschoolers' compliance. *Journal of Applied Behavior Analysis, 40*, 535–539.

Williams, J., Klinepeter, K., Palmes, G., Pulley, A., & Foy, J. M. (2004). Diagnosis and treatment of behavioral health disorders in pediatric practice. *Pediatrics, 114*(3), 601–606.

CHAPTER 12

Toward Behavior Analytic Practice in Augmentative and Alternative Communication (AAC)

Breanne J. Byiers[1], Joe E. Reichle[1,2]
[1]Department of Educational Psychology, University of Minnesota, Minneapolis, Minnesota, USA
[2]Department of Speech-Language-Hearing Sciences, University of Minnesota, Minneapolis, Minnesota, USA

Addressing deficits in functional communication is a challenging and enduring problem for those working with individuals with intellectual and developmental disabilities (IDD; Drasgow, Halle, & Sigafoos, 1999). Providing access to, and support for, effective communication intervention for individuals for whom spoken language is not possible should hold substantial interest for applied behavior analysts. There is a substantial and growing collection of evidence-based research that has contributed to the selection and implementation of spoken, gestural, and/or graphic communication modes with those with moderate and severe disabilities. Most recently, this conclusion was supported by Rispoli, Franco, van der Meer, Lang, and Camargo (2010) who reviewed 35 studies examining the use of speech generating devices (SGDs) for individuals with IDD and found that 86% of the articles reviewed reported positive outcomes with 54% providing conclusive evidence. However, as in much of the communication intervention literature, generalization and maintenance of intervention gains represent areas that have received far more modest attention among individuals with IDD. This is particularly an important area of inquiry with respect to Augmentative and Alternative Communication (AAC) technologies given that, overall, there may be a high rate of failure or abandonment (Phillips & Zhao, 1993).

Rather than attributing AAC abandonment or failure to the characteristics of the learners or their families, the failure of clinicians/educators to select AAC strategies that are most efficient for the learners or the environments in which they operate may contribute to challenges in establishing well-maintained and appropriately generalized functional communication skills. In support of this hypothesis, Schlosser and Lee (2000) conducted a

Clinical and Organizational Applications of Applied Behavior Analysis
http://dx.doi.org/10.1016/B978-0-12-420249-8.00012-5

273

meta-analysis of single-subject experimental studies of AAC intervention. They reported that most studies used a "train and hope" (Stokes & Baer, 1977) strategy to address generalization and maintenance. Although it is unclear whether the field has improved in recent years, revisiting some relevant principles of applied behavior analysis (ABA) may help address these issues in the functional use of communication by learners with IDD who rely on AAC. Consequently, the purpose of this chapter is to examine the application of ABA principles and procedures in improving long-term outcomes of AAC interventions for individuals with developmental and cognitive disabilities and to consider some areas from the experimental analysis of behavior that could play a further role in future advances. This chapter focuses primarily on strategies for teaching functional communication in the form of mands (i.e., requesting, rejecting/protesting) to beginning communicators (i.e., those with few or no forms of intentional communication) with IDD. After defining some key terminology, we will provide a brief overview of functional communication training (FCT), followed by a discussion of the role of functional equivalence and response efficiency in designing communication interventions. Subsequently, we will examine the role of single-subject experimental designs in identifying and selecting AAC strategies and address techniques for promoting the conditional use, generalization, and maintenance of different communicative functions. Finally, some possible directions for future research involving the application of ABA in teaching beginning communicators with IDD to use AAC communication strategies will be suggested.

DEFINING AUGMENTATIVE AND ALTERNATIVE COMMUNICATION

AAC refers to all strategies, devices, or forms that are used to replace or supplement speech when communicating thoughts, needs, or ideas (ASHA, 2002). It includes all unaided forms of communication, such as gestures, facial expressions, body movement, sign, and sign approximations, as well as aided communication applications from a range of high-tech SGDs to low-tech applications such as the Picture Exchange Communication System (PECS) with a number of applications in between this range. Although we all use some unaided forms of AAC to supplement our spoken communication (e.g., a head nod), individuals with IDD may benefit from access to a larger variety, or different forms of AAC. The range of AAC forms may depend, in part, on the context in which they are attempting to communicate in order to make their communicative behaviors meaningful to those around them and to maximize communicative efficiency. Doing so will maximize communication's reinforcement value for both the speaker and the listener involved in a communicative exchange.

INTRODUCTION TO FUNCTIONAL COMMUNICATION TRAINING

FCT is one area in which behavior analytic theory has had a significant impact on the strategies commonly accepted in teaching the use of a beginning AAC repertoire for individuals with IDD. FCT was developed as an intervention with a primary objective of reducing problem behaviors (e.g., aggression, property destruction, self-injury, tantrums) by teaching a functionally equivalent and socially acceptable communicative alternative to gain or maintain access to reinforcers that previously maintained the problem behavior (Carr & Durand, 1985; Reichle, & Wacker, 1993; Reichle, York, & Sigafoos, 1991). To successfully implement FCT, a prospective interventionist must successfully identify the source(s) of reinforcement maintaining the problem behavior (e.g., complete a functional analysis). These sources may include positive reinforcement in the form of access to attention, food, or preferred activities/objects, and negative reinforcement in the form of escape from task demands or other nonpreferred environments or events. Following identification of the maintaining reinforcer, the intervention targets the training and reinforcement of a novel communicative behavior. Many individuals experience multiple functions associated with problem behavior. For example, the learner who severely scratches himself to *escape* math may also receive dense *attention* from adults while treating the scratch. This, in turn, can result in a "double-dip" of both positive and negative reinforcements.

Nearly 30 years of research supports the effectiveness of FCT as an intervention for a variety of severe behavior problems in a wide range of populations (see Tiger, Hanley, & Bruzek, 2008). FCT has been implemented in in- and out-patient clinics (e.g., Fisher et al., 1993; Hagopian, Fisher, Sullivan, Acquisto, & LeBlanc, 1998), homes (e.g., Derby et al., 1997; Wacker et al., 2005), schools and community settings (e.g., Durand, 1999; Durand & Carr, 1991; Lalli, Browder, Mace, & Brown, 1993), and even through internet-based long-distance coaching (e.g., Wacker et al., 2013). Although much of the work to date has been conducted with individuals with IDD, there have been recent applications of the concepts of functional assessment and differential reinforcement of appropriate communicative responses to different populations, including individuals with language delays (e.g., Dunlap, Ester, Langhans, & Fox, 2006; Vollmer, Northup, Ringdahl, Leblanc, & Chauvin, 1996), attention-deficit hyperactivity disorder (ADHD; Flood & Wilder, 2002), and schizophrenia (Wilder, Masuda, O'Conner, & Baham, 2001), among others.

Despite the fact that the primary purpose of most FCT applications has been the reduction of problem behaviors, most applications also show concomitant collateral increases in appropriate communicative (and, in some cases, other relevant socially acceptable alternative) behaviors. This finding suggests that the foundational concepts of FCT could be used as a communication intervention strategy, in addition to being a treatment for problem behaviors. Recently, some researchers have implemented FCT as a strategy for increasing requesting among individuals with severe disabilities who did not engage in severe behavior problems. For example, Tait, Sigafoos, Woodyatt, O'Reilly, and Lancioni (2004) taught parents to use FCT to teach a range of graphic and gestural communicative behaviors with six young children with developmental and physical disabilities. Subsequent to intervention, all six children demonstrated increases in socially acceptable communicative behaviors that served the same functions as the prelinguistic behaviors for which baseline data were available. Regardless of the initial motivation for implementing FCT, the substantial evidence base supports the claim that it is one of the most visible applications of ABA to the communication intervention literature. Next, we will address the selection of a communicative alternative to teach during FCT that requires careful analyses of functional equivalence and response efficiency.

APPLYING BEHAVIORAL PRINCIPLES TO AAC
Functional Equivalence

One of the main reasons that FCT is so effective in increasing appropriate communicative behaviors among individuals with IDD is that it capitalizes on the learner's existing motivation to communicate (e.g., Dragsow & Halle, 1995). Using functional analysis methodology, researchers and practitioners can identify the function of inappropriate or idiosyncratic forms of communication (e.g., problem behavior), which leads to the identification of natural consequences that serve to maintain socially unacceptable communicative strategies used by a given learner. The inappropriate forms can then be replaced with more conventional, socially acceptable communicative behaviors.

A critical component of this process is that the function(s) of the behavior being replaced is/are correctly specified, meaning that the motivating operations (MOs) that increase the reinforcing value of the consequence are in place during intervention. In some cases, however, the specific MOs or discriminative stimuli that occasion the behavior are difficult to identify. For example, if a learner engages in behaviors to escape from tasks and the typical consequence during the school day is that he/she is removed from the classroom area, the function can be summarized as negative reinforcement. This characterization, although accurate, may not adequately describe the relevant stimuli to permit a determination of exactly what or whom the learner is escaping. For example, it is possible that the learner may engage in problem behavior to escape tasks that are either too difficult or those that are not difficult but take too long. Alternatively, the learner may be escaping from the teacher's attention that is associated with the task, rather than the task itself. It is also possible that the functional reinforcer is escape from classroom noise, peer interaction, or any number of other variables. If intervention involves teaching the learner a response that will result in all of the same consequences (removal from the environment) as the problem behavior, the intervention should, in theory, be effective. If, however, the true function of the behavior is escape from classroom noise, and the intervention involves teaching the student to ask for assistance with challenging tasks, the two responses are not truly functionally equivalent, and the intervention is unlikely to result in a substantial decrease in the problem behavior. Therefore, it is important that the interventionist correctly identifies the relevant MOs, discriminative stimuli, and functional reinforcer for the behavior being replaced in order to capitalize on the advantages of FCT.

Response Efficiency

In addition to ensuring functional equivalence, interventionists must consider the relative efficiency of the two responses when teaching a replacement communicative behavior. Matching theory dictates that when several functionally equivalent responses are available, individuals allocate the most responses to the alternative that they perceive as being the most efficient (Herrnstein, 1961; Mace & Roberts, 1993). Response efficiency is affected by at least four components, including response effort (Bauman, Shull, & Brownstein, 1975), rate of reinforcement (Martens & Houk, 1989), quality of reinforcement (Hollard & Davison, 1971; Miller, 1976), and immediacy of reinforcement (Logue, 1988). It should therefore be possible to bias an individual's responding toward or away from a particular behavior by altering one or more of these facets of response efficiency.

For example, if an interventionist is hoping that a learner is going to use an SGD to ask for a break from academic tasks in place of the problem behavior of tearing up worksheets when they are presented, use of the SGD must be more efficient, in terms of physical effort and parameters of reinforcement, than the current problem behaviors that serve the same purpose. In real life, these parameters often interact, and in almost all cases, different behaviors involve a trade-off. In our example, engaging in destructive behavior may be less effortful (from the learner's perspective) than searching for and selecting a "break" symbol on an SGD. It is also likely that, in most environments, the problem behavior is more likely to result in immediate reinforcement (the interventionist may not have another worksheet to present in order to follow through with a work instruction) than a socially acceptable request for a break. Therefore, in order to make using the SGD a more efficient response option, the interventionist would need to make the device as simple to use as possible (possibly easier than is really necessary during the early stages of intervention) and ensure that appropriate requests would result in at least as much (and preferably better) reinforcement in terms of the rate, immediacy, and quality as reinforcement that has resulted from the individual's history of problem behavioral emissions.

Even when an interventionist is teaching a new communicative behavior that is not designed to compete with or replace a problem behavior, response efficiency can directly affect an individual's acquisition rate or preference for one communication strategy over another (Johnston & Evans, 2005). Several researchers have manipulated one or more facets of response efficiency to assess the effects on the communicative behaviors of individuals with IDD. For example, Horner (1990) systematically altered the physical effort required for an adolescent to use an SGD to request assistance in place of challenging behavior. Specifically, two conditions were implemented that included "high" and "low effort." In the high-effort condition, the participant had to type out the full phrase "help please" on an SGD; in the low-effort condition, pressing a single key on the device emitted the spoken phrase "help please." The results demonstrated that the high-effort condition had no meaningful effect on the rates of challenging behavior, whereas the low-effort resulted in a significant and sustained decrease. During a second investigation, Horner and Day (1991) conducted analyses of the effects of three variables associated with response efficiency (physical effort, reinforcement schedule, and latency of reinforcement) on the rates of problem behaviors and appropriate replacement behaviors (mands or appropriate task completion) of three individuals with significant IDD. They found that when the replacement behaviors being reinforced were less efficient than problem behavior on any one of the variables, they did not successfully compete with the problem behaviors. However, when reinforcement was available for more efficient alternative behaviors, the new behaviors effectively competed with the problem behaviors. Overall, these studies suggest that response efficiency should be carefully considered when identifying AAC devices or strategies for beginning communicators.

Using Single-Subject Experimental Designs to Assist in Selecting AAC Strategies

In some cases, identifying the relevant facets of response efficiency for all of the potential modes being considered for an individual learner is not a feasible approach to selecting a communicative system. Regardless, behavior analytic technologies can be used to select an aided and/or unaided system that is going to be most functional and successful for him or her. Speech-language pathologists who specialize in supporting persons as they learn to use AAC modes should be taught to consider carefully the match between (a) the characteristics of the learner, (b) their communication partners, and (c) the environments in which the learner will need to communicate with the features of the device or strategy (often referred to as feature matching; e.g., Beukelman & Mirenda, 1998), but there are currently no clear evidence-based guidelines on which to base choices about which communication modes are likely to be most successful for an individual learner. In an effort to address this issue, Gregory, DeLeon, and Richman (2009) investigated whether potential prerequisite skills (i.e., matching and motor-imitation abilities) predicted which learners would rapidly acquire the use of manual signs and picture exchange-based communication. The authors hypothesized that learners who could imitate would be more likely to acquire manual signs, whereas learners who could match to sample would be more likely to acquire exchange-based communication. Of the six participants included in the study, however, three displayed both skills, and three displayed neither. All of the participants who had both skills learned both communicative forms. One of the participants with neither skill acquired the exchange-based system only, while the other two did not master either form. These results point to a potential direction for research in predicting which type of system is most likely to be successful for an individual learner, but a great deal of additional work is needed in this area.

Comparative AAC Studies

Because of the lack of clear decision rules for selecting AAC strategies for specific learners, several researchers have used single-subject experimental designs to compare how quickly a learner acquires new responses across different communicative modes. This type of research question has clear clinical applications, as identifying a mode that is efficient for an individual to learn could potentially lead to faster acquisition of functional communication and better long-term outcomes. Conducting comparative studies in AAC can be a challenging task, however, because the behaviors being taught may not be independent from one another and may therefore be susceptible to multiple treatment interference (see Schlosser, 1999 for a discussion of this issue, and methodological suggestions for addressing it). As a result, in comparative studies an interventionist must consider identifying sets of communicative behaviors that are: (a) unknown to the participants (to control for learning history), (b) independent from each other (to control for treatment carryover), and (c) of similar difficulty (in order to conduct direct comparisons). Reichle et al. (1991) suggested using an alternating treatment design to compare the relative ease of teaching graphic, gestural, and spoken symbols in informing which mode(s) to emphasize during early instruction.

Comparing Speed of Acquisition

A few studies have used single-subject designs to demonstrate a clear and consistent advantage of one communicative strategy or mode over another across participants, leading to clear generalizable recommendations. For example, in a seminal comparative study comparing different graphic communication symbol types, Hurlbut, Iwata, and Green (1982) assessed acquisition rates across two symbol types that were commonly used for communication boards for individuals with intellectual disabilities at the time. The symbol types evaluated were iconic symbols, which are readily recognizable visual representations of items or actions, and "Bliss" symbols (Bliss, 1965), which are combinations of geometric shapes, that may or may not bear any resemblance to the items or actions that they represent. Proponents of the Bliss symbol system argued that such nonrepresentational symbols might facilitate generalization and acquisition of abstract concepts, whereas proponents of iconic symbols argued that the similarity to referents would facilitate learning. There was, however, no empirical evidence to support or refute either of the arguments, and the Hurlbut study sought to directly compare acquisition rates using the two symbol types.

To directly compare acquisition across the two symbol types, Hurlbut and colleagues (1982) used an adapted alternating treatments design (AATD; Sindelar, Rosenberg, & Wilson, 1985). As with the traditional alternating treatments design, the AATD involves rapid alternation between two or more assessment or intervention conditions, so that the vertical separation between data paths can be assessed across the entire length of the phase. The adapted part of the design is that, rather than maintaining the same dependent variable across the conditions, a different set of responses is assigned to each intervention or assessment condition. In the Hurlbut study, the researchers identified common objects (e.g., sock, door) that were known to the participants (i.e., the participants could identify the correct label in a "yes" or "no" format), and assigned sets of five objects to the conditions, with assignment counterbalanced across participants. By maintaining the same instructional methods across the two conditions, the authors were able to determine that the iconic symbols were associated with substantially faster rates of acquisition for all three participants. In addition, the iconic symbols resulted in greater maintenance over time, more stimulus generalization, and more spontaneous use than the Bliss symbols for all the participants. These results led to the conclusion that the iconic system had several advantages over the Bliss symbols for beginning communicators.

This finding of a substantial and consistent advantage of one strategy over another across all of the participants in a study is relatively rare in comparative AAC studies; however, see van der Meer, Sigafoos, O'Reilly, and Lancioni (2011). Rather, in many cases, differences in rates of acquisition are idiosyncratic across participants. Single-subject comparative designs are even better suited to addressing this issue, however, and can be helpful in identifying effective modes for individual learners. For example, Hyppa Martin, Reichle, Dimian, and Chen (2013) compared the efficacy of teaching graphic and gestural mode communicative forms to a toddler with Angelman's syndrome. Further, this within-participant strategy can be extended within aided communication systems to consider the type of symbol that might best meet a learners needs. Consider Figure 12.1 which displays data implemented by Reichle and Parker-McGowan (2014) of a 4-year-old preschooler with moderate intellectual delay. The learner's interventionist wished to determine whether color photos, product logos, or line drawn symbols would be easiest for the learner to use. Using a three-choice array and the same referent items, each of three sessions occurred each day. During one session, the learner was taught a simple discrimination using only line drawings as symbol choices. In a second session, only product logos were presented. Finally, during the third

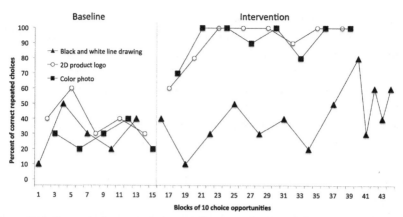

Figure 12.1 Percent of correct choices, defined as selection of the same option as on the first trial of the session using line drawings, product logos, and color photos. *From Reichle and Parker-McGowan (2014).*

session each day, three color photos were presented. In each of the three conditions, the interventionist placed three items (either color photos, product logos, or black and white line drawings) equally spaced and randomized in front of the learner. None of the three items that were depicted represented reinforcers. During the initial opportunity during a session, the learner was allowed to choose a symbol (it did not matter which was chosen). The symbol chosen by the learner set the standard for defining a correct response and was reinforced by allowing a choice among documented reinforcers. If, after the initial opportunity, the learner continued to select the same symbol choice, he continued to be reinforced with a choice of highly preferred items. If a different choice was selected, the learner was not reinforced and after 10s, he was given another opportunity. The three conditions were compared across opportunities via an alternating treatment design, and the order of sessions was counterbalanced across days. The symbol selections were treated as tacts, or labels, so that a choice of reinforcers could be offered to ensure reinforcer salience. As can be seen in Figure 12.1, as a result of examining learner performance, we concluded that either color photos or product logos would be more successful as symbol targets from the standpoint of accuracy during early phases of intervention. We hypothesized that this may have been the result of the learner having more exposure to these symbol types in his natural environment.

The Role of Preference in Selecting Modes

In addition to assessing differences in the speed of acquisition, some researchers have considered learners' preferences for different communicative modes when selecting systems. For example, Son, Sigafoos, O'Reilly, and Lancioni (2006) taught three children with autism to make requests using a speech-generating device, and the PECS (Bondy & Frost, 1994), a low-tech picture-based communication system. All participants met mastery criteria with both systems, and there were no clear differences across the systems in terms of acquisition rates, as assessed in an alternating treatments design. Follow-up assessments were conducted to determine whether participants preferred one system over the other. Two participants demonstrated a preference for PECS while one showed a preference for symbols displayed on the SGD. Similarly, Winborn-Kemmerer, Ringdahl, Wacker, and Kitsukawa (2009) taught two learners with IDD two different mand topographies (picture card and voice-output switch) for the same function as a part of an FCT intervention. They found that, although the two forms were equally effective in reducing problem behaviors, the two participants demonstrated distinct preferences for one form over the other. Cannella-Malone, DeBar, and Sigafoos (2009) found similar results when examining acquisition and preference of three different speech-generating devices with two children with IDD. One of the participants successfully acquired the target behaviors with only one device. The other participant successfully acquired the requesting skill across all three of the devices, but showed a clear preference for one device.

In many of the studies examining both acquisition and preference for communicative forms, the authors could not conduct direct comparisons of the acquisition rates across the forms, as they did not implement comparison designs, such as alternating treatments or AATD. One study (van Der Meer, Sutherland, O'Reilly, Lancioni, & Sigafoos, 2012) that did directly compare acquisition rates and preferences across manual signing, picture exchange, and speech-generating devices found that faster acquisition and better maintenance were associated with the preferred communication mode for all of the participants. The degree to which preference equates to more efficient learning and better generalization is currently not totally clear, however, and there is preliminary evidence that, when the purpose of communication training involves replacing problem behaviors, the learner's preference may not be a good indicator of the form to be used.

Other investigators have examined learners' use of new symbols and existing symbols used to mand within the context of FCT (Winborn, Wacker, Richman, Asmus, & Geier, 2002). They found that the participants allocated more responses to the familiar mands compared to the novel mands. However, when reinforcement was available for both responses, periods during which familiar mands were reinforced were associated with higher levels of problem behavior. Consequently, it is possible that preference alone may not be the most accurate indicator of the success of a communication strategy. Research examining whether preference is associated with better long-term outcomes (including generalization and maintenance) could represent a useful addition to the functional communication intervention literature. Regardless of the form of the communicative act, teaching learners to use their new skills in different environments, with a variety of communication partners, and over time requires careful consideration of the features of the learner's natural environment, especially the relevant discriminative stimuli that indicate when and where the behavior should and should not be produced.

TEACHING CONDITIONAL USE OF MANDS

Once an appropriate communication mode and the type of symbols to be taught have been selected, communication intervention for persons with significant developmental or cognitive disabilities moves to teaching functional use of the communication skills. In many cases, initial intervention with individuals for whom replacing problem behavior is not the focus of intervention has involved the introduction requesting (functions identified as "mands" in Skinner's *Verbal Behavior*, 1957), because mands are frequently among the first to be acquired by beginning communicators (Carpenter, Mastergeorge, & Coggins, 1983). To ensure efficient early stage acquisition, interventionists typically provide dense reinforcement schedules (Bondy & Frost, 1994; Harding, Wacker, Berg, Barretto, & Rankin, 2002; Johnston, Reichle, Feeley, & Jones, 2012; Sigafoos, O'Reilly, Drasgow, & Reichle, 2002; Sigafoos & Reichle, 1993).

Myriad studies demonstrating the effectiveness of FCT have shown how quickly learners with IDD can be taught to request access to preferred activities and objects. Once the skills have been mastered, typically the focus of intervention shifts to maintaining and generalizing the newly established behaviors. This, in turn, presents a new and particularly challenging set of issues. Take, for example, a learner who has been taught to activate an SGD to access caregiver attention. During acquisition, it is likely that the environment has been carefully controlled so that the switch is present only when the MO—in this case, diverted caregiver attention—is in place, and when the reinforcer (caregiver attention) is available, contingent on the learner's device activation (which likely involved prompts that were systematically faded). Following acquisition, however, the new communicative production is apt to be transferred to a range of natural environments. These environments may be far less controlled than the one that was associated with acquisition. As a result, the learner may produce the desired communicative symbol at times when it is unlikely to result in reinforcement. Such responses can occur because the learner (a) may attempt to use their new skills in contexts when it is not acceptable to do so and/or (b) may use the behavior in appropriate contexts, but at rates for which it is impossible to maintain a continuous schedule of reinforcement. Therefore, interventionists may need to thin the reinforcement schedules for the newly acquired communicative acts, either during or immediately following acquisition.

For example, a learner who is motivated by attention might quickly learn to use an SGD to request attention from his or her caregivers. During acquisition, especially in a controlled learning environment, such as one-on-one instruction with a teacher, this behavior would likely result in reinforcement every time it occurs. Once the teacher recognizes that the response is mastered, however, he/she may be less quick to respond to it if he/she is involved with other students or activities when it occurs. This change in responding might introduce delays to reinforcement that never occurred during the initial acquisition period, challenging the learner's persistence in producing the response. If, however, the teacher systematically thinned the reinforcement schedule (e.g., by using intermittent reinforcement schedules or delays to reinforcement) for the response during or immediately following acquisition training, the learner might be more likely to maintain the response in the face of such challenges.

Delay and Signaled Delay Schedules

Researchers have examined the effects of several different strategies to thin reinforcement schedules and make newly acquired communicative responses more resistant to extinction in the natural environment. One of the most commonly used strategies is a delay schedule. This type of schedule involves inserting a progressive time delay to reinforcement following the production of a communicative response. In the case of requests for preferred objects or activities, this may involve telling the learner to "wait" for the reinforcer or having the learner engage or continue to engage in an activity while waiting, and providing access to the object or activity following a progressively longer period of appropriate behavior (Hagopian et al., 1998). In the case of requests for breaks from task demands, the procedure involves "demand fading," or having the learner complete a progressively larger number of tasks before accessing the break (Fisher et al., 1993).

Delay schedules have the advantage of simulating many natural situations in which access to reinforcement may not be immediately available (Hagopian, Boelter, & Jarmolowicz, 2011; Johnston et al., 2012), such as when a caregiver is engaged in a task and cannot provide attention. On the other hand, the time delay between the response and the reinforcer also has the potential to undermine the functional relationship, thereby increasing the possibility of inadvertent reinforcement of other, potentially undesirable behaviors. According to a review by Hagopian et al. (2011), 50% of FCT studies reviewed that included delay schedules or demand fading required additional treatment components (e.g., noncontingent reinforcement or punishment) in order to obtain the desired outcomes, suggesting that delay schedules alone may be inadequate to transfer stimulus control of the behaviors to the natural environment. Some have hypothesized that signaling a delay in the delivery of reinforcement may be helpful in that it may provide the learner increased monitoring capability of when the delivery of reinforcement may be apt to occur (Johnston et al., 2012; Reichle, Johnson, Monn, & Harris, 2010).

Most of the studies reviewed by Hagopian et al. (2011) involved unsignaled delays to reinforcement, meaning that the learner was not informed regarding the amount of time to pass or number of tasks to complete prior to reinforcement. There is some evidence that using signaled delays to reinforcement resulted in better maintenance of the decreases in challenging behavior than were obtained with unsignaled delays. For example, Reichle et al. (2010) examined the effects of general and explicit delay cues on task engagement and escape-maintained problem behaviors exhibited by two school-aged children. They found that both types of delay cues resulted in decreases in problem behavior, but explicit delay cues resulted in higher rates of successful work completion than the general cues.

Similarly, Vollmer, Borrero, Lalli, and Daniel (1999) used signaled and unsignaled delays to reinforcement to evaluate self-control and impulsivity among children with severe behavior disorders. Both participants in the study engaged in aggression when it produced immediate but small rewards, even though mands produced larger, more delayed rewards. However, when the delay to reinforcement for mands was signaled, both participants displayed improved self control with respect to delayed reinforcement, in that they used mands to access the larger delayed rewards. These results are a promising addition to the delay schedule literature but do not indicate the degree to which signaling delays to reinforcement might facilitate schedule thinning in communication training contexts, and additional work in this area is needed.

Concurrent Reinforcement Schedules

While delay schedules are used to gradually introduce longer delays in reinforcement to facilitate the transfer of the newly taught communicative skill to a range of environments, other types of reinforcement schedules can be used to encourage discriminated or conditional use of responses. Concurrent schedules are one such method that can be used to bias responding to one response over another.

Reichle and McComas (2004) taught a 12-year-old child with a significant behavior disorder who engaged in a range of problem behaviors to escape difficult work to request assistance during the completion of math worksheets (that required carrying numbers in solving addition problems) by raising his hand as an alternative to problem behavior. Although the participant learned to request assistance for difficult problems the investigators noted a continued propensity to overuse assistance requests during tasks that the learner should have been able to complete independently. This outcome was likely attributable to issues involving response efficiency; that is, if the quality and quantity of reinforcement available for completing a task with assistance is equivalent to the reinforcement for independent completion, asking for assistance is likely to be an easier response to emit. To ensure that the learner could benefit from prompts delivered after he requested assistance that were designed to teach him to solve difficult math problems, a regularly occurring errorless tutorial session was established. Once the learner was successfully solving what originally had been difficult problems it was apparent that he was continuing to overuse his assistance request back in the classroom on math worksheets with the same problems. It was unclear whether this generalization problem was the result of failing to recognize the problems on a worksheet as a stimulus condition that should be associated with independent work, or alternatively, whether he realized that he could independently complete the problems but simply chose not to do them (see bottom cell Figure 12.2). Consequently, during Phase 3 (Figure 12.2) in an effort to bias the learner's responding away from assistance requests and toward independent task completion during easy tasks, competing concurrent schedules of reinforcement were implemented. This involved providing more substantial reinforcement contingent on independent problem solving than was available when the learner requested assistance. During this

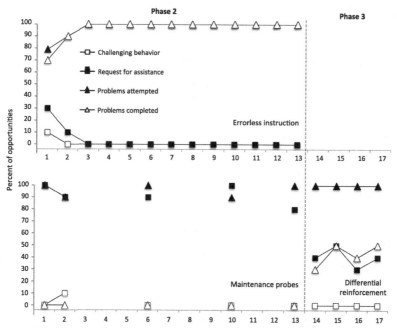

Figure 12.2 Percent of work opportunities with challenging behavior, assistance requests, math problems attempted, and problems completed across errorless instruction (top panel) and maintenance/generalization probes in the classroom during worksheet completion (bottom panel). During phase two, differential reinforcement for task completion was available for work completion in the "errorless instruction" environment, but not the "maintenance environment" (not displayed). During phase 3, differential reinforcement implemented in the "maintenance" environment. *Adapted from Reichle and McComas (2004). Copyright 2004 by Informa Healthcare. Adapted with permission of Informa Healthcare.*

phase, in each session, five problems were offered that represented new and very difficult problems for which the learner should have requested assistance and five problems that represented previously difficult problems that the participant had learned to solve independently. This additional intervention phase was successful in establishing more conditional use of the newly taught assistance requests with difficult problems and independent performance with problems that the learner had mastered during the intervention. Therefore, for this participant, the difficulty of the work appeared to serve as an effective discriminative stimulus for the conditional use of assistance requests. A particularly unique aspect to this investigation was the fact that the competing schedule demonstration was completed by defining easy tasks as those that during baseline had been identified as difficult problems. Over the course of the requesting intervention, the learner became able to solve the originally difficult problems as a result of prompts offered in the form of help that were contingent on a successful assistance request. In spite of the usefulness of competing schedules, other individuals may benefit from the application of specific stimulus control procedures.

Stimulus Control Procedures

Some of the problems that arise when using consequence-based strategies to facilitate the transfer of communicative behavior from an acquisition environment to other environments may be a function of not addressing a sufficient number of environmental features where the newly taught behavior should (and should not) occur. By arranging salient antecedent stimuli during functional communication interventions, interventionists may be able to facilitate the development of appropriate stimulus control and reduce complications associated with changes to reinforcement schedules. Stimulus control is based on Skinner's three-term contingency (Skinner, 1957) and refers to situations in which a behavior is emitted in the presence of a certain antecedent stimulus, but not emitted in its absence. Discussions of stimulus control typically refer to discriminative stimuli (S^D), or antecedent stimuli that signal the availability of reinforcement for a particular behavior (e.g., caregiver being nearby might signal the availability of reinforcement for requests using a communication board), and S-Deltas (S^Δ), or antecedent stimuli that signal the unavailability of reinforcement for the behavior (e.g., caregiver being in another room would signal the unavailability of reinforcement for communication board use).

Multiple Schedules

Some researchers have used stimulus control procedures to facilitate the thinning of reinforcement schedules by implementing multiple schedules, in which at least two distinct, signaled schedule components are alternated. The reinforcement component (periods when the communicative response will result in reinforcement) is signaled with some kind of S^D, and the extinction component (periods when the communicative response will not be reinforced) is signaled with an S^Δ (in some cases only the reinforcement component is signaled, which seems to be sufficient to establish stimulus control). For example, Hanley, Iwata, and Thompson (2001) compared the use of a multiple schedule to a mixed schedule without signals for thinning reinforcement schedules following FCT with two individuals with IDD. Prior to implementation of the schedule thinning, requests for attention occurred at high rates (five or more times per minute). The multiple schedule involved placing a white circular card on the table when the communicative response would result in reinforcement, and a red rectangular card during periods in which requests were on extinction. Initially, the reinforcement component was in effect for a much greater percentage of the time compared to the extinction component. Eventually, however, the duration of the extinction component was gradually increased, while the duration of the reinforcement component was decreased. They found that, by the end of training, both participants produced the communicative response most often when the reinforcement component was in effect, suggesting that the white card functioned as an S^D (and/or the red card functioned as an S^{Δ}), and the multiple schedule resulted in lower levels of problem behavior across the thinning process than the unsignaled mixed schedules.

Similar procedures have been used to reduce the frequency of mands for teacher attention among typically developing preschoolers (Cammilleri, Tiger, & Hanley, 2008; Tiger & Hanley, 2004). In these studies, teachers wore flowered leis in different colors to signal when teacher attention was or was not available. By alternating the schedules within a multielement design, the researchers were able to maintain student mands during desirable periods, while minimizing them during other times.

Research using multiple schedules to thin reinforcement schedules following FCT has been fairly promising. Hagopian et al. (2011) found that treatment goals were reached without requiring additional treatment components in the majority (5 of 8) studies using multiple schedules that they reviewed. Nevertheless, in three of the studies, additional intervention components were necessary. Additionally, in most of the existing studies in this area, researchers introduced contrived stimuli (e.g., cards of different shapes/colors) to serve as the S^D and S^{Δ}, rather than relying on salient features of the natural environment that could signal the availability or nonavailability of reinforcement. When relying on such artificial additions to the environment, generalization and maintenance may be compromised if the signals become lost or are not available in new environments.

Kuhn, Chirighin, and Zelenka (2010) attempted to address issues associated with the use of arbitrary stimuli by teaching individuals with IDD to respond to naturally occurring S^Ds, in this case caregiver behaviors. Specifically, the researchers arranged pairs of busy (e.g., cleaning or talking) and nonbusy (e.g., listening to music or reading) therapist behaviors in a multiple baseline across behaviors designed for each participant. Following a traditional FCT intervention, both participants produced communicative responses most often when the therapists were engaged in nonbusy activities. This study demonstrated that individuals with IDD can learn to use discriminated functional communication in response to natural salient stimuli. However, it did not assess whether the participants generalized to other, untrained activities. More recently, another study showed that one child with IDD did demonstrate generalized conditional use to novel therapists, activities, and settings (Leon, Hausman, Kahng, & Becraft, 2010).

These results are promising because they suggest that individuals with IDD can learn to respond to relatively subtle cues in the environment as discriminative stimuli, but, as these studies were conducted in relatively structured intervention settings, it is also clear that a very limited range of teaching exemplars may pose a significant challenge to interventionists teaching a beginning communicative repertoire to individuals with significant IDD. This challenge is somewhat magnified if the individual exhibits socially maintained problem behavior in that the learner already has (at least from his/her perspective) a relatively efficient communicative strategy in the form of challenging behavior in environments not addressed in FCT. As a result, the learner may see no need to extend the use of the more socially acceptable alternative to problem behavior. Such was the case in a study conducted by Drasgow, Halle, and Ostrosky (1998), in which three young children with severe language delays were taught to use appropriate mands to access preferred food, toys, and activities within a multiple-baseline across functions design. All of the participants acquired the new mands within the structured intervention environment. When posttraining probes were conducted in new settings, however, few instances of the new mands occurred. Differential reinforcement for the newly acquired mands was sufficient to promote generalization to the untrained settings for all of the participants. Results such as those reported by Drasgow et al. suggest that generalization failure for some learners may be less related to cognitive limitations and more related to a choice not to use a newly taught alternative to problem behavior. This finding suggests that generalization and conditional use of newly acquired communicative skills need to be carefully considered prior to the implementation of an intervention.

It Takes a Village of Dependent Measures to Teach Functional Communication Skills

It is not enough to have dependent measures on the new communicative alternative to be established and (in the case of FCT with persons engaging in problem behavior) problem behavior to be decelerated. A relatively limited number of investigations have carefully examined the learners' conditional use of the new communicative alternative. That is, few demonstrations have monitored both desired and undesired aspects of maintenance and generalized use. Further, few studies have acknowledged that learners who engage in problem behaviors for which communicative alternatives are an option automatically require a set of intervention support strategies aimed at the situations where the learner should refrain from using his/her new communicative alternative. For example, saying "no thanks" to green beans (an escape function can be reinforced) can become problematic when "no thanks" is extended to the offer of seizure control medication. For this latter situation, a range of other interventions that may involve powerful contingencies for participating in medication taking, a judicious arrangement of a learner's schedule, and a visual organizational aid to enhance predictability of the scheduled events might be components of a strategy for this latter occasion. Additionally, as a field, ABA is not particularly adept at addressing positive-teaching exemplars (i.e., difficult problems) that initially serve as a discriminative stimulus for a communicative alternative but later in training (once the learner becomes more competent) serve as an S^Δ for requesting assistance. Interestingly, there is an instructional technology to avoid a problematic over-narrowing of stimulus conditions associated with the discriminated use of a new communicative alternative. Next, we will address general case instruction, which is a strategy that has great potential in establishing the conditional use of desired communicative skills.

General Case Instruction

Instead of following up a successful instructional strategy with additional generalization training, as was done in many of the preceding examples, one potential instructional strategy builds in generalization training during the initial acquisition phase. As such, general case instruction is a promising proactive strategy for teaching beginning communicators to use new communicative skills conditionally by responding to natural environmental cues. This strategy involves providing teaching examples across the range of possible stimuli, from situations that call for the production of a particular communicative act (positive-teaching examples), to situations in which the communicative act would be inappropriate and would not result in reinforcement (i.e., negative-teaching examples; see O'Neill & Reichle, 1993 for a detailed description and examples). Theoretically, by concurrently providing positive- and negative-teaching examples, general case instruction should maximize the discriminative use of the new skill while also maximizing desired generalization. The utility of general case instruction for teaching individuals with IDD to use discriminated skills has been demonstrated across a variety of tasks, including vocational skills (Horner & McDonald, 1982) and personal hygiene (Stokes, Cameron, Dorsey, & Fleming, 2004). Applications of general case instruction to communication intervention, however, have been relatively few to date.

O'Neill and Reichle (1993) delineated a six-step procedure for using general case instruction for beginning communicators: (a) determine the range of stimulus conditions that should elicit the target response and the range of stimulus conditions that should not elicit the target response, (b) determine the range of relevant response variation and stimulus variation within each of the two conditions, (c) select positive-teaching examples (ones that should elicit the target response) and negative-teaching examples (ones that should not elicit the target response) for use in teaching and probe testing, (d) sequence the teaching examples, (e) teach the examples, and (f) test for acquisition with nontrained probe examples.

In reality, however, most studies that have applied the general case concept have focused on teaching either positive examples only, or a single positive and negative example, and assessing generalization across the spectrum of stimulus conditions. For example, Reichle and Johnston (1999) taught two beginning AAC users with severe disabilities to either request or reach for snack items, depending on the proximity of the items. When the items were nearby, reaching was the correct response. When the items were more distant, or in the possession of another person requesting the items by pointing to a graphic symbol was the correct response. Instruction was conducted across two conditions (near and far), and generalization to conditions with proximities between the two teaching distances was probed. Both learners quickly acquired the appropriate responses associated with the two stimulus conditions. In addition, the responses generalized differentially to the untrained distances.

Evaluation of Appropriate and Inappropriate Generalization: The Application of Generalization Gradients

In the Reichle and Johnston (1999) study described previously, data on the learners' generalization to novel distances were collected and reported in a table, which allowed for some examination of the allocation of responses across the distance values. Visual inspection is one of the hallmarks of applied behavior analysis, however, and a tool from the experimental analysis of behavior literature may be useful in such cases. Many basic studies investigating stimulus control and stimulus generalization have used figures called "generalization gradients" to assess how changes to stimulus

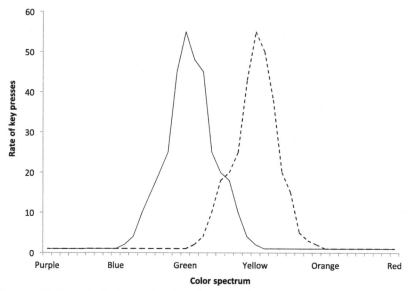

Figure 12.3 Hypothetical data showing the generalization gradients across the color spectrum for pigeons trained to respond to green (solid) and yellow (dashed) lights.

parameters affect generalization. For example, consider a pigeon that was trained to peck keys in the presence of yellow lights, but not orange or green. Following training, generalization was assessed by measuring the number of key presses in response to lights across the color spectrum. In this case, the generalization gradient that resulted might look like the solid line in Figure 12.3. If, on the other hand, the pigeon was taught to peck in the presence of green, but not yellow or blue, the gradient might look more like the dashed line in Figure 12.3. Such visual depictions of the degree of response strength (or probability of a response) as a function of stimulus value (or degree of similarity to the training stimulus or stimuli; Pierce & Cheney, 2013) have not been applied frequently in the applied literature. They could, however, be harnessed to allow for the visualization and analysis of a learner's performance across a range of stimuli and in order to determine the degree of appropriate and inappropriate generalizations.

As an example, Figure 12.4 shows a generalization gradient created using the generalization data from the Reichle and Johnston (1999) study. The figure clearly shows that, although both participants' gradients have similar shapes, with requests being least likely to occur at the closest distances, and

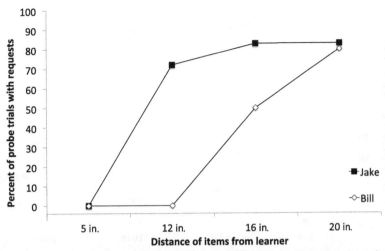

Figure 12.4 Generalization gradients showing appropriate conditional requests based on the distance from desired item. *Based on the data from Reichle and Johnston (1999). Copyright 2001 by the American Speech-Language-Hearing Association (ASHA). Adapted with permission.*

most likely at the furthest distances, the location of the gradients are shifted, so that Jake switched from reaching to requesting at a closer distance than Bill did.

Based on the generalization gradients, we can determine that stimulus generalization occurred for both participants, and overall, the degree of generalization appears to be appropriate for both participants. If, however, the generalization gradients looked like the hypothetical results presented in Figure 12.5, they would suggest that overgeneralization of the requesting and reaching behaviors occurred for Bill and Jake. In this case, it would indicate that conditional use had not been achieved, and additional interventions to bias responding towards the alternative behaviors would be necessary.

Considering the previous example from Reichle and McComas (2004) provides another good example of how general case instruction and generalization gradients can be used in combination to assess and teach appropriate conditional use of the assistance requests. Rather than teaching and reinforcing assistance requests only when challenging work was presented at the beginning of the intervention, the interventionists could have identified several positive examples (difficult work tasks) which would have been S^Ds for assistance requests, and interspersed trials with easy work in which the correct response would have resulted in reinforcement, and negative examples (easy work tasks) which would have been S^Δs for assistance requests, but S^Ds

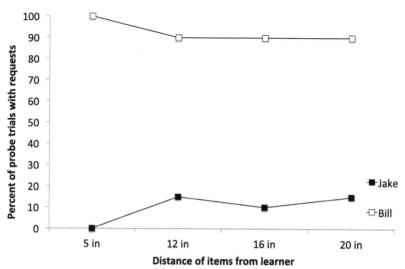

Figure 12.5 Hypothetical generalization gradients showing overgeneralized requests (Jake) and reaching (Bill) behaviors. *Based on the procedures from Reichle and Johnston (1999).*

for independent task completion. By teaching both the positive and negative examples together, this strategy could help address a significant challenge in teaching the use of assistance requests. In many cases, practice in a given task will reduce its difficulty over time. As a result (and as mentioned earlier in this chapter), what may initially serve as a discriminative stimulus for a request for assistance (e.g., difficult work) eventually becomes easier for the learner. Over time, the task should switch from being an S^D to an S^Δ for assistance requests. Instead, it should become a discriminative stimulus for independent work. That is, the assistance request should result in appropriate prompts to teach the skill that precipitated the request for assistance. In turn, the prompts associated with learning the task should be faded and eventually eliminated. Ideally, as the learner masters tasks that were initially challenging, one would expect to see a decline in the use of requests for assistance with this activity, yet continued use of the requests with difficult tasks not yet mastered. In many cases, however, the assistance requests will continue to be a less effortful response than independent task completion, even with mastered tasks. Therefore, using a generalization gradient could serve as a useful tool in assessing whether, and at what point, responding switches from assistance requests to independent task completion, and whether the location of the gradient shifts over time.

CONCLUSIONS

The instructional strategies developed within the science of ABA are particularly relevant for teaching individuals with IDD to produce functional communicative acts using AAC. As we have seen, many researchers have successfully applied single-subject experimental designs to determine which communication modes or symbol types are likely to be beneficial for individual learners. Beyond being an applied science that generates idiographic information, however, ABA is also a technological science that can generate conceptual knowledge to inform broader issues. In general, there has been less work in translating the basic knowledge generated through experimental behavioral analyses into evidence-based interventions in the field of AAC. Although basic strategies such as FCT have been effective in teaching individuals to use simple communicative responses in controlled situations, much more work is needed to address the more complex issues of conditional use and long-term maintenance. In particular, the basic and applied literatures on response efficiency, stimulus control, and generalization should be considered more frequently when designing AAC interventions for beginning communicators. This chapter has reviewed some preliminary work that has extended these concepts into the applied literature, but more work is needed in order to achieve the full potential of the field.

ACKNOWLEDGMENTS

Preparation of this chapter was supported in part by Grant #2-T73MC12835-03-00 from the Maternal & Child Health Bureau (MCHB) of the US Department of Health and Human Services awarded to the University of Minnesota.

REFERENCES

American Speech-Language Hearing Association (ASHA). (2002). *Augmentative and alternative communication: Knowledge and skills for service delivery.* Accessed from www.asha.org/policy.

Bauman, R. A., Shull, R. L., & Brownstein, A. J. (1975). Time allocation on concurrent schedules with asymmetrical response requirements. *Journal of the Experimental Analysis of Behavior, 24,* 53–57. http://dx.doi.org/10.1901/jeab.1975.24-53.

Beukelman, D., & Mirenda, P. (1998). Principles of assessment. In D. Beukelman & P. Mirenda (Eds.), *Augmentative and alternative communication* (2nd, pp. 145–169). Baltimore: Paul H. Brookes Publishing Company.

Bliss, C. K. (1965). *Semantography-Blissymbolics.* Sydney, Australia: Semantology Publications.

Bondy, A. S., & Frost, L. A. (1994). The picture exchange communication system. *Focus on Autism and Other Developmental Disabilities*, *9*, 1–19. http://dx.doi.org/10.1177/108835769400900301.

Cammilleri, A. P., Tiger, J. H., & Hanley, G. P. (2008). Developing stimulus control of young children's requests to teachers: Classwide applications of multiple schedules. *Journal of Applied Behavior Analysis*, *41*, 299–303. http://dx.doi.org/10.1901/jaba.2008.41-299.

Cannella-Malone, H. I., DeBar, R. M., & Sigafoos, J. (2009). An examination of preference for augmentative and alternative communication devices with two boys with significant intellectual disabilities. *Augmentative and Alternative Communication*, *25*, 262–273. http://dx.doi.org/10.3109/07434610903384511.

Carpenter, R. L., Mastergeorge, A. M., & Coggins, T. E. (1983). The acquisition of communicative intentions in infants eight to fifteen months of age. *Language and Speech*, *26*, 101–116. http://dx.doi.org/10.1177/002383098302600201.

Carr, E. G., & Durand, V. M. (1985). Reducing behavior problems through functional communication training. *Journal of Applied Behavior Analysis*, *18*, 111–126. http://dx.doi.org/10.1901/jaba.1985.18-111.

Derby, K. M., Wacker, D. P., Berg, W., DeRaad, A., Ulrich, S., Asmus, J., et al. (1997). The long-term effects of functional communication training in home settings. *Journal of Applied Behavior Analysis*, *30*, 507–531. http://dx.doi.org/10.1901/jaba.1997.30-507.

Drasgow, E., & Halle, J. W. (1995). Teaching social communication to young children with severe disabilities. *Topics in Early Childhood Special Education*, *15*, 165–186. http://dx.doi.org/10.1177/027112149501500203.

Drasgow, E., Halle, J. W., & Ostrosky, M. M. (1998). Effects of differential reinforcement on the generalization of a replacement mand in three children with severe language delays. *Journal of Applied Behavior Analysis*, *31*, 357–374. http://dx.doi.org/10.1901/jaba.1998.31-357.

Drasgow, E., Halle, J. W., & Sigafoos, J. (1999). Teaching communication to learners with severe disabilities: Motivation, response competition, and generalization. *Australasian Journal of Special Education*, *1*, 47–63. http://dx.doi.org/10.1080/1030011990230105.

Dunlap, G., Ester, T., Langhans, S., & Fox, L. (2006). Functional communication training with toddlers in home environments. *Journal of Early Intervention*, *28*, 81–96. http://dx.doi.org/10.1177/105381510602800201.

Durand, V. M. (1999). Functional communication training using assistive devices: Recruiting natural communities of reinforcement. *Journal of Applied Behavior Analysis*, *32*, 247–267. http://dx.doi.org/10.1901/jaba.1999.32-247.

Durand, G. M., & Carr, E. G. (1991). Functional communication training to replace challenging behavior: Maintenance and application to new settings. *Journal of Applied Behavior Analysis*, *24*, 251–264. http://dx.doi.org/10.1901/jaba.1991.24-251.

Fisher, W., Piazza, C., Cataldo, M., Harrell, R., Jefferson, G., & Conner, R. (1993). Functional communication training with and without extinction and punishment. *Journal of Applied Behavior Analysis*, *26*, 23–36. http://dx.doi.org/10.1901/jaba.1993.26-23.

Flood, W. A., & Wilder, D. A. (2002). Antecedent assessment and assessment-based treatment of off-task behavior in a child diagnosed with attention deficit-hyperactivity disorder (ADHD). *Education and Treatment of Children*, *25*, 331–339.

Gregory, M. K., DeLeon, I. G., & Richman, D. M. (2009). The influence of matching and motor-imitation abilities on rapid acquisition of manual signs and exchange-based communicative responses. *Journal of Applied Behavior Analysis*, *42*, 399–404. http://dx.doi.org/10.1901/jaba.2009.42-399.

Hagopian, L. P., Boelter, E. W., & Jarmolowicz, D. P. (2011). Reinforcement schedule thinning following functional communication training: Review and recommendations. *Behavior Analysis in Practice, 4*, 4–16.

Hagopian, L. P., Fisher, W. W., Sullivan, M. T., Acquisto, J., & LeBlanc, L. A. (1998). Effectiveness of functional communication training with and without extinction and punishment: A summary of 21 inpatient cases. *Journal of Applied Behavior Analysis, 31*, 211–235. http://dx.doi.org/10.1901/jaba.1998.31-211.

Hanley, G. P., Iwata, B. A., & Thompson, R. H. (2001). Reinforcement schedule thinning following treatment with functional communication training. *Journal of Applied Behavior Analysis, 34*, 17–38. http://dx.doi.org/10.1901/jaba.2001.34-17.

Harding, J. W., Wacker, D. P., Berg, W. K., Barretto, A., & Rankin, B. (2002). Assessment and treatment of severe behavior problems using choice-making procedures. *Education and Treatment of Children, 24*, 26–46.

Herrnstein, R. J. (1961). Relative and absolute strength of response as a function of frequency of reinforcement. *Journal of the Experimental Analysis of Behavior, 4*, 267–272. http://dx.doi.org/10.1901/jeab.1961.4-267.

Hollard, V., & Davison, M. C. (1971). Preference for qualitatively different reinforcers. *Journal of the Experimental Analysis of Behavior, 16*, 375–380. http://dx.doi.org/10.1901/jeab.1971.16-375.

Horner, R. H. (1990). The role of response efficiency in the reduction of problem behaviors through functional equivalence training: A case study. *Journal of the Association for Persons with Severe Handicaps, 15*, 91–97.

Horner, R. H., & Day, H. M. (1991). The effects of response efficiency on functionally equivalent competing behaviors. *Journal of Applied Behavior Analysis, 24*, 719–732. http://dx.doi.org/10.1901/jaba.1991.24-719.

Horner, R. H., & McDonald, R. S. (1982). Comparison of single instance and general case instruction in teaching a generalized vocational skill. *Journal of the Association for the Severely Handicapped, 7*, 7–20.

Hurlbut, B. I., Iwata, B. A., & Green, J. D. (1982). Nonvocal language acquisition in adolescents with severe physical disabilities: Blissymbol versus iconic stimulus formats. *Journal of Applied Behavior Analysis, 15*, 241–258. http://dx.doi.org/10.1901/jaba.1982.15-241.

Hyppa Martin, J., Reichle, J., Dimian, A., & Chen, M. (2013). Communication modality sampling for a toddler with Angelman syndrome. *Language, Speech, and Hearing Services in Schools, 44*, 327–336. http://dx.doi.org/10.1044/0161-1461.

Johnston, S. S., & Evans, J. (2005). Considering response efficiency as a strategy to prevent assistive technology abandonment. *Journal of Special Education Technology, 20*, 45–50.

Johnston, S., Reichle, J., Feeley, K., & Jones, E. (2012). *AAC strategies for individuals with moderate to severe disabilities.* Baltimore, MD: Paul H. Brookes Publishing Company.

Kuhn, D. E., Chirighin, A. E., & Zelenka, K. (2010). Discriminated functional communication: A procedural extension of functional communication training. *Journal of Applied Behavior Analysis, 43*, 249–264. http://dx.doi.org/10.1901/jaba.2010.43-249.

Lalli, J. S., Browder, D. M., Mace, F. C., & Brown, D. K. (1993). Teacher use of descriptive analysis data to implement interventions to decrease students' problem behaviors. *Journal of Applied Behavior Analysis, 26*, 227–238. http://dx.doi.org/10.1901/jaba.1993.26-227.

Leon, Y., Hausman, N., Kahng, S. W., & Becraft, J. L. (2010). Further examination of discriminated functional communication. *Journal of Applied Behavior Analysis, 43*, 525–530. http://dx.doi.org/10.1901/jaba.2010.43-525.

Logue, A. W. (1988). Research on self-control: An integrating framework. *Behavioral and Brain Sciences, 11*, 665–679. http://dx.doi.org/10.1017/S0140525X00053978.

Mace, C. F., & Roberts, M. L. (1993). Developing effective interventions: Empirical and conceptual considerations. In J. Reichle & D. P. Wacker (Eds.), *Communicative alternatives to challenging behaviors* (pp. 113–133). Baltimore, MD: Paul H. Brookes Publishing Company.

Martens, B. K., & Houk, J. L. (1989). The application of Herrnstein's law of effect to disruptive and on-task behavior of a retarded adolescent girl. *Journal of the Experimental Analysis of Behavior, 51*, 17–27. http://dx.doi.org/10.1901/jeab.1989.51-17.

Miller, H. L. (1976). Matching-based hedonic scaling in the pigeon. *Journal of the Experimental Analysis of Behavior, 26*, 335–347. http://dx.doi.org/10.1901/jeab.1976.26-335.

O'Neill, R., & Reichle, J. (1993). Addressing socially motivated challenging behaviors by establishing communicative alternatives: Basics of a general case approach. In J. Reichle, & D. P. Wacker (Eds.), *Communicative alternatives to challenging behaviors* (pp. 205–235). Baltimore, MD: Paul H. Brookes Publishing Company.

Phillips, B., & Zhao, H. (1993). Predictors of assistive technology abandonment. *Assistive Technology, 5*, 36–45. http://dx.doi.org/10.1080/10400435.1993.10132205.

Pierce, W. D., & Cheney, C. D. (2013). *Behavior analysis and learning* (5th). Sussex, UK: Psychology Press.

Reichle, J., Johnson, L., Monn, E., & Harris, M. (2010). Task engagement and escape maintained challenging behavior: Differential effects of general and explicit cues when implementing a signaled delay in the delivery of reinforcement. *Journal of Autism and Developmental Disorders, 40*, 709–720. http://dx.doi.org/10.1007/s10803-010-0946-6.

Reichle, J., & Johnston, S. S. (1999). Teaching the conditional use of communicative requests to two school-age children with severe developmental disabilities. *Language, Speech, and Hearing Services in Schools, 30*, 324–334.

Reichle, J., & McComas, J. (2004). Conditional use of a request for assistance. *Disability and Rehabilitation, 26*, 1255–1262. http://dx.doi.org/10.1080/09638280412331280262.

Reichle, J., & Parker-McGowan, Q. (2014). *Determining graphic symbol type to implement for a preschooler with ASD and a moderate intellectual delay.* Unpublished manuscript. Minneapolis: University of Minnesota.

Reichle, J., & Wacker, D. P. (1993). *Communicative alternatives to challenging behaviors* (pp. 205–235). Baltimore, MD: Paul H. Brookes Publishing Company.

Reichle, J., York, J., & Sigafoos, J. (1991). *Implementing augmentative and alternative communication: Strategies for learners with severe disabilities.* Baltimore, MD: Paul H. Brookes Publishing Company.

Rispoli, M. J., Franco, J. H., van der Meer, L., Lang, R., & Camargo, S. P. H. (2010). The use of speech generating devices in communication interventions for individuals with developmental disabilities: A review of the literature. *Developmental Neurorehabilitation, 13*, 276–293. http://dx.doi.org/10.3109/17518421003636794.

Schlosser, R. W., & Lee, D. L. (2000). Promoting generalization and maintenance in augmentative and alternative communication. *Augmentative and Alternative Communication, 16*, 208–226. http://dx.doi.org/10.1080/07434610012331279074.

Schlosser, R. W. (1999). Comparative efficacy of interventions in augmentative and alternative communication. *Augmentative and Alternative Communication, 15*, 56–68. http://dx.doi.org/10.1080/07434619912331278575.

Sigafoos, J., O'Reilly, M., Drasgow, E., & Reichle, J. (2002). Strategies to achieve socially acceptable escape and avoidance. In J. Reichle, D. Beukelman, & J. Light (Eds.), *Exemplary practices for beginning communicators* (pp. 157–186). Baltimore: Paul H. Brookes Publishing Company.

Sigafoos, J., & Reichle, J. (1993). Establishing spontaneous verbal behavior. In R. A. Gable, & S. F. Warren (Eds.), *Strategies for teaching students with mild to severe mental retardation* (Vol. 5, pp. 191–230). London: Jessica Kingsley Company.

Sindelar, P. T., Rosenberg, M. S., & Wilson, R. J. (1985). An adapted alternating treatments design for instructional research. *Education & Treatment of Children, 8*, 67–76.

Skinner, B. F. (1957). *Verbal behavior*. New York: Appleton-Century-Crofts.

Son, S. H., Sigafoos, J., O'Reilly, M., & Lancioni, G. E. (2006). Comparing two types of augmentative and alternative communication systems for children with autism. *Developmental Neurorehabilitation*, *9*, 389–395. http://dx.doi.org/10.1080/13638490500519984.

Stokes, T. F., & Baer, D. M. (1977). An implicit technology of generalization. *Journal of Applied Behavior Analysis*, *10*, 349–367. http://dx.doi.org/10.1901/jaba.1977.10-349.

Stokes, J. V., Cameron, M. J., Dorsey, M. F., & Fleming, E. (2004). Task analysis, correspondence training, and general case instruction for teaching personal hygiene skills. *Behavioral Interventions*, *19*, 121–135. http://dx.doi.org/10.1002/bin.153.

Tait, K., Sigafoos, J., Woodyatt, G., O'Reilly, M., & Lancioni, G. (2004). Evaluating parent use of functional communication training to replace and enhance prelinguistic behaviours in six children with developmental and physical disabilities. *Disability & Rehabilitation*, *26*, 1241–1254. http://dx.doi.org/10.1080/09638280312331280253.

Tiger, J. H., & Hanley, G. P. (2004). Developing stimulus control of preschooler mands: An analysis of schedule-correlated and contingency-specifying stimuli. *Journal of Applied Behavior Analysis*, *37*, 517–521. http://dx.doi.org/10.1901/jaba.2004.37-517.

Tiger, J. H., Hanley, G. P., & Bruzek, J. (2008). Functional communication training: A review and practical guide. *Behavior Analysis in Practice*, *1*, 16–23.

van der Meer, L., Sigafoos, J., O'Reilly, M. F., & Lancioni, G. E. (2011). Assessing preferences for AAC options in communication interventions for individuals with developmental disabilities: A review of the literature. *Research in Developmental Disabilities*, *32*, 1422–1431. http://dx.doi.org/10.1016/j.ridd.2011.02.003.

van Der Meer, L., Sutherland, D., O'Reilly, M. F., Lancioni, G. E., & Sigafoos, J. (2012). A further comparison of manual signing, picture exchange, and speech-generating devices as communication modes for children with autism spectrum disorders. *Research in Autism Spectrum Disorders*, *6*, 1247–1257. http://dx.doi.org/10.1016/j.rasd.2012.04.005.

Vollmer, T. R., Borrero, J. C., Lalli, J. S., & Daniel, D. (1999). Evaluating self-control and impulsivity in children with severe behavior disorders. *Journal of Applied Behavior Analysis*, *32*, 451–466. http://dx.doi.org/10.1901/jaba.1999.32-451.

Vollmer, T. R., Northup, J., Ringdahl, J. E., LeBlanc, L. A., & Chauvin, T. M. (1996). Functional analysis of severe tantrums displayed by children with language delays: An outclinic assessment. *Behavior Modification*, *20*, 97–115. http://dx.doi.org/10.1177/01454455960201005.

Wacker, D. P., Berg, W. K., Harding, J. W., Barretto, A., Rankin, B., & Ganzer, J. (2005). Treatment effectiveness, stimulus generalization, and acceptability to parents of functional communication training. *Educational Psychology*, *25*, 233–256. http://dx.doi.org/10.1080/0144341042000301184.

Wacker, D. P., Lee, J. F., Dalmau, Y. C. P., Kopelman, T. G., Lindgren, S. D., Kuhle, J., et al. (2013). Conducting functional communication training via telehealth to reduce the problem behavior of young children with autism. *Journal of Developmental and Physical Disabilities*, *25*, 35–48. http://dx.doi.org/10.1007/s10882-012-9314-0.

Wilder, D. A., Masuda, A., O'Conner, C., & Baham, M. (2001). Brief functional analysis and treatment of bizarre vocalization in an adult with schizophrenia. *Journal of Applied Behavior Analysis*, *34*, 65–68. http://dx.doi.org/10.1901/jaba.2001.34-65.

Winborn, L., Wacker, D. P., Richman, D. M., Asmus, J., & Geier, D. (2002). Assessment of mand selection for functional communication training packages. *Journal of Applied Behavior Analysis*, *35*, 295–298. http://dx.doi.org/10.1901/jaba.2002.35-295.

Winborn-Kemmerer, L., Ringdahl, J. E., Wacker, D. P., & Kitsukawa, K. (2009). A demonstration of individual preference for novel mands during functional communication training. *Journal of Applied Behavior Analysis*, *42*, 185–189. http://dx.doi.org/10.1901/jaba.2009.42-185.

CHAPTER 13

Treatment of Pediatric Obesity: An Opportunity for Behavior Analysts

Nicole L. Hausman[1], SungWoo Kahng[2]
[1]Department of Behavioral Psychology, The Kennedy Krieger Institute, Baltimore, Maryland, USA
[2]Department of Health Psychology, University of Missouri, Columbia, Missouri, USA

OVERVIEW OF PEDIATRIC OBESITY

The prevalence of obesity among children in the United States has increased since the 1970s and is an important public health concern. Classification of children between the ages of 2 and 19 years as overweight or obese is based on comparing a child's Body Mass Index (BMI) to the BMI of peers (i.e., same age and gender). BMI is a standardized measure of body composition (i.e., body fat) based upon factors such as age, height, weight, and gender. Children are classified as of a healthy weight if their BMI is between the 5th and 84th percentile, overweight if their BMI falls between the 85th and 94th percentile, and obese if their BMI is greater than the 95th percentile for their age and gender.

Obesity prevalence among children increased significantly in the 1980s and 1990s (Ogden, Carroll, Kit, & Flegal, 2012). Currently, an estimated 32% of children between the ages of 2 and 19 are overweight, 17% are obese, and 12% have a BMI above the 97th percentile for their age and gender (Ogden, Carroll, Curtin, Lamb, & Flegal, 2010; Ogden, Carroll, & Flegal, 2008; Ogden et al., 2012). Furthermore, 10% of infants and toddlers under the age of 2 are at or above the 95th percentile in weight (Ogden et al., 2010). Obesity prevalence is higher among Hispanic and non-Hispanic black children, indicating a racial/ethnic disparity in the prevalence of obesity (Ogden et al., 2012).

Obesity is associated with an overall higher risk of numerous health conditions, including heart disease, hypertension, asthma, sleep apnea, and Type 2 diabetes (Daniels, 2009). Adolescents who are overweight are 70% more likely to remain overweight in adulthood, increasing the probability that they will develop serious health conditions (Barlow & Dietz, 1998).

Clinical and Organizational Applications of Applied Behavior Analysis
http://dx.doi.org/10.1016/B978-0-12-420249-8.00013-7

303

For overweight children in particular, the risk of developing serious chronic illnesses at an early age as a result of their weight is a significant public health issue.

CAUSES OF OBESITY

Due to the rapid increase in the prevalence of individuals who are obese, an increasing number of studies have been conducted to determine the etiology of obesity, whether biological or environmental in nature (Chakravarthy & Booth, 2004; Hebebrand & Hinney, 2008). Although data suggest that genetics may play a large role in the development of obesity, the environment also exerts a strong influence. Much of the data supporting a genetic predisposition to obesity has been reported from twin studies. Heritability estimates in BMI between 0.60 and 0.90 have been found for twins raised in shared and unshared environments (Hebebrand & Hinney, 2008). Heritability coefficients as low as 0.60 among twins suggest that at least 40% of the variance of BMI may be due to external factors, presumably those present in the environment. Thus, a possible interaction between genetics and the environment must be considered when determining the cause of obesity. That is, a child with obese parents and siblings who is also living in an environment where calorically dense foods are readily available, and there is little opportunity for physical activity is more likely to become obese than a similar child with only one of these risk factors.

Although an interaction between genetic and environmental factors ultimately contributes to the development of obesity, only environmental factors are currently amenable to intervention. That is, although genetic factors likely play a role in the development of obesity, modifying environmental factors to promote healthier eating habits and engagement in physical activity are common targets for intervention. According to the expert committee recommendations, the primary goal of weight loss programs for children should be behavior change (Barlow & Dietz, 1998). Thus, clinicians should emphasize the importance of healthy eating habits and physical activity to children referred for weight loss programs. Environmental variables (e.g., eating unhealthy foods and engaging in more sedentary behavior) involved in the development of pediatric obesity are of importance to behavior analysts, who have particular expertise in identifying the antecedents and consequences of maintaining health-related behavior and subsequently developing behavioral interventions to decrease maladaptive behavior and increase healthier alternative behavior. In the area of pediatric obesity, there are three areas in which behavior analytic procedures may be particularly useful: changing eating habits, increasing physical activity, and developing comprehensive, behaviorally based treatment programs for overweight children.

PROMOTING HEALTHY EATING

Obesity can be conceptualized as a problem of positive energy balance in which individuals consume more calories than are expended through physical activity. Many researchers have attributed the rise in the prevalence of overweight and obesity over the last 30 years to an overall increase in caloric consumption rather than decreases in physical activity, suggesting that changing eating habits may be critical to successful treatment (Chandon & Wansink, 2007; Kopelman, 2000). This positive energy balance can be a function of eating foods that have a high energy density (i.e., are high in fat and calories) or eating portion sizes that are too large. Historically, treatment of obesity has focused on changing eating habits by providing participants with general information regarding dietary guidelines and educating participants on ways to reduce calorie intake (i.e., nutrition education). Essentially, nutrition education programs provide patients with information regarding what to eat and how much, and what foods to avoid. The primary purpose of nutrition education interventions is to decrease the caloric intake of participants and to help establish healthier eating habits (Epstein, Masek, & Marshall, 1978). However, the use of nutrition education alone to reduce BMI has had mixed results, necessitating the need for additional intervention components or more specific interventions to change eating habits. Behavior analysts have long been involved in the successful assessment and treatment of problematic food-related behavior (e.g., food refusal; Friman & Piazza, 2011). Chronic overconsumption of unhealthy, energy dense foods could be conceptualized as a type of feeding disorder that may be responsive to behavioral intervention, similar to food selectivity or refusal. Therefore, modifying the eating habits of overweight children should fall within the scope of applied behavior analysis yet has received little attention from researchers in the field.

Factors influencing choice: Researchers have demonstrated that obese individuals may find food more reinforcing than healthy weight individuals (Epstein, Lin, Carr, & Fletcher, 2012; Saelens & Epstein, 1996; Temple & Epstein, 2012). The relative reinforcing value (RRV) of high energy-density food is greater for overweight children than healthy weight peers, suggesting that overweight children may value energy-dense food over other potential reinforcers such as spending time with peers (e.g., Best et al., 2012; Epstein et al., 2007) and has subsequently been linked to greater weight gain (Hill, Saxton, Webber, Blundell, & Wardle, 2009).

Furthermore, higher BMI may be predictive of sensitization to the presentation of high energy-density snack foods (Temple & Epstein, 2012). Stated differently, obese individuals may work harder to obtain food and may become more sensitized to repeated exposures to high energy-density snack foods in laboratory experiments. This phenomenon is similar to what has been observed in studies on drug and alcohol addiction (e.g., Robinson & Berridge, 1993). Thus, obese individuals may need a higher "dose" of a particular food after several presentations of that food.

The critical questions for behavioral intervention for healthy eating are: How do individuals choose what to eat given a range of concurrently available alternative food items and how do we subsequently intervene to teach individuals to make healthier choices? Behavioral economics is a promising area in the study of pediatric obesity in that it allows us to better understand how individuals make choices within their environment. Furthermore, behavioral economics may provide an important framework for predicting success with weight loss interventions and how the environment may influence eating habits (Best et al., 2012).

Multiple studies in the area of behavioral economics have suggested that obese individuals may discount delayed rewards more than healthy weight peers (e.g., Epstein, Salvy, Carr, Dearing, & Bickel, 2010). That is, as the time to obtaining some reward increases, the subjective value of that reward decreases. In classic delayed discounting studies, participants are asked to choose between hypothetical rewards that are delivered immediately versus at later points in time. For example, a participant may be asked to choose between $1 immediately and $10 in a week. When individuals consistently allocate responding towards the smaller, sooner rewards (SSR) over the larger, later rewards (LLR), they are said to be more impulsive; self-control being associated with selection of the LLR and less discounting. Impulsive choice on delayed discounting tasks has been demonstrated across a variety of other at-risk populations such as substance abusers, cigarette smokers, and gamblers, suggesting that discounting of delayed rewards may underlie a wide variety of maladaptive behaviors (Bickel, Yi, Landes, Hill, & Baxter, 2011; Dixon & Holton, 2009).

Interventions to alter choice: Given that increased discounting of delayed rewards is common to a variety of disorders, an evaluation of individuals' allocation of responding under these delayed discounting paradigms may be important to the development of interventions to teach individuals self-control. For overweight individuals seeking treatment, the potential reinforcers for engaging in healthy behavior (e.g., losing weight, improved overall health) can be very delayed. Therefore, these individuals may be more likely to choose to engage in more immediate, unhealthy behavior (e.g., eating an unhealthy food now). Furthermore, high energy-density foods may be more readily available and more highly preferred, making it more likely for the individual to obtain a snack from a vending machine rather than seeking out a healthier alternative.

Researchers in the field have explored various methods to teach self-control to individuals who may be more likely to behave impulsively. In the previous studies, systematically increasing the delay to the LLR (e.g., Schweitzer & Sulzer-Azaroff, 1988), providing a distraction during the delay to the reinforcer (e.g., Mischel, Ebbesen, & Zeiss, 1972), and a combination of the procedures (e.g., Dixon et al., 1998) have all been effective at reducing impulsivity. Binder, Dixon, and Ghezzi (2000), for example, evaluated a progressive delay procedure with two verbal distraction tasks (i.e., repeating rules and flash cards) to teach self-control to three children diagnosed with Attention-Deficit Hyperactivity Disorder (ADHD). During the initial baseline delayed discounting task, all participants displayed an exclusive preference for the SSR; however, when the larger reinforcer was available immediately, all participants showed an exclusive preference for the larger, immediately available reward. During self-control training, participants continued to choose the LLR. These findings extended the research on teaching self-control and suggested that the type of verbal distraction task used may be irrelevant in the teaching of self-control.

Dixon and Holton (2009) evaluated past and future delayed discounting of pathological gamblers before and after a conditional discrimination training procedure. Baseline consisted of a delayed discounting task using hypothetical monetary rewards and was followed by conditional discrimination training consisting of stimulus sets that included monetary values, gambling stimuli, nonmonetary quantitative stimuli, and nonmonetary qualitative stimuli to teach relation of "better than" and "worse than." Training was followed by a delayed discounting posttest. For all five participants, greater discounting of delayed, hypothetical monetary rewards was observed during baseline. During the posttest, less discounting of delayed rewards was observed.

Finally, Bickel et al. (2011) compared the efficacy of two training methods to teach self-control to 27 stimulant addicts. Both training groups completed working memory tasks; however, participants assigned to the Active Training group were compensated for performance. By contrast, compensation in the Control Training group was yoked to an individual in the Active Training group (performance independent), and correct responses in the Control Training group were provided to participants such that they did not have to engage working memory to answer correctly. Delayed discounting tasks were conducted before and after training. Results suggested that individuals assigned to the Active Training group discounted the value of delayed, hypothetical rewards less than participants assigned to the Control Training group.

Research in the area of behavioral economics is important to the treatment of pediatric obesity in that it allows clinicians to better understand how overweight children may make choices between various concurrently available food options. Although delay discounting has been more widely applied to evaluate choice in areas outside of obesity and other health-related behaviors, behavior analysts have an opportunity to apply this technology to overweight children in an effort to inform the development of more effective interventions. Subsequently, research in the area of self-control training has the potential to improve the efficacy of behavioral treatment programs for weight loss. Although further research in the area is needed, it is possible that teaching children to engage in a simple distraction task (e.g., reciting a rule about what to eat) when making food selections may reduce more impulsive choices.

Teaching portion control: In addition to an analysis of how individuals make choices regarding what to eat, it is important to teach individuals how much to eat once they have selected a food item. Obesity research consistently suggests that there is a positive correlation between portion size and consumption (Freedman & Brochado, 2010; Rolls, Roe, Kral, Meengs, & Wall, 2004; Steenhuis & Vermeer, 2009; Wansink, Painter, & North, 2005; Wansink, van Ittersum, & Painter, 2006). Furthermore, individuals who are overweight may be even more likely to overeat when presented with larger portion sizes (Burger, Fisher, & Johnson, 2011). This trend is compounded as Americans dine out with increasing frequency. Current estimates suggest that Americans consume one-third of their calories each day from foods prepared outside of the home, and foods prepared outside of the home are generally presented as larger portion sizes (Young & Nestle, 2007).

Given the important role portion size plays in overconsumption of foods, it is important to teach individuals to consume appropriate portion sizes of even healthy foods. Much of the research on teaching individuals to consume smaller portion sizes has focused on teaching the use of Portion Size Measurement Aids (PSMAs) that serve as representations of various portion sizes (e.g., parts of the hand; Byrd-Bredbenner & Schwartz, 2004; Cypel, Guenther, & Petot, 1997). Research has generally supported the use of various PSMAs to teach individuals to identify portion sizes with greater accuracy (e.g., Byrd-Bredbenner & Schwartz, 2004; Weber, 1993); however, the few studies that have evaluated the effectiveness of PSMAs on the portion size estimations of children have not proven as successful (Foster, Adamson, Anderson, Barton, & Wrieden, 2009; Foster, Anderson, & Adamson, 2001; Frobisher & Maxwell, 2003; Young & Nestle, 1995).

To address some of the limitations in the literature pertaining to the use of PSMAs in pediatric populations, more intensive training methods may be necessary to teach children how to estimate portion sizes. One method for teaching individuals to use PSMAs may be through a stimulus equivalence paradigm. Stimulus equivalence procedures have been used to teach a variety of skills (Critchfield & Fienup, 2010; Toussaint & Tiger, 2010; Walker, Rehfeldt, & Ninness, 2010) and are applicable to a number of different populations (Hall, DeBernardis, & Reiss, 2006; LeBlanc, Miguel, Cummings, Goldsmith, & Carr, 2003; Toussaint & Tiger, 2010). In a stimulus equivalence procedure, specific sets of relations are taught, followed by a test to determine whether untrained relations between stimuli may emerge (Green & Saunders, 1998; Rehfeldt, 2011).

As of yet, stimulus equivalence paradigms have not been widely used to teach health-related behaviors such as those that may be related to estimating portion sizes using PSMAs. In a recent study, a stimulus equivalence paradigm was used to teach college students to more accurately estimate a target portion size (Hausman, Borrero, Fisher, & Kahng, 2014). During baseline and posttraining probes, participants were asked to estimate a one-half cup portion size of Cheerios® without the use of any aids. During training, a stimulus equivalence procedure was used to teach the specific relations between portion sizes of various foods, measuring cups depicting various portion sizes, and PSMAs representing these portion sizes (various sports balls). A test of untrained relations was then conducted to determine if untrained relations between the various stimuli had been established. Maintenance sessions at one-week posttraining and extension sessions with novel foods were also conducted. Results suggested that the majority of

participants more accurately estimated the target portion size of Cheerios®
during posttraining and maintenance sessions. Furthermore, some participants were able to accurately estimate the target portion size of a novel food
not used in training during the extension sessions.

The results of Hausman et al. (2014) suggest that the use of stimulus
equivalence procedures might be useful to help teach overweight individuals
seeking treatment how to more accurately estimate portion sizes of foods
they are eating, particularly when dining outside of the home when the
use of more specific measurement tools (e.g., measuring cups) may not be
practical or may be stigmatizing. However, it is unknown the extent to
which teaching individuals to estimate portion sizes accurately may translate
into direct changes in eating habits. That is, it remains untested whether providing individuals with the skills needed to accurately estimate the portion
size available may translate into actual reductions in calories consumed and
subsequent weight loss.

PROMOTING PHYSICAL ACTIVITY

In addition to increasing the consumption of healthy foods and decreasing
consumption of unhealthy foods, increasing physical activity is integral to
maintaining a healthy BMI. If eating is equivalent to the "energy in" side
of the energy balance equation, physical activity is equivalent to the "energy
out" side of the equation. It is recommended that children get at least 60 min
of physical activity each day (U.S. Department of Health and Human
Services, 2012). Although it is unclear just how much physical activity children are getting each day, most researchers suggest that it is not enough to
support a healthy lifestyle. Furthermore, an increase in sedentary behavior
no doubt contributes to the current obesity epidemic. Assessment of physical
activity has received more attention from behavior analysts, in part because it
is overt and easily observable. Additionally, physical activity may be more
sensitive to social contingencies than eating, making the application of
functional assessment methodology ideal.

Over the last decade, multiple studies have been published in the *Journal
of Applied Behavior Analysis* related to the assessment of, and interventions to
increase, physical activity. In a recent review of the extant literature on the
subject, Van Camp and Hayes (2012) suggested that although multiple studies have proposed technology to accurately collect data on physical activity
(e.g., observation systems, pedometers), few studies have focused on evaluating interventions to actually increase levels of physical activity.

Behavioral assessment of physical activity: One of the earlier studies in the area was to develop the Behaviors of Eating and Activity for Children's Health Evaluation System (BEACHES; McKenzie et al., 1991), an instrument designed to directly measure activity and eating behaviors and then relate those behaviors to environmental events. More recent research in the area of physical activity by behavior analysts has focused on conducting direct behavioral assessments of physical activity in an effort to understand the antecedent conditions that may better support increased physical activity, particularly among children. For example, researchers have evaluated activity context as a potential antecedent condition that may support or discourage physical activity (Hustyi, Normand, Larson, & Morley, 2012). In this study, the Observational System for Recording Physical Activity (OSRAC) was used to measure levels of moderate-to-vigorous physical activity across four typically developing four-year-old children. Physical activity was evaluated across four conditions: outdoor toys, fixed equipment, open space, and a control condition (i.e., table-top activities). Although the participants engaged in high levels of sedentary behavior across conditions, increased levels of physical activity were observed in the fixed-equipment condition for all participants, suggesting that the presence of playground equipment may occasion higher rates of physical activity for young children. It remains to be seen if similar results would be obtained with older children.

Exergaming has shown promise as a way to increase physical activity among children. Exergames are specific types of interactive video games designed to increase exercise behavior (Fogel, Miltenberger, Graves, & Koehler, 2010). In comparisons of exergaming and standard physical education, exergaming has been shown to be associated with relative increases in duration of physical activity and opportunities to engage in physical activity (Fogel et al., 2010; Shayne, Fogel, Miltenberger, & Koehler, 2012). Findings from these studies suggest that providing access to exergaming equipment may increase physical activity among children; however, additional research is necessary to determine whether similar findings would be obtained with overweight children and to evaluate the potential effects of exergaming on weight loss. Furthermore, it is unclear whether social contingencies inherent in exergaming may also contribute to increases in physical activity.

Larson, Normand, Morley, and Miller (2013) extended the literature by conducting a functional analysis of physical activity. Two healthy weight children participated, and physical activity was evaluated across multiple conditions. During baseline, no consequences were provided for physical activity, and participants were able to access outdoor toys and playground equipment. During the interactive play condition, the experimenter engaged in activity with the participants but ignored the participant if they did not engage in physical activity. During the attention condition, praise was provided contingent upon physical activity. During the escape condition, participants received brief escape from work contingent upon physical activity. During the alone condition, no consequences were provided for physical activity. Finally, during the control condition, an experimenter colored with the participant near the playground and provided no consequences for physical activity. Across experimental conditions, rules were provided to the participants regarding the contingencies in place for engaging in physical activity. Results suggested that increased physical activity was observed in the contingent attention and interactive play conditions, which may help to inform interventions targeting physical activity among children. That is, providing attention for engaging in physical activity or engaging in interactive play may result in higher levels of physical activity.

Interventions to increase physical activity: VanWormer (2004) evaluated the effects of providing pedometers and brief e-counseling to help three overweight adult participants increase physical activity and lose weight. In this study, participants self-recorded steps per day and weight each week at home. Brief e-counseling included a weekly 10-min session during which participants interacted with the experimenter and set weekly goals. All participants increased the daily number of steps taken during treatment, and only one participant's daily number of steps were higher in the self-monitoring plus e-counseling phase than in the self-monitoring phase. Generally, taking a greater number of steps per day was positively correlated with weight loss; however, one of the two participants who lost weight regained a portion of the weight lost during follow-up. Thus, the effects of the intervention may not have maintained overtime. Although this study included only a small number of participants, these findings suggest that providing overweight individuals with inexpensive pedometers may help to increase physical activity which may, in turn, contribute to weight loss.

Hustyi, Normand, and Larson (2011) measured physical activity in two overweight preschool children using direct observation and pedometers that the children wore to track the number of steps they took. During baseline, there were no programmed consequences for physical activity or the number of steps taken. During the intervention phase, goals were set using percentile schedules and participants who met their activity goals (i.e., number of steps) were provided with a small toy. Results suggested only modest increases in activity for one participant during the intervention phase and no increases in activity during the intervention phase for the other participant. Thus, additional research is warranted to evaluate more effective interventions to increase physical activity among overweight children.

COMPREHENSIVE WEIGHT MANAGEMENT PROGRAMS

The research discussed previously has the potential to inform the development and modification of comprehensive treatment programs for weight loss. Behaviorally based treatment programs typically consist of multiple components aimed at changing behaviors associated with weight-loss (i.e., eating and physical activity). Self-monitoring (e.g., food recording), contracting and contingency management (e.g., providing incentives/ rewards), goal setting, antecedent manipulations (e.g., environmental manipulation), and feedback are all examples of common behavioral interventions that have been included in behavioral treatment programs for weight loss. Generally, behaviorally based programs have been found to be superior at promoting weight change relative to conventional diets or no treatment controls, as well as to nutrition education programs (Aragona, Cassady, & Drabman, 1975; Epstein, Wing, Steranchak, Dickson, & Michelson, 1980; Weiss, 1977).

Family-based treatment: For pediatric populations, behaviorally based treatment programs are most effective when they are family-based. That is, children are most successful at losing weight when their caregivers also participate in the treatment program. Parents, especially parents of younger children, exert a great deal of control over the food environment via food shopping and preparation, as well as the frequency with which food is presented to children in the home. The goal of family-based, behavioral weight management programs is to educate parents and their children together to facilitate long-term behavioral changes.

Epstein, Wing, Koeske, Andrasik, and Ossip (1981) compared the relative effectiveness of a family-based treatment program on child weight loss. Participants were randomly assigned to one of the three groups (parent-child weight loss target group, a child only target group, and a nonspecific target group). Across groups, participants were taught to use the Traffic Light diet, in which foods are classified according to energy density (Epstein et al., 1978). Each family deposited $60 at the beginning of the program. Each week, a portion of the deposit was returned contingent upon meeting weekly weight loss goals for the parent and child (parent-child target group), child alone (child target group), or attendance (nonspecific target group).

Results suggested that the family-based treatment program (parent-child target group) was associated with the greatest weight loss. Most importantly, participants in family-based treatment programs may maintain weight-loss for longer periods of time relative to participants in other programs (Epstein, Valoski, Wing, & McCurley, 1994; Epstein, Wing, Koeske, & Valoski, 1987).

CONCLUSIONS

Although behavior analysts are starting to become more involved in the study of pediatric obesity, additional research is needed to gain a better understanding of the various behaviors involved in establishing a healthy lifestyle. Thus far, much of the research in the treatment of pediatric obesity has focused on typically developing children. Given that many behavior analysts work with children diagnosed with intellectual and developmental disabilities (IDD) in a variety of contexts (e.g., in school, in the home), it may be appropriate for behavior analysts to begin to develop interventions to target increased consumption of healthy foods and physical activity to improve the overall health of their clients.

Although the exact prevalence of obesity among children diagnosed with IDD is unknown, it is likely that obesity in this population is at least as great as the prevalence among their typically developing peers. Individuals with Down syndrome, for example, are at an increased risk for obesity (Whitt-Glover, O'Neill, & Stettler, 2006). Increased caloric intake and sedentary behavior contribute to the development of obesity in the IDD population; however, treatment may be complicated by increased use of medications that are associated with increased appetite and weight gain (e.g., antipsychotics), food selectivity, and the presence of problem behavior that may be maintained by nonpreferred tasks (e.g., physical activity). One program that focuses specifically on the treatment of obesity in the IDD population is Health U, which is a comprehensive, behaviorally based weight loss program for adolescents with Down syndrome that is extending the work on family-based treatment programs for obesity (Fleming et al., 2008). Although it is probable that early intervention to teach healthy eating habits and the promotion of physical activity would be similarly effective in the IDD population, little research exists. Future studies should begin to extend the current research in the area of pediatric obesity to the IDD population in an effort to inform the development of treatment programs for weight management.

Given the current prevalence of pediatric obesity, developing more effective, comprehensive interventions to teach healthier eating habits, increase physical activity, and promote weight loss is an important research priority. Behavior analysts have particular expertise in the assessment and treatment of a variety of problematic behaviors and may be well-suited to become more involved in the area of pediatric obesity. Research in the area of behavioral economics shows promise in understanding how overweight children may make choices between concurrently available foods which may, in turn, inform interventions to teach healthier eating habits. Similarly, research in the area of self-control training may have important implications for clinicians developing interventions targeting weight loss. Finally, multiple researchers in the field of behavior analysis are working to better understand how environmental variables affect physical activity in children. The application of functional assessment methodology to understand possible functional relations between activity and socially mediated reinforcers is a highly novel approach. Refinement and extension of this functional assessment methodology has the potential to inform further research on function-based interventions to increase and maintain physical activity in children.

REFERENCES

Aragona, J., Cassady, J., & Drabman, R. S. (1975). Treating overweight children through parental training and contingency contracting. *Journal of Applied Behavior Analysis*, *8*, 269–278. http://dx.doi.org/10.1901/jaba.1975.8-269.

Barlow, S. E., & Dietz, W. H. (1998). Obesity evaluation and treatment: Expert committee recommendations. *Pediatrics*, *102*, 1–11. http://dx.doi.org/10.1542/peds.102.3.e29.

Best, J. R., Theim, K. R., Gredysa, D. M., Stein, R. I., Welch, R. R., Saelens, B. E., et al. (2012). Behavioral economic predictors of overweight children's weight loss. *Journal of Consulting and Clinical Psychology*, *80*, 1086–1096. http://dx.doi.org/10.1037/a0029827.

Bickel, W. K., Yi, R., Landes, R. D., Hill, P. F., & Baxter, C. (2011). Remember the future: Working memory training decreases delay discounting among stimulant addicts. *Biological Psychiatry*, *69*, 260–265. http://dx.doi.org/10.1016/j.biopsych.2010.08.017.

Binder, L. M., Dixon, M. R., & Ghezzi, P. M. (2000). A procedure to teach self-control to children with attention deficit hyperactivity disorder. *Journal of Applied Behavior Analysis*, *33*, 233–237. http://dx.doi.org/10.1019/jaba.2000.33-233.

Burger, K. S., Fisher, J. O., & Johnson, S. L. (2011). Mechanisms behind the portion size effect: Visibility and bite size. *Obesity*, *19*, 546–551. http://dx.doi.org/10.1038/oby.2010.233.

Byrd-Bredbenner, C., & Schwartz, J. (2004). The effect of practical portion size measurement aids on the accuracy of portion size estimates made by young adults. *Journal of Human Nutrition and Dietetics*, *17*, 351–357. http://dx.doi.org/10.1111/j.1365-277x.2004.00534.x.

Chakravarthy, M. V., & Booth, F. W. (2004). Eating, exercise, and "thrifty" genotypes: Connecting the dots towards an evolutionary understanding of modern chronic diseases. *Journal of Applied Physiology*, *96*, 3–10. http://dx.doi.org/10.1152/japplphysiol.00757.2003.

Chandon, P., & Wansink, B. (2007). The biasing health halos of fast-food restaurant health claims: Lower calorie estimates and higher side-dish consumption intentions. *Journal of Consumer Research, 34*, 301–314. http://dx.doi.org/10.1086/519499.

Critchfield, T. S., & Fienup, D. M. (2010). Using stimulus equivalence technology to teach statistical inference in a group setting. *Journal of Applied Behavior Analysis, 43*, 763–768. http://dx.doi.org/10.1901/jaba.2010.43-763.

Cypel, Y. S., Guenther, P. M., & Petot, G. J. (1997). Validity of portion size measurement aids: A review. *Journal of the American Dietetic Association, 97*, 289–292. http://dx.doi.org/10.1016/S0002-8223(97)00074-6.

Daniels, S. R. (2009). Complications of obesity in children and adolescents. *International Journal of Obesity, 33*, S60–S65. http://dx.doi.org/10.1038/ijo.2009.20.

Dixon, M. R., Hayes, L. J., Binder, L. M., Manthey, S., Sigman, C., & Zdanowski, D. M. (1998). Using a self-control training procedure to increase appropriate behavior. *Journal of Applied Behavior Analysis, 31*, 203–210. http://dx.doi.org/10.1901/jaba.1998.31-203.

Dixon, M. R., & Holton, B. (2009). Altering the magnitude of delay discounting by pathological gamblers. *Journal of Applied Behavior Analysis, 42*, 269–275. http://dx.doi.org/10.1901/jaba.2009.42-269.

Epstein, L. H., Lin, H., Carr, K. A., & Fletcher, K. D. (2012). Food reinforcement and obesity. Psychological moderators. *Appetite, 58*, 157–162. http://dx.doi.org/10.1016/j.eppet.2011.09.025.

Epstein, L. H., Masek, B. J., & Marshall, W. R. (1978). A nutritionally based school program for control of eating in obese children. *Behavior Therapy, 9*, 766–788. http://dx.doi.org/10.1016/S0005-7894(78)80007-0.

Epstein, L. H., Salvy, S. J., Carr, K. A., Dearing, K. K., & Bickel, W. K. (2010). Food reinforcement, delay discounting, and obesity. *Physiology & Behavior, 100*, 438–445. http://dx.doi.org/10.1016/j.physbeh.2010.04.029.

Epstein, L. H., Temple, J. L., Neaderhiser, B. J., Salis, R. J., Erbe, R. W., & Leddy, J. J. (2007). Food reinforcement, the dopamine D_2 receptor genotype, and energy intake in obese and nonobese humans. *Behavioral Neuroscience, 121*, 877–886. http://dx.doi.org/10.1037/0735-7044.121.5.877.

Epstein, L. H., Valoski, A., Wing, R. R., & McCurley, J. (1994). Ten-year outcomes of behavioral family-based treatment for childhood obesity. *Health Psychology, 13*, 373–383. http://dx.doi.org/10.1037/0278-6133.13.5.373.

Epstein, L. H., Wing, R. R., Koeske, R., Andrasik, F., & Ossip, D. J. (1981). Child and parent weight loss in family-based behavior modification programs. *Journal of Consulting and Clinical Psychology, 49*, 674–685. http://dx.doi.org/10.1037/0022-006X.49.5.674.

Epstein, L. H., Wing, R. R., Koeske, R., & Valoski, A. (1987). Long-term effects of family-based treatment of childhood obesity. *Journal of Consulting and Clinical Psychology, 1*, 91–95. http://dx.doi.org/10.1037/0022-006X.55.1.91.

Epstein, L. H., Wing, R. R., Steranchak, L., Dickson, B. E., & Michelson, J. (1980). Comparison of family based behavior modification and nutrition education for childhood obesity. *Journal of Pediatric Psychology, 5*, 25–36. http://dx.doi.org/10.1093/jpepsy/5.1.25.

Fleming, R. K., Stokes, E. A., Curtin, C., Bandini, L. G., Gleason, J., Scampini, R., et al. (2008). Behavioral health in developmental disabilities: A comprehensive program of nutrition, exercise, and weight reduction. *International Journal of Behavioral Consultation and Therapy, 4*, 287–296.

Fogel, V. A., Miltenberger, R. G., Graves, R., & Koehler, S. (2010). The effects of exergaming on physical activity among inactive children in a physical education classroom. *Journal of Applied Behavior Analysis, 43*, 591–600. http://dx.doi.org/10.1901/jaba.2010.43-591.

Foster, E., Adamson, A. J., Anderson, A. S., Barton, K. L., & Wrieden, W. L. (2009). Estimation of portion size in children's dietary assessment: Lessons learnt. *European Journal of Clinical Nutrition, 63*, S45–S49. http://dx.doi.org/10.1038/ejcn.2008.64.

Foster, E., Anderson, A. S., & Adamson, A. J. (2001). Portion size estimation by primary school children. *Proceedings of the Nutrition Society, 60,* 205A. http://dx.doi.org/10.1017/S0029665101000684.

Freedman, M. R., & Brochado, C. (2010). Reducing portion size reduces food intake and plate waste. *Obesity, 18,* 1864–1866. http://dx.doi.org/10.1038/oby.2009.480.

Friman, P. C., & Piazza, C. C. (2011). Behavioral pediatrics: Integrating Applied Behavior Analysis with pediatric medicine. In W. W. Fisher, C. C. Piazza, & H. S. Roane (Eds.), *Handbook of applied behavior analysis* (pp. 433–450). New York, NY: The Guilford Press.

Frobisher, C., & Maxwell, M. (2003). The estimation of food portion sizes: A comparison between using descriptions of portion sizes and a photographic food atlas by children and adults. *Journal of Human Nutrition and Dietetics, 16,* 181–188. http://dx.doi.org/10.1046/j.1365-277X.2003.00434.x.

Green, G., & Saunders, R. R. (1998). Stimulus equivalence. In K. A. Lattal, & M. Perone (Eds.), *Handbook of research methods in human operant behavior* (pp. 229–262). New York: Plenum.

Hall, S. S., DeBernardis, G. M., & Reiss, A. L. (2006). The acquisition of stimulus equivalence in individuals with fragile X syndrome. *Journal of Intellectual Disability Research, 50,* 643–651. http://dx.doi.org/10.1111/j.1365-2788.2006.00814.x.

Hausman, N. L., Borrero, J. C., Fisher, A., & Kahng, S. (2014). Improving portion size estimations through a stimulus equivalence paradigm. *Journal of Applied Behavior Analysis, 47,* 485–499. http://dx.doi.org/10.1002/jaba.139.

Hebebrand, J., & Hinney, A. (2008). Environmental and genetic risk factors in obesity. *Child & Adolescent Psychiatric Clinics of North America, 18,* 83–94. http://dx.doi.org/10.1016/j.chc.2008.07.006.

Hill, C., Saxton, J., Webber, L., Blundell, L., & Wardle, J. (2009). The relative reinforcing value of food predicts weight gain in a longitudinal study of 7-10-year old children. *American Journal of Clinical Nutrition, 90,* 276–281. http://dx.doi.org/10.3945/ajcn.2009.27479.

Hustyi, K. M., Normand, M. P., & Larson, T. A. (2011). Behavioral assessment of physical activity in obese preschool children. *Journal of Applied Behavior Analysis, 44,* 635–639. http://dx.doi.org/10.1901/jaba.2011.44-653.

Hustyi, K. M., Normand, M. P., Larson, T. A., & Morley, A. J. (2012). The effect of outdoor activity context on physical activity in preschool children. *Journal of Applied Behavior Analysis, 45,* 401–405. http://dx.doi.org/10.1901/jaba.2012.45-401.

Kopelman, P. G. (2000). Obesity as a medical problem. *Nature, 404,* 635–643. http://dx.doi.org/10.1038/35007508.

Larson, T. A., Normand, M. P., Morley, A. J., & Miller, B. G. (2013). A functional analysis of moderate-to-vigorous physical activity in young children. *Journal of Applied Behavior Analysis, 46,* 199–207. http://dx.doi.org/10.1901/jaba.2013.46-199.

LeBlanc, L. A., Miguel, C. F., Cummings, A. R., Goldsmith, T. R., & Carr, J. E. (2003). The effects of three stimulus-equivalence testing conditions on emergent US geography relations of children diagnosed with autism. *Behavioral Interventions, 18,* 279–289. http://dx.doi.org/10.1002/bin.144.

McKenzie, T. L., Sallis, J. F., Nader, P. R., Patterson, T. L., Elder, J. P., Berry, C. C., et al. (1991). BEACHES: An observational system for assessing children's eating and physical activity behaviors and associated events. *Journal of Applied Behavior Analysis, 24,* 141–151. http://dx.doi.org/10.1901/jaba.1991.24-141.

Mischel, H. N., Ebbesen, E. B., & Zeiss, A. R. (1972). Cognitive and attentional mechanisms in delay of gratification. *Journal of Personality and Social Psychology, 16,* 204–218. http://dx.doi.org/10.1037/h0032198.

Ogden, C. L., Carroll, M. D., Curtin, L. R., Lamb, M. M., & Flegal, K. (2010). Prevalence of high body mass index in US children and adolescents, 2007-2008. *Journal of the American Medical Association, 303,* 242–249. http://dx.doi.org/10.1001/jama.2009.2012.

Ogden, C. L., Carroll, M. D., & Flegal, K. M. (2008). High body mass index for age among US children and adolescents, 2003-2006. *Journal of the American Medical Association, 299,* 2401–2405. http://dx.doi.org/10.1001/jama.299.20.2401.

Ogden, C. L., Carroll, M. D., Kit, B. K., & Flegal, K. M. (2012). Prevalence of obesity and trends in body mass index among US children and adolescents, 1999-2010. *The Journal of the American Medical Association, 307,* 483–490. http://dx.doi.org/10.1001/jama.2012.40.

Rehfeldt, R. A. (2011). Toward a technology of derived stimulus relations: An analysis of articles published in the Journal of Applied Behavior Analysis, 1992-2009. *Journal of Applied Behavior Analysis, 44,* 109–119. http://dx.doi.org/10.1901/jaba.2011.44-109.

Robinson, T. E., & Berridge, K. C. (1993). The neural basis of drug craving: An incentive-sensitization theory of addiction. *Brain Research, 18,* 247–291. http://dx.doi.org/10.1016/0165-0173(93)90013-P.

Rolls, B. J., Roe, L. S., Kral, T. V. E., Meengs, J. S., & Wall, D. E. (2004). Increasing the portion size of a packaged snack increases energy intake in men and women. *Appetite, 42,* 63–69. http://dx.doi.org/10.1016/S0195-6663(03)00117-X.

Saelens, B. E., & Epstein, L. H. (1996). Reinforcing value of food in obese and non obese women. *Appetite, 27,* 41–50. http://dx.doi.org/10.1006/appe.1996.0032.

Schweitzer, J. B., & Sulzer-Azaroff, B. (1988). Self-control: Teaching tolerance for delay in impulsive children. *Journal of the Experimental Analysis of Behavior, 50,* 173–186. http://dx.doi.org/10.1901/jeab.1988.50-173.

Shayne, R. K., Fogel, V. A., Miltenberger, R. G., & Koehler, S. (2012). The effects of exer-gaming on physical activity in a third-grade physical education class. *Journal of Applied Behavior Analysis, 45,* 211–215. http://dx.doi.org/10.1901/jaba.2012.45-211.

Steenhuis, I. H. M., & Vermeer, W. M. (2009). Portion size: Review and framework for interventions. *International Journal of Behavioral Nutrition and Physical Activity, 6,* 58. http://dx.doi.org/10.1186/1479-5868-6-58.

Temple, J. L., & Epstein, L. H. (2012). Sensitization of food reinforcement is related to weight status and baseline food reinforcement. *International Journal of Obesity, 36,* 1102–1107. http://dx.doi.org/10.1038/ijo.2011.210.

Toussaint, K. A., & Tiger, J. H. (2010). Teaching early braille literacy skills within a stimulus equivalence paradigm to children with degenerative visual impairments. *Journal of Applied Behavior Analysis, 43,* 181–194. http://dx.doi.org/10.1901/jaba.2010.43-181.

U.S. Department of Health and Human Services. (2012). *The Surgeon General's vision for a healthy and fit nation.* Rockville, MD: U.S. Department of Health and Human Services.

Van Camp, C. M., & Hayes, L. B. (2012). Assessing and increasing physical activity. *Journal of Applied Behavior Analysis, 45,* 871–875. http://dx.doi.org/10.1901/jaba.2012.45-871.

VanWormer, J. J. (2004). Pedometers and brief e-counseling: Increasing physical activity for overweight adults. *Journal of Applied Behavior Analysis, 37,* 421–425. http://dx.doi.org/10.1901/jaba.2004.37-421.

Walker, B. D., Rehfeldt, R., & Ninness, C. (2010). Using the stimulus equivalence paradigm to teach course material in an undergraduate rehabilitation course. *Journal of Applied Behavior Analysis, 43,* 615–633. http://dx.doi.org/10.1901/jaba.2010.43-615.

Wansink, B., Painter, J. E., & North, J. (2005). Bottomless bowls: Why visual cues of portion size may influence intake. *Obesity Research, 13,* 93–100. http://dx.doi.org/10.1038/oby.2005.12.

Wansink, B., van Ittersum, K., & Painter, J. E. (2006). Ice cream illusions: Bowls, spoons, and self-served portion sizes. *American Journal of Preventative Medicine, 31,* 240–243. http://dx.doi.org/10.1016/j.amepre.2006.04.003.

Weber, J. L. (1993). *Effects of training on portion size estimation.* Dissertation. Tucson, AZ: University of Arizona. Retrieved from: http://hdl.handle.net/10150/186506.

Weiss, A. R. A. (1977). A behavioral approach to the treatment of adolescent obesity. *Behavior Therapy, 8*, 720–726. http://dx.doi.org/10.1016/S0005-7894(77)80204-9.

Whitt-Glover, M. C., O'Neill, K. L., & Stettler, N. (2006). Physical activity patterns in children with and without Down syndrome. *Pediatric Rehabilitation, 9*, 158–164. http://dx.doi.org/10.1080/13638490500353202.

Young, L. R., & Nestle, M. (1995). Portion sizes estimations in dietary assessment: Issues and policy implications. *Nutrition Review, 53*, 149–158. http://dx.doi.org/10.1111/j.1753-4887.1995.tb01542.x.

Young, L. R., & Nestle, M. (2007). Portion sizes and obesity: Responses of fast-food companies. *Journal of Public Health Policy, 28*, 238–248. http://dx.doi.org/10.1057/palgrave.jphp.3200127.

CHAPTER 14

Evidence-Based Application of Staff and Caregiver Training Procedures

Dorothea C. Lerman[1], Linda A. LeBlanc[2], Amber L. Valentino[2]
[1]Department of Clinical, Health, and Applied Sciences, University of Houston—Clear Lake, Houston, Texas, USA
[2]Trumpet Behavioral Health, Lakewood, Colorado, USA

Applied behavior analysis is unique among the helping professions because of its reliance on others to implement the procedures that are critical to effective intervention. As such, behavioral skills training (BST) of parents, teachers, staff, and other care providers is an integral component of research and practice in the field. Behavioral researchers have created a substantial literature on strategies to promote the acquisition, maintenance, and generalization of treatment implementation by others in various community settings, including private homes, residential treatment facilities, and schools. Much of this literature has focused on staff training in human–service settings for individuals with developmental disabilities (Parsons, Reid, & Green, 1996; Reid & Green, 1990; Reid, Parsons, Lattimore, Towery, & Reade, 2005; Reid et al., 2003; Schepis & Reid, 1994). However, a variety of populations have participated in training research, including parents and teachers of children in home, school, and foster care settings; nursing staff caring for aged individuals; and rehabilitation staff working with individuals with acquired brain injury (Franks et al., 2013; Guercio & Dixon, 2011; Miles & Wilder, 2009; Pangborn, Borrero, & Borrero, 2013; Van Camp et al., 2008).

A range of caregiver skills has been targeted in this research, including positive interactions with clients (Finn & Sturmey, 2009); data collection procedures (Mozingo, Smith, Riordan, Reiss, & Bailey, 2006); functional assessment and behavioral intervention procedures for problem behavior (Lambert et al., 2013; Shore, Iwata, Vollmer, Lerman, & Zarcone, 1995); strategies for teaching language, social, and academic skills (Lafasakis & Sturmey, 2007); and environmental modifications and client care procedures to promote safety and organization in treatment centers and classrooms

Clinical and Organizational Applications of Applied Behavior Analysis
http://dx.doi.org/10.1016/B978-0-12-420249-8.00014-9

(Schmidt, Urban, Luiselli, White, & Harrington, 2013). A burgeoning literature also has targeted the skills needed to train others when adopting a train-the-trainer approach to program dissemination (Shore et al., 1995).

Research on staff and caregiver training has demonstrated the importance of providing effective initial training (whether live, video, or Web-based; Macurik, O'Kane, Malanga, & Reid, 2008) and clear and potentially public feedback (Parsons & Reid, 1995; Wilson, Reid, & Korabek-Pinkowski, 1991). In addition, curriculum manuals are available for training both direct support staff and supervisory staff to provide effective positive behavior supports (Reid & Parsons, 2007).

This chapter covers the literature and best practices on behavior analytic caregiver and staff training procedures. The same behavioral principles and procedures are applicable in both of these training situations, and the same individual and group instructional procedures are often effective. However, important differences often exist in the scope of the training and motivational variables across the two situations. Consider the scope of skills taught to natural caregivers versus employed staff. Natural caregivers are often taught a few specific strategies that are likely to prove useful for their child's needs and challenges. For example, a parent may be taught how to implement three-step-guided compliance or to incorporate requesting opportunities during targeted times of the day (e.g., snack times). Parents also may be taught a few basic behavioral principles and terms, although the terms may be more layperson friendly (e.g., reward) than those taught to employed staff (e.g., reinforcement). In contrast, employed staff in human services or educational settings typically must implement a large number of instructional and assessment procedures with a high degree of procedural integrity. For example, staff working in early intensive behavioral intervention programs are often taught to implement discrete trial teaching procedures as criterion for every individual component of the discrete trial. The same staff may need to know how to conduct assessment procedures, how to collect multiple types of data on problem behaviors and targeted skills for acquisition and how to implement a wider range of instructional procedures (e.g., video modeling, chaining, direct instruction). Staff members are also likely to experience training in areas such as professionalism and ethical issues including confidentiality, dual relationships, and protection of the client.

Important distinctions also should be made about the nature of the relationship between the trainer and trainee in these contexts and the motivational variables that come into play in those relationships. Parents, caregivers, and teachers have a clear role as consumers of behavioral services. They can elect to discontinue services, decline to participate fully, or choose not to implement parts of a treatment. Behavior analysts have an ethical obligation not to abandon clients even if implementation is not optimal; therefore, behavior analysts continue working in partnership to help caregivers achieve their goals and to give them a voice in setting the goals even if they do not always completely align with the professional's purposes. For natural caregivers, the child's progress and the overall improvement in their own lives is the likely reinforcer for consistent and correct implementation, although effective professionals can establish their own social interactions as powerful reinforcers as well. Fear, fatigue, and family dynamics are the most likely barriers to optimal implementation. In contrast, employed staff members are accountable for income, evaluation, promotion, and liability and generally must participate and implement procedures correctly to prosper in their job. Trainers and supervisors can set clear goals for performance and implement contingencies to support that performance or terminate the relationship if performance is consistently sub-par. Thus, in addition to reinforcers based on child progress, other tangible reinforcers such as income, positive evaluation, and professional progress can be brought to bear to impact staff performance during and after training. In the following sections, we describe evidence-based application of caregiver and staff training procedures.

WHAT TO TEACH
Factors to Consider When Selecting Training Targets

Although the needs and the goals of clients are major considerations, a variety of other factors often influence the type and complexity of the procedures that behavior analysts teach to caregivers and staff. These factors include the existing skills, roles, and responsibilities of the trainee; amount of time available for the training; and the preferences of the trainee. Suppose a primary goal is to reduce a child's self-injury at home; the behavior is maintained by parental attention, and the child's parents will be responsible for implementing the intervention. The parents have no prior experience implementing behavioral interventions, work multiple jobs that consume most of the available training time, and must also care for the child's three young siblings. Instead of targeting complex skills, such as determining the function of self-injury, selecting and teaching an appropriate replacement behavior, and identifying and modifying motivating operations, the behavior analyst should consider the simplest intervention for attention-maintained self-injury that is likely to be effective. In contrast, if the primary goal is to reduce a child's self-injury in a classroom with a low student–teacher ratio and with a teacher who has prior training in behavioral interventions, the behavior analyst might target the more complex skills described previously. Not only would the multiple treatment components enhance the efficacy of the intervention, but also the teacher would acquire a more sophisticated behavioral repertoire that would benefit other students in the classroom.

As this latter example illustrates, considerations related to the maintenance and generalization of the trainees' skills also may dictate the types of skills targeted. A caregiver, for example, might be expected to target a range of client behaviors under multiple stimulus conditions without the continued support of the consulting behavior analyst. In this case, the behavior analyst might target a more general skill repertoire. Koegel, Glahn, and Nieminen (1978) demonstrated the benefit of this approach by first training caregivers how to teach specific skills to children with autism (e.g., how to teach a child to follow the instruction, "Touch your head"). However, when asked to teach the child a new skill, caregivers did so with low procedural integrity. Integrity improved after caregivers were taught more general teaching procedures, such as how to deliver effective instructions, prompts, and reinforcement. Professionals who work with multiple learners and who individualize interventions to ensure success will require an even larger repertoire of skills. For example, when training public school teachers on effective instructional practices, Lerman, Vorndran, Addison, and Kuhn (2004) targeted instruction delivery in both discrete trial and incidental teaching formats, three different types of preference assessments, and three different prompt-fading approaches. Chok, Shlesinger, Studer, and Bird (2012) taught staff how to conduct functional analyses (FAs) of problem behavior, how to interpret FA data, how to proceed when the FA data were undifferentiated, and how to choose appropriate interventions based on the FA results. This behavioral repertoire includes most of the critical elements for developing function-based treatments, regardless of the client, response topography, or function.

Behavior analysts also might consider staff and caregiver preferences when selecting among several potentially effective interventions. This approach recently was illustrated in a study by Gabor, Fritz, Roath, Rothe, and Salazar (in press). The experimenters evaluated the preferences of parents who requested interventions for their children's attention–maintained problem behavior. First, they taught the parents how to implement three reinforcement-based treatments that are appropriate for problem behavior maintained by attention (differential reinforcement of alternative behavior [DRA], differential reinforcement of other behavior [DRO], and noncontingent reinforcement [NCR]). The experimenters then permitted the parents to select among the three interventions, along with no intervention, during additional practice sessions after the parents demonstrated high levels of procedural integrity with all three procedures. Of the five parents, three demonstrated a preference for DRA, one demonstrated a preference for DRA and DRO, and one parent showed no preference. This study provides a model for objectively evaluating caregiver preference within the context of training.

Train-the-Trainer Targets

Professionals with supervisory responsibilities, including behavior analysts, also benefit from direct instruction on how to train and supervise others (e.g., how to provide feedback effectively, how to model correct responses; McGimsey, Greene, & Lutzker, 1995; Parsons & Reid, 1995). Such targets are an essential part of pyramidal training, or train-the-trainer models, which have been extended beyond supervisors to give behavior analysts a more efficient way to train multiple people. Behavior analysts have included peers, family members, teachers, and staff supervisors in research on pyramidal training. These individuals acquired the skills necessary to teach others a variety of behavioral procedures, such as how to implement FAs of problem behavior (Pence, St. Peter, & Giles, 2014), how to increase children's adaptive behavior (Neef, 1995), how to manage behavior in the classroom (Jones, Fremouw, & Carples, 1977), how to interact appropriately with clients (Finn & Sturmey, 2009), and how to implement individualized treatments for problem behavior (Kuhn, Lerman, & Vorndran, 2003; Shore et al., 1995).

Previous research has identified a number of essential components of pyramidal training. First, the behavior analyst must teach the trainer how to implement the targeted behavioral procedures or intervention with the client. Trainers should meet a performance-based criterion when implementing the procedures themselves before attempting to teach those procedures to someone else. Next, the behavior analyst must teach the trainer how to implement BST with the trainees. Typically, behavior analysts teach the trainer to describe the intervention, model its correct implementation, and set up opportunities for the trainee to practice the intervention via role-play and/or *in situ* with the client(s). Other critical trainer skills include how to

(a) provide feedback to the trainee, (b) collect data on the trainee's integrity, (c) monitor the trainee's progress, (d) determine when the trainee has mastered the skills, and (e) ensure that the trainees maintain their skills. Behavior analysts who employ pyramidal training might consider trainer skills that go beyond the basics of BST. For example, in Jones et al. (1977), the experimenters taught the trainers how to manage potential anxiety of the trainee as a result of participating in the role play portion of the training and how to respond to negative comments made by trainees about the training.

Ideally, behavior analysts employing pyramidal training should observe their trainers' initial teaching sessions with trainees to provide corrective feedback on their use of BST. However, in many studies, the experimenters were not present when the trainers taught the trainees. As a key element of training, the behavior analyst should evaluate the performance of the trainees to ensure they have been properly trained to high integrity. The most effective evaluation includes measurement of client behavior prior to and following pyramidal training to further confirm that trainees are implementing the intervention in a successful manner (i.e., produces behavior change in the client).

Additional Targets to Consider

Some relatively complex skills that rarely receive attention in the training literature also may be important to teach staff and caregivers. For example, it may be helpful for staff or parents to detect, report, and/or solve emerging difficulties related to the acquisition of new skills or the development of problem behavior. Such a skill requires the discrimination of behavioral patterns and environmental conditions that suggest emerging problems. A caregiver might learn to detect frequently occurring error patterns when teaching conditional discriminations to a child (e.g., left-side bias) so that such problems can be corrected quickly and successfully. Caregivers also might learn to detect the presence of environmental conditions that commonly evoke problem behavior (e.g., low levels of attention) or precursors to severe behavior problems so that they can implement preventative strategies before problems arise. Teaching caregivers to notice how and when their own responses could potentially reinforce problem behavior is another useful skill that could potentially prevent the development of problem behavior in the first place.

Another frequently overlooked area of training that is critical for human-service providers is how to behave ethically with clients. Ethics training is particularly important for staff members that do not hold licenses or certification in behavior analysis. Licensed or certified behavior analysts must demonstrate some knowledge of ethical issues directly related to the provision of behavior analytic services and maintain competency through continuing education. Staff without such credentials may receive little, if any, exposure to guidelines for ethical conduct with vulnerable populations and, thus, may place their clients and organization at risk when difficult situations arise. However, licensed or credentialed behavior analysts also may benefit from ethics training that is specific to the population, setting, or focus of their practice and that may not be covered in general continuing education classes (Brodhead & Higbee, 2012). Staff who provide services to adults with severe behavior disorders in residential treatment settings tend to encounter different ethical issues than do staff who consult with parents about programs to increase self-care skills in children with autism.

Training in ethical behavior may take a variety of forms. Opportunities to provide informal training may arise during the course of normal service provision as the staff encounters situations that could lead to ethical dilemmas. For example, a parent may invite a direct therapist to join his or her family for dinner. Such an invitation provides an opportunity for the therapist's supervisor to discuss how, when, and why it is important to avoid dual relationships. Trainers also should arrange formal ethics instruction to review relevant portions of the ethical guidelines with staff, describe scenarios that illustrate ethical situations, and discuss ways to respond ethically in those situations. Trainers should create opportunities to model ethical behavior for the trainees and to arrange for trainees to role play ethical behavior. In the next section, we provide further discussion about evidence-based approaches for training staff and caregivers.

HOW TO TEACH

Verbal instruction is generally included as one component of staff and caregiver training; however, verbal instruction by itself is usually insufficient to produce mastery in implementation (Parsons, Rollyson, & Reid, 2012). Many of the skills that behavior analysts target for caregivers and staff members are complicated chains of behavior that must be emitted with some degree of fluency. A verbal description alone is unlikely to produce accuracy or fluency. Accordingly, training must be explicit, practice-oriented, careful, and precise (Miltenberger, 2003). The most commonly used evidence-based approach to staff training is BST, which will be described in this section. In addition, we will review strategies to promote generalization and maintenance of acquired skills and strategies for increasing the number of individuals who can be trained with limited person resources or logistical barriers to live training (i.e., technology-based training).

Components of Behavioral Skills Training

BST is an active-response training procedure that has proven effective for teaching individuals a variety of new skills (e.g., Fleming, Oliver, & Bolton, 1996). BST has been effectively used to train parents to implement various procedures such as incidental teaching (Hsieh, Wilder, & Abellon, 2011), guided compliance (Miles & Wilder, 2009), feeding protocols (Pangborn et al., 2013), and correct implementation of functional assessment and treatment protocols (Shayne & Miltenberger, 2013). BST is also effective in teaching staff skills such as how to conduct specific behavioral assessments (Barnes, Mellor, & Rehfeldt, 2014), and how to teach peer-to-peer manding (Madzharova, Sturmey, & Jones, 2012) among many others (e.g., Love, Carr, LeBlanc, & Kisamore, 2013).

BST involves four critical components: instruction, modeling, rehearsal, and feedback (Miltenberger, 2003). These components are typically implemented until a pre-set performance criterion is met (e.g., 80% accurate for multiple sessions; 100% accurate on a critical component; see section on How to Evaluate and Monitor Progress). Parsons et al. (2012) described a six-step BST protocol for conducting training with a group of staff members with precise details for each phase of BST. Instructions can be oral or written, but should be clear, brief, and limited in number (e.g., include no more than five specific items or steps per instructional bout). Written reminders or "aids" should be used to supplement the oral instructional portion. Instructions often include what to do, when to do it, and things to avoid doing. Instructions should include visuals to support text and response opportunities about the information (e.g., answering questions, restating, performing part of the task) to check for understanding of the material. The next step of BST, modeling, can be implemented live or via video and should include multiple, clear demonstrations of the target in different settings, with different performers, and with different materials and responses as appropriate. The model can include nonexemplars and the consequences associated with the procedural error, explicitly described as such. Modeling can include active participation such as having individuals describe what is occurring (i.e., the steps of the procedure, errors that occur). Finally, during the rehearsal and feedback phase, the easiest component might be trained to mastery first with prompts and praise as needed. The instructor can then slowly increase the level of difficulty while continuing to praise and prompt accurate performance and then fading prompts and making the schedule of praise intermittent. It is important for individuals to continue practicing the skill at increasingly difficult levels until no prompts are needed and accuracy scores are high (e.g., 80% or higher of steps completed correctly on multiple consecutive attempts).

The following clinical case example illustrates the effective use of BST to teach the mother and 11-year-old sister of an 8-year-old female with developmental delay to implement an effective intervention to cross driveways safely (Veazey, Valentino, & LeBlanc, 2014). A behavior analyst met directly with the family in their home approximately three times per week for 2-h sessions to develop the intervention and provide training. The behavioral intervention for the child consisted of a rule plus differential reinforcement of alternative behavior (DRA) with response blocking. Specifically, the therapist stated the rule "When you get to a driveway, look to see if a car is moving, and then let me know if it is safe to cross." A preferred tangible item was provided for looking both ways before crossing and for correctly labeling whether it was "safe" or "not safe" to cross. Attempts to cross the driveway without looking were blocked. An ABAB reversal design was utilized to assess the effectiveness of the intervention (see Figure 1, left panel). During the initial baseline phase, she did not cross any driveways safely. During treatment, the percentage of driveways crossed safely quickly increased, reaching a final percentage of 100. A brief reversal indicated she crossed only 50% and 30% of driveways safely. When treatment was reinstated, safe driveway crossing increased to 100% and the results maintained at a 4-month maintenance probe. The schedule of reinforcement for safe driveway crossing was successfully faded from an edible or sticker provided on a fixed-ratio (FR 1) schedule during the first phase of treatment, to tokens (conditioned after the reversal phase) on an FR-1 schedule, to social praise only on an FR-1 schedule.

When the intervention was demonstrated effective, BST was implemented at session 19 to teach the mother and sister to implement the effective intervention. Training consisted of describing the intervention, modeling the intervention with the child while the mother and sister observed, and providing multiple opportunities for the mother and sister to practice implementing the intervention with immediate feedback on performance. Procedural integrity data were collected on the percentage of all steps of the procedure implemented correctly for each training session and subsequent implementation session. See Figure 2 for the procedural integrity data sheet

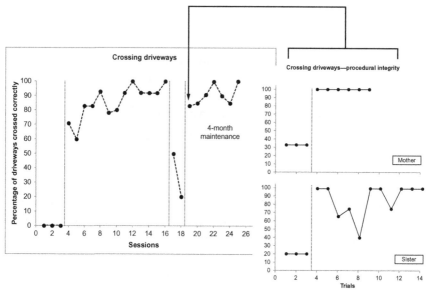

Figure 1 Percentage of driveways crossed (left panel) and percentage of intervention steps completed correctly by the mother (top panel) and sister (bottom panel).

Procedural integrity data sheet for crossing driveways safely

Key:
Y = Completed correctly
N = Not completed correctly
N/A = Step not needed
DO = Direct observation
RP = Role play
BL = Baseline

TX initials:					
Date:					
Caregiver observed:	**Mom sister**	**Mom sister**	**Mom sister**	**Mom sister**	**Mom sister**
Trial number:					
Trial type:	BL RP O	BL RP O	BL RP O	BL RP O	BL RP O
1. If at the beginning of the outing, **state the rule**, "Check the driveways before crossing them so see if they are safe."	Y N N/A	Y N N/A	Y N N/A	Y N N/A	Y N N/A
2. During the outing, walk within reaching distance to MA and between her and the street side of the sidewalk.	Y N N/A	Y N N/A	Y N N/A	Y N N/A	Y N N/A
3. Following a correctly crossed driveway, provide tangible/token reinforcer + social praise statement.	Y N N/A	Y N N/A	Y N N/A	Y N N/A	Y N N/A
4. Following a driveway where she has walked 1 foot into the driveway, block further walking and restate the rule.	Y N N/A	Y N N/A	Y N N/A	Y N N/A	Y N N/A
a. If she looks into the drive and labels that it is safe to cross, provide behavior specific praise	Y N N/A	Y N N/A	Y N N/A	Y N N/A	Y N N/A
b. If she does not look into the driveway or tact, provide a model prompt.	Y N N/A	Y N N/A	Y N N/A	Y N N/A	Y N N/A
c. If she imitates the model prompt provide social praise only, provide social praise.	Y N N/A	Y N N/A	Y N N/A	Y N N/A	Y N N/A
5. Correctly record data	Y N N/A	Y N N/A	Y N N/A	Y N N/A	Y N N/A
% Correct:					

Figure 2 Procedural integrity data sheet used to assess the mother and sister's implementation of the driveway crossing protocol.

and steps of the protocol. During the baseline phase, the mother and sister did not implement any steps of the intervention correctly. Once BST was conducted, correct implementation increased immediately with the mother to 100% and remained perfect for six consecutive sessions. Correct responding for the sister was more variable, but with continued training she too implemented the intervention with 100% integrity across three consecutive sessions (see Figure 1, right panel).

Strategies to Promote Generalization and Maintenance

It is important to explicitly program for maintenance and generalization of the newly acquired skills to ensure that the training efforts result in sustained and robust effects. After the necessary skills have been acquired, the environment must include natural contingencies to support their continued use without substantial additional costs or effort. Skills are described as maintaining when the previously trained person continues to independently perform the skills accurately some amount of time after training without ongoing prompts, error correction, or consistent, specific consequences for performance (LeBlanc, Gravina, & Carr, 2009). We provide an example in the maintenance probes that occurred for the mother and sister's implementation of the street crossing protocol in the above clinical case example at 4 months postintervention.

Stimulus and response generalizations are also equally important; that is, performing the same procedure in a different environmental context or a similar procedure with a slightly different skill (Baer, Wolf, & Risley, 1968). Specific opportunities to assess and teach generalization skills should be embedded into training to ensure these two types of generalization occur. We review strategies to promote generalization and maintenance of acquired skills in this section.

Maintenance

Low-cost incentives such as intermittent supervisor feedback and praise are highly effective at improving and maintaining staff performance (Alvero, Bucklin, & Austin, 2001) and have no additional monetary cost beyond that associated with the supervisor's time commitment. Praise is most effective when it directly follows monitoring of performance and when it is directly contingent upon, and descriptive of, aspects of the performance (Komaki, Desselles, & Bowman, 1989). Performance-contingent feedback and praise are closely linked with job satisfaction (Podsakoff & Schriescheim, 1985), and job satisfaction is often associated with employee retention

(Eskildsen & Dahlgaard, 2000). Therefore, praise of effective performance can be a high-impact organizational tool because it directly relates to improving and maintaining performance, improving job satisfaction, and minimizing turnover without extensive additional cost to the employer.

Other low-cost incentives that can be utilized to reinforce maintenance of skills include access to ongoing training, schedule flexibility, small tangible rewards, and small bonus payments. Research on monetary incentives has indicated that even very small financial incentives produce increases in performance equivalent to those produced by comparatively larger financial incentives (Dickinson & Gillette, 1993). Therefore, small bonus payments or entering staff into a raffle for an opportunity to win a desirable prize are reasonable alternatives when funding for incentives is negligible. If performance-based pay is a possibility for an organization, Abernathy (2011) provided a guide to creating pay-for-performance systems. For example, staff members may earn bonus pay for each observation in which their procedural integrity exceeds a target level (i.e., specific target performance) or for the number of the consumer-acquired skills that maintain with a novel tester (i.e., outcome-based measure). Abernathy describes a system for including multiple operationalized metrics at various weightings in a performance evaluation system. Two authors of this chapter have developed this type of system at Trumpet Behavioral Health to evaluate the performance of therapists each quarter to determine eligibility for raises and bonuses. As illustrated in Figure 3, procedural integrity measures from sessions constitute 50% of the performance evaluation, accurate and timely documentation constitutes another 25%, and effective and professional interactions with families and teams constitutes the remaining 25%. Performance ranges are determined, and weighted performance scores are calculated. The company can then set a performance target for raises to ensure that all employees have an equal opportunity for performance-based compensation increases.

The above suggestions for maintenance are well suited to situations in which the individual is an employee, but may not be relevant for maintenance of skills for caregivers since financial motivation is not a factor in initial acquisition or maintenance of skills. In these cases, it is important to design programming so that the contingencies for correct implementation support continued use of the programs. For example, in the case example above, the mother and sister were taught to implement the DRA procedure for the child to safely cross the driveway. This resulted in an increase in child safety and in the caregiver feeling more confident about her child crossing driveways with her. These improved conditions and repertoires for the child

Therapist

Quarterly Performance

THERAPY SESSIONS		Last Quarter's Score:			This Quarter's Score:		0%

Avg. percent accuracy score on procedural integrity during overlaps by Clinicians

Date:	mmdd								
Score:	0%								
Date:									
Score:									

NPA & FORMS	Last Quarter's Score:		This Quarter's Score:	100%
100%	% of weeks on time, accurate, rendering of hours in NPA works (-7.7 each week missed)			
100%	% of SVF or other signature forms completed accruately and appropriately (-7.7 each week missed)			

PROFESSIONALISM	Last Quarter's Score:		This Quarter's Score:	0.00

(3) Excellent   (2) Satisfactory   (1) Needs Improvement

0	Arrives to sessions and meetings on time, appropriately following schedule time period
0	Exhibits appropriate dress and demeanor in professional situations
0	Responds in a timely manner to phone calls, emails and other requests
0	Behaves ethically (e.g. confidentiality, minimizing dual role relationships)
0	Responds appropriately to feedback; seeks and welcomes feedback
0	Works effectively with teams
0	Keeps supervisor(s) informed of issues and problems

BONUS!!!	MAX BONUS:	10	This Quarter's Score:	0.00
0.00	Volunteer on project for Clinician, Senior Clinician or Clinical Director (1 hour= .5) Max 2			
0	Volunteer to cover session within 24 hours of the appointment notice (1 session= 1 point)			

Performance Levels

	4	5	6	7	8	9	10	11	12	Weight	Total	Score
Therapy Sessions	60%	70%	80%	85%	90%	93%	95%	98%	100%	50%	0%	
NPAWorks/FORMS	69%	77%		84%			92%	96%	100%	25%	100%	
Professionalism	1.50	2.00	2.29	2.36	2.43	2.57	2.71	2.86	3.00	25%	0.00	
Bonus										10.00%	0.00	
TOTAL												0.00%

Figure 3 A performance matrix used at Trumpet Behavioral Health to evaluate the performance of therapists each quarter to determine eligibility for raises and bonuses.

served as natural contingencies that may have maintained the mother and sister's implementation of the DRA procedure in the absence of other oversight or consequences. The improved outcome may have also eliminated avoidance of driveway crossing that occurred prior to the intervention. Although not implemented in this case study, an intermittent schedule of reinforcement during the training phase may increase the likelihood that caregiver or staff behavior will be resistant to extinction once the behavior analyst no longer provides direct oversight and consequences for accuracy.

Naturally occurring consequences are the only thing that can promote maintenance for caregivers when the training is completed, and the behavior analyst is no longer providing services. Planning for these contingencies should occur during the active training phase to ensure success. Just as improved repertoires of the child could maintain caregiver implementation of the procedure, extinction bursts, and spontaneous recovery of problem behavior could have a punishing effect on implementation. A behavior analyst might prepare a caregiver for these potential undesirable effects and provide instruction on how to proceed with the intervention if they should occur (see Allen & Warzak, 2000, for a thorough analysis of the contingencies that affect parental adherence beyond the supervised clinic environment and recommendations for solving problems with adherence).

Generalization

Stimulus generalization occurs when the same behavior is evoked by similar but not identical antecedents (Catania, 2012). In the above case example, stimulus generalization occurred when the mother and sister correctly implemented the same DRA procedure to teach the 8-year-old child how to cross a variety of driveways that differed in stimulus features (e.g., some had curbs while others did not, width of the crossing varied, bushes partially blocked the view of some but not others). Response generalization happens when untrained responses occur that are functionally equivalent to the trained behavior (Catania). In the above case example, response generalization would occur if the mother and sister gave a slightly different rule that functioned in the same way. For example, instead of saying "If you cross the driveway safely, you'll get a token," they might say "Remember to look both ways when you cross the driveway." The words changed, but these phrases are functionally equivalent.

It is important to specifically program for generalization because the trained person is likely to respond to new situations and to implement new functionally equivalent teaching procedures after the behavior analyst is no longer providing close oversight. Therefore, during initial training, the behavior analyst should have staff or caregivers practice implementation in new settings and under slightly different antecedent conditions, providing feedback and reinforcement under these generalization conditions. Additionally, multiple exemplar training consisting of implementation of the same procedure but with slightly different skills may prove useful. Periodic probes can occur to ensure the skill is durable over time, occurs in a variety of contexts, and spreads to a variety of behaviors.

Ducharme and Feldman (1992) provided an excellent example of programming for generalization in a training setting. In this study, the authors compared the use of programming with multiple stimuli and with multiple learners to an overall general case training approach (i.e., multiple exemplar training). General case training consisted of multiple exemplar training with multiple client programs in a simulated situation and was successful in promoting generalized use of teaching skills across clients, settings, and client programs. Single case training involved a single client program exemplar with simulated clients and performance-based training using real clients as the trainees. This general case training was found to be the most effective in the promotion of generalization.

Use of Technology

Interactive computer training, or computer-based instruction, involves the presentation of training material via a computer or internet site and requires the learner to answer questions about the material or engage in some activity related to the material (Williams & Zahad, 1996). It is proposed to be an effective alternative when face-to-face instruction is not possible (LeBlanc et al., 2009). Technology (e.g., Web- and video-based training) is becoming a more common means to train staff and caregivers when face-to-face instruction is not feasible. Interactive computer training that requires the viewer to answer questions and make evaluations has been demonstrated to be more effective than lecture (Williams & Zahad, 1996) and reading (Eckerman et al., 2002). Additionally, video presentation has proven as effective as, and more efficient than, live training for behavioral intervention plan implementation, although staff who received training rated live training more highly (Macurik et al., 2008). Technology can also be integrated into the various steps of the BST model to increase efficiency and standardize training procedures. For example, Catania, Almeida, Liu-Constant, and DiGennaro Reed (2009) demonstrated the effectiveness of video modeling in training staff to implement discrete trial instruction.

Telehealth, or the use of online communication, is becoming more commonly used to train parents of children with autism on effective implementation of procedures (Wainer & Ingersoll, 2013). For example, Vismara, McCormick, Young, Nadhan, and Monlux (2013) used video conferencing and a self-guided Web site to provide parent training to families of children with autism. The parents learned new skills and child behavior improved for some families through the use of this technology. Similarly, Wacker et al. (2013) assessed the effectiveness of coaching via telehealth on correct parent implementation of FAs and functional communication training for 17 families of children with autism. The results indicated that problem behavior was reduced by an average of 93.5% for all participants. Although these authors did not directly measure correct parent implementation, the dramatically improved child outcomes are unlikely to have occurred without effective implementation of the treatment. Acceptability measures indicated that parents found the intervention to be highly acceptable. Suess et al. (2014)

successfully demonstrated that instructions and feedback provided from a distance could produce high parent-implemented treatment fidelity and changes in targeted child behaviors.

Geiger (2013) directly compared live BST to an interactive computer-based instruction (CBI) module for teaching undergraduate students to implement receptive language programming in a role-play with a confederate adult. Participants were randomly assigned to either the BST or the CBI condition. The BST condition was conducted individually to ensure that group versus individual instruction would not introduce a confounding variable. The CBI module used the same basic instructions and video models as the BST condition but incorporated active responding in the computer platform *in lieu* of rehearsal and feedback. For example, participants moved images with their computer mouse to create an accurate stimulus array, and feedback was provided by the computer based on their accuracy of placement. Similarly, they clicked in the appropriate location on an image of a data sheet as an analogue to data collection on responses in video footage. The two training conditions took a similar amount of time to complete (~50 min) and produced mastery during role play with a confederate for the vast majority of participants, with a greater percentage meeting the mastery criterion of 85% accuracy in the live BST condition (23/25 participants) compared to the CBI condition (16/25 participants). An additional 5-min live feedback and rehearsal session produced mastery for all of the participants who were not initially successful. A follow-up study was conducted with therapists in a provider agency and the children with autism that they served (Geiger & LeBlanc, 2013). All participants immediately met the mastery criterion after the CBI module. Thus, prior experience teaching children with autism alleviated the minor performance problems that remained for undergraduate students in the first study. A breakeven analysis indicated that the costs to produce the CBI module were recouped once approximately 65 people were trained using the module.

The examples provided herein illustrate the importance of establishing performance criteria and monitoring the progress of trainees during staff and caregiver training. We provide a more detailed discussion about best practices for evaluating and monitoring the progress of trainees in the next section.

HOW TO EVALUATE AND MONITOR PROGRESS

As indicated previously, behavior analysts evaluate the accuracy with which staff and caregivers implement prescribed interventions throughout the training process, and they continue to do so while monitoring treatment outcomes. Collecting data on implementation accuracy, typically called treatment integrity or fidelity, is necessary for determining whether caregivers acquire the targeted skills and whether those skills generalize and maintain over time. Data on treatment integrity also is critical for determining what do to if an intervention is ineffective or loses effectiveness over time. Behavior analysts should rule out problems with treatment integrity before modifying or replacing seemingly ineffective treatments. Ultimately, the most important measure of training outcomes is the change in client behavior as a result of caregiver treatment implementation. As such, behavior analysts measure the behavior of both clients and caregivers to evaluate progress.

Behavior analysts should collect data on caregiver performance prior to training, if possible. Baseline data on treatment integrity not only provide a point of comparison for determining the impact of training, but they permit behavior analysts to focus on components of the intervention that caregivers are not implementing correctly. As they do for all consumers, behavior analysts use some type of performance criteria to make decisions about training progression and modifications. For example, initial training may continue until a caregiver implements all intervention components with a certain level of accuracy across three different settings. Following initial mastery, the behavior analyst should periodically monitor performance and implement some type of remediation if caregivers fail to maintain a certain level of accuracy over time.

Data Collection

A data collection system, consisting of objectively defined caregiver responses (correct versus incorrect responses), the data recording method, and a plan for summarizing and graphing the data, must be developed for each training program (Vollmer, Sloman, & Pipkin, 2008). Data on treatment integrity are difficult to interpret without information about the opportunities for staff or caregivers to implement the treatment components, so the data collection system must capture this type of information as well. Client behavior establishes an opportunity for caregiver behavior in the form of a consequence for many treatments (e.g., response to appropriate behavior versus problem behavior; Shore et al., 1995). Suppose a behavior analyst has taught a parent to withhold attention for at least 20 s following instances of problem behavior; data indicating that the parent correctly withheld attention four times during an observation would be difficult to evaluate without knowing the number of times the child engaged in problem behavior. If the child engaged in problem behavior four times, we could determine that the parent always responded accurately. However, we would draw a different conclusion about the parent's implementation accuracy if the child engaged in problem behavior 10 times.

Caregivers or staff also may need to implement some intervention components independent of child behavior (e.g., antecedent-based interventions). Suppose a behavior analyst has instructed a teacher to deliver 10 s of attention to a student every 5 min (i.e., NCR); in this case, the number of 5-min intervals must be considered when evaluating data on the teacher's correct use of NCR.

Data collection systems for use during training tend to be particularly complex, given the number of different responses that behavior analysts must track (i.e., multiple responses of the caregiver, responses of the client, other opportunities for treatment implementation). As such, recording systems must be practical and reliable yet still permit observers to obtain the information needed to evaluate training outcomes. For example, when training teachers to implement discrete trial teaching with students, one of the authors of this chapter taught observers to score the teacher's delivery of instructions, prompts, and reinforcement; management of problem behavior; data collection; and intertrial interval length, along with the performance of the student, on each instructional trial (Lerman et al., 2004). The observers were able to use the data collection system reliably only by scoring videotaped teaching sessions, a labor-intensive practice that required them to repeatedly stop and replay portions of the session to ensure that they recorded data on all of the responses. The goal, however, was to disseminate a practical training program for public school district personnel. Thus, the next step was to evaluate a recording method that would be easier to use although necessarily less precise (Lerman, Tetreault, Hovanetz, Strobel, & Garro, 2008). Instead of scoring correct and incorrect teacher responses on each instructional trial, observers scored whether or not the teacher performed each response correctly across a block of trials (e.g., 10). Observers simply observed the teacher working with a student during an instructional session and used a checklist, as shown in Figure 4, to note any responses that the teacher performed incorrectly at least once. The remaining responses then could be scored as correct (or having no opportunity) at the end of the session. Results of this research indicated that this recording method had adequate reliability and was sensitive enough to show teachers' mastery of discrete trial teaching as a result of the training.

DTT monitoring checklist

Session #:_____ _____immediate feedback OR _____ delayed feedback
Teacher _____   Student: _____
Skill:_____ _____ Prompting Proc._____
Observer:_____ Date_____

Check one   **Percentage correct:** _____(# Yes / # Yes + # No)

___ _____ Materials ready/organized prior to teaching
Yes   No N/A
___ _____ Instructions delivered when child attending.
Yes   No N/A
___ _____ Instructions clear, concise, and consistent.
Yes   No N/A
___ _____ Appropriate and consistent prompting strategy used for no
Yes   No N/A   responses or incorrect responses
___ _____ Reinforcement delivered immediately for correct responses
Yes   No N/A
___ _____ Highly preferred tangible reinforcers paired with praise
Yes   No N/A
___ _____ Varied reinforcers used.
Yes   No N/A
___ _____ Reinforcement delivered periodically for on-task behavior.
Yes   No N/A
___ _____ Reinforcement withheld until desired behavior occurred.
Yes   No N/A
___ _____ Distractions removed
Yes   No N/A
___ _____ Problem behavior managed appropriately.
Yes   No N/A
___ _____ Brief interval between instructional trials
Yes   No N/A
___ _____ Data collected appropriately.
Yes   No N/A

Figure 4 Procedural integrity checklist used during teacher training in Lerman et al., 2008.

Graphing

Like data on consumer performance, data on treatment integrity should be graphed and evaluated via visual inspection. Integrity data typically may be converted to a percentage for summary purposes. In most cases, data on correct use will be converted to a percentage based on the number of opportunities to exhibit the response, regardless of accuracy. Suppose a teacher correctly delivers reinforcement following seven of eight instances of appropriate student behavior; converting this to a percentage, the behavior analyst would plot an accuracy score of 87.5% for this observation on the graph. For some intervention components, it is helpful to calculate the percentage of total responses (correct and incorrect) that a caregiver performed accurately. Suppose a behavior analyst has taught a parent how to word instructions in a particular manner to increase the likelihood of child compliance; data on the percentage of total instructions that the parent delivered in the prescribed manner would be useful for evaluating the outcome of training. If the parent delivered 5 of 10 instructions correctly, the behavior analyst would plot an accuracy score of 50% for this observation on the graph.

When a treatment has multiple components (e.g., delivering instructions, responding to incorrect responses, and responding to correct responses), integrity data can be summarized by averaging the percentage accuracy scores for each component. For example, a behavior analyst might plot an average accuracy score of 83% if a teacher delivered 60% of instructions correctly, provided reinforcement correctly for 90% of correct responses, and delivered prompts correctly for 100% of incorrect responses. However, summary data may obscure different integrity levels across the individual treatment components. Inspecting performance on individual components permits behavior analysts to focus their training and remediation on aspects of the treatment that caregivers are implementing with less-than-desirable accuracy. In the example data above, the teacher would benefit from more focused training on how to deliver instructions correctly.

Performance Criteria

Behavior analysts use performance-based criteria to determine when a trainee has successfully mastered the procedures for the prescribed intervention and whether the trainee maintains these skills over time. For example, a minimum performance criterion might be established for each intervention component, such as completing each component with at least 90% accuracy. Because research findings indicate that procedural drift commonly occurs following training (Noell et al., 2000), behavior analysts should consider setting a fairly stringent mastery criteria before concluding that the caregiver has been successfully trained.

Nonetheless, a number of factors should be considered when setting goals for the acquisition, maintenance, and generalization of intervention implementation (Vollmer et al., 2008). These factors include the complexity of the procedures and the potential impact of the integrity level on the efficacy of the treatment. For example, some research suggests that low levels of treatment integrity may be less likely to compromise outcomes, depending on the treatment component (Carroll, Kodak, & Fisher, 2013; St. Peter Pipkin, Vollmer, & Sloman, 2010). Although integrity must be near perfect accuracy to ensure that problem behavior extinguishes when using extinction, providing reinforcement for alternative behavior more intermittently than prescribed may be adequate to maintain treatment effects. Some research also suggests that a reduction in integrity over time may not necessarily lead to treatment relapse if caregivers initially implement the intervention with high levels of integrity (e.g., Stephenson & Hanley, 2010). However, research on the relation between integrity and treatment outcomes is still in its infancy. The best approach for behavior analysts is to regularly monitor both treatment integrity and client outcomes to determine if retraining or supplemental instruction is warranted.

Social Validity

A final important measure for behavior analysts to consider is the extent to which a caregiver or staff member likes the training procedures, the treatment, and the outcomes (Wolf, 1978). These social validity data are typically collected by obtaining verbal reports from caregivers about the acceptability of the procedures and outcomes. A number of surveys, rating scales, and questionnaires have been developed for this purpose, making it relatively easy for behavior analysts to incorporate social validity measures into their training programs (see Fuqua & Schwade, 1986, for a review). For example, one of the authors of this chapter modified the Treatment Evaluation Inventory (Kazdin, 1980) to evaluate a summer teacher training program (Lerman et al., 2008). Social validity data might be used to select or modify training procedures before the training begins by asking caregivers to rate the acceptability of various training modalities (e.g., video versus live modeling). Although the acceptability of the treatment itself also might be evaluated prior to training, research findings suggest that direct experience with implementation can alter caregiver ratings of acceptability (Gabor et al., in press). Thus, behavior analysts might consider collecting social validity data during or immediately following the initial training. Finally, data on staff or caregiver acceptability of treatment outcomes can be a useful supplement to objective data on client behavior change. If staff or caregivers are not satisfied with the outcomes of treatment, they may be less willing to implement the prescribed interventions; furthermore, they may seek assistance elsewhere if the behavior analyst is not responsive to their goals for the consumer.

In the previous sections, we have described evidence-based approaches for selecting targets, training staff and caregivers, and evaluating the outcomes of training. In the final section, we describe how these elements might be integrated into large-scale training systems for organizations employing human-service providers.

TRAINING SYSTEMS AND PERFORMANCE MANAGEMENT

The growing demand for applied behavior analysis services exceeds the capacity of the number of qualified individuals able to provide these services, making access to individual single-event training by a behavior analyst less likely over time. Thus, behavior analysts need to create standardized training systems and ensure those systems are sustainable and require minimal effort to reach a greater number of consumers. Training systems must include components that target pivotal repertoires of trainers themselves and ensure maintenance of the system over time. In addition, sometimes individuals are trained adequately but other barriers interfere with accurate and consistent use of the new skills (e.g., faulty or missing equipment, competing contingencies). In these instances, performance management strategies are employed to minimize barriers and increase performance to the desired level. The following section presents a model for the development of effective training systems and an overview of basic performance management strategies for improving and maintaining performance over time.

Training Systems

An important distinction can be made between single-event training and a training system. *Single-event training* involves teaching an individual or group of individuals a very specific set of skills (e.g., to conduct a preference assessment, to implement a specific protocol). For example, a clinical supervisor may conduct a training to teach his or her supervisees how to conduct an FA. The training may include written instruction on the conditions involved in an FA, conducting the actual sessions, and analyzing the collected data. Another example of single-event training includes a behavior analyst training a parent or group of parents to implement toilet training with their child. The training might consist of instruction on how to fluid load, use a scheduled sit routine, and use positive reinforcement for continence. Such trainings may take several sessions to complete and are common in the delivery of applied behavior analysis services. Although single-event training can be very useful for teaching caregivers new skills in the context of time limited service delivery, this approach typically targets a limited set of skills and cannot be implemented readily with large numbers of individuals due to time and manpower constraints for the trainer.

Alternatively, *training systems* involve the use of a standardized curriculum to teach individuals a greater number of skills applicable to a wide range of treatment concerns. A training system also includes infrastructure and procedures for training others to deliver the original curriculum such that the capacity for impact increases over time. Systems also target sustainability of the model over time. Reid, Parsons, and Green (2011) provided an excellent example of a training system for teaching managers how to effectively supervise their staff who provide services to individuals with intellectual and developmental disabilities. The curriculum did not focus on teaching a particular intervention technique such as chaining. Instead, the curriculum focused on teaching supervisors to use behavioral strategies (e.g., modeling, reinforcement) to change the performance of the people who implement any intervention techniques. Curriculum topics included clearly defining performance expectations, creating job duty checklists, assessing work performance through formal and informal monitoring, and implementing a positive work environment. The materials included the specific curriculum and a trainee workbook as well as an extensive manual and PowerPoint® presentations for the trainers who teach the managers how to be more effective supervisors. Thus, the curriculum could be delivered by a core group of trainers to train an entire company of effective supervising managers who improve the performance of all direct service providers in the agency. The curriculum was a 2-day, competency-based system, employing BST to teach others to implement BST to teach their staff any new skill or to improve performance in any area (e.g., keeping a clean, safe workplace).

Two authors of this chapter have implemented this type of system at Trumpet Behavioral Health (TBH), a large provider agency that serves individuals with special needs in more than 10 states. TBH purchased the curriculum and modified it slightly to include additional leadership components and practice activities pertinent to educational and early intensive behavioral intervention settings. The Executive Director of Clinical Services and a Senior Clinician from one division prepared all materials and delivered a 2-day train-the-trainer version of the curriculum with all Clinical Leaders in the organization. That is, the 2-day event included the primary instructional material as well as instructions and modeling on how to conduct the training. Those clinical leaders were then given all instructional slides, activities, training videos, and a manual to conduct the same training for all supervising team members in their home division. A subcommittee was formed to create a group of lead trainers who could help across multiple divisions and create new materials for future trainings. Over the next 9 months, the training occurred in all divisions of the organization. This type of system development greatly increased the capacity of the agency to train their team compared to if the two primary trainers had attempted to train all 800 team members across all states. In addition, such a system ensures the sustainability of training even if critical people leave the organization.

The TBH example illustrates how behavior analysts can create training systems within their own organizations; however, behavior analysts have also used training systems to influence separate provider systems. For example, child welfare systems already exist in every state and serve a large number of vulnerable children who are at high risk for negative outcomes. In at least three states, behavior analysts have partnered with the existing child welfare agency to create a system to conduct effective parent training with a large number of biological and foster parents (Berard & Smith, 2008; Dunlap & Vollmer, 2008; Franks et al., 2013). The *Tools for Positive Behavior Change* curriculum is a 5–7 week program designed to teach parents' core skills for creating positive home environments and responding to child appropriate and inappropriate behaviors. The curriculum uses parent-friendly terms to refer to basic behavioral concepts and procedures such as reinforcement, rules, and noncontingent-positive attention (e.g., Stoutimore, Williams, Neff, & Foster, 2008). Instead of directly teaching parents a specific strategy for a specific situation (e.g., how to use positive reinforcement to increase functional communication), the curriculum focuses on teaching parents general strategies applicable to a variety of situations (e.g., using empathy statements, asking open-ended positive questions, redirecting actions, praising positive actions). The trainers undergo a multi-week program to learn the content and how to deliver the content via BST and to develop effective interpersonal skills to effectively manage the groups of parents who may not be excited to participate in state-mandated training (Franks et al., 2013). Professionals (who are sometimes behavior analysts) employed by the child welfare organization then deliver the training classes at regular intervals to reach a large number of families throughout each year.

The development and first implementation of this model occurred in Florida (Stoutimore et al., 2008). Families in the state of Florida were assigned a designated behavior analyst who partnered with social workers to teach regular parent-training courses and to provide support and feedback to families. Initial implementation of this parent-training system resulted in a decrease in placement disruptions for families (Stoutimore et al., 2008) and substantial improvements in the targeted skills from pretest to posttest role play (Van Camp et al., 2008). A very similar curriculum was implemented and evaluated in Texas with similar increases in parent performance on role play and a quiz on the information (Berard & Smith, 2008). More recently, a similar system was implemented in Alabama to deliver services in the four most populated counties. Franks et al. (2013) evaluated the effects of the parent-training program on child placement outcomes for biological parents with children in the child welfare system. An archival analysis was conducted to compare the outcomes for families who completed the *Tools of Choice* curriculum or declined to participate in the training but received all other services in identical fashion through the child welfare system. Families were matched on county of service, time of referral to the service, and age of the child at entry into the system. The 171 families who participated in the parent-training classes were more likely to have their children residing with them and more likely to no longer require close monitoring by the system at follow up than the 171 families who did not participate. The families who did not participate in training were more likely to have had their child permanently removed from the home or to have continued temporary out-of-home placement and close monitoring by the system.

Any training system must be designed to minimize the effort required to deliver the training and the variability evident in the execution of the training. Once the primary training curriculum exists, the remaining effort involves repeated delivery of the training and ensuring consistency of the delivery across implementations and trainers. Ongoing oversight of the trainers focuses on ensuring continued consistent implementation, teaching the trainers to problem-solve novel and challenging situations, and developing new training materials as needed. For example, a trainer may fluently deliver the Reid et al. (2011) supervisor's curriculum over the course of several months. He or she may encounter a situation with a trainee that is not covered in the existing training material (i.e., how to handle erratic behavior of the trainee). Oversight and support from the advanced trainer would focus on teaching the other trainers to respond effectively to these situations and on developing new content and supports to enhance the original training (i.e., a systems feedback loop).

Performance Management

When competency-based training is complete, the behavior analyst must ensure that the trained care providers maintain the skills over time.

Performance management refers to the application of behavior analysis in work settings to functionally diagnose performance problems and arrange environmental contingencies to sustain effective performance (Daniels & Daniels, 2004). Diagnosis of the functional determinants of the performance deficit becomes the first step in treatment of performance issues. The Performance Diagnostic Checklist for Human Services (PDC-HS; Carr, Wilder, Majdalany, Mathisen, & Strain, 2013) assesses potential causes of performance issues and constitutes a functional assessment of poor performance in the workplace.

The functional assessment tool samples four main areas: (a) training; (b) task clarification and prompting; (c) resources, materials, and processes; and (d) performance consequences, effort, and competing contingencies. Note that poor training procedures or outcomes are an important area but are not the only area that might contribute to poor implementation and performance. The remaining items on the checklist identify challenges related to unclear expectations and reminders, inadequate resources and materials, excessive difficulty and response effort of the task, lack of reinforcement for effective performance, and available reinforcers for behaviors that compete with the desired and previously trained behaviors. An individual who obtained "training" may be underperforming for one or more of those other reasons. The items that are identified as critical contributors to underperformance are then directly linked to function-based interventions (e.g., inadequate prompts → posted prompts; lack of reinforcement for effective performance → increased supervisor presence and reinforcement).

In one example of the use of this type of performance tool, a therapist inconsistently implemented "three-step guided compliance," a common behavioral procedure used with children with autism. The most common issues were not providing an adequate amount of time between levels, repeating steps, and skipping some steps of the procedure. The completed PDC indicated that instructions and modeling had occurred but rehearsal to criterion had not been a part of the initial training procedure. The supervisor arranged an opportunity for the therapist to rehearse with performance feedback, and the performance problem was immediately remedied. In another example, a clinician had difficulty maintaining an adequate number of teaching programs for consumers and completing treatment integrity checks with all therapists implementing the programs. The completed PDC revealed that training had been completed according to best practices, expectations were clear, and materials (e.g., checklists) were available.

Performance was adequate when a supervisor was present; however, performance decreased whenever the supervisor was not in the immediate vicinity and off-task behavior related to the clinician's home life increased. The prescribed interventions were increased supervisor presence and a decrease to 75% employment to allow management of family events.

SUMMARY

The voluminous literature on staff and caregiver training provides behavior analysts with a variety of evidence-based practices to successfully disseminate behavioral technologies to caregivers and staff. Key features of effective training programs include careful consideration of the most appropriate targets: design of practical, reliable, and sensitive performance monitoring systems; precise implementation of BST components; and strategies to promote maintenance and generalization of caregiver and staff skills. More recent research has demonstrated the benefits of technology (i.e., Web- and video-based training programs) for broadening the reach of behavior analysts to large groups of consumers and those who live some distance from qualified trainers. Combining elements of effective training practices with system-wide curricula and functional approaches to performance management have enabled behavior analysts to address the training needs of burgeoning organizations charged with providing services to consumers with special needs.

REFERENCES

Abernathy, W. B. (2011). *Pay for profit: Designing an organization-wide performance-based compensation system*. Atlanta, GA: Performance Management Publications.

Allen, K. D., & Warzak, W. J. (2000). The problem of parental nonadherence in clinical behavior analysis: Effective treatment is not enough. *Journal of Applied Behavior Analysis*, *33*, 373–391. http://dx.doi.org/10.1901/jaba.2000.33-373.

Alvero, A. M., Bucklin, B. R., & Austin, J. (2001). An objective review of the effectiveness and essential characteristics of performance feedback in organizational settings. *Journal of Organizational Behavior Management*, *21*, 3–29.

Baer, D. M., Wolf, M. M., & Risley, T. R. (1968). Some current dimensions of applied behavior analysis. *Journal of Applied Behavior Analysis*, *1*, 91–97.

Barnes, C. S., Mellor, J. R., & Rehfeldt, R. A. (2014). Implementing the verbal behavior milestones assessment and placement program (VBMAPP): Teaching assessment techniques. *The Analysis of Verbal Behavior*, *30*, 36–47.

Berard, K. P., & Smith, R. G. (2008). Evaluating a positive parenting curriculum package: An analysis of the acquisition of key skills. *Research on Social Work Practice*, *18*, 442–452.

Brodhead, M. T., & Higbee, T. S. (2012). Teaching and maintaining ethical behavior in a professional organization. *Behavior Analysis in Practice*, *5*, 82–88.

Carr, J. E., Wilder, D. A., Majdalany, L., Mathisen, D., & Strain, L. A. (2013). An assessment-based solution to a human-service employee performance problem: An initial evaluation of the performance diagnostic checklist—Human services. *Behavior Analysis in Practice, 6,* 16–32.

Carroll, R. A., Kodak, T., & Fisher, W. W. (2013). An evaluation of programmed treatment-integrity errors during discrete-trial instruction. *Journal of Applied Behavior Analysis, 46,* 379–394. http://dx.doi.org/10.1002/jaba.49.

Catania, C. A. (2012). *Learning* (5th). Cornwall-on-Hudson, New York: Sloan Publishing.

Catania, C., Almeida, D., Liu-Constant, B., & DiGennaro Reed, F. D. (2009). Video modeling to train staff to implement discrete-trial instruction. *Journal of Applied Behavior Analysis, 42,* 387–392.

Chok, J. T., Shlesinger, A., Studer, L., & Bird, F. L. (2012). Description of a practitioner training program on functional analysis and treatment development. *Behavior Analysis in Practice, 5,* 25–36.

Daniels, A. C., & Daniels, J. D. (2004). *Performance management: Changing behavior that drives organizational effectiveness.* Atlanta, GA: Performance Management Publications.

Dickinson, A. M., & Gillette, K. L. (1993). A comparison of the effects of two individual monetary incentive systems on productivity: Piece rate pay versus base pay plus incentives. *Journal of Organizational Behavior Management, 14,* 3–82.

Ducharme, J. M., & Feldman, M. A. (1992). Comparison of staff training strategies to promote generalized teaching skills. *Journal of Applied Behavior Analysis, 25,* 165–179.

Dunlap, G., & Vollmer, T. R. (2008). Introduction to the special issue on the Florida Behavior Analysis Services Program. *Research on Social Work Practice, 18,* 365–366.

Eckerman, D. A., Lundeen, C. A., Steele, A., Fercho, H., Ammerman, T., & Anger, W. K. (2002). Interactive training versus reading to teach respiratory protection. *Journal of Occupational Health Psychology, 7,* 313–323.

Eskildsen, J. K., & Dahlgaard, J. J. (2000). A causal model for employee satisfaction. *Total Quality Management, 11,* 1081–1094.

Finn, L. L., & Sturmey, P. (2009). The effect of peer-to-peer training on staff interactions with adults with dual diagnoses. *Research in Developmental Disabilities, 30,* 96–106. http://dx.doi.org/10.1016/j.ridd.2007.11.004.

Fleming, R. K., Oliver, J. R., & Bolton, D. M. (1996). Training supervisors to train staff: A case study in a human service organization. *Journal or Organizational Behavior Management, 16,* 3–25.

Franks, S. B., Mata, F. C., Wofford, E., Briggs, A. M., LeBlanc, L. A., & Carr, J. E. (2013). The effects of behavioral parent training on placement outcomes of biological families in a state child welfare system. *Research on Social Work Practice, 23,* 377–382.

Fuqua, R. W., & Schwade, J. (1986). Social validation of applied behavioral research: A selective review and critique. In A. Poling & R. W. Fuqua (Eds.), *Research methods in applied behavior analysis* (pp. 265–292). New York: Plenum Press.

Gabor, A. M., Fritz, J.N., Roath, C. T., Rothe, B. R., & Salazar, D. A. (in press). Caregiver preference for reinforcement-based behavioral interventions. *Journal of Applied Behavior Analysis.*

Geiger, K. B. (2013). A comparison of staff training methods for effective implementation of discrete trial teaching for learners with developmental disabilities. *Dissertation Abstracts International: Section B: The Sciences and Engineering, 73*(12-B(E)), 0419–4217.

Geiger, K. B., & LeBlanc, L. A. (2013). A comparison of staff training methods for effective implementation of discrete trial teaching for learners with developmental disabilities. In L. A. LeBlanc (Chair), *Staff training in delivery of applied behavior analysis intervention services. Presented at the association for professional behavior analysts,* Las Vegas, NV.

Guercio, J. M., & Dixon, M. R. (2011). The observer effect and its impact on staff behavior in an acquired brain injury neurobehavioral treatment setting. *Journal of Organizational Behavior Management, 31,* 43–54. http://dx.doi.org/10.1080/01608061.2010.520142.

Hsieh, H. H., Wilder, D. A., & Abellon, E. O. (2011). The effects of training on caregiver implementation of incidental teaching. *Journal of Applied Behavior Analysis, 44*, 199–203.

Jones, F. H., Fremouw, W., & Carples, S. (1977). Pyramid training of elementary school teachers to use a classroom management 'skill package'. *Journal of Applied Behavior Analysis, 10*, 239–253. http://dx.doi.org/10.1901/jaba.1977.10-239.

Kazdin, A. E. (1980). Acceptability of alternative treatments for deviant child behavior. *Journal of Applied Behavior Analysis, 13*, 259–273. http://dx.doi.org/10.1901/jaba.1980.13-259.

Koegel, R. L., Glahn, T. J., & Nieminen, G. S. (1978). Generalization of parent-training results. *Journal of Applied Behavior Analysis, 11*, 95–109.

Komaki, J. L., Desselles, M. L., & Bowman, E. D. (1989). Definitely not a breeze: Extending an operant model of effective supervision to teams. *Journal of Applied Psychology, 74*, 522–529.

Kuhn, S. A. C., Lerman, D. C., & Vorndran, C. M. (2003). Pyramidal training for families of children with problem behavior. *Journal of Applied Behavior Analysis, 36*, 77–88. http://dx.doi.org/10.1901/jaba.2003.36-77.

Lafasakis, M., & Sturmey, P. (2007). Training parent implementation of discrete-trial teaching: Effects on generalization of parent teaching and child correct responding. *Journal of Applied Behavior Analysis, 40*, 685–689. http://dx.doi.org/10.1901/jaba.2007.685-689.

Lambert, J. M., Bloom, S. E., Kunnavatana, S., Shanun, C., Shawnee, D., & Casey, J. (2013). Training residential staff to conduct trial-based functional analyses. *Journal of Applied Behavior Analysis, 46*, 296–300.

LeBlanc, L. A., Gravina, N., & Carr, J. E. (2009). Training issues unique to autism spectrum disorders. In J. Matson (Ed.), *Practitioner's guide to applied behavior analysis for children with autism spectrum disorders* (pp. 225–235). New York: Springer.

Lerman, D. C., Tetreault, A., Hovanetz, A., Strobel, M., & Garro, J. (2008). Further evaluation of a brief, intensive teacher training model. *Journal of Applied Behavior Analysis, 41*, 243–248.

Lerman, D. C., Vorndran, C. M., Addison, L., & Kuhn, S. C. (2004). Preparing teachers in evidence-based practices for young children with autism. *School Psychology Review, 33*, 510–526.

Love, J. R., Carr, J. E., LeBlanc, L. A., & Kisamore, A. N. (2013). Training behavioral research methods to staff in an early and intensive behavioral intervention setting: A program description and preliminary evaluation. *Education & Treatment of Children, 36*, 139–160.

Macurik, K. M., O'Kane, N. P., Malanga, P., & Reid, D. H. (2008). Video training of support staff in intervention plans for challenging behavior: Comparison with live training. *Behavioral Interventions, 23*, 143–163.

Madzharova, M. S., Sturmey, P., & Jones, E. A. (2012). Training staff to increase manding in students with autism: two preliminary case studies. *Behavioral Interventions, 27*, 224–235.

McGimsey, J. F., Greene, B. F., & Lutzker, J. R. (1995). Competence in aspects of behavioral treatment and consultation: Implications for service delivery and graduate training. *Journal of Applied Behavior Analysis, 28*, 301–315. http://dx.doi.org/10.1901/jaba.1995.28-301.

Miles, N. I., & Wilder, D. A. (2009). The effects of behavioral skills training on caregiver implementation of guided compliance. *Journal of Applied Behavior Analysis, 42*, 405–410.

Miltenberger, R. G. (2003). *Behavior modification: Principles and procedures*. Belmont, CA: Wadsworth Publishing.

Mozingo, D. B., Smith, T., Riordan, M. R., Reiss, M. L., & Bailey, J. S. (2006). Enhancing frequency recording by developmental disabilities treatment staff. *Journal of Applied Behavior Analysis, 39*, 253–256. http://dx.doi.org/10.1901/jaba.2006.55-05.

Neef, N. (1995). Pyramidal parent training by peers. *Journal of Applied Behavior Analysis, 28*, 333–337. http://dx.doi.org/10.1901/jaba.1995.28-333.

Noell, G. H., Witt, J. C., LaFleur, L. H., Mortenson, B. P., Ranier, D. D., & LeVelle, J. (2000). Increasing intervention implementation in general education following consultation: A comparison of two follow-up strategies. *Journal of Applied Behavior Analysis, 33*, 271–284. http://dx.doi.org/10.1901/jaba.2000.33-271.

Pangborn, M. M., Borrero, C. S., & Borrero, J. C. (2013). Initial application of caregiver training to implement pediatric feeding protocols. *Behavioral Interventions, 28*, 107–130.

Parsons, M. B., & Reid, D. H. (1995). Training residential supervisors to provide feedback for maintaining staff teaching skills with people who have severe disabilities. *Journal of Applied Behavior Analysis, 28*, 317–322.

Parsons, M. B., Reid, D. H., & Green, C. W. (1996). Training basic teaching skills to community and institutional support staff for people with severe disabilities: A one-day program. *Research in Developmental Disabilities, 17*, 467–485.

Parsons, M. B., Rollyson, J. H., & Reid, D. H. (2012). Evidence-based staff training: A guide for practitioners. *Behavior Analysis in Practice, 5*, 2–11.

Pence, S. T., St. Peter, C. C., & Giles, A. F. (2014). Teacher acquisition of functional analysis methods using pyramidal training. *Journal of Behavioral Education, 23*, 132–149. http://dx.doi.org/10.1007/s10864-013-9182-4.

Podsakoff, P. M., & Schriescheim, C. A. (1985). Field studies of French and Raven's bases of power: Critique, reanalysis, and suggestions for future research. *Psychological Bulletin, 97*, 387–411.

Reid, D. H., & Green, C. W. (1990). Staff training. In J. L. Matson (Ed.), *Handbook of behavior modification with the mentally retarded* (2nd, pp. 71–90). New York: Plenum Press.

Reid, D. H., & Parsons, M. B. (2007). *Positive behavior support training curriculum* (2nd). Washington, DC: AAIDD.

Reid, D. H., Parsons, M. B., & Green, C. W. (2011). *The supervisor training curriculum: Evidence-based ways to promote work quality and enjoyment among support staff*. Washington, DC: AAIDD.

Reid, D. H., Parsons, M. B., Lattimore, L. P., Towery, D. L., & Reade, K. K. (2005). Improving staff performance through clinician application of outcome management. *Research in Developmental Disabilities, 26*, 101–116.

Reid, D. H., Rotholz, D. A., Parsons, M. B., Morris, L., Braswell, B. A., Green, C. W., et al. (2003). Training human service supervisors in aspects of PBS: Evaluation of a statewide, performance-based program. *Journal of Positive Behavior Interventions, 5*, 35–46.

Schepis, M. M., & Reid, D. H. (1994). Training direct service staff in congregate settings to interact with people with severe disabilities: A quick, effective and acceptable program. *Behavioral Interventions, 9*, 13–26.

Schmidt, J. D., Urban, K. D., Luiselli, J. K., White, C., & Harrington, C. (2013). Improving appearance, organization, and safety of special education classrooms: Effects of staff training in a human services setting. *Education & Treatment of Children, 36*, 1–13.

Shayne, R., & Miltenberger, R. G. (2013). Evaluation of behavioral skills training for teaching functional assessment and treatment selecton skills to parents. *Behavioral Interventions, 28*, 4–21.

Shore, B. A., Iwata, B. A., Vollmer, T. R., Lerman, D. C., & Zarcone, J. R. (1995). Pyramidal staff training in the extension of treatment for severe behavior disorders. *Journal of Applied Behavior Analysis, 28*, 323–332.

St. Peter Pipkin, C., Vollmer, T. R., & Sloman, K. N. (2010). Effects of treatment integrity failures during differential reinforcement of alternative behavior: A translational model. *Journal of Applied Behavior Analysis, 43*, 47–70. http://dx.doi.org/10.1901/jaba.2010.43-47.

Stephenson, K. M., & Hanley, G. P. (2010). Preschoolers' compliance with simple instructions: A descriptive and experimental evaluation. *Journal of Applied Behavior Analysis, 43* (2), 229–247. http://dx.doi.org/10.1901/jaba.2010.43-229.

Stoutimore, M. R., Williams, C. E., Neff, B., & Foster, M. (2008). The Florida child welfare behavior analysis services program. *Research on Social Work Practice, 18,* 36–376.

Suess, A. N., Romani, P. W., Wacker, D. P., Dyson, S. M., Kuhle, J. L., Lee, J. F., et al. (2014). Evaluating the treatment fidelity of parents who conduct in-home functional communication training with coaching via tele-health. *Journal of Behavioral Education, 23,* 34–59.

Van Camp, C. M., Vollmer, R. R., Goh, H., Whitehouse, C. M., Reyes, J. R., Montgomery, J. L., et al. (2008). Behavioral parent training in child welfare: Evaluations of skills acquisition. *Research on Social Work Practice, 18,* 377–391.

Veazey, S., Valentino, A. L., & LeBlanc, L. A. (2014). Teaching community safety skills to a pre-adolescent with developmental delay. In *Presented at the California association for behavior analysis annual conference,* Burlingame, CA.

Vismara, L. A., McCormick, C., Young, G. S., Nadhan, A., & Monlux, K. (2013). Preliminary findings of a telehealth approach to parent training in autism. *Journal of Autism and Developmental Disorders, 43,* 2953–2969. http://dx.doi.org/10.1007/s10803-013-1841-8.

Vollmer, T. R., Sloman, K. N., & Pipkin, C. (2008). Practical implications of data reliability and treatment integrity monitoring. *Behavior Analysis in Practice, 1,* 4–11.

Wacker, D. P., Lee, J. S., Padilla Dalmau, Y. C., Kopelman, T. G., Lindgren, S. D., Kuhle, J., et al. (2013). Conducting functional communication training via telehealth to reduce the problem behavior of young children with autism. *Journal of Developmental and Physical Disabilities, 25,* 35–48.

Wainer, A. L., & Ingersoll, B. R. (2013). Disseminating ASD interventions: A pilot study of a distance learning program for parents and professionals. *Journal of Autism and Developmental Disorders, 43,* 11–24.

Williams, T. C., & Zahad, H. (1996). Computer-based training versus traditional lecture: Effect on learning and retention. *Journal of Business and Psychology, 11,* 297–310.

Wilson, P. G., Reid, D. H., & Korabek-Pinkowski, C. A. (1991). Analysis of public verbal feedback as a staff management procedure. *Behavioral Residential Treatment, 6,* 263–277.

Wolf, M. M. (1978). Social validity: The case for subjective measurement or how applied behavior analysis is finding its heart. *Journal of Applied Behavior Analysis, 11,* 203–214. http://dx.doi.org/10.1901/jaba.1978.11-203.

CHAPTER 15

Conceptual, Experimental, and Therapeutic Approaches to Problem Gambling

Jacob H. Daar, Mark R. Dixon
Rehabilitation Institute, Southern Illinois University, Carbondale, Illinois, USA

OVERVIEW

Gambling has become a common pastime in our culture. Over the course of 2012, commercial casinos grossed 37.34 billion dollars: an increase of 4.8% from the previous year. The 76.1 million patrons who visited commercial casinos to produce this income represent 32% of the United States' adult population (American Gaming Association, 2013). According to the National Gambling Impact Study Commission (1999), an estimated 86% of Americans have engaged in some sort of gambling behavior during their lifetime. For many, gambling is considered an acceptable activity for themselves, 47%, and if not for themselves personally, for others, 38% (AGA, 2013). However, despite the seemingly popular acceptance of casinos and gambling in general, activities involving the wagering of money are not only problematic for some but also addictive. According to the DSM-IV, individuals who have difficulties with gambling may acquire a preoccupation with gambling; feel the need to increase wager sizes to maintain excitement levels when gambling; attempt repeated, unsuccessful efforts to control gambling; experience restlessness or irritability when trying to stop gambling; use gambling as a means of escaping problems or depressed moods; attempt to regain losses through continued betting; attempt to conceal the extent of their gambling activities; engage in illegal acts to finance gambling; jeopardize relationships or job opportunities; or rely on others to help manage financial situations caused by gambling (APA, 1994). Based on these criteria, as much as 4% of the American population can be classified as problem gamblers with an additional 2% diagnosable as pathological according to DSM-IV (Petry, 2005; Shaffer & Hall, 2001). Due to the similarities in presentation of symptoms and high comorbidity of pathological gambling with substance abuse disorders, the DSM-5 has reclassified pathological gambling as an

Clinical and Organizational Applications of Applied Behavior Analysis
http://dx.doi.org/10.1016/B978-0-12-420249-8.00015-0

addictive disorder under the term "Gambling Disorder." This reclassification, along with the removal of the illegal activity criteria and a reduction in the diagnostic threshold to four characteristics, was made to increase credibility of gambling as a psychiatric disorder, to encourage awareness and screening for those with a gambling disorder, and to promote research into effective treatment options (Petry, Bowden-Jones, & George, 2013).

Important to the latter of these goals is our understanding of the factors and conditions that lead to the development and maintenance of gambling behaviors in those persons who are classified with a gambling disorder. According to Porter and Ghezzi (2006), conceptualizations of pathology play a large role in the construction of therapeutic procedures. Treatments for pathological gambling that are derived from integrated approaches have provided only varying degrees of effectiveness, possibly due to differences in underlying assumptions about the etiology. Additionally, new hybrid treatments that are constituted of eclectic theoretic conceptualizations of pathological gambling serve to confuse questions of why some people have trouble with gambling and why treatments are often ineffective. Porter and Ghezzi concluded that the study of pathological gambling may benefit from an approach that does not assume causal relations between hypothetical constructs and instead places an emphasis on the experimental analysis of contingencies that predict and control gambling behaviors directly; such an approach would be explicitly behavioral in philosophy.

In an effort to achieve this parsimony of theoretical analysis and clinical application, this chapter explores the theoretic and empirical work conducted by behavioral scientists on the subject of pathological gambling and the identification of specific conditions under which behavior patterns of gambling are established, maintained, and extinguished. Analysis is eventually provided regarding the three generations of behavioral treatments for pathological gambling produced by such experimental work.

BEHAVIORAL UNDERSTANDINGS

Behavior analytic conceptualizations of gambling behavior have traditionally focused on the nature of the exchange between gambling participants and the evaluation of schedules of reinforcement in gambling contexts. For example, Skinner (1957) described gambling as a "system of economic control in which the individual is induced to pay money for a reinforcement the value of which is too small to lead to exchange under other schedules" (p. 397). In other words, the noteworthy characteristic of gambling is that individuals who gamble learn to exchange relatively large amounts of money for payouts that are less than the amount spent, despite the fact that such exchanges would generally cease over time due to ratio-strain. Skinner (1957, p. 396) likened gambling to a dishonest vendor who often fails to provide his paying customer with the items they had purchased. In general, a vendor such as this would soon find himself without customers as those he tricked would seek restitution or look elsewhere for trade. However, if this same vendor randomly provided double or even triple the amount of items purchased whenever he did complete a transaction, it is likely that patrons may continue to shop with him on the chance that they would benefit from the vendor's seemingly random miscalculations. Despite having to periodically give away three times the value in items he has agreed to provide, the sly vendor could easily maintain a margin of profit by simply completing fewer transactions than he left uncompleted (i.e., keep a greater ratio of money collected than money paid-out). The vendor in this example would also need to involve more than one patron, as the system would eventually collapse when the single patron realized that the vendor was taking in more money than he was giving out. By involving many patrons, however, the vendor would be able to reinforce any single patron's participation with a greater value of items at the expense of all other patrons who did not receive the items paid for. When patrons enter into business with this vendor fully informed of his poor follow-through but random overcompensation, the product being bought could better be described as a "chance to win." This example may seem unlikely in today's litigious society but consider its resemblance to the raffles and lotteries commonly employed in traditional gambling settings and in fundraiser events. In a raffle, an item such as a car that could not be sold to a single individual for $50,000 could be sold to 50,000 individuals for a single dollar provided that the culture has taught the individuals to take chances (Skinner, 1957, p. 396). When viewed from a behavioral perspective, the behavior of buying a raffle ticket is left unreinforced by any tangible return because only one individual out of many receives the reward.

Schedules of Reinforcement

Skinner (1953) acknowledged that many variables, such as the size of the stake, might influence how and when a gambler may participate in a game of chance, and also posited that the "important factor contributing to the probability that an individual will turn over money, either for other money or for goods, is the schedule on which he is reinforced for doing so"

(p. 396). Gambling scenarios are typified by the unequal ratio of bets to payouts, and thus a degree of unpredictability is necessary else each gambler would only contribute to the pot when he/she was sure to win. Insofar as schedules of reinforcement go, this arrangement rules out the continuous-ratio schedule, as each gambler would always win more money than they had contributed. Likewise, fixed-schedules would lead gamblers to strategically bet small on trials leading up to a win and bet high on the winning trial. Thus, the necessity of unpredictability in gambling systems led Skinner (1953) to suggest that all gambling systems were based on the variable-ratio (VR) schedule of reinforcement as a gambler's probability of winning is not determined by a set number of bets or the passage of time, but instead manifests as an average frequency of wins across a number of wagers. Skinner frequently used the example of a slot machine when explaining the pattern of behavior produced by VR schedules (Skinner, 1953, 1961, 1974). The players of a slot machine engage in gambling in much the same way that a laboratory animal is conditioned to repeatedly press a lever for food. In both instances, a "cost" is paid, whether it is energy required to push the lever in the case of the animal or depositing a coin in the case of the gambler, and the machine provides reinforcement on a given average number of trials. Skinner (1961) noted that the VR schedule of reinforcement could be used with laboratory animals to produce and maintain relatively high rates of activity while only providing a slight net of reinforcement. He extended this observation to the behaviors of gamblers in which a player will steadily lose money while being provided a mean ratio of pay-outs that fails to keep up with his expenditure (Skinner, 1953). For example, an American roulette wheel contains 38 possible numbered outcomes, all of which have an equal likelihood of being produced when the wheel is spun. Furthermore, each of these outcomes is organized into 18 red, 18 black, and 2 green outcomes. Among the various types of bets allowed in roulette, a player might wager on a black outcome, red outcome, or a single number. Winning on a black or red bet will occur, on average, 18 out of 38 spins and will win the player a payout equal to their bet. The greatest payout, 35 times the bet, is provided for betting that the ball will come to rest on a particular number. It can be expected that a new player might begin by betting primarily on red or black since winning outcomes will appear to occur with some frequency. Over-time, this same player may become encouraged by perceived gains or desperate due to continued losses and begin to play on the less likely but better paying bet of a single number. If a player continued to bet on one number all night, he could expect to win, on average, one out of 38 times. Inevitably, continued gambling under this arrangement would lead to a steady loss of money, as the odds do not equal the payout. However, this ultimate loss, or "negative-utility," does not offset the effect of the schedule (Skinner, 1974), which is to establish an otherwise weak reinforcer as very effective (Skinner, 1953, 1971).

The argument that "all gambling systems are based on variable-ratio schedules of reinforcement" (Skinner, 1971, p. 67) is, in fact, technically inaccurate (Hurlburt, Knapp, & Knowles, 1980). This inaccuracy lies in the specifics of how a VR schedule of reinforcement is provided. Technically, a VR schedule is arranged such that reinforcers are delivered "contingent upon a given average number of responses but the numbers are allowed to vary roughly at random" (Skinner, 1961, p. 106). In practice, VR schedules are produced by creating a sequence of numbers of which the average value equals a predetermined ratio (e.g., a sequence that required 1, 2, 3, 4, 5, and then 6 responses would produce a VR-3.5 schedule). The same numbers in a different order would produce the same VR-3.5 schedule because the average would remain the same (Hurlburt et al., 1980). This VR sequencing differs from the manner in which all casino games work. In the example of the roulette wheel, no predetermined sequence of numbers exists that specifies how many times a gambler must bet before receiving a winning outcome; each spin of the wheel produces outcomes based on the same probabilities as the spin before it. This probability is not true for the VR schedule, as each loss brings the player one spin closer to an eventual win (i.e., the probability of a win following each loss increases, whereas a real slot-machine produces no such change in probability). For this reason, gambling games that include an independent assortment of outcomes, such as slots and roulette, are better described as random-ratio (RR) schedules of reinforcement as reinforcement is provided after a random number of responses. While both VR and RR schedules may produce reinforcement at equal rates over time, the implication is that a VR schedule becomes a game of skill in which a gambler can maintain a net gain by either guessing when a win is coming or increasing the size of his bets after each loss as the eventual win will recoup the previous lost bets (Hurlburt et al., 1980). This same strategy, sometimes referred to as maximizing on the VR schedule, can lead to devastating losses for the deceived gambler as an RR schedule may not provide a win before the gambler runs out of money.

In order to assess whether gamblers were sensitive to the differences in VR and RR schedules, Hurlburt et al. (1980) asked 20 subjects to play on two different pairs of slot machines. Each pair of slots was expected to provide wins, on average, after 6 or 20 trials. However, one slot machine operated on a VR schedule while the other operated on an RR schedule. Subjects were asked to play each slot within the available pair prior to being allowed to freely allocate choices. The results indicated that subjects did not statistically prefer one schedule to the other but did choose to play the slot on which wins were experienced more frequently during initial training. The authors suggested that eventually the subjects may have learned to discriminate between the two available schedules but did not do so during the study. A perhaps more interesting finding was that the number of coins bet per trial was observed to be a function of the number of trials since the last payoff (i.e., participants bet increasingly more following successive losses). This finding indicated that subjects were attempting to apply a strategy consistent with maximization on the VR schedule to both the VR and RR machines. The implication of this lack of discrimination between schedules is that gamblers were likely to incorrectly respond as though a win on the RR schedule was more probable following a string of losses, a negative-recency effect, or, as it is colloquially called, the "gamblers fallacy" (Jarvik, 1951).

As gambling, from Skinner's perspective, is characterized by persistent engagement in an activity that produces less value than the cost of the activity itself, it is not surprising that those engaging in gambling behavior demonstrate a lack of sensitivity to differing schedules of reinforcement. The observation of Hurlburt et al. (1980) that individuals were more likely to allocate their time to the slot machine that produced the most frequent wins in the training phase of their study further suggested that the overall schedule of reinforcement may be less important than the general distribution of wins (Dixon, MacLin, & Daugherty, 2006). In a study designed to explore the importance of win distributions, Dixon et al. asked student volunteers to choose between two concurrently available slot machines that provided either a 10-credit win every 10 trials or a 50-credit win every 50 trials. Despite producing an equal net utility (i.e., both conditions produced the same overall magnitude of reinforcement), students were significantly more likely to allocate their time to the slot machine that produced the more frequent wins. The tendency for individuals to allocate more time to slot machines with higher frequencies of pay-outs, rather than those with greater payout magnitudes, may explain why individuals often prefer slot machines that allow for simultaneous betting across multiple lines as this increases the overall ratio of wins to spins (Dixon, Miller, Whiting, Wilson, & Hensel, 2012; Harrigan, Dixon, MacLaren, Collins, & Fugelsang, 2011). Similarly, the preference for more frequent wins may also lead gamblers of other games, such as online-poker, to play multiple hands at a time as this too would increase the frequency of wins (Witts & Lyons, 2013). In contrast to this observation, Weatherly and Brandt (2004) found that differing payout rates did not produce differences in the number of bets placed or bet sizes when win rates were manipulated between 75%, 83%, and 95%. However, Weatherly and Brandt did observe differences when the value of credits was manipulated. This finding was replicated by Haw (2008) who found that slot machine preferences were not affected by payout rate but rather players were more likely to choose a slot machine if it provided a relatively higher density of wins in training phases.

Similar to the effects of shaping procedures used to increase responding under VR schedules with laboratory animals, frequent and early wins in gambling was predicted by Skinner (1974) to condition gamblers to continue responding at thinner schedules in later play. Skinner supposed that a professional gambler (i.e., a provider of gambling opportunities) might allow for a high rate of wins initially, and then thin the schedule of reinforcement as the victim (i.e., the patron of a gambling game) begins to place bets more frequently. The supposition that a player will gamble more persistently after winning early in a gambling game, sometimes called the "big win effect" (Custer, 1984), has been questioned because players exposed to a big win early are more likely to quit playing when faced with extinction conditions (Weatherly, Sauter, & King, 2004).

Collectively, these findings provide inconsistent support for Skinner's suggestion that the schedule of reinforcement is the primary factor in establishing gambling behavior despite the fact that such schedules are a major determinant in operant behavior in general.

Conditioned Reinforcers

One reason why gambling behavior may predictably differ as a function of payout schedules is that payouts are not the only reinforcing outcome presented by gambling games. Conditioned reinforcers are suspected to play a large role in the maintenance of gambling behavior. According to Skinner (1953), "gambling devices make an effective use of conditioned reinforcers which are set up by pairing certain stimuli with economic reinforcers which occasionally appear" (p. 397).

The Near-Miss Outcome

Gambling outcomes that appear to be similar to payouts may also contribute to the maintenance of gambling behavior by functioning as a conditioned reinforcer. Skinner (1953) provided the example of a slot machine that pays out when three identical symbols are on the payout line. Skinner suggested that over time, the generous payout of three identical symbols will establish an "almost jackpot" (e.g., two matching symbols with a third identical symbol just above the payout) outcome as a conditioned reinforcer. According to Skinner, providing "almost jackpots" as reinforcers allow gambling establishments to provide a greater frequency of reinforcement without having to actually payout any additional funds. Outcomes that approximate a win, sometimes called a "near-win" or "near-miss," have been hypothesized to function as conditioned reinforcers due to their formal similarity to a win and, therefore, are produced not through pairing but through stimulus generalization (Reid, 1986). Under this principle, gamblers who had previously learned to discriminate winning outcomes as being desirable might also mistakenly discriminate losing outcomes that share a formal similarity to a win as also being a win. This generalization of losing outcomes to winning outcomes would then evoke further investment from the gambler much the same as a win would have. According to Reid, a near-miss outcome may elicit the same sort of excitement and physiological arousal as that of a win. Alternatively, the near-miss effect has also been hypothesized as an aversive event that frustrates the player leading him/her to play faster to escape the current trial (Dixon & Schreiber, 2002; Hineline, 1977; Schreiber & Dixon, 2001). Whether a conditioned reinforcer or an aversive event, numerous studies have demonstrated that gambling behavior is sensitive to near-miss outcomes. For example, Kassinove and Schare (2001) observed that individuals who played slot machines with a 30% probability of a near-miss outcome persisted longer during extinction procedures than individuals exposed to near-miss probability of 15% and 45%. Ghezzi, Wilson, and Porter (2006) further examined the impact of near-miss frequency on slot-machine play by asking individuals to engage with a slot machine for a specified number of trials (i.e., 25, 50, 75, or 100 trials) with different probabilities of near-miss outcomes (i.e., 0%, 33%, 66%, and 100%). After each participant had completed the required number of trials, they were allowed to continue playing for as long as they wanted. Individuals were observed to play longer if they had been exposed to the 25-trial conditions or the 66% near-miss probability; no interaction effect was observed.

Implicit and subjective behavioral measures have also been associated with near-miss outcomes. In a study examining the near-miss effect, Dixon and Schreiber (2004) asked 12 participants to play 100 trials on a standard three-reel slot machine. After each losing outcome, participants were asked to "estimate the degree to which your losing spin was close to a win," on a 10-point Likert-type scale. In addition to this subjective rating, response latencies between the presentation of each trial (spin) outcome and the next spin were determined. Results of this study showed that despite functionally being no different from a loss, near-miss outcomes were erroneously rated as being closer to a win than non-near-miss losses. Furthermore, the specific arrangement of symbols comprising the near-miss outcome (i.e., matching symbols on the left, right, or where the left and right symbol are matching but the center is not) was also shown to influence subjective ratings for 11 of the 12 participants. Response latencies following near-misses were also shown to be longer than those of total losses for 9 of the 12 participants; a result that lends support to the assertion that near-misses function as conditioned reinforcers (i.e., producing post-reinforcement pauses), rather than an aversive stimulus which the player seeks to escape by playing more quickly.

Losses Disguised as Wins

One need spend very little time in a modern casino to note that most slot machines are no longer the traditional three-reel machines of yesteryear. Modern slot machines typically offer five or more reels in addition to the option to play on multiple pay lines. Where the traditional slot machines were mechanical devices in which you put a token and pulled a lever, modern slot machines are termed "electronic gaming machines" capable of delivering many forms of audio/visual stimuli and symbol arrangements, and thus conditioned reinforcers. Among other aspects, modern slot machines offer the player the opportunity to bet across multiple lines. For example, a traditional slot machine may offer a single pay-line meaning that all three matching symbols must appear in the center of the display for a win to be registered. Additionally, some mechanical models offer pay-lines across the top, bottom, or on the diagonal. For each additional pay-line activated, the player places an additional bet equal to the bet made on the primary pay-line (i.e., the player must risk a bet on each line played). While this betting strategy effectively increases the player's chances to win on at least one line per spin due to a greater diversity of possible symbol arrangements, it also multiplies the potential losses as each pay line that does not win costs the player a wager. Because the most common winning outcomes on a multiline slot machine pay out at a relatively small ratio such as 5× or 10× the bet wagered, a win on a single line may not recoup the losses of the entire trial. For example, if an individual were to bet a penny on each line of a 20-line slot machine, the player potentially risks losing 20 cents per spin. If this same player won 5 × his bet on a single line, the player would win only 5 cents on his 20-cent bet. Due to the negative net utility of such outcomes, the end result can clearly be considered a loss. However, in the context of a slot machine, such outcomes are very different than the quiet of a total loss; it is typically accompanied by chimes, flashing lights, and a payout indicator that states the player won "5 cents!" Because the slot machine designates any successful pay line arrangement as a win, despite the net loss for that trial, some researchers have referred to this outcome as a "loss disguised as a win" (LDW; Dixon, Harrigan, Sandhu, Collins, & Fugelsang, 2010).

LDWs are an especially useful outcome for providers of gambling games. LDWs not only allow for the obfuscation of the net loss of bets, but also decrease the overall proportion of total losses without significantly decreasing the take. This is accomplished by decreasing the values of jackpots and other large wins so as to accommodate more frequent LDW outcomes. The result is a slot machine that can deliver frequent "hits" without providing a net win (Harrigan et al., 2011). As previously discussed, the frequency of wins was associated with greater persistence of play and preference for individual slot machines (Dixon, Miller, et al., 2012; Harrigan et al., 2011). Because LDWs are formally similar to a win (i.e., the slot machine celebrates a 5-cent win despite a net loss of 15 cents), it is predicted that individuals are more likely to prefer and persist on slot machines with frequent LDW outcomes. As such, slot machines will appear to provide more frequent wins. Currently, few studies have investigated the influence of LDWs on gambling behavior; however, Dixon et al. (2010) have demonstrated that LDWs and actual wins produce similar patterns of skin conductance, response amplitudes, and heart-rate changes.

Discounting Values

As suggested in the works describing losses disguised as wins, frequent payouts may obfuscate the overall net utility of the game. As an expression of the overall ratio of bets to winnings, the expected net utility is a function of payout ratio and the probability of a win. For example, a player who places a $1 bet on black 15 at a roulette table can expect to win, on average, 1 out of 38 bets or 2.63%. However, since the payout rate of the bet is $35 dollars for every $1 bet, the odds do not keep up with the probability of winning. This disparity between the payout and the odds is called the "house edge" and is calculated by taking the probability of a win times the payout, minus the probability of a loss. For an American roulette wheel on a single number bet, the house edge is -5.26% ($35 * (1/38) - (37/38)$). Thus, on average, a roulette wheel will lose a player 5.26 cents for every dollar bet. The house edge is synonymous with the expected net utility of the game. As one can imagine, the house edge is always in the house's favor. Thus, the proverb "The house always wins," is more than moral heuristic; it is a statistical inevitability. So why then would anyone, knowing that the game is rigged, continue to gamble? One reason may be that the pathological gambler improperly discounts the odds of the game.

From a behavioral economic standpoint, discounting describes any situation in which the value of an outcome is depreciated due to factors relating to its delivery. When based on a temporal delay, discounting occurs when an individual is more likely to choose a sooner but smaller outcome over a larger but later outcome. For example, if one were offered the choice between $100 now or $1000 now, the rational choice is $1000 dollars now. However, if the same values were given but with different delays, such as $100 now or $1000 in 10 years, the choice becomes somewhat more difficult. Even though the $1000 is monetarily more than the $100, many people would rather have the money that is available now, thus discounting the value of the $1000. Likewise, probabilistic discounting is said to occur when an individual is more likely to choose a smaller, but more certain outcome over a larger, but less likely outcome. An example of probabilistic discounting would be if you were given the choice between a guaranteed $100 or a 10% chance for $1000 dollars. Because discounting generally reflects a preference for more immediate or certain gratification, discounting is seen as a marker of impulsivity or risk-taking. Discounting is typically expressed as a hyperbolic curve in which the subjective value of the reinforcer becomes shallower as the delay increases or the probability decreases (see Green & Myerson, 2004 for a general review of discounting).

In the context of gambling, inappropriate discounting may help to describe why a gambler would continue to engage in a game that has a known negative net utility. For instance, Rachlin (1990) suggested that the compulsive gambler might inappropriately reevaluate a new bet after each loss thus assuming a short delay to a win and a net utility based on the odds of the immediate bet. By doing so, the compulsive gambler does not take into account the stochastic nature of gambling that invariably negative house-edge plays out over a large number of trials. Thus, the gambler discounts the value of the delayed cumulative losses in favor of the immediate payout. Petry and Casarella (1999) further examined this issue with individuals with substance abuse and problematic gambling histories by asking participants to choose between hypothetical monetary rewards that were concurrently available but varying in the delay to delivery. It was found that individuals with either substance abuse issues or problems with gambling discounted monetary rewards to a greater extent than did their nonsubstance abuse or nongambling controls (i.e., those with addictive disorders were more likely to accept a smaller immediate reward over a larger delayed reward). These findings were further replicated by a study by Petry (2001) in which delay discounting among pathological gamblers with and without substance abuse disorders were compared to control participants. Again, higher impulsivity as indicated by steeper discounting curves was presented by pathological gamblers when compared to nonpathological controls. Pathological gamblers who also had substance abuse disorders were shown to discount to an even greater extent than nonsubstance-abusing gamblers. As a behavioral indicator, delay discounting has also been shown to better predict variances on measures of pathological gambling, such as the South Oaks Gambling Scale, than age, gender, years of education, substance abuse treatment history, or cigarette smoking history (Alessi & Petry, 2003).

The implication that pathological gamblers generally engage in more impulsive behavior than nonpathological individuals was challenged by findings that showed that while pathological gamblers might display greater patterns of discounting when faced with delayed reinforcers, significantly less discounting was shown than nonpathological gamblers displayed during probabilistic tasks (Holt, Green, & Myerson, 2003; Petry & Madden, 2010). In other words, when given the choice between a small but certain prospect, the pathological gamblers were more likely to select a greater payout despite increasingly poor chances. This finding indicated that pathological gamblers did not have trouble delaying gratification so much as judging the appropriateness of a risk. Furthermore, contextual control of discounting among pathological gamblers was demonstrated when gamblers were asked to complete delay-discounting tasks in an off-track betting facility and in a nongambling setting (Dixon, Jacobs, & Sanders, 2006). When surrounded by the gambling environment, 16 of the 20 participants displayed greater delay discounting than when surrounded by nongambling stimuli. Differences in the degree to which pathological gamblers discount rewards has also been seen in a greater degree of discounting of monetary gains but not in nonmonetary gains (Weatherly & Derenne, 2010). The presence of such contextual control over discounting suggests that the propensity toward impulsive decisions is not a trait characteristic of the individual but rather a malleable state.

The concept that discounting is a conditionable state has important implications within the field of clinical practice. If discounting was a personality trait, it would manifest as a global and consistent difficulty in avoiding impulsive choices. However, as a behavior under contextual control, procedures could be developed to condition or uncondition appropriate discriminative stimuli to influence gambling behaviors. One such procedure, reported by Dixon and Holton (2009), demonstrated that delay discounting was susceptible to such behavior change approaches. In this study, a multiple baseline design across five pathological gamblers was implemented. Participants were asked to engage in baseline delay discounting tasks across several sessions followed by a matching-to-sample training procedure designed to produce the conditional discrimination of contextual stimuli. Various stimuli with ordinal qualities, such as letter grades, dollar amounts, playing cards, and superlative word sequences, were presented along with a colored background. Participants were provided feedback for selecting the "better than" or "worse than" stimuli based on which colored background was presented. For example, under the context of a purple background, the selection of the card with the highest quantitative value was reinforced. Once appropriate contextual responding was observed, the participants were again exposed to several sessions of delay discounting tasks; however, this time the sooner/smaller option was presented with the "worse than" contextual cue and the later/larger option with the "better than" contextual cue. Area under the curve (AUC) was calculated for each session and plotted for visual analysis. Visual inspection of the AUCs in the pretest sessions revealed consistently high levels of delay discounting (i.e., low AUCs, prior to implementation of the contextual trainings). After training, all five participants displayed relatively low levels of delay discounting that maintained across multiple sessions (Dixon & Holton, 2009).

The Impact of Verbal Behaviors

Outside of the field of behavior analysis, various mentalistic biases have been used to describe the irrational behaviors of pathological gamblers. For instance, the inclination of gamblers to believe that a win is around the corner, the "gambler's fallacy" (Jarvik, 1951), has been used to describe why individuals tend to place larger wagers following a string of losses despite the fact that no change in overall probability has occurred (Leopard, 1978). Alternatively, players may make larger bets following a string of wins due to the belief that they are on a lucky streak, a bias called the "hot hand fallacy" (Ayton & Fischer, 2004; Gilovich, Vallone, & Tversky, 1985).

Individuals may falsely attribute successful outcomes to their own personal skill when participating in gambling games that provide choices, such as in roulette, craps, or blackjack; thus, further betting is more of a function of their internal "illusion of control" (Dixon, Hayes, & Ebbs, 1998; Ladouceur, Gaboury, Dumont, & Rochette, 1988; Langer, 1975). Likewise, the gambler's desire to express a degree of control over luck may explain why so many slot machine gamblers carry lucky totems such as four leaf clovers and rabbit feet.

Superstition

Within the scope of behavior analysis, several theories have been put forth to explain how such cognitive distortions may develop and subsequently impact gambling behavior. In their most simple form, each of the above-described biases could have emerged as a result of accidental consequences. Skinner (1948, 1953) described such adventitious pairings of stimuli associated with a win and behavior as superstitious because the behavior itself does nothing to increase the coordinated outcome. For example, an individual may seek to reenact the behaviors of a previously successful betting trip by asking a pretty lady to blow on the dice or always sit at the third slot machine in the row because last time this strategy was correlated with big wins. Superstitious behavior conditioned in this manner may persist despite extinction for lengthy periods of time, especially if the behavior is low in response effort and more effective behaviors do not contact reinforcement (e.g., Skinner, 1948). Because most gambling games operate on the RR schedule of reinforcement, few behaviors exist that can effectively alter the odds and therefore gambling contexts are ripe for the emergence of superstitious behaviors. Although superstition does not necessarily need to involve language (as nonhumans demonstrate these effects regularly due to temporal proximity), in the context of gambling, language is a participating factor in the eventual superstition.

For humans, as verbally capable organisms, language may play a large role in the irrational behaviors and insensitivity to consequences displayed by gamblers. Extending his observances of superstitious responses to verbal behavior, Skinner (1957, p. 47) provided the common example of the craps player whose verbal expressions of "come on seven" appear to ask, or "mand," the dice for a specific outcome. Because verbal behaviors require a listener to enact the consequences of the speaker's utterance, and the dice, as inanimate objects, cannot provide such interaction, the behavior of requesting assistance from such stimuli can only be seen as a generalization of previously taught manding repertoires. Because the outcome of the dice roll may, on occasion, come up sevens following the player's request for them to do so, the player's mand may in some way be strengthened, even if the player himself admits to knowing that no such mechanical relation exists between his behavior and the dice outcome.

Rule-Governed Behaviors

Previously successful verbal repertoires of rule following have also been implicated in the emergence of misguided gambling beliefs (Dixon & Hayes, 1998; Dixon, Hayes, Rehfeldt, & Ebbs, 1998). Rule following describes a distinct form of operant behavior in which a past history of consequences for following instructions produces a conditioned repertoire of following rules, regardless of whether the individual has ever contacted the contingencies specified within the present rule (Hayes, Zettle, & Rosenfarb, 1989). For example, an individual who has never gambled before could be told "always bet big on red 21," and without any previous experience with the roulette wheel proceed to place a large bet on 21. The distinction between following this rule and a topographically similar contingency shaped behavior is that in the case of the former, the player requires no previous experience with the roulette wheel to maintain his betting strategy, whereas the latter form would only be predicted if the player had previously won frequently when betting on red 21. Rule-governed behaviors are categorized into three distinct forms based on the contingencies that are specified in the rule: pliance, tracking, and augmentals (see Hayes, Zettle, et al., 1989 for a more thorough description of rule units). Pliance rules are instructions that specify a behavior to be engaged in, or to be avoided, that will produce a socially-mediated consequence. In the context of the "bet big on red 21" rule, the naïve player may engage in the specified betting behavior because he was told to do so by someone who has some importance in his life. While it is not directly stated in the rule "bet big on red 21," the implied consequence may be "or I will be disappointed with you." Even though the latter half of the rule may be unspecified, a long history of following rules and receiving appropriate reinforcement or punishment from another person based on performance may adequately produce rule following of this kind. The second type of rule following consists of instructions that specify a behavior and its presumed outcome in the environment. This form of rule following is called "tracking," as in the following of a path. Tracking, therefore, is more akin to advice than pliance, which better exemplifies a demand. Therefore, an example of a track may include our inexperienced gambler betting big on red 21 not because he is seeking the approval of another person, but because the croupier informs the player that most people win on red 21. The implied consequence then is "bet big on red 21 and you will win big." The last type of rule following is augmenting. This form of rule following specifies a relation between the potential outcome of a behavior and another stimulus function. For example, if our player was told "only the best bet big on red 21," the contingency of following the rule has been transformed from simply winning a bet to something far more glamorous. In this augmental statement, the consequence of betting big on red 21 has been endowed with the positive functions of being the "best." In this way, augmenting is similar to the concept of motivating operations (Laraway, Snycerski, Michael, & Poling, 2003; Michael, 1982) in that it enhances the preference for a specified consequence and establishes the reinforcing or punishing function of outcome.

The likelihood that an individual will follow a given rule depends on multiple factors such as the plausibility of the rule, the credibility of the speaker, and the authority of the person delivering the rule (Barnes-Holmes, Hayes, & Dymond, 2001; Barnes-Holmes, O'Hora, et al., 2001). Individuals can also generate their own rules and follow them. Self-generated rules are products of a learned history of rules in appropriate situations and the contingencies experienced in those environments (Poppen, 1989). For example, the roulette player who observes that he usually wins on a black number may formulate the rule: "bet big on black to win." The problem with a reliance on self-formulated rules is that the individual may fail to generate a rule when a rule is worthwhile. Or, alternatively, he may develop a rule in a situation in which a rule needlessly restricts the individual's behavioral repertoire. An additional problem with self-formulated rules is that the rule may be inaccurate or irrational (Hayes, Kohlenberg, & Melancon, 1989).

The conceptual and clinical importance of rules in the context of gambling is that rules can be employed to explain the emergence of patterns of behavior usually described as cognitive biases (Poppen, 1989). Each of the cognitive biases presented earlier in this chapter can easily be interpreted as inaccurate rules that specify a behavior to be performed and a perceived consequence for acting upon the rule. For example, the "gamblers fallacy" specifies that one should keep gambling after a loss because a "win is around the corner" or because "my luck has got to change sometime." The "hot hand" bias expresses a similar rule, "you got to bet big while the dice are hot," or "can't quit on a winning streak." Illusions of control may also be described by gamblers in statements such as "bet big when you're the shooter," "as long as I have my lucky bracelet," or "come on, you can do better." Furthermore, the patterns of betting behavior used to substantiate the presence of such cognitive biases are consistent with the decreased sensitivity to actual consequences and persistent responding seen in demonstrations of rule-governed behavior (Dixon, Hayes, & Aban, 2000). As a case in point, Dixon et al. (2000) demonstrated the effect of rules on the gambling behavior by asking 45 participants to play a simulated roulette game across three phases. In the first phase, participants were exposed to 75 trials of completely random game play. The second phase consisted of manipulating the probability of a win such that participants either received wins at 20%, 80%, or RRs. Additionally, some participants were given accurate rules that reflected the nature of roulette, some were given inaccurate rules that expressed untrue aspects of the game, and some received no rules at all. Within the accurate and inaccurate rules given, were the statements "if you have been losing for a while, there is no reason to believe that your luck will change," and "if you have been losing for a while, there is every reason to believe that your luck will change," respectively. The third phase of the experiment consisted of adjusting the probability of a win to 20% for all participants as well as offering the option to quit playing. The results of this study indicated that those who received inaccurate rules regarding roulette placed higher bets, placed riskier bets, and left the table later. No significant effect was observed in relation to reinforcement density.

A second benefit of approaching gambling biases as inaccurate rules is that rules, as verbal behaviors, can be modified via the same processes that produce them. This aspect of rule-governed behavior was demonstrated by Dixon (2000) in the context of roulette play. For this experiment, five participants engaged in an alternating treatment design that consisted of placing their own chips on the board or having the croupier place bets for them. In this way, the presence of an "illusion of control" could be assumed if participants placed larger wagers when they themselves picked the numbers as compared to having the numbers but not the wagers picked for them. Participants were taught how to play roulette and instructed that they could quit at any time following the first trial. After a baseline level of responding across the two conditions was established, the croupier provided players with inaccurate rules, in the form of advice, regarding the game of roulette and the illusion of control. These rules included "People that win more pick their own numbers," "if you want to win big, you have to bet big," and "I will try to pick numbers that will make you lose." After each session, players were asked to answer a survey regarding their own perception of the game. Following the inaccurate rule phase, the croupier provided accurate advice such as "it does not make a difference if I pick the numbers or if you pick the numbers," "if you want to win big, you do not have to bet big," and "I cannot pick numbers that make you lose." Participants were again asked questions related to their subjective experience. Follow-up surveys were provided 1 week after the experiment as well. Results of this study showed that during baseline, four of the five participants wagered more chips when they controlled chip placement compared to when the croupier selected their bet. This disparity of wager size between control and illusion of control conditions was further widened when inaccurate rules were provided. When accurate rules were provided, two of the five participants showed an overall decrease in wagers in both conditions, two participants showed a decrease in the illusion of control condition, and the last participant paradoxically increased wagers in both conditions. Because participants were allowed to quit playing after the first trial, the overall impact of rules on persistence of play could be evaluated. In all five cases, participants chose to play more trials of roulette during the inaccurate rules condition than in the accurate rules condition. In addition to the findings related to wager size and persistence of play, comparisons including the subjective estimations of winnings versus actual winnings and the probability of wins during the inaccurate rule condition showed that most subjects tended to overestimate their winnings and the probability of wins when they were allowed to place their own bets; however, this differentiation was not observed in the accurate rule condition. Follow-up estimations of winnings and win probability were again differentiated between the control/illusion of control conditions. The results of this study support the idea that gambling behavior is susceptible to illusions of control and inaccurate rules following, but also that such rule following can be utilized to mediate the impact of illusory control. This study also provides an example of the feasibility that within-individual analysis of rule-governed behavior is possible within the gambling context.

Transformation of Stimulus Functions

Casino goers are inundated with evocative stimuli. Bells and whistles, flashing lights, advertisements that promise big winnings, loose slots, a better life, or a sexier companion; all carefully placed within the casino environment with the intention of keeping you gambling. Yet, few of these stimuli are directly related to the gambling games themselves and even fewer still ever appear simultaneously along with winning outcomes, as would typical conditioned reinforcers. For example, imagine that our naïve player is considering playing a slot machine game but is faced with having to choose from among the many options provided by the casino. Should he choose the "Wheel of Fortune," the "Queen of the Wild," or "Glitter Kitty?" After viewing the myriad of possibilities he eyes the "Robin Hood and The Golden Arrow" slot machine. As it happens, our naïve player is a fan of the legendary Sherwood bandit and his swashbuckling adventures. The player thinks to himself that it would be ironic if he beat the "one arm bandit" which features a real bandit who was known for robbing the rich and giving to the poor; only in this case our player hopes Robin Hood will steal from the rich casino and give to the poor player. Furthermore, the naïve gambler wishes he were more like the famous archer: brave, skilled, and charming. And with that, the naïve gambler, confident that this machine will bring him luck, sits down at the Robin Hood slots and proceeds to hand over his money to a machine that provides exactly the same probabilities of winning as every other machine surrounding it.

Slot machines' themes are not arbitrarily selected decoration, but rather carefully selected arrangements of stimuli that are designed to evoke a complex form of verbal behavior referred to as arbitrarily applicable derived relational responding (see Hayes et al., 2001 for a more thorough description of relational frame theory, RFT). Relational responding describes a repertoire of behavior in which one stimulus event is responded to in terms of another (e.g., a quantity of money can only be said to be greater if it is compared to another). This act becomes "derived" when the relational response is not due to a directly trained relationship but rather due to a learned history of reversing relations (e.g., deriving that A is greater than B if taught B is less than A), or indirectly relating stimuli across multiple relations (e.g., knowing that A is greater than C, if taught that A is greater than B and that B is greater than C). These types of derived relational responding become arbitrarily applicable when the relations being brought to bear are not dependent on the physical features of the participating stimuli, but rather are under the control of contextual cues. For example, the relation of greater than or less than can be arbitrarily applied to almost any two stimuli given that an additional contextual cue is provided that specifies exactly what function or value the individual is meant to compare. In this case, a contextual cue that specifies what relation is to be applied is referred to as a contextual relata (Crel) and the cue specifying the function to be related, the contextual function (Cfunc). When stimuli are related in these ways, the psychological functions of the related stimuli are transformed in accordance with the specific relations applied (e.g., if B is less than A and B is a reinforcer, then A may come to function as a greater reinforcer than B; Hayes et al., 2001). In the Robin Hood slot machine example, multiple stimulus functions of Robin Hood were brought into a frame of coordination (sameness) with the player's perception of the probability of a win from that particular slot machine. For the player, the brave, skilled, and charming qualities of Robin Hood have now become attributes of the slot machine itself. Because these qualities are also coordinated with success, so too do the functions of the slot machine become more desirable. Additionally, by relating the lauded philanthropic exploits of Robin Hood with the potential future of taking money from the casino, the player has now transformed the consequences of winning on this particular machine to having an increased value beyond its monetary outcome.

In an experiment conducted by Zlomke and Dixon (2006), contextual control of arbitrarily applicable relations was demonstrated by using conditional discriminations to influence the preference of slot machine players for concurrently available slots. In this experiment, nine participants were exposed to a pretest baseline in which they were asked to play two concurrently available slot machine simulators that provided reinforcement on the same 50% RR, with the magnitude of reinforcement held constant at one credit. Next, participants worked through a conditional discrimination training program in which the relations of "greater than" and "less than" were trained to be applied in the presence of specific color based contextual cues (e.g., in the presence of a yellow background select the greater of the three stimuli and in the presence of a blue background select the lesser). Stimuli used in the conditional discrimination training involved images of paper money, coin money, and letter grades. When mastery criteria were reached for the conditional discrimination training, participants again engaged with the concurrent slot machines. However, this time each slot machine was also presented with colored backgrounds previously taught as contextual cues. Results of this experiment showed that despite the fact that most participants showed little or no preference between the concurrently available slot machines in the pretest, and no direct history of differential reinforcement was provided for slot play given any specific colored background, eight out of the nine participants allocated a majority of their responses to the slot machine with the "greater than" colored background following conditional discrimination training (Zlomke & Dixon, 2006). These findings were further extended with modified relational training procedures (Hoon, Dymond, Jackson, & Dixon, 2008), using different functions, and across different gambling contexts. For instance, Dixon, Wilson, and Whiting (2012) demonstrated that temporal functions associated with rates of responding could be used to transform the functions of gambling stimuli in a simulated horse track scenario. In this study, 10 participants engaged in simulated horse track gambling by allocating bets across eight differently colored horses. Once a baseline of response allocation was established, a pretraining to establish responding to a conjuctive schedule was presented. Under this format, an FR-5 schedule and a temporal schedule were independently required to be met before reinforcement was provided. The FR-5 schedule was trained by providing each participant the opportunity to earn reinforcement for engaging in trials that required clicking five consecutive times on one of three arbitrary images. Next, participants were exposed to a temporal differentiation training procedure in which the three new arbitrary stimuli, designated A1, A2, and A3, were presented again. However, now the participants were required to click the images at a specific speed, e.g., stimuli A1 and A2 might require the five clicks to have less than an inter-response time between 0.5 and 1.5 s while stimulus A3 required all five clicks to occur with a comparably slower 1.5-3 s inter-response time requirement. Following successful acquisition of the temporal differentiation functions for each of the three A stimuli, a matching to sample training was employed to teach participants to select an appropriate arbitrary three word stimuli (B stimuli) when presented with an appropriate A stimuli (e.g., "select B1 when presented with A1"). A second block of conditional discriminations was provided following the A-B training in order to train B-C relations where C stimuli consisted of colored square images. After reaching the required mastery criterion and completing a test for the presence of derived relational responding, each participant again completed the horse track assessment. Results of this experiment showed that following the conditional discrimination training, 7 of the 10 participants were more likely to allocate bets toward the horse that shared the formal feature of the color that was indirectly trained into coordination with the fastest temporal differentiation speed. Concomitantly, 7 of the 10 participants also increased betting directed toward the horses who shared formal similarities with the temporally trained slower colors. In order to clarify these results, the researchers replicated the previous procedure with three additional participants while blocking participants from viewing the results of each race during the pretraining assessment in order to account for reinforcement histories with respect to horse color. The results of this experiment showed that two of the three participants preferred to bet on the horse that was the color indirectly associated with the fastest clicking speed during the temporal differentiation training.

Dixon, Miller, et al. (2012) and Dixon, Wilson, et al. (2012) likened this process of transforming stimulus functions of gambling stimuli, via derived relational responding, to the preference for the arbitrary names given to race horses. Names such as "speedy," "lightning," or "quicksilver" facilitate the application of rules and relations that coordinate networks of meaning with the otherwise unobserved capabilities of the present horse. It should be noted, however, that extended exposure to the actual consequences of gambling will weaken the contextual control of derived cues to influence preference (Hoon & Dymond, 2013).

From the RFT perspective, self-directed rules are a product of arbitrarily applicable relational responding (Barnes-Holmes, Hayes, et al., 2001; Barnes-Holmes, O'Hora, et al., 2001). According to RFT, rules are antecedent verbal events that gain evocative potential from the relations existing between the specified verbal references and the transformation of subsequent consequential functions. For example, the rule "Always bet big on red 21 to win big," could spur a player to follow the rule as the sentence structure implies that a cause and effect relationship exists between betting on red 21 and winning. Furthermore, the rule links the necessity of "always" betting big with the causal relation of winning big. Because rules have been implicated in the maintenance of problematic gambling behaviors, arbitrarily applicable derived relational responding, and the subsequent transformations of stimulus functions that lead to the antecedent qualities of such rules should be further explored in the behavioral literature.

Gambling as an Outcome, Not a Cause

The field of applied behavior analysis (ABA) has largely come to focus on function-based approaches to clinical problems (Cooper, Heron, & Heward, 2007). This approach suggests that problem behaviors exist because they produce an outcome that is relevant to the one behaving and because the behavior is more efficient than appropriate alternatives. ABA addresses the presentation of problematic behaviors by identifying the contingencies that maintain behavior and then rearranging the environment such that appropriate behaviors produce a similar or more reinforcing outcome. As such, behavior analysts typically discount topographical descriptions of behavior and instead categorize behaviors based on the general outcome that the behavior produces (i.e., automatic sensory, attention maintained, tangible, or escape). This approach allows behavior analysts to experimentally evaluate the variables that contribute to the maintenance of problematic behavior and program individualized treatment packages that address these variables. As gambling for escape is a diagnostic characteristic of problematic gambling (American Psychiatric Association, 2013), identifying the contingencies that maintain gambling may have important value for both the identification and treatment of pathological gambling.

From a behavior analytic standpoint, problematic gambling describes a topography of behaviors associated with the wagering of some commodity for a probabilistic chance of earning a reinforcer of a comparably greater magnitude. However, this description does not necessarily address the function of gambling. For example, three roulette players may sit next to each other at the table. Each player may engage in nearly identical patterns of betting, yet the specific consequence that maintains these patterns may be different. For the first player, perhaps earning money is the most important aspect of the game; a consequence that suggests a tangible function. The second player may simply be using the context of the game to access attention from the attractive croupier running the table; a form of positive attention. The third player may not be interested in either the money or the company, but instead be playing because gambling provides a desperately needed reprieve from the stress of the work day.

In order to identify possible differences in the maintaining variables leading to pathological gambling, the gambling functional assessment (GFA) was developed. This 20-item questionnaire presents statements related to gambling behavior and asks that participants respond using a seven-point Likert scale that signifies the frequencies with which that individual engages in the specified behavior. Each item on the GFA corresponds to one of four functions: sensory, escape, attention, or tangible. The GFA is scored by calculating the sum of ratings for each category; the category with the highest summation is considered to be the most likely maintaining function for gambling (Dixon & Johnson, 2007). Evaluation of the GFA revealed that the assessment tool mainly assessed two categories, positive reinforcement and escape. Therefore, the GFA was revised to more accurately discriminate between these two functions (Miller, Meier, Muehlenkamp, & Weatherly, 2009; Miller, Meier, & Weatherly, 2009). The resulting GFA-R consisted of only 16 questions designed to identify the degree to which gamblers sought out positive reinforcement or escape. Conceptually, these two categories present a difficulty in that most gamblers "believe" that their behavior is maintained by positive reinforcement and may not be aware of the influence of escape contingencies. This hypothesis was supported by researchers evaluating the construct validity of the GFA-R who found that the majority of participants indicated a high level of endorsement for positive behaviors (Weatherly, Miller, & Terrell, 2011). While scores indicating positive reinforcement remained high across the board, higher scores in statements related to escape were associated with higher problem gambling (e.g., Weatherly, 2013; Weatherly & Derenne, 2012; Weatherly et al., 2011). Additionally, young people are more likely to endorse escape-related statements than older participants.

BEHAVIORAL TREATMENT APPROACHES
Early Behavioral Approaches

Some of the earliest explicitly behavioral approaches to the treatment of problem gambling focused on the conditioning gambling stimuli as aversives, or punishing gambling behavior directly (Barker & Miller, 1966, 1968; Goorney, 1968; Koller, 1972; Seager, 1970; Seager, Pkorny, & Black, 1966). Barker and Miller (1966), for instance, presented a case study in which a subject was asked to watch films of either himself gambling or himself at home with his wife. Over the course of 10 days of half-hour treatments, 450 shocks were delivered while he watched himself gamble; no shocks were delivered while watching himself at home. Barker and Miller reported that the subject's orientation toward gambling appeared to change and that he expressed a deep sense of shame while watching himself gamble. Following this phase, the subject was asked to play on an actual slot machine while receiving shocks. The authors noted that as of 2 months following treatment, the subject had not returned to gambling. Similarly, Seager (1970) applied electrical shocks to gamblers when they viewed newspaper pages with horse track information, slides of betting shops, or poker cards. Like Barker and Miller, relief stimuli including pictures of the gambler's home, wife, or children were used in conjunction with the gambling stimuli; however, no shocks were applied in the their presence. Of the 14 compulsive gamblers treated, five remained free of gambling at a 12-month follow up. Greenberg and Rankin (1982) described methods that, along with advice on how to avoid gambling contexts, included having a therapist accompany the client into gambling inducing situations and then gradually fading the presence of the therapist. While in these situations, the participant was asked to resist the urge to bet by snapping a rubber band on their wrist or by introducing a fantasy of a disastrous sequence (covert-sensitization). Of the 26 participants, only five participants were reported to have maintained control of their gambling after follow-ups of 9 months to 5 years. Similarly, patients exposed to aversive shock treatments were 26% less likely to demonstrate cessation or control when compared to subjects who were taught to relax when thinking about gambling (McConaghy, Blaszczynski, & Frankova, 1991). While these early studies generally expressed optimism regarding outcomes, limitations in outcome measures, small sample sizes, and the absence of controlled research designs do not support the use of aversive treatments as a primary approach (Petry & Roll, 2006).

Other behavioral approaches, such as those used to treat impulse control issues related to substance abuse, have been appropriated in the treatment of pathological gambling. For instance, Symes and Nicki (1997) employed cue-exposure, response-prevention treatment, a treatment previously demonstrated to reduce urges to engage in cigarette smoking (Self, 1989), to reduce the elicitation of conditioned responses in the presence of gambling stimuli. Unlike the previous case studies involving respondent extinction and aversive conditioning in which participants were passively exposed to gambling stimuli (i.e., Greenberg & Marks, 1982; Greenberg & Rankin, 1982; McConaghy et al., 1991), Symes and Nicki asked participants to actively observe stimulus cues and the subsequently elicited responses. In this study, participants were instructed to stop at particular points in the process of gambling (e.g., while entering the building, while entering the gambling setting, while exchanging money for the machine, while standing in front of the gambling machine, while putting money in the machine, etc.). At each of these points, the participant was asked to focus on his or her physiological reactions, to think about the feelings in that moment, to look at the surrounding stimuli, and to listen to the sounds around them. In addition to the active cues-exposure, participants were allowed to engage with the gambling machine but not to actually gamble (i.e., response prevention). Each wager on the machine was returned regardless of the outcome of the game. Examination of the frequency of self-reported gambling urges, both within and outside of the treatment procedure, and the frequency of gambling behavior outside of treatment suggested that for both cases presented, cue-exposure response prevention treatment reduced pathological gambling. According to Symes and Nicki, the results supported the concept that exposure to the environmental, cognitive, and physiological cues in gambling situations without the monetary outcomes serves to extinguish the elicitation of gambling behaviors in the presence of salient gambling stimuli.

Cognitive Behavior Therapy

Cognitive approaches to pathological gambling place emphasis on cognitive distortions as the causal mechanism of pathological gambling. As cognitive distortions and perceptual inaccuracies are thought to contribute to the development of pathological gambling, structured correction of such erroneous beliefs should help to reduce symptoms (Ladouceur, Boisvert, & Dumont, 1994). For example, simply pointing out the negative utility of gambling or the inability to predict outcomes during simulated gambling play may lead to greatly reduced gambling as the gambler no longer incorrectly believes they will come out on top (Toneatto & Sobell, 1990). Cognitive correction, techniques focused on modifying erroneous perceptions toward notions of randomness, have been associated with clinically significant decreases in diagnostic criteria and self-reported measures relating to pathological gambling (Ladouceur et al., 2003, 2001; Ladouceur, Sylvain, Letarte, Giroux, & Jacques, 1998). Measures of erroneous gambling attitudes and beliefs have also been shown to decrease following cognitively oriented treatments (Breen, Kruedelbach, & Walker, 2001). However, the cognitive behavioral perspective incorporates behavioral learning theories and behavioral processes as fundamental causal mechanisms and methods of treatment. As put forward by Sharpe and Tarrier (1993), irrational gambling cognitions are thoughts or associations that are conditioned during prolonged exposure to the continuous autonomic arousal, experienced by the gambler as excitement, during the unpredictably partial or variable schedules of reinforcement found in gambling environments. Once established, relevant gambling stimuli and the internal gambling-related cognitions become cues that trigger heightened autonomic arousal and the distorted gambling-related cognitions such as "I feel lucky today," or "I know I can win." If gambling behavior is evoked by such cognitions then any subsequent winning may serve to adventitiously reinforce the faulty cognitions and perpetuate a cycle of cognitively evoked behavior. It is proposed within this heuristic, or "cognitive-behavioral model," that the difference between a controlled-gambler and a pathological gambler is the individual's repertoire of coping skills that allow him or her to control or manage autonomic arousal, problem solve situations, and to challenge gambling-related cognitions. General traits of impulsivity and the difficulty in delaying responses are also implicated.

Sylvain, Ladouceur, and Boisvert (1997) investigated a cognitive behavior treatment (CBT) package designed to address such deficits in coping skills by providing individuals with training in cognitive correction, problem-solving training, social skills training, and relapse prevention. Cognitive correction involved four targets: understanding the concept of randomness and the lack of control in gambling, understanding the erroneous beliefs held by gamblers, awareness of inaccurate perceptions, and correction of erroneous perceptions. Therapists provided explanations and feedback to the participants in order to achieve these targets. Problem-solving training involved the presentation of a problem-solving method that taught participants to define the problem, collect information, generate different solutions, list advantages and disadvantages of each solution, and implement and evaluate the solution. This training focused on problems that presumably lead the individual to gambling. The social skills training involved discussions related to the potential link between poor social skills and the lack of resistance to peer pressure. Role-playing was used to improve communication skills. The fourth component, relapse prevention, involved discussion of high-risk situations and reasons individuals return to gambling. Participants were asked to describe past relapses, to identify their own high-risk situations, and develop strategies for dealing with those situations. After an average of 16.7 h of treatment (60-90 min/week), 8 of the 14 subjects who received CBT improved by at least 50% on dependent measures involving the number of DSM-III-R diagnostic criteria met, South Oaks Gambling Scale, participant ratings of perception of control over gambling, and self-reported desire to gamble. Self-reported ratings of the participant's belief that they could refrain from gambling also increased while the same could be said for only 1 of 15 subjects who were assigned to a waitlist control group. Twelve of the 15 treatment participants improved by 50% on at least three of the five dependent variables with only 1 of the 15 doing so from the control group. Of the 14 participants in the treatment group, 86% fell below diagnostic criteria, compared to 1 of the 15 participants in the control group, for pathological gambling. Only one of nine participants reported as having relapsed at a 12-month follow-up.

Other CBT approaches have placed more attention on the environmental influence and behavioral processes contributing to pathological gambling than on cognitive correction alone. Petry (2005) described an eight-session CBT approach that places reinforcement of nongambling behaviors as a central component of treatment. In this approach, the gambler and the therapist track the gambling and nongambling behavior on a graph throughout the course of treatment. The gambler is taught to arrange for individually selected praise and reward for each day of nongambling. Greater lengths of abstinence are to be reinforced with greater rewards and gambling behavior with the withholding of the rewards. Each session begins with review and graphing of the previous week's gambling and nongambling behavior. Over the course of the eight sessions, the gambler is also taught to recognize his or her own pattern of behavior and identify triggers of gambling; evaluate episodes in terms of the triggers, behaviors, and consequences; develop checklists of leisure type behaviors; problem solve situations that trigger gambling; employ techniques for coping with, and reducing, cravings such as gradual relaxation; explore interpersonal styles and role-play difficult social interactions; understand cognitive biases and erroneous beliefs; and to consider how changes in his or her life may affect triggering situations and coping strategies. This approach to treatment was evaluated in a large-scale randomized group design study that compared both individual therapy and self-help workbook formats of Petry's (2005) CBT with referral to Gambler's Anonymous (GA) as a control (Petry et al., 2006). Gambling measures included diagnostic interviews, scores on assessments designed to assess risk of gambling pathology, service utilization, addiction severity, and symptom severity. In addition, self-report measures of gambling behaviors were taken that included days gambled and amounts lost. Collaterals identified by the participant were used to verify self-reported behavior frequencies. Overall, reductions in gambling-related measures were seen across all groups with the greatest reductions observed in those from the individual therapy group followed by the workbook group. However, 12-month follow-up measures did not indicate differences between groups. Dose effects, in the form of attendance to either GA, individual CBT, or completion of the CB workbook, were also observed to influence posttreatment abstinence and treatment efficacy.

Acceptance and Commitment Therapy

Although the two general therapeutic approaches to gambling pathology, treatments derived from traditional behavior analytic procedures and those addressing cognitive behavioral targets, have demonstrated some degree of efficacy, neither is entirely adequate. Specifically, traditional behavior approaches lack an empirically adequate account of the private, cognitive biases that appear to derail patterns of behavior in the presence of programmed contingencies. Likewise, cognitive behavioral approaches appear to lack a conceptually systematic account for the development and influence of cognitive biases or explicit methodologies to validate the role of direct cognitive change strategies on behavior (c.f. Hayes, Luoma, Bond, Masuda, & Lillis, 2006). In the wake of these basic and applied inadequacies, "third wave" therapies have emerged. Generally considered to be contextual in nature, "third wave" therapies such as dialetical behavior therapy, mindfulness therapy, and acceptance and commitment therapy (ACT) focus on the function of psychological events and provide strategies for individuals to influence how they experience them. Of these therapies, ACT is of particular note in that it is rooted in radical behaviorism and extends the principles of behavior analysis to complex human behavior via the basic theoretical concepts of RFT. ACT, like RFT, is focused on how language affects experiences and suggests that a primary source of some psychopathology can be found in the interaction between direct contingencies and relational responding (i.e., language and cognition). According to ACT, individuals fail to behave in accordance with their own values due to a sort of "cognitive fusion," or overregulation of behavior by means of verbal processes such as rules and relational networks. ACT therefore seeks to help individuals achieve a degree of "psychological flexibility" in which they are able to make contact with the present moment and in turn make appropriate decisions (Hayes et al., 2006). Psychological flexibility is encouraged by means of six psychological concepts; contact with the present moment, acceptance, cognitive defusion, self-as-context, committed action, and values (Hayes, Strosahl, & Wilson, 2012). Contact with the present moment involves engaging in active observance of the immediate environment and any pragmatically important psychological functions. Acceptance involves being willing to engage with these functions even when they may be painful or unpleasant. Cognitive defusion describes the process of disassociating, or making less salient, the psychological functions of verbal events that serve to hinder persistence or change in behavior patterns toward a pragmatic end. Self-as-context involves taking the perspective that you are the setting in which events such as thoughts, labels, or experiences take place and therefore are not the events themselves. Committed action is the process of choosing to engage in behaviors that produce valued outcomes. Values are chosen qualities that equate patterns of behavior with psychological function. For example, "being a good provider" is a value that associates the psychological functions of reinforcement with any pattern of behavior that produces outcomes that are consistent with providing for one's family. It should be noted, however, that values are not outcomes themselves and therefore can never be achieved in their own right.

The concepts of ACT translate well to the context of pathological gambling. Consider the pathological gambler who routinely returns to the slot machines every night. Despite being tens of thousands of dollars in debt he continues to play, excited by the prospect of a big win that will solve all of his problems, that will make him a winner that others like and respect, and that will allow him to return home as the great provider. This individual is not living in the present moment, he is not focused on his immediate surroundings; instead, he is fixated on his thoughts about the future. He does not see the house edge taking effect; instead, he sees the potential of a win and therefore discounts the contingencies that are present. This individual is unwilling to confront the feelings that he is unhappy, ashamed, or running away from an unpleasant home life. He instead avoids these stressful thoughts by engaging in behaviors that are only supported by erroneous rules such as "winners always bet on red." He may value supporting his family, but his behaviors do not represent committed actions that produce outcomes in line with this preferred evaluation of behavior. He is, in a word, inflexible and thus locked into a persistent pattern of experiential avoidance that continually leads to worsening contingencies and a greater need for escape.

ACT approaches have been successfully employed and compared to other therapies designed to alleviate symptoms related to numerous psychopathologies such as smoking (Gifford et al., 2004), chronic pain and pain tolerance (Dahl, Wilson, & Nilsson, 2004; Hayes et al., 1999), depression (Zettle & Hayes, 1986; Zettle & Rains, 1989), anxiety (Zettle, 2003), and psychosis (Bach & Hayes, 2002). However, few studies to date have explored the potential of ACT-based therapies on pathological gambling. A brief ACT-based intervention was employed to alter responses to near-miss outcomes in pathological gamblers (Nastally & Dixon, 2012). Using a multiple baseline design, this study exposed three participants with a history of pathological gambling to a slot machine game. After each spin, the participants rated the outcome of the trial based on how close they felt they were to a win. Mean subjective ratings per 10-trial block showed that each participant rated near-miss outcomes as being closer to a win than total loss outcomes despite the fact that both outcomes were essentially equally a loss. Participants then viewed a PowerPoint presentation that provided descriptions and instructions for practicing the six core ACT processes. For defusion, the participants viewed a flashing screen with two statements, "almost a win" and "almost a win is just another loss," above images of near-miss outcomes. Self-as-context involved two slides including questions that prompted perspective taking. Acceptance was taught by presenting pictures of both near-miss outcomes and total loss outcomes with text describing stimuli paired with both winning and losing. Instructions to accept and contact feelings of loss were also presented. Contact-with-the-present moment was addressed by a short description and instruction for a mindfulness exercise incorporating slot machine outcomes. Values were taught using pictures of material wealth and slot machine outcomes with text that instructed participants to recall their past and personal values. Lastly, committed action involved pictures of near-miss outcomes and questions surrounding goal set-ting such as "are you ready to start making a change right here, right now?" Following the exposure to this 10-min brief ACT treatment, participants returned to the slot machine previously played. Mean subjective ratings of closeness to a win for near-miss outcomes were greatly disrupted for two of the three participants. For one participant, ratings for total losses and near-misses both declined following treatment. For the second partic-ipant, who prior to treatment rated near-miss outcomes as being closer to a win than losses which were rated at the bottom of the scale, post-treatment measures indicated that near-misses were now equally far from a win as losses. The third participant's mean ratings for both total losses and near-misses remained stable following treatment.

In another study evaluating the potential efficacy of brief ACT-based interventions for pathological gambling, participants were exposed to function-based or nonfunction-based ACT protocols (Wilson, 2012). Prior to being assigned to either group, each participant completed the GFA. When these assessments were completed, each participant com-pleted a gambling task that involved rating how close the participant thought slot machine outcomes were to a win. Following completion of the gambling task assessment, participants were provided with one of two ACT-based therapies. For the function-based ACT therapy group, participants received a treatment protocol that specifically targeted behaviors that led to the consequence for which his or her GFA indicated as the most likely maintaining function. For the nonfunction-based ACT therapy group, participants received a generic ACT protocol that targeted gambling behaviors in general. After completing the treatment protocol, participants again completed the gambling task. Results indicated that prior to treatment all participants rated near-miss outcomes as being closer to a win than a total loss. Following treatment, all seven of the function-based treatment group rated near-miss outcomes as being closer to a loss than a win, while only four of the nine nonfunction-based par-ticipants improved.

Current research on the effectiveness of ACT-based approaches to prob-lem gambling has helped to produce an 8-week treatment protocol specif-ically for pathological gambling (Dixon & Wilson, 2014). According to this protocol, ACT is especially suited to pathological gambling as it is effectively a function-based approach that targets the consequence of gambling rather than the topographical aspects of gambling play. Clients are taught to iden-tify potential functions of their own gambling such as avoidance of going home, escape from stressful feelings, access to attention from others, and access to tangibles and monetary awards. Each week of this protocol is designed to train the six ACT processes by providing gambling specific metaphors, thought exercises, and information that promotes psychological flexibility. For example, present-moment awareness is taught to clients by asking them to be actively aware of their physiological sensations and thoughts in the presence of gambling-related stimuli. One exercise to promote acceptance and willingness to experience unpleasant thoughts involves asking the individual to avoid thinking about gambling while in the presence of a gambling machine and then to sit with the resulting urges. Clarification of values and lack of committed action are addressed by having the individual indicate how much they feel they have lived up to their values in the past day, week, month, or year. Self-as-context and defusion are taught by having the individual identify the thoughts and rules they feel control them and then using metaphors to help them create distance between their sense of self and the specific thoughts thereby reducing the evocative function these thoughts have over their own behavior. One method suggested to help foster committed action is to have the client identify outcomes they consider to be consistent with their own values and then list the barriers that keep them from achieving these goals. The therapist then might engage in further defusion by helping the individual to see that most of the obstacles are verbal rules and not physical realities that values can always be worked toward even when goals cannot be completed.

SUMMARY

Pathological gambling has been a topic of academic and clinical interest in behavior analysis for over 60 years. Conceptualizations of gambling behavior initially focused on contingencies of reinforcement that were thought to select for and maintain continued wagers even when the net utility of such wagering is untenable. Early conceptualizations of gambling theorized that variable schedules of reinforcement were not only responsible for gambling in general, but that adventitious exposure to improbable winning streaks would shape obsessive gambling behavior. Such theories were challenged on the grounds that variable schedules were only ostensibly present in gambling and that the actual schedules of reinforcement were RRs. Research comparing preference and performance between RRs and variable schedules did not produce differentiated gambling patterns. However, despite the lack of sensitivity to such ratios, those playing on RR machines demonstrated patterns of gambling that were consistent with effective strategy on VR machines (i.e., betting higher after subsequent losses), thus suggesting inappropriate generalizations of games of skill upon chance-based gambling games. Further manipulation of contingencies and schedules of reinforcement revealed that gambling behaviors were less sensitive to the distribution of wins and more to the overall frequency of wins thus predicting greater persistence in gambling.

As predicted by Skinner (1953), outcomes that approximate or appear close to a win were shown to function as conditioned reinforcers. So-called "near-misses" or "near-wins" are a natural aspect of mechanical games and allow gambling games to provide high frequencies of conditioned reinforcers without actually providing monetary compensation. Alternatively, some gambling games have been suggested to provide outcomes that have the characteristics of a win but return less money than was wagered, thereby disguising losses as wins. Game characteristics, such as deceptive outcomes, may contribute to inaccurate discriminations of outcome probabilities or inappropriate discounting of the probabilities. Additionally, the immediacy of gambling outcomes has been attributed to the apparent discounting of short-term gains irrespective of the overall negative net utility of gambling. Hypothetical monetary discounting has been correlated with addictive disorders in general, and pathological gambling specifically. While sometimes suggested as a trait characteristic (e.g., gamblers are impulsive people), monetary discounting has been shown to be a contextually controlled behavior in which stimuli associated with gambling serve to evoke discounting where nongambling situations do not).

Verbal behaviors, such as superstitious tacting or rule following, have been implicated as both origins and maintaining factors of gambling behavior. For example, many players present behaviors suggestive of generalizations of manding repertoires in gambling contexts (e.g., asking "Please, Lady Luck, help me roll a seven"). Behaviors learned from such social contexts bear no causal influence on gambling outcomes, yet may lead to the obfuscation of actual outcome probabilities and contribute discriminative strength to outcomes when they appear to reinforce the mand. Inaccurate rule-generation and rule-following have also been identified as verbal behaviors that may lead to increased gambling problems. Rules, such as "Winners always bet on black," may introduce new outcomes to the event field, thus resulting in conditioned reinforcement as a function of rule completion or by making salient instances in which the rule seemed to be accurate. In the same manner that inaccurate rules contribute to inappropriate gambling, accurate rules may help to produce less persistent gambling patterns. Transformations of stimulus functions may also contribute to inappropriate gambling by virtue of the relatedness of gambling stimuli with other preferred stimuli. This account provides a model for the development of preferences and inaccurate discrimination of odds in games that include features that are salient to the player yet unrelated to the actual performance of the game itself (e.g., picking "Speedy the Horse" over "Fat Joe").

Approaching problem gambling as a single topography of behavior rather than repeated engagement in wagering within a session has helped researchers to identify the differences in functions that maintained the overall act of gambling. Specifically, high endorsements of escape contingencies on questionnaires have been seen to correlate to higher propensities toward problematic gambling. Because behavior analytic treatments are generally function-based, tools and procedures that allow clinicians to identify functions of gambling can be used to design individualized programs.

Taken together, the behavior literature suggests that pathological gambling is a complex topography of contingency-based and rule-governed behavior that is greatly influenced by verbal behaviors and the transformation of stimulus functions. Additionally, these conditions may only reach clinically critical levels when the behaviors they reinforce also begin to function as a means of obtaining escape. While the complexity of pathological gambling may seem daunting, these findings reflect that pathological behavior is indeed sensitive to experimental analysis (i.e., prediction and control). Furthermore, whereas experimental procedure may produce alterations in gambling behaviors, so to can clinical practice target the environmental stimuli and events.

Early attempts to influence pathological gambling behavior focused upon the pairing of aversive stimulus functions with gambling-related activities. Respondent extinction procedures were also employed in an effort to decrease the individual's urge to gamble when confronted with gambling cues. While these behavior modification techniques were reported to be successful, limitations in the methodologies utilized did not support the generalization of these techniques or their ability to be replicated. Furthermore, these traditional behavior approaches did little to address, either conceptually or clinically, the cognitive biases which appeared to present in manifestations of pathological gambling. As a result, cognitive behavioral approaches began to appear. These approaches attempted to correct cognitive distortions and reduce deficits in problem-solving and coping skills. Although these approaches have produced a number of quality studies concerned with treating gambling behaviors, cognitive approaches have generally failed to produce conceptually systematic frameworks for basic research or methodologies for validating the constructs thought to mediate behavior. As a result, "third wave" approaches such as ACT have emerged. ACT, in particular, may warrant attention from the behavior analytic community as its underlying philosophy, theoretic basis, and principles of behavior change are based on the radical behaviorism. When applied to the treatment of problem gambling, ACT affords behavior scientists a conceptually systematic approach that does not appeal to mental constructs. Instead, it maintains that gambling pathology represents a repertoire of physical and verbal behaviors that produce experiential avoidance and escape from stressful thoughts. Additionally, individuals who struggle with gambling do so because they have become psychologically inflexible with respect to verbal rules and relational frames that constitute cognitive biases. In this way, ACT is the most comprehensive behavioral approach to treating the many variables that contribute to pathological gambling. ACT addresses insensitivities to direct contingencies by asking clients to be mindful. ACT helps individuals to accept uncomfortable feelings and thus reduce the need for escape. Defusion of rules and relational networks that comprise the irrational biases of gamblers is addressed through various metaphors, thought exercises, and with exposure to gambling-related stimuli. And perhaps the most important component of ACT to the treatment of pathological gambling, the identification of values and the planning of committed actions provide clients with functionally based alternative behaviors to replace gambling.

Several conclusions can be drawn from these points. First, gambling has been, and will continue to be, a fruitful field for behavior researchers whether they are seeking to explore basic behavioral principles or highly developed cognitive phenomena. This may be due in large part to the ease with which most participants engage with gambling games and with the similarities between gambling games and operant preparations. For example, most gambling games involve arbitrary behaviors, such as pulling a lever or pressing a button, so as to produce an outcome that can easily be manipulated by an experimenter. As is the hope of gambling providers, games often produce discrete behaviors that are sufficiently high in frequency and persist even in the face of extinction. These frequencies are often high enough to allow for gambling to be evaluated for changes in rates of play or post reinforcement pauses. Other aspects of gambling behavior, such as the magnitude of wagers or the number of lines played, can also be measured in order to evaluate other phenomena of interest such as choice allocation. The payout of gambling games is also a form of conditioned reinforcement that can be delivered immediately and with little cost to the experimenter. Gambling machines also allow for the incorporation of many other stimuli such as lights, sounds, videos, and even vibrations; all of which can be paired to condition discriminative or consequential functions. Gambling games are also easy to acquire. Many casino type games can be replicated cheaply by buying a pack of cards, dice, poker chips, or a table felt at your local party supply store. If preselecting outcomes is necessary, one can simply stack the deck or use loaded dice. Where more sophisticated operations are required, computerized gambling games can be purchased or even programmed by following already available task analyses (Dixon & Schreiber, 2002; MacLin & Dixon, 2004). Lastly, gambling games are just that, games. Participants may be more motivated to attend to experimental tasks if they are embedded within games. In applied domains, pathological gamblers represent a population of clients whose primary diagnostic criteria are expressed as easily objectified behaviors (e.g., dollars gambled or the number of trips to the casino). Such behaviors may be easily incorporated into treatment goals, contracts, or contingency management strategies. Additionally, the availability of gambling stimuli ensures that treatment protocols can incorporate actual exposure to gambling-related stimuli and allows for the potential use of *in situ* training.

Second, our understanding of gambling has come a long way since simple variable schedules of reinforcement were suggested as the causal mechanism. Behavioral theories about gambling now constitute increasingly complex conceptualizations that include not only direct contingencies but also verbally mediated cognitive repertoires and neurobehavioral correlates. While such complexity may seem daunting, this very feature makes research in the area of pathological gambling an excellent opportunity to extend the scope and application of behavior analysis into the generally cognitive dominated field of clinical psychology. Research on gambling has allowed behavior analysts to identify, predict, and influence verbal behaviors directly and subsequently the behaviors that are mediated by such verbal repertoires. However, the influence of complex verbal behaviors by means of counseling or talk therapy has remained taboo within traditional behavior analytic training programs. This issue is even more evident in the Model act for licensing/regulating behavior analysts, as put forward by the Behavior Analysis Certification Board (2012), the primary credentialing agency for applied behavior analysts, which expressly identifies psychotherapy, cognitive therapies, and long-term counseling as treatment modalities outside of the scope of practice for behavior analysts. As the study of pathological gambling provides behavior analysts with the chance to explore complex human behaviors that are socially and clinically significant, the inclusion of "third wave" therapeutic approaches, such as ACT, in the therapeutic toolbox of the next generation of behavior analysts may be a logical next step.

REFERENCES

Alessi, S. M., & Petry, N. M. (2003). Pathological gambling severity is associated with impulsivity in a delay discounting procedure. *Behavioral Processes, 64*(3), 345–354. http://dx.doi.org/10.1016/S0376-6357(03)00150-5.

American Gaming Association. (2013). *2013 state of the states: The AGA survey of casino entertainment.* May 24, 2013. Retrieved from: http://www.americangaming.org/sites/default/files/uploads/docs/aga_sos2013_fnl.pdf.

American Psychiatric Association. (1994). *Diagnostic and statistical manual of mental disorders* (4th). Washington, DC: American Psychiatric Association.

American Psychiatric Association. (2013). *Diagnostic and statistical manual of mental disorders* (5th). Arlington, VA: American Psychiatric Publishing.

Ayton, P., & Fischer, I. (2004). The hot hand fallacy and the gambler's fallacy: Two faces of subjective randomness? *Memory & Cognition, 32*(8), 1369–1378. http://dx.doi.org/10.3758/BF03206327.

Bach, P. B., & Hayes, S. C. (2002). The use of acceptance and commitment therapy to present the rehospitalization of psychotic patients: A randomized controlled trial. *Journal of Consulting and Clinical Psychology, 70,* 1129–1139.

Barker, J. C., & Miller, M. (1966). Aversion therapy for compulsive gamblers. *British Journal of Medicine, 2*(5505), 115.

Barker, J. C., & Miller, M. (1968). Aversion therapy for compulsive gambling. *Journal of Nervous and Mental Disease, 146*(5), 286–302. http://dx.doi.org/10.1097/00005053-196804000-00002.

Barnes-Holmes, D., Hayes, S. C., & Dymond, S. (2001). Self and self-directed rules. In S. C. Hayes, D. Barnes-Holmes, & B. Roche (Eds.), *Relational frame theory: A post-Skinnerian account of human language and cognition* (pp. 119–139). New York, NY: Kluwer Academic/Plenum Publishers.

Barnes-Holmes, D., O'Hora, D., Roche, B., Hayes, S. C., Bissett, R. T., & Lyddy, F. (2001). Understanding and verbal regulation. In S. C. Hayes, D. Barnes-Holmes, & B. Roche (Eds.), *Relational frame theory: A post-Skinnerian account of human language and cognition* (pp. 103–117). New York, NY: Kluwer Academic/Plenum Publishers.

Behavior Analysis Certification Board. (2012). *Model act for licensing/regulating behavior analysts.* Retrieved from: http://www.bacb.com/Downloadfiles/BACB_Model_Act.pdf.

Breen, R., Kruedelbach, N., & Walker, H. (2001). Cognitive changes in pathological gamblers following a 28-day inpatient program. *Psychology of Addictive Behaviors: Journal of the Society of Psychologists in Addictive Behaviors, 15*(3), 246–248. Available from: PsycINFO, Ipswich, MA. Accessed June 1, 2014.

Cooper, J. O., Heron, T. E., & Heward, W. L. (2007). *Applied behavior analysis* (2nd). Upper Saddle River, NJ: Pearson Prentice-Hall.

Custer, R. L. (1984). Profile of the pathological gambler. *Journal of Clinical Psychology, 45,* 35–38.

Dahl, J., Wilson, K. G., & Nilsson, A. (2004). Acceptance and commitment therapy and the treatment of persons at risk for long-term disability resulting from stress and pain symptoms: A preliminary randomized trial. *Behavior Therapy, 35,* 785–802.

Dixon, M. R. (2000). Manipulating the "Illusion of Control": Variations in risk-taking as a function of perceived control over chance outcomes. *The Psychological Record, 50*, 705–720.

Dixon, M. J., Harrigan, K. A., Sandhu, R., Collins, K., & Fugelsang, J. A. (2010). Losses disguised as wins in modern multi-line video slot machines. *Addiction, 105*(10), 1819–1824. http://dx.doi.org/10.1111/j.1360-0443.2010.03050.x.

Dixon, M. R., & Hayes, L. J. (1998). Effects of different instructional histories on the resurgence of rule-following. *The Psychological Record, 48*, 275–292.

Dixon, M. R., Hayes, L. J., & Aban, I. B. (2000). Examining the roles of rule following, reinforcement, and preexperimental histories on risk-taking behavior. *The Psychological Record, 50*(4), 687–704.

Dixon, M. R., Hayes, L. J., & Ebbs, R. E. (1998). Engaging in illusionary control during repeated risk-taking. *Psychological Reports, 83*, 959–962.

Dixon, M. R., Hayes, L. J., Rehfeldt, R. A., & Ebbs, R. E. (1998). An adjusting procedure for studying outcomes of risk-taking. *Psychological Reports, 82*, 1047–1050.

Dixon, M. R., & Holton, B. (2009). Altering the magnitude of delay discounting by pathological gamblers. *Journal of Applied Behavior Analysis, 42*(2), 269–275. http://dx.doi.org/10.1901/jaba. 2009.42-269.

Dixon, M. R., Jacobs, E. A., & Sanders, S. (2006). Contextual control of delay discounting by pathological gamblers. *Journal of Applied Behavior Analysis, 39*(4), 413–422. http://dx.doi.org/10.1901/jaba. 2006.173-05.

Dixon, M. R., & Johnson, T. E. (2007). The gambling functional assessment (GFA): An assessment device for identification of the maintaining variables of pathological gambling. *Analysis of Gambling Behavior, 1*, 44–49.

Dixon, M. R., MacLin, O. H., & Daugherty, D. (2006). An evaluation of response allocations to concurrently available slot machine simulations. *Behavior Research Methods, 38*, 232–236.

Dixon, M. R., Miller, J. R., Whiting, S. W., Wilson, A. N., & Hensel, A. M. (2012). Evaluating preference and rate of ambling on video slot machines. *Analysis of Gambling Behavior, 6*(2), 66–82.

Dixon, M. R., & Schreiber, J. B. (2002). Utilizing a computerized video poker simulation for the collection of data on gambling behavior. *The Psychological Record, 52*(4), 417–428.

Dixon, M. R., & Schreiber, J. B. (2004). Near-miss effects on response latencies and win estimations of slot machine players. *The Psychological Record, 54*, 335–348.

Dixon, M. R., & Wilson, A. N. (2014). *Acceptance and commitment therapy for pathological gamblers*. Carbondale, IL: Shawnee Scientific Press. ISBN: 978-0991484607.

Dixon, M. R., Wilson, A. N., & Whiting, S. W. (2012). A preliminary investigation of relational network influence on horse-track betting. *Analysis of Gambling Behavior, 6*(1), 23–26.

Ghezzi, P. M., Wilson, G. R., & Porter, J. C. K. (2006). The near-miss effect in simulated slot machine play. In P. M. Ghezzi, C. A. Lyons, M. R. Dixon, & G. R. Wilson (Eds.), *Gambling: Behavior theory, research and application* (pp. 155–170). Reno, NV: Context Press.

Gifford, E. V., Kohlenberg, B. S., Hayes, S. C., Antonuccio, D. O., Piasecki, M. M., Rasmussen-Hall, M. L., & Palm, K. M. (2004). Acceptance-based treatment for smoking cessation. *Behavior Therapy, 35*(4), 689–705.

Gilovich, T., Vallone, R., & Tversky, A. (1985). The hot hand in basketball: On the misperception of random sequences. *Cognitive Psychology, 17*, 295–314.

Goorney, A. B. (1968). Treatment of a compulsive horse race gambler by aversion therapy. *The British Journal of Psychiatry: The Journal of Mental Science, 114*(508), 329–333.

Green, L., & Myerson, J. (2004). A discounting framework for choice with delayed and probabilistic rewards. *Psychological Bulletin, 130*, 769–792.

Greenberg, D., & Marks, I. (1982). Behavioural psychotherapy of uncommon referrals. *The British Journal of Psychiatry: The Journal of Mental Science, 141*, 148–153.

Greenberg, D., & Rankin, H. (1982). Compulsive gamblers in treatment. *The British Journal of Psychiatry: The Journal of Mental Science, 140,* 364–366. http://dx.doi.org/10.1192/bjp.140.4.364.

Harrigan, K., Dixon, M., MacLaren, V., Collins, K., & Fugelsang, J. (2011). The maximum rewards at the minimum price: Reinforcement rates and payback percentages in multi-line slot machines. *Journal of Gambling Issues, 26,* 2611–2629. http://dx.doi.org/10.4309/jgi.2011.26.3.

Haw, J. (2008). The relationship between reinforcement and gambling machine choice. *Journal of Gambling Studies, 24,* 55–61.

Hayes, S. C., Bissett, R. T., Korn, Z., Zettle, R. D., Rosenfarb, I. S., Cooper, L. D., et al. (1999). The impact of acceptance versus control rationales on pain tolerance. *The Psychological Record, 49*(1), 33–47.

Hayes, S. C., Fox, E., Gifford, E. V., Wilson, K. G., Barnes-Holmes, D., & Healy, O. (2001). Derived relational responding as learned behavior. In S. C. Hayes, D. Barnes-Holmes, & B. Roche (Eds.), *Relational frame theory: A post-Skinnerian account of human language and cognition* (pp. 21–49). New York, NY: Kluwer Academic/Plenum Publishers.

Hayes, S. C., Kohlenberg, B. S., & Melancon, S. M. (1989). Avoiding and altering rule-control as a strategy of clinical intervention. In S. C. Hayes (Ed.), *Rule-governed behavior: Cognition, contingencies, and instructional control* (pp. 359–385). New York, NY: Plenum Press.

Hayes, S. C., Luoma, J. B., Bond, F. W., Masuda, A., & Lillis, J. (2006). Acceptance and commitment therapy: Model, processes and outcomes. *Behaviour Research and Therapy, 44*(1), 1–25. http://dx.doi.org/10.1016/j.brat.2005.06.006.

Hayes, S. C., Strosahl, K. D., & Wilson, K. G. (2012). *Acceptance and commitment therapy: The process and practice of mindful change* (2nd). New York, NY: Guilford Press.

Hayes, S. C., Zettle, R. D., & Rosenfarb, I. (1989). Rule-following. In S. C. Hayes (Ed.), *Rule-governed behavior: Cognition, contingencies, and instructional control* (pp. 191–220). New York, NY: Plenum Press.

Hineline, P. N. (1977). Negative reinforcement and avoidance. In W. K. Honig & J. E. R. Staddon (Eds.), *Handbook of operant behavior.* New York: Prentice-Hall.

Holt, D. D., Green, L., & Myerson, J. (2003). Is discounting impulsive? Evidence from temporal and probability discounting in gambling and non-gambling college students. *Behavioural Processes, 64*(3), 355–367. http://dx.doi.org/10.1016/S0376-6357(03)00141-4.

Hoon, A. E., & Dymond, S. (2013). Altering preferences for concurrently available simulated slot machines: Nonarbitary contextual control over gambling choice. *Analysis of Gambling Behavior, 6*(2), 35–52.

Hoon, A., Dymond, S., Jackson, J. W., & Dixon, M. R. (2008). Contextual control of slot machine gambling: Replication and extension. *Journal of Applied Behavior Analysis, 41,* 467–470.

Hurlburt, R. T., Knapp, T. J., & Knowles, S. H. (1980). Simulated slot-machine play with concurrent variable ratio and random ratio schedules of reinforcement. *Psychological Reports, 47*(2), 635–639. http://dx.doi.org/10.2466/pr0.1980.47.2.635.

Jarvik, M. E. (1951). Probability learning and a negative recency effect in the serial anticipation of alternative symbols. *Journal of Experimental Psychology, 41*(4), 291–297. http://dx.doi.org/10.1037/h0056878.

Kassinove, J. I., & Schare, M. L. (2001). Effects of the "near miss" and the "big win" on persistence at slot machine gambling. *Psychology of Addictive Behaviors, 15,* 155–158.

Koller, K. M. (1972). Treatment of poker-machine addicts by aversion therapy. *The Medical Journal of Australia, 1,* 742–745.

Ladouceur, R., Boisvert, J., & Dumont, J. (1994). Cognitive-behavioral treatment for adolescent pathological gamblers. *Behavior Modification, 18*(2), 230–242. http://dx.doi.org/10.1177/01454455940182006.

Ladouceur, R., Gaboury, A., Dumont, M., & Rochette, P. (1988). Gambling: Relationship between the frequency of wins and irrational thinking. *Journal of Psychology, 122*(4), 409–414.

Ladouceur, R., Sylvain, C., Boutin, C., Lachance, S., Doucet, C., & Leblond, J. (2003). Group therapy for pathological gamblers: A cognitive approach. *Behaviour Research and Therapy, 41*(5), 587–596. http://dx.doi.org/10.1016/S0005-7967(02)00036-0.

Ladouceur, R., Sylvain, C., Boutin, C., Lachance, S., Doucet, C., Leblond, J., et al. (2001). Cognitive treatment of pathological gambling. *Journal of Nervous and Mental Disease, 189* (11), 774–780. http://dx.doi.org/10.1097/00005053-200111000-00007.

Ladouceur, R., Sylvain, C., Letarte, H., Giroux, I., & Jacques, C. (1998). Cognitive treatment of pathological gamblers. *Behaviour Research and Therapy, 36*(12), 1111–1119. http://dx.doi.org/10.1016/S0005-7967(98)00086-2.

Langer, E. J. (1975). The illusion of control. *Journal of Personality and Social Psychology, 32*, 311–328.

Laraway, S., Snycerski, S., Michael, J., & Poling, A. (2003). Motivating operations and terms to describe them: Some further refinements. *Journal of Applied Behavior Analysis, 36*(3), 407–414. http://dx.doi.org/10.1901/jaba. 2003.36-407.

Leopard, A. (1978). Risk preference in consecutive gambling. *Journal of Experimental Psychology: Human Perception and Performance, 4*(3), 521–528. http://dx.doi.org/10.1037/0096-1523.4.3.521.

MacLin, O. H., & Dixon, M. R. (2004). A computerized simulation for investigating gambling behavior during roulette play. *Behavior Research Methods, Instruments, & Computers, 36*(1), 96–100. http://dx.doi.org/10.3758/BF03195554.

McConaghy, N., Blaszczynski, A., & Frankova, A. (1991). Comparison of imaginal desensitisation with other behavioural treatments of pathological gambling. A two- to nine-year follow-up. *The British Journal of Psychiatry: The Journal of Mental Science, 159*, 390–393.

Michael, J. (1982). Distinguishing between discriminative and motivational functions of stimuli. *Journal of the Experimental Analysis of Behavior, 37*(1), 149–155. http://dx.doi. org/10.1901/jeab. 1982.37-149.

Miller, J. C., Meier, E., Muehlenkamp, J., & Weatherly, J. N. (2009). Testing the validity of Dixon & Johnson's (2007) gambling functional assessment. *Behavior Modification, 33*, 156–174.

Miller, J. C., Meier, E., & Weatherly, J. N. (2009). Assessing the reliability of the gambling functional assessment. *Journal of Gambling Studies, 25*, 121–129.

Nastally, B. L., & Dixon, M. R. (2012). The effect of a brief acceptance and commitment therapy (ACT) intervention on the near miss effect in problem gamblers. *The Psychological Record, 62*, 677–690.

National Gambling Impact Study Commission. (1999). *National Gambling Impact Study Commission final report.* Retrieved from: http://govinfo.library.unt.edu/ngisc/reports/finrpt. html.

Petry, N. M. (2001). Pathological gamblers, with and without substance abuse disorders, discount delayed rewards at high rates. *Journal of Abnormal Psychology, 110*(3), 482–487. http://dx.doi.org/10.1037/0021-843X.110.3.482.

Petry, N. M. (2005). *Pathological gambling: Etiology, comorbidity, and treatment.* Washington, DC: American Psychological Association.

Petry, N. M., Ammerman, Y., Bohl, J., Doersch, A., Gay, H., Kadden, R., et al. (2006). Cognitive-behavioral therapy for pathological gamblers. *Journal of Consulting and Clinical Psychology, 74*(3), 555–567. http://dx.doi.org/10.1037/0022-006X.74.3.555.

Petry, N. M., Bowden-Jones, H., & George, S. (2013). Proposed changes for substance use and gambling disorders in DSM-5: Impact on assessment and treatment in the UK. *The Psychiatrist, 37*(2), 41–43. http://dx.doi.org/10.1192/pb.bp.112.040063.

Petry, N. M., & Casarella, T. (1999). Excessive discounting of delayed rewards in substance abusers with gambling problems. *Drug and Alcohol Dependence, 56*(1), 25–32. http://dx. doi.org/10.1016/S0376-8716(99)00010-1.

Petry, N. M., & Madden, G. J. (2010). Discounting and pathological gambling. In G. J. Madden & W. K. Bickel (Eds.), *Impulsivity: The behavioral and neurological science of discounting* (pp. 273–294). Washington, DC: American Psychological Association.

Petry, N. M., & Roll, J. M. (2006). Cognitive-behavioral treatments for pathological gambling. In P. Ghezzi, C. A. Lyons, M. R. Dixon, & G. R. Wilson (Eds.), *Gambling: Behavior theory, research, and application* (pp. 249–260). Reno, NV, USA: Context Press.

Poppen, R. L. (1989). Some clinical implications of rule-governed behavior. In S. C. Hayes (Ed.), *Rule-governed behavior: Cognition, contingencies, and instructional control* (pp. 325–357). New York, NY, USA: Plenum Press.

Porter, J. K., & Ghezzi, P. M. (2006). Theories of pathological gambling. In P. Ghezzi, C. A. Lyons, M. R. Dixon, & G. R. Wilson (Eds.), *Gambling: Behavior theory, research, and application* (pp. 19–43). Reno, NV, USA: Context Press.

Rachlin, H. (1990). Why do people gamble and keep gambling despite heavy losses? *Psychological Science, 1*(5), 294–297. http://dx.doi.org/10.1111/j.1467-9280.1990.tb00220.x.

Reid, R. L. (1986). The psychology of the near miss. *Journal of Gambling Behavior, 2*(1), 32–39. http://dx.doi.org/10.1007/BF01019932.

Schreiber, J., & Dixon, M. R. (2001). Temporal characteristics of slot machine play in recreational gamblers. *Psychological Reports, 89*(1), 67–72. http://dx.doi.org/10.2466/PR0.89.5.67-72.

Seager, C. P. (1970). Treatment of compulsive gamblers by electrical aversion. *The British Journal of Psychiatry: The Journal of Mental Science, 117*(540), 545–553. http://dx.doi.org/10.1192/bjp.117.540.545.

Seager, C. P., Pkorny, M. R., & Black, D. (1966). Aversion therapy for compulsive gambling. *The Lancet, 1*(7436), 546.

Self, R. (1989). The effect of cue-exposure response prevention on cigarette smoking—A single case. *Behavioural Psychotherapy, 17*, 151–159.

Shaffer, H. J., & Hall, M. N. (2001). Updating and refining prevalence estimates of disordered gambling behaviour in the United States and Canada. *Canadian Journal of Public Health, 92* (3), 168–172.

Sharpe, L., & Tarrier, N. (1993). Towards a cognitive-behavioural theory of problem gambling. *The British Journal of Psychiatry: The Journal of Mental Science, 162*, 407–412. http://dx.doi.org/10.1192/bjp.162.3.407.

Skinner, B. F. (1948). 'Superstition' in the pigeon. *Journal of Experimental Psychology, 38*(2), 168–172. http://dx.doi.org/10.1037/h0055873.

Skinner, B. F. (1953). *Science and human behavior.* New York: Macmillan.

Skinner, B. F. (1957). *Verbal behavior.* East Norwalk, CT, USA: Appleton-Century-Crofts.

Skinner, B. F. (1961). *The cumulative record.* East Norwalk: Appleton-Century-Crofts. http://dx.doi.org/10.1037/11324-012.

Skinner, B. F. (1971). *Beyond freedom and dignity.* New York: Bantam/Vintage.

Skinner, B. F. (1974). *About behaviorism.* New York: Knopf.

Sylvain, C., Ladouceur, R., & Boisvert, J. (1997). Cognitive and behavioral treatment of pathological gambling: A controlled study. *Journal of Consulting and Clinical Psychology, 65*(5), 727–732. http://dx.doi.org/10.1037/0022-006X.65.5.727.

Symes, B. A., & Nicki, R. A. (1997). A preliminary consideration of cue-exposure, response-prevention treatment for pathological gambling behavior: Two case studies. *Journal of Gambling Studies, 13*, 145–157.

Toneatto, T., & Sobell, L. C. (1990). Pathological gambling treated by cognitive-behavior therapy: A case report. *Addictive Behaviors, 15*, 497–501.

Weatherly, J. N. (2013). The relationship between endorsing gambling as an escape and the display of gambling problems. *Journal of Addiction. 2013*, http://dx.doi.org/10.1155/2013/156365, Article ID 156365, 7 p.

Weatherly, J. N., & Brandt, A. E. (2004). Participants' sensitivity to percentage payback and credit value when playing a slot-machine simulation. *Behavior and Social Issues, 13*(1), 33–50.

Weatherly, J. N., & Derenne, A. (2010). SOGS scores correlate with rates of delay discounting of hypothetical monetary amounts, but not non-monetary outcomes. *Analysis of Gambling Behavior, 4,* 103–112.

Weatherly, J. N., & Derenne, A. (2012). Investigating the relationship between the contingencies that maintain gambling and probability discounting of gains and losses. *European Journal of Behavior Analysis, 13,* 39–46.

Weatherly, J. N., Miller, J. C., & Terrell, H. K. (2011). Testing the construct validity of the gambling functional assessment-revised (GFA-R). *Behavior Modification, 35,* 553–569.

Weatherly, J. N., Sauter, J. M., & King, B. M. (2004). The 'big win' and resistance to extinction when gambling. *Journal of Psychology: Interdisciplinary and Applied, 138*(6), 495–504. http://dx.doi.org/10.3200/JRLP. 138.6.495-504.

Wilson, A. N. (2012). Behavioral and neurological investigations into pathological gambling as a behavioral addiction. Doctoral dissertation. Retrieved from, http://opensiuc.lib.siu.edu/dissertations/524.

Witts, B., & Lyons, C. (2013). Factors correlated with persistence in online Texas Hold'em poker play. *Analysis of Gambling Behavior, 7*(1), 17–24.

Zettle, R. D. (2003). Acceptance and commitment therapy (ACT) vs. systematic desensitization in the treatment of mathematics anxiety. *The Psychological Record, 53,* 197–215.

Zettle, R. D., & Hayes, S. C. (1986). Dysfunctional control by client verbal behavior: The context of reason giving. *The Analysis of Verbal Behavior, 4,* 30–38.

Zettle, R. D., & Rains, J. C. (1989). Group cognitive and contextual therapies in treatment of 'depression. *Journal of Clinical Psychology, 45*(3), 436–445.

Zlomke, K. R., & Dixon, M. R. (2006). Modification of slot-machine preferences through the use of a conditional discrimination paradigm. *Journal of Applied Behavior Analysis, 39,* 351–361.

CHAPTER 16

Contingency Management to Promote Drug Abstinence

Jesse Dallery[1], Anthony Defulio[2], Steven E. Meredith[2]
[1]Department of Psychology, University of Florida, Gainesville, Florida, USA
[2]Department of Psychiatry and Behavioral Sciences, Johns Hopkins University School of Medicine, Baltimore, Maryland, USA

INTRODUCTION

Substance abuse remains a challenging problem in the United States. Over 22 million individuals aged 12 or older use illicit drugs, and nearly one in four smokes cigarettes (Substance Abuse and Mental Health Services Administration, 2012). The National Institutes of Health estimates that cigarette, alcohol, and illicit drug use account for more deaths than all other preventable causes combined, and the cost to society is about $599 billion per year (National Institute on Drug Abuse, 2014).

One of the most effective procedures to promote drug abstinence is contingency management (CM; Dutra et al., 2008). Under CM procedures, patients receive alternative, nondrug consequences contingent on providing objective evidence of drug abstinence. A large number of studies over the past 30 years have established the broad applicability and efficacy of CM (for a review see Higgins, Silverman, & Heil, 2008). A meta-analysis of CM effects on abstinence across a range of drug classes concluded that the data "provide strong support for CM as being among the more effective approaches to promoting abstinence during and after the treatment of drug dependence disorders" (Prendergast, Podus, Finney, Greenwell, & Roll, 2006, p. 1556).

In this chapter, we discuss the history and contemporary applications of CM interventions to initiate and maintain drug abstinence. We also highlight innovations in CM that promise to increase its access and cost-effectiveness. We conclude with a brief discussion of considerations for implementation in clinical contexts and of methods to broaden the dissemination and implementation of CM.

Clinical and Organizational Applications of Applied Behavior Analysis
http://dx.doi.org/10.1016/B978-0-12-420249-8.00016-2

HISTORY OF TRANSLATIONAL RESEARCH ON DRUGS AS REINFORCERS

Early laboratory research demonstrated that the drugs commonly abused by humans served as highly effective reinforcers in other animals (Griffiths, Bigelow, & Henningfield, 1980; Johanson, 1978; Johanson & Schuster, 1981; Pickens & Thompson, 1968). This laboratory research employed the drug self-administration procedure, in which drug delivery was contingent upon a response, such as a rat pressing a lever (Schuster & Thompson, 1969). The potency of drug reinforcement was illustrated by studies showing that, under certain conditions, animals would self-administer a drug even if it meant forfeiting access to food (e.g., Aigner & Balster, 1978). Although drug use is a complex and multidetermined phenomenon, the studies on drug reinforcement in animals supported the view that drug use in humans may be acquired and maintained through operant processes. Later research on animal drug self-administration also revealed some of the conditions under which drug use in humans may be suppressed (e.g., Carroll, 1996). In particular, the availability of alternative, nondrug reinforcers attenuated the acquisition and maintenance of drug self-administration (e.g., Carroll, 1996). These findings provided a strong empirical rationale for CM.

In addition, several theoretical frameworks emerged from behavior analysis and behavioral economics that dovetailed with the emerging empirical work on drug reinforcement (Herrnstein, 1970; Herrnstein & Prelec, 1992; Heyman, 2009; Rachlin, 1997; Vuchinich & Heather, 2003). Under these theories, drug use is viewed as operant behavior, or behavior influenced by its consequences (i.e., contingencies of reinforcement and punishment), and the context in which those consequences occur (Bigelow, Brooner, & Silverman, 1998; Johanson & Schuster, 1981). The theories also provided compelling accounts of how choice can be influenced by the dynamic competition between reinforcing (or punishing) consequences for drug use and the reinforcing (or punishing) consequences for alternative behavior.

It was not long until operant principles were translated into a novel intervention to promote abstinence. The general procedure was to increase the availability of alternative, nondrug reinforcement contingent on evidence of abstinence. For example, Miller (1975) used a CM procedure to decrease public drunkenness among "skid row" alcoholics. Abstinence from alcohol was verified via negative breath-alcohol tests and staff observation. Based on this evidence of abstinence, individuals could receive shelter, employment, food, clothing, and other services from local social agencies. Similar contingencies were arranged in a number of clinical contexts. For instance, in methadone clinics, a "take-home" dose was used as a consequence for abstaining from secondary drugs of abuse (i.e., not opiates). A number of studies have demonstrated that making take-home doses contingent on abstinence from secondary drugs is an effective method for reducing drug use (e.g., Stitzer & Bigelow, 1978; Stitzer et al., 1977). Take-home privileges have also been used to enhance attendance at counseling sessions (Iguchi et al., 1996; Stitzer et al., 1977), as well as compliance with clinic regulations, vocational training, and payment of clinic fees (Stitzer & Bigelow, 1984).

DEFINING AND MONITORING A TARGET BEHAVIOR

The first step in a CM procedure is specifying a measurable target behavior to be increased or decreased. Most CM interventions target drug abstinence, but other goals have been counseling attendance, medication adherence, or a specific treatment goal or homework task (Higgins et al., 2008). There are two core elements of a CM program to promote drug abstinence: a monitoring system to detect the presence or absence of a drug, and a delivery system to consequate drug use or abstinence. Most monitoring systems involve biochemical confirmation of a drug's metabolite. For example, the cocaine metabolite benzoylecgonine can be detected in urine, and morphine in urine can signify the presence of opiates. Several on-site test cups are available to detect these and other illicit drugs (e.g., amphetamine, benzodiazepine, THC). Although detection times vary depending on dose, route of administration, metabolism, and characteristics of the drug assay (Vandevenne, Vandenbussche, & Verstraete, 2000), most urinalysis-based sampling procedures are scheduled three times per week to detect even low amounts of drug use and to provide a reasonably frequent schedule of reinforcement.

Biochemical measures of licit drug use, such as cigarette smoking and alcohol ingestion, are also available. There are two common approaches to monitoring smoking: measuring breath carbon monoxide (CO) levels and measuring cotinine levels found in urine, plasma, or saliva. Breath CO levels are typically measured using hand-held meters into which the smoker exhales. The elimination half-life of CO averages about 4 h, therefore, abstaining smokers can achieve a CO level in the nonsmoker range within 12-24 h (Javors, Hatch, & Lamb, 2005; Marrone et al., 2011; Perkins, Karelitz, & Jao, 2013). Recent studies suggest that CO cutoffs of 3-6 parts per million (ppm) provide an appropriate level of sensitivity. Also, CO samples must be taken several times per day to provide a valid index of smoking status. If nicotine replacement therapy (e.g., a nicotine patch) is not used, then cotinine, a metabolite of nicotine, can be used to detect smoking over longer durations (e.g., up to about a week; see Sigmon, Lamb, & Dallery, 2008). Relatively low-cost dip sticks may be a practical way to measure cotinine (e.g, Parker et al., 2002).

Alcohol can also be detected noninvasively in breath (Alcohol Monitoring Systems, 2013; see also Leffingwell et al., 2013). Alcohol measured in breath peaks approximately 1 h following consumption and is eliminated rapidly, which means that several tests must be conducted each day to detect use. Sweat-based assessment is another possibility (Gambelunghe et al., 2013). For example, the Secure Continuous Remote Alcohol Monitoring (SCRAM, Alcohol Monitoring Systems, 2013) bracelet detects approximately 1% of ingested alcohol that is excreted through the skin (Swift, 2003). Although potentially more costly, new biomarkers of alcohol ingestion may increase the time window for detection relative to breath-based markers. For example, McDonell et al. (2012) used ethyl glucuronide (EtG) in urine, which has a two-day detection period, in a CM intervention to promote abstinence from alcohol.

Selecting an appropriate monitoring system and the frequency of monitoring will depend on a number of factors such as the drug(s) targeted, costs, and acceptability. A complete discussion of these issues is beyond the scope of this chapter. In the remainder of this chapter, we discuss variations of CM delivery systems.

VOUCHER-BASED CONTINGENCY MANAGEMENT

A research team at the University of Vermont led by Stephen Higgins furthered the translation of operant principles into treatment settings by developing voucher-based CM. Statements of monetary earnings, or vouchers, could be earned based on the evidence of abstinence (Higgins et al., 1994, 1993, 1991), and the vouchers could be exchanged for goods and services.

Voucher-based CM was developed during the height of the cocaine epidemic in the United States, at a time when psychotherapeutic and pharmacological approaches to the treatment of cocaine dependence were equally ineffectual. The AIDS epidemic, together with the growing understanding of the importance of injection drug use and crack cocaine in the transmission of HIV (e.g., Booth, Watters, & Chitwood, 1993; Chiasson et al., 1991; Edlin et al., 1994), added further urgency to the problem. In the first voucher-based study, injection cocaine users were offered either a behavioral treatment that included the Community Reinforcement Approach (CRA; Azrin, 1976; Hunt & Azrin, 1973) and a voucher-based CM intervention, or a 12-step program (Higgins et al., 1991). This study also introduced many of the features that have become the standard for voucher-based interventions, including thrice weekly urine testing, an ascending schedule of vouchers as cocaine abstinence is maintained, a reset to the initial voucher value if a required urine sample is missed or if the target metabolite is detected in the urine, and a voucher bonus each time three drug-free samples are provided consecutively (i.e., per week of continuous abstinence). Figure 16.1 illustrates these features. Results suggested that the behavioral approach was superior on measures of treatment engagement, treatment retention, and promotion of cocaine abstinence. These findings were confirmed in a later randomized controlled trial (Higgins et al., 1993) that was similar to the first study. The results from Higgins et al. are presented in Figure 16.2.

An additional randomized controlled trial evaluated the effects of abstinence-contingent monetary vouchers in promoting cocaine abstinence (Higgins et al., 1994). Participants were randomly assigned to a control group that received CRA treatment, thrice-weekly urine testing, and feedback regarding test results, or a CM group that received an identical set of services plus monetary vouchers contingent on provision of cocaine-negative urine samples. The study evaluation period was 24 weeks. In weeks 1-12, CM participants received monetary vouchers according to an

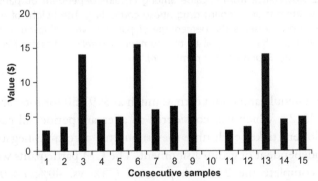

Figure 16.1 An illustration of the basic features of the ascending schedule of reinforcement used in many CM interventions. For each negative sample, the voucher value increases, and bonuses are awarded for three consecutive negative samples. The missing or positive sample at sample number 10 results in no voucher, and then a "reset" to the initial voucher value with the next negative sample. Voucher values are for illustrative purposes only.

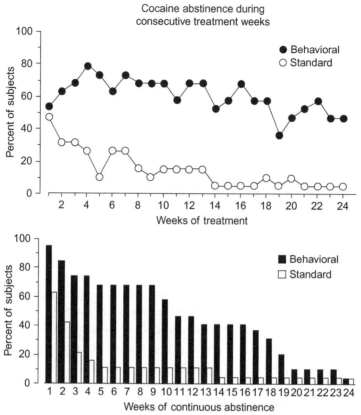

Figure 16.2 Abstinence from cocaine among cocaine-dependent outpatients given behavioral treatment or standard drug abuse counseling. The height of each bar in the lower graph represents the percentage of patients who achieved a duration of abstinence greater than or equal to the number of weeks indicated. *(From Higgins et al. (1993, p. 766). Reprinted with permission).*

ascending schedule and could earn as much as $997.50 for total abstinence. In weeks 13-24, which was considered an aftercare period, all participants earned a lottery ticket each time they submitted a cocaine-negative urine sample, independent of group assignment. The CM participants were more likely to complete the 24-week program (75% vs. 40%; $p=0.03$) and achieved longer durations of continuous cocaine abstinence on average compared to controls (11.7 weeks vs. 6.0 weeks; $p=0.03$). Because the abstinence-contingent vouchers were combined with CRA in the earlier studies, this trial is thus the first report to isolate the unique contribution of voucher-based CM to clinical outcomes and remains the most frequently cited paper in the CM literature.

Extensions of Voucher-Based Contingency Management

The success of voucher-based CM set the stage for the dozens of subsequent trials that investigated this general approach in treating every major kind of substance use disorder in a wide variety of populations. Voucher-based CM has been applied with success in inner-city and rural settings, with all major drug problems including poly-substance use, and in special populations such as adolescents, pregnant women, and individuals with co-occurring mental health disorders (e.g., Downey, Helmus, & Schuster, 2000; Piotrowski & Hall, 1999; Silverman, Chutuape, Bigelow, & Stitzer, 1996; Silverman, Higgins, et al., 1996; Silverman, Wong, et al., 1996). The broad potency of CM has been described in literature reviews and meta-analyzes (Dutra et al., 2008; Lussier, Heil, Mongeon, Badger, & Higgins, 2006). Voucher-based CM currently holds the dual distinctions of being the most rigorously tested application of behavior analytic principles in randomized controlled trials, and the most effective psychosocial approach to drug abuse treatment (Dutra et al., 2008).

Long-Term and Postintervention Effects

For many individuals, drug dependence continues over decades and often persists until death (Hser, Hoffman, Grella, & Anglin, 2001; Dennis, Scott, Funk, & Foss, 2005). It is also recognized that a propensity to relapse is a fundamental feature of drug use disorders (Hunt, Barnett, & Branch, 1971; Kirshenbaum, Olsen, & Bickel, 2009; Shah, Galai, Celentano, Vlahov, & Strathdee, 2006), independent of treatment modality. For these reasons, evaluating long-term application of CM, as well as its postintervention effects, is of utmost clinical importance.

To evaluate the long-term application of voucher-based CM in the treatment of drug dependence, Silverman, Robles, Mudric, Bigelow, and Stitzer (2004) conducted a year-long study in which methadone patients who continued to inject drugs and use cocaine were randomly assigned to one of the three groups. All participants submitted urine samples on Mondays, Wednesdays, and Fridays. Participants assigned to the control group received standard methadone treatment, which included a daily dose of methadone delivered at a clinic. Participants assigned to the Take-Home Only group received the standard methadone treatment, but were also allowed to take-home the next day's dose of methadone each time their urine sample indicated cocaine and opiate abstinence. Take-Home & Voucher group participants received the same services and contingencies as the Take-Home Only group but also received monetary vouchers contingent on cocaine and opiate abstinence. The voucher contingencies were similar to those used in other studies (e.g., an ascending schedule that reset to the original value if a sample was missed or positive; see Figure 16.1), and at their highest value paid $130 per week of continuous abstinence. Results showed that the Take Home & Voucher group had sustained high rates of cocaine- and opiate-negative samples over the course of the year and that the rates of drug abstinence were highest (and significantly higher than the other two groups) during the last three quarters of the year. This and other demonstrations of long-term application of CM (see Employment-based Contingency Management later), suggest that, for at least as long as the contingencies are maintained, they can successfully sustain drug abstinence, even in refractory drug users.

Despite growing consensus within the addiction research community that long-term care strategies are required to produce lasting and meaningful change, most treatments are still delivered under the acute care model (McLellan, Lewis, O'Brien, & Kleber, 2000; McLellan, McKay, Forman, Cacciola, & Kemp, 2005). The need for long-term care stems from poor postintervention outcomes, independent of treatment modality or approach (e.g., Burtscheidt, Wolwer, Schwarz, Strauss, & Gaebel, 2002; Hajek et al., 2013; O'Brien, 2008; Scott, Foss, & Dennis, 2005). The woeful results with respect to postintervention outcomes in the studies of addiction treatments may be best captured by noting what is missing from the literature rather than what is present. For example, a comprehensive textbook on substance abuse for medical students written by 178 leading researchers and clinicians (Ruiz & Strain, 2011) includes a section on clinical relapse prevention interventions that lacks reference to (or description of) any controlled trial demonstrating the effectiveness of a particular intervention in a clinical sample. With respect to voucher-based CM intervention, there are limited successes. For example, in the Silverman et al. (2004) study described previously, the effects of the vouchers appeared to persist throughout a 9-week postintervention follow-up period, and Take Home & Voucher participants who completed treatment submitted significantly more cocaine- and opiate-negative urine samples than their counterparts in the two nonvoucher groups during the nine weeks after the contingencies were discontinued. Because of the need for long-term care strategies and limitations on treatment funding, efforts must be made to increase access and reduce the costs of voucher-based CM interventions.

EMPLOYMENT-BASED CONTINGENCY MANAGEMENT

One promising method to increase access and reduce costs is employment-based CM, wherein access to work is contingent upon a therapeutically relevant behavior such as drug abstinence. Silverman and colleagues identified employment as a potentially ideal vehicle for implementing an intervention because it is typically open-ended, and because even relatively low wages result in pay rates that are much higher than what is typically offered in CM programs (Silverman et al., 2004). In addition, although the intervention features large-magnitude reinforcement, the cost of maintaining the intervention could be reduced to the cost of drug testing because wages from work are a standard part of any business enterprise. The only rigorously evaluated employment-based CM intervention developed to date is the Therapeutic Workplace.

The Therapeutic Workplace

The Therapeutic Workplace intervention is delivered in two phases (Silverman et al., 2005). In Phase 1, the goals are to initiate drug abstinence and build job skills. This latter goal is important because many drug dependent adults lack requisite job skills and because extensive research shows that the long-term outcomes of employment interventions are better among individuals who receive human capital development services than those receiving services that focus on quick entry to the workplace (e.g., Freedman et al., 2000). During Phase 1, payments are made in the form of monetary vouchers. Mandatory urine samples are collected thrice weekly to monitor drug taking. During an initial reinforcer sampling period, access to the Therapeutic Workplace is granted independent of the results of urinalysis. Drug abstinence contingencies are introduced individually (e.g., an opiate abstinence contingency may be introduced first, and after a period of sustained opiate abstinence, a cocaine abstinence contingency could be added). Once abstinence to all target drugs has been initiated and sufficient job skills are in place, a patient-employee can progress to Phase 2. In Phase 2, the goals are to maintain drug abstinence and engage in gainful employment. The frequency of aperiodic mandatory urine sample collection decreases as drug abstinence is maintained, and payments are made in the form of regular biweekly paychecks. It is noteworthy that in both phases of the intervention, total pay for patient-employees is determined partly by an hourly rate, and partly by various measures of workplace productivity.

The Therapeutic Workplace was evaluated in a series of three randomized controlled trials (Silverman, Svikis, Robles, Stitzer, & Bigelow, 2001; Silverman et al., 2002, 2007). Each of these studies featured chronically unemployed adults who continued to use cocaine and heroin while enrolled in methadone treatment in Baltimore, MD. In the first study, Therapeutic Workplace participants submitted significantly and substantially higher rates of cocaine-negative urine samples over the first 6 months (54% vs. 32%, $p=0.04$; Silverman et al., 2001) and 3 years (54% vs. 28%, $p=0.04$; Silverman et al., 2002) of the intervention compared to usual care. Subsequent studies isolated the effect of the abstinence contingency; Silverman et al. (2007) showed that participants attempting to initiate cocaine abstinence submitted higher rates of cocaine-negative urine samples when access to the workplace and the highest rate of pay were contingent on opiate and cocaine abstinence than when they were available independent of drug use (29% vs. 10%, $p=0.004$). Finally, DeFulio, Donlin, Wong, and Silverman (2009) investigated the role of the contingency in the maintenance of long-term drug abstinence. Participants who successfully initiated opiate and cocaine abstinence and who acquired requisite job skills during Phase 1 of the Therapeutic Workplace intervention were hired for 1 year as data entry operators in a Phase 2 Therapeutic Workplace business and randomly assigned to conditions in which the drug abstinence contingencies were retained throughout the year, or discontinued, respectively. As shown in Figure 16.3, the continuation of the drug abstinence contingency during the phase 2 period produced a significantly and substantially higher rate of cocaine-negative urine samples (79% vs. 51%; $p=0.004$). Collectively, the three core studies show that the Therapeutic Workplace initiates and maintains cocaine abstinence better than usual care and noncontingent employment, and that the Therapeutic Workplace can be effectively implemented as a long-term intervention.

Other Populations and Behavioral Targets

In addition to the original series of studies, several randomized controlled trials have demonstrated the effectiveness and utility of the Therapeutic Workplace in the treatment of homeless alcoholics (Koffarnus et al., 2011) and out-of-treatment injection drug users (Holtyn et al., 2015). Another series of three studies evaluated the Therapeutic Workplace as a means of promoting adherence to the opioid antagonist naltrexone (DeFulio et al., 2012; Dunn et al., 2013; Everly et al., 2011). Naltrexone blocks the subjective and physiological effects of opioids, but its clinical utility has been limited because most patients refuse to take it. In all three of the Therapeutic Workplace naltrexone studies, recently detoxified opiate-dependent participants were provided with naltrexone at no cost and randomly assigned to either a prescription group that could participate

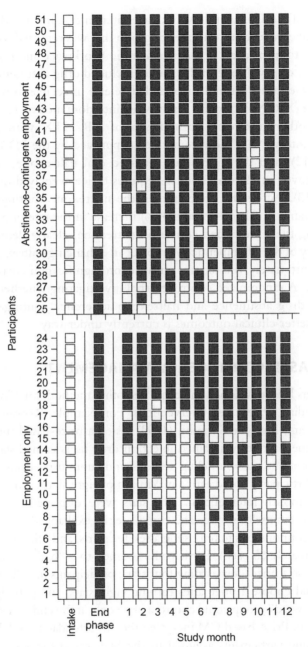

Figure 16.3 Cocaine urinalysis results at intake, end of phase 1, and across consecutive months during the intervention (phase 2). Within each panel, rows of data represent the cocaine urinalysis results for individual participants. Filled squares indicate cocaine-negative urine samples, and open squares indicate cocaine-positive urine samples. Empty sections indicate missing samples. Within each panel, participants are arranged from those showing the least abstinence (fewest cocaine-negative urine samples) on the bottom to those with the most abstinence on top. *(From DeFulio et al. (2009, p. 1534). Reprinted with permission).*

in Phase 1 of the Therapeutic Workplace intervention independent of naltrexone adherence, or a contingency group that was required to adhere to naltrexone to gain access to the Therapeutic Workplace and maintain the highest rate of pay. None of the studies included drug abstinence contingencies. One study featured an extended-release injectable formulation of naltrexone (XR-NTX) with a three-week interdose interval (Everly et al., 2011), another featured a formulation of XR-NTX with a 4-week interdose interval that had recently been approved by the FDA (DeFulio et al., 2012), and the third study featured oral naltrexone, which was FDA approved in 1984 and which requires thrice-weekly dosing (Dunn et al., 2013). Across the three studies, the naltrexone contingency produced a dramatic (31%, 48%, and 38%) increase in the rate of participants completing their prescribed course of naltrexone, clearly demonstrating the efficacy of the Therapeutic Workplace in enhancing naltrexone adherence. Unfortunately, this did not translate into significant increases in drug abstinence. A randomized controlled trial investigating whether a combination of drug abstinence and naltrexone adherence contingencies can produce better clinical outcomes is currently under way.

PRIZE-BASED CONTINGENCY MANAGEMENT

Researchers have developed and evaluated other methods for administering CM, including prize-based interventions. For example, Rowan-Szal, Joe, Chatham, and Dwayne Simpson (1994) tested a prize-based intervention in which methadone-maintained injection drug users earned stars contingent upon attending counseling sessions and submitting drug-free urine samples. Participants could earn a maximum of eight stars each month during the 3-month intervention. The stars were displayed on a bulletin board in the counselor's office and could later be exchanged for small prizes (i.e., food coupons, bus tokens, sunglasses, tee shirts, and other prizes valued at approximately $5 each). Participants assigned to a "high reward" group could choose a prize after earning four stars, participants in a "low reward" group could choose a prize after earning eight stars, and participants in a "delayed reward" group could choose a prize only at the end of the 3-month intervention. Prize-based CM increased therapy attendance and drug abstinence among participants assigned to the high reward group. Thus, this study was the first to demonstrate that relatively low-cost prizes could be used to increase compliance with substance abuse treatment goals in a community-based treatment program.

Petry, Martin, Cooney, and Kranzler (2000) later extended the findings of Rowan-Szal et al. (1994) to a group of alcohol–dependent US military veterans. This study is one of only a handful of empirical reports to demonstrate that CM can be used to promote abstinence from alcohol. Petry et al. showed that prizes contingent upon blood alcohol content (BAC) indicative of abstinence significantly increased the number of participants retained in treatment relative to a standard treatment condition (84% vs. 22%; $p < 0.001$) and increased the number of participants who demonstrated continuous alcohol abstinence (69% vs. 39%; $p < 0.05$).

The intervention developed by Petry et al. (2000) was particularly noteworthy because the researchers made several modifications to prize-based CM that helped lower treatment costs and increase the dissemination potential of CM. For example, they used an intermittent, lottery-based schedule of reinforcement in which each negative BAC sample resulted in an opportunity to earn a prize of variable magnitude, but not every opportunity resulted in a prize. Participants could draw a slip of paper from a fishbowl each time they submitted a Breathalyzer sample indicative of abstinence. About 25% of the slips were nonwinning slips, which stated, "Sorry, try again," and 75% of the slips were winning slips that could be exchanged for small prizes (e.g., bus tokens, $1 McDonald's gift certificates), medium prizes (e.g., radios, watches, and $20 gift certificates at various retail outlets), and large prizes (e.g., handheld televisions or boom boxes valued at approximately $100).

Subsequent studies by Petry and other researchers have shown that the "fishbowl" method of prize-based CM can be used to promote abstinence in a variety of substance-dependent populations (e.g., Lott & Jencius, 2009; Peirce et al., 2006; Petry & Alessi, 2010). The procedures for implementing prize-based CM are described in detail in Petry (2012). Briefly, contingencies are arranged such that the probability of earning a large prize is low, the probability of earning an intermediate or small prize is higher, and the probability of not winning a prize is highest. For example, in a typical intervention, 500 slips of paper are added to a prize bowl. One slip (i.e., 0.2% of the slips) can be exchanged for a large prize valued at $100, more slips (e.g., 40 slips; 8%) can be exchanged for medium prizes valued at $20, a much greater number of slips (e.g., 209; 41.8%) can be exchanged for small prizes valued at $1, and the greatest number of slips (e.g., 250; 50%) are nonwinners, which state, "Good job!" Although the probability of earning a prize may vary between interventions, this probability should be relatively high in order for the schedule of reinforcement to be maximally effective

(Ghitza et al., 2007). In addition, contingencies similar to those used in voucher-based CM should be included to promote continuous abstinence. In other words, consecutive negative samples should result in additional opportunities to win prizes such that the first sample indicative of drug abstinence might result in one prize draw, the second consecutive negative sample might result in two prize draws, the third consecutive negative sample might result in three draws, and so on. This ascending schedule of reinforcement combined with the variable-ratio-like properties of prize-based CM has been shown to generate high rates of behavior at relatively low costs (e.g., Peirce et al., 2006; Petry, Alessi, Hanson, & Sierra, 2007; Petry, Alessi, Marx, Austin, & Tardif, 2005).

TECHNOLOGY-BASED CONTINGENCY MANAGEMENT

One potential limitation of CM interventions is that both drug monitoring and reward delivery are typically conducted in person. That is, a researcher or clinician must be physically present to perform these procedures. The limitation is that access to treatment clinics that provide CM may be restricted, either due to transportation difficulties or to geographical distance. One way to circumvent these difficulties is to harness advances in digital and information technologies to monitor and reinforce drug abstinence (Dallery & Raiff, 2011; Marsch & Dallery, 2012).

Dallery and colleagues developed and evaluated the first Internet-based CM intervention to promote smoking cessation (Dallery, Glenn, & Raiff, 2007; Dallery, Meredith, & Glenn, 2008; Dallery & Raiff, 2011; Stoops et al., 2009). Smokers used web-cameras to record themselves blowing into breath CO monitors, which provided evidence of smoking status. Consequences in the form of money and social feedback were delivered immediately to individuals who met CO cutpoints for abstinence using an automated, web-based program called Mōtiv8. Results suggested that Internet-based CM can promote smoking cessation in heavy (Dallery et al., 2007), rural (Stoops et al., 2009), and adolescent (Reynolds, Dallery, Shroff, Patak, & Leraas, 2008) smokers. Dallery, Raiff, and Grabinski (2013) conducted a randomized trial of Internet-based CM. Participants ($n = 39$) assigned to the Contingent Group earned vouchers contingent on submitting web-camera recorded videos of breath carbon monoxide (CO) samples < 4 ppm. Voucher earnings for participants assigned to the Noncontingent Group ($n = 38$) were yoked to participant earnings in the Contingent Group. The median percentages of negative samples during the intervention phases in the Noncontingent and Contingent Groups were 25.0% and 66.7%, respectively. Group differences in abstinence, however, were not maintained at 3- and 6-month follow-up assessments.

To partially offset the costs associated with monetary-based CM, Dallery et al. (2008) used the Internet-based CM model in combination with a deposit contract procedure (see also Paxton, 1980, 1981, 1983; Winett, 1973). The procedure required an up-front deposit by the participant, which could be earned back based on the evidence of abstinence. Eight smokers were randomly assigned to a deposit contract ($50) or to a nondeposit group. The nondeposit group experienced a traditional CM program, in which the maximum amount for continued abstinence was $78.80. Participants in the deposit group could recoup their $50 deposit for smoking reductions and abstinence (breath carbon monoxide ≤ 4 ppm) during treatment phases, plus an additional $28.80 in vouchers (total of $78.80). As expected, there were no differences between groups in terms of abstinence (and amount of money earned), with 65% ($156.90) and 63% ($178.90) negative samples for the deposit and nondeposit groups, respectively. However, because $200 was paid to researchers by participants in the deposit group, a $43.10 surplus remained in this group. The surplus was used to supplement experimental costs in the nondeposit group (e.g., vouchers). As another strategy to offset costs, Raiff, Jarvis, and Rapoza (2012) proposed a novel method to deliver reinforcers in the context of a video game. Game-based consequences such as points, badges, and leveling to new game environments would be accessible based on the evidence of smoking abstinence. Such a program would represent an innovative integration of CM with game-based procedures (King, Greaves, Exeter, & Darzi, 2013; McCallum, 2012).

The Internet-based CM model has also been used to incorporate group contingencies, where small groups of smokers must collectively achieve cessation goals to receive consequences (Meredith & Dallery, 2013; Meredith, Grabinski, & Dallery, 2011; see also Kirby, Kerwin, Carpenedo, Rosenwasser, & Gardner, 2008). Participants can also provide and/or receive encouragement, feedback, and support via a discussion board integrated into the Mōtiv8 architecture. Using a multiple baseline design, Meredith et al. found that fewer than 1% of CO samples submitted during baseline were negative for smoking, compared to 57% submitted during the treatment phase. In addition, 65% of participants' comments on the online peer support forum were rated as positive by independent observers. The group contingency model could aid in the sustainability of the intervention after monetary consequences are withdrawn. That is, the group could continue to interact and provide social consequences for continued mainte-nance of abstinence, lapses to smoking, and so on with no increase in the costs of the intervention.

In addition to smoking cessation, two technology-based CM interven-tions have been used to promote alcohol abstinence. In the first intervention, Barnett, Tidey, Murphy, Swift, and Colby (2011) used SCRAM to monitor alcohol intake. Compared to a SCRAM-monitoring phase during the first week of the study, average transdermal alcohol concentrations decreased by 72% when Internet-based CM was used during the second and the third weeks. In the second intervention, Alessi and Petry (2013) used video-based monitoring via mobile phones to assess abstinence from alcohol. For 4 weeks, researchers texted participants one to three times daily to indicate that a breathalyzer test was due within the hour. Participants were randomized to either a monitoring alone or to a monitoring plus CM condition. Adherence was high and equivalent between groups (88.6% of the scheduled videos were submitted), and the CM group submitted significantly more negative breath samples than the monitoring alone group (87.1% vs. 66.9%).

Overall, the use of technology can enable broad access to CM. In an ongoing clinical trial, qualified smokers from anywhere in the United States can access the intervention. In addition, Alessi and Petry (2013) and Hertzberg et al. (2013) demonstrated the feasibility of using mobile phones to collect objective evidence of alcohol and smoking status, respectively, using video. Mobile phone-based CM has the potential to further increase access beyond the capacity of computer plus Internet methods. Thus, Meredith, Jarvis, et al. (2014) developed and tested the first, integrated mobile phone-based breath CO meter. These developments suggest that technology can both increase access and decrease the response burden to maintain adherence. Furthermore, technology may increase the sustainability of the intervention for long durations, particularly in concert with low-cost contingencies (e.g., deposit contracts, group contingencies, prize-based consequences).

DESIGNING A CONTINGENCY MANAGEMENT INTERVENTION: PARAMETERS AND PROCEDURES

CM interventions are comprised of a number of components that can be implemented in a variety of ways (Meredith, Robinson, et al., 2014; Petry, 2000). Once a reliable and valid monitoring system is selected, the researcher or clinician must select a CM intervention (e.g., voucher- or prize-based). In addition, a number of specific parameters of the CM intervention must be selected to maximize cost effectiveness and access to treatment. For example, the clinician must select parameters of reinforcement (e.g., delay, magnitude) to maximize the probability of successful outcomes. Selection of "incorrect" parameters may render the intervention ineffective, which could lead to the erroneous conclusion that the principles underlying the intervention do not work or that they will not work for a particular population or individual. In clinical practice, the parameters of a specific CM program may need to be modified iteratively, using experimental methods, to reveal the optimal program for a specific population or treatment setting.

One variable that has been shown to influence CM outcomes is reinforcer magnitude (Lussier et al., 2006). In general, interventions that have relatively larger reinforcer magnitudes (e.g., monetary values) produce relatively larger increases in drug abstinence. For example, Silverman and colleagues (Silverman, Chutuape, Bigelow, & Stitzer, 1999) investigated the efficacy of three different voucher magnitudes in initiating cocaine abstinence among participants who were previously treatment resistant in a CM intervention. The authors compared no vouchers, a low magnitude schedule (total possible earnings = $382), and a high magnitude schedule (total possible earnings = $3480). Significantly more participants provided cocaine abstinent samples during the high magnitude condition (46%), versus the control (8%) and low (14%) magnitude conditions (Dallery, Silverman, Chutuape, Bigelow, & Stitzer, 2001; Silverman et al., 1999). Similar outcomes have been shown with tobacco smoking (Stitzer & Bigelow, 1983). Counseling and job-training attendance rates are also sensitive to the magnitude of reinforcement provided for engaging in these clinical activities (Kidorf, Stitzer, & Brooner, 1994; Silverman, Chutuape, et al., 1996).

Another consideration in designing a CM intervention in a clinical setting is the schedule of reinforcement. The most common schedule of reinforcement used in CM interventions is the ascending schedule of reinforcer delivery with resets of the voucher value for the evidence of lapses or missed samples (Roll & Higgins, 2000; Roll et al., 2006; Roll, Reilly, & Johanson, 2000; Roll & Shoptaw, 2006; see Figure 16.1). One study found that a schedule that included ascending values plus resets resulted in greater rates of smoking abstinence than an ascending schedule without resets, and greater rates of abstinence compared to a fixed schedule in which the same amount was available for each negative sample (Roll & Higgins, 2000).

One potential problem with an ascending schedule of reinforcement is the low initial value of the consequence for abstinence. Several researchers

have noted that a number of participants never contact the monetary reinforcers for abstinence (Correia, Sigmon, Silverman, Bigelow, & Stitzer,
2005). It is possible that the low initial value is not high enough to promote
initial abstinence. One study suggested that increasing the initial voucher
earnings did not result in a higher rate of cocaine abstinence compared to
the standard ascending schedule of reinforcement (Silverman et al., 1998).
Another study, however, found that participants who received a high magnitude voucher immediately upon demonstrating abstinence showed longer
periods of sustained cocaine abstinence, relative to the traditional ascending
schedule with a reset contingency (Kirby, Marlowe, Festinger, Lamb, &
Platt, 1998). A number of parameters may have been confounded in this
study (e.g., immediacy, frequency, and overall magnitude), so it is unclear
whether the higher rates of abstinence were a result of the initial higher magnitude or because of some other variables.

Another possible reason why some participants do not achieve abstinence
is that most CM interventions require an abrupt transition to complete abstinence. Gradual reductions in drug use may permit greater contact with monetary reinforcers for changing drug use behavior. Several studies suggest that
gradual reductions in drug use, or shaping procedures, can generate high initial
rates of abstinence in cocaine- (Correia et al., 2005) and nicotine-dependent
individuals (Lamb, Kirby, Morral, Galbicka, & Iguchi, 2004, 2010; Lamb
et al., 2007). Shaping procedures are only possible if some quantitative or
semiquantitative monitoring of drug status is available. These monitoring procedures may also permit reinforcement of briefer periods of abstinence (e.g., a
day) compared to monitoring procedures that require longer durations of drug
clearance before a negative sample can be detected.

A number of resources are available for clinicians and administrators who
are interested in implementing a CM procedure. Several excellent resources
for implementing CM can be found online at http://www.bettertxoutcomes.
org/bettertxoutcomes/. In addition, Petry et al. (2001) described a series of
case studies that illustrate the versatility of CM across a range of settings, target
behaviors, and reinforcers. For example, one case describes an individual with
cocaine-induced psychotic episodes on a regimen of methadone maintenance.
The CM intervention reinforced abstinence from opioids and cocaine by
using the chance to win prizes. Another case describes an individual with
cocaine dependence and paranoid schizophrenia who was chronically misus-
ing psychiatric emergency room services. The CM plan involved using portions of his disability payments as reinforcers contingent upon drug abstinence,
medication compliance, and appropriate use of therapeutic services.

DISSEMINATION OF CONTINGENCY MANAGEMENT: CHALLENGES AND OPPORTUNITIES

Challenges to Dissemination

Like many other evidence-based psychotherapies and behavioral interventions, CM has been slow to diffuse to the clinic (McGovern, Fox, Xie, & Drake, 2004). One barrier to dissemination is treatment acceptability. Despite dozens of empirical reports demonstrating the efficacy of CM, many clinicians believe that CM-based treatment approaches are ineffective (Herbeck, Hser, & Teruya, 2008) and that such approaches fail to address the underlying causes of substance abuse (Kirby, Benishek, Dugosh, & Kerwin, 2006). However, treatment providers' negative opinions and misperceptions about CM can be corrected through education and training. Recent studies have shown that exposure to CM or experience with this evidence-based intervention is associated with more positive provider beliefs about the treatment (Benishek, Kirby, Dugosh, & Padovano, 2010; Hartzler, Jackson, Jones, Beadnell, & Calsyn, 2014; Kirby et al., 2012) and that education and training are positively associated with acceptance and adoption of CM by community-based treatment providers (Kirby et al., 2006; McCarty et al., 2007; Rash, Dephilippis, McKay, Drapkin, & Petry, 2013).

Unfavorable opinions of CM and insufficient training and experience with this treatment approach are not the only barriers to dissemination. Treatment providers often report that the cost of monetary consequences is the most substantial barrier to dissemination (Benishek et al., 2010; Kirby et al., 2006). To circumvent this barrier, researchers have developed and tested a variety of innovative strategies to reduce or offset incentive costs without compromising treatment efficacy. Many of these strategies have been discussed throughout this chapter. For example, deposit contracts can be used to offset incentive costs (e.g., Dallery et al., 2008), and creative contingency arrangements, such as harnessing the reinforcing potential of wages from work (e.g., Silverman et al., 2001), prize-based CM (e.g., Petry, 2012), and group CM (e.g., Meredith & Dallery, 2013; Meredith et al., 2011), can be used to reduce incentive costs. In addition, treatment providers can solicit donations from the community. For instance, Amass and Kamien (2004) secured $161,000 in donations over a 34-month period from the Los Angeles community to fund CM for pregnant, postpartum, and parenting drug users. Notably, when cash and prizes are not an option for treatment providers, clinicians can choose from whatever other potential reinforcers they have at their disposal (e.g., clinic privileges; Chutuape,

Silverman, & Stitzer, 1998). However, treatment providers should use preference assessments to increase the probability that particular consequences will function as reinforcers (Amass, Bickel, Crean, Higgins, & Badger, 1996; Chutuape et al., 1998).

Recent Dissemination Efforts

A major goal of the Clinical Trials Network (CTN) of the National Institute on Drug Abuse (NIDA) is to disseminate evidence-based interventions into community-based treatment centers. Collaboration between researchers working with the CTN and leadership within the New York City Health and Hospitals Corporation (HHC) led to the adoption of CM by the HHC Chemical Dependency Treatment Services. A report by Kellogg and colleagues indicated that CM adoption by the HHC increased patient motivation for recovery, facilitated treatment goal attainment, improved staff morale, and enhanced relationships between patients and staff (Kellogg et al., 2005). Although CM was initially met with resistance by clinicians, attitudes began to change when the treatment providers observed improvements in patients' behavior. Whereas counselors and staff once viewed positive consequences as bribes, after experience with CM, they viewed them as opportunities to praise patients for meeting treatment goals. Counselors began congratulating patients for meeting their goals, rather than criticizing them when they failed to do so. Thus, clinicians not only developed more favorable opinions of CM, the overall culture of the clinics changed.

Other reports also highlight attempts to integrate CM into community-based substance use disorder clinics (e.g., Henggeler et al., 2008; Lott & Jencius, 2009; Petry, Alessi, & Ledgerwood, 2012; Walker et al., 2010). In addition, recent efforts have been made to integrate CM into juvenile drug courts (Henggeler, McCart, Cunningham, & Chapman, 2012) and veterans' health care (Hagedorn et al., 2013). For example, in 2011, the Department of Veterans Affairs (VA) sponsored CM training and implementation in over 100 outpatient VA programs around the country (Rash et al., 2013). Initial reports indicated that trainers, clinicians, and patients found training and implementation to be highly successful, and the VA committed additional funds to CM dissemination efforts in the summer of 2012 (Petry, DePhilippis, Rash, Drapkin, & McKay, 2014). Overall, however, CM adoption remains relatively low at community-based substance abuse treatment clinics (Gifford et al., 2012; Roman, Abraham, Rothrauff, & Knudsen, 2010).

To promote CM dissemination, more research is needed to improve sustainability. One way to enhance sustainability may be to increase treatment duration without increasing costs. This strategy can be accomplished by increasing the response requirements placed on patients by gradually thinning the schedule of reinforcement. Once behavior is established, basic and applied behavior analytic research has shown that relatively small and infrequent reinforcers can sustain behavior change over an extended duration (Baer, Blount, Detrich, & Stokes, 1987; Ferster & Skinner, 1957; Freeland & Noell, 2002).

CONCLUSIONS

Over the past three decades, CM procedures have evolved substantially to increase efficacy, access, and cost effectiveness. This chapter has described innovations in monitoring systems and CM delivery systems across a range of drug classes, populations, and settings. CM represents one of the most successful translational applications of behavior analytic principles and procedures to a diverse range of public health problems including substance abuse (see also the Chapter 22).

Several challenges remain, however, such as prolonging postintervention effects. Addressing the challenges associated with CM interventions will entail continued translational and applied research on CM procedures and parameters. Several examples of such translations to the clinic already exist, such as assessments of effects of reinforcement rate, delay, and magnitude on drug abstinence (e.g., Festinger, Dugosh, Kirby, & Seymour, 2014; Ghitza et al., 2007; Kirby et al., 1998; Packer, Howell, McPherson, & Roll, 2012). In addition, innovative animal and human laboratory models of CM will help inform CM interventions (e.g., Bouton & Schepers, 2013; Dallery & Raiff, 2007; Kearns & Weiss, 2007; Lesage, 2009). For example, Bouton and Schepers developed an animal model of relapse that can occur following termination of a CM intervention. Their model suggests new methods to prevent relapse, such as developing techniques to promote generalization between the intervention and relapse situations. Indeed, more research is needed on behavioral technologies to promote generalization of treatment effects across situations and time (Stokes & Baer, 1977).

Although this chapter focused on contingencies of reinforcement to promote drug abstinence, such a focus should not belie the considerable complexity of the environmental, sociocultural, and biological influences on substance abuse. CM is just one of many evidence-based behavioral and pharmacological treatments, and in practice several treatments are used together in a complementary fashion to address these influences. Furthermore, in addition to promoting drug use reductions and abstinence, the goals of substance abuse treatment can include decreasing high risk behavior (e.g., sharing needles, unprotected sex) and increasing occupational, social, and recreational functioning. CM targeting drug outcomes can aid in reaching these goals, and also help enhance treatment engagement and the patient-clinician relationship. CM can also be used to target some of these other outcomes directly (e.g., Iguchi, Belding, Morral, Lamb, & Husband, 1997). Overall, behavior analytic principles and procedures have been quite successful in addressing substance abuse, but there remains considerable work to be done to refine and disseminate CM interventions to impact public health in a sustainable, cost-effective manner.

REFERENCES

Aigner, T. G., & Balster, R. L. (1978). Choice behavior in rhesus monkeys: Cocaine versus food. *Science, 201*, 534–535.

Alcohol Monitoring Systems. (2013). Retrieved from http://www.alcoholmonitoring.com/index/scram/scram-remote-breath.

Alessi, S. M., & Petry, N. M. (2013). A randomized study of cellphone technology to reinforce alcohol abstinence in the natural environment. *Addiction, 108*, 900–909.

Amass, L., Bickel, W. K., Crean, J. P., Higgins, S. T., & Badger, G. J. (1996). Preferences for clinic privileges, retail items and social activities in an outpatient buprenorphine treatment program. *Journal of Substance Abuse Treatment, 13*, 43–49.

Amass, L., & Kamien, J. (2004). A tale of two cities: Financing two voucher programs for substance abusers through community donations. *Experimental and Clinical Psychopharmacology, 12*(2), 147.

Azrin, N. H. (1976). Improvements in the community-reinforcement approach to alcoholism. *Behaviour Research and Therapy, 14*(5), 339–348.

Baer, R. A., Blount, R. L., Detrich, R., & Stokes, T. F. (1987). Using intermittent reinforcement to program maintenance of verbal/nonverbal correspondence. *Journal of Applied Behavior Analysis, 20*, 179–184.

Barnett, N. P., Tidey, J., Murphy, J. G., Swift, R., & Colby, S. M. (2011). Contingency management for alcohol use reduction: A pilot study using a transdermal alcohol sensor. *Drug and Alcohol Dependence, 118*(2), 391–399.

Benishek, L. A., Kirby, K. C., Dugosh, K. L., & Padovano, A. (2010). Beliefs about the empirical support of drug abuse treatment interventions: A survey of outpatient treatment providers. *Drug and Alcohol Dependence, 107*(2-3), 202–208. http://dx.doi.org/10.1016/j.drugalcdep.2009.10.013; 10.1016/j.drugalcdep.2009.10.013.

Bigelow, G. E., Brooner, R. K., & Silverman, K. (1998). Competing motivations: Drug reinforcement vs non-drug reinforcement. *Journal of Psychopharmacology (Oxford, England), 12*(1), 8–14.

Booth, R. E., Watters, J. K., & Chitwood, D. D. (1993). HIV risk-related sex behaviors among injection drug users, crack smokers, and injection drug users who smoke crack. *American Journal of Public Health, 83*(8), 1144–1148.

Bouton, M. E., & Schepers, S. T. (2013). Resurgence of instrumental behavior after an abstinence contingency. *Learning and Behavior, 42*, 131–143.

Burtscheidt, W., Wolwer, W., Schwarz, R., Strauss, W., & Gaebel, W. (2002). Out-patient behaviour therapy in alcoholism: treatment outcome after 2 years. *Acta Psychiatrica Scandinavica, 106*(3), 227–232.

Carroll, M. E. (1996). Reducing drug abuse by enriching the environment with alternative nondrug reinforcers. In L. Green & J. H. Kagel (Eds.), *Advances in behavioral economics: Substance use and abuse* (Vol. 3, pp. 37–68). Norwood, NJ: Ablex Publishing.

Chiasson, M. A., Stoneburner, R. L., Hildebrandt, D. S., Ewing, W. E., Telzak, E. E., & Jaffe, H. W. (1991). Heterosexual transmission of HIV-1 associated with the use of smokable freebase cocaine (crack). *AIDS, 5*(9), 1121–1126.

Chutuape, M. A., Silverman, K., & Stitzer, M. L. (1998). Survey assessment of methadone treatment services as reinforcers. *The American Journal of Drug and Alcohol Abuse, 24*, 1–16.

Correia, C. J., Sigmon, S. C., Silverman, K., Bigelow, G., & Stitzer, M. L. (2005). A comparison of voucher-delivery schedules for the initiation of cocaine abstinence. *Experimental and Clinical Psychopharmacology, 13*(3), 253–258. http://dx.doi.org/10.1037/1064-1297.13.3.253.

Dallery, J., Glenn, I. M., & Raiff, B. R. (2007). An internet-based abstinence reinforcement treatment for cigarette smoking. *Drug and Alcohol Dependence, 86*(2–3), 230–238. http://dx.doi.org/10.1016/j.drugalcdep.2006.06.013.

Dallery, J., Meredith, S., & Glenn, I. M. (2008). A deposit contract method to deliver abstinence reinforcement for cigarette smoking. *Journal of Applied Behavior Analysis, 41*(4), 609–615.

Dallery, J., & Raiff, B. R. (2007). Delay discounting predicts cigarette smoking in a laboratory model of abstinence reinforcement. *Psychopharmacology, 190*, 485–496.

Dallery, J., & Raiff, B. R. (2011). Contingency management in the 21st century: Technological innovations to promote smoking cessation. *Substance Use & Misuse, 46*(1), 10–22. http://dx.doi.org/10.3109/10826084.2011.521067.

Dallery, J., Raiff, B. R., & Grabinski, M. (2013). Internet-based contingency management to promote smoking cessation: a randomized, controlled study. *Journal of Applied Behavior Analysis, 46*, 750–764.

Dallery, J., Silverman, K., Chutuape, M. A., Bigelow, G. E., & Stitzer, M. L. (2001). Voucher-based reinforcement of opiate plus cocaine abstinence in treatment-resistant methadone patients: Effects of reinforcer magnitude. *Experimental and Clinical Psychopharmacology, 9*(3), 317–325.

DeFulio, A., Donlin, W. D., Wong, C. J., & Silverman, K. (2009). Employment-based abstinence reinforcement as a maintenance intervention for the treatment of cocaine dependence: A randomized controlled trial. *Addiction, 104*(9), 1530–1538.

DeFulio, A., Everly, J. J., Leoutsakos, J. M., Umbricht, A., Fingerhood, M., Bigelow, G. E., et al. (2012). Employment-based reinforcement of adherence to an FDA approved extended release formulation of naltrexone in opioid-dependent adults: a randomized controlled trial. *Drug and Alcohol Dependence, 120*(1–3), 48–54.

Dennis, M. L., Scott, C. K., Funk, R., & Foss, M. A. (2005). The duration and correlates of addiction and treatment careers. *Journal of Substance Abuse Treatment, 28*(Suppl. 1), S51–S62.

Downey, K. K., Helmus, T. C., & Schuster, C. R. (2000). Treatment of heroin-dependent poly-drug abusers with contingency management and buprenorphine maintenance. *Experimental and Clinical Psychopharmacology, 8*(2), 176–184. http://dx.doi.org/10.1037/1064-1297.8.2.176.

Dunn, K. E., DeFulio, A., Everly, J. J., Donlin, W. D., Aklin, W. M., Nuzzo, P. A., et al. (2013). Employment-based reinforcement of adherence to oral naltrexone treatment in unemployed injection drug users. *Experimental and Clincial Psychopharmacology, 21*(1), 74–83.

Dutra, L., Stathopoulou, G., Basden, S. L., Leyro, T. M., Powers, M. B., & Otto, M. W. (2008). A meta-analytic review of psychosocial interventions for substance use disorders. *The American Journal of Psychiatry*, *165*(2), 179–187. http://dx.doi.org/10.1176/appi. ajp.2007.06111851.

Edlin, B. R., Irwin, K. L., Farugue, S., McCoy, C. B., Word, C., Serrano, Y., et al. (1994). Intersecting epidemics—crack cocaine use and HIV infection among inner-city young adults. Multicenter cocaine and HIV infection study team. *The New England Journal of Medicine*, *331*(21), 1422–1427.

Everly, J. J., DeFulio, A., Koffarnus, M. N., Leoutsakos, J. M., Donlin, W. D., Aklin, W. M., et al. (2011). Employment-based reinforcement of adherence to depot naltrexone in unemployed opioid-dependent adults: A randomized controlled trial. *Addiction*, *106* (7), 1309–1318.

Ferster, C. B., & Skinner, B. (1957). *Schedules of reinforcement.* New York: Appleton-Century-Crofts.

Festinger, D. S., Dugosh, K. L., Kirby, K. C., & Seymour, B. L. (2014). Contingency management for cocaine treatment: Cash vs. vouchers. *Journal of Substance Abuse Treatment*, *47*, 168–174.

Freedman, S., Friedlander, D., Hamilton, G., Rock, J., Mitchell, M., Nudelman, J., et al. (2000). *Evaluating alternative welfare-to-work approaches: Two-year impacts for eleven programs. National evaluation of welfare-to-work strategies.* Washington, DC: U.S. Department of Education. Retrieved from: http://www.mdrc.org/sites/default/files/full_93.pdf.

Freeland, J. T., & Noell, G. H. (2002). Programming for maintenance: An investigation of delayed intermittent reinforcement and common stimuli to create indiscriminable contingencies. *Journal of Behavioral Education*, *11*, 5–18.

Gambelunghe, C., Rossi, R., Aroni, K., Bacci, M., Lazzarini, A., De Giovanni, N., et al. (2013). Sweat testing to monitor drug exposure. *Annals of Clinical and Laboratory Science*, *43*(1), 22–30.

Ghitza, U. E., Epstein, D. H., Schmittner, J., Vahabzadeh, M., Lin, J. L., & Preston, K. L. (2007). Randomized trial of prize-based reinforcement density for simultaneous abstinence from cocaine and heroin. *Journal of Consulting and Clinical Psychology*, *75*, 765–774.

Gifford, E. V., Tavakoli, S., Weingardt, K. R., Finney, J. W., Pierson, H. M., Rosen, C. S., et al. (2012). How do components of evidence-based psychological treatment cluster in practice? A survey and cluster analysis. *Journal of Substance Abuse Treatment*, *42*, 45–55.

Griffiths, R. R., Bigelow, G. E., & Henningfield, J. E. (1980). *Similarities in animal and human drug-taking behavior. Advances in substance abuse* (Vol. 1, pp. 1–90). USA: JAI Press Inc.

Hagedorn, H. J., Noorbaloochi, S., Simon, A. B., Bangerter, A., Stitzer, M. L., Stetler, C. B., et al. (2013). Rewarding early abstinence in veterans health administration addiction clinics. *Journal of Substance Abuse Treatment*, *45*, 109–117.

Hajek, P., Stead, L. F., West, R., Jarvis, M., Hartmann-Boyce, J., & Lancaster, T. (2013). Relapse prevention interventions for smoking cessation. *Cochrane Databse Systematic Reviews*, *8*, CD003999.

Hartzler, B., Jackson, T. R., Jones, B. E., Beadnell, B., & Calsyn, D. A. (2014). Disseminating contingency management: Impacts of staff training and implementation at an opiate treatment program. *Journal of Substance Abuse Treatment*, *46*(4), 429–438. http://dx.doi. org/10.1016/j.jsat.2013.12.007; 10.1016/j.jsat.2013.12.007.

Henggeler, S. W., Chapman, J. E., Rowland, M. D., Halliday-Boykins, C. A., Randall, J., Shackelford, J., et al. (2008). Statewide adoption and initial implementation of contingency management for substance-abusing adolescents. *Journal of Consulting and Clinical Psychology*, *76*(4), 556–567. http://dx.doi.org/10.1037/0022-006X.76.4.556; 10.1037/0022-006X.76.4.556.

Henggeler, S. W., McCart, M. R., Cunningham, P. B., & Chapman, J. E. (2012). Enhancing the effectiveness of juvenile drug courts by integrating evidence-based practices. *Journal of Consulting and Clinical Psychology*, *80*(2), 264–275. http://dx.doi.org/10.1037/a0027147; 10.1037/a0027147.

Herbeck, D. M., Hser, Y. I., & Teruya, C. (2008). Empirically supported substance abuse treatment approaches: A survey of treatment providers' perspectives and practices. *Addictive Behaviors*, *33*(5), 699–712. http://dx.doi.org/10.1016/j.addbeh.2007.12.003; 10.1016/j.addbeh.2007.12.003.

Herrnstein, R. J. (1970). On the law of effect. *Journal of the Experimental Analysis of Behavior*, *13*, 243–266.

Herrnstein, R. J., & Prelec, D. (1992). A theory of addiction. In J. Elster (Ed.), *Choice over time* (pp. 331–360). New York, USA: Russell Sage Foundation.

Hertzberg, J. S., Carpenter, V. L., Kirby, A. C., Calhoun, P. S., Moore, S. D., Dennis, M. F., et al. (2013). Mobile contingency management as an adjunctive smoking cessation treatment for smokers with posttraumatic stress disorder. *Nicotine & Tobacco Research*, *15*(11), 1934–1938. http://dx.doi.org/10.1093/ntr/ntt060.

Heyman, G. M. (2009). *Addiction: A disorder of choice*. Cambridge, MA, USA: Harvard University Press.

Higgins, S. T., Budney, A. J., Bickel, W. K., Foerg, F. E., Donham, R., & Badger, G. J. (1994). Incentives improve outcome in outpatient behavioral treatment of cocaine dependence. *Archives of General Psychiatry*, *51*(7), 568–576.

Higgins, S. T., Budney, A. J., Bickel, W. K., Hughes, J. R., Foerg, F., & Badger, G. (1993). Achieving cocaine abstinence with a behavioral approach. *The American Journal of Psychiatry*, *150*(5), 763–769.

Higgins, S. T., Delaney, D. D., Budney, A. J., Bickel, W. K., Hughes, J. R., Foerg, F., et al. (1991). A behavioral approach to achieving initial cocaine abstinence. *The American Journal of Psychiatry*, *148*(9), 1218–1224.

Higgins, S. T., Silverman, K., & Heil, S. H. (2008). *Contingency management in substance abuse treatment*. New York, USA: Guilford Press.

Holtyn, A. F., DeFulio, A., & Silverman, K. (2015). Academic skills of chronically unemployed drug-addicted adults. *Journal of Vocational Rehabilitation*, *42*, 67–74.

Hser, Y. I., Hoffman, V., Grella, G. E., & Anglin, M. D. (2001). A 33-year follow-up of narcotics addicts. *Archives of General Psychiatry*, *58*(5), 503–508.

Hunt, G. M., & Azrin, N. H. (1973). A community-reinforcement approach to alcoholism. *Behaviour Research and Therapy*, *11*(1), 91–104. http://dx.doi.org/10.1016/0005-7967(73)90072-7.

Hunt, W. A., Barnett, L. W., & Branch, L. G. (1971). Relapse rates in addiction programs. *Journal of Clinical Psychology*, *27*(4), 455–456.

Iguchi, M. Y., Belding, M. A., Morral, A. R., Lamb, R. J., & Husband, S. D. (1997). Reinforcing operants other than abstinence in drug abuse treatment: An effective alternative for reducing drug use. *Journal of Consulting and Clinical Psychology*, *65*(3), 421–428. http://dx.doi.org/10.1037/0022-006X.65.3.421.

Iguchi, M. Y., Lamb, R. J., Belding, M. A., Platt, J. J., Husband, S. D., & Morral, A. R. (1996). Contingent reinforcement of group participation versus abstinence in a methadone maintenance program. *Experimental and Clinical Psychopharmacology*, *4*(3), 315–321. http://dx.doi.org/10.1037/1064-1297.4.3.315.

Javors, M. A., Hatch, J. P., & Lamb, R. J. (2005). Cut-off levels for breath carbon monoxide as a marker for cigarette smoking. *Addiction*, *100*(2), 159–167. http://dx.doi.org/10.1111/j.1360-0443.2004.00957.x.

Johanson, C. E. (1978). Drugs as reinforcers. In D. E. Blackman, & D. J. Sanger (Eds.), *Contemporary research in behavioral pharmacology* (pp. 325–390). New York: Plenum Press.

Johanson, C. E., & Schuster, C. R. (1981). Animal models of drug self-administration. *Advances in Substance Abuse, 2,* 219–297.

Kearns, D. N., & Weiss, S. J. (2007). Contextual renewal of cocaine seeking in rats and its attenuation by the conditioned effects of an alternative reinforcer. *Drug and Alcohol Dependence, 90,* 193–202.

Kellogg, S. H., Burns, M., Coleman, P., Stitzer, M., Wale, J. B., & Kreek, J. (2005). Something of value: The introduction of contingency management interventions into the new york city health and hospital addiction treatment service. *Journal of Substance Abuse Treatment, 28,* 57–65.

Kidorf, M., Stitzer, M. L., & Brooner, R. K. (1994). Characteristics of methadone patients responding to take-home incentives. *Behavior Therapy, 25*(1), 109–121. http://dx.doi.org/10.1016/S0005-7894(05)80148-0.

King, D., Greaves, F., Exeter, C., & Darzi, A. (2013). 'Gamification': Influencing health behaviours with games. *Journal of the Royal Society of Medicine, 106*(3), 76–78. http://dx.doi.org/10.1177/0141076813480996; 10.1177/0141076813480996.

Kirby, K. C., Benishek, L. A., Dugosh, K. L., & Kerwin, M. E. (2006). Substance abuse treatment providers' beliefs and objections regarding contingency management: Implications for dissemination. *Drug and Alcohol Dependence, 85*(1), 19–27. http://dx.doi.org/10.1016/j.drugalcdep.2006.03.010.

Kirby, K. C., Carpenedo, C. M., Stitzer, M. L., Dugosh, K. L., Petry, N. M., Roll, J. M., et al. (2012). Is exposure to an effective contingency management intervention associated with more positive provider beliefs? *Journal of Substance Abuse Treatment, 42*(4), 356–365. http://dx.doi.org/10.1016/j.jsat.2011.09.004; 10.1016/j.jsat.2011.09.004.

Kirby, K. C., Kerwin, M. E., Carpenedo, C. M., Rosenwasser, B. J., & Gardner, R. S. (2008). Interdependent group contingency management for cocaine-dependent methadone maintenance patients. *Journal of Applied Behavior Analysis, 41*(4), 579–595.

Kirby, K. C., Marlowe, D. B., Festinger, D. S., Lamb, R. J., & Platt, J. J. (1998). Schedule of voucher delivery influences initiation of cocaine abstinence. *Journal of Consulting and Clinical Psychology, 66*(5), 761–767. http://dx.doi.org/10.1037/0022-006X.66.5.761.

Kirshenbaum, A. P., Olsen, D. M., & Bickel, W. K. (2009). A quantitative review of the ubiquitous relapse curve. *Journal of Substance Abuse Treatment, 36*(1), 8–17.

Koffarnus, M. N., Wong, C. J., Diemer, K., Needham, M., Hampton, J., Fingerhood, M., et al. (2011). A randomized clinical trial of a Therapeutic Workplace for chronically unemployed, homeless, alcohol-dependent adults. *Alcohol and Alcoholism, 46*(5), 561–569.

Lamb, R. J., Kirby, K. C., Morral, A. R., Galbicka, G., & Iguchi, M. Y. (2004). Improving contingency management programs for addiction. *Addictive Behaviors, 29*(3), 507–523. http://dx.doi.org/10.1016/j.addbeh.2003.08.021.

Lamb, R. J., Kirby, K. C., Morral, A. R., Galbicka, G., & Iguchi, M. Y. (2010). Shaping smoking cessation in hard-to-treat smokers. *Journal of Consulting and Clinical Psychology, 78*(1), 62–71. http://dx.doi.org/10.1037/a0018323.

Lamb, R. J., Morral, A. R., Kirby, K. C., Javors, M. A., Galbicka, G., & Iguchi, M. (2007). Contingencies for change in complacent smokers. *Experimental and Clinical Psychopharmacology, 15*(3), 245–255. http://dx.doi.org/10.1037/1064-1297.15.3.245.

Leffingwell, T. R., Cooney, N. J., Murphy, J. G., Luczak, S., Rosen, G., Dougherty, D. M., et al. (2013). Continuous objective monitoring of alcohol use: Twenty first century measurement using transdermal sensors. *Alcoholism, Clinical and Experimental Research, 37*(1), 16–22.

Lesage, M. G. (2009). Toward a nonhuman model of contingency management: effects of reinforcing abstinence from nicotine self-administration in rats with an alternative non-drug reinforcer. *Psychopharmacology, 203,* 13–22.

Lott, D. C., & Jencius, S. (2009). Effectiveness of very low-cost contingency management in a community adolescent treatment program. *Drug and Alcohol Dependence, 102,* 162–165.

Lussier, J. P., Heil, S. H., Mongeon, J. A., Badger, G. J., & Higgins, S. T. (2006). A meta-analysis of voucher-based reinforcement therapy for substance use disorders. *Addiction*, *101*(2), 192–203. http://dx.doi.org/10.1111/j.1360-0443.2006.01311.x.

Marrone, G. F., Shakleya, D. M., Scheidweiler, K. B., Singleton, E. G., Huestis, M. A., & Heishman, S. J. (2011). Relative performance of common biochemical indicators in detecting cigarette smoking. *Addiction*, *106*(7), 1325–1334.

Marsch, L. A., & Dallery, J. (2012). Advances in the psychosocial treatment of addiction: The role of technology in the delivery of evidence-based psychosocial treatment. *Psychiatric Clinics of North America*, *35*(2), 481–493.

McCallum, S. (2012). Gamification and serious games for personalized health. *Studies in Health Technology and Informatics*, *177*, 85–96.

McCarty, D., Fuller, B. E., Arfken, C., Miller, M., Nunes, E. V., Edmundson, E., et al. (2007). Direct care workers in the national drug abuse treatment clinical trials network: Characteristics, opinions, and beliefs. *Psychiatric Services (Washington, DC)*, *58*(2), 181–190. http://dx.doi.org/10.1176/appi.ps.58.2.181.

McDonell, M. G., Howell, D. N., McPherson, S., Cameron, J. M., Srebnik, D., Roll, J. M., et al. (2012). Voucher-based reinforcement for alcohol abstinence using the ethyl-glucuronide alcohol biomarker. *Journal of Applied Behavior Analysis*, *45*(1), 161–165; Retrieved from Meredith et al. (2011).

McGovern, M. P., Fox, T. S., Xie, H., & Drake, R. E. (2004). A survey of clinical practices and readiness to adopt evidence-based practices: Dissemination research in an addiction treatment system. *Journal of Substance Abuse Treatment*, *26*(4), 305–312. http://dx.doi.org/10.1016/j.jsat.2004.03.003.

McLellan, A. T., Lewis, D. C., O'Brien, C. P., & Kleber, H. D. (2000). Drug dependence, a chronic medical illness: implications for treatment, insurance, and outcomes evaluation. *JAMA*, *284*(13), 1689–1695.

McLellan, A. T., McKay, J. R., Forman, R., Cacciola, J., & Kemp, J. (2005). Reconsidering the evaluation of addiction treatment: from retrospective follow-up to concurrent recovery monitoring. *Addiction*, *100*(4), 447–458.

Meredith, S. E., & Dallery, J. (2013). Investigating group contingencies to promote brief abstinence from cigarette smoking. *Experimental and Clinical Psychopharmacology*, *21*(2), 144–154. http://dx.doi.org/10.1037/a0031707; 10.1037/a0031707.

Meredith, S. E., Grabinski, M. J., & Dallery, J. (2011). Internet-based group contingency management to promote abstinence from cigarette smoking: A feasibility study. *Drug and Alcohol Dependence*, *118*(1), 23–30. http://dx.doi.org/10.1016/j.drugalcdep.2011.02.012.

Meredith, S. E., Jarvis, B. P., Raiff, B. R., Rojewski, A., Kurti, A., Cassidy, R. N., et al. (2014). The ABCs of incentive-based treatment in health care: A behavior analytic framework to inform research and practice. *Psychology Research and Behavior Management*, *7*, 103–114.

Meredith, S. E., Robinson, A., Erb, P., Spieler, C. A., Klugman, N., Dutta, P., et al. (2014). A mobile-phone-based breath carbon monoxide meter to detect cigarette smoking. *Nicotine & Tobacco Research*, *16*(6), 766–773. http://dx.doi.org/10.1093/ntr/ntt275.

Miller, P. M. (1975). A behavioral intervention program for chronic public drunkenness offenders. *Archives of General Psychiatry*, *32*(7), 915–918.

National Institute on Drug Abuse. (2014). *Drug facts: Nationwide trends*. Retrieved 3/17/14 from: http://www.drugabuse.gov/publications/drugfacts/nationwide-trends.

O'Brien, C. P. (2008). Evidence-based treatments of addiction. *Philosophical Transactions of the Royal Society B*, *363*(1507), 3277–3286.

Packer, R. R., Howell, D. N., McPherson, S., & Roll, J. M. (2012). Investigating reinforcer magnitude and reinforcer delay: A contingency management analog study. *Experimental and Clinical Psychopharmacology*, *20*(4), 287.

Parker, D. R., Lasater, T. M., Windsor, R., Wilkins, J., Upegui, D. I., & Heimdal, J. (2002). The accuracy of self-reported smoking status assessed by cotinine test strips. *Nicotine and Tobacco Research*, *4*, 305–309.

Paxton, R. (1980). The effects of a deposit contract as a component in a behavioural programme for stopping smoking. *Behaviour Research and Therapy*, *18*(1), 45–50. http://dx.doi.org/10.1016/0005-7967(80)90068-6.

Paxton, R. (1981). Deposit contracts with smokers: Varying frequency and amount of repayments. *Behaviour Research and Therapy*, *19*(2), 117–123. http://dx.doi.org/10.1016/0005-7967(81)90035-8.

Paxton, R. (1983). Prolonging the effects of deposit contracts with smokers. *Behaviour Research and Therapy*, *21*(4), 425–433. http://dx.doi.org/10.1016/0005-7967(83)90012-8.

Peirce, J. M., Petry, N. M., Stitzer, M. L., Blaine, J., Kellogg, S., Satterfield, F., et al. (2006). Effects of lower-cost incentives on stimulant abstinence in methadone maintenance treatment: A national drug abuse treatment clinical trials network study. *Archives of General Psychiatry*, *63*, 201–208.

Perkins, K. A., Karelitz, J. L., & Jao, N. C. (2013). Optimal carbon monoxide criteria to confirm 24-hr smoking abstinence. *Nicotine & Tobacco Research*, *15*(5), 978–982.

Petry, N. M. (2000). A comprehensive guide to the application of contingency management procedures in clinical settings. *Drug and Alcohol Dependence*, *58*, 9–25.

Petry, N. M. (2012). *Contingency management for substance abuse treatment: A guide to implementing this evidence-based practice*. New York, USA: Routledge.

Petry, N. M., & Alessi, S. M. (2010). Prize-based contingency management is efficacious in cocaine-abusing patients with and without recent gambling participation. *Journal of Substance Abuse Treatment*, *39*, 282–288.

Petry, N. M., Alessi, S. M., Hanson, T., & Sierra, S. (2007). Randomized trial of contingent prizes versus vouchers in cocaine-using methadone patients. *Journal of Consulting and Clinical Psychology*, *75*, 983–991.

Petry, N. M., Alessi, S. M., & Ledgerwood, D. M. (2012). A randomized trial of contingency management delivered by community therapists. *Journal of Consulting and Clinical Psychiatry*, *80*, 286–298.

Petry, N. M., Alessi, S. M., Marx, J., Austin, M., & Tardif, M. (2005). Vouchers versus prizes: Contingency management treatment of substance abusers in community settings. *Journal of Consulting and Clinical Psychology*, *73*, 1005–1014.

Petry, N. M., DePhilippis, D., Rash, C. J., Drapkin, M., & McKay, J. R. (2014). Nationwide dissemination of contingency management: The Veterans Administration initiative. *The American Journal on Addictions*, *23*, 205–210.

Petry, N. M., Martin, B., Cooney, J. L., & Kranzler, H. R. (2000). Give them prizes, and they will come: Contingency management for treatment of alcohol dependence. *Journal of Consulting and Clinical Psychology*, *68*, 250–257.

Petry, N. M., Petrakis, I., Trevisan, L., Wiredu, G., Boutros, N. N., Martin, B., et al. (2001). Contingency management interventions: From research to practice. *American Journal of Psychiatry*, *158*, 694–702.

Pickens, R., & Thompson, T. (1968). Cocaine-reinforced behavior in rats: Effect of reinforcement magnitude and fixed-ratio size. *Journal of Pharmacology and Experimental Therapeutics*, *161*, 122–129.

Piotrowski, N. A., & Hall, S. M. (1999). Treatment of multiple drug abuse in the methadone clinic. In K. Silverman (Ed.), *Motivating behavior change among illicit-drug abusers: Research on contingency management interventions* (pp. 183–202). Washington, DC, USA: American Psychological Association. http://dx.doi.org/10.1037/10321-009.

Prendergast, M., Podus, D., Finney, J., Greenwell, L., & Roll, J. (2006). Contingency management for treatment of substance use disorders: A meta-analysis. *Addiction (Abingdon, England)*, *101*(11), 1546–1560. http://dx.doi.org/10.1111/j.1360-0443.2006.01581.x.

Rachlin, H. (1997). Four teleological theories of addiction. *Psychonomic Bulletin and Review, 4*, 462–473.

Raiff, B. R., Jarvis, B. P., & Rapoza, D. (2012). Prevalence of video game use, cigarette smoking, and acceptability of a video Game–Based smoking cessation intervention among online adults. *Nicotine & Tobacco Research, 14*(12), 1453–1457.

Rash, C. J., Dephilippis, D., McKay, J. R., Drapkin, M., & Petry, N. M. (2013). Training workshops positively impact beliefs about contingency management in a nationwide dissemination effort. *Journal of Substance Abuse Treatment, 45*(3), 306–312. http://dx.doi.org/10.1016/j.jsat.2013.03.003; 10.1016/j.jsat.2013.03.003.

Reynolds, B., Dallery, J., Shroff, P., Patak, M., & Leraas, K. (2008). A web-based contingency management program with adolescent smokers. *Journal of Applied Behavior Analysis, 41*(4), 597–601.

Roll, J. M., & Higgins, S. T. (2000). A within-subject comparison of three different schedules of reinforcement of drug abstinence using cigarette smoking as an exemplar. *Drug and Alcohol Dependence, 58*(1–2), 103–109. http://dx.doi.org/10.1016/S0376-8716(99)00073-3.

Roll, J. M., Huber, A., Sodano, R., Chudzynski, J. E., Moynier, E., & Shoptaw, S. (2006). A comparison of five reinforcement schedules for use in contingency management-based treatment of methamphetamine abuse. *The Psychological Record, 56*(1), 67–81.

Roll, J. M., Reilly, M. P., & Johanson, C. (2000). The influence of exchange delays on cigarette versus money choice: A laboratory analog of voucher-based reinforcement therapy. *Experimental and Clinical Psychopharmacology, 8*(3), 366–370. http://dx.doi.org/10.1037/1064-1297.8.3.366.

Roll, J. M., & Shoptaw, S. (2006). Contingency management: Schedule effects. *Psychiatry Research, 144*(1), 91–93. http://dx.doi.org/10.1016/j.psychres.2005.12.003.

Roman, P. M., Abraham, A. J., Rothrauff, T. C., & Knudsen, H. K. (2010). A longitudinal study of organizational formation, innovation adoption, and dissemination activities within the national drug abuse treatment clinical trials network. *Journal of Substance Abuse Treatment, 38*(Suppl 1), S44–S52. http://dx.doi.org/10.1016/j.jsat.2009.12.008; 10.1016/j.jsat.2009.12.008.

Rowan-Szal, G., Joe, G. W., Chatham, L. R., & Dwayne Simpson, D. (1994). A simple reinforcement system for methadone clients in a community-based treatment program. *Journal of Substance Abuse Treatment, 11*, 217–223.

Ruiz, P., & Strain, E. C. (2011). *Lowinson and Ruiz's substance abuse: A comprehensive textbook* (Fifth Edition). Philadelphia PA: Lippincott, Williams & Wilkins. ISBN: 1605472778.

Schuster, C. R., & Thompson, T. (1969). Self administration of and behavioral dependence on drugs. *Annual Review of Pharmacology, 9*, 483–502.

Scott, C. K., Foss, M. A., & Dennis, M. L. (2005). Pathways in the relapse—treatment—recovery cycle over 3 years. *Journal of Substance Abuse Treatment, 28*(Suppl 1), S63–S72.

Shah, N. G., Galai, N., Celentano, D. D., Vlahov, D., & Strathdee, S. A. (2006). Longitudinal predictors of injection cessation and subsequent relapse among a cohort of injection drug users in Baltimore, MD, 1988-2000. *Drug and Alcohol Dependence, 83*(2), 147–156.

Sigmon, S. C., Lamb, R. J., & Dallery, J. (2008). Tobacco. In S. H. Heil (Ed.), *Contingency management in substance abuse treatment* (pp. 99–119). New York, USA: Guilford Press.

Silverman, K., Chutuape, M. A., Bigelow, G. E., & Stitzer, M. L. (1996). Voucher-based reinforcement of attendance by unemployed methadone patients in a job skills training program. *Drug and Alcohol Dependence, 41*(3), 197–207.

Silverman, K., Chutuape, M. A., Bigelow, G. E., & Stitzer, M. L. (1999). Voucher-based reinforcement of cocaine abstinence in treatment-resistant methadone patients: Effects of reinforcement magnitude. *Psychopharmacology, 146*(2), 128–138.

Silverman, K., Higgins, S. T., Brooner, R. K., Montoya, I. D., Cone, E. J., Schuster, C. R., et al. (1996). Sustained cocaine abstinence in methadone maintenance patients through voucher-based reinforcement therapy. *Archives of General Psychiatry, 53*(5), 409–415.

Silverman, K., Robles, E., Mudric, T., Bigelow, G. E., & Stitzer, M. L. (2004). A randomized trial of long-term reinforcement of cocaine abstinence in methadone-maintained patients who inject drugs. *Journal of Consulting and Clinical Psychology, 72*(5), 839–854.

Silverman, K., Svikis, D., Robles, E., Stitzer, M. L., & Bigelow, G. E. (2001). A reinforcement-based therapeutic workplace for the treatment of drug abuse: Six-month abstinence outcomes. *Experimental and Clinical Psychopharmacology, 9*(1), 14–23.

Silverman, K., Svikis, D., Wong, C. J., Hampton, J., Stitzer, M. L., & Bigelow, G. E. (2002). A reinforcement-based therapeutic workplace for the treatment of drug abuse: Three-year abstinence outcomes. *Experimental and Clinical Psychopharmacology, 10*(3), 228–240.

Silverman, K., Wong, C. J., Grabinski, M. J., Hampton, J., Sylvest, C. E., Dillon, E. M., et al. (2005). A web-based therapeutic workplace for the treatment of drug addiction and chronic unemployment. *Behavior Modification, 29*(2), 417–463.

Silverman, K., Wong, C. J., Higgins, S. T., Brooner, R. K., Montoya, I. D., Contoreggi, C., et al. (1996). Increasing opiate abstinence through voucher-based reinforcement therapy. *Drug and Alcohol Dependence, 41*(2), 157–165.

Silverman, K., Wong, C. J., Needham, M., Diemer, K. N., Knealing, T., Crone-Todd, D., et al. (2007). A randomized trial of employment-based reinforcement of cocaine abstinence in injection drug users. *Journal of Applied Behavior Analysis, 40*(3), 387–410.

Silverman, K., Wong, C. J., Umbricht-Schneiter, A., Montoya, I. D., Schuster, C. R., & Preston, K. L. (1998). Broad beneficial effects of cocaine abstinence reinforcement among methadone patients. *Journal of Consulting and Clinical Psychology, 66*(5), 811–824. http://dx.doi.org/10.1037/0022-006X.66.5.811.

Stitzer, M. L., & Bigelow, G. (1978). Contingency management in a methadone maintenance program: Availability of reinforcers. *International Journal of the Addictions, 13*(5), 737–746.

Stitzer, M. L., & Bigelow, G. E. (1983). Contingent payment for carbon monoxide reduction: Effects of pay amount. *Behavior Therapy, 14*(5), 647–656. http://dx.doi.org/10.1016/S0005-7894(83)80057-4.

Stitzer, M. L., & Bigelow, G. E. (1984). Contingent methadone take-home privileges: Effects on compliance with fee payment schedules. *Drug and Alcohol Dependence, 13*(4), 395–399.

Stitzer, M., Bigelow, G., Lawrence, C., Cohen, J., D'Lugoff, B., & Hawthorne, J. (1977). Medication take-home as a reinforcer in a methadone maintenance program. *Addictive Behaviors, 2*(1), 9–14.

Stokes, T. F., & Baer, D. M. (1977). An implicit technology of generalization. *Journal of Applied Behavior Analysis, 10*, 349–367.

Stoops, W. W., Dallery, J., Fields, N. M., Nuzzo, P. A., Schoenberg, N. E., Martin, C. A., et al. (2009). An internet-based abstinence reinforcement smoking cessation intervention in rural smokers. *Drug and Alcohol Dependence, 105*(1–2), 56–62. http://dx.doi.org/10.1016/j.drugalcdep.2009.06.010.

Substance Abuse and Mental Health Services Administration. (2012). *Results from the 2011 National Survey on Drug Use and Health: Summary of national findings, NSDUH Series H-44, HHS Publication No. (SMA) 12-4713.* Rockville, MD: Substance Abuse and Mental Health Services Administration.

Swift, R. (2003). Direct measurement of alcohol and its metabolites. *Addiction, 98*(s2), 73–80.

Vandevenne, M., Vandenbussche, H., & Verstraete, A. (2000). Detection time of drugs of abuse in urine. *Acta Clinica Belgica, 55*, 323–333.

Vuchinich, R. E., & Heather, N. (2003). *Choice, behavioural economics and addiction.* Amsterdam, Netherlands: Pergamon/Elsevier Science Inc.

Walker, R., Rosvall, T., Field, C. A., Allen, S., McDonald, D., Salim, Z., et al. (2010). Disseminating contingency management to increase attendance in two community substance abuse treatment centers: Lessons learned. *Journal of Substance Abuse Treatment, 39* (3), 202–209. http://dx.doi.org/10.1016/j.jsat.2010.05.010; 10.1016/j.jsat.2010.05.010.

Winett, R. A. (1973). Parameters of deposite contracts in the modification of smoking. *The Psychological Record, 23*(1), 49–60.

CHAPTER 17

Behavioral Gerontology: Research and Clinical Considerations

Jonathan C. Baker, Kathleen M. Fairchild, Dawn A. Seefeldt
Rehabilitation Institute, Southern Illinois University, Carbondale, Illinois, USA

Researchers within the field of behavior analysis, as well as in other human services areas, have highlighted the impending changes to older adult populations across the world. For instance, the proportion of older adults continues to increase along with the frequency and severity of disability in this population and the need for care (Brault, 2008; Werner, 2011). Before the growing concerns about gaps in care for aging populations, behavior analysis had been applying existing behavioral technologies for older adults in need since the publication of "Geriatric Behavioral Prosthetics" approximately 50 years ago (Lindsley, 1964). A scientific framework based on the addressing behaviors of "…importance to men and society" was also published in the 1960s (Baer, Wolf, & Risley, 1968, p. 92).

In the time since Lindsley's publication (1964), behavior analysts have spent the majority of their efforts applying the framework established by Baer et al. (1968) to children with autism spectrum disorders (ASDs) and individuals with intellectual disabilities (ID). Children with ASD and ID have become the hallmark population of Applied Behavior Analysis services, based on the support offered by decades of effective interventions (Virués-Ortega, 2010). Nonetheless, behavior analysts and related scholars have also demonstrated that behavior analytic techniques developed for working with individuals with ASD and ID are just as effective at addressing age-related behavior changes (Adkins & Mathews, 1999; Burgio & Burgio, 1986; Carstensen, 1988; LeBlanc, Raetz, & Feliciano, 2011; Trahan, Kahng, Fisher, & Hausman, 2011; Turner & Mathews, 2013; Williamson & Ascione, 1983).

Much of the research addressing age-related changes has shown that consideration must be used with regard to the procedures and design of research as well as treatment development and implementation. This chapter will focus on the empirical support for these considerations by first discussing the model of care and context in which behavior analytic services occur,

Clinical and Organizational Applications of Applied Behavior Analysis
http://dx.doi.org/10.1016/B978-0-12-420249-8.00017-4
425

followed by hurdles for behavior analysts, research design decisions, and clinical case management and implications for elder-care settings. Numerous parallels exist between working with older adults and individuals with ASD or ID. The remainder of the chapter will focus heavily on behavior analytic considerations for typically developing older adults, with some comparisons between individuals with ASD and ID and the older adult population.

GENERAL CONSIDERATIONS AND SIMILARITIES
Medical Model

Currently the predominant paradigm in the area of aging is the medical model (Adkins & Mathews, 1999; Burgio & Burgio, 1986; Carstensen, 1988; Trahan et al., 2011; Wisocki, 1991). This model focuses on identifying the physiological causes of age-related disorders in order to develop an effective treatment. The foothold of the medical model, which can be contrasted with a behavioral or psychosocial model of care (Burgio & Fisher, 2000), represents a challenge to providing behavioral services in an elder-care setting because many behavioral problems are hypothesized to be the result of age-related physiological changes rather than environmental factors (Turner & Mathews, 2013).

Much of the existing care that has been designed for older adults has stemmed from the need to address medical changes associated with aging. As such, behavior analysts will have to become aware of the impact of the medical model and present behavior analysis in conjunction with the medical model (Burgio & Burgio, 1986). Dementia care is one of the best examples of this issue. Elderly persons have significant health conditions that cause progressive dementia and inevitably lead to functional limitations (e.g., short-term memory, language, reasoning, computation, and self-care). A common assumption among practitioners working with this population is that behavioral interventions are ineffective because medical conditions cause a continuous deterioration in skills. Therefore, medical providers assume nothing can be done until a medical cure is found to stop disease progression. Although there are biological bases for many age-related changes, it is unlikely that a medical cure will be found anytime soon due to the unknown etiology of the medical conditions that cause progressive dementia (Buchanan, Christenson, Houlihan, & Ostrom, 2011). In contrast with this bleak prognosis, a behavioral model is applicable because behavior analysis has been effective in developing efficacious interventions without fully understanding the underlying cause of progressive dementia. As Skinner (1975) noted:

> The physiologist of the future will provide an account of genetic endowment changes during the lifetime of the individual and why, as a result, the individual then responds in a given occasion. However, we do not need to wait for further progress of that sort. We can analyze a given instance of behavior in relation to the current setting and to antecedent events in the history of the species and the individual. Thus, we do not need an explicit account of the anatomy and physiology of genetic endowment in order to describe the behavior, or the behavioral processes, characteristics of a species, or to speculate about the contingencies of survival under which they might have evolved. (p. 42)

Historically, behavior analysts have demonstrated that a behavioral approach can supplant the medical model and lead to empirically supported treatments. For instance, in the area of ASD, underlying physiological causes are unknown, and the medical model has not resulted in effective treatment options (Thompson, 2005).

As behavior analysts continue to increase their involvement in treating behavioral excesses and deficits, it is incumbent to assess the acceptability and adoptability of intervention procedures for older adults. Regardless of a treatment's effectiveness, many procedures remain unused because they are unacceptable to participants, caregivers, or consumers (Burgio & Burgio, 1986). Researchers have examined a range of acceptability issues in applying behavioral interventions with children and adults with severe ID because these populations usually neither provide direct consent nor have immediate recourse to those who administer treatment (Kazdin, 1981). These issues also apply with elderly individuals with cognitive impairments that are living in the community and in institutionalized settings. Even more imperative than treatment acceptability is treatment adoption. Interventions must not only be acceptable, but also adoptable by caregivers, as they carry the responsibility of treatment implementation as cognitive impairment increases (Baker & LeBlanc, 2011).

Identifying the Population in Need

At least two general strategies seem practical for preventing or compensating for age-related declines, which also lead to two distinct service possibilities: (1) teaching behavioral management skills to the elderly and (2) training caregivers in the use of behavior management procedures (Burgio & Burgio, 1986). Clearly, behavioral procedures can be used to prepare the elderly for life changes and to attempt to prevent the development of self-protective or challenging behavior. Buchanan and colleagues (2011) proposed that the selective compensation model from Baltes and Baltes (1990) provides a useful framework for behavior analysts to use when attempting to work with this population. This model proposes that older adults best adapt to age-related declines through a process of selection, which involves restricting their daily life to fewer activities that are of higher importance; optimization, which involves efforts to maximize successful execution and satisfaction with chosen life domains; and compensation, which involves implementing new adaptive strategies when abilities are lost or are insufficient for adequate functioning (Buchanan et al., 2011).

Behavior analysts can help with the selection process through behavior analytic assessments (e.g., preference, reinforcer, or engagement assessments). They can then help with optimization through skill acquisition and maintenance procedures (e.g., developing antecedent and performance management procedures to help an individual to engage in preferred activities who struggles with scheduling but wants to stay active in the community). Finally, the behavior analyst can assist the individual in compensating for declines by restructuring the environment to increase the likelihood of behaviors that are occurring at a low rate or not at all (e.g., creating reminders in the home for activities, such as turning off the stove or locking the front door) (Burgio & Burgio, 1986). Behavioral self-management procedures have been used to effectively treat behavioral deficits in a number of clinical and nonclinical populations (Kanfer & Karoly, 1982). These types of procedures are particularly attractive because, once learned, strategy generalization to other challenging areas can occur with intermittent therapist contact (Burgio & Burgio, 1986).

At a certain point, however, caregivers will need to not only sustain a selective optimization with compensation approach, but also address behavioral excesses. As cognitive or physical impairment increases in the elderly individual, the caregiver becomes the primary individual that assists the client in his/her daily activities and observes potentially challenging behavior. A large percentage of elderly individuals over the age of 65 live in homes of family members and are dependent on them to some degree. However, the emergence of challenging behaviors in elderly clients is a leading factor in caregiver stress as well as a family's decision to institutionalize an elderly relative (Burgio & Burgio, 1986). Behavior analysts need to assess the training needs and the acceptability as well as adoptability of behavioral treatments by caregivers in the community (Burgio & Burgio, 1986). Therefore, behavior analysts can assist elderly individuals age in place by teaching family caregivers behavioral procedures that reinforce independent behaviors rather than dependent behaviors.

Staffing Considerations

In addition to training family members, behavior analysts can develop procedures for teaching behavioral skills to care providers in other settings such as adult day care centers (ADCs), assisted living facilities (ALFs), supportive living facilities (SLFs), and nursing homes (Burgio & Burgio, 1986). Staffing has emerged as a key focus of quality of care in various residential long-term care settings. The annualized turnover rate is found to be the highest among certified nursing assistants at 74.5%, followed by registered nurses at 56.1%, and licensed practical nurses at 51.0% (Donoghue, 2010). Castle, Wagner, Ferguson, and Handler (2014) demonstrated that low staffing levels in nursing homes were associated with more frequent facility deficiency citations during routine state survey visits. Hunt, Corazzini, and Anderson (2014) have also shown that upper-level management turnover in nursing homes was detrimental to resident safety and can destabilize the quality care delivered.

Staff training in geriatric long-term care is often brief and relies heavily on didactic techniques that frequently are insufficient for changing staff behavior (Rahman, Applbaum, Schnelle, & Simmons, 2012). Behavior analysts have developed and evaluated a number of effective staff training and management procedures that are employed in facilities for individuals with ID and, to a lesser extent, in psychiatric facilities. Researchers should focus on adapting these procedures to the needs of long-term care aging settings (Burgio & Burgio, 1986).

Family and professional nursing aides have limited understanding of how their behavior can affect the behavior of the elderly individual (Burgio & Burgio, 1986). In addition, family caregivers and professionals working in long-term care settings are not usually trained or prepared to effectively manage the behavioral and psychological symptoms of dementia (BPSD) (Brodaty, Draper, & Low, 2003) such as depression, wandering, verbal aggression, and physical aggression (Buchanan et al., 2011). Lack of appropriate training is also an issue in ALFs and SLFs. These facilities are limited by the amount of care that can be provided and usually have regulations that require them to discharge individuals with BPSDs because they do not have adequately trained staff to manage these behaviors.

In summary, the first step in becoming involved with behavioral geron-tology is to become familiar with the paradigm and the target populations. Once familiar, there are still many considerations that behavior analysts must be aware of with regard to research and clinical work. These considerations fall into three general categories that are discussed in the following material. The first category, hurdles for behavior analysts, highlights considerations that span across both research and clinical work in elder-care settings. The second category, single-case research design, addresses those considerations that are unique to conducting and publishing important behavior analytic findings for an aging population. Finally, the third category, considerations in clinical services, addresses how to transition from consuming the empirical support for an intervention to beginning to implement behavior analytic clinical services in an elder-care setting.

HURDLES FOR BEHAVIOR ANALYSTS

Although the categories discussed previously, including staff retention, training, and education considerations are aging-related hurdles, there are many hurdles specific to behavior analytic research and clinical work. This section will focus on hurdles that, in our experience, are important to both research and clinical work. Many of the hurdles listed are based on the state regulations and therefore may be unique to each state. The state of Illinois, where we are currently practicing and conducting research, will be used as an example in most cases, although other states (e.g., Montana) may be used to illustrate issues that do not exist in Illinois but may exist in other states. Later, we discuss issues that are specific to either research or clinical work in respective sections.

Data Collection

To begin to appreciate the challenges related to data collection in elder-care settings, it is first important to note the type of data that behavior analysts are collecting or have access to, along with the regulations that support such data. Treatment plans, behavior support plans (BSPs), or individualized edu-cation plans (IEPs) for individuals with ID include defined goals and required measurement for both academic and functional goals, as well as plans for how those goals will be measured (Department of Education Assis-tance to States for the Education of Children with Disabilities & Preschool

Grants for Children with Disabilities Rule, 2006). In a school setting, behavior analysts may target verbal aggression if a student (we'll call him Martin) displays verbal aggression when presented with demands. Verbal aggression may be defined as any derogatory or belittling utterance, including profanity. Behavior analysts may complete an Antecedent-Behavior-Consequence data sheet or individualized data sheet specifically designed for Martin's verbal aggression. Behavior analysts are also likely to record adaptive target behaviors that assist in an individual's daily and social functioning given general ethical guidelines as well as specific state requirements (Bailey & Burch, 2011; Minnesota Division of Mental Health Developmental Disabilities Addictive Diseases, 2005). For instance, behavior analysts may record that Martin completed 50 math problems on a data sheet if targeting academic behavior. Initial data collection is eased by mandatory record keeping requirements for larger, state-operated residential placements as well as smaller, not-for-profit community residential placements. For example, in Montana, service providers must record individual limitations, needs, activities, incident reports, mental and physical health records, financial arrangements, as well as a treatment plan which includes implementation procedures, goals, duration of service, and training programs that must be provided (Montana Public Health et al., 1987).

In elder-care settings, inherent issues arise due to the lack of requirements for staff data collection procedures. There is no analogous elder-care legislation that requires the content or documentation of services similar to IEPs or BSPs. States create requirements for documentation, yet only focus on medical changes. For example, in the State of Illinois, the Department of Aging created a Community Care Program (CCP), with the goal to help "senior citizens, who might otherwise need nursing home care, to remain in their own homes by providing in-home and community-based services" (Illinois Department on Aging, 2012). The data utilized in the CCP are taken from the Determination of Need (DON), an assessment that determines the level of support an individual needs (Illinois Department on Aging, Care Program, & Determination of Need Rule, 1999). The DON focuses on demographics, number of chronic diseases, activities of daily living (ADLs), instrumental activities of daily living, and score on the Mini Mental State Exam (MMSE; Folstein, Folstein, & McHugh, 1975).

Care plans are developed based on the results of the DON assessment, and changes to the plan are based on the changes in the data. There are state regulations on collecting data on each of the DON focus areas. Subsequently, the State of Illinois provides disciplinary actions when such data are not properly and regularly documented. However, there are no data expectations related to behavior and, therefore, no regulation within Illinois elder-care facilities to document behavior (unless used as the justification for the administration of a medication, but this is limited to nursing homes). As such, finding data on behaviors in an elder-care setting becomes a challenge. If data exist, direct care providers typically describe behavior using hypothetical constructs and anecdotal observations, as opposed to using operational definitions and systematic data recording procedures. For instance, staff may report "Earl is more agitated lately," or "Martha is always unhappy," without explaining the behaviors that comprise "agitated" or "unhappy." Staff members also neglect to consistently and uniformly collect behavioral data on occurrences of "agitation" and "unhappiness." If given a questionnaire about a resident's challenging behavior, two direct care workers are likely to describe divergent types, frequencies, and intensities of behavior. Discrepancy in the reports of behavior amongst care providers is expected, as each employee has a unique history with each resident. However, discrepancies may be minimized with the use of operational definitions and systematic data recording. Uniform data collection practices could also incorporate interobserver agreement (IOA) to further refine behavioral descriptions.

When behavioral data collection occurs, staff members are likely to record instances of challenging behavior or medical concerns in case notes and communication logs. As noted earlier, in the state of Illinois, SLFs are mandated to keep records on improvement or deterioration in a resident's condition, but there are no requirements for including well-defined and quantified measurements of behavior (Illinois Department of Healthcare & Services, 2009). In a review of each state's regulations for ALFs, it was found that Missouri and Rhode Island included that behaviors that could result in harm to self or others should be recorded beneath the regulations for move-in/move-out procedures (National Center for Assisted Living, 2012). Numerous states speak about recording the reason of nonadmittance or termination of residential placement, which could include challenging, dangerous, or socially inappropriate behavior, but a method of behavior tracking is not specified (National Center for Assisted Living, 2012). A few instances of challenging behavior become magnified, which may lead to excessive scrutiny of said behavior and avoidance of the particular older adult.

In clinical experience in working with nursing homes, ALFs, SLFs, and day centers, socially appropriate behaviors that are recorded usually relate to the daily routine (e.g., "Wanda came for breakfast and played bingo.").

Other adaptive behaviors are typically not recorded, especially for the individuals who display challenging behavior. Staff rarely record that "agitated" Earl "socialized with other residents," "opened the door for Martha" or "thanked me when I brought him supper." The paucity of data recording related to appropriate behaviors shifts the agency's focus from a rehabilitative to a punitive and potentially avoidant culture.

Behavior analysts conduct direct behavioral observations of, and assessments with, clients and perform indirect assessments with caregivers to create well-designed data collection systems (Kazdin, 2011; Neef & Peterson, 2007). In elder-care settings, direct observation can prove problematic due to reactivity from residents and caregivers. Behavior analysts must effectively collect unobtrusive data within the environment. If possible, it may be best to interact with numerous residents while carrying around a clipboard without collecting data. Interacting with multiple residents helps to avoid singling out individuals. Repeated presence in the environment without collecting data may be necessary to reduce reactivity. Props may be used, such as a laptop, to disguise behavior analysts whilst collecting data. Video cameras may be used, after obtaining consent (from any individual who may come into the shot, which may require consent from all residents), to reduce the number of behavior analysts needed on site.

Additionally, reactivity may prove more of an obstacle for male behavior analysts, as elder-care settings are primarily comprised of female residents and service workers (Caffrey et al., 2012). Female residents may attend more to male students or professionals given the paucity of male residents and staff. Distribution of the sexes among consumers as well as caregivers is more equal in settings designed for ID (Bershadsky et al., 2012). A more even balance of male and female individuals may decrease reactivity towards and special attention garnered from male behavior analysts, although the previously mentioned steps may be applied to reduce reactivity in these settings.

Ethical Concerns

Sole focus on challenging behaviors in elder-care settings can present an ethical challenge for behavior analysts. Staff at residential facilities may refer a client for disruptive vocalizations, noncompliance with health regulations, such as wearing a lifeline, or physical agitation or aggression. Direct service workers may request that we "fix Earl" or "make Earl better," as if referring to a broken arm or the common cold. These requests relate to the prevalence of the medical model in elder-care settings, as discussed earlier within General Considerations and Similarities. Recently, within the field of gerontology, there has been a push to describe challenging behaviors that occur during care tasks as self-protective behaviors (e.g., Fisher, Drossel, Kyle, Cherup, & Sylvester, 2010). This approach is encouraged because it not only emphasizes that behavior serves a function, self-protection, but also questions if the target behavior is challenging for the individual or staff who are caring for the individual. Behavior analysts must be clear that services will not only be rendered to address behavioral excesses, but will also focus on identifying staff behaviors that must change along with supporting individual adaptive behaviors, which will improve the individual's quality of life and/or maintain the client's current level of functioning (Bailey & Burch, 2011). The targets and goals of the treatment plan should be created based on the data from all relevant caregivers but must conform to the ethical guidelines for behavior analysts (Bailey & Burch, 2011) and the dimensions of behavior analysis (Baer et al., 1968).

Before selecting target behaviors and treatment goals, another ethical consideration may arise as behavior analysts identify the client's current level of cognitive functioning, and if the client is his/her own representative or has a medical power of attorney (MPOA; someone responsible for medical decisions should the individual be deemed unable to make independent competent decisions; American Bar Association, The Commission on Law and Aging, 2011) or legal guardian. When working with someone at a long-term care facility, the individual's file may contain existing diagnoses of Alzheimer's disease or dementia. There may also be previous assessment records indicating higher cognitive scores. Common cognitive assessment measures, such as the MMSE or St. Louis University Mental Status Examination, may indicate impairment (Tariq, Tumosa, Chibnall, Perry, & Morley, 2006), suggesting an older adult should have an MPOA. Either a formal diagnosis or evidence of cognitive impairment should serve as an indicator that the behavior analysts should take additional measures to ensure informed consent (see BACB Guidelines 1.05 Professional and Scientific Relationships, 2.04 Consultation, 3.04, Consent-Client Records, & 10.4 Informed Consent, 2013; http://www.bacb.com/Downloadfiles/BACBguidelines/BACB_Conduct_Guidelines.pdf).

Data Analysis

In addition to the challenges to data collection and ethical considerations noted above, a third general hurdle encountered by behavior analysts working in elder-care centers is the analysis of data to determine treatment effectiveness. Visual analysis of data comes with special considerations. In both research and clinical work, behavior analysts use analytic designs (Baer et al., 1968) that allow for a demonstration of the effect. First, this typically requires stability of the data across phases and a long enough baseline to assess any trends in those data. However, the lack of control over how individuals' days are structured (due to the lack of behavior plans that enforce structured, facilitative services), coupled with the high probability of pharmacological interventions, extended baselines may prove difficult to justify. Behavior analysts might consider shortening longer observations (e.g., entire day or shift) into multiple shorter observations (30 min to 1 h), assuming that the behaviors occur at a high enough frequency, to capture the behavior (Bailey & Burch, 2002). Also, there may be specific times when the behavior is more or less likely to occur, which should be taken into account and ideally held constant when considering session length and duration.

The goal of stable baseline data is to allow for the application of baseline logic when evaluating intervention impact. Although baseline logic is still applicable in an elder-care setting, it is important to know what an appropriate prediction of baseline would entail. Typically baseline performance would be extended at a similar level, trend, and variability and behavior analysts would determine if the data collected deviate enough from the predicted baseline. However, improvements in performance beyond baseline levels may not be possible when working with older adults with a moderate to severe limitation, such as a degenerative cognitive or physical disorder, or clients with comorbid conditions (Buchanan et al., 2011). An accurate prediction, even for stable data, is often a decline in performance over time. Intervention efficacy may not occur through the demonstration of higher levels of responding, but maintenance of stable responding. Although the accurate prediction of future baseline data requires incorporating a potential decline in functioning, there are numerous behavior analytic aging publications demonstrating an improvement in performance above baseline levels (e.g., Brenske, Rudrud, Schulze, & Rapp, 2008; LeBlanc, Cherup, Feliciano, & Sidener, 2006; Nolan, Mathews, & Harrison, 2001). Reductions in challenging behavior are also achievable, though not expected in a medical model, similar to results garnered using behavioral technology with other populations (Baker, LeBlanc, Raetz, & Hilton, 2011; Buchanan & Fisher, 2002), though once again, an effective demonstration of behavior-analytic interventions may be found in simply keeping the behaviors from increasing along some dimension.

In review, the focus of the behavior analyst should be in conveying to caregivers that learning adaptive behaviors may become more difficult in the later stages of cognitive impairment, which should be discussed at the onset of services, so treatment goals may be related to maintaining the client's current level of functioning. Additionally, it is more crucial to maintain shorter baselines, as attrition due to mortality becomes a consideration. A multiple baseline design with prolonged baselines may not be feasible, but may be modified by lowering criteria for moving into treatment on a second baseline depending on the health and functioning level of the client.

Considerations in Single-Case Research Design

Several reviews have both discussed the efficacy of behavior analytic approaches in elder-care settings and called for more basic and applied research in this area (Buchanan et al., 2011; Buchanan, Hustfeldt, Berg, & Houlihan, 2008; Burgio & Burgio, 1986; Carstensen, 1988; LeBlanc et al., 2011; Rosenthal & Carstensen, 1988; Turner & Mathews, 2013; Williamson & Ascione, 1983; Wisocki, 1991). However, very few (e.g., Adkins & Mathews, 1999; Burgio & Kowalkoski, 2011) have addressed the unique research considerations inherent in an elder-care context. Therefore, instead of reviewing the efficacy of existing behavior analytic research, the following section discusses a few major adjustments that we have come across in our research. We have organized these adjustments into these areas: (a) participants, settings, and materials; (b) dependent variables; and (c) procedures.

Participants and Settings

Research participants typically involve the individual (Buchanan & Fisher, 2002; Durkin, Prescott, Furchtgott, Cantor, & Powell, 1993; Dwyer-Moore & Dixon, 2007; Fisher & Noll, 1996; Woodruff-Pak, 2001), their caregivers (Burgio, 1991; Burgio & Burgio, 1990; Burgio et al., 2002; Engelman, Altus, & Mathews, 1999; Mathews & Altus, 1997), and/or a combination of both (Baker, Hanley, & Mathews, 2006). Given that most aging research is aimed at addressing aging-related changes, the older adult is selected as the primary participant to show that the intervention is effective. Older adult research participants may be 65 years old or older and have one or more age related problems including: (a) declines in physical abilities; (b) sensory deficits; and (c) memory problems (Burgio & Burgio, 1986). Researchers should screen for age-related changes and include results of any screens or assessments in the description of the participants.

As noted above, caregivers are common research participants, either along with the elder or as the sole type of participant. Caregivers may include unpaid family members or paid direct care staff working in nursing homes,

ADCs, or ALFs (e.g., certified nursing assistants, direct care staff, etc.). The training caregivers receive may be very limited, and many will lack requisite knowledge about behavioral changes associated with age-related declines. Many will possibly require a great deal of training when learning intervention procedures (which should be documented for generalization purposes). Researchers should be aware that behavioral problems in elderly clients frequently lead to caregiver stress and burnout (Burgio & Burgio, 1986). Caregiver stress should be assessed whenever possible prior to implementing an intervention (Chou, Chu, Tseng, & Lu, 2003). When attempting to recruit caregivers, researchers should explain how their work might help to reduce caregiver stress and workload to increase "buy-in" from caregivers. Experimental procedures should be adapted to fit the current workload that caregivers have, as procedures that significantly increase their workload may produce additional issues related to recruitment, implementation, and maintenance.

In nursing homes, ADCs, and ALFs, researchers should be knowledgeable of staff-to-resident ratios and where staff allocates a majority of their time while at work. Baltes, Orzech, Barton, and Lago (1983) examined where the majority of resident behavior occurred compared to where staff spent most of their time. They found that staff did not spend a majority of their time in the same places where older adults spent most of their time. For example, 67% of the older adults' behavior occurred in their bedrooms, but staff was in residents' bedrooms only 27% of the time. Being knowledgeable of how staff spends their time is important for choosing an intervention. Settings with a low staff-to-resident ratio or where staff members do not spend most of their time in the same locations as the residents, research on differential reinforcement procedures may not result in generalizable effects. It is unrealistic that a setting would implement a procedure that would require staff to observe the client continuously. Researchers might instead focus on a noncontingent reinforcement protocol.

Nursing homes continue to be the most common aging experimental setting, but recently there has been an increasing number of studies conducted in additional settings (e.g., assisted living facilities, and home residences; Trahan et al., 2011). In these settings, researchers need to be aware of the legal requirements regarding the type of care provided because this may influence the design of the study. Regulations may include: (a) who can be alone with an individual; (b) who can be present during certain care tasks; (c) activity and diet restrictions; and (d) requirements about event participation. For example, when developing a treatment for elopement from the building, a trial-based functional analysis (Thomason-Sassi, Iwata, Neidert, & Roscoe, 2011) may be more appropriate if it is not possible to allow multiple instances of the behavior. Additionally, functional analysis conditions that are common for other populations may not be appropriate due to regulations. For example, if the participant is in a wheel chair, an alone condition may not be possible due to the potential fall risk. In that case, a no-interaction condition may be more appropriate (Hanley, Iwata, & McCord, 2003).

In summary, researchers wanting to conduct research in elder-care settings will want to properly investigate participant and setting characteristics to adequately design a research protocol that will be feasible and to control for environmental factors that could potentially confound the study's results. Researchers will want to meet with facility administrators to discuss the research studies and facility regulations prior to developing the study.

Materials

Typically, behavior analytic research involves some combination of assessments, data collection systems, utilization of existing data, etc. When conducting research in an elder-care setting, it is unlikely that researchers will find many of the needed materials to conduct their study in the natural environment. Researchers should be prepared to bring any needed materials and consider how interventions may need to be modified to account for an environment that was not specifically designed to accommodate research. IOA (reliability) is typically obtained by having two independent observers collect data and then comparing their records in a way that quantifies agreement related to the occurrence of targeted behavior that occurred at specific times (Adkins & Mathews, 1999). However, very few elder-care settings have two-way mirrors, making it more difficult to observe clients without them seeing the researchers (which may result in reactivity). As mentioned earlier in the Hurdles for Behavior Analysts section, researchers might bring video recording devices to help collect data.

A combination of indirect assessments and direct behavioral observations are commonly used by behavior analysts in many different settings to create well-designed data collection systems (Kratchowill & Shapiro, 2000). Indirect assessments should be obtained ahead of time because it is uncommon for them to be readily available on site. Some of the most commonly used assessments include the MMSE, Cohen Mansfield Agitation Inventory (Cohen-Mansfield, 1991), Adaptive Behavior Dementia Questionnaire (Prasher, Farooq, & Holder, 2004), and Questions About Behavioral

Function (Matson & Vollmer, 1995). Unfortunately, in the event that such assessments are available on site, it is possible that staff with insufficient training may have administered the assessments. It is important for researchers to be aware of this and not simply to rely on scores that have been recorded by staff. Instead, the researcher should administer the assessments him- or herself to ensure that assessments are administered correctly (Molloy & Standish, 1997).

Dependent Variables

Common dependent variables in aging research include: urinary incontinence (Burgio et al., 1998), smoking cessation (Dale et al., 1997), diabetes management (McHorney, 1996), increasing exercise (Simmons, Ferrell, & Schnelle, 2002), weight reduction (Weisfeldt, Gerstenblith, & Lakatta, 1985), agitation (Burgio et al., 2002), aggression (Baker et al., 2006), increasing activity attendance and engagement (Brenske et al., 2008), disruptive vocalizations (Buchanan & Fisher, 2002), and way-finding (Nolan et al., 2001).

As mentioned in the Hurdles for Behavior Analysts section earlier, it is common for staff to describe a client's behaviors using hypothetical constructs and anecdotal observations when describing behaviors that may be the dependent variables of interest for research. Researchers must ensure that the characteristics of specific procedures and dependent variables be identified in an objective manner so that they can be replicated. Providing a detailed procedural description of an intervention and the dependent variables will allow other researchers to replicate the treatment strategies used in published research (Adkins & Mathews, 1999).

Procedures

As mentioned in the Medical Model section, behavior changes (behavioral excesses and deficits) are often attributed to some sort of medical condition that does not have a known medical cure. The common misconception is that as the disorder progresses, these behaviors will increase and are frequently hypothesized to be untreatable (Buchanan et al., 2011). Therefore, it is important to present the context of the behavior-related changes when publishing in behavioral journals. Researchers must ensure that it is clear to the reader why the area being studied is important and why the data should be published.

The most common types of age-related research (see Buchanan et al., 2011; Burgio & Kowalkoski, 2011; Trahan et al., 2011; Turner & Mathews, 2013 for recent reviews) have focused on reducing behavioral excesses (e.g., disruptive vocalizations, agitation, elopement, wandering, and verbal and physical aggression), increasing behavioral deficits (e.g., engagement in socialization, ADL, and decreased abilities in recognition and recall), and staff training. Existing research has used both single-subject and group experimental designs to demonstrate functional control (i.e., when a predictable change in an individual's behavior can be reliably and repeatedly produced by the systematic manipulation of some aspect of a person's environment; Adkins & Mathews, 1999). Reversal and multiple baseline designs are frequently used in behavioral gerontology along with traditional experimental group designs with single-subject analyses embedded within them (Adkins & Mathews, 1999).

The type of research design and the level of experimental control should be considered when choosing where to publish research. When publishing in a behavior analytic journal, researchers will have to carefully choose designs that result in a reasonable demonstration of experimental control to demonstrate internal validity. Such research is necessary to advance the science of behavior with older adults. However, there is much that can also be done with regard to external validity. Burgio and Kowalkoski (2011) encourage behavioral gerontology researchers to attempt to publish not only in behavioral journals but also in nonbehavioral journals. They indicated that publishing in behavioral journals is, in a sense, "preaching to the choir," and that it is important for behavioral gerontology to begin to get more recognition from other fields. If researchers want to do this, it is important to be aware of their audience and to use terms that are easily understood by the type of audience that they are seeking. Therefore, if a researcher attempts to publish in a nonbehavioral journal, s/he may want to consider revising the terms used in the document (e.g., use the term "incentive" rather than "reinforcer"; Burgio & Kowalkoski, 2011). Burgio and Kowalkoski argue that doing so does not mean the researcher should fall into the habit of using hypothetical constructs or large, abstract terms. Rather, using terms that are understood in a larger community may be the better approach to take when disseminating outside of the behavior analytic community. Researchers trying to reach a wider audience may want to conduct research using experimental group designs. Group designs may reach a larger portion of the professionals that have more experience reviewing these types of research. Regardless of the type of audience researchers are targeting when selecting their interventions, it is imperative that researchers consider all of the aforementioned areas: participants and setting, materials, dependent variables, and procedures. This approach will help to ensure that they have gathered enough information to develop a study that will capture the population, target behavior, and procedure of interest while controlling for potential confounds and hurdles that are inherently found when conducting research with an aging population.

CONSIDERATIONS IN CLINICAL SERVICES

Although behavior analytic interventions have been demonstrated in community settings across a wide range of behavior changes (LeBlanc et al., 2011), the majority of empirical support for behavior analytic interventions is related to interventions conducted in long-term care settings. Behavioral changes such as wandering, inability to manage personal hygiene, resistance to assistance or care, and aggression are the most common factors that lead to a person being placed in a nursing home (Turner & Mathews, 2013). The most frequently cited reasons for referral include: (a) physical and verbal aggression, (b) disruptive vocalization, (c) resistance to care, (d) intrusiveness, (e) chronic psychotic behaviors (responding to auditory hallucinations, or acting on delusional beliefs), (f) sleep disturbances, and (g) incontinence (Turner & Mathews, 2013). Behavior analysis has been very successful in developing and implementing effective interventions for (a) physical and verbal aggression (Baker et al., 2006), (b) disruptive vocalization (Buchanan & Fisher, 2002), (c) resistance to care (Sloane et al., 2004), (d) chronic psychotic behaviors (Zimmerman, Favrod, Trieu, & Pomini, 2005), (e) sleep disturbances (Schnelle et al., 1998), and (f) incontinence (Burgio et al., 1990). As such, readers are encouraged to read any of the many reviews noted in this chapter (Adkins & Mathews, 1999; Buchanan et al., 2011, 2008; Burgio & Burgio, 1986; Carstensen, 1988; LeBlanc et al., 2011; Trahan et al., 2011; Turner & Mathews, 2013; Williamson & Ascione, 1983) for a more detailed account of the efficacy of clinical applications of behavior analysis in elder-care settings. These reviews note the empirical support of applied behavior analytic procedures across a wide array of settings and clinical issues. Given the relatively high number of quality reviews published in the past 5 years alone, the empirical support for behavioral approaches in elder-care settings has been well documented. Therefore, the remainder of this chapter will depart from previous reviews and will instead highlight the challenges of providing clinical behavior analytic services in elder-care settings, as well as discuss an example of a model for beginning to provide such services in the state of Illinois.

Behavior Analysis and Clinical Integration

The paradigm shift from the medical to the behavioral model, which has largely been achieved in the area of ASD, is unlikely to occur in geriatric long-term care. As mentioned previously, many elderly persons suffer from significant health problems that require the constant presence of medical and nursing staff. Unlike behavior analysts working in the area of ASD and ID, in most nursing home settings, interdisciplinary teams that do not include a behavior analyst make the majority of treatment decisions rather than a single person. Typically, medical professionals or occupational therapists lead these teams and treatment decisions often involve medication- and sensory-based interventions (Baker & LeBlanc, 2011). It would be naïve and perhaps harmful for behavior analysts to attempt to work with this population without the consideration of the special needs of this population (Burgio & Burgio, 1986).

The ever-present reliance on the medical model also directly affects a major challenge for behavior analysts' integration into clinical elder-care services: a lack of funding or reimbursement for behavioral services. Currently there is no funding readily available for applied behavior analysis to receive compensation for services because the services covered are usually medical in nature (e.g., skilled nursing, physical therapy, and prescription medications). Administrators of residential settings are often unaware that a behavior analyst might have the appropriate background and training to provide expertise in designing BSPs. Under these circumstances, a coexistence of the medical and behavioral training models is more appropriate because the medical model is appropriate for some age-related diseases that can be effectively treated with medications or surgical operations. If behavior analysts are to increase their participation in geriatric care, it is crucial that they collaborate with geriatricians and geriatric nurses (Burgio & Burgio, 1986).

Historically, behavior analysts have developed collaborations and achieved entry into new settings demonstrating that their presence would in some way benefit the facility or program. There will need to be reforms in existing legislature to begin to fund behavioral services to make them more readily available. Behavior analysts in the area of ASDs have shown that these types of reforms are possible. As of November 4, 2014, 29 states (Speaks, 2014) had enacted ASD insurance laws that specifically included applied behavioral analysis as a covered service. The increasing number of older adults that are able to vote and advocate for themselves puts behavior analysts in an optimum time period to begin to shift the existing funding streams for their services and expand their consumer base (LeBlanc et al., 2012). Until these reforms are implemented, effective consultation in residential facilities might provide the opportunity to convince the organization of the need for a behavior analyst to coordinate behavioral programming, data collection and analysis, and staff training as a strategy for complying with federal mandates to minimizing problem behavior without excessive pharmacological sedation (LeBlanc et al.). In the following section, we detail how the authors have utilized the method outlined by LeBlanc et al. to begin to create an opportunity for behavior analytic services in an elder-care setting by demonstrating that elderly residents might benefit from behavioral interventions, devising procedures that reduce financial expenditure, and convincing administrators that collaboration with behavior analysts is desirable (Burgio & Burgio, 1986).

Steps to Provide Clinical Services in an Elder-Care Setting

LeBlanc et al. (2012) provided a general framework for behavior analysts to expand into underrepresented areas of behavior analysis and expound on that framework in the context of traumatic brain injury and elder-care services. The general framework included two main components: (a) increasing professional competence with the population and (b) identifying and managing employment opportunities. In the following paragraphs we detail how we developed the Behavioral Residential In-home Care and Supports (BRICS) program to provide behavior analytic services in Illinois.

The first of LeBlanc et al.'s (2012) recommendations, increasing professional competence with the populations, includes several subcomponents: (a) contacting the literature, (b) contacting relevant professional groups, (c) pursuing retraining and supervision, and (d) identifying professional credentials. The current authors had the unique opportunity to receive graduate training specific in behavioral gerontology, which meant that all had contacted the literature and received the necessary training and supervision to work with older adults. This training included contacting behavior analytic research in behavioral journals, behavior analytic research in gerontology journals, and aging specific research in gerontology journals. As noted by LeBlanc et al., there is no specific credential necessary to provide elder-care services per se, but the first author does hold a post baccalaureate certificate in gerontology, and the second and third authors are working toward their own postbaccalaureate certificates in gerontology. The first author began work in Southern Illinois in the fall of 2009, at which point he began contacting professional groups. He worked with the Area Agency on Aging, the Department of Aging, and the Alzheimer's Association to become familiar with the services provided in the area, as well as to begin to spread the word about the behavior analytic research he was conducting. He also contacted the medical school at Southern Illinois University to become involved in a dementia assessment initiative in Southern Illinois. As such, our road to providing clinical services in an elder-care setting was somewhat smoother due to our familiarity with the aging population. Other behavior analysts who are new to elder-care services might require more time before moving into elder care. Readers are referred to LeBlanc et al. for more details about completing this first component of branching into a new area.

The second component of LeBlanc et al.'s (2012) recommendation, identifying and managing employment options, also includes several sub-components: (a) developing effective communication skills, (b) increasing your professional profile, (c) determining employment options, (d) locating funding sources, and (e) marketing the power of behavior analysis. LeBlanc et al. noted that the importance of communication skills is paramount in aging due to the ubiquity of interdisciplinary care. Once again, each of us have had several years of experience working in interdisciplinary settings with medical doctors, nurses, facility administrators, certified nursing assistants, social workers, dieticians, activity coordinators, and case managers. All of these professionals played a role in our expansion of behavior analytic services and we benefited from training opportunities working with such professionals. As LeBlanc et al. noted, effective communication requires not only avoiding technical jargon, but also knowing the technical terms of these professions, including elder-care providers. For example, in our discussions, local care providers would talk about the DON (see the DON referenced in the section on data collection, under hurdles), SLFs versus ALFs (referencing different types of living arrangement with different rules and regulations about how staff can and cannot provide supports), care plans (which are tied to the CCP), care coordinators versus assistant care coordinators (different staff working in a case management role), in-home assessments versus intakes (different types of assessments resulting in different types of care plans), etc. It was clear during our interactions that using such terms incorrectly was a "mark" that we were not a part of the elder-care team and were outsiders. As we refined our "aging" repertoire, we found that we could achieve buy in to our approaches must faster.

Many of our efforts to increase our professional profile came from the first author's position as a faculty member in a behavior analytic graduate training program. Required BACB© training opportunities were developed in nursing homes, where older adults experience many behavioral excesses and deficits. Additionally, student and faculty research was conducted at the sites. All clinical and research work was provided at no cost to the sites. After several students had completed projects at the sites, the first author reached out to the administrators of a company (the Chief Executive Officer (CEO) and Chief Operating Officer) with a combination of five ALFs and SLFs to discuss expanding services that might help those elders who are still in the community. This was done because: (a) due to regulations about providing basic care, staff at nursing homes had little time to implement interventions when the behavior analysts were not present and facility staff would not implement any supports or contingencies to maintain implementation and (b) it was possible to show a cost savings if individuals could be kept from moving into a nursing home (nursing home care costs close to $7000 per month per person, compared to less than $4000 if individuals can stay in the community), but behavior analytic services actually cost more when provided in nursing homes (due to the current lack of Medicaid or Medicare reimbursement for behavior analytic services). In conjunction with the administrators for the ALF and SLF company, the first author began pursuing funding sources, another recommendation of LeBlanc et al. (2012). Initially, the company pursued funding graduate students on a graduate assistantship, but the company was a nonprofit company and funding was not in their budget beyond funding a single summer semester.

During that summer and into the fall (once again, providing pro-bono support), the three authors worked together conducting functional assessments and developing function-based treatments for eight individuals, all of whom were close to being discharged from the facility due to behavioral excesses, including elopement, aggression, hoarding, and disruptive vocalizations. We were able to develop interventions, train staff, and demonstrate the efficacy of those interventions when staff treatment integrity was high. The first author and the CEO of the company used the data collected to put together a proposal for more funding. That proposal was eventually funded in 2013 as a 2-year program demonstration through the Illinois Department on Aging to provide behavior analytic services at SLFs, ALFs, in home settings, and ADCs, in the Southern Illinois Region. The CEO of the company played a major role in helping to secure the funding, using her contacts with the Department of Aging to set up a meeting where the first author was able to pitch the idea. She also provided compelling testimony about the efficacy of behavior analysis at her site and the need for such data-based care throughout the state. The Director of the Department of Aging noted that it was the data-based focus of applied behavior analysis, along with the clear cost savings from keeping people from entering a nursing home, that made his decision to fund the program easy, even at a time when the Department on Aging was facing budget cuts. As of the writing of this chapter, more than half of those individuals we initially served are still residents at the facilities (a full 2 years later), a cost savings to the Department of Aging of over $288,000 when compared to if those individuals had been admitted to nursing homes at the time of their referral.

We hope that through marketing the power of behavior analysis (the final recommendation of LeBlanc et al., 2012), we may begin to create employment opportunities for behavior analysts in the state of Illinois. Both the Department of Aging and the administrators of the sites are hoping to present data from the BRICS program at several state conferences. The director of the Department on Aging has said that this would be the first evidence-based approach to elder care for the state of Illinois and an initiative that he would like to see funded similarly to how the state currently provides funding for behavior analytic services to individuals with ID.

The BRICS program is not the first of its kind. Burgio et al. (2009) created a similar program called the REACH (and REACH out) program. As more and more individuals experience advanced age and the failure of the medical model to effectively address aging-related changes, the opportunity for behavior analytic services to be a part of aging care is available. However, there are many hurdles that behavior analysts face in both research and clinical work. Through perseverance and data-based decisions, behavior analysts can begin to provide services and make their mark in yet another area that is greatly in need of our technologies.

REFERENCES

Adkins, V. K., & Mathews, R. M. (1999). Behavioral gerontology: State of the science. *Journal of Clinical Geropsychology, 5*, 39–49. http://dx.doi.org/10.1023/A:1022990829485.

American Bar Association, The Commission on Law and Aging. (2011). *Giving someone a power of attorney for your health care.* Retrieved from: http://www.americanbar.org/content/dam/aba/uncategorized/2011/2011_aging_hcdec_univhcpaform.authcheckdam.pdf.

Autism Speaks. (2014). *FAQs: State autism insurance reform laws.* Retrieved from: http://www.autismspeaks.org/advocacy/insurance/faqs-state-autism-insurance-reform-laws.

Baer, D. M., Wolf, M. M., & Risley, T. R. (1968). Some current dimensions of applied behavior analysis. *Journal of Applied Behavior Analysis, 1*, 91–97.

Bailey, J., & Burch, M. (2002). *Research methods in applied behavior analysis.* Thousand Oaks, CA: Sage.

Bailey, J., & Burch, M. (2011). *Ethics for behavior analysts* (2nd). New York: Routledge.

Baker, J. C., Hanley, G. P., & Mathews, R. M. (2006). Staff administered functional analysis and treatment of aggression by an elder with dementia. *Journal of Applied Behavior Analysis, 39*, 469–474.

Baker, J. C., & LeBlanc, L. A. (2011). Acceptability of interventions for aggressive behavior in long-term care settings: Comparing ratings and hierarchical selection. *Behavior Therapy, 42*, 30–41. http://dx.doi.org/10.1016/j.beth.2010.04.005.

Baker, J. C., LeBlanc, L. A., Raetz, P. B., & Hilton, L. C. (2011). Assessment and treatment of hoarding in an individual with dementia. *Behavior Therapy, 42,* 135–142. http://dx. doi.org/10.1016/j.beth.2010.02.006.

Baltes, P. B., & Baltes, M. M. (1990). Psychological perspectives on successful aging: The model of selective optimization with compensation. In P. B. Baltes & M. M. Baltes (Eds.), *Successful aging: Perspectives from the behavioral sciences.* New York: Cambridge University Press.

Baltes, M. M., Orzech, M. J., Barton, E. M., & Lago, D. (1983). The microecology of residents and staff: Behavioral mapping in a nursing home. *Zeitschrift für Gerontologie, 16,* 18–26.

Behavior Analyst Certification Board. (2013). *Guidelines for responsible conduct for behavior analysts.* Retrieved from: http://www.bacb.com/Downloadfiles/BACBguidelines/ BACB_Conduct_Guidelines.pdf.

Bershadsky, J., Taub, S., Engler, J., Moseley, C. R., Lakin, K. C., Stancliffe, R. J., et al. (2012). Place of residence and preventive health care for intellectual and developmental disabilities services recipients in 20 states. *Public Health Reports, 127,* 475–485. Retrieved from: http://www.publichealthreports.org/.

Brault, M. W. (2008). Americans with disabilities: 2005. Household economic studies, current population reports, December. U.S. Department of Commerce. Retrieved from: www.census.gov.

Brenske, S., Rudrud, E. H., Schulze, A., & Rapp, J. T. (2008). Increasing activity attendance and engagement in individuals with dementia using descriptive prompts. *Journal of Applied Behavior Analysis, 41,* 273–277. http://dx.doi.org/10.1901/ jaba.2008.41-273.

Brodaty, H., Draper, B., & Low, L. F. (2003). Behavioural and psychological symptoms of dementia: A seven-tiered model of service delivery. *Medical Journal of Australia, 178*(5), 231–234.

Buchanan, J. A., Christenson, A., Houlihan, D., & Ostrom, C. (2011). The role of behavior analysis in the rehabilitation of persons with dementia. *Behavior Therapy, 42,* 9–21. http://dx.doi.org/10.1016/j.beth.2010.01.003.

Buchanan, J. A., & Fisher, J. E. (2002). Functional assessment and noncontingent reinforcement in the treatment of disruptive vocalizations in elderly dementia patients. *Journal of Applied Behavior Analysis, 35,* 99–103.

Buchanan, J., Hustfeldt, J., Berg, T., & Houlihan, D. (2008). Publication trends in behavioral gerontology in the past 25 years: Are the elderly still an understudied population in behavioral research? *Behavioral Interventions, 23,* 65–74. http://dx.doi.org/10.1002/ bin.254.

Burgio, L. (1991). Behavioral staff training and management in geriatric long-term care facilities. In P. A. Wisocki (Ed.), *Handbook of clinical behavior therapy with the elderly client* (pp. 423–438). New York: Plenum Press.

Burgio, L. D., & Burgio, K. L. (1986). Behavioral gerontology: Application of behavioral methods to the problems of older adults. *Journal of Applied Behavior Analysis, 19,* 231–328. http://dx.doi.org/10.1901/jaba.1986.19-321.

Burgio, L., & Burgio, K. (1990). Institutional staff training and management: A review of the literature and a model for geriatric long-term facilities. *International Journal of Aging and Human Development, 30,* 287–302.

Burgio, L. D., Collins, I. B., Schmid, B., Wharton, T., McCallum, D., & DeCoster, J. (2009). Translating the REACH caregiver intervention for use by area agency on aging personnel: The REACH OUT program. *Gerontologist, 49,* 103–116. http://dx.doi.org/ 10.1093/geront/gnp012.

Burgio, L. D., Engel, B. T., Hawkins, A., McCormick, K., Scheve, A., & Jones, L. T. (1990). A staff management system for maintaining improvements in continence with elderly nursing home residents. *Journal of Applied Behavior Analysis, 23,* 111–118.

Burgio, L. D., & Fisher, S. E. (2000). Application of psychosocial interventions for treating behavioral and psychosocial symptoms of dementia. *International Psychogeriatrics, 12,* 351–358.

Burgio, L., & Kowalkoski, J. D. (2011). Alive and well: The state of behavioral gerontology in 2011. *Behavior Therapy, 42,* 3–8.

Burgio, K. L., Locker, J. L., Goode, P. S., Hardin, J. M., McDowell, B. J., Dombroski, M., et al. (1998). Behavioral vs. drug treatment for urge urinary incontinence in older women. *Journal of American Medical Association, 280,* 1995–2000.

Burgio, L., Stevens, A., Burgio, K., Roth, D., Paul, P., & Gerstle, J. (2002). Teaching and maintaining behavior management in the nursing home. *Gerontologist, 42,* 487–496.

Caffrey, C., Sengupta, M., Park-Lee, E., Moss, A., Rosenhoff, E., & Harris-Kojetin, L. (2012). *Residents living in residential care facilities: United States, 2010. NCHS data brief, no. 91* (pp. 1–8). Retrieved from: http://www.cdc.gov/nchs/data/databriefs/db91. pdf.

Carstensen, L. L. (1988). The emerging field of behavioral gerontology. *Behavior Therapy, 19,* 259–281. http://dx.doi.org/10.1016/S0005-7894(88)80002-9.

Castle, N., Wagner, L., Ferguson, J., & Handler, S. (2014). Hand hygiene deficiency citations in nursing homes. *Journal of Applied Gerontology, 33,* 24–50.

Chou, K. -R., Chu, H., Tseng, C. -L., & Lu, R. -B. (2003). The measurement of caregiver burden. *Journal of Medical Science, 23*(2), 73–82. Retrieved from: http://jms.ndmctsgh. edu.tw/2302073.pdf.

Cohen-Mansfield, J. (1991). *Instruction manual for the Cohen-Mansfield Agitation Inventory (CMAI).* Rockville, MD: Research Institute of the Hebrew Home of Greater.

Dale, L. C., Olsen, D. A., Patten, C. A., Schroeder, D. R., Croghan, I. T., Hurt, R. D., et al. (1997). Predictors of smoking cessation among elderly smokers treated for nicotine dependence. *Tobacco Control, 6,* 181–187.

Department of Education Assistance to States for the Education of Children with Disabilities and Preschool Grants for Children with Disabilities Rule. (2006). 34 C.F.R. § 300.

Donoghue, C. (2010). Nursing home staff turnover and retention: An analysis of national level data. *Journal of Applied Gerontology, 29*(1), 89–106. http://dx.doi.org/10.1177/ 0733464809334899.

Durkin, M., Prescott, L., Furchtgott, E., Cantor, J., & Powell, D. A. (1993). Concomitant eyeblink and heart rate classical conditioning in young middle aged and elderly human subjects. *Pschology and Aging, 8,* 571–581.

Dwyer-Moore, K. J., & Dixon, M. R. (2007). Functional analysis and treatment of problem behavior of elderly adults in long-term care. *Journal of Applied Behavior Analysis, 40,* 679–683.

Engelman, K. K., Altus, D. E., & Mathews, R. M. (1999). Increasing engagement in daily activities by older adults with dementia. *Journal of Applied Behavior Analysis, 32,* 107–110.

Fisher, J. E., Drossel, C., Kyle, K., Cherup, S., & Sylvester, M. (2010). Treating persons with dementia in context. In D. Gallagher-Thompson, A. Steffen, & L. Thompson (Eds.), *Handbook of cognitive therapies with older adults* (pp. 200–215). New York: Springer.

Fisher, J. E., & Noll, J. (1996). Age-associated differences in sensitivity to reinforcement frequency. *Journal of Clinical Geropsychology, 2,* 297–306.

Folstein, M. F., Folstein, S. E., & McHugh, P. R. (1975). Mini-mental state: A practical method for grading the cognitive state of patients for the clinician. *Journal of Psychiatric Research, 12,* 221–231.

Hanley, G. P., Iwata, B. A., & McCord, B. E. (2003). Functional analysis of problem behavior: A review. *Journal of Applied Behavior Analysis, 36,* 147–185.

Hunt, S. R., Corazzini, K., & Anderson, R. A. (2014). Top nurse-management staffing collapse and care quality in nursing homes. *Journal of Applied Gerontology, 33,* 51–74.

Illinois Department of Healthcare and Family Services, Supportive Living Facilities: Records and Reporting Requirements Rule. (2009). 89 § 146.265.

Illinois Department on Aging. (2012). *Community care plan.* Retrieved from: http://www.state.il.us/aging/1athome/ccp.htm.

Illinois Department on Aging, Community Care Program, Determination of Need Rule. (1999). 89 § 240.715.

Kanfer, F. H., & Karoly, P. (1982). *Self-management and behavior change: From theory to practice.* New York: Pergamon.

Kazdin, A. E. (1981). Acceptability of child treatment techniques of treatment efficacy and adverse side effects. *Behavior Therapy, 12,* 493–506.

Kazdin, A. E. (2011). *Single-case research designs* (2nd). NY: Oxford University Press.

Kratchowill, T. R., & Shapiro, E. S. (2000). Conceptual foundations of behavioral assessment in schools. In R. S. Shapiro & T. R. Kratochwill (Eds.), *Behavioral assessment in schools.* (2nd). New York: The Guilford Press.

LeBlanc, L. A., Cherup, S. M., Feliciano, L., & Sidener, T. M. (2006). Choice-making opportunities to increase activity engagement in individuals with dementia. *American Journal of Alzheimer's Disease and Other Dementias, 21,* 318–325. http://dx.doi.org/10.1177/1533317506292183.

LeBlanc, L. A., Heinkicke, M. R., & Baker, J. C. (2012). Expanding the consumer base for behavior-analytic services: Meeting the needs of consumers in the 21st century. *Behavior Analysis in Practice, 5,* 4–114.

LeBlanc, L. A., Raetz, P. B., & Feliciano, L. (2011). Behavioral gerontology. In W. W. Fisher, C. C. Piazza, & H. S. Roane (Eds.), *Handbook of applied behavior analysis* (pp. 472–488). NY: The Guilford Press.

Lindsley, O. R. (1964). Geriatric behavioral prosthetics. In R. Kastenbaum (Ed.), *New thoughts on old age* (pp. 41–60). NY: Springer.

Mathews, M., & Altus, H. (1997). Teaching nurse aides to promote independence in people with dementia. *Journal of Clinical Geropsychology, 3,* 149–156.

Matson, J. L., & Vollmer, T. R. (1995). *User's guide: Questions about behavioral function (QABF).* Baton Rouge, LA: Scientific Publishers, Inc.

McHorney, C. A. (1996). Measuring and monitoring general health status in elderly persons: Practical and methological issues using the SF-36 Health Survey. *Gerontologist, 36,* 571–583.

Minnesota Division of Mental Health Developmental Disabilities Addictive Diseases. (2005). *Guidelines for supporting adults with challenging behaviors in community settings.* Retrieved from: http://mn.gov/mnddc/positive_behavior_supports/pdf/guidelines_supporting_adults_challenging_behaviors1.pdf.

Molloy, D. W., & Standish, T. I. (1997). A guide to the standardized Mini-Mental State Examination. *International Psychogeriatrics, 9*(1), 87–94.

Montana Public Health and Human Services, Community Homes for Persons with Developmental Disabilities: Record Keeping Rule. (1987). 37 § 100.340.

National Center for Assisted Living. (2012). Assisted living state regulatory review: 2012. Washington, DC. Retrieved from: http://www.ahcancal.org/ncal/resources/Documents/Final%2012%20Reg%20Review.pdf.

Neef, N., & Peterson, S. (2007). Functional behavior assessment. In J. O. Cooper, T. E. Heron, & W. L. Heward (Eds.), *Applied behavior analysis* (2nd, pp. 500–524). Upper Saddle River, NJ: Pearson Education, Inc.

Nolan, B. A. D., Mathews, R. M., & Harrison, M. (2001). Using external memory aids to increase room finding by older adults with dementia. *American Journal of Alzheimer's Disease and Other Dementias, 16*(4), 251–254.

Prasher, V., Farooq, A., & Holder, R. (2004). The adaptive behaviour dementia questionnaire (ABDQ): Screening questionnaire for dementia in Alzheimer's disease in adults with Down syndrome. *Research in Developmental Disabilities, 25*(4), 385–397.

Rahman, A. N., Applbaum, R. A., Schnelle, J. F., & Simmons, S. F. (2012). Translating research into nursing homes: Can we close the gap? *Gerontologist*, *52*(5), 597–606. http://dx.doi.org/10.1093/geront/gnr157.

Rosenthal, T. L., & Carstensen, L. L. (Eds.), (1988). Aging: Clinical needs and research opportunities. *Behavior Therapy*, *19*(3), 257–258 [Special section].

Schnelle, J. F., Cruise, P. A., Alessi, C. A., Ludlow, K., Al-Samarrai, N. R., & Ouslander, J. G. (1998). Sleep hygiene in physically dependent nursing home residents: Behavioral and environmental intervention implications. *Sleep*, *21*, 515–523.

Simmons, S. F., Ferrell, B. A., & Schnelle, J. F. (2002). The effects of a controlled exercise trial on pain in nursing home residents. *Clinical Journal of Pain*, *18*, 380–385.

Skinner, B. F. (1975). The steep and thorny way to a science of behavior. *American Psychologist*, *30*(1), 42–49.

Sloane, P. D., Hoeffer, B., Mitchell, M., McKenzie, D. A., Barrick, A., Rader, J., et al. (2004). Effect of person-centered showering and the towel bath on bathing-associated aggression, agitation, and discomfort in nursing home residents with dementia: A randomized, controlled trial. *Journal of the American Geriatrics Society*, *52*, 1795–1804. http://dx.doi.org/10.1111/j.1532-5415.2004.52501.x.

Tariq, S. H., Tumosa, N., Chibnall, J. T., Perry, H. M., III, & Morley, J. E. (2006). The Saint Louis University Mental Status (SLUMS) Examination for detecting mild cognitive impairment and dementia is more sensitive than the Mini-Mental Status Examination (MMSE)—A pilot study. *American Journal of Geriatric Psychology*, *14*, 900–910.

Thomason-Sassi, J. L., Iwata, B. A., Neidert, P. L., & Roscoe, E. M. (2011). Response latency as an index of response strength during functional analysis of problem behavior. *Journal of Applied Behavior Analysis*, *44*, 51–67.

Thompson, T. (2005). Paul E. Meehl and B. F. Skinner: Autitaxia, autitypy, and autism. *Behavior and Philosophy*, *33*, 101–131.

Trahan, M. A., Kahng, S., Fisher, A. B., & Hausman, N. L. (2011). Behavior-analytic research on dementia in older adults. *Journal of Applied Behavior Analysis*, *44*, 687–691. http://dx.doi.org/10.1901/jaba.2011.44-687.

Turner, J., & Mathews, R. M. (2013). Behavioral gerontology. In G. J. Madden, W. V. Dube, T. D. Hackenberg, & G. P. Hanley (Eds.), *Translating principles into practice. APA handbook of behavior analysis: Vol. 2*. Washington, DC: American Psychological Association.

Virués-Ortega, J. (2010). Applied behavior analytic intervention for autism in early childhood: Meta-analysis, meta-regression and dose-response meta-analysis of multiple outcomes. *Clinical Psychology Review*, *30*, 387–399.

Weisfeldt, M. L., Gerstenblith, M. L., & Lakatta, E. G. (1985). Alterations in circulatory function. In R. Andrea, E. L. Seirman, & W. R. Hazzard (Eds.), *Principles of geriatric medicine* (pp. 248–279). New York: McGraw Hill.

Werner, C. A. (2011). The older population: 2010. 2010 census briefs. U.S. Department of Commerce. Retrieved from: www.census.gov.

Williamson, P. N., & Ascione, F. R. (1983). Behavioral treatment of the elderly: Implications for theory and therapy. *Behavior Modification*, *7*, 583–610. http://dx.doi.org/10.1177/01454455830074008.

Wisocki, P. A. (Ed.) (1991). Behavioral gerontology. In *Handbook of clinical behavior therapy with the elderly client* (pp. 3–51). New York: Plenum Press.

Woodruff-Pak, D. (2001). Eyeblink classical conditioning differentiates normal from Alzheimer's disease. *Integrative Psychological and Behavioral Science*, *36*, 87–108.

Zimmerman, G., Favrod, J., Trieu, V. H., & Pomini, V. (2005). Cognitive behavior therapy for schizophrenia: Effect sizes, clinical models, and methodological rigor. *Schizophrenia Bulletin*, *34*, 523–537. http://dx.doi.org/10.1093/schul/sbm114.

CHAPTER 18

Behavior Analysis and the Treatment of Human Psychological Suffering

Yvonne Barnes-Holmes, Ciara McEnteggart
Department of Psychology, National University of Ireland Maynooth, Co., Kildare, Ireland

For decades, clinical psychology has organized behavior and individuals within categorical symptom-based systems of classification, most notably as in the Diagnostic and Statistical Manual (DSM; e.g., American Psychiatric Association (APA), 1994). This topographically based method of categorization does not resonate easily with the behavior-analytic tradition, which is deeply rooted in functional contextualism (Hayes, Long, Levin, & Follette, 2013). Indeed, topographies offer little direction on the function of any behavior, and, thus, organizing behavior along topographical dimensions says little about how behavior comes to emerge, is maintained, or can be altered. For the behavior analyst, this limitation applies equally to appropriate and "dysfunctional" behavior.

Applied behavior analysis (ABA), as the dominant application of behavioral principles and its focus on developmental disabilities in particular, often relies on a simple distinction between behavioral excesses and deficits. And, perhaps surprisingly, this simple distinction has proven very useful in guiding categorizations of behavior and directing programs of behavior change. For example, if a child with autism shows deficits in eye contact, and eye contact is an essential prerequisite to socialization, then establishing eye contact is an obvious place to start gaining social aptitude. Hence, the categorization of lack of eye contact as a *deficiency* in a broad social repertoire is helpful. A range of intervention tools (similar to those used to train other behaviors) then become available for establishing this skill.

Interestingly, however, no functional analysis is involved in the type of diagnostic process just described. What occurred clinically was a simple set of working assumptions: eye contact is essential for socialization; the frequency

Clinical and Organizational Applications of Applied Behavior Analysis
http://dx.doi.org/10.1016/B978-0-12-420249-8.00018-6

451

of eye contact was deemed to be at a level that was inappropriately low (e.g., by virtue of age), and likely to reduce access to reinforcers; hence the frequency of that behavior needed to be increased; and this was likely needed before more complex social skills could be established. The primary functional-analytic piece of this puzzle concerns two aspects. First, there may be an alternative behavior which is currently reinforced (and thus may be categorized as excessive) and which provides reinforcement that would otherwise follow eye contact. Second, one needs to ensure that eye contact is established with appropriate (social) reinforcers and that when the behavior occurs, this is what maintains it in the child's repertoire.

As can be seen from the point just discussed, an excessive behavior often accompanies a deficiency but is more functional in nature. That is, as soon as one suspects that a child engages in a behavior which she/he should not, or should do so to a much lesser extent, this immediately begs the question about what contingency maintains the behavior. Again, in most cases, a more appropriate alternative behavior occurs at a low rate (i.e., is deficient), and the observed behavior provides access to reinforcement not enabled by the deficient response. For example, a child might tantrum for attention instead of manding. Much of ABA is like this, and operating this simple model has been hugely successful for establishing those types of target behaviors in developmentally disabled populations.

There is little evidence that such a simple distinction between behavioral excesses and deficits would have similar benefits with the complex problems that characterize psychological suffering. In other words, perhaps this latter clinical context requires sophisticated functional analyses because topographies are so varied, and the histories of the individuals in question are already so well established (Barnes-Holmes, Barnes-Holmes, McHugh, & Hayes, 2004). We are not proposing that the simple distinction between behavioral excesses and deficits has *no* utility in this context, we are simply suggesting that it alone is not enough. Indeed, the proliferation of extensive fine-grained systems of categorical classifications, such as DSM, appears to support this suggestion.

As a result, one might assume that the behavior therapies traditionally used as applications of behavioral principles to complex clinical problems rely heavily on sophisticated functional analyses. Interestingly, however, this is not as much the case as one would think. Section "Developing Behavior Therapy" of the current chapter offers a potted history of how behavioral principles have been used to understand and treat clinical or psychiatric problems, and to what extent these applications have been successful.

The history of what is collectively referred to as "behavior therapy" has been loosely summarized as "three waves" (Moran, 2008). The first wave was mostly influenced by the principles of classical conditioning and largely comprised counter-conditioning techniques. The second wave[1] moved forward with the newly discovered principles of operant conditioning and mainly comprised exposure techniques. Although they represent a clear progression toward greater behavioral complexity, neither of these waves rested upon particularly complex accounts of human behavior, nor did they suggest that there was anything different at the level of process about psychological suffering versus more typically observed behavior. For example, classical and operant conditioning processes are both readily observed in nonhuman behavior.

Section "Developing Behavior Therapy" thereafter summarizes the third wave of behavior therapies, including functional analytic psychotherapy (FAP; Kohlenberg & Tsai, 1991), dialectical behavior therapy (DBT; Linehan, 1993), and acceptance and commitment therapy (ACT; Hayes, Strosahl, & Wilson, 1999). These appear to represent a fundamental shift in thinking from their second-wave predecessors, with a new approach to complex behavior that was stimulated, at least in part, by Skinner's account of verbal behavior. According to this perspective, classical and operant conditioning principles, such as those observed with nonhumans, cannot fully explain the types of behaviors that are psychologically problematic.

While even greater behavioral complexity can be accounted for by this shift upwards to verbal behavior, it is interesting that all three therapeutic approaches that comprise the third wave of behavior therapy also possess elements that are not germane to the behavioral tradition. For example, DBT, FAP, and ACT all focus heavily on facilitating psychological acceptance, and DBT is directly influenced by Buddhism. Our key point from Section "Developing Behavior Therapy" of the present chapter is that, although Skinner's account of verbal behavior (1957) clearly moved the field forward in its ability to tackle greater complexity, the various transitions evident in the third wave of behavior therapies suggest that even this was not adequate in accounting for the types of complex behavioral problems that comprise psychological suffering. In other words, it appears that behavior

---

[1] We would like to highlight that some authors might include the cognitive revolution within the second wave of behavior therapies (i.e., the introduction of cognitive behavioral therapy [CBT]), however, the present classification is simply another way of organizing the history of behavior therapy for the purposes of this chapter.

therapy has difficulty adhering only to its behavioral roots when trying to generate comprehensive accounts of human suffering and how it can be alleviated.

In Section "The Radical Rethink of Verbal Behavior and Human Suffering: A Relational Frame Perspective", we introduce relational frame theory (RFT)—a radical rethink of language and cognition from a functional and behavioral perspective. Although the theory has not specifically generated clinical applications (i.e., it is a scientific account, not an application), the deeply rooted functionality inherent in its concepts appears to suggest functional analytic ways in which clinically relevant behavior can be understood and manipulated. Indeed, the latter end of the chapter explores some interesting examples of ways in which RFT concepts can be translated directly into clinical application, thereby offering the type of functional bottom-up approach to psychological suffering that even behavior therapy has not seen before.

We would like to be explicit from the outset about our choice of using the phrase "psychological suffering" over the standard term "psychopathology." In truth, we do not believe that there is much "pathological" about psychological suffering, and even if there are physiological elements to this, they would not be of interest to behavioral psychologists or behavior therapists whose job it is to understand and manipulate behavior directly. Furthermore, we believe that the pathology model of this type of suffering has done the science of understanding and sufferers a great deal more harm than good. Hence, in functional-analytic terms, nothing is to be gained from continuing to operate this model. Indeed, *novel* (nonpathology-oriented) behavior by scientists and clinicians in terms of identifying new models and approaches is to be strongly encouraged. The current chapter is a move toward this aim.

DEVELOPING BEHAVIOR THERAPY

First-Wave Behavior Therapy

As a direct result of a massive body of evidence in support of the basic principles of learning, it was not long before someone asked about whether these principles, although largely abstracted from work with nonhumans, could be applied to the understanding and treatment of various patterns of psychological suffering. And this application of principles is precisely what Watson and Rayner (1920) did, even before operant learning principles were fully articulated. While there are few or no other psychological therapies against which Watson and Rayner's suggestions can be compared, what is important to note is their emphasis on directly applying basic learning principles with nonhumans to human problems. This translation or abstraction appears to rest on two basic assumptions that may or may not be correct (Barnes-Holmes et al., 2004). First, the continuity assumption states that the principles observed with nonhuman behavior operate somewhat similarly in the context of human behavior (Hayes, Barnes-Holmes, & Roche, 2001; Skinner, 1938). Indeed, this assumption proved particularly useful in the development of ABA as a therapy for autism (e.g., Lovaas, 1981), which rests primarily on operant conditioning principles abstracted by Skinner from animal behavior. Second, all behaviors (normal and "abnormal") involve the same behavioral processes, such as classical and operant conditioning. Watson and Rayner's account of phobia as conditioned fear responding to previously neutral stimuli is a classic example. However, in spite of enormous support for the basic principle of classical conditioning, the concept saw little translation into applied settings beyond Watson and Rayner's account of phobia, and even that had many critics (e.g., Harris, 1979; Samelson, 1980).

Second-Wave Behavior Therapy

Within 40 years, even greater scope and depth were promised with the emergence of the new broader learning principles that governed operant responding. This suggested a wholly novel method of tackling the complexity of human behavior and suffering, and how they might be influenced. For example, Wolpe (1958) proposed systematic desensitization and counterconditioning for the treatment of anxiety and phobia. Mowrer (1960) proposed that repeated exposure to a feared stimulus extinguishes the fear response and reduces avoidance. Bandura and Menlove (1968) proposed the concept of modeling as an explanation for the development of substance abuse and phobia. Seligman (1974) proposed the learned hopelessness model of depression.

What coordinates each of these approaches is that they tried at their core to remain close to the basic scientific principles of operant learning, much the same as these principles applied to nonhumans. Indeed, although Skinner's account of verbal behavior was available to them, this was not readily harnessed in any of these second-wave approaches. This transition did not fully occur until the emergence of the third wave of behavior therapies.

Third-Wave Behavior Therapy
Functional Analytic Psychotherapy

The core techniques of FAP are firmly rooted in radical behaviorism, particularly a behavior analytic account of the therapeutic relationship (Kanter, Tsai, & Kohlenberg, 2010). These techniques are not normally packaged as a therapeutic program but are rather designed to be used in conjunction with other behavior therapies *or* to be introduced specifically when a client's relationship skills are problematic. The basic principle of FAP is that therapeutic benefits are maximized when problematic behaviors are activated *in vivo* (Kohlenberg & Tsai, 2002). This principle arises from two traditional behavioral assumptions. First, behavior is most likely to be changed when the context is changed, rather than trying to change responding directly. Second, shaping is more likely to be effective when consequences are immediate rather than delayed. As such, FAP focuses more on in-session behaviors, rather than talking about behaviors that occur elsewhere, as is common in therapy. As a result, the therapeutic relationship lies at the core of this contextual contingency-based approach.

FAP's strict adherence to its behavioral roots is readily illustrated by its five core rules (Kohlenberg & Tsai, 2002). First, therapists should identify clinically relevant behaviors in terms of: (a) problematic behavior *in-session* that relates to the client's reported problem; (b) absence of behavior that would alleviate the problem; and (c) how the client *describes* the problem and its cause. Second, therapists should create an environment in which the likelihood of these behaviors occurring in-session is increased. Third, therapists should reinforce behaviors that will alleviate the problem, preferably with natural reinforcers to aid generalization outside of therapy. Fourth, therapists should be aware of the influence of their own behavior on the client's clinically relevant behavior. Fifth, repertoires for describing their own behavior in functional terms should be developed with clients. Although, not as behaviorally consistent, FAP argues that it promotes acceptance through improved self-observation, reduced self-criticism, and more consistent reinforcement of positive behavior in-session. Specifically, the change of context increases the likelihood of the acceptance of aversive situations outside of therapy. With the exception of the middle-level term "acceptance," FAP is otherwise an almost entirely functional-analytic form of therapy, with functional analyses required by all of its core principles.

While there are no current randomized-controlled trials investigating the efficacy of FAP, there are a vast number of case studies which support FAP's effectiveness in treating human suffering—for example, depression, smoking cessation, obsessive compulsive disorder, sex offending, personality disorders, and panic (Holman et al., 2012; Lopez Bermudez, Ferro, & Calvillo, 2010; Manduchi & Schoendorff, 2012; McClafferty, 2012; Newring & Wheeler, 2012; Pankey, 2012).

Dialectical Behavior Therapy

DBT operates a much broader biopsychosocial model that is most often applied to parasuicidal behavior and borderline personality disorder (BPD; Linehan, 1993). Specifically, the core psychological problems targeted by the therapy are emotional dysregulation and invalidation of one's sense of self (Linehan, 2001). The treatment model's primary focus concerns the dialectic between acceptance and behavior change across four main therapeutic stages. Stage 1 seeks to reduce life-threatening behavior and increase mindfulness, interpersonal skills, emotional regulation, distress tolerance, and self-management. Stage 2 focuses on exposure to emotional difficulties. Stage 3 focuses on life skills, including employment, education, and relationships. Finally, Stage 4 promotes the acceptance and normality of human suffering and enhances the life skills necessary to live with contentment and difficulties simultaneously. This final stage includes contingency management, where individuals learn to observe consequences of their own behavior such that workable, adaptive responding is increased, and maladaptive responding is decreased (Linehan et al., 2006). In spite of this strong behavioral focus, at least the language and techniques of DBT borrows heavily from fields far beyond behavior analysis and traditional behavior therapy (e.g., influences from Zen Buddhism; Robins, 2002).

To date, the efficacy of DBT has been investigated in a number of meta-analyses. First, Öst (2008) investigated the efficacy of all third-wave behavior therapies, in which DBT yielded a significant effect size. Notably, for randomized controlled trials (RCTs) that recruited waiting-list control participants, the effect size for DBT was largest, whereas those using treatment-as-usual (TAU) or active treatment controls yielded only moderate effect sizes. Second, in a more recent meta-analysis, Panos, Jackson, Hasan, and Panos (2014) investigated the efficacy of DBT for suicidal and depressive symptoms, and also treatment attrition in BPD. The authors reported that DBT effectively stabilized self-destructive behavior and was marginally better than TAU in reducing treatment attrition; however, there was no significant difference in reducing depressive symptoms. Third, Clarkin (2013) conducted a meta-analysis of DBT for BPD that demonstrated a significant benefit over TAU for anger, parasuicidality, and mental health. And finally, Frazier and Vela (2014) reported similar effects for anger and aggression in various populations (not solely BPD participants) in their meta-analysis. Overall, in a review, Burmeister et al. (2014) concluded that the effects from these meta-analyses are robust and stable, and the effects of individual RCTs and small-scale studies support the promise of DBT adaptations for wider aspects of human suffering.

Acceptance and Commitment Therapy

The roots of ACT lie in functional contextualism, although, similar to DBT and to a lesser extent to FAP, a number of its core concepts (e.g., acceptance) are not germane to that tradition. The full ACT treatment model specifies six related concepts organized centrally around psychological flexibility. First, acting in the present moment promotes an ongoing awareness of internal and external events and minimizes other influences over behavior. Second, acceptance (used synonymously with willingness) is promoted as a superior strategy for dealing with private events (positive and negative) over avoidance. Third, defusion techniques (that target emotional and/or cognitive fusion) attempt to separate individuals from their literal psychological content (i.e., thoughts and feelings). The ability to achieve this in the context of previously avoided psychological content is referred to as operating in self-as-context—the fourth concept in the ACT model. Individuals should fully discriminate their content as only content (without evaluation) for fusion and avoidance to be minimized. Fifth, values are a highly personalized and potentially unique set of objectives that are pivotal to one's sense of self. In short, in suffering, avoidance predominates and interferes with valued action. Sixth, ACT relies heavily on the concept of behavior change to emphasize the need to alter patterns of behavior toward personal values—this is referred to as committed action.

ACT strongly advocates its roots in functional contextualism, while recognizing the tension between this and the need to employ terms not germane to the behavioral tradition (Barnes-Holmes, Hussey, McEnteggart, Barnes-Holmes, & Foody, 2015). In wrestling with this tension, authors of ACT propose that middle-level terms, such as acceptance and fusion, are essential at least in the interim to allow therapeutic developments while more basic scientific terms emerge (Hayes et al., 2013). There is nothing inherently problematic with this approach at a clinical level, and clinicians from almost all traditions employ a mix of concepts that serve their purposes best (e.g., acceptance is used in many therapeutic traditions). However, some recent ACT authors have argued that clinicians, especially from the behavioral tradition (whose philosophical roots are purely prediction and influence) should be clear about when they are and are not using behavioral terms (Barnes-Holmes et al., 2015).

The efficacy of ACT has been investigated in a small number of meta-analyses. First, in the Öst (2008) review, ACT yielded a significant effect size and followed the same pattern as DBT, where the effect size was largest when compared to waiting list controls and moderate when compared to TAU or active treatment controls. Second, Ruiz (2012) conducted a meta-analysis of RCTs comparing ACT to traditional CBT. Overall, ACT was found to yield a greater effect size, specifically for depression, quality of life posttreatment (PT), but not anxiety. Notably, ACT had a large impact on its proposed processes of change; however, this finding was absent for CBT. Third, Ducasse and Fond (in press) reported that in controlled-outcome studies, ACT had a moderate overall effect size both at PT and at follow-up (FU). Indeed, when compared to waiting list controls, TAU, or placebo, the effect was stronger both at PT and FU, than when compared to active treatments. Finally, in a meta-analysis of component analyses of ACT's core concepts, Levin, Hildebrandt, Lillis, and Hayes (2012) reported that significant effect sizes were found when compared to inactive comparison conditions, with greater effect sizes for theoretically specified outcomes (i.e., targeted by the model of psychological flexibility) and components that included metaphors and exercises. Notably, these effects were stable between at-risk (i.e., distressed) and convenience samples.

Behavior Therapy: The Successes and Shortcomings

The third wave of behavior therapies clearly represented a more sophisticated, although in some cases less obviously behavioral, approach to psychological suffering and its treatment. For example, ACT emphasizes acceptance and cognitive defusion, while DBT emphasizes dialectics. On the other hand, these therapies include a number of core principles of operant condition, such as functional analysis, skills building, and shaping (for a review, see Hayes, Masuda, Bissett, Luoma, & Guerrero, 2004). As a result, one might question why this more eclectic mix of behavioral and nonbehavior concepts appeared necessary, at least to all three contemporary behavior therapies?

Chomsky's (1959) indictment of the limitations of Skinner's (1957) account of verbal behavior inflicted little direct damage on the second-wave behavior therapies because, as noted above, they were not built on Skinner's account of language, only his account of operant conditioning. In fact, the second-wave behavior therapies declined precisely because the dominance of behavioral psychology had begun to seriously unravel, and Eysenck's (1952) seminal paper undermined the whole perception of the benefits of talking therapy (see Zimmermann & Pomini, 2013). As a result, it was not necessarily the case that behavior therapy declined because it was limited in scope (although this was undoubtedly the case; Chomsky, 1959). It was more the case that the professional appetite for behavioral psychology was enormously undermined (see Watrin & Darwich, 2012). Hence, any therapy based on the behavioral principles was disregarded by virtue of dislike for these principles. Indeed, this was all somewhat ironic given that behavior therapy's initial strength was the very fact that applications translated basic principles directly from the lab to the treatment room, and it was these basic principles that ultimately caused their demise. It is perhaps not surprising, therefore, that even when the new third-wave behavior therapies emerged, they looked much less behavioral than their predecessors.

But, behavior therapies did have their limitations, at least conceptually, and these too played an important role in the types of alternative approaches that would ultimately succeed them. Consider Chomsky's (1959) core criticism of Skinner's account of verbal behavior as falling short of complex psychological phenomena such as language and cognition, thus massively undermining the continuity assumption from nonhumans. For Chomsky, the two species were fundamentally distinguishable by language and cognition, and principles in nonhumans would have limited accounts of complex human behavior. Consider also the implications of this criticism for psychological suffering. Exposure techniques are used to overcome avoidance responding, such as those that appear to operate in phobia. In short, exposure to the *conditioned* stimulus is said to extinguish avoidance responding that has been acquired in the context of that stimulus. But there has long been debate about the conditioning history that gave rise to fear, which is believed to be the source of the avoidance (for a review, see Rachman, 2002). In other words, individuals become highly fearful and avoidant of stimuli in the absence of a history of direct fear conditioning. This is not observed in nonhumans. So, how did that stimulus acquire those fear and avoidant functions, if not by direct training? There is indeed very little in Skinner's account of verbal behavior that can adequately account for these novel effects. And yet, they occur for a sizeable number of individuals across a whole manner of stimuli (including, for example, sub-mechanophobia in which individuals fear underwater man-made objects, see Doctor, Kahn, & Adamec, 2008).

As a result, we suggest that this limited scope results directly from the limits within the traditional Skinnerian account of verbal behavior. In short, our thesis is that behavior-therapy interventions were limited in terms of both scientific understanding and clinical outcomes because they were not based on a coherent functional account of complex behavior. Put another way, complex (but not necessarily "abnormal") processes are at work in complex organisms, and complex interventions will be needed to alter these complex processes, if the organisms are to behave differently. Indeed, the almost complete absence of clinical suffering in nonhumans, relative to its pervasiveness in humans, suggests that there is something fundamentally very different between these two species. As a result, the traditional behavioral approach of abstracting principles from nonhumans to humans is unlikely to offer much that will help clinicians to understand uniquely human patterns of psychological suffering.

As an alternative, in Section "The Radical Rethink of Verbal Behavior and Human Suffering: A Relational Frame Perspective" we propose RFT which posits itself specifically as a *post-Skinnerian* account of human language and cognition (Hayes, Barnes-Holmes, et al., 2001). If this is the case, and theory does indeed offer that level of depth and breadth, then by definition it must have conceptual implications for human suffering. These implications may be summarized as follows. First, for RFT, human behavior is predominantly verbal from approximately childhood onwards. Second, these verbal processes can be defined behaviorally. Third, psychological problems are manifestations of these typical verbal processes. Fourth, therapy interventions need to target these verbal processes. In Section "The Radical Rethink of Verbal Behavior and Human Suffering: A Relational Frame Perspective", we explore the implications of RFT for psychological suffering and its remediation through functional behavioral means.

THE RADICAL RETHINK OF VERBAL BEHAVIOR AND HUMAN SUFFERING: A RELATIONAL FRAME PERSPECTIVE

The current section firstly comprises an overview of the radical rethink of language that separates RFT from Skinner. We will briefly review RFT's core concepts, but readers are referred to the original book on RFT by Hayes, Barnes-Holmes, et al. (2001). Although the theory has not specifically generated clinical applications (i.e., it is a scientific account, not an application), the deeply rooted functionality inherent in its concepts of verbal behavior appears to suggest directly functional ways in which clinically relevant behavior can be understood and manipulated. Toward the end, the chapter explores some interesting ways in which these concepts can be translated into direct application, thereby offering the type of functional bottom-up approach to psychological suffering that even behavior therapy has not seen before. We will then close the section with some RFT-based suggestions for specific therapeutic techniques (e.g., metaphor) that may complement contemporary behavior therapies, but which fundamentally do not require integration with nonbehavioral concepts.

Relational Responding

For RFT, the bidirectional nature of stimulus relations is a defining feature of language and cognition and is likely in turn to be central to its account of human suffering and its alleviation. For example, in reporting a traumatic event, the bidirectional relations between words and the event allow the reporting to acquire many of the aversive and painful functions of the actual event (Hayes & Gifford, 1997). In RFT terms, the words and the events to which they refer are in a relation of coordination, and as a result the original functions attached to the event now transform through the coordination relation to the words. Hence, saying the words can bring almost all of the features and trauma of the past event into the present.

Coordination relations are synonymous with Sidman's concept of equivalence (e.g., Sidman & Tailby, 1982), and both terms critically refer to the ability to relate two stimuli as "the same" *without direct training of that behavior*. For RFT, the types of coordination relations noted above are based on a developmental history that is full of object-word and word-object exemplars. For example, imagine a child is told that another word for "teddy" is "kino" and there is a direct history of saying "teddy" in the presence of the teddy (e.g., by showing the teddy and saying the word and/or by saying the word and showing the teddy). When the child hears the word "kino," she will be able to select the teddy and could also select the word "teddy," even though the word "kino" has never been directly associated with the physical object teddy (i.e., this word-object relation is novel or derived).

Another defining feature of RFT is its focus on multiple stimulus relations, above and beyond coordination. This is where RFT parts company with the concept of equivalence. For RFT, other types of stimulus relations include: difference, opposition, comparison, hierarchy, and perspective-taking, although this list is not definitive. For example, if a verbally able child is taught that $A > B$, she can readily derive then that $B < A$. Similarly, if she is then instructed that $C < D$, she will derive that $D > C$. If sufficient exemplars of these types of training exist, now simply telling the child that $X > Y$ will readily enable her to derive that $Y < X$, even though explicit training in this relation among these two stimuli has never occurred. RFT pivots heavily on this concept of derived relational learning (often called derivation) in its attempt to account for the generativity and complexity of language and cognition.

Essential Features of Relational Framing

According to RFT, the various patterns in which derived relational responding can emerge are referred to as relational frames. All frames are believed to share three common properties: mutual entailment, combinatorial entailment, and the transfer or transformation of stimulus functions. Mutual entailment refers to the relations between two stimuli. For example, if you are told that $A = B$, you can derive that $B = A$. That is, the specified $A = B$ relation mutually entails the (symmetrical) $B = A$ relation. Combinatorial entailment refers to the relations among three or more stimuli. For example, if $A > B$ and $B > C$, then you will derive that $A > C$ and $C < A$. That is, the A-B and B-C relations combinatorially entail the A-C and C-A relations.

Perhaps the most important property of relational frames is the transfer or transformation of stimulus functions that provide the psychological content for derived relations. For example, if $A > B$, and a reinforcing function is attached to B, then A will acquire an even greater reinforcing function than B, even though the function was directly attached to B but not to A; although at one level this outcome would seem paradoxical in that one could argue that a stronger function would emerge for B not A because of the direct history in which the function came to be attached to B. For RFT, however, this outcome is easily explained by the transformation of the reinforcing function through the comparative relation between A and B (Dymond & Barnes, 1995). Specifically, the reinforcing function of A is transformed by virtue of its comparative (more-than) relation with B, hence any functions attached to B will be stronger with A.

Given the incredible complexity and specificity that is available with derived relational responding, the theory would have to account for the very precise ways in which language appears to control the derived relations among stimuli and the functions that transform accordingly. And contextual control is RFT's answer to this (Hayes, Fox, et al., 2001). For RFT, derived relational responding is under the control of contextual cues, and everyday language provides these cues. For example, if you are asked to imagine that B is A, the word "is" now acts a contextual cue to control a coordination relation between A and B (i.e., "is" means that A and B are hypothetically the same). Of course, for the theory it is irrelevant that you do not actually know what A and B are or that you may have never seen either. Instead, what is crucial is that, with an adequate history of language training, the word "is" permits you to coordinate the stimuli and functions of one will transfer to the other. Indeed, RFT relies heavily on the concept of arbitrarily applicable relational responding to indicate that this coordination relation and the fact that the word "is" are both arbitrarily applied. In other words, there is nothing about the actual word "is" that implies coordination. The verbal community could just have easily come to use an alternative word for this. Furthermore, because A and B are completely verbal, there is nothing about their physical form (even if they had one) that suggests that the two stimuli are the same. In other words, the relating of these two stimuli together is an entirely verbal behavior. For RFT, contextual cues, usually in the spoken environment but not necessarily, control the specificity and arbitrariness of derived relational responding.

RFT as an Account of Psychological Suffering

It is not surprising that the concept of the transformation of functions seems vital to understanding human suffering from the perspective of RFT. Consider a simple example of an early, relatively minor traumatic event. Imagine a boy who went horse riding for the first time and experienced a traumatic fall off the horse; thus, a fear of horses is now classically conditioned through aversive consequences. When the boy is told that donkeys are like horses (i.e., frame of coordination), he will also likely fear donkeys despite having no direct negative experience with a donkey. In this case, the fear functions of horses are transferred to donkeys via the relations of coordination between horses and donkeys. And the same would occur if he is told that camels are like horses, and zebras are a type of horse, and so on. With only a small number of coordination relations, the class of animals that instill fear in the child might be so great that, for example, a trip to the zoo could become a potentially terrifying event, even though the zoo might not contain a single horse.

But again, there are more complex derived relations than coordination, and a whole range of psychological functions will also be transformed in accordance with these. For example, imagine a man who has intrusive cleaning obsessions and a history of panic attacks. In therapy, he is asked to describe the dirtiest imaginable scene that would, in principle, make him have a full-blown panic attack. Paradoxically, the man describes a slum in India, which he has never visited. For RFT, the slums in India are likely to be in a number of comparative frames with dirty scenes in daily life for this man such as: dirtier than; more risk of disease than; less control over, etc. Therefore, the functions of the Indian slum transform in accordance with these multiple stimulus relations and the functions that have indirectly or directly become attached to scenes from daily life. Indeed, it is easy to imagine that this man would have difficulty in going on holidays, using public toilets, eating at restaurants, taking his children to recreational facilities, etc. And all of these limitations could exert their own strain on his interpersonal relationships with his family.

While RFT is now well established and soundly supported by empirical evidence, it is only in the last decade that the full implications of the theory for psychological suffering are being explored. And it is important to add here that the empirical basis for this extension remains limited (see Hussey & Barnes-Holmes, 2012; Nicholson & Barnes-Holmes, 2012). However, there are a number of aspects of RFT that appear to have clear conceptual implications for how we understand human suffering, as well as clear practical implications for how this might be alleviated. The three most obvious such areas at present are the perspective-taking relations, rule-governed behavior, and metaphor. In the following paragraphs, we address these three areas and their clinical implications.

Deictic Relations

According to RFT, the deictic relations provide a functional way of talking about perspective-taking and self more broadly. RFT research has demonstrated functional distinctions among: interpersonal I-you relations, spatial here-there relations, and temporal now-then relations (Barnes-Holmes, 2001). This also appears to be the order in which these relations develop in our natural learning histories (McHugh, Barnes-Holmes, & Barnes-Holmes, 2004) and appears to reflect increasing levels of relational complexity (McHugh, Barnes-Holmes, O'Hora, & Barnes-Holmes, 2004).

Deictic frames appear to be more complex than other types of relations, in part because they do not have persistent formal or nonarbitrary counterparts. For example, if I say "here," I only mean where I am at that point in time, whereas if I say "here" later, I mean a different place. In other words, there is no formal property of "here," it is always only the place in which I am at present. As a result, learning to respond to and from "here" in terms of acquiring a constant perspective (i.e., I am always responding from here) likely requires many multiple exemplars (e.g., "What were you doing there?"). Indeed, what appears to be abstracted across these exemplars is the ability to respond from a constant perspective (Barnes-Holmes, Foody, Barnes-Holmes, & McHugh, 2013). It is not surprising that the I–you relations would likely be established before the here–there relations, because one needs to have an interpersonal (I) perspective along with which the constancy of the perspective here can develop.

As one's perspective becomes more established, the integration of I-here as noted earlier appears to increasingly incorporate constancy with regard to time, as the temporal relations develop. Specifically, the perspective of verbally sophisticated individuals appears to be anchored I-here-now, even though the realities of now are ever-changing. For example, if I say "now" I am referring to this specific and current point in time, whereas if I say "then," I am referring to a different time. Again, there is no formal property of "now"; it is always only the time at present. So again, what appears to be abstracted across exemplars is the ability to respond from a constant temporal perspective (Barnes-Holmes et al., 2013).

In a broader definition of self that incorporated the importance of perspective-taking, Hayes (1995) referred to the dual functions of self in terms of "functioning both as a doer (content) and as an observer (perspective) of the doing" (p. 95). Foody, Barnes-Holmes, and Barnes-Holmes (2012) used this distinction to propose an RFT account of ways in which psychological problems emerge. Specifically, these authors proposed that one's perspective as doer is constant in terms of always operating from I-here-now, as would be entirely consistent with one's developmental history, as noted earlier. However, one's relationship with regard to one's psychological content is more variable. That is, when one's psychological content is located here-now, and given that one's perspective is always I-here-now, this coordination of perspective and content (both here and now) leads to problematic transformations of function, for example, such that you can believe that you are what you think (rather than just being the person who is doing the thinking). For instance, if I am having the thought that I am depressed, then I must be depressed. When these relations between perspective and content are coordinated, an individual would have no control over the transformation of psychological functions between them. A synonymous way of describing this using the language of ACT is "self-as-content." Indeed, ACT employs the concept of "fusion" to denote the fact that this level of attachment of one's content to one's self is obstructive to psychological wellbeing.

Foody et al. (2012) described a second place from which you can relate to your psychological content. They proposed that psychological content at this level is also located here-now, but fusion or attachment can be considerably reduced if one responds to one's content in a dynamic and on-going way. This serves to minimize the transformations of psychological functions even though the relations are still coordinated. This proposition is synonymous with ACT's concept of "self-as-process" that refers to the ongoing and experiential description of thoughts, feelings, and behavior. Operating at this level likely increases psychological flexibility because psychological content is less likely to control behavior. As a result, both RFT and ACT would argue that this is a much more psychologically healthy place from which to operate. Nonetheless, given that the perspective and content remain coordinated, the individual would need to be wary because functions can transfer readily through these (and you would be operating in self-as-content).

Foody et al. (2012) described a third place from which you can relate to your psychological content. They proposed that psychological content only at this level is located there-then, hence fusion or attachment are unlikely. This is because the perspective and content are now in a relation of distinction (possibly even opposition), hence psychological functions will transform accordingly. For example, if I can see that I just had an unpleasant thought about myself and can notice that this was only a thought, then the content of the thought will have little or no impact on who I am at that time. For instance, I can have the thought that I am depressed while discriminating from my experience that I have achieved a great deal, hence an opposition relation between the thought and experience, making it likely that I will completely disregard the thought rather than believing it. This proposition is synonymous with ACT's concept of "self-as-context" or "defusion." Operating at this level likely facilitates maximum psychological flexibility because psychological content is unlikely to control behavior. Indeed, Hayes (1995) referred to self-as-context as follows: "*I* in some meaningful sense is the location that is left behind when all of the content differences are subtracted out" (p. 96).

As you can see, although our developmental histories establish complex perspective-taking abilities that are essential for the development of the self, the same histories also make psychological suffering inevitable because it occurs through the same "normal" verbal processes. For ACT and RFT, learning to switch perspective on your content from here-now to there-then is a key feature of psychological flexibility and an important index of psychological well-being, although at one level it goes against your developmental history. As a result, one can easily see why psychological suffering is almost unavoidable.

Rule-governed Behavior

From an early age, we learn to follow the rules given to us by influential others (e.g., parents). And these rules provide us with useful strategies for controlling our own behavior and predicting the behavior of others (e.g., "If you're a good boy at the party, you can have ice-cream when you get home"). For RFT, rule-governed behavior is a type of complex verbal regulation (Törneke, Luciano, Barnes-Holmes, & Bond, 2015) that has both advantages and disadvantages (Törneke, Luciano, & Salas, 2008).

In an RFT articulation of rules, Törneke et al. (2015) suggested that excessive rule following may be obstructive to psychological wellbeing, because the behavior continues even when the consequences cease to occur, have never occurred, and are aversive. Furthermore, excessive rule-following is particularly problematic when one attempts to apply it to one's psychological content, because content by its very nature is so complex that even a series of rules on how to manage it is unlikely to be helpful, even if one could adhere to them all the time.

Consider an individual who verbally constructs the rule "I must always appear strong." Now consider the additional rules generated by this: "I mustn't let my guard down," "People can't see me upset," "I shouldn't be so sensitive," etc. If this was a man, it is not difficult to see how this type of rule-following would potentially work well in his professional environment, especially for example if he was the leader of a team. But consider a different aspect of his life, such as his relationship with his wife. In this context, some aspects of following the rule might be beneficial at times when his wife needs support or needs her husband to act like a strong father for their unruly children. However, following the rule excessively in this context could equally be problematic, if it means, for example, that he perceives that he cannot openly share negative or vulnerable experiences with her.

ACT employs various interventions to facilitate an awareness of one's own rule-following and the various contexts in which this occurs, often unknowingly. In this case, the therapist seeks to have the client abstract exemplars of rule-following in relation to discriminating whether this worked in the various contexts in which it occurred. This relationship between the rule-following and its consequences is often referred to as "workability" that provides clients with a defused perspective from which to view their own behavior (Barnes-Holmes et al., 2004). Specifically, Törneke et al. (2015) proposed that the safest place from which to operate regarding self-rules is in a relation of hierarchy (rather than coordination) between one's perspective and one's psychological content. They also argued that this type of flexible, workable discrimination of one's own behavior is critical to psychological flexibility and wellbeing.

Metaphor (Relating Relations)

According to RFT, complex relational networks and the relations among these lie at the root of metaphors (Stewart, Barnes-Holmes, Hayes, & Lipkens, 2001). While this complexity may not be obvious when metaphors are apparently simple, for RFT the same complex verbal process is at work.

In a paper applying RFT's basic account of metaphors to the development and use of *clinical* metaphors, Foody et al. (2015) explained why metaphors have such well-established clinical utility, as well as what needs to be considered in the construction of metaphors that work in a clinical context. To illustrate the extent to which RFT's basic account provides a useful approach to the clinical context, the authors took one of ACT's stock metaphors "Struggling with anxiety is like struggling in quicksand." This example contains two relational networks: the target (struggling with anxiety) and the vehicle (struggling with quicksand). The vehicle relational network illustrates metaphorically and in relational terms a critical aspect of the client's situation, as represented by the target network.

The key therapeutic aims of coordinating these two relational networks may be summarized as follows:
- What the client is doing with her anxiety can be collectively called "struggling," and this will contain various topographies that refer to all of the ways in which she tries to deal with or manage all of the feelings, etc. that she collectively refers to as "anxiety."
- The therapist will use the metaphor to encourage the client to discriminate and tact these various experiences, both in terms of what is felt and in terms of how she behaves when these events occur.
- There is something about struggling with anxiety that, from the therapist's perspective, suggests that it is similar to struggling with quicksand.

- Talking about one's psychological content in a new metaphorical way helps to alter one's perspective on it and reduce fusion and attachment. This is, in part, because the client can discriminate that she is talking about her content in an external way, rather than dealing with it in a primarily internal way (i.e., a strong feature of struggling).
- The metaphor can be used to highlight the fact that just as struggling physically in quicksand can lead to drowning, so too can struggling with anxiety lead to panic attacks (assuming panic attacks are an issue for this client).
- That is, the client had probably not before discriminated that her attempts to avoid anxiety had *caused* her panic attacks. Rather, she will likely have believed that avoiding anxiety also helped her avoid panic attacks.
- As a result, the therapist is encouraging the client to more accurately discriminate the consequences of her own actions.
- Part of the power of this particular metaphor rests in the coordination of panic attacks and drowning through the metaphor. That is, panic attacks are coordinated with not being able to breathe, while drowning is coordinated with choking and not being able to breathe. Not only does this coordination indicate to the client that the therapist fully appreciates how serious it feels when it seems that she cannot breathe (i.e., it feels like dying), it also highlights for the client that this severity is caused by her own actions.

For Foody et al. (2015), the use of metaphor in therapy may simply allow the therapist to provide an alternative metaphorical perspective for the client on her situation, and as such metaphors need have no obvious "solution." For example, in the quicksand metaphor, the solution indirectly is for the client to stop struggling with anxiety and to expose herself to anxiety much the same way as one survives quicksand by exposing oneself to it as fully and calmly as possible. Even without this, the metaphor may have utility by virtue of the fact that it offers a shift in perspective.

Constructing the target relational network forces the therapist to make a *functional* assessment of the client's situation. That is, the therapist first needs to ask herself what is the client's specific problem, otherwise the therapist will have difficulty identifying the target relational network. For example, if the type of anxiety experienced by a particular client does not include a sense of struggling to breathe, then the coordination with drowning in quicksand may not work at all. Similarly, only accurate functional analyses will permit a string match between the vehicle and target networks. For example, if a client has never heard of quicksand, then there is no point in trying to create a relational network around this. Critically, the closer the vehicle matches the target relationally, the greater will be the transformation of functions (e.g., exposing oneself to anxiety, just as one would do with quicksand) and the greater the likelihood of behavior change.

Behavior Therapies: Getting Back to Functionality

Many contemporary therapies advocate the use of protocols in their treatment of psychological problems, as a means of guiding therapists generally to deal with broad symptom-based categories or to target therapeutically-designated problems. But we would argue that from a functional-analytic perspective this is a bit like using a sledge hammer to insert a thumb tack. That is, in order to target the highly complex nature of psychological suffering, and the problematic relational networks at play, a highly individualized set of functional analyses is required. Imagine a client comes into therapy and the therapist concludes that the client struggles often with the thought "I am not clever enough," and much of her behavior is an attempt to remove or reduce this thought. For instance, she might engage in distraction or may attempt to remind herself with a self-generated rule that she is a good person deep down. From a functional-analytic RFT perspective, the client's problem here is much more than uncertainty about intellectual attainment (i.e., cleverness). While the topography of clever may be relevant to the client, and thoughts about this may indeed be part of her struggles, for RFT this is more likely to be a problem with the deictic relations. That is, it is likely that this client struggles with *all psychological content that is negative* because her perspective is coordinated with it. In other words, she is what she thinks and when much of that is evaluated negatively, that would be a pretty awful psychological space in which to live. Furthermore, when one is coordinated with one's negative content, it is likely that others appear comparatively better or superior on many fronts (e.g., cleverer than, richer than, more attractive, etc.). As a result, a strong comparative relation may emerge between the self and others, in which others are always better. This, in turn, generates more negative content, hence more to be avoided, and so on. As a result, one can easily see how the very relations that give us healthy development also bring us very unhealthy adulthood.

While RFT appears to offer remarkable precision and clinical applicability, these can only be harnessed through adequate functional analyses. Part of one's clinical narrative (especially with clients directly) will of course involve many middle and higher level terms, even folk psychology terms. But critically, the clinician does not *need* to incorporate these into the analyses. The analyses can be conducted in a bottom-up way, using scientifically generated, purely functional concepts (e.g., deictic relations). Indeed, a functional or relational analysis can be conducted by the therapist using the client's verbal and other behavior as it is relayed.

Concluding Comments

Even in describing the analyses in the current chapter, we have found ourselves providing alternative descriptions using concepts, such as acceptance, fusion. This is often as helpful for readers as for clients in terms of exemplar training. But critically, when engaged in the therapeutic process, RFT appears to offer the clinician a possible language for conducting functional analyses that are highly individualized in a way that may facilitate lasting behavior change. This bottom-up analysis is something, we would argue, that has been missing in behavior therapy for some time. It should be noted that we are not proposing bottom-up thinking for the sake of it. If therapeutic outcomes across the board were uniformly positive and the majority of sufferers achieved long-term valued living, there would be no urgency in seeking alternative ways to understand and change suffering. However, the fact is that clinical outcomes still indicate that a great many clients are not helped (Steinert, Hofmann, Kruse, & Leichsenring, 2014). Looking metaphorically to our counterparts in ABA, one can readily see the incredible success a simplistic, functional, bottom-up analysis has had in that field. While the application of behavioral principles seems to have stumbled in its account of complex verbal behavior thus far, that limitation is now relieved with RFT and the fact that it appears to account for both complexity and generativity. The strength of RFT lies in the very fact that it is a basic science, only constrained by its philosophical roots in functional contextualism. But, paradoxically, these two very facts may also be the theory's greatest assets as it may lead the way for precise functional analyses that explain human suffering and its alleviation in purely behavioral, functional, and effective ways.

REFERENCES

American Psychiatric Association (APA). (1994). *Diagnostic and statistical manual of mental disorders* (4th). Washington, DC: American Psychiatric Association.

Bandura, A., & Menlove, F. L. (1968). Factors determining vicarious extinction of avoidance behavior through symbolic modeling. *Journal of Personality and Social Psychology, 8,* 99–108.

Barnes-Holmes, Y. (2001). *Analysing relational frames: Studying language and cognition in young children.* Unpublished doctoral thesis. Maynooth: National University of Ireland.

Barnes-Holmes, Y., Barnes-Holmes, D., McHugh, L., & Hayes, S. C. (2004). Relational frame theory: Some implications for understanding and treating human psychopathology. *International Journal of Psychology and Psychological Therapy, 4*, 355–375.

Barnes-Holmes, Y., Foody, M., Barnes-Holmes, D., & McHugh, L. (2013). Advances in research on deictic relations and perspective-taking. In S. Dymond, & B. Roche (Eds.), *Advances in relational frame theory: Research and application* (pp. 127–150). Oakland, CA: New Harbinger.

Barnes-Holmes, Y., Hussey, I., McEnteggart, C., Barnes-Holmes, D., & Foody, M. (2015). Scientific ambition: The relationship between relational frame theory and middle-level terms in acceptance and commitment therapy. In S. C. Hayes, D. Barnes-Holmes, R. D. Zettle, & A. Biglan (Eds.), *Handbook of contextual behavioral science*. Nevada: Blackwell-Wiley.

Burmeister, K., Höschel, K., von Auer, A. K., Reiske, S., Schweiger, U., Sipos, V., et al. (2014). Dialectical behavior therapy (DBT)—Developments and empirical evidence. *Psychiatrische Praxis, 41*(5), 242–249.

Chomsky, N. (1959). A review of B.F. Skinner's verbal behavior. *Language, 35*, 26–58.

Clarkin, J. F. (2013). Review: Some evidence of benefit for psychotherapies in borderline personality disorder. *Evidence-Based Mental Health, 16*(1), 17.

Doctor, R. M., Kahn, A. P., & Adamec, C. (2008). *The encyclopedia of phobias, fears and anxieties* (3rd). New York: Facts on File.

Ducasse, D., & Fond, G. (in press). Acceptance and commitment therapy. *Encephale*. Retrieved from: http://www.scopus.com/inward/record.url?eid=2-s2.0-84887544604& partnerID=40&md5=0ca06dac474807b6fb67e52296130542.

Dymond, S., & Barnes, D. (1995). A transformation of self-discrimination response functions in accordance with the arbitrarily applicable relations of sameness, more-than, and less-than. *Journal of the Experimental Analysis of Behavior, 64*, 163–184.

Eysenck, H. J. (1952). The effects of psychotherapy: An evaluation. *Journal of Consulting Psychology, 16*, 319–324.

Foody, M., Barnes-Holmes, Y., & Barnes-Holmes, D. (2012). The role of self in acceptance and commitment therapy (ACT). In L. McHugh, & I. Stewart (Eds.), *The self and perspective taking: Research and applications* (pp. 125–142). Oakland, CA: New Harbinger.

Foody, M., Barnes-Holmes, Y., Barnes-Holmes, D., Törneke, N., Luciano, C., Stewart, I., & McEnteggart, C. (2015). RFT for clinical use: The example of metaphor. *Journal of Contextual Behavioral Science, 3*(4), 305–313.

Frazier, S. N., & Vela, J. (2014). Dialectical behavior therapy for the treatment of anger and aggressive behavior: A review. *Aggression and Violent Behavior, 19*(2), 156–163.

Harris, B. (1979). What ever happened to little Albert? *American Psychologist, 34*, 151–160.

Hayes, S. C. (1995). Knowing selves. *The Behavior Therapist, 18*, 94–96.

Hayes, S. C., Barnes-Holmes, D., & Roche, B. (Eds.), (2001). *Relational frame theory: A post-Skinnerian account of language and cognition*. New York: Plenum Press.

Hayes, S. C., Fox, E., Gifford, E. V., Wilson, K. G., Barnes-Holmes, D., & Healy, O. (2001). Derived relational responding as learned behavior. In S. C. Hayes, D. Barnes-Holmes, & B. Roche (Eds.), *Relational frame theory: A post-Skinnerian account of language and cognition* (pp. 21–50). New York: Plenum Press.

Hayes, S. C., & Gifford, E. V. (1997). The trouble with language: Experiential avoidance, rules, and the nature of verbal events. *Psychological Science, 8*, 170–173.

Hayes, S. C., Long, D. M., Levin, M. E., & Follette, W. C. (2013). Treatment development: Can we find a better way? *Clinical Psychology Review, 33*(7), 870–882.

Hayes, S. C., Masuda, A., Bissett, R., Luoma, J., & Guerrero, L. F. (2004). DBT, FAP, and ACT: How empirically oriented are the new behavior therapy technologies? *Behavior Therapy, 35*, 35–54.

Hayes, S. C., Strosahl, K. D., & Wilson, K. G. (1999). *Acceptance and commitment therapy: An experiential approach to behavior change*. New York: Guilford Press.

Holman, G., Kohlenberg, R. J., Tsai, M., Haworth, K., Jacobson, E., & Liu, S. (2012). Functional analytic psychotherapy is a framework for implementing evidence-based practices: The example of integrated smoking cessation and depression treatment. *International Journal of Behavioral Consultation and Therapy, 7*(2), 58–62.

Hussey, I., & Barnes-Holmes, D. (2012). The implicit relational assessment procedure as a measure of implicit depression and the role of psychological flexibility. *Cognitive and Behavioral Practice, 19*(4), 573–582.

Kanter, J., Tsai, M., & Kohlenberg, R. J. (Eds.), (2010). *The practice of functional analytic psychotherapy.* New York: Springer.

Kohlenberg, R. J., & Tsai, M. (1991). *Functional analytic psychotherapy.* New York: Plenum Press.

Kohlenberg, R. J., & Tsai, M. (2002). Functional analytic psychotherapy. In M. Hersen, & W. Sledge (Eds.), *Encyclopedia of psychotherapy* (pp. 841–845). New York: Academic Press.

Levin, M. E., Hildebrandt, M., Lillis, J., & Hayes, S. C. (2012). The impact of treatment components suggested by the psychological flexibility model: A meta-analysis of laboratory-based component studies. *Behavior Therapy, 43,* 741–756.

Linehan, M. M. (1993). *Cognitive-behavioral treatment of borderline personality disorder.* New York: Guilford.

Linehan, M. M. (2001). Dialectical behavior therapy. In N. J. Smelser & P. B. Baltes (Eds.), *International encyclopedia of the social and behavioral sciences* (pp. 3631–3634). Pergamon: Oxford.

Linehan, M. M., Comtois, K., Murray, A. M., Brown, M. Z., Gallop, R. J., Heard, H. L., et al. (2006). Two-year randomized controlled trial and follow-up of dialectical behavior therapy vs. therapy by experts for suicidal behaviors and borderline personality disorder. *Archives of General Psychiatry, 63*(7), 757–766.

Lopez Bermudez, M. A., Ferro, R., & Calvillo, M. (2010). An application of functional analytic psychotherapy in a case of anxiety panic disorder without agoraphobia. *International Journal of Behavioral Consultation and Therapy, 6*(4), 356–372.

Lovaas, O. I. (1981). *Teaching developmentally disabled children: The ME book.* Texas: Pro-ed.

Manduchi, K., & Schoendorff, B. (2012). First steps in FAP: Experiences of beginning functional analytic psychotherapy with an obsessive-compulsive personality disorder client. *International Journal of Behavioral Consultation and Therapy, 7*(2), 72–77.

McClafferty, C. (2012). Expanding the cognitive behavioural therapy traditions: An application of functional analytic psychotherapy treatment in a case study of depression. *International Journal of Behavioral Consultation and Therapy, 7*(2), 90–95.

McHugh, L., Barnes-Holmes, Y., & Barnes-Holmes, D. (2004). Perspective-taking as relational responding: A developmental profile. *Psychological Record, 54*(1), 115–144.

McHugh, L., Barnes-Holmes, Y., O'Hora, D., & Barnes-Holmes, D. (2004). Perspective-taking: A relational frame analysis. *The Experimental Analysis of Human Behavior Bulletin, 22,* 4–10.

Moran, D. J. (2008). The three waves of behavior therapy: Course corrections or navigation errors? *The Behavior Therapist,* (Winter), 147–157 [Special issue].

Mowrer, O. H. (1960). *Learning theory and behavior.* New York: Wiley.

Newring, K. A. B., & Wheeler, J. G. (2012). Functional analytic psychotherapy (FAP) with juveniles with sexual offense behaviors. *International Journal of Behavioral and Cognitive Therapy, 7*(2–3), 102–110.

Nicholson, E., & Barnes-Holmes, D. (2012). Developing an implicit measure of disgust propensity and disgust sensitivity: Examining the role of implicit disgust-propensity and -sensitivity in obsessive-compulsive tendencies. *Journal of Behavior Therapy and Experimental Psychiatry, 43,* 922–930.

Öst, L. G. (2008). Efficacy of the third wave of behavioral therapies: A systematic review and meta-analysis. *Behaviour Research and Therapy, 46*(3), 296–321.

Pankey, J. (2012). Functional analytic psychotherapy (FAP) for cluster B personality disorders: Creating meaning, mattering, and skills. *International Journal of Behavioral Consultation and Therapy, 7*(2), 117–124.

Panos, P. T., Jackson, J. W., Hasan, O., & Panos, A. (2014). Meta-analysis and systematic review assessing the efficacy of dialectical behavior therapy (DBT). *Research on Social Work Practice, 24*(2), 213–223.

Rachman, S. (2002). Fears born and bred: Non-associative fear acquisition? *Behaviour Research and Therapy, 40*(2), 121–126.

Robins, C. J. (2002). Zen principles and mindfulness practice in dialectical behavior therapy. *Cognitive and Behavioral Practice, 9*(1), 50–57.

Ruiz, F. (2012). Acceptance and commitment therapy versus traditional cognitive behavioral therapy: A systematic review and meta-analysis of current empirical evidence. *The International Journal of Psychology and Psychological Therapy, 12*(2), 333–357.

Samelson, F. (1980). Watson's little Albert, Cyril Burt's twins, and the need for a critical science. *American Psychologist, 35*, 619–625.

Seligman, M. E. P. (1974). Depression and learned helplessness. In R. J. Friedman & M. M. Katz (Eds.), *The psychology of depression: Contemporary theory and research* (pp. 83–126). Washington, DC: Winston-Wiley.

Sidman, M., & Tailby, W. (1982). Conditional discrimination versus matching to sample: An expansion of the testing paradigm. *Journal of the Experimental Analysis of Behavior, 37*, 5–22.

Skinner, B. F. (1938). *Behavior of organisms.* New York: Appelton-Century-Crofts.

Skinner, B. F. (1957). *Verbal behavior.* New York: Appleton-Century-Crofts.

Steinert, C., Hofmann, M., Kruse, J., & Leichsenring, F. (2014). Relapse rates after psychotherapy for depression—Stable long-term effects? A meta-analysis. *Journal of Affective Disorders, 168*, 107–118. http://dx.doi.org/10.1016/j.jad.2014.06.043.

Stewart, I., Barnes-Holmes, D., Hayes, S. C., & Lipkens, R. (2001). Relations among relations: Analogies, metaphors and stories. In S. C. Hayes, D. Barnes-Holmes, & B. Roche (Eds.), *Relational frame theory: A post-Skinnerian account of language and cognition* (pp. 73–86). New York: Plenum Press.

Törneke, N., Luciano, C., Barnes-Holmes, Y., & Bond, F. (2015). Relational frame theory and three core strategies in understanding and treating human suffering. In S. C. Hayes, D. Barnes-Holmes, R. D. Zettle, & A. Biglan (Eds.), *Handbook of contextual behavioral science.* Nevada: Blackwell-Wiley.

Törneke, N., Luciano, C., & Salas, S. V. (2008). Rule-governed behavior and psychological problems. *International Journal of Psychology and Psychological Therapy, 8*(2), 141–156.

Watrin, J., & Darwich, R. (2012). On behaviorism in the cognitive revolution: Myth and reactions. *Review of General Psychology, 16*(3), 269–282.

Watson, J. B., & Rayner, R. (1920). Conditioned emotional reactions. *Journal of Experimental Psychology, 3*, 1–14.

Wolpe, J. (1958). *Psychotherapy by reciprocal inhibition.* Stanford, CA: Stanford University Press.

Zimmermann, G., & Pomini, V. (2013). Meta-analysis and psychotherapy efficacy: Facts and fictions. *Psychologie Française, 58*(3), 167–175.

CHAPTER 19

Teaching Safety Skills to Children

Raymond G. Miltenberger, Sindy Sanchez, Diego A. Valbuena
Department of Child and Family Studies, University of South Florida, Tampa, Florida, USA

Throughout their lives, children may be exposed to a variety of safety threats that can result in harm or even death. Although some safety threats occur on a regular basis and afford children the opportunity to repeatedly practice safe behavior (e.g., wearing a safety belt in a vehicle, wearing a helmet when riding a bike, crossing streets safely, not touching the stovetop), others occur less frequently yet pose extreme danger. These safety threats include abduction, sexual abuse, finding a loaded firearm, or finding poisons such as medications or cleaning products (e.g., Miltenberger & Gross, 2011). Researchers have evaluated these safety threats and identified the skills children need to respond safely (Miltenberger & Gross, 2011; Miltenberger & Hanratty, 2013).

Studies by Marchand-Martella, Huber, Martella, and Wood (1996), Poche, Yoder, and Miltenberger (1988), and Holocombe, Wolery, and Katzenmeyer (1995) suggest that perpetrators of abduction typically use lures to entice children to leave with them; four types of abduction lures include simple, authority, incentive, and assistance lures. According to the National Center for Missing and Exploited Children (2009) (NCMEC), over 50,000 children are victims of nonfamilial abductions in a 1-year period. Nonfamily abduction may lead to death, exploitation, human trafficking, or sexual abuse.

Sexual abuse refers to children being physically molested (e.g., from inappropriate touching to intercourse) or used in other ways for the pleasure of adults (e.g., being photographed or filmed; Finkelhor, Hotaling, Lewis, & Smith, 1990). Most sexual abuse is perpetrated by a known individual and occurs through a gradual process in which the child is "groomed" to comply with increasingly more inappropriate adult requests. Through December of 2010, the NCMEC received over 2.4 million calls from individuals asking for help in cases related to missing and sexually abused children and asking for advice for protecting their families.

Another type of safety threat that children may encounter when not in the direct supervision of an adult is finding a loaded firearm. Although

Clinical and Organizational Applications of Applied Behavior Analysis
http://dx.doi.org/10.1016/B978-0-12-420249-8.00019-8
477

proper storage of firearms would eliminate or diminish accidental firearm injury to children, a survey of 5238 parents revealed that 21.5% of parents stored their firearm loaded and unlocked (Stennies, Ikeda, Leadbetter, Houston, & Sacks, 1999). Furthermore, Hardy, Armstrong, Martin, and Strawn (1996) suggested that, contrary to parents' beliefs, children had difficulties discriminating real from fake guns and many had played with their parents' guns without their parents' knowledge. Hardy et al. (1996) also showed that when kids find guns, they are likely to play with them. According to Eber, Annest, Mercy, and Ryan (2004), more than one hundred children are killed and more than one thousand children are injured each year as a result of playing with unattended firearms.

Yet another safety threat children may encounter is finding a poison hazard. The National Capital Poison Center (2013) reported that a leading source of injury for children under 6 years old is unintentional poisoning, and that rates of nonfatal poisoning are steadily increasing, with 44% of exposures involving children less than 6 years of age. Although precautions can be taken at home to avoid accidental poisoning in children (i.e., storing medications or cleaning products safely), the possibility remains that children may come in contact with a poisonous substance (or a loaded gun) in their own home or while visiting someone else's house.

From this discussion, it is clear that safety threats may arise from a variety of situations, both social (e.g., abduction, sexual abuse) and nonsocial (e.g., firearm injury, poisoning). Research highlights the need for effective strategies to teach children to recognize a safety threat and engage in behaviors that will increase their chances of escaping safely. The purpose of this chapter is to discuss the research on teaching safety skills to children. The chapter will discuss different approaches to assessment and training with an emphasis on active learning approaches as the most effective strategies.

SAFETY SKILLS

Researchers have focused on teaching age-appropriate, observable, and measurable skills in response to the various safety threats. Although procedures differ slightly with respect to the safety threat being addressed, a common feature of all the training programs is the emphasis on recognizing a dangerous situation and avoiding contact with the safety threat, immediately leaving the area, and telling an adult (e.g., Himle, Miltenberger, Flessner, & Gatheridge, 2004; Himle, Miltenberger, Gatheridge, & Flessner, 2004). According to Miltenberger and Hanratty (2013), the essential safety skills, applicable to any of the safety threats described, are to recognize, avoid, escape, and report when encountering a safety threat. It is important to note that it is not the goal of safety skills research to make children afraid of people or their environment; rather, the goal is to teach children to recognize dangerous situations and to behave accordingly. Fortunately, research has consistently shown that children do not experience fear or other negative side effects of participating in research on teaching safety skills (as reported by participants and caregivers on answers to questionnaires, e.g., Beck & Miltenberger, 2009; Johnson et al., 2005).

The skills taught in abduction and sexual abuse prevention programs are the same because the child is responding to a threat from another person (in most cases, an adult). The child is taught to say "no" when presented with the respective lure, get away, and tell a trusted adult. The importance of this combination of behaviors as explained by Miltenberger and Hanratty (2013) is as follows: saying "no" is a way for the child to clearly refuse the perpetrator's lure and diminish the chances of further contact. Getting away creates distance between the child and the perpetrator, thereby decreasing the probability that the perpetrator will use force or coercion to make the child engage in the requested behavior. Finally, telling an adult warns the caregivers of the threat so they can ensure the safety of the child and prevent the incident from happening again.

In the case of a nonsocial threat such an unattended gun or poison hazard, a verbal refusal is not required as the child is responding to danger in the physical environment. In the presence of these threats, the child is required to refrain from touching or approaching the safety hazard so as to prevent possible life threatening injuries, leave the area immediately to decrease the time exposed to the dangerous situation, and report the incident to an adult so that he/she can take the necessary precautions to eliminate the threat at that moment and in the future. With regard to any safety threat, social or nonsocial, it is imperative for the child to discriminate the presence of the safety threat so he or she will then initiate the safety skills (the threat should function as an S^D and evoke the safety skills).

ASSESSMENT

The literature on safety skills training describes three types of assessments: verbal report assessments, role-play assessments, and in situ assessments.

Verbal Report Assessment

In a verbal report assessment, the researcher describes a scenario involving a safety threat and asks the child to say how he or she would behave in that situation (Miltenberger & Hanratty, 2013). For example, to assess a child's knowledge of abduction prevention skills, a researcher might say, "Pretend you were at the playground and a man walked up to you and asked you to come with him to help him find his lost puppy. What would you do?" The child describes his or her behavior but the experimenter does not provide any praise or feedback for the child's answer. The child is simply thanked for answering. Saslawasky and Wurtele (1986) developed the Personal Safety Questionnaire (PSQ), which requires children to answer by saying "yes," "no," or "I'm not sure" and the What If Situations Test which assesses answers to a series of questions related to inappropriate sexual requests made by an adult. Similar to the PSQ, the What I Know About Touching Scale, developed by Hazzard, Webb, Kleemeier, Angert, and Pohl (1991), uses "yes," "no," or "I don't know" responses to questions about sexual abuse. In another approach, Miltenberger and Thiesse-Duffy (1988) and Miltenberger, Thiesse-Duffy, Kozak, and Bruellman (1990) read abusive and non-abusive scenarios to children and asked them what they would do in response to each.

Carrol-Rowan and Miltenberger (1994) used verbal report assessment as one measure of the effectiveness of a teacher-directed group training of abduction prevention skills with 4- and 5-year-old children. The children's verbal reports of what they would do in response to abduction scenarios were scored using a 0-4 scale (0 = went with the abductor; 1 = stayed near the abductor but did not refuse; 2 = stayed near the abductor, but said "no" to the request; 3 = ran away from abductor; 4 = ran away from the abductor and reported the incident to the parent). Verbal reports have also been used to assess firearm safety skills (e.g., Gatheridge et al., 2004; Himle, Miltenberger, Gatheridge, et al., 2004; Kelso, Miltenberger, Waters, Egemo-Helm, & Bagne, 2007) and sexual abuse prevention skills (e.g., Harvey, Forehand, Brown, & Holmes, 1988; Hazzard et al., 1991; Kenny, Wurtele, & Alonso, 2012; Miltenberger & Thiesse-Duffy, 1988). Although many of these studies found improvements in responding compared to baseline, not all studies assessed the children's use of the safety skills in situ (e.g., Hazzard et al., 1991; Kenny et al., 2012) and thus, without an actual measure of the children's behavior in the presence of the safety threat, one cannot determine whether the program is effective. In fact, Carrol-Rowan and Miltenberger (1994), Olsen-Woods, Miltenberger, and Foreman (1998), Gatheridge et al. (2004), and Himle, Miltenberger, Gatheridge, et al. (2004) showed poor correspondence between the results of verbal report assessments and in situ assessments. Furthermore, the results of Gatheridge et al. (2004)

and Himle, Miltenberger, Gatheridge, et al. (2004) showed that while most children described the safety skills during the verbal report assessments, they did not demonstrate the skills during in situ assessments.

Due to ethical concerns associated with presenting sexual abuse lures to children, verbal report assessments are typically used in the sexual abuse prevention literature (Miltenberger & Hanratty, 2013). This reliance on verbal report is particularly problematic because of the poor correspondence between children's verbal reports and their use of the appropriate safety skills in real-life scenarios (Miltenberger et al., 1990). Future research on teaching sexual abuse prevention skills should develop better assessment strategies that do not rely on verbal reports.

Role-Play Assessment

Role plays are another type of assessment used in the safety skills literature (Gatheridge et al., 2004; Himle, Miltenberger, Gatheridge, et al., 2004; Kelso et al., 2007). Researchers using role-play assessments evaluate safety skills by presenting children with a scenario and asking them to demonstrate or "act out" what they would do. For example, a researcher might say, "Let's pretend we are in your kitchen and you see this gun on the table" (the researcher places the disabled gun on the table). "Let's also pretend I am your father and I am in the other room. I want you to show me exactly what you would do if you found the gun on your kitchen table." (The researcher then walks across the room to be the "dad" in the other room.) During a role-play assessment, the researcher records the child's behavior but does not provide any praise or corrective feedback. The child is simply thanked for participating. Gatheridge et al. (2004) used role-play assessments to evaluate the efficacy of the Eddie Eagle GunSafe Program and behavioral skills training (BST) with 6- and 7-year-old children. Similarly, Himle, Miltenberger, Gatheridge, et al. (2004) used role-play assessments to evaluate the same programs with children aged 4 to 5 years. Children's responses on the role plays were evaluated using a 4-point scoring scale (0 = the child touched the gun; 1 = the child did not touch the gun but did not get away from the gun; 2 = the child did not touch the gun and got away from the gun but did not report the incident to an adult; and 3 = the child did not touch the gun, but did leave the area and tell an adult).

Role-play assessments were also used by Miltenberger and Thiesse-Duffy (1988) and Miltenberger et al. (1990) to evaluate the acquisition of sexual abuse prevention skills with 4- to 7-year-old children. Because the literature on sexual abuse suggests that inappropriate sexual requests typically originate from a known individual, role-play assessments would need to depict a sexual abuse lure from a known individual (Kopp & Miltenberger, 2009). Because the content of such role plays might be controversial, Kopp and Miltenberger (2008) assessed the validity and social acceptability of scenarios with known individuals that could be used as possible role-play assessments (for example, "Your teacher asks you to stay after class because he has something important to tell you". When you are alone with him he says, "you're doing so well, can I give you a hug and kiss?"). All scenarios were regarded by child protection workers as socially acceptable for use in role plays.

Although role-play assessment is superior to verbal report assessment because the children are actually performing the behavior of interest, role-play assessments are still limited in that they do not assess how the child will actually behave when an adult is not present. The adult's presence may lead to reactivity in the role-play assessment because the adult, rather than the safety threat alone, may be a discriminative stimulus (S^D) for the correct response. In fact, research suggests that children's demonstration of the safety skills during role-play assessments does not always correspond with correct responses during in situ assessments (e.g., Gatheridge et al., 2004; Himle, Miltenberger, Gatheridge, et al., 2004).

In Situ Assessment

In-situation or in situ assessments test the child's response to a safety threat in the natural environment. Because research suggests a disparity between children's behavior during a role-play assessment when they know they are being watched and what they are likely to do in the presence of a safety threat when alone (e.g., Carrol-Rowan & Miltenberger, 1994; Gatheridge et al., 2004; Miltenberger et al., 1990), in situ assessments are conducted without the child's knowledge. This necessary deception ensures that the child is responding with respect to the specific safety threat (S^D) and not with respect to the setting or the presence of an adult such as the researcher or parents.

During an in situ assessment, the safety threat experienced by the child must seem real to the child so that the assessment measures the child's behavior as it would occur in a real situation. To conduct an in situ assessment: (a) a safety threat is simulated in the natural environment, (b) the child has no knowledge of the assessment, and (c) a trusted adult is not in proximity to the safety threat (the child is alone; Miltenberger & Hanratty, 2013). Beck and Miltenberger (2009) used in situ assessments to evaluate the effectiveness of in situ training (IST) and the Stranger Safety abduction prevention program. This study evaluated two types of abduction situations, a knock on the door at home and an approach by a stranger in a public place. During the door-knock scenario, a confederate knocked on the front door three times while the child was in the room near the door and the parent was in a different room. The child was expected to go to the parent and tell the parent about the knock on the door. In the approach scenario, a confederate approached the child in a community setting, got within 1 m of the child, and talked to the child. The child was then expected to get away from the confederate and tell the parent who was nearby but out of sight. Responses to both scenarios were evaluated using a 3-point rating scale similar to the one described earlier. It is important to mention that in studies evaluating abduction prevention skills, either the researcher or another adult (e.g., parent) is present but out of sight, and the confederate never actually leaves the area with the child. If the child fails to demonstrate the safety skills, the confederate creates an excuse and leaves.

Gatheridge et al. (2004) conducted in situ assessments with 6- and 7-year-old children in an after school program to evaluate a gun safety program. During in situ assessments, the child was asked to go to a room where the researchers had placed a hidden camera and disabled firearm (the child was not aware he or she was being assessed). Upon finding the gun, the child was expected to stop immediately, refrain from touching the gun, leave the area, and tell an adult.

Because safety threats can occur in a variety of settings, in situ assessments have been conducted in schools or after school programs (e.g., Miltenberger et al., 2004, 2005), community settings (e.g., Gatheridge et al., 2004; Miltenberger et al., 2013), and family homes (e.g., Gross, Miltenberger, Knudson, Bosch, & Brower-Breitwieser, 2007). In situ assessments have been used to evaluate programs to prevent firearm injury (e.g., Gatheridge et al., 2004), abduction (e.g., Miltenberger et al., 2013), poisoning (Dancho, Thompson, & Rhoades, 2008), and sexual abuse (Miltenberger et al., 1999). In situ assessments also have been extended to evaluate safety skills in the presence of peers. In a study by Miltenberger et al. (2009), both the participant and a peer found a gun, but the peer was trained to entice the participant to play with the gun. Incorporating the peer challenge increased the "realness" of the situation, as children may find guns while they are playing together. Other studies that have conducted in situ assessments with dyads are Hardy (2002), Hardy et al. (1996), Jackman, Farah, Kellermann, and Simon (2001), and Miltenberger et al. (2005).

Because research indicates that most sexual abuse is perpetrated by known individuals, a known individual must present the sexual abuse lure for the assessment to be a realistic simulation of the actual safety threat

(Miltenberger & Hanratty, 2013). However, due to ethical concerns regarding a known person delivering a sexual abuse lure, in situ assessments have not been used in the child sexual abuse prevention literature. Miltenberger and Hanratty (2013) suggested that a possible solution to this problem might be to adopt a procedure similar to that used by Miltenberger et al. (1999) with adults with intellectual disabilities. In this study, the researchers used BST and IST to teach sexual abuse prevention skills to five women diagnosed with intellectual disabilities. During in situ assessments, a male confederate was introduced as a new group home staff, built rapport with the women for approximately 15 min, and subsequently presented an inappropriate sexual request. Because the confederate was introduced as a new staff member and first spent time building rapport, he became a "known" individual to the women participating in the study. Until some type of in situ assessment is also used in the research on sexual abuse prevention for children, there is no evidence to demonstrate that the training programs that have been developed thus far are effective for teaching these critical safety skills. Further research is required in this area.

Although self-report, role-play, and in situ assessment have been used to evaluate the effects of safety skills training, the most valid assessment of safety skills is an in situ assessment. Verbal report assessments are limited because they only assess the child's verbal responses or knowledge of the safety skills. Role-play assessments are valuable because they assess safety skills in response to a simulated safety threat. However, role-play assessments are limited because the child performs the behavior in the presence of the researcher and thus it is not known if the child would perform the behavior in the presence of the safety threat when alone. An in situ assessment is the only form of assessment that provides this valuable information. Therefore, it is recommended that researchers and practitioners continue to use in situ assessments for evaluating safety skills.

TEACHING SAFETY SKILLS

Research on teaching safety skills to children has focused on two main approaches: informational and active learning. The informational, or passive, learning approach consists of the teacher providing information about the safety threat and describing or modeling the correct response to the threat. In this approach, the learner does not rehearse the skills but may practice the correct response verbally (e.g., saying, "If I find a gun, I will not touch it, leave the room, and tell an adult"). On the other hand, in the active learning approach, the learner practices the correct response to the threat (e.g., in a role play, the learner refrains from touching a gun, leaves the room, and tells an adult) while the teacher provides reinforcement and corrective feedback on the performance. The key distinction between the two approaches is that the active approach provides the opportunity for the child to repeatedly engage in the actual safety skills while receiving reinforcement and feedback for his or her response to a simulated safety threat.

Informational Approaches

Informational approaches have been evaluated for teaching a number of safety skills to children including gun safety, abduction prevention, and sexual abuse prevention. These informational approaches include a variety of media to deliver information and model the appropriate responses for the learners, including in-person (e.g., Hardy et al., 1996), books (e.g., Miltenberger & Thiesse-Duffy, 1988), and videos (e.g., Beck & Miltenberger, 2009). Although these approaches are widely used (e.g., Wurtele & Kenny, 2010), the majority of studies evaluating the effectiveness of these passive approaches have only used verbal report assessments, which have demonstrated an increase in the learner's knowledge of the safety threat and their ability to describe the correct responses (e.g., Kenny et al., 2012; Roberts & Miltenberger, 1999; Wurtele & Kenny, 2010). The use of verbal report assessments is concerning, given that numerous studies have demonstrated the lack of correspondence between verbal report and observed behaviors during in situ assessments (e.g., Carrol-Rowan & Miltenberger, 1994; Himle, Miltenberger, Gatheridge, et al., 2004; Miltenberger et al., 1990). Therefore, although these assessments have shown an improvement in the children's knowledge of the safety skill, verbal report does not measure how the children will actually behave when they encounter a real threat. Fortunately, many of these informational approaches have been evaluated using in situ assessments.

Studies using in situ assessments to evaluate informational approaches have found that in general, informational approaches are not effective for teaching safety skills. Hardy evaluated two informational programs for teaching gun safety skills. In one, children listened to instructions from the researchers and a police officer on how to respond to finding a gun and signed a certificate promising not to touch the gun (Hardy et al., 1996). The other evaluated the STAR program, which is commonly used to teach children about the dangers of firearms, making smart decisions, and preventing aggressive conflicts (Hardy, 2002). In addition Gatheridge et al. (2004) and

Himle, Miltenberger, Gatheridge, et al. (2004) evaluated the Eddie Eagle program in which children received instruction from a trainer, watched a video, and completed a coloring book which instructed them to "stop, don't touch, leave the area and tell an adult" when they found a gun. In situ assessments following these informational programs showed that the children did not exhibit the safety skills despite engaging in the correct verbal responses during training sessions.

Similar results have been found when evaluating informational approaches with other safety skills such as abduction prevention and sexual abuse prevention. For example, Beck and Miltenberger (2009) evaluated the commercially available Safe Side Stranger Safety program for teaching children abduction prevention skills. This program consists of a 42-min DVD that provides instructions and models the appropriate responses to abduction threats across a variety of situations. The investigators conducted in situ assessments of the children's performance of the safety skills within a week of having watched the video. This study found that the children did not exhibit the safety skills after watching the Stranger Safety DVD. This finding was further supported in a replication using a group design, where 12 out of 13 children did not display the safety skills during an in situ assessment after watching the Stranger Safety DVD (Miltenberger et al., 2013). In an earlier study, Poche et al. (1988) also showed that an informational approach to teaching abduction prevention skills was ineffective. Wurtele, Marrs, and Miller-Perrin (1987) reached similar conclusions when comparing programs for teaching sexual abuse prevention with and without a rehearsal component. One group received instructions followed by the opportunity to rehearse the skill and receive feedback, while the other group only watched a video model perform the skill without an opportunity to practice. Despite not assessing the skills through in situ assessments, the group that had the rehearsal component scored higher than the video-modeling group on the self-report measures. Similarly, Wurtele, Saslawsky, Miller, Marrs, and Britcher (1986) found that programs that incorporated active learning (BST) were superior to a video-based program for sexual abuse prevention according to self-report measures.

Overall, findings are consistent that informational or passive learning approaches are not effective for teaching safety skills to children as assessed in situations where the child actually has to perform the skills in response to the safety threat during in situ assessments. Although these commercially available programs have the potential to increase accessibility to safety skills training, they do not represent successful alternatives to active learning approaches for teaching safety skills.

Active Learning Approaches

In contrast to passive or informational approaches, which are limited to the provision of information and modeling, active approaches incorporate rehearsal of the safety skills being trained. The advantage of these approaches is that the child executes the safety skills in the presence of the S^D so the trainer can reinforce correct responses and provide further instruction (feedback) for incorrect or partially correct responses. In this way, the trainer can assure the acquisition of the safety skills. The two active learning approaches to teaching safety skills are BST and IST.

Behavioral skills training. BST consists of instruction (the instructor describes the safety threat and appropriate safety skills), modeling (the instructor demonstrates the safety skills), rehearsal (the child practices the safety skills), and feedback (the child receives praise for correct responses, and further instruction to improve the performance followed by an immediate opportunity for further rehearsal). In order for children to respond correctly in the presence of the different safety threats, Miltenberger and Hanratty (2013) emphasized the importance of rehearsal during multiple training sessions. With multiple rehearsals of the safety skills in the presence of the simulated safety threat, responding is more likely to come under the control of the safety threat (rather than the parent or researcher). The goal is for the safety threat to function as an S^D in the presence of which the correct safety skill is demonstrated and reinforced.

Poche et al. (1988) conducted one of the first studies to highlight the importance of the rehearsal component for training safety skills. This study extended the findings from a previous study by Poche, Brouwer, and Swearingen (1981), which found that BST was effective for teaching abduction prevention skills to three children as measured by their responses during in situ assessments. The investigators compared a 60-min safety presentation from a police officer, a 25-min videotape modeling the safety skills (during which the children verbally rehearsed the safety skills), a videotape plus behavioral rehearsal group (same videotape plus the opportunity to rehearse the safety skills while receiving feedback until executed correctly), and a control group that received no training. The children were expected to say "no" and get away when presented with an abduction lure. During in situ assessments, only 12.5% of the children in the 60-min safety presentation ran away from the perpetrator, whereas 47.4% in the videotape group ran away, and 73.7% in the videotape plus behavioral rehearsal group ran away.

Several studies have further examined the utility of BST for teaching a number of safety skills to children (e.g., Miltenberger, 2008; Miltenberger & Olsen, 1996). For example, Carrol-Rowan and Miltenberger (1994) compared two variations of BST for teaching preschoolers abduction prevention skills. One intervention consisted of instructions and modeling provided via video followed by behavioral rehearsal and feedback from the teacher. The other intervention consisted of instructions and modeling provided by the teacher followed by behavioral rehearsal with feedback from the teacher. For both training groups, the performance of the safety skills during in situ assessments was superior to the control group.

Despite being effective for teaching safety skills to some children, the general finding in studies evaluating BST is that it may not be effective for all children. For example, Himle, Miltenberger, Gatheridge, et al. (2004) implemented BST with groups of two to five 4- and 5-year-old children to teach them to respond appropriately to finding a gun. The authors found that following BST, 10 out of 10 children performed the correct response during a role-play assessment; however, only 2 out of 10 demonstrated the skills during an in situ assessment. Gatheridge et al. (2004) replicated this study with 6 and 7 year olds. The group that received BST scored significantly higher in the in situ assessment than did the group receiving the informational approach or the control group. Specifically, 11 out 15 children who received BST in small groups displayed the safety skills when finding a gun. Similar results, showing that BST is effective for teaching safety skills to some but not all children, were shown by Himle, Miltenberger, Flessner, et al. (2004) with 4 and 5 year olds and Miltenberger et al. (2004) with 6 and 7 year olds.

The use of BST was also evaluated for teaching 3- to 5-year-old children to avoid poison hazards (Dancho et al., 2008). During BST, the children were taught to ask an adult before consuming anything and were given a small snack as an alternative. Following training, in situ assessments were conducted in which the children were placed in a room in the presence of containers resembling poison hazards typically found in the natural environment (e.g., pills, liquids). The results of this study showed that BST was somewhat effective at decreasing the frequency of opening unknown containers for some of the children compared to baseline and that further IST was needed to reach zero levels of the unsafe behavior.

The finding that BST can be an effective training method for teaching safety skills has been shown with a variety of safety threats such as abduction (Poche et al., 1981, 1988), firearms (Gatheridge et al., 2004;

Miltenberger et al., 2004), and poison hazards (Dancho et al., 2008). Overall, findings suggest that BST is superior to informational approaches for teaching safety skills. However, the results also show that, although it is effective for teaching the safety skills to some children, some children do not perform the safety skill with complete accuracy following BST alone and require the inclusion of an IST component (e.g., Dancho et al., 2008; Himle, Miltenberger, Flessner, et al., 2004; Jostad, Miltenberger, Kelso, & Knudson, 2008; Miltenberger et al., 2004).

In situ training. IST consists of a training session in the actual context where the safety skill should be performed. That is, when the safety threat is simulated during an in situ assessment, if the participant does not engage in the correct safety response, the trainer intervenes and immediately starts a BST session. IST incorporates the active learning components of BST and enhances generalization of the effects of BST as it is conducted in the natural environment in the presence of the "actual" safety threat the child experienced while alone. Numerous studies have evaluated IST for teaching safety skills to children following or combined with BST (e.g., Dancho et al., 2008; Himle, Miltenberger, Flessner, et al., 2004; Johnson et al., 2005; Jostad et al., 2008; Miltenberger et al., 2004, 2005), following informational approaches (e.g., Beck & Miltenberger, 2009; Gatheridge et al., 2004), or as a stand-alone procedure (Miltenberger et al., 2013).

Gatheridge et al. (2004) implemented IST with the 6 and 7 year olds who failed to use the safety skills following BST. To implement IST, the investigators interrupted the in situ assessment the moment the participant failed to engage in the correct response in the presence of the safety threat and provided instruction, modeling, rehearsal, and feedback. The researchers found that after implementing IST, all participants correctly displayed the safety skills during the subsequent in situ assessments. Similar findings were reported by Himle, Miltenberger, Flessner, et al. (2004) with 4 and 5 year olds and Miltenberger et al. (2004) with 6 and 7 year olds. The researchers reported that half of the children engaged in the safety skills following BST but all the children engaged in the safety skills once IST was implemented.

Based on the studies showing that IST is effective when it follows the use of BST, several researchers evaluated IST in combination with BST to teach safety skills. Johnson et al. (2005) examined the effectiveness of BST with IST to teach abduction prevention skills to 4- and 5-year-old children. A secondary purpose of the research was to assess the maintenance of the safety skills following this program. The researchers conducted three BST sessions in which the children were taught to say no to the lure posed by the stranger, get away, and tell an adult. Safety skills were recorded using a 4-point scale similar to the one used by Carrol-Rowan and Miltenberger (1994). Unlike training programs in which IST is implemented after the failure of BST, in this study, the two training approaches were used concurrently. That is, as in situ assessments were conducted following each training session, IST was implemented each time the children failed to demonstrate the correct safety skills. The results of this study indicate that all children engaged in the correct responses following training, although the number of training sessions varied across children; some children exhibited the skills after one session, whereas others required multiple training sessions. Furthermore, most children performed all the safety skills during follow-up assessments. Similar results were reported by Miltenberger et al. (2005) when evaluating BST and IST for teaching firearm safety skills. In another investigation of BST and IST, Johnson et al. (2006) compared BST alone to BST combined with IST for training abduction prevention skills to children. Using a group design, the researchers found that both approaches were effective for teaching abduction prevention skills but that the BST plus IST group performed significantly better at the 3-month follow-up.

Beck and Miltenberger (2009) also evaluated IST for teaching abduction prevention skills, but they implemented IST following the failure of the Stranger Safety DVD. After viewing the DVD, all children failed to perform the safety skills during in situ assessments. Their parents then implemented IST, and all children engaged in the safety skills after one or more sessions. Similar results were shown by Miltenberger et al. (2013) who evaluated the Stranger Safety DVD and parent-conducted IST and showed that IST was effective after the Stranger Safety DVD was not. Gatheridge et al. (2004) also demonstrated the effectiveness of IST following the failure of an informational program (Eddie Eagle Gunsafe Program) for teaching safety skills to avoid gunplay. These researchers found that only after the implementation of IST did the children exhibit the safety skills during in situ assessments.

Miltenberger et al. (2009) evaluated BST with simulated IST to teach gun safety skills to 6- and 7-year-old children. Simulated IST consisted of the use of training videos in which children were depicted engaging in the safety skills and receiving praise or failing to engage in the safety skills and experiencing IST paired with the loss of a reinforcer. The authors reasoned that seeing IST simulated in a video might have an effect similar to that of actual IST. The results showed that simulated IST was not effective and that IST was needed for the participants to engage in the correct behaviors during in situ assessments. An interesting finding from this study is that children in a control group who did not receive any other safety skills training benefitted from IST as a stand-alone procedure.

The majority of studies have implemented IST following the failure of BST or passive training approaches, which limit conclusions that can be drawn about its efficacy as a stand-alone procedure. However, some studies have examined IST independently of BST or informational approaches. Similar to Miltenberger et al. (2009), Miltenberger et al. (2013) showed that IST was effective as a stand-alone procedure. The authors compared two groups who received parent-implemented IST, one that watched the Stranger Safety DVD and one that received no training (control group). The parents implemented IST when their child failed to use the safety skills during an in situ assessment. Results showed that the treatment group and the control group displayed significantly higher scores during the in situ assessments following IST. These results suggest that IST may be effective as a stand-alone procedure and, consistent with the findings of Beck and Miltenberger (2009), that parents can be taught to teach safety skills to children.

Although researchers have not evaluated exactly which behavioral process is responsible for the effectiveness of IST, researchers suggest that it may be a combination of positive punishment as well as positive and negative reinforcement (Miltenberger & Gross, 2011; Miltenberger & Hanratty, 2013). It is possible that being caught engaging in the incorrect behaviors during an in situ assessment is an aversive event that decreases the likelihood that the children will engage in the incorrect behaviors in the future when the safety threat is present. In addition, avoidance of this aversive event may negatively reinforce engaging in the correct safety skills in appropriate situations. Finally, the praise received for engaging in the safety skills may positively reinforce the safety skills and thus increase the probability of the children engaging in these behaviors in the future (e.g., Miltenberger & Hanratty, 2013).

INCREASING ACCESSIBILITY

Given that active learning approaches have been found to be effective for teaching a number of safety skills, recent emphasis has been placed on increasing the accessibility of these effective approaches (e.g., Miltenberger & Gross, 2011). Increasing accessibility is important because in most successful studies, trained investigators conduct the BST and IST procedures with individual children. Although this approach is successful, it is inefficient, requiring substantial time and professional resources. For example, Vanselow and Hanley (2014) concluded that due to the time required for individual rehearsal, implementing BST for only one safety skill would take around 20 h for the average elementary school. Consequently, a number of studies have evaluated the efficacy of active training approaches for teaching safety skills to children without the need for investigators to implement the training procedures with individual children.

Group Training

One approach for reducing the cost and resources required to teach children safety skills is to conduct group training rather than individual training. Although Miltenberger and Olsen (1996) concluded that individualized training was superior to group training, a number of studies continued to evaluate group trainings as a way to increase the accessibility of effective training approaches. For example, Carrol-Rowan and Miltenberger (1994) and Olsen-Woods et al. (1998) showed that BST implemented in the classroom was effective for teaching abduction prevention skills to most children. In addition, Himle, Miltenberger, Gatheridge, et al. (2004), Gatheridge et al. (2004), and Kelso et al. (2007) evaluated the effectiveness of BST implemented in small groups to teach children gun safety skills. The results of these studies showed that group-implemented BST was effective for teaching some of the children to respond appropriately to finding a gun, while some of the children required IST to perform at criterion levels (Gatheridge et al., 2004).

Despite some inconsistency in the effectiveness of group BST, this approach may be a useful first step for teaching safety skills in the classroom or to groups of children in other settings (e.g., a camp or after school program). If BST is implemented in a group format, the trainer should assure that (a) all children are paying attention to instructions and modeling, (b) all children get an opportunity to rehearse the skills with feedback until correct, and (c) all children observe other children's rehearsals and the feedback they receive (Miltenberger, 2012). However, because it cannot be determined in advance which children will benefit from group BST, in situ assessments must be conducted following training to identify children for whom more individualized training with IST is necessary. Researchers should investigate strategies for increasing the effectiveness of BST implemented with groups of children.

Parent-Implemented Training

Another approach to making training more accessible is the use of parents or caregivers to teach safety skills to their children. Gross et al. (2007) investigated the effectiveness of a program in which parents taught their own children gun safety skills. In this study, the parents read a training manual and watched a training video to learn how to conduct BST and IST sessions. The parents then implemented BST and IST with no further training from the researchers to teach their own children the gun safety skills. The results showed that parent-implemented BST and IST were effective for three of the four children who participated, and they were rated favorably by the parents in terms of ease of implementation and satisfaction. The authors suggested that implementation fidelity was a key factor in the success of parent training; the parents of the three children who performed the safety skills correctly implemented the program with 100% fidelity. A subsequent study by Beck and Miltenberger (2009) evaluated the effectiveness of the Stranger Safety DVD and parent-implemented IST for teaching children abduction prevention skills. The researchers used written and vocal instructions and modeling along with rehearsal and feedback (BST) to teach the parents to conduct IST. A researcher also observed the first IST session and provided feedback to the parents (praise and instructions for improvement if needed). The parents implemented IST if their child did not respond correctly to a stranger's approach in a public place and to a knock on the door at home. Although children did not respond appropriately to the safety threats following the Stranger Safety DVD, all participants performed the safety skills correctly following parent-implemented IST and maintained the skills at follow-up assessments ranging from 4 to 22 weeks after training. Miltenberger et al. (2013) extended the findings from this study using a group design with 27 participants. A control group and a group that watched the Stranger Safety DVD both received parent-implemented IST. The authors used video modeling and BST to teach the parents to conduct IST. They found no significant difference in the safety skills for the children in the Stranger Safety DVD group and the control group prior to IST. After parent-implemented IST, both the control and treatment groups showed significant improvements in the safety skills, with no significant differences between the two groups. The results of these studies suggest that parents can learn to conduct BST and IST and that parent-implemented BST and IST are effective for teaching safety skills to children when the parents implement the procedures with fidelity. More research should establish the type and amount of training needed for parents to successfully teach safety skills to their own children.

Peer-Implemented Training

Another promising approach for increasing the accessibility of BST and IST is the use of peer tutoring. Jostad et al. (2008) trained 6- and 7-year-old children to teach gun safety skills to 4- and 5-year-old children. After the 6- and 7-year-old trainers participated in BST to learn how to conduct BST and IST with the younger children, they used BST and IST successfully with little adult assistance to teach the skills to the younger children. All children who were trained by a peer demonstrated the skills during in situ assessments, confirming suggestions by Jostad and Miltenberger (2004) that peer training of safety skills may be both feasible and practical. Consistent with findings from Himle, Miltenberger, Flessner, et al. (2004) and Miltenberger et al. (2004), half of the children demonstrated the skills following BST, and half demonstrated the skills only after IST. These findings have been further extended to abduction prevention skills by Tarasenko, Miltenberger, Brower-Breitwieser, and Bosch (2010). In this study, two child trainers effectively trained three peers to say "no," leave the area, and tell an adult when lured by a stranger. Although the research examining the utility of peer trainers is limited, it appears that peer-implemented training approaches can be effective and practical for teaching safety skills to children. The use of peers as trainers merits further research.

Simulated Training

Another tactic for increasing accessibility of safety skills training has been the incorporation of computer simulations into training. Advancements in technology have allowed for computer simulations where participants can engage in the target behaviors through virtual reality (VR). Some researchers have already demonstrated the effectiveness of VR for teaching such skills as safe street-crossing to children (e.g., Arbogast et al., 2014; McComas, MacKay, & Pivik, 2002; Schwebel & McClure, 2014; Schwebel, McClure, & Severson, 2014). Vanselow and Hanley (2014) evaluated the effectiveness and generality of a computerized version of BST (CBST) for teaching safety skills. CBST consisted of a computer game in which the participants completed modules that incorporated BST components (it provided information on the safety threat, showed videos demonstrating correct and incorrect responses to threats, and provided the opportunity for the children to rehearse the correct response in the appropriate context within the virtual simulation). This approach may be superior to traditional video modeling approaches because the participant controls the character as the character rehearses the correct response. Through a series of studies, the investigators used in situ assessments to evaluate the effectiveness of CBST for teaching abduction prevention skills, poison prevention skills, and lighter safety skills. In situ assessments were also conducted to assess generalization for some skills that were not explicitly trained. IST was conducted for the skills that were not performed correctly during in situ assessments. The authors found that only a few participants acquired the skill after CBST alone. However, when CBST was combined with IST, it resulted in correct performance of the safety skills and generalization of the skills to different categories of threats. CBST may be useful for increasing the availability of effective training programs, particularly for such skills that are difficult to simulate in role plays (e.g., sexual abuse prevention, fire safety, or pedestrian safety). However, IST may still be necessary for children who do not benefit from CBST. Future research is recommended to examine the effectiveness of VR training programs and examine the validity of VR assessments by comparing results with in situ assessments across a wide range of safety skills.

SUMMARY

The growing body of research on teaching safety skills to children shows that an active learning approach is most successful. Children who participate in programs that are informational in nature do not exhibit the safety skills during in situ assessments following training. However, children who learn the skills through instructions and modeling and then rehearse the skills multiple times with feedback in response to simulated safety threats are more likely to demonstrate the safety skills during in situ assessments. The research shows BST to be effective in many but not all cases. Some children demonstrate the safety skills following BST but some do not. Fortunately, children who fail to demonstrate the safety skills following BST subsequently engage in the skills following IST (see Table 19.1). Furthermore, IST is effective following the failure of informational approaches such as the Eddie Eagle GunSafe program and the Stranger Safety program. Research even shows that IST is effective as a stand-alone program. Researchers should continue to investigate ways to make successful safety skill training programs more accessible so more children can benefit. Promising approaches include group-implemented BST, parent-implemented programs, peer-implemented programs, and computer-assisted programs using VR applications. More research should investigate these promising approaches for increasing the accessibility of safety skills training. At the same time, parents, teachers, and others should be discouraged from using informational approaches that have been shown to be ineffective for teaching safety skills to children.

Table 19.1 Steps in teaching safety skills to children

1. Conduct in situ assessment
   (a) Assess safety skills in the presence of the simulated safety threat that appears real to the child
   (b) While the child is alone
   (c) With no knowledge of the assessment
2. Implement BST with individual child or small group of children
   (a) Describe the safety threat and the safety skills (describe all variations of the safety threat, e.g., types of abduction lures)
   (b) Model the safety skills in realistic role plays depicting each variation of the safety threat
   (c) Have child rehearse the safety skills in realistic role plays depicting each variation of the safety threat
   (d) Provide immediate feedback—praise for correct performance, further instruction for incorrect performance
   (e) Provide multiple opportunities for rehearsal and feedback until skills are exhibited with fluency (if group training, all children should have multiple opportunities for rehearsal with feedback)
   (f) Incorporate common stimuli in training so role plays are as realistic as possible (e.g., use disabled firearms or actual medicine containers, conduct abduction prevention training on the playground)
3. Conduct posttraining in situ assessment
   (a) If child exhibits the skills, training is complete (move to follow-up)
   (b) If child fails to use the skills implement IST
      (i) Trainer (or parent) shows up in the assessment situation and conducts BST
      (ii) Child practices the safety skills multiple times with feedback in the presence of the simulated safety threat in the natural environment
4. Conduct further in situ assessment and IST until child exhibits skills
   (a) Each assessment situation is different from the previous assessments
   (b) The child is not cued to the assessment
   (c) In situ assessment is turned into an IST session if child fails to use the skills
   (d) If child uses the skills, training is complete (move to follow-up)
5. Conduct follow-up assessments at periodic intervals (weeks, months) and implement booster IST if needed

REFERENCES

Arbogast, H., Burke, R., Muller, V., Ruiz, P., Knudson, M., & Upperman, J. (2014). Randomized controlled trial to evaluate the effectiveness of a video game as a child pedestrian educational tool. *Journal of Trauma and Acute Care Surgery, 76*, 1317–1321.

Beck, K., & Miltenberger, R. (2009). Evaluation of a commercially available program and in situ training by parents to teach abduction prevention skills to children. *Journal of Applied Behavior Analysis, 42*, 761–772.

Carrol-Rowan, L., & Miltenberger, R. (1994). A comparison of procedures for teaching abduction prevention to preschoolers. *Education and Treatment of Children*, *17*, 113–128.

Dancho, K., Thompson, R., & Rhoades, M. (2008). Teaching preschool children to avoid poison hazards. *Journal of Applied Behavior Analysis*, *41*, 267–271.

Eber, G. B., Annest, J. L., Mercy, J. A., & Ryan, G. W. (2004). Nonfatal and fatal firearm-related injuries among children aged 14 years and younger: United States, 1993-2000. *Pediatrics*, *113*(6), 1686–1692.

Finkelhor, D., Hotaling, G., Lewis, I. A., & Smith, C. (1990). Sexual abuse in a national sample of adult men and women: Prevalence, characteristics, and risk factors. *Child Abuse & Neglect*, *14*, 19–28.

Gatheridge, B., Miltenberger, R., Huneke, D., Satterlund, M., Mattern, A., Johnson, B., et al. (2004). Comparison of two programs to teach firearm injury prevention skills to 6-and 7-year old children. *Pediatrics*, *114*, 294–299.

Gross, A., Miltenberger, R., Knudson, P., Bosch, A., & Brower-Breitwieser, C. (2007). Preliminary evaluation of a parent training program to prevent gun play. *Journal of Applied Behavior Analysis*, *40*, 691–695.

Hardy, M. S. (2002). Teaching firearm safety to children: Failure of a program. *Journal of Developmental and Behavioral Pediatrics*, *23*, 71–76.

Hardy, M. S., Armstrong, F. D., Martin, B. L., & Strawn, K. N. (1996). A firearm safety program for children: They just can't say no. *Journal of Developmental and Behavioral Pediatrics*, *17*, 216–221.

Harvey, P., Forehand, R., Brown, C., & Holmes, T. (1988). The prevention of sexual abuse: Examination of the effectives of a program with kindergarten—age children. *Behavior Therapy*, *19*, 429–435.

Hazzard, A., Webb, C., Kleemeier, C., Angert, L., & Pohl, J. (1991). Child sexual abuse prevention: Evaluation and one year follow-up. *Child Abuse & Neglect*, *15*, 123–138.

Himle, M., Miltenberger, R., Flessner, C., & Gatheridge, B. (2004). Teaching safety skills to children to prevent gun play. *Journal of Applied Behavior Analysis*, *37*, 1–9.

Himle, M., Miltenberger, R., Gatheridge, B., & Flessner, C. (2004). An evaluation of two procedures for training skills to prevent gun play in children. *Pediatrics*, *113*, 70–77.

Holocombe, A., Wolery, M., & Katzenmeyer, J. (1995). Teaching preschoolers to avoid abduction by strangers: Evaluation of maintenance strategies. *Journal of Child and Family Studies*, *4*, 177–191.

Jackman, G. A., Farah, M. M., Kellermann, A. L., & Simon, H. K. (2001). Seeing is believing: What do boys do when they find a real gun? *Pediatrics*, *107*, 1247–1250.

Johnson, B., Miltenberger, R., Egmo-Helm, C., Jostad, C., Flessner, C., & Gatheridge, B. (2005). Evaluation of behavioral skills training for teaching abduction-prevention skills to young children. *Journal of Applied Behavior Analysis*, *38*, 67–78.

Johnson, B. M., Miltenberger, R. G., Knudson, P., Egemo-Helm, K., Kelso, P., Jostad, C., et al. (2006). A preliminary evaluation of two behavioral skills training procedures for teaching abduction prevention skills to school children. *Journal of Applied Behavior Analysis*, *39*, 25–34.

Jostad, C. M., & Miltenberger, R. G. (2004). Firearm injury prevention skills: Increasing the efficiency of training with peer tutoring. *Child and Family Behavior Therapy*, *26*, 21–35.

Jostad, C., Miltenberger, R., Kelso, P., & Knudson, P. (2008). Peer tutoring to prevent gun play: Acquisition, generalization, and maintenance of safety skills. *Journal of Applied Behavior Analysis*, *41*, 117–123.

Kelso, P. D., Miltenberger, R. C., Waters, M. A., Egemo-Helm, K., & Bagne, A. C. (2007). Teaching Skills to second and third grade children to prevent gun play: A comparison of procedures. *Education and Treatment of Children*, *30*, 29–48.

Kenny, M. C., Wurtele, S. K., & Alonso, L. (2012). Evaluation of a personal safety program with Latino preschoolers. *Journal of Child Sexual Abuse*, *21*, 368–385.

Kopp, B., & Miltenberger, R. G. (2008). Evaluating the validity and social acceptability of child sexual abuse prevention skill measures. *Child and Family Behavior Therapy, 30*, 1–11.

Kopp, B., & Miltenberger, R. (2009). Evaluating the acceptability of four versions of a child sexual abuse prevention program. *Child and Family Behavior Therapy, 31*, 192–202.

Marchand-Martella, N., Huber, G., Martella, R. C., & Wood, W. S. (1996). Assessing the long-term maintenance of abduction prevention skills by disadvantaged preschoolers. *Education and Treatment of Children, 19*, 55–68.

McComas, J., MacKay, M., & Pivik, J. (2002). Effectiveness of virtual reality for teaching pedestrian safety. *Cyberpsychology & Behavior, 5*, 185–190.

Miltenberger, R. (2008). Teaching safety skills to children: Prevention of firearm injury as an exemplar of best practice in assessment, training, and generalization of safety skills. *Behavior Analysis in Practice, 1*, 30–36.

Miltenberger, R. G. (2012). *Behavior modification: Principles and procedures* (5th). Pacific Grove, CA: Cengage/Wadsworth.

Miltenberger, R., Flessner, C., Gatheridge, B., Johnson, B., Satterlund, M., & Egemo, K. (2004). Evaluation of behavioral skills training to prevent gun play in children. *Journal of Applied Behavior Analysis, 37*, 513–516.

Miltenberger, R., Fogel, V., Beck, K., Koehler, S., Graves, R., Noah, J., et al. (2013). Examining the efficacy of the Stranger Safety abduction prevention program and parent conducted in situ training. *Journal of Applied Behavior Analysis, 46*, 817–820.

Miltenberger, R. G., Gatheridge, B. J., Satterlund, M., Egemo-Helm, K., Johnson, B. M., Jostad, C., et al. (2005). Teaching safety skills to children to prevent gun play: An evaluation of in situ training. *Journal of Applied Behavior Analysis, 38*, 395–398.

Miltenberger, R. G., & Gross, A. (2011). Teaching safety skills to children. In W. Fisher, C. Piazza, & H. Roane (Eds.), *Handbook of applied behavior analysis* (pp. 417–432). New York: Guilford.

Miltenberger, R., Gross, A., Knudson, P., Jostad, C., Bosch, A., & Brower-Breitwieser, C. (2009). Evaluating behavioral skills training with and without simulated in situ training for teaching safety skills to children. *Education and Treatment of Children, 32*, 63–75.

Miltenberger, R., & Hanratty, L. (2013). Teaching sexual abuse prevention skills to children. In D. Bromberg & W. O'Donohue (Eds.), *Handbook of child and adolescent sexuality: Developmental and forensic psychology* (pp. 419–447). London: Elsevier.

Miltenberger, R., & Olsen, L. (1996). Abduction prevention training: A review of findings and issues for future research. *Education and Treatment of Children, 19*, 69–82.

Miltenberger, R., Roberts, J., Elligson, S., Galensky, T., Rapp, J., Long, E., et al. (1999). Training and generalization of sexual abuse prevention skills for women with mental retardation. *Journal of Applied Behavior Analysis, 32*, 385–388.

Miltenberger, R., & Thiesse-Duffy, E. (1988). Evaluation of home-based programs for teaching personal safety skills to children. *Journal of Applied Behavior Analysis, 21*, 81–88.

Miltenberger, R., Thiesse-Duffy, E., Kozak, C., & Bruellman, J. (1990). Teaching prevention skills to children: The use of multiple measures to evaluate parent versus expert instruction. *Child and Family Behavior Therapy, 12*(4), 65–87.

National Capital Poison Center. (2013). *Poisonings: The local picture.* http://www.poison.org/stats/#Poisonings:_The_National_Picture_, Retrieved 02 April 2014.

National Center for Missing and Exploited Children. (2009). *NCMEC timeline.* http://www.missingkids.com, Retrieved 02 April 2014.

Olsen-Woods, L., Miltenberger, R., & Foreman, G. (1998). The effects of correspondence training in an abduction prevention training program. *Child and Family Behavior Therapy, 20*, 15–34.

Poche, C., Brouwer, R., & Swearingen, M. (1981). Teaching self protection to young children. *Journal of Applied Behavior Analysis, 14*, 169–176.

Poche, C., Yoder, P., & Miltenberger, R. (1988). Teaching self-protection to children using television techniques. *Journal of Applied Behavior Analysis, 21*, 253–261.

Roberts, J., & Miltenberger, R. (1999). Emerging issues in the research on child sexual abuse prevention. *Education and Treatment of Children, 22,* 84–102.

Saslawasky, D. A., & Wurtele, S. K. (1986). Educating children about sexual abuse: Implications for pediatric intervention and possible prevention. *Journal of Pediatric Psychology, 11,* 235–245.

Schwebel, D., & McClure, L. (2014). Training children in pedestrian safety: Distinguishing gains in knowledge from gains in safe behavior. *Journal of Primary Prevention, 35,* 151–162.

Schwebel, D., McClure, L., & Severson, J. (2014). Usability and feasibility of an internet-based virtual pedestrian environment to teach children to cross streets safely. *Virtual Reality, 18,* 5–11.

Stennies, G., Ikeda, R., Leadbetter, S., Houston, B., & Sacks, J. (1999). Firearm storage practices and children in the house, United States, 1994. *Archives of Pediatrics and Adolescent Medicine, 153,* 586–590.

Tarasenko, M. A., Miltenberger, R. G., Brower-Breitwieser, C., & Bosch, A. (2010). Evaluation of peer training for teaching abduction prevention skills. *Child and Family Behavior Therapy, 32,* 219–230.

Vanselow, N. R., & Hanley, G. P. (2014). An evaluation of computerized behavior skills training to teach safety skills to young children. *Journal of Applied Behavior Analysis, 47,* 51–69.

Wurtele, S. K., & Kenny, M. C. (2010). Partnering with parents to prevent childhood sexual abuse. *Child Abuse Review, 19*(2), 130–152.

Wurtele, S., Marrs, S., & Miller-Perrin, C. (1987). Practice makes perfect? The role of participant modeling in sexual abuse prevention programs. *Journal of Consulting and Clinical Psychology, 55,* 599–602.

Wurtele, S. K., Saslawsky, S. K., Miller, C. L., Marrs, S. R., & Britcher, J. C. (1986). Teaching personal safety skills for potential prevention of sexual abuse: A comparison of treatments. *Journal of Consulting and Clinical Psychology, 54,* 688–692.

CHAPTER 20

Clinical Application of Behavior Analytic Social Work Practice

Alyssa N. Wilson, Monica M. Matthieu
School of Social Work, St Louis University, St Louis, Missouri, USA

Cooperation with workers in other fields is often a useful source of support
Skinner (1987, p. 198)

Clinical social work and clinical behavior analysis have been considered a good fit for interdisciplinary practice (c.f., Thyer, 1999). Recent interdisciplinary interest in behavior analysis and social work is beginning to emerge across university training programs (e.g., St Louis University) and clinical employment opportunities (e.g., schools, hospitals, community health centers, psychiatric institutions). The intersection between the two disciplines has been discussed as a "mutually reinforcing relationship" (Thyer, 1999), with social workers endorsing behavioral methods for over 40 years (Bronson & Thyer, 2001). Social work and behavioral analysis share equivalent value systems such as a theoretical perspective between person and environment and the individualized assessment and treatment of socially relevant problem behaviors (Gambrill, 1995). While the two disciplines have similar (e.g., principle of parsimony, pragmatism) and distinct philosophical tenants (e.g., metaphysical vs. natural selection), empirical support for this interdisciplinary practice is currently evolving.

Common applications of behavior analysis and social work are identified within social systems, perhaps most notably child welfare. For example, the Behavior Analysis Services Program (BASP) is a statewide program in Florida that provides behavioral parent training to foster parents and caregivers of dependent children (Stoutimore, Williams, Neff, & Foster, 2008; see also the 2008 special issue of *Research on Social Work Practice* on the various outcomes of the BASP program). Likewise, Project 12 Ways is a multifaceted program that provides in-home parent training for prevention and intervention of child abuse and neglect (Lutzker & Rice, 1984). Both the BASP and Project 12 Ways programs infuse behavioral principles with clinical social work.

Clinical and Organizational Applications of Applied Behavior Analysis
http://dx.doi.org/10.1016/B978-0-12-420249-8.00020-4

A more recent relationship between disciplines is evident in environmental sustainability (e.g., Alavosius & Mattaini, 2011; Gray, Coates, & Hetherington, 2013). For instance, special issues of *The Behavior Analyst* and *Behavior and Social Issues* have discussed the urgency for behavioral scientists to attend to climate change and environmental degradation. Further, Behavior Analysis for Sustainable Societies (BASS) and Behaviorists for Social Responsibility (BFSR) are recently formed special interest groups within the Association for Behavior Analysis-International, collaborating with other behavioral scientists and community service providers dedicated to enhancing social responsibility as a key feature of cultural behavior (Alavosius & Mattaini, 2011).

While an interdisciplinary approach may appear promising, behavior analysts have maintained distance from social work, given the perception of otherwise weak methodological standards adhered to in social work practice (Adkins, 1999). Minimal empirical evidence has been discussed between clinical behavior analysis and clinical social work, particularly as applied to the treatment of mental health disorders. The purpose of the current chapter is (1) to expose disciplinary myths that may preclude behavior analysts from infusing social work into their practice and vice versa, (2) to provide a procedural overview of the phases of clinical intervention for behavior analytic social work practice, (3) to present clinical case studies as exemplars for treating clients with mental health disorders, and (4) to identify key characteristics of both social work and behavior analysis to enhance during interventions to improve evidence-based mental health care.

EXPOSING INTERDISCIPLINARY MYTHS

Applied behavior analysis and social work each have a unique history of misrepresentations, particularly across the disciplines. For example, Jon Bailey once wrote of social workers as "do-gooders" who often "stood in the way of effective behavioral treatment" (as discussed in Bronson & Thyer, 2001, p. 192). Behavior analysts also hold that social work practice has little experimental control with high regards for subjective data collection techniques (Thyer, 2012). Use of subjective or qualitative data is a common concern for behavior analysts, as "subjective data may not have any relationship to actual events" leading to a potential danger "that subjective data will seriously mislead" (Wolf, 1978, p. 212). Concomitantly, behavior analysts differentiate between certified behavior analysts and individuals providing client services who use a behavior-analytic orientation (e.g., Hawkins & Anderson, 2002). Those utilizing a behavior-analytic orientation with clients may not necessarily follow underlying behavioral philosophies, such as determinism, and worldviews of autonomy or agency.

Skinner (1953) attested that the science of human behavior focuses on objective and reliable data, rather than on subjective introspective perspectives from an initiating actor. For Skinner (1987), the field of behavior analysis was resisted and rejected "precisely because it has no place for a person as an initiating agent" (p. 62). He argued,

> ...the proper recognition of the selective action of the environment will require a change in our conception of the origin of behavior, a change perhaps as extensive as that of our former conceptions of the origin of species. As long as we cling to the view that a person is an initiating doer, actor, or causer of behavior, we shall probably continue to neglect the conditions that must be changed if we are to solve our problems.
>
> Skinner (1987, p. 62–63)

Instead of rejecting the existence of inner states completely, like some of his earlier counterparts (e.g., Watson), Skinner urged behavioral researchers to measure observable events without referring to inner states. Behavioral scientists were expected to include the world within the skin into their experimental analyzes of behavior (Skinner, 1974).

Similar misunderstandings abound in professional circles about applied behavior analysis. For instance, in 2011, two social work professionals suggested that behavior analysts "do not acknowledge the importance or 'reality' of an internal mental life" (as discussed by Gambrill, 2012, p. 124). Additional misconceptions are disseminated in social work texts, classrooms, and practice areas where behavior analysts are depicted as "ignoring client feelings and relationship variables in treatment," "treating only symptoms of underlying problems, not the real issues," or as practicing an outdated "stimulus-response theory" (Thyer, 1999, p. 24). Quantitative methods were seen by social workers as inappropriate "for the purposes of social advocacy and activism" and as "too blunt an instrument to understand human affairs in general, and subjective experiences in particular" (Thyer, 2012, p. 115). While perhaps convenient, qualitative measures (particularly those measuring private events or events taking place within the skin) can be ambiguous and unreliable (Wolf, 1978), yet valuable for maladaptive behaviors such as suicidal rumination.

While each discipline has a unique history and philosophical worldview (including methodological considerations), there are salient commonalities shared across disciplines that warrant further discussion. Contrary to popular convention, social workers reliably implement behavioral treatments (see

Thyer, 1981, 1991 for review), and often agree with behavioral theory and philosophical underpinnings. For example, the National Association of Social Workers (NASW) supports evidence-based practice and is currently working to integrate the evidence-based process into social work training (National Association of Social Workers, 2015). Social work university programs currently provide quantitative and qualitative research requirements for graduate trainings. Even though social work still holds qualitative research as an important aspect of the discipline (e.g., Thyer, 2012 for a similar argument), primary disciplinary focus has recently shifted toward the use of mixed methods, with increased valuing of objective and quantitative methods.

Both disciplines also consider the environment as a mediating factor for behavior (Skinner, 1953; Thyer, 1999). Skinner (1953) often referred to the environment as a key variable in the science of human that the environment gives significant contribution to the evolution of a species, but "exerts a different kind of effect during the lifetime of the individual...any available information about either contribution helps in the prediction and control of human behavior and in its interpretation in daily life" (p. 19). The historical development of social work as a discipline has focused on a person-in-environment perspective (Greene, 2008) derived from general systems theory (von Bertalanffy, 1962), and informed later by the ecological perspective (Germain, 1973) and social learning theory (e.g., Bandura, 1977). By creating a common structured approach to the helping process, social workers assess and intervene effectively across a multifaceted theoretical orientation, regardless of the field of specialization (Meyer, 1987). For example, Bandura (1969, 1977) social learning theory has been used to understand psychiatric conditions and has been adapted in social work training programs to model and modify behavior. Postmodern social work practice has redefined and grounded itself based on a performance of successful working (i.e., effective intervention), rather than on the specific idiosyncratic theoretical position adapted during the intervention process (see also Greene, 2008, for similar historical conceptualization).

Perhaps the most obvious connection between the two disciplines is the continued focus on socially relevant target behaviors. Applied behavior analysis has a rich history of theoretical and experimental identifications of socially relevant behaviors (Baer, Wolf, & Risley, 1968; 1987; Skinner, 1974; Wolf, 1978), with the premise that all of human behavior is important and socially relevant for scientific study (Skinner, 1953). Interdisciplinary behavior analytic social work research has investigated a range of populations (e.g., developmental disabilities, Lovaas, 1987; Malone, McKinsey, Thyer, & Straka, 2000, and foster children, Clark et al., 2008; Witherup et al., 2008), interventions (e.g., job-skill training; Koffarnus et al., 2013), and target behaviors (e.g., environmental sustainability; McKinnon, 2008).

Behavioral researchers also identify social importance and acceptability of interventions by assessing social validity (Schwartz & Baer, 1991). Social validation of treatments is equally important for both behavior analytic and social work disciplines. In behavior analysis, social validity of treatment is assessed across three levels: the significance of the treatment goals, the appropriateness of the procedures, and the importance of the effects (Wolf, 1978). Social validity of treatment is just as important as the treatment outcomes themselves (Kazdin, 1977a). By including opinions of society (or those being affected or impacted by the treatment or outcomes of treatment), researchers can be responsive to the perspectives of the consumers or communities directly affected by the treatment or intervention (e.g., Fields et al., 2009; Hanley, Piazza, Fisher, Contrucci, & Maglieri, 1997). Together, it would appear that the combination of socially relevant target behaviors and the application of effective, socially valid treatments would yield successful outcomes for both the clinician and client, who often have differing perspectives of treatment "success."

The ethical code of conduct for both social workers and behavior analysts requires use of the most effective treatment options in the least restrictive way (Bailey & Burch, 2011; National Association of Social Workers, 2008). The history of both disciplines suggests such interdisciplinary or interprofessional practice may be advantageous for the production of successful interventions (World Health Organization, 2010). However, limited literature exists outlining the process of how to incorporate both disciplines into a single practice. The following provides a framework for how to proceed with delivering interdisciplinary practice to assist with the development of behavior analytic social work practice.

PHASES OF CLINICAL INTERVENTION

Phases of clinical intervention, as discussed here, highlight overarching themes of treatment from start to finish. By taking an idiosyncratic (and person-in-environment) approach to clinical practice (e.g., Greene, 1998/2008), each client will need a specialized treatment plan, with variations across treatment approach and length of treatment. The phases of clinical interventions (see Figure 20.1) use Greene's (1998/2008) phases of social

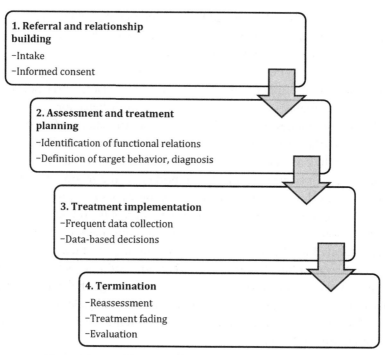

1. Referral and relationship building
–Intake
–Informed consent

2. Assessment and treatment planning
–Identification of functional relations
–Definition of target behavior, diagnosis

3. Treatment implementation
–Frequent data collection
–Data-based decisions

4. Termination
–Reassessment
–Treatment fading
–Evaluation

Figure 20.1 Phases of clinical intervention.

work practice as a model for general guidelines related to the use of inter-disciplinary behavior analytic social work practice.

The first phase of the intervention is Referral and Relationship Building. Here, clients have made some contact with the clinical organization or clinician for help with a specific symptom or challenge. During intake, the client may be asked to complete informed consent or similar intervention-related contracts (e.g., agreements on treatment, cancelation policies, payment rates, etc.). Following contractual agreements, the pre-senting problem(s) are discussed, usually incorporating a bio-psycho-social interview and retrospective baseline assessment of the problem. The prob-lem behavior(s) are also explored across a range of behavioral dimensions, including frequency, intensity, duration, time of occurrence, outcomes, etc.

Assessment and Treatment Planning is the second phase of intervention. During this phase, the clinician defines the target behaviors for treatment and may diagnose the client if appropriate. After defining the target behav-ior(s), the clinician explores the functional relations between the target behavior(s) and relevant environmental events. Questions such as "what happens before (the behavior)" and "what happens right after (the behavior)" are useful to determine the antecedents and consequences that precede and follow the target behavior(s), respectively. Functional assessments can also be achieved through psychometrics testing or through direct manipulation of environmental events. Once the clinician has enough information, a clinical hypothesis can be formed to assist the clinician and client to form treatment goals and objectives (see also Dougher & Hayes, 2000, for an overview of clinical functional assessments derived through clinical interviews).

After identification of functional relations, the Treatment Implementation phase can begin. During implementation, the clinician and client work together to develop more adaptive behaviors rather than continuing to engage in maladaptive behaviors. Regardless of the specific treatment paradigm used, the intervention should be specifically tailored from the information gathered during the first and second phases. Further, frequent data assessment and monitoring should continue throughout the third phase to ensure that the clinician can make data-based decisions. The duration of the intervention phase should be specifically tailored to the individual client, with the goal of eventually fading and terminating services.

The final, or Termination, phase should evolve from the intervention phase, where the clinician and client discuss and make decisions together regarding the end of treatment. During reassessment, the client completes the same psychometrics or other data collection items (e.g., interview questions, rating scales) as completed during the referral phase. Treatment fading should be implemented following reassessment. Treatment fading can vary based on the dose (e.g., length of treatment sessions) and duration between sessions (e.g., weekly to bi-monthly sessions). Treatment evaluation should occur on the final day of treatment and should assess achievement of clinical outcomes, social validity, client satisfaction of treatment goals, and whether there are new treatment goals to target for future services. Treatment termination should be considered if both clinician and client find behavior change to be acceptable.

Applications of social work and behavior analytic clinical practice may follow the four phases of clinical intervention as previously outlined. Given the limited empirical evidence on the effectiveness of interdisciplinary clinical practice, behavior analysts and social workers may benefit from knowing how to incorporate both disciplines across these intervention phases. Lack of empirical evidence may be a residual of the ambiguity of behavioral science, combined with an evolving social work framework concerned with effective intervention rather than theoretical lore. Therefore, the following clinical case formulations are provided as evidence to the utility of an interdisciplinary approach to providing mental health treatment. These cases were developed by an interdisciplinary team of behavior analysts, clinical social workers, and case managers. The clinical wisdom of these professionals in treating individuals with disordered gambling and posttraumatic stress disorder has been represented here for the demonstration of how to integrate behavior analysis and social work into clinical practice. Given the novelty and limited empirical evidence to draw upon, each case presentation will provide insight into a shared clinical approach for assessing and treating mental health disorders.

Both case studies begin with Phase 1 and Phase 2 of treatment. Phases 3 and 4 are discussed in the section on Fundamental Features, to highlight the idiosyncrasies of treatments implemented for each case. Across both case presentations, clinical behavior analytic and social work techniques are identified and discussed, including the use of single-subject design and the identification of relationships between the independent variable and measures of interest (e.g., target behavior, treatment goals). Each case is conceptualized across indirect and direct observational methods, to assist clinicians with collecting information to incorporate the whole person. Key case examples will be presented across the four phases of intervention as exemplars. The goal of the case presentations is to demonstrate how to combine behavior analysis and social work into an interdisciplinary model for mental health professional practice. The descriptive analysis provided herein has been modified to ensure client confidentiality.

Case Presentations
Susan
Phase 1: Baseline Psychological Functioning and Assessment
Susan was a 69-year-old African American female diagnosed with obsessive/compulsive disorder (OCD), adult onset attention-deficit disorder (ADD), borderline-personality disorder, and chronic pain. She was a grandmother of nine, did not complete college, and worked as a bank teller for almost 20 years until she was fired when the bank downsized. After losing her job, Susan started going to the casino with friends as a way to "cheer up" and forget about her troubles. Susan reported psychological difficulties as

related to her OCD and adult onset ADD and did not report any difficulties with her personality. She reported that her pain escalated only when she was stressed, and a trip to the casino could "cure" it better than her medication. Her family history revealed substance use disorders on her maternal and paternal side and personality disorders on her maternal side. She reported a history of physical trauma as a young child, particularly as a result of her drunkard father. When Susan self-referred for gambling services, she had gambled away her life savings, her family home, and her grandchildren's college funds. Her preferred game was multiline slot machines. A retrospective baseline of her gambling behaviors over the preceding 60 days was collected during intake. Within the 60 days prior to intake, Susan had gambled around 45-50 days on various gaming activities and had wagered over $5000.

Phase 2: Functional Assessment and Treatment Planning

Susan's gambling proclivity was initially assessed using the South Oaks Gambling Screen (SOGS; Lesieur & Blume, 1987), where scores of 5 or higher indicate disordered or pathological gambling (highest total score = 20). Gambling severity was assessed using the Gambling Severity Assessment Scale (GSAS; Kim, Grant, Adson, Shin, & Young, 2001). Susan also completed the Gambling Functional Assessment II (GFA-II; Dixon, Wilson, & Schrieber, under review) to identify potential variables maintaining her gambling (e.g., access to social attention, tangible items, sensory or neurochemical changes, and escape/avoidance from aversive stimulation). Gambling assessments revealed a high proclivity toward gambling (SOGS > 5), high severity (G-SAS > 40), and high probability of escape/avoidance as maintaining gambling behaviors (highest GFA-II component was escape).

Barry

Phase 1: Baseline Psychological Functioning and Assessment

Barry was a 24-year-old married, Caucasian man, with two young children. Barry served two tours of duty in Afghanistan, where he was wounded twice in improvised explosive device (IED) attacks and firefights. He sustained a range of injuries including loss of consciousness, short-term memory loss, and traumatic brain injury (TBI) and was involved in collecting human remains including his battle buddy and close friends. About 6 months following his second injury from an IED attack, Barry returned to the states, where he had difficulty sleeping, finding and keeping a job and found himself consumed with thoughts about the buddies he lost in the war. He presented to a Department of Veterans Affairs outpatient counseling center in the southern part of the United States. Barry reported no prior history of trauma outside of his military service and reported having supportive family and peer relationships. His family history revealed alcohol use disorders on his paternal side and depression on his maternal side. A retrospective baseline of Barry's traumatic symptoms over the preceding 60 days was collected during intake. Within the 60 days prior to intake, Barry reported feeling extremely depressed across the entire 60-day period, experienced repeated intrusive thoughts of his tours in Afghanistan almost every day, flashbacks nearly every week, heavy drinking every night to help him get to sleep, and only sleeping about 2-3 h at a time.

Phase 2: Functional Assessment and Treatment Planning

Barry was initially assessed using the self-report Post-Traumatic Stress Disorder (PTSD) Checklist-Military Version (PCL-M; Blanchard, Jones-Alexander, Buckley, & Forneris, 1996) and Patient Health Questionnaire-9 (PHQ-9; Kroenke, Spitzer, & Williams, 2001) to evaluate PTSD and depression symptoms severity, respectively. Barry met criteria for PTSD and scored in the clinical range on the PCL and endorsed a number of PTSD symptoms in the extreme range in the month prior to his arrival at the VA (e.g., daily and nightly repeated disturbing memories, thoughts, or images of a stressful experience from the military; avoiding thinking about, talking about, or similar activities or situations that remind him of his military experience; and feeling jumpy or easily startled, or being "super alert" or watchful and on guard). Barry's PHQ-9 score indicated significant depressive symptoms, although a diagnosis of major depressive disorder was deferred as secondary to his PTSD severity. Barry's ruminations about suicide and his own death included a sense of a foreshortened future in that he was living on borrowed time; yet the survivor guilt was a constant reminder that he lived and his buddies did not. Clinical interviews were completed to identify functional relations between Barry's symptoms and environmental events.

FUNDAMENTAL FEATURES OF INTERDISCIPLINARY CLINICAL PRACTICE

The aforementioned exemplars are represented here given the similarities in cases with regards to targeting comorbid mental health concerns (e.g., a veteran presenting with PTSD; gambler presenting with borderline personality disorder and OCD). With each case, clinicians are required to evaluate client symptoms in order to develop functional treatment. We have identified five defining features of interdisciplinary social work and behavior analytic practice to assist clinicians with case conceptualization: (1) identification of clinically relevant target behaviors; (2) use of reliable and valid measurements; (3) relationship between target behaviors, measures, and treatment; (4) data-based treatment decisions; and (5) social validity of treatment process and outcomes. In the following section, each feature will be discussed as they specifically relate to Susan and Barry's case conceptualization and progression across phases of clinical intervention.

IDENTIFICATION OF TARGET BEHAVIORS

Target behaviors are an important first step in treatment for both behavior analysts and social work practitioners. Current disciplinary myths suggest that social workers and behavior analysts only attend to covert and overt behaviors, respectively. Covert behaviors that occur within the skin (Skinner, 1974) are difficult to directly observe and are easily discarded by behavior analysts (c.f., Skinner, 1953, for inclusionary argument of covert behavior within an analysis of human behavior). Conversely, overt behaviors occur in ways that are easier to directly observe, often increasing the ability to establish reliability between multiple observers. Both Susan and Barry presented with a specific behavior of concern (e.g., gambling and insomnia, respectively), and both had a series of comorbid mental health diagnoses ranging from OCD and adult onset ADD to PTSD and depression. For instance, Susan's primary behavior of concern was her gambling, even though she reported negative thoughts and depressive symptoms during intake. Barry presented with insomnia, in addition to PTSD, depression, suicidality, and current alcohol use. Given the high rates of mental health comorbidity (e.g., Ledgerwood & Petry, 2004; McCormick, Russo, Ramirez, & Taber, 1984), secondary target behaviors (e.g., self-reported and clinician reported covert symptoms) should be selected to create a balance between covert and overt behaviors.

Target behaviors should be idiosyncratically identified based on the client self-report and clinician observation during intake. Treatment outcomes for each selected target behavior are most effective when developed with client input. Further, the combination of both client self-report and clinician assessment can be useful when targeting covert events as target behaviors. Potential target behaviors for Susan included gambling-related thoughts and urges, gambling episodes, and perceived control over gambling episodes. A range of potential target behaviors for Barry included frequency of insomnia, avoidance of activities that reminded him of his traumas from his military service, survivor guilt mixed with suicidal thoughts, and frequency/intensity of depressive symptoms.

USE OF RELIABLE AND VALID MEASUREMENT

Behavior analytic measures usually target a single individual's overt behavior; therefore, traditional measures are not standardized and are judged as "valid" based on the nature of the applied setting and conditions under which the behavior has been directly observed. As a result, behavior analytic measures of reliability and validity are commonly assessed through interobserver agreement and procedural reliability (Kazdin, 1977a, 1977b). Common psychometric assessments, however, are usually standardized and assessed for test-retest reliability and validity across settings, populations, and sometimes symptomology. Therefore, when creating an interdisciplinary approach, using both psychometric assessments in addition to more traditional behavior analytic measures requires different reliability and validity assessments. For Susan and Barry, measures were identified based on the existing evidence suggesting high rates of reliability and validity.

Indirect Psychometric Measures

Indirect measures, useful in identifying target behaviors as displayed by Susan and Barry, include the SOGS, G-SAS, and the GFA-II for gambling-related issues and the PCL and PHQ-9 for trauma and depression, respectively. A brief overview of each measure is provided. *The SOGS* is a 26-item assessment (20 of which are scored) that includes questions as to the type of gambling event typically engaged in, frequency of gambling events, the severity of money gambled and/or borrowed from friends or family, subjective interpretation of the emotional aspects of gambling, and history of gambling. The SOGS was originally derived from items in the diagnostic manual on gambling disorders and has good internal and convergent validity (Stinchfield, 2002; Stinchfield & Winters, 2001) for both clinical and general populations (Gambino & Lesieur, 2006; Stinchfield & Winters, 2001). *The G-SAS* (Kim et al., 2001) is a 12-item assessment designed to measure changes across four subcategories of gambling severity: gambling-related urges across severity, frequency, duration, and control; gambling-related thoughts across severity, frequency, duration, and control; duration of gambling-related behavior; and emotional experience caused by gambling including anticipatory tension, excitement, mental pain/anguish, and personal trouble. Each item is scored on a 4-point Likert scale, with higher scores reflecting higher severity of symptoms (highest total score = 48). The G-SAS has been found to have good test-retest reliability (Kim et al., 2001), internal consistency, and validity (Kim, Grant, Potenza,

Blanco, & Hollander, 2009). *The GFA-II* is a 15-item assessment based on the Gambling Functional Assessment (GFA; Dixon & Johnson, 2007) that identifies four potential maintaining variables of gambling: access to social attention, access to tangible items, sensory experience, and escape/avoidance. While the original GFA yielded acceptable test-retest reliability (Miller, Meier, & Weatherly, 2009), the GFA-II has been found to have good construct validity, accounting for 64% of the variance (Dixon et al., under review).

The *PCL* is a brief, 17-item self-report screening assessment tool for PTSD. The PCL has strong internal consistency, test-retest reliability, and correlations with other established PTSD diagnostic instruments (Blanchard et al., 1996). As a diagnostic instrument targeting trauma symptoms experienced over the past month, each item is scored from 1 (not at all) to 5 (extremely), the highest score is 85, with the standard cut off score of 50 indicative of a PTSD diagnosis (Blanchard et al., 1996). *The PHQ-9* is a psychometrically sound, brief screening assessment instrument targeting depression severity over the past 2 weeks with nine items. Each item is rated from "not at all," to "several days," to "more than half the days," to "nearly every day," with scores greater than 20 indicating severe depression. The measure is considered reliable with high internal consistency paired with strong criterion and diagnostic validity for Major Depressive Disorder (Kroenke et al., 2001).

Direct Observational Measures

Direct observational measures are the hallmark of behavioral research and practice. Given that both Susan and Barry first reported stress from negative thoughts (either about their gambling, obsessions, avoidance, urges to misuse, or depression), direct observational measure of private events should incorporate a self-report component (e.g., diary or journal). For Susan and Barry, thoughts were tracked across intervention sessions, where they completed questions about thoughts related to their target behaviors each day in a journal. Thoughts were reported across a range of dimensions, including frequency, believability, intensity, and workability.

Additional direct observational measures are needed when the primary target behavior occurs within the client's skin. One approach for gambling disorders is to allow clients to play on computerized slot machines or casino-replica gaming devices (e.g., Dixon & Wilson, 2014; Nastally & Dixon, 2012). During gambling play, clients are never provided with real money to wager, nor do they receive any payment during the gaming session.

Rather, clients wager meaningless points or tokens while talking aloud and subjectively rating each gaming outcome (e.g., closeness to win scales, emotions/feeling scales, etc.). One approach for PTSD is to engage clients in imaginary exposure to process the traumatic event (Tuerk, Brady, & Grubaugh, 2009; VA/DoD Management of Post-Traumatic Stress Working Group, 2010). During this section of exposure therapy, clients replay traumatic events, while clinicians rate the client's physiological and affective responses during sessions.

Whenever using direct observational methods or measures, obtained data should be subjected to interobserver agreement (IOA). Interobserver agreement refers to the extent that two or more observers agree in terms of their scoring of behavior and ensures that the assessment is a function of the client being observed, rather than the individual observer (Kazdin, 1977a, 1977b). For clinical interventions, point-by-point agreement is useful for behaviors occurring within sessions that are easily tracked (e.g., verbal statements, wagering and magnitude of bet during gaming, participation in exposure exercise). This type of IOA assesses agreement across every behavior observed and number of agreements are divided by number of agreements plus number of disagreements multiplied by 100 (Kazdin, 2011). Generally, agreement is regarded as acceptable at or above 80%.

RELATIONSHIP BETWEEN TARGET BEHAVIORS, MEASURES, AND TREATMENT

Best behavior analytic practice endorses a functional approach, wherein maintaining variables are identified and manipulated to alter the probability of behaviors to occur in the future (Skinner, 1953). As previously suggested, treatment development should follow information gathered during the second phase of clinical intervention. Functional assessments can be conducted either by paper-pencil (e.g., GFA-II) or by structured diagnostic interview (DSM-5; American Psychiatric Association, 2013). In practice, paper-and-pencil measures are preferred for measurement reliability and can be supplemented with structured interviews. Identifying relations between target behaviors and environmental variables through a systematic process increases the probability of developing a functional treatment for behavior change.

Maladaptive behaviors, such as those reported by Susan and Barry, are common response topographies for escaping or avoiding aversive stimulation (Hayes, Strosahl, & Wilson, 1999/2011). Escape-maintained behaviors have been the recent focus of clinical behavior analysts (e.g., Dougher &

Hayes, 2000). Research on escape-maintained maladaptive behaviors has supported exposure-based treatments in which new behaviors are shaped to provide access to similar reinforcers obtained by engaging in the maladaptive behaviors. For example, PTSD symptoms including intrusive thoughts, nightmares, and co-occurring insomnia improve through exposure-based treatment (see also Rauch, Eftekhari, & Ruzek, 2012 for a review). Modern variations of exposure therapy include variations of acceptance and mindfulness interventions, including Acceptance and Commitment Therapy (ACT; Hayes et al., 1999/2011). ACT is a behavioral therapy that combines exposure, mindfulness, and cognitive dissonance, with value clarification and behavioral activation. Adaptive values–centered replacement behaviors, such as meditation and physical activities, are often targeted and rehearsed during treatment sessions. ACT has been shown to be an effective treatment approach for substance use disorders such as gambling (Nastally & Dixon, 2012) and PTSD (Batten & Hayes, 2005; Orsillo & Batten, 2005).

For Susan and Barry, identification of escape would require exposure interventions. An ACT for gambling protocol (Dixon & Wilson, 2014) was identified and used during the treatment phase with Susan. For Barry, however, the VA/DoD Clinical Practice Guideline for the Management of Post-Traumatic Stress (VA/DoD Management of Post-Traumatic Stress Working Group, 2010) determined that Barry's traumatic and secondary depressive symptoms were a result of his attempts to avoid thinking about the traumas and the losses he experienced during direct combat in Afghanistan. As a part of the VA/DoD best practice guideline, a suicide risk assessment and behavioral contract on an agreed-upon safety plan was included in the second phase for Barry. Functional treatment for Barry's PTSD and depression targeted intrusive thoughts, nightmares, and insomnia through exposure-based treatment (e.g., Tuerk et al., 2009).

DATA-BASED TREATMENT DECISIONS

Data-based decision making, particularly with clients presenting with multiple psychological and physical symptoms, is an important aspect of clinical services. First, data-based decisions give clinicians a foundation for clinical case conceptualization and hypothesis testing. Data can assist clinicians in answering all types of clinically relevant questions: *Is the treatment working? When should I target a different problem behavior? Do I need to change what I'm doing? How do I know when to terminate treatment?* In general, and particularly with comorbid mental health disorders, it is critical that clinicians understand the difference between function and topography across multiple response classes.

For example, Barry presented with behaviors common to PTSD; however, the relationships between his presenting behaviors and specific environmental events are worth noting, given the symptom similarities of each. Barry's depressive thoughts were more intense during periods of stress and rumination over past losses. The relationship between Barry's target behaviors to environmental events (e.g., escape from aversive stimuli) should be identified across various response topographies (e.g., insomnia, aggression, depression) to assist in data collection across response classes. If depression and PTSD symptoms are conceptualized as a response class, then functionally equivalent behaviors such as suicidality, depression, and insomnia would naturally occur when PTSD-related symptoms are suppressed. Tracking response classes, rather than just selected symptoms, may be important when considering cluster classes of maladaptive behaviors. While the concept of response class is well known in behavior analysis, clinical social workers are beginning to see the utility of response classes, particularly with new changes ascribed to the Diagnostic Statistical Manual (DSM-5). While more research on the relationship of cluster disorders is needed, the current case examples demonstrate how the suppression of one response engaged in as a way to escape aversive stimulation, may lead to the emergence of other functionally equivalent maladaptive behaviors.

The identification of when to alter treatment can be made in congruence with frequent data collection and analysis of behavioral patterns. Target behaviors recorded each session throughout the intervention process will ensure continued data-driven decision making by clinicians. For example, Susan tracked her gambling-related thoughts and urges every day. During each session, Susan would discuss her week by going through the diary ratings before completing the ACT intervention. The intervention was separated into four modules: present moment focus, value clarification and identification, deliteralization of language and avoidance, and committed values-based action. Session content was derived from Susan's presenting concerns from the week and shifted depending on the trends of her self-report. After eight treatment sessions, the termination phase started by reducing total duration of sessions (e.g., 90-50 min) while increasing length between sessions (e.g., 1-4 weeks).

For Barry, extra time in the functional assessment and treatment-planning phase was conducted to ensure a complete history was collected prior to starting treatment. Exposure treatment has been demonstrated as an effective treatment for PTSD (VA/DoD Management of Post-Traumatic Stress Working Group, 2010). Exposure interventions assisted Barry with desensitization of avoidant behaviors, identification of survivor guilt, and extinguishing maladaptive responses to aversive stimuli and cues. Appropriate coping skills were also targeted and rehearsed during sessions, after noticing stability patterns in frequency of self-directed aggression.

SOCIAL VALIDITY OF TREATMENT PROCESS AND OUTCOMES

During the termination phase, a social validity questionnaire should be administered to systematically assess the client's perspectives of treatment process and treatment outcomes. For example, a 7-point Likert scale (1 = not at all, 4 = somewhat, 7 = completely) presented as a part of the termination phase at the final session may include items such as:

- How enjoyable were the experiential exercises?
- Do you feel like you are closer to living a valued life?
- How confident do you feel that you have the skills to cope with life events?
- How willing are you to accept your thoughts, feelings, or urges?
- How confident were you in your counselor?

For Susan, at the end of treatment, she reported herself as very confident in the treatment process and outcomes of her newly acquired skills. She reported that the experiential exercises were completely appropriate, attributed the treatment to helping her get back on track in her life, and felt completely satisfied about the progress made during treatment. Interestingly, she reported herself as only somewhat confident about never gambling again and somewhat confident in accepting her gambling-related thoughts/urges. Results from her responses suggest that exposure-based interventions may not be desirable in the moment (i.e., she was only somewhat confident that the experiential exercises were appropriate) but may yield higher satisfaction of treatment outcomes (i.e., she was completely confident of never gambling again).

CONCLUSION

When developing interdisciplinary applications for clinical interventions, there are many discipline-specific factors to consider. In combining behavior analytic principles and social work practice, important variables often include research–practice harmonization, experimental analyzes, using single-subject design, collecting objective data, and using data to inform treatment decisions. The current case examples provide a clear overview of how members of both disciplines can work together as scientist practitioners (c.f., Hayes, Barlow, & Nelson-Gray, 1999) who combine empirical evidence across disciplines to create multimodal treatment approaches. Without a scientific foundation for clinical practice (e.g., experimental designs and use of valid or reliable psychometric assessments for outcomes measurement), practitioners will be unable to make data-based decisions. Further, they may be ill equipped to properly assess the appropriateness of an intervention or procedure, particularly when applied to a single client.

Across research laboratories and clinical community centers, basic and applied applications of behavioral principles have been utilized through a range of disciplines spanning from education (Cooper, 1982) and economics (Kagel & Winkler, 1972) to social work (Thyer, 1999). For, the application of behavioral analytic investigation involves a

process of applying sometimes tentative principles of behavior to the improvement of specific [socially relevant] behaviors, and simultaneously evaluating whether or not any changes noted are indeed attributable to the process of application—and if so, to what parts of that process.

Baer et al. (1968, p. 91)

Today, there is a broad spectrum of analytic behavioral application, ranging from basic and translational research (Mace & Critchfield, 2010) to applied behavioral analysis (Deitz, 1983) and behavioral service delivery (see also Moore & Cooper, 2003). The distinction between applications is not what is discovered or applied during the experimental analysis; rather, it is the manipulation of variables, measurements of change, and overall goals of the application, which distinguishes the type of behavioral application. Baer et al. (1968) argued that applied research is constrained to identifying "variables which can be effective in improving the behavior under study" and to examining "behaviors which are socially important, rather than convenient for study" (pp. 91-92). Social work clinicians are examining similar behaviors as behavior analysts, and they often can work together to identify maintaining variables and successful treatments, as evident in the current case examples.

With an interdisciplinary approach to solving socially relevant target behaviors, we exponentially increase the probability of developing successful treatments and protocols. According to Thyer (1993) or Gallant and Thyer (2011), social work theory includes a comprehensive, empirically and conceptually systematic research agenda across a range of social problems. Behavior analysis has followed similar characteristics specifically programmed to improve socially relevant behaviors while simultaneously assessing whether or not the changes were the result of the manipulated program (Baer et al., 1968). Social work applies similar standards by using standardized assessment instruments and structured diagnostic clinical interviews. While a handful of professionals are beginning to embark on interdisciplinary research agendas by combining social work with behavior analytic principles and vice versa, the existing relationship between these fields is underrecognized yet largely expansive in possibilities for future interdisciplinary achievement (see Gambrill, 2012; Thyer, 1999 for similar arguments).

The current chapter describes how individuals may proceed with integrating behavior analytic principles into clinical social work. Perhaps social work and behavior analytic practice can assist with bridging the gap between research and practice through the development of new relationships and collaborations that lead to developing innovative measurements for behaviors occurring within the skin. The cases discussed in the current chapter demonstrate how to identify and target covert behaviors during sessions. It is our hope that this chapter may serve as a catalyst for behavior analysts and social workers to continue working toward the betterment of our clients and world at large.

REFERENCES

Adkins, V. K. (1999). Clinical behavior analysis and clinical social work: A mutually reinforcing relationship (as long as science is included). *The Behavior Analyst, 2*(22), 159–160.

Alavosius, M., & Mattaini, M. A. (2011). Editorial: Behavior analysis, sustainability, resilience, and adaptation. *Behavior and Social Issues, 20*, 1–5. http://dx.doi.org/10.5210/bsi.v20i0.3782.

American Psychiatric Association. (2013). *Diagnostic and statistical manual of mental disorders* (5th). Arlington, VA: American Psychiatric Publishing.

Baer, D. M., Wolf, M. M., & Risley, T. R. (1968). Some current dimensions of applied behavior analysis. *Journal of Applied Behavior Analysis, 1*(1), 91–97. http://dx.doi.org/10.1901/jaba.1968.1-91.

Baer, D. M., Wolf, M. M., & Risley, T. R. (1987). Some still-current dimensions of applied behavior analysis. *Journal of Applied Behavior Analysis, 20*(4), 313–327. http://dx.doi.org/10.1901/jaba.1987.20-313.

Bailey, J., & Burch, M. (2011). *Ethics for behavior analysts* (2nd). New York: Routledge.

Bandura, A. (1969). *Principles of behavior modification.* New York: Holt, Rinehart & Winston.

Bandura, A. (1977). *Social learning theory.* New York: General Learning Press.

Batten, S. V., & Hayes, S. C. (2005). Acceptance and commitment therapy in the treatment of comorbid substance abuse and post-traumatic stress disorder: A case study. *Clinical Case Studies, 4*(3), 246–262. http://dx.doi.org/10.1177/1534650103259689.

Blanchard, E. B., Jones-Alexander, J., Buckley, T. C., & Forneris, C. A. (1996). Psychometric properties of the PTSD checklist (PCL). *Behavioral Research & Therapy, 34*, 669–673. http://dx.doi.org/10.1016/0005-7967(96)00033-2.

Bronson, D. E., & Thyer, B. A. (2001). Behavioral social work: Where has it been and where is it going? *The Behavior Analyst Today, 2*(3), 192–195.

Clark, H. B., Crosland, K. A., Geller, D., Cripe, M., Kenney, T., Neff, B., et al. (2008). A functional approach to reducing runaway behavior and stabilizing placements for adolescents in foster care. *Research on Social Work Practice, 18*(5), 429–441. http://dx.doi.org/10.1177/1049731508314265.

Cooper, J. O. (1982). Applied behavior analysis in education. *Theory into Practice, 21*(2), 114–118. http://dx.doi.org/10.1080/00405848209542992.

Deitz, S. M. (1983). Two correct definitions of "applied". *The Behavior Analyst, 6*, 105–106.

Dixon, M. R., & Johnson, T. E. (2007). The gambling functional assessment (GFA): An assessment device for identification of the maintaining variables of pathological gambling. *Analysis of Gambling Behavior, 1*, 44–49.

Dixon, M. R., & Wilson, A. N. (2014). *Acceptance and commitment therapy for pathological gamblers*. Carbondale, IL: Shawnee Scientific Press.

Dixon, M. R., Wilson, A. N., & Schrieber, J. (under review). Gambling Functional Assessment II: Construct validity.

Dougher, M. J., & Hayes, S. C. (2000). *Clinical behavior analysis*. NV, USA: Context Press.

Fields, L., Travis, R., Roy, D., Yadlovker, E., de Aguiar-Rocha, L., & Sturmey, P. (2009). Equivalence class formation: A method for teaching statistical interactions. *Journal of Applied Behavior Analysis, 42*, 575–593. http://dx.doi.org/10.1901/jaba. 2009.42-57.

Gallant, J. P., & Thyer, B. A. (2011). Usefulness of general systems theory in social work practice. In R. R. Greene (Ed.), *Human behavior theory and social work practice* (pp. 250–259). New Jersey: Transaction Publishers.

Gambino, B., & Lesieur, H. (2006). The south oaks gambling screen (SOGS): A rebuttal to critics. *Journal of Gambling Issues, 17*, 1–16. http://dx.doi.org/10.4309/jgi.2006.17.10.

Gambrill, E. (1995). Behavioral social work: Past, present, and future. *Research on Social Work Practice, 5*, 460–484. http://dx.doi.org/10.1177/104973159500500406.

Gambrill, E. (2012). Birds of a feather: Applied behavior analysis and quality of life. *Research on Social Work Practice, 23*(2), 121–140. http://dx.doi.org/10.1177/1049731512465775.

Germain, C. B. (1973). An ecological perspective in casework practice. *Social Casework, 54*, 323–330.

Gray, M., Coates, J., & Hetherington, T. (Eds.). (2013). *Environmental social work*. New York: Routledge.

Greene, R. R. (2008). Human behavior theory, person-in-environment, and social work method. In R. R. Greene (Ed.), *Human behavior theory and social work practice* (3rd, pp. 1–28). New Jersey: Transaction Publishers.

Hanley, G. P., Piazza, C. C., Fisher, W. W., Contrucci, S. A., & Maglieri, K. A. (1997). Evaluation of client preference for function-based treatment packages. *Journal of Applied Behavior Analysis, 30*, 459–473. http://dx.doi.org/10.1901/jaba. 1997.30-459.

Hawkins, R. P., & Anderson, C. M. (2002). On the distinction between science and practice: A reply to Thyer and Adkins. *The Behavior Analyst, 25*(1), 115–119.

Hayes, S. C., Barlow, D. H., & Nelson-Gray, R. O. (1999). *The scientist practitioner: Research and accountability in the age of managed care*. MA, USA: Allyn & Bacon.

Hayes, S. C., Strosahl, K. D., & Wilson, K. G. (1999/2011). *Acceptance and commitment therapy: An experiential approach to behavior change*. New York: Guilford.

Kagel, J. H., & Winkler, R. C. (1972). Behavioral economics: Areas of cooperative research between economics and applied behavior analysis. *Journal of Applied Behavior Analysis, 5*(3), 335–342. http://dx.doi.org/10.1901/jaba. 1972.5-335.

Kazdin, A. E. (1977a). Assessing the clinical or applied importance of behavior change through social validation. *Behavior Modification, 1*, 427–452. http://dx.doi.org/10.1177/014544557714001.

Kazdin, A. E. (1977b). Artifact, bias, and complexity of assessment: The ABCs of reliability. *Journal of Applied Behavior Analysis*, *10*(1), 141–150. http://dx.doi.org/10.1901/jaba. 1977.10-141.

Kazdin, A. E. (2011). *Single-case research designs: Methods for clinical and applied settings*. UK: Oxford University Press.

Kim, S. W., Grant, J. E., Adson, D. E., Shin, Y. C., & Young, C. (2001). Double-blind naltrexone and placebo comparison study in the treatment of patho-logical gambling. *Biological Psychiatry*, *49*, 914–921. http://dx.doi.org/10.1016/S0006-3223(01)01079-4.

Kim, S. W., Grant, J. E., Potenza, M. N., Blanco, C., & Hollander, E. (2009). The Gambling Symptom Assessment Scale (G-SAS): A reliability and validity study. *Psychiatry Research*, *166*(1), 76–84. http://dx.doi.org/10.1016/j.psychres.2007.11.008.

Koffarnus, M. N., Wong, C. J., Fingerhood, M., Svikis, D. S., Bigelow, G. E., & Silverman, K. (2013). Monetary incentives to reinforce engagement and achievement in a job-skills training program for homeless, unemployed adults. *Journal of Applied Behavior Analysis*, *46*(3), 582–591. http://dx.doi.org/10.1002/jaba.60.

Kroenke, K., Spitzer, R., & Williams, W. (2001). The PHQ-9: Validation of a brief screening depression severity measure. *Journal of General Internal Medicine*, *16*, 606–616. http://dx.doi.org/10.1046/j.1525-1497.2001.016009606.x.

Ledgerwood, D. M., & Petry, N. M. (2004). Gambling and suicidality in treatment-seeking pathological gamblers. *The Journal of Nervous and Mental Disease*, *192*(10), 711–714. http://dx.doi.org/10.1097/01.nmd.0000142021.71880.ce.

Lesieur, H. R., & Blume, S. B. (1987). The South Oaks Gambling Screen (The SOGS): A new instrument for the identification of pathological gamblers. *American Journal of Psychiatry*, *144*, 1184–1188.

Lovaas, O. I. (1987). Behavioral treatment and normal educational and intellectual functioning in young autistic children. *Journal of Consulting and Clinical Psychology*, *55*(1), 3.

Lutzker, J. R., & Rice, J. M. (1984). Project 12-ways: Measuring outcome of a large in-home service for treatment and prevention of child abuse and neglect. *Child Abuse & Neglect*, *8* (4), 519–524.

Mace, F. C., & Critchfield, T. S. (2010). Translational research in behavior analysis: Historical traditions and imperative for the future. *Journal of the Experimental Analysis of Behavior*, *93*(3), 293–312. http://dx.doi.org/10.1901/jeab. 2010.93-293.

Malone, D. M., McKinsey, P. D., Thyer, B. A., & Straka, E. (2000). Social work early intervention for young children with developmental disabilities. *Health Social Work*, *25*(3), 169–180. http://dx.doi.org/10.1093/hsw/25.3.169.

McCormick, R. A., Russo, A. M., Ramirez, L. F., & Taber, J. I. (1984). Affective disorders among pathological gamblers seeking treatment. *The American Journal of Psychiatry*, *141* (2), 215–218.

McKinnon, J. (2008). Exploring the nexus between social work and the environment. *Australian Social Work*, *61*(3), 256–268.

Meyer, C. (1987). Direct practice in social work: Overview. In A. Minahan (Ed.), *Encyclopedia of social work* (Vol. 1, pp. 409–422). Silver Spring, MD: National Association of Social Workers.

Miller, J. C., Meier, E., & Weatherly, J. N. (2009). Assessing the reliability of the gambling functional assessment. *Journal of Gambling Studies*, *25*(1), 121–129.

Moore, J., & Cooper, J. O. (2003). Some proposed relations among the domains of behavior analysis. *The Behavior Analyst*, *26*, 69–84.

Nastally, B. L., & Dixon, M. R. (2012). The effect of a brief acceptance and commitment therapy intervention on the near-miss effect in problem gamblers. *Psychological Record*, *62* (4), 677–690.

National Association of Social Workers. (2008). *Code of ethics of the national association of social workers*. Washington, DC: NASW Press.

National Association of Social Workers (2015). NASW practice snapshot: Evidence-based practices-for social workers. Retrieved from: http://www.socialworkers.org/practice/clinical/csw081605snapshot.asp

Orsillo, S. M., & Batten, S. V. (2005). Acceptance and commitment therapy in the treatment of posttraumatic stress disorder. *Behavior Modification, 29*(1), 95–129. http://dx.doi.org/10.1177/0145445504270876.

Rauch, S. A., Eftekhari, A., & Ruzek, J. I. (2012). Review of exposure therapy: A gold standard for PTSD treatment. *Journal of Rehabilitation Research and Development, 49*(5), 679–688.

Schwartz, I. S., & Baer, D. M. (1991). Social validity assessments: Is current practice state of the art? *Journal of Applied Behavior Analysis, 24*(2), 189–204. http://dx.doi.org/10.1901/jaba. 1991.24-189.

Skinner, B. F. (1953). *Science and human behavior.* USA: The Macmillan Company.

Skinner, B. F. (1974). *About behaviorism.* New York: Alfred Knopf.

Skinner, B. F. (1987). *Upon further reflection.* Englewood Cliffs, NJ: Prentice-Hall.

Stinchfield, R. (2002). Reliability, validity, and classification accuracy of the south oaks gambling screen (SOGS). *Addictive Behaviors, 27,* 1–19.

Stinchfield, R., & Winters, K. (2001). Outcome of Minnesota's gambling treatment programs. *Journal of Gambling Studies, 17,* 217–245. http://dx.doi.org/10.1023/A:1012268322509.

Stoutimore, M. R., Williams, C. E., Neff, B., & Foster, M. (2008). The Florida child welfare behavior analysis services program. *Research on Social Work Practice, 18*(5), 367–376. http://dx.doi.org/10.1177/1049731508318654.

Thyer, B. A. (1981). Behavioral social work: A bibliography. *International Journal of Behavioral Social Work and Abstracts, 1,* 229–251.

Thyer, B. A. (1991). Behavioral social work: It's not what you think. *Arete, 16*(2), 1–9.

Thyer, B. A. (1993). Social work theory and practice research: The approach of logical positivism. *Social Work and Social Sciences Review, 4,* 5–26.

Thyer, B. A. (1999). Clinical behavior analysis and clinical social work: A mutually reinforcing relationship. *The Behavior Analyst, 22*(1), 17–29.

Thyer, B. A. (2012). The scientific value of qualitative research for social work. *Qualitative Social Work, 11*(2), 115–129. http://dx.doi.org/10.1177/1473325011433928.

Tuerk, P., Brady, K. T., & Grubaugh, A. L. (2009). Clinical case discussion: Combat PTSD and substance use disorders. *Journal of Addiction Medicine, 3*(4), 189–193. http://dx.doi.org/10.1097/ADM.0b013e3181a9d276.

VA/DoD Management of Post-Traumatic Stress Working Group. (2010). *VA/DoD Clinical practice guideline for management of post traumatic stress.* Washington, DC: Department of Veterans Affairs and Department of Defense.

von Bertalanffy, L. (1962). *Modern theories of development.* New York: Harper.

Witherup, L. R., Vollmer, T. R., Van Camp, C. M., Goh, H., Borrero, J. C., & Mayfield, K. (2008). Baseline measurement of running away among youth in foster care. *Journal of Applied Behavior Analysis, 41*(3), 305–318. http://dx.doi.org/10.1901/jaba. 2008.41-305.

Wolf, M. M. (1978). Social validity: The case for subjective measurement or how applied behavior analysis is finding its heart. *Journal of Applied Behavior Analysis, 11*(2), 203–214. http://dx.doi.org/10.1901/jaba. 1978.11-203.

World Health Organization. (2010). *Framework for action on interprofessional education & collaborative practice.* Geneva, Switzerland: World Health Organization. *http://www.who.int/hrh/resources/framework_action/en.*

CHAPTER 21

Applied Behavior Analysis and Sports Performance

James K. Luiselli[1], Derek D. Reed[2]
[1]Clinical Solutions, Inc. and North East Educational and Developmental Support Center, Tewksbury, Massachusetts, USA
[2]Department of Applied Behavioral Science, University of Kansas, Lawrence, Kansas, USA

In 1974, McKenzie and Rushall published one of the first studies using applied behavior analysis (ABA) methods to improve sports performance. About 40 years later ABA continues to play a vital role in sports with youth, collegiate, and elite athletes (Luiselli & Reed, 2011; Luiselli, Woods & Reed, 2011; Martin, 2011). Behavioral intervention and research has focused on many sports, including football, basketball, swimming, tennis, soccer, and others. ABA applications have also been used to increase exercise and physical activity in normative and at-risk populations (DeLuca & Holborn, 1992; Fitterling, Martin, Gramling, Cole, & Milan, 1988; Wack, Crosland, & Miltenberger, 2014). In this chapter, we review ABA and sports performance by describing seminal and contemporary studies, highlighting key areas that impact practice and research, and summarizing future directions.

OVERVIEW

Martin and Thomson (2011) identified several characteristics of ABA–sports performance, which they subsumed under the category of *behavioral sport psychology*. First, the specialty area of ABA and sports "involves identifying target behaviors of athletes and/or coaches to be improved, defining those behaviors in a way so that they can be reliably measured, and using changes in the behavioral measure as the best indicator of the extent to which the recipient of an intervention is being helped" (p. 5). A second characteristic is that ABA interventions with athletes rely on principles and procedures of both respondent and operant conditioning. Third, most ABA–sports research has relied on single-case experimental methods as a strategy for evaluating intervention effectiveness (Luiselli, 2011; Martin, Thompson, & Regehr, 2004). Finally, social validation assessment emphasizes how the

Clinical and Organizational Applications of Applied Behavior Analysis
http://dx.doi.org/10.1016/B978-0-12-420249-8.00021-6

recipients of ABA-sports interventions value the goals, procedures, and results of the services they received. We explore each of these characteristics in more detail later in the chapter.

Martin and Thomson (2011) also commented that many interventions with athletes "have been developed by practitioners with a cognitive-behavioral orientation" (p. 7). Although some behavior analysts dismiss the influence of cognitive processes in human learning, cognitively focused sport psychologists have demonstrated that manipulating an athlete's thoughts and attitudes can improve performance (Brown, 2011; Zinsser, Bunker, & Williams, 2006). In effect, "from an applied behavior analysis (ABA) perspective...it is assumed that the behavioral principles and techniques that apply to overt behaviors are also applicable to covert behaviors" (Martin & Thomson, 2011, p. 7). As revealed in our subsequent research review, goal setting, imagery training, and self-talk are cognitive-behavioral procedures sometimes included with ABA-sports interventions.

Several other characteristics of ABA-sports intervention should be highlighted. One prominent concern is the distinction between skills and performance deficits. Some children and adults, for example, receive intervention to teach them new athletic skills or skills that have yet to be mastered. In other cases, the focus of intervention is to improve and perfect performance of acquired skills. Accordingly, skills and performance objectives may involve different intervention methods. Additionally, skill acquisition is usually the purview of practice and training sessions, whereas improving performance is in the domain of competitive events.

Whether skills- or performance-focused, ABA-sports interventions must include procedures for motivating athletes during practice and competition. Motivation is influenced by several factors such as (a) positive and negative reinforcement contingencies arranged for athletic behaviors, (b) manipulation of establishing operations (Michel, 1982), and (c) proper identification of reinforcing stimuli, ideally through preference assessment (Tiger & Kliebert, 2011). Virtually all of the studies reviewed in this chapter illustrate the influence of motivational processes when intervening with athletes at every level.

Behavioral assessment is fundamental within sport psychology in general (Tkachuk, Leslie-Toogood, & Martin, 2003) and a cornerstone of ABA across multiple disciplines (Kazdin, 2013). Within sports, behavioral assessment is principally focused on evaluating effectiveness by measuring intervention-targeted responses. However, behavioral assessment has other objectives as well, namely, selecting skill and performance objectives, identifying functional influences on responding, and informing intervention planning. Ideally, behavioral assessment should encompass multiple methods to provide the broadest possible documentation of critical measures.

ABA-SPORTS RESEARCH

This section of the chapter describes ABA intervention research in several sports. The representative studies are not inclusive of the extant literature; instead, we selected sports that have the largest research base or have been studied recently with promising results. We also reference less frequently studied sports to illustrate the full extent of ABA work in the athletic arena. For each sport, we highlight procedural methodology in light of the intervention objectives and some of the commonalities and differences among the studies.

Football

Allison and Ayllon (1980) evaluated a behavioral coaching intervention with four youth football players (11–12 years old) to teach them line blocking skills. The responses constituting a correct block were identified and described in an 8-step task analysis. The dependent measure in the study was the percentage of trials in which each player demonstrated all of the steps correctly. During a standard coaching (baseline) phase, the coach instructed players in what he wanted them to do, praised correct execution, and "loudly informed the player and, at times, commented on the player's stupidity, lack of courage, awareness, or even worse" (p. 300). With intervention, the coach was taught to (a) give explicit instructions to the players about executing the blocking responses, (b) evaluate and provide feedback to the players following trials, (c) model correct performance of a block, and (d) request the players to imitate his model. As evaluated in a multiple baseline design across players, this combination of procedures effectively increased the percentage of blocks executed correctly from near-zero levels during baseline to averages of 50–70%. This study is noteworthy in being one of the first to evaluate ABA procedures with football players.

In a study with five linebackers (19–21 years old) on a Division II football team, Ward and Carnes (2002) implemented goal setting and public posting to improve "reads" (covering a specific area of the field during a pass or run), "drops" (moving to the correct field position before each offensive snap), and "tackles" (bringing a runner to the ground). These dependent measures were recorded as percentage of correct execution during 10 trials per player at practices and games. Under baseline conditions, the coach met with the players before practice, reviewed expectations, and gave them in-practice feedback and error correction. Intervention started with a researcher speaking to each player about his baseline performance for drops, reads, and tackles. The players were then requested to set goals that exceeded their mean performance during practices (they did not set goals for games). All of the players selected a goal of 90% correct execution for the three performance measures. The public posting component of intervention featured a chart that was displayed in the locker room on which each player's daily practice results were depicted as him achieving ("yes") or not achieving ("no") the 90% goal-setting criterion. Similar to the goal-setting procedure in practice, public posting was not implemented for performance during games.

Ward and Carnes (2002) intervened with each player according to a multiple baseline design across the three dependent measures. All of the players had relatively stable performance during baseline, ranging from 60% to 80% correct execution of reads, drops, and tackles. Average performance during intervention increased to 90-100%, again for all of the players and the three dependent measures. Notably, players uniformly improved their baseline game performance during the time that intervention was implemented in practice.

In another study with Division II college football players, Smith and Ward (2006) intervened with three wide receivers (ages not specified) to improve their percentage of correct blocks, routes run, and releases from the line of scrimmage during practice. Following a baseline phase in which the coach met with the players, reviewed performance expectations, and gave verbal feedback and error correction in practice drills, the researchers implemented three intervention phases, each phase separated by a brief return-to-baseline condition. With *public posting plus verbal feedback*, the players were informed before each practice about their previous day's performance of the three target skills. Also, their performance data were presented in a chart on the door leading to the locker room. The next intervention phase, *goal setting plus verbal feedback*, imposed a 90% performance criterion for each skill and positive verbal feedback to the players when they were successful. The third intervention phase was *public posting plus verbal feedback plus goal setting*, in effect a combination of the previously implemented procedures. Identical to baseline, the coach continued to give verbal feedback and error correction during intervention practice phases.

The results of the Smith and Ward (2006) intervention were that all three players improved their performance of blocks, routes, and releases from

50-80% correct during baseline to 80-100% during intervention with each combination of verbal feedback, goal setting, and public posting. Game performance, which was included as a generalization measure, also improved similarly over baseline levels, something that would be expected given the advanced football competence of the players. Unfortunately, the comparative effectiveness of the procedures could not be determined because the three intervention phases were introduced sequentially in the same order with each player.

Several studies have highlighted behavioral coaching methods with high school football athletes. Stokes, Luiselli, Reed, and Fleming (2010) developed a 10-step task analysis to improve offensive line blocking of five players (15-17 years old). Five offensive line coaches (not associated with the study) were surveyed to validate the steps that comprised the task analysis. Normative data were also acquired by using the task analysis to record pass blocking execution of the three highest rated starting offensive linemen from the previous season. The dependent measure throughout the study was the percentage of task analysis steps the players executed correctly during one pass blocking drill in practice and 3-4 pass blocking sequences during a single game. Under baseline conditions, the offensive line coach implemented conventional procedures that entailed instructing the players about proper positional technique and staying focused. The coach typically praised good performance ("That's the way to hit!"), responded negatively to poor execution, and sometimes modeled the desired blocking responses.

During intervention, Stokes, Luiselli, Reed, and Fleming (2010) exposed the players to the following procedures: (1) *Descriptive feedback*: The coach reviewed the task analysis steps with each player after the pass blocking drill. Correctly executed steps received praise and nonverbal approval (e.g., slapping a "high five"). The coach responded to incorrect steps by explaining how they should be executed, having the player repeat the steps correctly, and praising performance accordingly. (2) *Descriptive feedback plus video feedback*: The coach continued to deliver descriptive feedback following pass blocking drills. Each player then watched a videotape of his performance, completed task analysis ratings with the coach, and performed missed steps one time correctly. Players could also question the coach about how to further refine their pass blocking skills. (3) *Teaching with acoustical guidance (TAG)*: During this phase, the coach selected task analysis steps that each player continued to execute inconsistently. When a player performed these steps correctly in the pass blocking drill the coach sounded a bullhorn that produced a siren lasting 1-5 s. The audible stimulus was intended to function as immediate feedback (reinforcement; Pryor, 1999). TAG was the only procedure implemented.

Stokes, Luiselli, Reed, and Fleming (2010) found that descriptive feedback alone did not improve pass blocking. However, all five players improved with video feedback, and four of the five players that received TAG enhanced their performance further. Another finding was that, with intervention, the players pass blocked at a level of proficiency that was comparable to more experienced linemen. They also showed this improvement during games. However, for three of the five players returning for a second season, descriptive and video feedback, and in one case, TAG, had to be implemented again because their line blocking skills deteriorated in the absence of practice and behavioral coaching.

Two additional studies with high school football players targeted tackling skills. Stokes, Luiselli, and Reed (2010) intervened with two linebackers (16–17 years old) to improve their performance in practice and during games. Based on a 10-step task analysis, the coach presented the players with a colorful helmet sticker each time they matched or exceeded the percentage of correctly executed steps during preceding tackling drills. Although no contingencies were programmed for their behavior, teammates also responded positively. This relatively simple intervention was associated with improved tackling during practice and in each player's first postintervention varsity game. Harrison and Pyles (2013) reported similar results with three linebackers (16–17 years old) using verbal instructions and TAG, initially to train four-component tackling skills at walking speed. Subsequently, the intervention procedures were applied successfully with the players during progressive speed drills that advanced from walking, to jogging, and then, running. However, the skills acquired during practice were not measured in games.

Soccer

Ziegler (1994) employed a multiple baseline design across four Division I college soccer players (ages were not specified) to study the effects of "an attention-training program" on their execution of four passing and kicking skills. In baseline, player performance was measured under conventional practice conditions. The training program included an information phase, in which attention shifting skills were taught via lecture and "laboratory attention shift exercises," then an application phase that consisted of using attention shifting skills while executing soccer drills. The players also received performance feedback during drills. With intervention, each player performed the soccer skills more accurately compared to consistently lower baseline levels. Ziegler (1994) acknowledged that these effects were difficult to interpret because the attention-training program combined simulated and *in vivo* procedures, and she did not assess intervention integrity. Also, the study did not evaluate game performance.

Brobst and Ward (2002) evaluated the effects of public posting, goal setting, and verbal feedback on three behaviors executed by three female soccer players (15-17 years old) during practices and games: movement with the ball, movement during restarts, and movement after a player passed the ball. In the baseline phase of a multiple baseline design across behaviors, the coach conducted practice drills with the team and gave performance feedback through praise and error correction. Several procedures were implemented during intervention in which (a) the players were expected to perform each behavior at a minimum of 90% accuracy, (b) practice performance data were posted on a chart each day, and (c) one of the researchers met individually with the players to review the performance data, praise goal-achievement, and encourage effort to improve sub-goal execution. The two main effects from this study were that intervention improved soccer skills during practice and the positive findings generalized to games for movement with the ball but not the other two skills.

Swimming

Koop and Martin (1983) described a behavioral coaching strategy that was implemented to decrease swimming errors of five children (7-12 years old) who were members of a competitive swim club. The researchers identified specific swim stroke errors within freestyle (9 errors), backstroke (7 errors), and breaststroke (11 errors) categories. The dependent measure was the percentage of errors each swimmer committed during 10 stroke trials per category. Following a "standard coach" baseline phase, the swimmers participated in a training phase in which a coach first referenced "large checklists containing drawings and instructions for correct behaviors on each stroke" (p. 451). Other components of the training phase featured (a) out-of-pool instructions about stroke execution, verbal prompting, modeling, and swimmer role-playing; (b) in-pool practice of correct strokes; and (c) in-pool consequences for correct (praise) and incorrect (contingent tactile cues and instructions) strokes. After the training phase, the coach introduced maintenance procedures consisting of an initial prompt during practice and performance feedback.

Koop and Martin (1983) evaluated an intervention using a multiple baseline design across swimmers for each of the three stroke categories. Their results were extensive, which they interpreted as demonstrating "that the error correction package resulted in a decrease in errors on swimming strokes to a low rate during training sessions, stimulus generalization to regular practice with three of four swimmers, and maintenance of improved performance with minimal prompting and feedback under normal practice conditions" (p. 458). Furthermore, intervention did not disrupt practice, and the swimmers and coach rated the procedures favorably.

Dragen and Austin (2008) reported another combination of behavioral procedures to improve performance of youth swimmers. The participants were three girls (15-18 years old) on a high school swimming and diving team. In this study, the dependent measure was the duration of freestyle "flip turns" during swim meets. The swimmers received standard training during baseline practices and then two intervention phases within an A (baseline)-B (intervention 1)-A (baseline)-C (intervention 2) experimental design. The first intervention phase consisted of graphic feedback in the form of a bar graph showing each swimmer's average flip turn in seconds for preceding swim meets. The coach also delivered accompanying verbal feedback. In the second intervention phase, the swimmers were instructed to use self-talk, for example, "explode" when pushing off the pool walls, and "reach" to remain in a streamlined position after pushing off. They were also taught to record their performance at swim meets on self-monitoring forms that the coach reviewed with them. Although the results were modest, each swimmer improved her flip turn speed while receiving graphic and verbal feedback, engaging in self-talk, and self-monitoring her swim performance.

Tennis

Allison and Ayllon (1980) compared a behavioral coaching intervention with standard coaching procedures for 12 students (18-35 years old) enrolled in a tennis instruction program. A detailed task analysis was created to measure forehand, backhand, and service strokes. The researchers described standard coaching as a combination of verbal instruction, modeling, feedback, and encouragement. Similar to their behavioral coaching protocol for football players described previously, Allison and Ayllon had the tennis coach deliver behavior-specific instructions about stroke position, evaluate correct and incorrect executions, and guide the students to assume proper positioning with further instruction. Multiple baseline designs across students and tennis strokes demonstrated that behavioral coaching increased the percentage of trials in which the students executed strokes correctly. Eventually, the standard coaching procedures were able to maintain the performance improvement that had been achieved with intervention. This finding is particularly relevant where there is concern about sustaining the more intensive and time-consuming demands that characterize most behavioral coaching applications.

Ziegler (1987) studied the effects of a self-directed stimulus cueing technique on the skill acquisition of 20 beginning tennis players (19-31 years old) attending a university-based physical education service program. Each day their forehand and backhand strokes were measured during ball-machine-generated drills. Performance was quantified as the percentage of task analysis steps executed correctly. The players were assigned to three groups, each group receiving general directions from a tennis instructor as well as ball-machine supervision from two assistants. The self-directed stimulus cueing intervention occurred in a multiple baseline design across groups. Intervention taught the players to (a) track the ball and say "ball" as soon as it was fired from the ball-machine, (b) say "bounce" as the ball contacted the court surface, (c) say "hit" upon striking the ball with the racket, and (d) say "ready" to prepare physically for the next ball. Reported as group data, the average percentage of correct forehand and backhand strokes increased dramatically, from 13-33% during baseline to 43-83% during intervention. Ziegler (1987) concluded that the performance improvement effects from self-directed stimulus cueing derived from "focusing on the ball as a form of preparation for skill execution" (p. 410), but the study was not planned to test this hypothesis.

One additional tennis study, reported by Allen (1998), is of interest because the objective was to *reduce negative behavior* during matches. The participant was a 14-year-old tennis player with a history of uncomplimentary outbursts (loud vocalizing, striking racket on the court, waving arms) when competing during state and regional tennis events. Baseline data documented numerous outbursts despite parental efforts to curtail the behavior. Intervention started with awareness training that had the boy describe outbursts, identify precursor behaviors, and pinpoint the most common provoking conditions. He was also taught to perform diaphragmatic breathing whenever he recognized the precursor behaviors and in response to an audible cue from his parents in the stands. Finally, he was able to earn points (exchanged for new stereo compact discs) when he was observed engaging in the competing response. This combination of procedures reduced the number of outbursts per tennis match but they continued at an unacceptable frequency.

Thereafter, any outburst resulted in the boy having to withdraw from the current match and forfeit his next event. This response cost procedure essentially eliminated outbursts. Unfortunately, a 12-month follow-up assessment revealed that the boy was again displaying outbursts, although his parents opined that behavior *intensity* had diminished.

Basketball

Kladopoulos and McComas (2001) used instructions and feedback to refine foul-shooting form and increase accuracy of three Division II female, college basketball players (19-20 years old). Foul-shooting form was measured as percentage of task-analyzed steps executed correctly on practice trials. The percentage of those shots falling through the hoop without touching the backboard was also recorded. In baseline, the players took 10 foul shots without instructions or feedback. During intervention, they continued taking 10 practice foul shots but a researcher instructed them in proper shooting form by (a) reviewing the task-analyzed steps, (b) having the players take 10 more foul shots, and (c) praising each shot made with reference to form (e.g., "Good job keeping your feet in the same position throughout the shot."). If a player missed a shot, the researcher gave corrective feedback about form but not accuracy. A multiple baseline analysis across players demonstrated that intervention simultaneously improved the percentage of trials with correct form as well as foul-shooting accuracy. This study did not evaluate whether improved performance could be maintained without ongoing form training or whether practice effects generalized to games.

Baseball

Osborne, Rudrud, and Zezoney (1990) conducted a study to determine whether adding distinctive visual cues to baseballs would improve curveball hitting of five collegiate players (ages not specified). A pitching machine set at a standard speed delivered curveballs to each player, and it was adjusted to accommodate their personal strike zone. There were 20 pitches per practice session. Only unmarked balls were pitched in the first phase of a multiele-ment design. In the next two phases the unmarked balls were mixed with balls that had either 1/4 in. or 1/8 in. orange highlighting strips around the seams. The researchers recorded the percentage of "well-hit" balls according to exacting criteria that encompassed distance, location, and swing. Results were that adding visual cues to the baseballs improved curveball hitting proficiency over unmarked balls, with the 1/4 in. color stimulus slightly better than the 1/8 color stimulus. The ultimate effect of such training would obviously have to be evaluated by gradually fading the baseball cues under live pitching conditions. Nevertheless, a stimulus control intervention may be an effective strategy for quickly improving athletic skills, which subsequently can be withdrawn to support performance in competitive games.

Track and Field

A study by Scott, Scott, and Goldwater (1997) incorporated prompting and shaping with a 21-year-old collegiate pole vaulter. The intervention objective was to improve his arm extension at take-off, a critical step that could lead to increased vaulting height. To start, his percentage of vaults with correct arm extension was recorded before intervention. After calculating his mean hand height on the pole (2.25 m), procedures were introduced to gradually shape maximum positioning at 2.54 m. The researchers installed a photoelectric beam that delivered an audible tone when his hand height on the pole achieved a specified criterion, beginning at 2.30 m (5 cm above the mean baseline height), and advanced over successive vaults to a terminal hand height of 2.52 m. A coach also verbalized "reach" as the vaulter progressed down the runway and preceding his take-off. Plotted as a changing criterion design (Hartmann & Hall, 1976), the performance data revealed that his hand height improved with the gradual increase in criterion, and it corresponded with higher bar height clearance. One caveat when interpreting these findings is that the data were highly variable and the duration of intervention lasted 200 sessions over a period of 18 months.

Gymnastics

Wolko, Hrycaiko, and Martin (1993) compared standard coaching with two self-management interventions among five female gymnasts (10-13 years old). This study consisted of an alternating treatments design in which frequency of attempted and completed balance beam skills were recorded within practice sessions. The baseline (standard coaching) phase had several procedures in effect, namely coach verbal goal setting, performance feedback, technique correction, encouragement, reprimands, and spotting. These procedures continued during both self-management intervention phases. One of these phases included public coach-written goal setting combined with public self-recording and graphing with coach feedback. Additionally, the gymnasts could select from a list of "rewards" if they achieved coach-written goals for both skill attempts and completions. The second intervention phase differed from the first in that the gymnasts engaged in private self-goal setting and self-recording plus graphing without coach feedback. The same reinforcement contingencies remained in effect.

The supplement of self-management to standard coaching in Wolko et al. (1993) improved balance beam performance of the gymnasts. This improvement was gradual, possibly because "the time span allotted for each condition to show its effect may have been too brief" (p. 220). The results also suggested that the private self-goal setting and self-monitoring combination was marginally more effective than the publically implemented procedures. This study also reported social validity assessment indicating that the gymnasts liked both self-management interventions more than standard coaching.

Another approach to gymnastics training, by Boyer, Miltenberger, Batsche, and Fogel (2009), incorporated video modeling and feedback with four girls (7–10 years old) at a local club. The dependent measures were three skills (backward giant circle to hand stand, hip cast, clean hip circle), executed on the uneven bars, which were sequenced in a 28-item checklist per skill. In a multiple baseline design across motor skills, a coach provided verbal feedback to the girls after they dismounted from the uneven bars during practice sessions. With intervention, the girls watched a computer screen showing a video clip of an expert gymnast performing one of the three targeted skills that was paired with their own practice performance. Next, (a) a technician freeze-framed each video clip at select emphasis-points for the skill, (b) the video clips were shown one time at normal speed, and (c) the girls attempted the target skill two more times. In summary, the results suggested "that adding video modeling by experts with video feedback to typical coaching and practice techniques could reduce the number of practice sessions required to improve a difficult physical skill" (Boyer et al., 2009, p. 857). Follow-up measures demonstrated generally positive maintenance of skills without further intervention. Both the gymnasts and coaches gave high approval ratings for the video modeling and feedback procedures.

Other Sports

In rounding out this description of ABA-sports research, we briefly cite other studies of interest, focusing on athletic areas that have less supportive data but nonetheless positive results. For example, Anderson and Kirkpatrick (2002) measured the percentage of correct relay tags executed by four female youth (12-16 years old) on a competitive inline roller speed skating team. Relative to baseline conditions, each skater improved her percentage of correct tags in response to intervention that included skill clarification, descriptive praise, and performance feedback. Harding, Wacker, Berg, Rick, and Lee (2004) taught two adults (33 and 40 years old) who were beginning students in the Kenpo system of martial arts to execute punching and kicking techniques through differential reinforcement and performance feedback. In work with five male rugby players (21-25 years old), Mellalieu, Hanton, and O'Brien (2006) used a three-phase intervention of goal-determination, goal setting, and goal reviewing to improve game performance of ball carries, tackles, successful kicks, and turnovers. Finally, Fogel, Weil, and Burris (2010) implemented TAG and other behavioral procedures to train five behaviors comprising a proper golf swing by a 30-year-old novice golfer.

Summary of ABA-Sports Research

The preceding review of research reveals that ABA methodology and procedures have been implemented with many sports, for individuals and teams, and among beginning, developing, and advanced athletes. Virtually every study featured direct measurement of skill acquisition and performance, although data gathered from video recording and self-report were also used on occasion. Certain procedures such as shaping, positive reinforcement, and goal setting were common, whereas methods such as TAG have been evaluated less frequently. One largely consistent finding is that ABA-sports interventions integrate multiple procedures—it is rare that a single method accounts for success.

The studies previously emphasized usually conducted intervention evaluation during practice sessions and routines, particularly when the objective was to train new skills. In some of the research, measurement was extended to postintervention games and competitive events in order to assess response generalization. The most complete and robust research measured game and competitive performance before, during, and following intervention. Notably, some maintenance evaluations were completed with intervention procedures ongoing while other studies had removed them.

Some intervention methods were evaluated with several sports but implemented differently. For example, in the case of goal setting, participants sometimes selected their own goals or were so instructed by coaches. Goals were also determined privately and publically, occasionally with accompanying performance feedback, in group or individual formats, either verbally, graphically, or both. From a research perspective, it is desirable to standardize procedures and keep them uniform across participants. However, the legitimate concern for experimental rigor must be tempered with the reality of practical sports coaching and training. That is, most athletes and performers demand individualized interventions that conform to their unique learning histories, skill level, performance expectations, and motivation. Therefore, the professional community should carefully consider the limitations of research-to-practice translation when applying evidence-based procedures.

RESEARCH INFORMED PRACTICE STANDARDS, IMPLICATIONS, AND FUTURE DIRECTIONS

This section of the chapter expands on several key issues that were consistent in the research literature and have practice implications, namely assessment-derived intervention, behavioral coaching, intervention integrity, social validity, and single-case evaluation designs. We also discuss emerging translational research and ABA–sports intervention with special populations.

Assessment-Derived Intervention

Beyond measuring the effects of intervention on skill acquisition and performance, behavior assessment should inform procedural decision-making. With regard to positive reinforcement, for example, current convention dictates that reinforcers be selected based on the results of preference assessment (Tiger & Kliebert, 2011). We noted previously that all ABA–sports research included some type of positive reinforcement to motivate and support critical behaviors and skills. Indeed, it is difficult to imagine any coach or trainer that does not recognize the importance of positively reinforcing athletes when they perform correctly! As such, behavioral sports practitioners should not choose social and tangible "rewards" arbitrarily. Rather, preintervention assessments should be initiated to more closely align programmed reinforcers with empirically selected, athlete-specific preferences. However, in preparing this chapter we did not locate any studies that included formal standardized preference assessment in the context of ABA–sports research.

Other foundations of ABA, functional behavioral assessment and functional analysis, have rarely been reported in ABA–sports research (Tkachuk et al., 2003). Certainly, there are antecedent and consequence influences on skill execution and problem behaviors, including but not limited to particular coaching strategies, an athlete's physical status, practice conditions, response effort, and so on. In the only published exemplar of functional analysis in ABA-sports research, Stokes and Luiselli (2010) evaluated procedures with a 17-year-old high school football player to improve his tackling skills. The functional analysis targeted the percentage of steps in a 10-step task analysis he executed correctly during one-on-one tackling drills. There were four functional analysis conditions, implemented over 2 days at a preseason camp:

No attention: With the other defensive players present during tackling drills, the coach praised the participant ("Good job!") when he tackled the ball carrier but otherwise did not give him specific feedback.

Coach attention: Only the coach was present during tackling drills. Contingent on a successful tackle he praised the participant enthusiastically ("Great work, that's how to hit!"), clapped, and delivered a "high five" or pat on the helmet.

Peer attention: The team captains and defensive players were present during the tackling drills, they shouted excitedly when the participant tackled the ball carrier and responded with "high fives" while the coach did not react.

Escape: Without other players present, the coach started the tackling drills by vigorously instructing the participant to use proper technique and "make a good tackle." Upon tackling the ball carrier, the coach did not praise the participant but allowed him to move on to the next practice activity.

Figure 21.1 presents the results of the functional analysis. These data showed that the participant had the highest percentage of correct tackling during the escape condition ($M = 56.6\%$), followed by no attention ($M = 45.0\%$), peer attention ($M = 30.0\%$), and coach attention ($M = 25.0\%$). Hypothesizing that coach avoidance instead of public commentary was responsible for the highest percentage of correct tackling during the functional analysis, Stokes and Luiselli (2010) intervened with the participant by having the coach present him with a one-page written checklist of correctly executed steps following practice and without verbal comment. Conceived as a type of delayed written performance feedback (Balcazar, Hopkins, & Suarez, 1985), the participant increased his correct tackling from an average of 33% at baseline to an average of 72% with intervention. Correct tackling was recorded at 75% during a one-game postintervention assessment. This study, although preliminary, suggests a model of functional analysis with

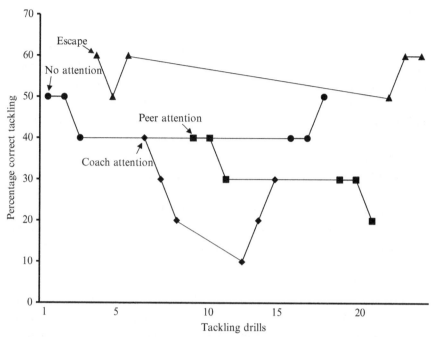

Figure 21.1 Percentage of correct tackling during a functional analysis with a high school football player.
From Stokes and Luiselli (2010).

athletes that is consistent with generally accepted ABA standards and recommendations (Cipani & Schock, 2011; Hanley, 2012).

Behavior checklists (Martin, Toogood, & Tkachuk, 1997) can also inform intervention planning and implementation in several ways. Apropos to preference assessments, athletes can complete checklists that identify pleasurable social and tangible stimuli to be incorporated into self- or coach-directed intervention plans. Similarly, sport-specific behavior checklists help highlight "identifiable psychological skills and strategies which differentiate between any athlete's best and worst performances, as well as those athletes who do and do not perform up to their potential at competitions" (Tkachuk et al., 2003, p. 108). In effect, athletes can verify skills and performance concerns that, in their judgment, should be the focus of intervention. At the same time, athletes could complete behavior checklists to inform coaches and trainers about the types of procedures that have high acceptance and satisfaction. Such data would be extremely informative because positively rated procedures by athletes are likely to be associated with intervention effectiveness (Smith & Smoll, 2011).

Behavioral Coaching

James Naismith—the inventor of basketball—is a household name in sports aficionados' circles. It may be surprising, however, to learn that Naismith vehemently opposed the notion of coaching basketball squads (Kerkhoff, 1996). Forrest "Phog" Allen challenged this premise and ultimately went on to become the father of coaching in basketball. "Phog" Allen recognized that effective coaching produces results far superior to letting athletes merely demonstrate their raw talent on the court. Many decades later, formalized coaching of sports performance has been a mainstay in nearly all popularized forms of athletics. It is not surprising that at the time of this writing, a Google search of "behavioral coaching" and "sports" yielded over 31,000 hits; a review of the various websites contained in those hits demonstrates the multiplicity of this term's interpretation.

The ABA-sports studies we reviewed in this chapter illustrated many combinations of procedures falling under the term "behavioral coaching." Behavior analysts have identified a common set of components that comprise the behavioral coaching approach (see review by Seniuk, Witts, Williams, & Ghezzi, 2013), but there are currently no standard implementation guidelines. The Seniuk et al. review revealed six components that we endorse and most behavior analysts would recognize as essential for effective coaching:

1. *Behavioral measurement*: The dependent variable should entail athletic performance that is observable, definable, and countable.
2. *Differentiation between acquisition and maintenance of athletic performance*: Coaching should approach skill acquisition differently than the maintenance of performance, using empirically supported positive reinforcement strategies for both.
3. *Within-athlete comparison*: Athletes' skills at the initiation of coaching should serve as the baseline comparison for eventual acquisition and maintenance procedures initiated by the coach.
4. *Use coaching procedures derived from rigorous experimentation*: Coaches must let data inform their practices, whether from published studies, or replications of procedures previously described and used (and that were effective) that were not necessarily published in peer-reviewed outlets.
5. *Recognize the role of the coach in athlete behavior change*: Like any other behavior analytic interventions, the behavior change agent—in this case, the coach—must change their behavior to affect change in the target client.

6. *Behavioral coaching must be socially valid*: The procedures comprising the coaching approach should be deemed acceptable by all relevant sports stakeholders, including, but not limited to, the athlete, the fans, the teammates (if relevant), and the broader athletic community.

Behavior analysts may see many parallels between behavioral coaching and behavior skills training, and for good reason; both derive from organizational behavior management. Behavioral skills training (BST) is a packaged intervention containing (a) instructions, (b) modeling and rehearsal, and (c) feedback (e.g., Sarokoff & Sturmey, 2004), three of the most popular ABA methods in sport training and consultation. Collectively, the research on BST and behavioral sport psychology suggests that BST should play an integral role in behavioral coaching.

Intervention Integrity

Intervention procedures in educational and clinical settings are most successful when practitioners implement them with high integrity (Fiske, 2008; Noell, Gresham, & Gansle, 2002; Wilder, Atwell, & Wine, 2006). The same conclusion can be drawn for ABA-sports applications but, unfortunately, intervention integrity assessment is conspicuously absent in the extant literature. A notable exception is the study by Koop and Martin (1983) in which they assessed "procedural compliance" in a program to reduce stroke errors by beginning swimmers. The assessment protocol required an observer to independently record the swim trainer's implementation of intervention procedures against an identical procedural checklist. A percentage compliance measure was calculated from these two data sets. Similarly, in their martial arts training study, Harding et al. (2004) recorded the procedural fidelity of instructor feedback to participants during sessions.

The rationale for conducting the intervention integrity assessment is ensuring proper evaluation of intervention procedures. That is, if practitioners apply procedures inaccurately it is not possible to determine whether poor intervention effects are the result of inconsistent implementation or the procedures themselves. Assessing intervention integrity is certainly a prerequisite for applied sports research but just as important in day-to-day coaching. To illustrate, Luiselli (2012) presented an intervention integrity recording form applicable to youth lacrosse coaching drills. Shown in Figure 21.2, the form designates eight coaching behaviors making up a

Intervention integrity recording form

Date of observation:
Setting: Lacrosse Practice-Smith Field
Observer:
Coach-implementer:
Target: Two-lane passing drills
Instructions: Record steps 1-7 one time (start of drill) and step 8 for the first 10 two-player passing exchanges

Coach behaviors	Integrity ratings		
	Implemented accurately	Implemented inaccurately	Not implemented
1: Divides players into 2 groups			
2: Arranges groups into 2, head-to-head vertical lines			
3: Spaces lines 15+ feet apart			
4: Calls for attention ("eyes on me")			
5. Describes purpose of drill			
6: Demonstrates expected behavior during drill			
7: Assumes monitoring position			
8: Whistles start of, and comments verbally following, each two-player passing exchange			
Player 1 >Player 2			
Player 3 >Player 4			
Player 5>Player 6			
Player 7 >Player 8			
Player 9 >Player 10			
Player 11>Player 12			
Player 13>Player 14			
Player 15>Player 16			
Player 17>Player 18			
Player 1 9>Player 20			

Implementation accuracy score (accurate ratings/total ratings scored x 100):

Figure 21.2 Intervention integrity recording form.
From Luiselli (2012).

practice passing drill. To evaluate intervention integrity, an observer, such as a behavioral consultant or assistant coach, records whether the coach displayed each behavior accurately, inaccurately, or not at all. Summing the number of accurate ratings and dividing by the total ratings scored produces an overall implementation accuracy score. Less than desirable intervention integrity would be corrected by isolating the misapplied behaviors, giving the coach respective training, and repeating intervention integrity assessment.

Social Validity

Broadly defined, social validity concerns the appropriateness and accept-ability of ABA interventions as both process and outcome measures (Kazdin, 1977; Wolf, 1978). One type of social validity, expert validation, has to do with the selection of intervention objectives, skills, and procedures. Thus, as an initial step in their program to reduce swimming stroke errors, Koop and Martin (1983) developed lists of possible errors from swimming instruction books and distributed the lists to team coaches "who indepen-dently rank-ordered the errors according to their relative importance in detracting from swimming speed," refining the lists further "by deleting errors on which coaches strongly disagreed, as well as errors that were unan-imously considered unimportant" (p. 449).

In the same vein, Stokes, Luiselli, and Reed (2010), Stokes, Luiselli, Reed, and Fleming (2010) and Harrison and Pyles (2013) referred to recommenda-tions from the American Football Coaches Association (1995) and sought ver-ification by active high school and collegiate coaches when developing task analyses for improving blocking and tackling skills. Boyer et al. (2009) pro-vided another example of expert validation by constructing their video modeling intervention with child gymnasts from videotaped performances of USA National Team members in competition, advice from a high-ranking gymnastics judge, and consultation with coaches of elite athletes.

A second type of social validity assessment compares preintervention, intervention, and postintervention measures against a high-performing nor-mative sample. Such assessment enables practitioners to select reasonable intervention-targeted criteria. Furthermore, the resulting data can confirm that intervention results matched or exceeded an acceptable standard. In the previously cited football study by Stokes, Luiselli, Reed, and Fleming (2010), the participants were five offensive linemen that coaches judged as having the poorest pass blocking skills on a high school varsity team. After preparing a 10-step task analysis and recording protocol for the study, the researchers documented the pass blocking performance of the three highest rated starting offensive linemen from videotaped games against opposing teams during the preceding season. The average correct pass blocking accu-racy for these linemen was 80%, and the range of 70-90% was adopted as the practice and game performance criteria in the study.

A further goal of social validity assessment in ABA-sports research asks athletes and coaches to rate the acceptability of intervention procedures they received and how satisfied they were with implementation and outcomes. Smith and Ward (2006) noted that beyond acquiring measures of acceptability and satisfaction, this type of social validity assessment may uncover unanticipated intervention effects and enable researchers to adjust procedures in future studies. On the most practical level, social validity assessment allows sports practitioners to select intervention procedures that have the greatest appeal and by extension will be implemented with good integrity.

A few research examples show the usual process of socially validating procedural acceptability and satisfaction. Following the gymnastics intervention, Boyer et al. (2009) gave a 5-point Likert-style questionnaire to the gymnasts, coach, and assistant coaches to assess "how much they liked the procedure, whether they would recommend it to others, how easy it was, how helpful it was, and how effective it was in skill development" (p. 857). Koop and Martin (1983) had a swimming coach determine the degree to which he considered intervention to be effective, useful, and easy to implement. The swimmers also documented how much they liked the procedures or found them useful. In Stokes, Luiselli, Reed, and Fleming (2010), the football players rated their satisfaction with baseline and intervention procedures on a number-coded questionnaire as poor (1), fair (2), good (3), and excellent (4). The social validity assessment with a novice golfer by Fogel, Weil, et al. (2010) required her to complete 6-point ratings (strongly disagree, disagree, slightly disagree, slightly agree, agree, strongly agree) for questions such as "My swing is better after this training," and "Learning the pivot via TAG is contributing to my long term golf goal."

The benefits of social validity assessment notwithstanding, it is possible that some respondents may not view the most effective procedures favorably. For example, young and beginning athletes might prefer procedures that are not highly strenuous or difficult independent of how quickly they learn target skills. More established performers are likely to discount procedures that do not produce rapid results and competitive success. Coaches, too, will likely judge procedures differently based on the level of play they are instructing, implementation complexity, familiarity, and so on. We suggest that these and similar variables be considered when designing and interpreting the data from social validity assessment questionnaires.

Single-Case Evaluation Designs

Single-case evaluation methodology is a mainstay of ABA research (Kazdin, 2011) and the basis of many sports related studies (Luiselli, 2011; Martin et al., 2004). The publications we reviewed in this chapter are testimony to the variety of single-case designs available to researchers. Of course, these designs are intended to control for internal validity through time series analysis and replication of effects through experimental manipulation of independent variables. Repeated evaluation of procedures that produce similar outcomes contributes to the external validity of single-case studies.

Briefly, reversal designs have value in quickly evaluating stimulus control and antecedent interventions (Osborne et al., 1990) but may not fit well with consequence-based interventions targeting skill acquisition (i.e., learned skills may not "reverse"). Multiple baseline designs are particularly adaptable, in part because of versatility. For example, the multiple baseline design across behaviors adequately meets the common coaching objective of training more than one skill in a single athlete (Boyer et al., 2009; Brobst & Ward, 2002; Ward & Carnes, 2002). For team sports, interventions can be evaluated efficiently in a multiple baseline design across players (Harrison & Pyles, 2013; Kladopoulos & McComas, 2001). In a changing criterion design, the steps within a task analysis naturally serve as the criteria for measuring the effects of shaping procedures (Scott et al., 1997). One additional strategy, the alternating treatments design, makes it possible to compare two or more procedures (Wolko et al., 1993), thereby enhancing coaching and training efficiency.

Independent of research, single-case evaluation designs should have considerable appeal to practitioners. Whether training athletes directly or consulting with coaches, professionals working in the sports arena can employ single-case designs to evaluate learning trends and make necessary procedural revisions that improve performance. Tkachuk et al. (2003) also commented that single-case methodology can be used to demonstrate "to the consumers of sport psychology services that measurable improvements in athletic performance are due to the interventions" (p. 112). Their suggestion is consistent with Gee's (2010) assertion that applied sport psychology research plays a vital role in educating athletes and coaches about the mechanisms by which professional consultation can positively influence performance.

Translational Research

In one sense of the term, *translational* research constitutes a transfer of technologies developed in the basic operant lab to frontline interventions that address issues of societal concern (Lerman, 2003). This technology transfer interpretation suggests that most, if not all, published experiments on behavioral applications for sports (or anything else, for that matter) could be considered translational. For the sake of this section, we will shift our focus to the middle portion of the basic-applied research continuum; that is, "bridge studies" involving novel applications of behavioral technologies informed directly from the experimental analysis of behavior (EAB).

As described earlier, sports performance constitutes a unique social behavior that is comprised of easily identifiable behavioral components, even for laypersons with no direct training in the science of behavior. Novice consumers of sport have little difficulty identifying quantifiable reinforcers that might maintain performance (e.g., points scored, shots attempted, speeds, times). More advanced consumers can identify specific sporting events that modulate reinforcers and behavioral allocation (e.g., throw a pass on third and long situations in American-rules football). As advocated elsewhere (Reed, 2011), the objective and quantifiable nature of sport performance provides scientists an excellent platform to test behavioral theories using easily accessible databases (e.g., online box scores). Using sport to test behavioral theory advances the generality of basic behavioral phenomena to everyday human events while simultaneously advancing the field's understanding of the operant principles underlying athletic performance. We will discuss two prime areas of bridge research emanating from behavior analytic perspectives on sport: behavioral momentum and matching theory.

Behavioral Momentum

Calling time outs during strategic periods in sporting events have been assumed to disrupt the momentum of the game. Whether the opponent has a "hot hand" in basketball, or a placekicker is about to attempt a crucial field goal in football, coaches rely on the notion of behavioral momentum to introduce a disruption to an unacceptable rate of reinforcement influencing an opponent's success. This concept of *behavioral momentum*—or resistance to extinction—derives from EAB studies on how rates of response persist in the presence of a disruption related to shifts in reinforcement contingencies or discriminable alternations in stimulus control (see Nevin & Grace, 2000). Like most behavioral phenomena, the origin of behavioral momentum theory (BMT) originated from infrahuman research. In perhaps the most defining paper on BMT, Nevin, Mandell, and Atak (1983) likened the maintenance of operant responding to an object in motion under Newton's second law of motion; behavior, like a rolling object, has velocity and mass (response rate and a history of reinforcement that produces resistance to change). Analogous to a rolling object under Newton's second law, behavioral response rates are impacted by an imposing disruptive force. In an excellent translation to the everyday world, Mace and Lalli (1992) demonstrated that NCAA men's basketball teams' ability to maintain performance in the face of adversities (turnovers, fouls, missed shots) was proportional to the rate of reinforcement (shots made) prior to the adversity, in line with BMT. Interestingly, the researchers found that time-outs served as effective disruptors to opposing teams' momentum, lending additional support to BMT while simultaneously offering an operant perspective on the widely appreciated perspective that coaches should call timeouts when the other team "gets hot." These findings have been replicated with NCAA women's basketball (Roane, Kelley, Trosclair, & Hauer, 2004) as well (for an extended discussion on this topic, see Roane, 2011).

Matching Theory

Perhaps the most widely studied concept in EAB is the quantitative model of choice known as *matching theory,* derived from Herrnstein's (1961) classic study demonstrating that relative rates of reinforcement for pigeons' key pecks predicted pigeons' relative allocation of pecking between keys. Over the past several decades, matching theory has been formalized into numerous quantitative models that can be used to describe molar accounts of behavior (for a review, see McDowell, 2013). Translational researchers soon discovered the utility in testing the explanatory flexibility (Stilling & Critchfield, 2010) of matching theory through the use of sports data. In this approach, sports researchers compare the relative ratio of play calls—such as passes or rushes in American-rules football (analogous to different colored illuminated keys in an operant chamber)—to the relative ratio of reinforcement—yards gained in those plays—for those plays (analogous to a pigeons' access to grain for key pecks). Toward this end, some of the most recent advances in the applied utility of the matching law have emanated from bridge studies on matching theory using basketball (Alferink, Critchfield, Hitt, & Higgins, 2009; Romanowich, Bourret, & Vollmer, 2007; Vollmer & Bourret, 2000) and American-rules football (Reed, Critchfield, & Martens, 2006; Reed, Skoch, Kaplan, & Brozyna, 2011; Stilling & Critchfield, 2010), given the easily identifiable concurrent behavior-reinforcement alternatives of 2-pt versus 3-pt shots and pass plays versus rush plays, respectively. These bridge studies have greatly advanced the applied utility of the matching theory, while also providing a unique perspective on the variables affecting play calling in elite sport competition.

Given the proliferation of, and public interest in, sports analytics (e.g., Winston, 2009), operant contributions to the understanding of sports performance via BMT or matching theory may serve as a catalyst to promoting behavior analytic influences to sport psychology. Unfortunately, the status quo in sports analytics is a strong reliance on multivariate statistical modeling that focuses more on fitting equations to data than parsimonious accounts of performance. Operant approaches to sports analytics, however, are firmly rooted in basic science and present a theoretically driven account of performance based on decades of operant studies. We believe that further research into the translational contributions of behavior analysis to sports performance will aid in the science of sports strategy while concurrently advancing behavioral theory. For a primer on how to begin analyzing sports from a translational behavior analytic lens, see Reed (2011).

Special Populations

Children and adults who have intellectual and developmental disabilities (IDD) can benefit greatly from sports as well as planned exercise and increased physical activity (Luiselli, 2014) for promoting health (Fleming, 2011; Yilmaz, Yanardag, Birkan, & Bumin, 2004) and enhancing quality of life (Elliot, Dobbin, Rose, & Soper, 1994; Gabler-Halle, Halle, & Chung, 1993; Rosenthal-Malek & Mitchell, 1997). Parents and caregivers of people with IDD also acknowledge the desirable effects of athletic and exercise activities on learning and socialization (Glidden, Bamberger, Draheim, & Kersh, 2011; Luiselli, Woods, Keary, & Parenteau, 2013). Systematic reviews have revealed that running, jogging, and swimming were the most frequently targeted activities in the extant literature (Lang et al., 2010; Sowa & Meulenbroek, 2012). However, this research is not extensive, and there are very few ABA-specific studies concerning sports. Additional research would contribute greatly to the lives of children and adults who have IDD, their families, and practitioners responsible for delivering high quality habilitation services.

Most of the ABA research with people who have IDD has addressed jogging and running (Allison, Basile, & MacDonald, 1991; Elliot et al., 1994; Rosenthal-Malek & Mitchell, 1997). However, these studies were not concerned with athletic performance *per se* but rather the effects of jogging and running as antecedent exercise to reduce problem behaviors. And yet, running in the context of track and field events has been an intervention objective. One example was reported by Cameron and Cappello (1993) who implemented an 11-step instructional program with a 21-year-old man preparing to run hurdles in a Special Olympics event. The program combined stimulus shaping that gradually raised the hurdle bar off the floor to a maximum height of 12 in. More recently, Luiselli, Duncan et al. (2013) improved the 100 m sprint times of two Special Olympics athletes (20 and 21 years old) through different combinations of goal setting, positive reinforcement, performance feedback, and video modeling.

Two other sports have shown the modest results from behavioral intervention. Luyben, Funk, Morgan, Clark, and Delulio (1986) taught three adults with IDD (24-52 years old) to execute a side-of-the-foot soccer pass using a most-to-least prompting hierarchy combined with forward chaining, a supportive device, and visual cueing. For instructing foundational swimming skills to three children with autism (10-12 years old), Rogers, Hemmeter, and Wolery (2010) employed a constant time-delay prompting procedure within a multiple probe design for flutter kicking, front-crawl arm stroking, and side-to-side head turning. In total, ABA-sports research in IDD is encouraging but needs to be expanded further so that more children and adults can experience the advantages of physical training and planned exercise. One avenue of innovative research is *exergaming* in which "video games or various auditory or visual stimuli are paired with different types of exercise equipment and activities, and the individual must engage in physical activity to play the game or produce the auditory or visual stimulation" (Fogel, Miltenberger, Graves, & Koehler, 2010, p. 592). This virtual sports format can be applied in a controlled setting, with individuals or peer groupings, and individualized to fit the activity interests of each player.

REFERENCES

Alferink, L. A., Critchfield, T. S., Hitt, J. L., & Higgins, W. J. (2009). Generality of the matching law as a descriptor of shot selection in basketball. *Journal of Applied Behavior Analysis, 42*, 595–608. http://dx.doi.org/10.1901/jaba.2009.42-595.

Allen, K. D. (1998). The use of an enhanced simplified habit-reversal procedure to reduce disruptive outbursts during athletic performance. *Journal of Applied Behavior Analysis, 31*, 489–492.

Allison, M. G., & Ayllon, T. (1980). Behavioral coaching in the development of skills in football, gymnastics, and tennis. *Journal of Applied Behavior Analysis, 13*, 297–314.

Allison, D. B., Basile, V. C., & MacDonald, R. B. (1991). Brief report: Comparative effects of antecedent exercise and lorazepam on the aggressive behavior of an autistic man. *Journal of Autism and Developmental Disorders, 21*, 89–94.

American Football Coaches Association. (1995). *Football coaching strategies*. Champaign, IL: Human Kinetics.

Anderson, G., & Kirkpatrick, M. A. (2002). Variable effects of a behavioral treatment package on the performance of inline roller speed skaters. *Journal of Applied Behavior Analysis, 35,* 195–198.

Balcazar, F. E., Hopkins, B., & Suarez, Y. (1985). A critical objective review of performance feedback. *Journal of Organizational Behavior Management, 7,* 65–89.

Boyer, E., Miltenberger, R. G., Batsche, C., & Fogel, V. (2009). Video modeling by experts with video feedback to enhance gymnastics skills. *Journal of Applied Behavior Analysis, 42,* 855–860.

Brobst, B., & Ward, P. (2002). Effects of public posting, goal setting, and oral feedback on the skills of female soccer players. *Journal of Applied Behavior Analysis, 35,* 247–257.

Brown, J. L. (2011). Cognitive-behavioral strategies. In J. K. Luiselli & D. D. Reed (Eds.), *Behavioral sport psychology: Evidence-based approaches to performance enhancement* (pp. 113–126). New York: Springer.

Cameron, M. J., & Cappello, M. J. (1993). "We'll cross that hurdle when we get to it": Teaching athletic performance within adaptive physical education. *Behavior Modification, 17,* 136–147.

Cipani, E., & Schock, K. M. (2011). *Functional behavioral assessment, diagnosis, and treatment: A complete system for education and mental health settings.* New York: Oxford University Press.

DeLuca, R. V., & Holborn, S. W. (1992). Effects of a variable-ratio reinforcement schedule with changing criteria on exercise in obese and non-obese boys. *Journal of Applied Behavior Analysis, 25,* 671–679.

Dragen, J., & Austin, J. (2008). Using graphic and verbal feedback with self-talk and self-monitoring to improve high school swim performance. *Journal of Behavior Analysis in Health, Sports, Fitness, and Medicine, 1,* 96–102.

Elliot, R. O., Dobbin, A. R., Rose, G. D., & Soper, H. V. (1994). Vigorous, aerobic exercise versus general motor training activities: Effects of maladaptive and stereotypic behaviors of adults with both autism and mental retardation. *Journal of Autism and Developmental Disorders, 24,* 565–576.

Fiske, K. E. (2008). Treatment integrity of school-based behavior analytic interventions: A review of the research. *Behavior Analysis in Practice, 1,* 19–25.

Fitterling, J. M., Martin, J. E., Gramling, S., Cole, P., & Milan, M. A. (1988). Behavioral management of exercise training in vascular headache patients: An investigation of exercise adherence and headache activity. *Journal of Applied Behavior Analysis, 21,* 9–19.

Fleming, R. K. (2011). Obesity and weight regulation. In J. K. Luiselli (Ed.), *The handbook of high-risk challenging behaviors in people with intellectual and developmental disabilities* (pp. 195–205). Baltimore, MD: Brookes.

Fogel, V. A., Miltenberger, R. G., Graves, R., & Koehler, S. (2010). The effects of exergaming on physical activity among inactive children in a physical education classroom. *Journal of Applied Behavior Analysis, 43,* 591–600.

Fogel, V. A., Weil, T. M., & Burris, H. (2010). Evaluating the efficacy of TagTeach as a training strategy for teaching a golf swing. *Journal of Behavioral Health and Medicine, 1,* 25–41.

Gabler-Halle, D., Halle, J. W., & Chung, Y. B. (1993). The effects of aerobic exercise on psychological and behavioral variables of individuals with developmental disabilities: A critical review. *Research in Developmental Disabilities, 14,* 359–386.

Gee, C. J. (2010). How does sport psychology actually improve athletic performance? A framework to facilitate athletes' and coaches' understanding. *Behavior Modification, 34,* 386–402.

Glidden, L. M., Bamberger, K. T., Draheim, A. R., & Kersh, J. (2011). Parent and athlete perceptions of Special Olympics participation: Utility and danger of proxy responding. *Intellectual and Developmental Disabilities, 49,* 37–45.

Hanley, G. P. (2012). Functional assessment of problem behavior: Dispelling myths, overcoming implementation obstacles, and developing new lore. *Behavior Analysis in Practice, 5*, 54–67.

Harding, J. W., Wacker, D. P., Berg, W. K., Rick, G., & Lee, J. F. (2004). Promoting response variability and stimulus generalization in martial arts training. *Journal of Applied Behavior Analysis, 37*, 185–195.

Harrison, A. M., & Pyles, D. A. (2013). The effects of verbal instruction and shaping to improve tackling by high school football players. *Journal of Applied Behavior Analysis, 46*, 518–522.

Hartmann, D. P., & Hall, R. V. (1976). The changing criterion design. *Journal of Applied Behavior Analysis, 9*, 527–532.

Herrnstein, R. J. (1961). Relative and absolute strength of response as a function of frequency of reinforcement. *Journal of the Experimental Analysis of Behavior, 4*, 267–272. http://dx.doi.org/10.1901/jeab.1961.4-267.

Kazdin, A. E. (1977). Assessing the clinical or applied importance of behavior change through social validation. *Behavior Modification, 1*, 427–452.

Kazdin, A. E. (2011). *Single-case research designs: Methods for clinical and applied settings* (2nd). New York: Oxford University Press.

Kazdin, A. E. (2013). *Behavior modification in applied setting* (7th). Long Grove, IL: Waveland Press, Inc.

Kerkhoff, B. (1996). *Phog Allen: The father of basketball coaching*. Indianapolis, IN: Masters Press.

Kladopoulos, C. N., & McComas, J. J. (2001). The effects of form training on foul-shooting performance in members of a women's college basketball team. *Journal of Applied Behavior Analysis, 34*, 329–332.

Koop, S., & Martin, G. L. (1983). Evaluation of a coaching strategy to reduce swimming stroke errors with beginning age-group swimmers. *Journal of Applied Behavior Analysis, 16*, 447–460.

Lang, R., Koegel, L. K., Ashbaugh, K., Regester, A., Ence, W., & Smith, W. (2010). Physical exercise and individuals with autism spectrum disorders: A systematic review. *Research in Autism Spectrum Disorders, 4*, 565–576.

Lerman, D. C. (2003). From the laboratory to community application: Translational research in behavior analysis. *Journal of Applied Behavior Analysis, 36*, 415–419. http://dx.doi.org/10.1901/jaba.2003.36-415.

Luiselli, J. K. (2011). Single-case evaluation of behavioral coaching interventions. In J. K. Luiselli, & D. D. Reed (Eds.), *Behavioral sport psychology: Evidence-based approaches to performance enhancement* (pp. 61–78). New York: Springer.

Luiselli, J. K. (2012). Behavioral sport psychology consulting: A review of some practice concerns and recommendations. *Journal of Sport Psychology in Action, 3*, 41–51.

Luiselli, J. K. (2014). Exercise, physical activity, and sports. In J. K. Luiselli (Ed.), *Children and youth with autism spectrum disorder (ASD): Recent advances and innovations in assessment, education, and intervention* (pp. 193–204). New York: Oxford University Press.

Luiselli, J. K., Duncan, N. G., Keary, P., Nelson, E. G., Parenteau, R. E., & Woods, K. E. (2013). Behavioral coaching of track athletes with developmental disabilities: Evaluation of sprint performance during training and Special Olympics competition. *Journal of Clinical Sport Psychology, 7*, 264–274.

Luiselli, J. K., & Reed, D. D. (2011). *Behavioral sport psychology: Evidence-based approaches to performance enhancement*. New York: Springer.

Luiselli, J. K., Woods, K. E., Keary, P., & Parenteau, R. E. (2013). Practitioner attitudes and beliefs about exercise, athletic, and recreational activities for children and youth with intellectual and developmental disabilities. *Journal of Developmental and Physical Disabilities, 25*, 485–492.

Luiselli, J. K., Woods, K. E., & Reed, D. D. (2011). Review of sports performance research with youth, collegiate, and elite athletes. *Journal of Applied Behavior Analysis, 44*, 999–1002.

Luyben, P. D., Funk, D. M., Morgan, J. K., Clark, K. A., & Delulio, D. W. (1986). Team sports for the severely retarded: Training a side-of-the-foot soccer pass using a maximum-to-minimum prompt reduction strategy. *Journal of Applied Behavior Analysis, 19*, 431–436.

Mace, F. C., & Lalli, J. S. (1992). Behavioral momentum in college basketball. *Journal of Applied Behavior Analysis, 25*, 657–663.

Martin, G. L. (2011). *Applied sport psychology: Practical guidelines for applied behavior analysts* (4th). Winnipeg, Canada: Sport Science Press.

Martin, G. L., Thompson, K., & Regehr, K. (2004). Studies using single-subject designs in sport psychology: 30 years of research. *The Behavior Analyst, 27*, 123–140.

Martin, G. L., & Thomson, K. (2011). Overview of behavioral sport psychology. In J. K. Luiselli, & D. D. Reed (Eds.), *Behavioral sport psychology: Evidence-based approaches to performance enhancement* (pp. 3–21). New York: Springer.

Martin, G. L., Toogood, A., & Tkachuk, G. A. (1997). *Behavioral assessment forms for sport psychology consulting.* Winnipeg, Canada: Sport Science Press.

McDowell, J. J. (2013). On the theoretical and empirical status of the matching law and matching theory. *Psychological Bulletin, 139*, 1000–1028. http://dx.doi.org/10.1037/a0029924.

McKenize, T. L., & Rushall, B. S. (1974). Effects of self-recording on attendance and performance in a competitive swimming training environment. *Journal of Applied Behavior Analysis, 7*, 199–206.

Mellalieu, S. D., Hanton, S., & O'Brien, M. (2006). The effects of goal setting on rugby performance. *Journal of Applied Behavior Analysis, 39*, 257–261.

Michel, J. (1982). Distinguishing between discriminative and motivational functions of stimuli. *Journal of the Experimental Analysis of Behavior, 37*, 149–155.

Nevin, J. A., & Grace, R. C. (2000). Behavioral momentum and the law of effect. *Behavioral and Brain Sciences, 23*, 73–90, discussion 90–130.

Nevin, J. A., Mandell, C., & Atak, J. R. (1983). The analysis of behavioral momentum. *Journal of the Experimental Analysis of Behavior, 39*, 49–59.

Noell, G. H., Gresham, F. M., & Gansle, K. A. (2002). Does treatment integrity matter? A preliminary investigation of instructional implementation and mathematics performance. *Journal of Behavioral Education, 11*, 51–67.

Osborne, K., Rudrud, E., & Zezoney, F. (1990). Improved curveball hitting through the enhancement of visual cues. *Journal of Applied Behavior Analysis, 23*, 371–377.

Pryor, K. (1999). *Don't shoot the dog: The new art of teaching and training.* New York: Bantam.

Reed, D. D. (2011). Quantitative analysis of sports. In J. K. Luiselli, & D. D. Reed (Eds.), *Behavioral sport psychology: Evidence-based approaches to performance enhancement* (pp. 43–59). New York: Springer.

Reed, D. D., Critchfield, T. S., & Martens, B. K. (2006). The generalized matching law in elite sport competition: Football play calling as operant choice. *Journal of Applied Behavior Analysis, 39*, 281–297. http://dx.doi.org/10.1901/jaba.2006.146-05.

Reed, D. D., Skoch, J. J., Kaplan, B. A., & Brozyna, G. A. (2011). Defensive performance as a modulator of biased play calling in collegiate American-rules football. *Revista Mexicana de Análisis de la Conducta, 37*, 51–57.

Roane, H. S. (2011). Behavioral momentum in sports. In J. K. Luiselli, & D. D. Reed (Eds.), *Behavioral sport psychology: Evidence-based approaches to performance enhancement* (pp. 143–155). New York: Springer.

Roane, H. S., Kelley, M. E., Trosclair, N. M., & Hauer, L. S. (2004). Behavioral momentum in sports: A partial replication with women's basketball. *Journal of Applied Behavior Analysis, 37*, 385–390. http://dx.doi.org/10.1901/jaba.2004.37-385.

Rogers, L., Hemmeter, M. L., & Wolery, M. (2010). Using a constant time delay procedure to teach foundational swimming skills to children with autism. *Topics in Early Childhood Special Education, 30*, 102–111.

Romanowich, P., Bourret, J., & Vollmer, T. R. (2007). Further analysis of the matching law to describe two- and three-point shot allocation by professional basketball players. *Journal of Applied Behavior Analysis*, *40*, 311–315. http://dx.doi.org/10.1901/jaba.2007.119-05.

Rosenthal-Malek, A., & Mitchell, S. (1997). Brief report: The effects of exercise on the self-stimulatory behaviors and positive responding of adolescents with autism. *Journal of Autism and Developmental Disorders*, *27*, 193–202.

Sarokoff, R. A., & Sturmey, P. (2004). The effects of behavioral skills training on staff implementation of discrete-trial teaching. *Journal of Applied Behavior Analysis*, *37*, 535–538. http://dx.doi.org/10.1901/jaba.2004.37-535.

Scott, D., Scott, L. M., & Goldwater, B. (1997). A performance improvement program for an international-level track and field athlete. *Journal of Applied Behavior Analysis*, *30*, 573–575.

Seniuk, H. A., Witts, B. N., Williams, W. L., & Ghezzi, P. M. (2013). On terms: Behavioral coaching. *The Behavior Analyst*, *36*, 167–172.

Smith, R. E., & Smoll, F. L. (2011). Cognitive-behavioral coach training: A translational approach to theory, research, and intervention. In J. K. Luiselli, & D. D. Reed (Eds.), *Behavioral sport psychology: Evidence-based approaches to performance enhancement* (pp. 227–248). New York: Springer.

Smith, S. L., & Ward, P. (2006). Behavioral interventions to improve performance in collegiate football. *Journal of Applied Behavior Analysis*, *39*, 385–391.

Sowa, M., & Meulenbroek, R. (2012). Effects of physical exercise on autism spectrum disorders: A meta-analysis. *Research in Autism Spectrum Disorders*, *6*, 46–57.

Stilling, S. T., & Critchfield, T. S. (2010). The matching relation and situation-specific bias modulation in professional football play selection. *Journal of the Experimental Analysis of Behavior*, *93*, 435–454. http://dx.doi.org/10.1901/jeab.2010.93-435.

Stokes, J. V., & Luiselli, J. K. (2010). Functional analysis and behavioral coaching intervention to improve tackling skills of a high school football athlete. *Journal of Clinical Sport Psychology*, *4*, 150–157.

Stokes, J. V., Luiselli, J. K., & Reed, D. D. (2010). A behavioral intervention for teaching tackling skills to high school football athletes. *Journal of Applied Behavior Analysis*, *43*, 509–512.

Stokes, J. V., Luiselli, J. K., Reed, D. D., & Fleming, R. K. (2010). Behavioral coaching to improve offensive line pass blocking skills of high school football athletes. *Journal of Applied Behavior Analysis*, *43*, 463–472.

Tiger, J. H., & Kliebert, M. L. (2011). Stimulus preference assessment. In J. K. Luiselli (Ed.), *Teaching and behavior support for children and adults with autism spectrum disorder: A practitioner's guide* (pp. 31–37). New York: Oxford University Press.

Tkachuk, G., Leslie-Toogood, A., & Martin, G. L. (2003). Behavioral assessment in sport psychology. *The Sport Psychologist*, *17*, 104–117.

Vollmer, T. R., & Bourret, J. (2000). An application of the matching law to evaluate the allocation of two- and three-point shots by college basketball players. *Journal of Applied Behavior Analysis*, *33*, 137–150. http://dx.doi.org/10.1901/jaba.2000.33-137.

Wack, S. R., Crosland, K. A., & Miltenberger, R. G. (2014). Using a goal-setting and feedback procedure to increase running distance. *Journal of Applied Behavior Analysis*, *47*, 181–185.

Ward, P. (2011). Goal setting and performance feedback. In J. K. Luiselli & D. D. Reed (Eds.), *Behavioral sport psychology: Evidence-based approaches to performance enhancement* (pp. 99–112). New York: Springer.

Ward, P., & Carnes, M. (2002). Effects of posting self-set goals on collegiate football players' skill execution during practice and games. *Journal of Applied Behavior Analysis*, *35*, 1–12.

Wilder, D. A., Atwell, J., & Wine, B. (2006). The effects of varying levels of treatment integrity on child compliance during a three-step prompting procedure. *Journal of Applied Behavior Analysis, 39,* 369–373.

Winston, W. L. (2009). *Mathletics: How gamblers, managers, and sports enthusiasts use mathematics in baseball, basketball, and football.* Princeton, NJ: Princeton University Press.

Wolf, M. M. (1978). Social validity: The case for subjective measurement or how applied behavior analysis is finding its heart. *Journal of Applied Behavior Analysis, 11,* 203–214.

Wolko, K. L., Hrycaiko, D. W., & Martin, G. L. (1993). A comparison of two self-management packages to standard coaching for improving practice performance of gymnasts. *Behavior Modification, 17,* 209–223.

Yilmaz, I., Yanardag, M., Birkan, B. A., & Bumin, G. (2004). Effects of swimming training on physical fitness and water orientation in autism. *Pediatrics International, 46,* 624–626.

Ziegler, S. G. (1987). Effects of stimulus cueing on the acquisition of ground strokes by beginning tennis players. *Journal of Applied Behavior Analysis, 20,* 405–411.

Ziegler, S. G. (1994). The effects of attentional shift training on the execution of soccer skills: A preliminary investigation. *Journal of Applied Behavior Analysis, 27,* 545–552.

Zinsser, N., Bunker, L., & Williams, J. M. (2006). Cognitive techniques for building confidence and enhancing performance. In J. M. Williams (Ed.), *Applied sport psychology: Personal growth to peak performance* (5th, pp. 349–381). New York: McGraw-Hill.

CHAPTER 22

Applied Behavior Analysis for Health and Fitness

Matthew P. Normand[1], Jesse Dallery[2], Triton Ong[1]
[1]Department of Psychology, University of the Pacific, Stockton, California, USA
[2]Department of Psychology, University of Florida, Gainesville, Florida, USA

Health promotion is among the foremost concerns of modern society. As with so many problems of considerable social significance, most health problems are caused by what people do and what people do not do. People eat too much, exercise too little, and visit healthcare providers too infrequently, among many other things. Understanding and solving these problems is a task for the behavioral sciences and, more specifically, for applied behavior analysis (ABA).

Most choices about health are made during everyday activities. Thus, as Schroeder (2007) noted, influencing these choices constitutes the "single greatest opportunity to improve health and reduce premature deaths" in the United States (p. 1222). Even chronically ill patients spend only a few hours per year with a doctor or nurse, leaving approximately 5000 h per year in which they are engaged in other health-related activities, including "deciding whether to take prescribed medications or follow other medical advice, deciding what to eat and drink and whether to smoke, and making other choices about activities that can profoundly influence their health" (Asch, Muller, & Volpp, 2012, p. 1). Because choices about health occur in naturalistic settings, the information is this chapter will pertain primarily to efforts to promote healthy behavior outside of the formal healthcare system.

The ABA literature contains examples of research addressing a myriad of health-related issues dating back to the 1960s, including tooth brushing (e.g., Lattal, 1969), behavior management during dental visits (e.g., Allen & Stokes, 1987), attendance at dental (e.g., Reiss & Bailey, 1982) or medical (e.g., Benjamin-Bauman, Reiss, & Bailey, 1984) appointments, and biofeedback (e.g., Shapiro & Surwit, 1979), to name just a few. The range of behavior analytic contributions to understanding health promotion spans basic and applied research, as well as practice. The primary focus of this chapter, however, will

Clinical and Organizational Applications of Applied Behavior Analysis
http://dx.doi.org/10.1016/B978-0-12-420249-8.00022-8

be applied research related to health promotion through diet, exercise, and medication adherence, as addressing these issues would significantly improve health across many populations (Schroeder, 2007).

There are two primary avenues to health promotion: prevention and treatment. However, there can be considerable overlap in the approaches used to prevent and to treat health problems. For example, eating a healthy diet and being physically active are ways both to prevent the onset of overweight and obesity and to treat these conditions if they already are present. Likewise, visiting a healthcare provider can be preventative if done on a regular basis for annual checkups and wellness visits and can constitute treatment if the visits occur because of pain or illness. Some controlling variables may differ across prevention and treatment situations, but the same kinds of contingencies of reinforcement and punishment can be involved in both situations. Thus, a common intervention strategy can often be used across settings. As such, this chapter will be organized by health topic rather than by prevention or treatment efforts.

GENERAL CHARACTERISTICS OF BEHAVIORAL INTERVENTIONS TO PROMOTE HEALTH

Most activities related to health can be conceptualized as operant behavior. That is, health-related behavior such as taking medication, eating healthy foods, or exercising can be changed by altering relevant antecedent and consequent variables. Antecedents can include stimuli such as prompts, verbal instructions, or changes in an environment to make a health-related activity more or less likely (e.g., placing a medication vial in an accessible location). Consequences can include desirable outcomes such as social praise, monetary reinforcement, or tangible goods to increase some behavior, or the loss of desirable items or outcomes to decrease some behavior. These consequences are delivered contingent on some target behavior, or, as often is the case, contingent on a behavior product related to healthy behavior (e.g., weight). Arranging consequences in these ways is referred to generally as contingency management (CM), but there are also specific CM procedures that have been derived from research in substance abuse.

In the CM procedures derived from research in substance abuse, desirable consequences are delivered based on the occurrence or nonoccurrence of some behavior. There are two main elements of these procedures: an objective *monitoring system* to record the presence or absence of behavior and a *delivery system* to provide positive consequences based on the evidence of the desirable behavior. For example, the monitoring system in the case of drug use is typically urinalysis for the presence or absence of drugs, and the delivery system could be vouchers (statements of monetary earnings exchangeable for goods or services) delivered by clinic staff. The literature on substance abuse is covered in Chapter 16. Many of the interventions described in this chapter also involve CM similar to, if not derived specifically from, the procedures used in treating substance abuse.

WEIGHT LOSS

The prevalence of obesity in the United States has been well documented (e.g., Flegal, Carroll, Ogden, & Curtin, 2010; Flegal, Carroll, Ogden, & Johnson, 2002; Ogden, Carroll, Curtin, Lamb, & Flegal, 2010; Ogden, Carroll, Curtin, McDowell, et al., 2010; Ogden, Flegal, Carroll, & Johnson, 2002), and a number of health problems are associated with obesity, including cardiovascular disease, type 2 diabetes mellitus, hypertension, stroke, dyslipidemia, osteoarthritis, some cancers, and even death (Must et al., 1999). Recent epidemiological forecasts predict that 51% of the adult US population will be obese by 2030 with associated healthcare costs as high as $956 billion annually if efforts to reduce obesity are unsuccessful (Finkelstein et al., 2012; Wang, Beydoun, Liang, Caballero, & Kumanyika, 2008). Clearly, the problem is of great social significance, and we have yet to find a solution.

Some of the earliest applications of behavior analysis to health promotion focused on weight as the primary-dependent variable (e.g., Aragona, Cassady, & Drabman, 1975; Mann, 1972), even before the onset of the current obesity epidemic. Although it is not a direct measure of behavior, weight is a behavioral product that is closely related to diet and physical activity. Moreover, weight is a clinically relevant treatment outcome because it is associated with a variety of health conditions, both good and bad. Weight also has the benefit of being relatively easy to measure and track over time with good reliability.

Typically, behavior analytic interventions targeting weight loss involve some combination of task clarification, goal setting, and feedback. The importance of maintaining a healthy weight is explained, usually with instructions for how to do so. Clear and manageable goals for weight loss are established, and clear consequences for meeting or not meeting these goals are arranged. For example, Mann (1972) used contingency contracting to promote weight loss with overweight and obese adults. The contingency contracting required participants to deposit personal items of some value with the experimenter at the outset of the study. These items could subsequently be "earned" by meeting weight loss goals or permanently lost by failing to meet these goals. Thus, a combined reinforcement and punishment (response cost) intervention was used to provide consequences both for meeting and failing to meet agreed-upon goals, respectively. Mann reported that all of the participants lost weight during the contingency-contract intervention and most subjects gained weight during the returns to baseline conditions.

Similar work by Aragona et al. (1975) demonstrated that task clarification and contingency contracts involving response cost and reinforcement procedures could be used with parents to promote weight loss in their overweight children. The loss of previously deposited money for failing to attend weekly meetings, submit weekly homework, or when the children did not meet their weight goals resulted in all children losing weight over the course of the intervention. This basic task-clarification and contingency-contracting strategy is part of a number of successful behavior-based interventions targeting healthy behavior and weight loss (e.g., Epstein, Valoski, Wing, & McCurley, 1994; Turner, Pooly, & Sherman, 1976; Vance, 1976; Wysocki, Hall, Iwata, & Riordan, 1979).

CM has also been employed to promote weight loss (e.g., Jeffery, 2012; Petry, Barry, Pescatello, & White, 2011). Most notably, a series of experiments conducted by Jeffrey and colleagues between 1978 and 1993 suggest that creative applications of CM can be delivered at low cost (reviewed in Jeffery, 2012). All participants in these studies were overweight but in otherwise good health, and all expressed interest in committing money to be used in a deposit contract for weight loss. The studies typically lasted between 10 and 25 weeks, during which participants met with a therapist weekly in a small group format. Participants were told to keep energy intake goals to about 1000 kcal per day below estimated weight maintenance needs, and exercise goals were about 1000 kcal per week. During the weekly group sessions, participants were weighed, received cash based on the meeting goals, and discussed behavioral strategies to meet intake and energy goals. Several general conclusions can be drawn from the series of studies reported by Jeffrey and colleagues: (a) financial rewards increase the effectiveness of weight loss programs in the short term, (b) larger and progressively increasing rewards are more effective than smaller or constant reward values, (c) deposit contract procedures are more effective than procedures that only provide positive reinforcement, and (d) deposit contracts involving groups of individuals are more effective than contracts based on an individual's behavior.

Although targeting weight loss or maintenance as the primary intervention goal seems logical, there are some important limitations to doing so. To start, weight is not perfectly correlated with healthy behavior. For example, a sedentary adult who begins a workout program might, at least initially, gain weight because of a gain in muscle mass or, perhaps even more likely, because they will also eat more in response to the increased caloric demand. Still, exercise is important even if these kinds of circumstances lead to some weight gain. However, there are ways to lose weight that are unhealthy. For example, one could reduce daily calorie intake to unhealthy levels or consume only unhealthy foods. Even more, some individuals might resort to using diuretics or to purging, especially if there are powerful consequences (e.g., monetary or social incentives) for losing weight. Subjects in Mann's (1972) study, for example, reported using diuretics and laxatives prior to being weighed throughout the study.

The problems with using behavioral products as proxies for direct observation of the behavior of interest should not be surprising to behavior analysts. For the most part, recording the products of behavior in lieu of the actual behavior is justified when the products of behavior are reliably produced by the behavior of interest and only by that behavior. Weight is a problematic behavior product because it is the consequence of several different behaviors (e.g., eating, activity), and weight change is a slow process, making it somewhat insensitive as an indicator of behavior change. In the following sections, the two primary classes of behavior influencing weight—diet and physical activity—will be addressed, both because of their relationship to weight and because of their relationship to health even independent of weight.

DIET AND HEALTHY EATING

Eating too much or eating the wrong foods can lead to weight gain and health problems such as diabetes, coronary heart disease, and cancer (Crawford, 2014; Willett, 2012). Although the role of food in physical health is complex, one can safely assert that moderation is a useful goal. To maintain weight and overall health, it is important not to consume more calories than burned, and it is important not to consume too much sugar and fat. Unfortunately, the immediate, powerful, and (mostly) automatically reinforcing effects of eating make moderation difficult for many people (Epstein, Leddy, Temple, & Faith, 2007; Epstein, Lin, Carr, & Fletcher, 2011; Epstein, Temple, et al., 2007).

Eating is an observable behavior that can be operationalized and quantified, but, as it turns out, not very easily. It is difficult to objectively measure eating in free-living conditions because doing so requires that an observer be available during all or most waking hours for a given subject. Self-reports of eating are problematic because, even under ideal circumstances, it can be difficult for a subject to accurately report what they have eaten prior to giving the report, especially if they were not instructed to monitor their eating beforehand. Self-reports tend to result in underestimates of the amount eaten (Hill & Davies, 2001; Schoeller, 1995). Even when someone does monitor their eating across a specified period of time, it is difficult or impossible to determine the nutritional content (e.g., calories, fat, sugar) consumed based on the general descriptions of the food eaten. Nutritional information is important for determining how healthy a diet might be. Even a vigilant observer would not be able to determine the actual nutritional content of the food consumed unless they prepared the food themselves.

In an attempt to address the problems with using dietary self-reports while still assessing eating across normal daily routines, Normand and Osborne (2010) incorporated point-of-sale technology into a feedback-based intervention designed to decrease the amount of calories and fat purchased, and presumably consumed, by college students at meal times. Rather than rely on self-reports of eating, Normand and Osborne collaborated with a university-affiliated dining program to monitor food purchases made by students using their pre-paid food plans. The general strategy of recording food purchases in a dining facility has been reported in a number of studies (e.g., Mayer et al., 1986; Stock & Milan, 1993; Winett, Kramer, Walker, Malone, & Lane, 1988); however, the Normand and Osborne methods involved automated data collection using modern technology. Students were able to purchase food by swiping their student identification card at the cash register. This produced an electronic record of the food purchased off the dining menu. The dining program provided the average nutritional content of each of the menu items they prepared so that reasonable estimates of the fat and calories purchased could be made.

Participants were students enrolled in the dining program, living on campus, and who self-reported not having access to a car (thusly eating most of their meals on campus). Based on the information from the electronic point-of-sale records, individualized daily feedback was provided to participants. The feedback consisted of a comparison of the amount of fat and calories they purchased that day as compared to the daily fat and calories recommended by the United States Department of Agriculture MyPyramid

Plan (USDA, 2005). Although participants purchased fewer calories and fat during the intervention, it was impossible to know how much food they consumed, or if they consumed more food outside of the dining facilities. Still, and although it was a single study with only four participants, the Normand and Osborne (2010) methodology might be a promising one for future research, especially as technology continues to improve (e.g., Lopez-Meyer, Schuckers, Makeyev, Fontana, & Sazonov, 2012; Makeyev, Lopez-Meyer, Schuckers, Besio, & Sazonov, 2012).

The Food Dudes

Directly observing and recording eating in more controlled settings is another feasible research strategy that can produce more accurate dietary information than food purchase records alone. For example, The Food Dudes program (Tapper, Horne, & Lowe, 2003) is a successful program that involves, among other things, direct observation of eating in school cafeterias. Developed by the Bangor Food Research Unit (BFRU) of Bangor University in the United Kingdom, the Food Dudes program is a school-wide intervention designed to increase children's consumption of fruits and vegetables (Tapper et al., 2003), as early research by the BFRU on child food preferences suggested that children rarely ate recommended amounts of fruits and vegetables and instead chose snack foods high in sugar and fat (Horne, Lowe, Bowdery, & Egerton, 1998). The Food Dudes program has been refined through research and applied evaluations since 1992 and has now been successfully implemented in more than 200 schools with the support of government agencies throughout the UK (Tapper et al., 2003).

The BFRU researchers began development of the Food Dudes program by reviewing the published literature across disciplines to identify key patterns in children's diets. The researchers then established that children's insufficient consumption of fruits and vegetables is strongly related to risks for cardiovascular disease, cancer, and weight-related health issues. Traditional approaches to increasing children's fruit and vegetable consumption (e.g., informational campaigns) were also reviewed and evaluated as ineffective. The BFRU later proposed its own model of intervention based on the principles of operant conditioning, arguing that "almost any child can learn to eat almost any food and that we could use known learning principles to bring about major shifts in eating behavior" (Horne et al., 1998, p. 75).

The main intervention of the Food Dudes program is composed of three key behavioral principles (Tapper et al., 2003). The first principle involves modeling. Children are exposed to peers (i.e., hero characters in the Food Dudes videos) who eat, talk favorably about, and encourage the consumption of fruits and vegetables. Second, the children are exposed to—and encouraged to try eating—small amounts of fruits and vegetables. Third, consumption of a set amount of fruits and vegetables is rewarded with praise, tokens, small school supplies, and Food Dudes toys—positive reinforcement. These combined principles of the Food Dudes intervention have consistently produced large increases in fruit and vegetable consumption (Horne, Hardman, Lowe, Tapper, et al., 2009; Horne et al., 2011; Lowe, Horne, Tapper, Bowdery, & Egerton, 2004).

Researchers have begun replicating the Food Dudes' success in the United States. Wengreen, Madden, Aguilar, Smits, and Jones (2013) conducted a pilot evaluation of the Food Dudes program funded by the USDA. The results of the study showed the same large increases in fruit and vegetable consumption. Additionally, parents and teachers rated the program highly and reported that children consumed more fruits and vegetables at home following intervention.

PHYSICAL ACTIVITY

Physical activity is an important behavioral target for interventions designed to improve health and fitness. For starters, physical activity plays an important role in promoting and abating the trends of obesity (Daniels et al., 2005; Janssen & LeBlanc, 2010); however, the benefits of physical activity extend beyond weight management, with movement being important for musculoskeletal development and coordination, especially in young children (Janz et al., 2010). Additionally, physical activity is correlated with a host of health benefits (Janssen & LeBlanc, 2010) and increasing physical activity to levels associated with health benefits is, therefore, an important clinical goal. Although the Centers for Disease Control and Prevention (CDC, 2011) recommend that children engage in 60 min of moderate-to-vigorous physical activity (MVPA) every day of the week, current estimates suggest that many children fail to meet this goal (Strong et al., 2005; Troiano et al., 2008).

Physical Activity Assessment

Understanding the environmental variables related to physical activity is important, as these variables must be changed if physical activity is to be increased. Research suggests that the social (e.g., McKenzie, Crespo, Baquero, & Elder, 2010; Morrissey, Wenthe, Letuchy, Levy, & Janz, 2012; cf.,

Hastmann, Foster, Rosenkranz, Rosenkranz, & Dzewaltowski, 2013) and physical (e.g., Brink et al., 2010; Brown, Sheeran, & Reuber, 2009; see Ding, Sallis, Kerr, Lee, & Rosenberg, 2011 for a review) environments influence activity levels, with the physical environment being potentially more influential for young children, as their ability to move among different environments is limited (Ding et al., 2011). Additionally, as with any behavior problem, the specific environmental variables that are most influential are likely to differ from child to child, suggesting a need for individualized assessment methods. To date, however, few studies have investigated the role of the physical environment on the physical activity of young children (Ding et al., 2011).

A number of strategies can be used to assess potential functional relations between environmental variables and behavior, including descriptive (correlational) and functional (experimental) analyses (see Beavers, Iwata, & Lerman, 2013; Hanley, Iwata, & McCord, 2003). Of these assessment strategies, descriptive methods are the most commonly reported in the physical activity literature. For example, Brown et al. (2006) and McIver, Brown, Pfeiffer, Dowda, and Pate (2009) developed an observational system called the Observational System for Recording Physical Activity in Children-Preschool Version (OSRAC-P). The OSRAC-P uses five activity categories to code varying levels of physical intensity as well as a variety of environmental events (e.g., activity type, location, indoor activity context, outdoor activity context, activity initiator, group composition, prompts, engagement, and television use). Subsequently, Brown et al. (2009) conducted a descriptive analysis using the OSRAC-P as a means of determining predictors of various levels of physical activity by analyzing changes in physical activity levels across observations when environmental stimuli were allowed to vary naturally. Their results indicated that, among other things, the availability of outdoor toys and open play space were correlated with increased activity for the children observed.

Descriptive information about the predictors and consequences of physical activity might prove useful in guiding social and physical manipulations for increasing physical activity. However, there is reason to be concerned about the emphasis on descriptive analyses of physical activity because the resulting data are correlational and, as such, do not constitute an empirical demonstration of functional relations. Studies comparing descriptive and functional analyses of problem behavior have consistently reported disagreement in the outcomes of the two assessment methods (e.g., Lerman & Iwata, 1993; Pence, Roscoe, Bourret, & Ahearn, 2009; Thompson & Iwata, 2007).

The degree to which such disagreements might be seen with physical activity assessments is not known, but it stands to reason that disagreements would be evident. Only recently have functional analyses of physical activity been reported (Hustyi, Normand, Larson, & Morley, 2012; Larson, Normand, Morley, & Hustyi, 2014; Larson, Normand, Morley, & Miller, 2013, 2014); however, there is voluminous literature reporting the success of pretreatment experimental analyses for problem behavior (Hanley et al., 2003).

To evaluate the influence of the physical environment on physical activity, Hustyi et al. (2012) experimentally manipulated several environmental contexts that were previously reported (e.g., Brown et al., 2009) to correlate with MVPA exhibited by young children. Four preschool children were provided controlled access to an open grassy play area, a play area containing outdoor toys, a play area containing fixed playground equipment (i.e., jungle gym), and a play area containing a table and indoor activities (i.e., coloring books and army guys). Participants were exposed to each activity context several times according to a multielement experimental design. Results indicated that MVPA was a function of the activity contexts evaluated, with the most MVPA observed when the participants were in the fixed equipment condition, suggesting that increasing access to the fixed equipment would be a prudent strategy to induce more physical activity by those children.

Determining the extent to which functional analysis methods can be used across differing group contexts (i.e., with one or more peers present) also is important, because children are likely to play with other children and might even be expected to play more actively when playing together. To do this, Larson, Normand, Morley, and Hustyi (2014) and Larson, Normand, Morley, and Miller (2014) evaluated the utility of the method reported by Hustyi et al. (2012) across different group compositions. The same procedures reported by Hustyi et al. were conducted across three different group compositions (solitary, one peer present, and a group of peers) with eight preschool children. The highest levels of MVPA were observed when fixed playground equipment was available, and at least one peer was present, and differential responding was observed across group compositions.

Because aspects of the social environment also warrant attention, Larson et al. (2013), Larson, Normand, Morley, and Hustyi (2014), and Larson, Normand, Morley, and Miller (2014) used a functional analysis methodology, similar to that reported by Iwata, Dorsey, Slifer, Bauman, and Richman (1994) for the assessment of problem behavior, to assess the role of social and nonsocial consequences on levels of MVPA exhibited by two preschool children. Larson et al. (2013) observed the amount of MVPA exhibited by two preschool children in four experimental conditions: alone, attention contingent on MVPA, adult interaction contingent on MVPA, and escape from task demands contingent on MVPA. The amount of MVPA observed in these four conditions was compared to the amount of MVPA observed in a naturalistic baseline and a control condition. Their results indicated that contingent interactive play and adult attention resulted in the highest levels of MVPA for both participants. Larson, Normand, Morley, and Hustyi (2014) and Larson, Normand, Morley, and Miller (2014) further demonstrated that MVPA remained elevated when the interactive play condition was continued following the functional analysis.

Physical Activity Interventions

One strategy to promote physical activity is to take advantage of environments in which physical activity already is expected to occur. For example, in an early study targeting increased physical activity, Wysocki et al. (1979) used contingency contracting to increase exercise in college students. The students were able to exercise in a variety of locations, but they had to specify the location and time they would exercise in advance, permitting observers to directly observe the physical activity. Using contracting procedures similar to Mann (1972) in which points were earned for exercising at specified levels, Wysocki et al. incorporated direct observation of exercise by using the subjects as trained peer observers for other subjects in the study, with reliability checks conducted by the experimenters. Thus, Wysocki et al. addressed a major limitation of the Mann study in that direct observations of healthy behavior (physical activity) were conducted and the contingencies were tied to the observed behavior rather than the product of that behavior (i.e., weight). The contract contingencies produced increases in the number of aerobic points earned per week for seven of eight subjects.

A later series of studies also demonstrated that reinforcement contingencies could increase physical activity occurring under even more controlled conditions. De Luca and Holborn examined the effects of fixed-interval (De Luca & Holborn, 1985) and fixed-ratio (De Luca & Holborn, 1990) schedules of reinforcement on the rate obese and nonobese boys pedaled a stationary exercise bicycle. Overall, both schedules increased pedaling rate, but fixed-ratio schedules produced somewhat higher rates of pedaling. Subsequently, De Luca and Holborn (1992) examined the effects of a variable-ratio schedule of reinforcement on pedaling a stationary exercise bicycle in the same population using a changing-criterion design in which each successive criterion was increased over mean performance rate in the previous phase by approximately 15%. The contingencies of the successive criteria resulted in systematic increases in rate of exercise for all children. Ultimately, the variable-ratio rates were higher than those under fixed ratios found in their previous research.

Physical education (PE) classes provide another context in which physical activity is expected to occur, even though research suggests that activity levels during PE classes are lower than they could or should be. Recent technologies provide opportunities to remedy this situation. For example, exergaming is a strategy that capitalizes on a technology that has the potential to reduce physical activity levels—video games—and uses it instead to promote physical activity by requiring exercise to play the games. Preliminary studies suggest that exergaming increases energy expenditure in children and adults in ways that avoid many of the classic motivational difficulties of prescribed exercise regimens (Lieberman et al., 2011). That is, many people appear to simply enjoy exergaming and the associated improvements in balance, muscle tone, and coordination (Harvard Heart Letter, 2012).

Fogel, Miltenberger, Graves, and Koehler (2010) reported that exergaming increased physical activity among four otherwise inactive children attending a PE classroom and that the exergames provided more opportunity to be active than did the typical PE activities. A follow-up study (Shayne, Fogel, Miltenberger, & Koehler, 2012) replicated the results of Fogel et al. and demonstrated that different exergames produced different levels of activity, underscoring the role of activity preference in promoting physical activity. Although exergames have many exciting and potentially impactful qualities, exergaming and formal investigations into their effectiveness are relatively new. However, medical expert consensus and preliminary studies have been remarkably favorable for exergaming as an intervention for increasing physical activity (Harvard Heart Letter, 2012; Lieberman et al., 2011).

Limiting the times and locations for exercise does permit direct observation of participant behavior. Although feasible, such arrangements impose additional response effort on an already effortful task because the participant not only has to be more active, they have to plan the times and places they will exercise. Fortunately, there are a number of mechanical devices that permit physical activity, or the products thereof, to be measured in free-living conditions. One of the more common mechanical measures used in physical activity research and intervention is the pedometer. A pedometer is a mechanical device typically worn at the waist to record the number of steps taken by the wearer, with many models being relatively inexpensive and accurate enough for research purposes (e.g., Schneider, Crouter, & Bassett, 2004; Tudor-Locke, 2002).

VanWormer (2004) used pedometers to measure the daily physical activity of three overweight adults who participated in a self-monitoring and a multicomponent intervention. In the multicomponent intervention phase, self-monitoring was combined with e-counseling involving performance reviews, weekly goal setting, and descriptive praise. All participants took more steps during intervention phases, although self-monitoring alone appeared to be more effective than the multicomponent intervention. All participants lost weight, though the weight loss was relatively small.

Although the results of VanWormer (2004) were suggestive, there were several methodological limitations to the study, including that the participants self-reported the pedometer data (with a family member conducting reliability checks), and the pedometers stored only the total steps taken in a given week so that baseline data had to be averaged rather than reported as daily totals, resulting in a comparison of two different behavioral measures. Because of these limitations, the degree of behavior change actually produced by the intervention was not clearly demonstrated. Normand (2008) extended the work of VanWormer by using pedometers with a 7-day recording feature to measure daily step totals across all experimental phases and permit reliability estimates of the participant-reported step totals, with intervention integrity monitored throughout the study. With the limitations of VanWormer addressed, the intervention still increased the number of steps taken by three nonobese adults who participated, but there were no changes in participant weights during the intervention. Similar procedures were used in a subsequent study targeting heart rate as the primary-dependent measure with overweight and obese adults participating in a hospital-affiliated fitness program, with increases in energy expenditure observed but without any corresponding weight loss (Donaldson & Normand, 2009).

Applications of CM to promote physical activity also have taken advantage of advances in technology to monitor activity. For example, wearable accelerometers collect information about physical activity and inactivity by measuring changes in velocity over time (acceleration; Intille et al., 2011; King et al., 2013; Van Camp & Hayes, 2012). This permits quantification of the intensity of physical activity. The reliability and validity of these devices in measuring energy expenditure depends on several factors, such as the location of the accelerometer on the body, the type of activity (ambulatory versus isometric exercise), and the particular equation used to convert acceleration counts to energy expenditure (Rothney, Schaefer, Neumann, Choi, & Chen, 2008). One way to enhance the reliability and validity of accelerations is to require one type of activity, such as walking. For example, Kurti and Dallery (2013) implemented an Internet-based CM intervention in which monetary consequences were delivered contingent on participants meeting a gradually increasing series of walking goals over successive 5–day blocks. Accelerations were converted to a measure of steps per day, which was calculated by a Fitbit®. Progressively increasing goals were arranged according to a changing-criterion design. All six participants increased their activity according to experimenter-arranged criteria.

Recent research by the BFRU has expanded the established Food Dudes program to address physical activity. Combining a variation of the Food Dudes peer-modeling videos with parental praise and reinforcement for meeting pedometer step count goals, the Fit "n" Fun Dudes program has produced large step count increases with children (Hardman, Horne, & Lowe, 2009, 2011; Horne, Hardman, Lowe, & Rowlands, 2009) with several additional effects. In one study, parents' step counts increased modestly even though their physical activity was not directly targeted in the intervention (Hardman et al., 2009). The children with the greatest sustained increase in step counts after a tapering phase in another study were those who were shown the Fit "n" Fun Dudes videos without tangible reinforcers (Hardman et al., 2011). While the Fit "n" Fun Dudes program has not yet been refined to the same degree as the Food Dudes program, BFRU researchers have specified long-term maintenance of effects as a goal for future research, and the early research looks promising.

ADHERENCE TO MEDICATION AND OTHER MEDICAL REGIMENS

A challenge in developing CM interventions for medication adherence is developing a reliable and valid monitoring system. The most straightforward method is to simply observe pill ingestion. This can be accomplished during visits to a clinic, by parents at home, or by health care professionals in institutional settings. A recent meta-analysis of CM for medication adherence reviewed effects of CM in the context of a range of conditions including tuberculosis, HIV, drug abuse, hepatitis, stroke prevention, and psychosis

(Petry, Rash, Byrne, Ashraf, & White, 2012). A total of 21 studies were included in the analysis. Across all studies, CM improved medication adherence relative to control conditions and produced an overall effect size of 0.77. Results also suggested that interventions that were "longer in duration, provided an average reinforcement of $50 or more per week, and reinforced patients at least weekly resulted in larger effect sizes than those that were shorter, provided lower reinforcers, and reinforced patients less frequently" (Petry et al., 2012, p. 888).

Additionally, a number of technology-based tools have been developed to monitor adherence performed in participants' natural environments (Bosworth, 2012; Granger & Bosworth, 2011). For example, medication event monitoring systems (MEMS) are pill bottles or containers that are fitted with microcircuitry that records the time and date of each opening and closing of the container (Acosta et al., 2009; Brown et al., 2009; Charach, Gajaria, Skyba, & Chen, 2008; Krummenacher, Cavassini, Bugnon, & Schneider, 2011; Lee, Kim, Chung, Demirici, & Khademhosseini, 2010; Oldenmenger et al., 2007; Remington et al., 2013; van Onzenoort et al., 2012; Zeller, Schroeder, & Peters, 2007). This information can be transmitted to research or medical personnel to track medication adherence and provide prompts, monetary consequences, or social consequences to promote adherence. CM has been used to promote adherence for highly active antiretroviral therapy (HAART) using MEMS in HIV-infected drug users (Rigsby et al., 2000; Rosen et al., 2007; Sorensen et al., 2007; see also Carroll & Rounsaville, 2007). In one study, patients in CM HAART adherence demonstrated lowered viral load compared to a control group (Rosen et al., 2007). Notably, the effect sizes for HAART adherence in several CM studies (Rosen et al., 2007; Sorensen et al., 2007) are among the highest produced by behavioral interventions to promote adherence among HIV-infected drug users.

In addition, Volpp et al. (2008) used MEMS to promote warfarin adherence. Warfarin is used to manage thromboembolism (Gulløv et al., 1998; Hyers et al., 2001), and adherence is often a problem (Kimmel et al., 2007). The intervention involved CM and an audible prompt to occasion adherence. Adherence was monitored, and consequences were delivered based on the MEMS openings. In two experiments, the proportion of time that anticoagulation levels were outside the therapeutic range decreased by 23-25% (Volpp et al., 2008). It is not clear whether reductions were due to CM or due to the use of the audible prompt.

One limitation of MEMS is that researchers or clinicians cannot verify pill ingestion, *per se*. There are several alternatives that may entail more valid monitoring systems. First, pill ingestion can be observed via video-enabled phones (Hoffman et al., 2010; Wade, Karnon, Eliott, & Hiller, 2012). The in-person equivalent to this process is called directly observed therapy (DOT), which is the model recommended by the World Health Organization to promote adherence to medication regimens such as tuberculosis treatment. In a pilot study, DeMaio, Schwartz, Cooley, and Tice (2001) used videophones to observe patients swallowing medication for tuberculosis. Adherence using video-based DOT (95%) was equivalent to adherence using traditional DOT (97.5%). Second, new technologies are being explored to verify pill ingestion. For example, digital pills contain small microchips that interact with gastric juices to produce a voltage. The voltage can be detected by a small, Band-Aid sized sensor adhered to the skin (Zullig, Shaw, & Bosworth, 2015). Third, paper microfluidics can be used to detect biomarkers of medication adherence (Lee et al., 2010; see Li, Ballerini, & Shen, 2012 for a review of new applications of microfluidics). Paper microfluidics involves a small test strip embedded with chemicals that react with the urine of individuals that adhere to a medication regimen (e.g., Barclay, 2009). One advantage of paper microfluidics is that the technology is relatively low cost. Fourth, medication adherence can be verified through breath output. Specifically, a food additive, 2-butanol, can be combined with a medication, and after ingestion the additive is converted to 2-butanone, which can be detected in breath output (Morey et al., 2013).

CM has also been used to increase adherence to regimens that require regular monitoring of health-status. For example, measuring lung function using peak expiratory flow (PEF) must occur regularly to prevent asthmatic episodes (Kamps, Roorda, & Brand, 2001; Legorreta et al., 1998). Burkhart, Rayens, Oakley, Abshire, and Zhang (2007) used an AccuTrax Personal Diary Spirometer (Ferraris Medical and Pulmonary Data Services Instrumentation, Louisville, CO) to time- and date-stamp PEF measurements. Children in the CM group demonstrated higher adherence for daily electronically monitored PEF at week 16 (during the maintenance period).

CM has also been employed to improve diabetics' adherence to glucose monitoring and other diabetes management (Carney et al., 1983; Raiff & Dallery, 2010; Wysocki, Green, & Huxtable, 1989; see Petry et al., 2013 for a review). Carney and colleagues (1983) promoted adherence to diabetes regimen recommendations when parents of diabetic children were instructed to deliver praise, as well as points exchangeable for privileges, contingent on glucose monitoring. During baseline, participants adhered approximately 5% of the time, compared to approximately 90% during

CM. Similarly, Raiff and Dallery (2010) showed that Internet-based CM improved adherence to blood glucose monitoring in four teenagers (aged 12-17) diagnosed with type 1 diabetes. In Internet-based CM, both the monitoring system and the delivery system are web-based. Participants were observed via web camera as they engaged in the blood glucose test, and monetary consequences were delivered via a web site. Prior to the intervention, participants tested their blood glucose an average of 1.7 times per day (range 0-4), which falls below the 4-6 times per day recommended for teenagers (Silverstein et al., 2005). During the intervention, all participants increased their frequency of testing to an average of 5.7 per day (range 4-8 days). When the intervention was removed, testing decreased to an average of 3.1 tests per day (range 2-5 days). Although more research will be necessary to initiate and maintain long-term adherence to self-management regimens, the results from these CM studies are promising.

SUMMARY AND CONCLUSIONS

One way to develop programmatic lines of research in a new area of investigation is to capitalize on examples of successful research in other areas. ABA-based research on health and fitness has done just this. To date, applied behavior analysts have used well-established intervention strategies (e.g., task clarification, goal setting, feedback, incentives) to address various problems related to health and fitness. Most often, powerful reinforcement contingencies are arranged to induce healthy behavior without respect to the function of the target behavior. Alternatively, powerful punishment contingencies are sometimes used to decrease unhealthy behavior, also without respect to the function of the target behavior.

Recently, however, functional behavior assessment methods have been used to identify the operant contingencies that will evoke and maintain, if not increase, physical activity. The same strategy might prove useful for other health behaviors, especially in cases where superimposing somewhat arbitrary reinforcement or punishment contingencies proves ineffective. Still, there has been little research involving the coordination of functional behavior assessment with the development of behavioral interventions. That is, much of the research on health and fitness has focused on interventions without any systematic analysis of the variables related to the behavior under investigation. With the exception of recent functional assessment research on physical activity (Larson, Normand, Morley, & Hustyi, 2014; Larson, Normand, Morley, & Miller, 2014), there has been little preintervention assessment reported in the health and fitness literature. The systematic assessment of relevant controlling variables has proven remarkably effective in what is arguably the most studied area in ABA: severe problem behavior (Hanley et al., 2003). It seems wise to learn from our successes with severe problem behavior when attempting to address the problems related to health and fitness; however, the extent to which we can generalize from the problem behavior literature to health and fitness remains to be seen.

There are two major difficulties with trying to change health behavior that are easily understood from a behavior analytic perspective. Put simply, unhealthy behavior often produces powerful immediate reinforcers, and healthy behavior can sometimes produce powerful and immediate punishers. For example, eating is a reinforcing activity, and exercising can be physically aversive, at least in the short term. The natural outcomes of these two important health-related behaviors work against healthy moderation. Similarly, medication adherence may be challenging due to natural yet unpleasant side effects, or to social attention derived from nonadherence (e.g., a parent reprimanding a child based on nonadherence). Anderson, Ruggiero, and Adams (2000) illustrated the utility of identifying the determinants of pill refusal in a child with HIV. Only by identifying the determinants—in this case fear of choking and attention from his mother—could the researchers make appropriate and effective treatment recommendations. There is scant research of this nature, particularly idiographic (as opposed to group averaged) assessment of medication refusal and adherence.

Looking ahead, Epstein and colleagues (e.g., Epstein, 1992, 1998; Epstein, Myers, Raynor, & Saelens, 1998; Epstein, Salvy, Carr, Dearing, & Bickel, 2010) have suggested that behavioral economics might prove a useful way of framing the problems of overeating and inadequate physical activity. Moreover, behavioral economic interventions typically do not provide information about the determinants of an individuals' problem behavior to guide treatment recommendations. In some cases this can be a limitation, but in other cases arranging environments to promote health behavior can be accomplished without such information. For example, in a school setting, increasing consumption of water and decreasing consumption of soft drinks may be accomplished by increasing the prevalence of water fountains and decreasing the prevalence of soda machines. This is one of many procedures that can be derived from behavioral economic theory and research that might promote public health without regard to assessment of the determinants of behavior for each individual. Thus, the lack of functional assessment needs not be a roadblock to developing and implementing effective and scalable behavioral interventions. Behavioral economic analysis of health behavior is an emerging theme in behavioral research (e.g., Asch et al., 2012; Carr & Epstein, 2011; Epstein et al., 2012; Loewenstein, Brennan, & Volpp, 2007; Salvy, Nitecki, & Epstein, 2009), but more work is needed, especially in terms of developing effective and efficient interventions that can be widely disseminated.

Another emerging theme in research on health behavior is the growing use of technology to assess and manage health behavior (for a review see Dallery, Kurti, & Erb, 2014). The use of technology could broaden substantially the reach of behavioral interventions (Dallery & Raiff, 2011). Many behavior analysts have lamented the limited scope of behavioral interventions, despite their potential to address a wide range of socially relevant behavior (e.g., Friman, 2010; Normand & Kohn, 2013). Technology has already started to revolutionize other fields that address health behavior (Asch et al., 2012; Kaplan & Stone, 2013; Kumar, Nilsen, Pavel, & Srivastava, 2013). Further, there are scores of health applications (apps) available via mobile devices, the vast majority of which have not been evaluated scientifically. Behavior analysts stand poised to embrace technology, both for assessment and treatment, in ways that could lead to marked improvements in public health.

Many of the CM interventions discussed in this chapter demonstrate that CM can help initiate a variety of health behaviors (e.g., medication adherence, physical activity). Initiation of these behaviors is an obvious prerequisite to maintaining them. However, there are limited demonstrations of post-CM maintenance of behavior. A variety of possibilities could help maintain a CM intervention for extended durations such as by using low cost, intermittent reinforcement (Petry et al., 2011), or by using deposit contract procedures (Dallery, Meredith, & Glenn, 2008). In addition, CM interventions to promote health behavior could be broadened and maintained by harnessing changes in health policy in the United States. One interesting and potentially momentous change in insurance policy is the recent passing of the Patient Protection and Affordable Care Act. One section of the act (Section 2705) specifies that up to 30% of an employee's health insurance premium can be used in the form of outcome-based wellness incentives. There are already several examples of how these programs can be implemented, and results to date are mixed (e.g., Hand, Heil, Sigmon, & Higgins, 2014). Several authors have described how research on CM can inform such programs. Indeed, Hand and colleagues suggested that variables such as reinforcer delay and magnitude may need to be manipulated to increase efficacy of health promotion programs. Integrating science-based procedures with sustainable insurance-based incentive programs has substantial promise.

In closing, applied behavior analysts have been addressing problems related to health and fitness since the earliest days of the field and continue to do so. Advances in behavioral and computer technology promise to enhance future efforts to get people to engage in more healthy behavior and less unhealthy behavior. The field of ABA has a strong track record of addressing difficult and, in some cases, seemingly intractable behavior problems. Health promotion is a problem that we have started to address, but we have considerable work to do in fleshing out the determinants of, and solutions for, unhealthy behavior. Fortunately, we have a well-stocked conceptual and empirical tool chest at our disposal.

REFERENCES

Acosta, F. J., Bosch, E., Sarmiento, G., Juanes, N., Caballero-Hidalgo, A., & Mayans, T. (2009). Evaluation of noncompliance in schizophrenia patients using electronic monitoring (MEMS®) and its relationship to sociodemographic, clinical and psychopathological variables. *Schizophrenia Research*, *107*, 213–217.

Allen, K. D., & Stokes, T. F. (1987). Use of escape and reward in the management of young children during dental treatment. *Journal of Applied Behavior Analysis*, *20*, 381–390. http://dx.doi.org/10.1901/jaba.1987.20-381.

Anderson, C. M., Ruggiero, K. J., & Adams, C. D. (2000). The use of functional assessment to facilitate treatment adherence: A case of a child with HIV and pill refusal. *Cognitive and Behavioral Practice*, *7*, 282–287.

Aragona, J., Cassady, J., & Drabman, R. S. (1975). Treating overweight children through parental training and contingency contracting. *Journal of Applied Behavior Analysis*, *8*, 269–278. http://dx.doi.org/10.1901/jaba.1975.8-269.

Asch, D. A., Muller, R. W., & Volpp, K. G. (2012). Automated hovering in health care—Watching over the 5000 hours. *The New England Journal of Medicine*, *367*, 1–3. http://dx.doi.org/10.1056/NEJMp1203869.

Barclay, E. (2009). Text messages could hasten tuberculosis drug compliance. *The Lancet*, *373*, 15–16.

Beavers, G. A., Iwata, B. A., & Lerman, D. C. (2013). Thirty years of research on the functional analysis of problem behavior. *Journal of Applied Behavior Analysis*, *46*, 1–21. http://dx.doi.org/10.1002/jaba.30.

Benjamin-Bauman, J., Reiss, M. L., & Bailey, J. S. (1984). Increasing appointment keeping by reducing the call-appointment interval. *Journal of Applied Behavior Analysis*, *17*, 295–301.

Bosworth, H. B. (2012). How can innovative uses of technology be harnessed to improve medication adherence? *Expert Review of Pharmacoeconomics & Outcomes Research*, *12*, 133–135. http://dx.doi.org/10.1586/erp.12.6.

Brink, L. A., Nigg, C. R., Lampe, S. M., Kingston, B. A., Mootz, A. L., & van Vliet, W. (2010). Influence of schoolyard renovations on children's physical activity: The learning landscapes program. *American Journal of Public Health*, *100*, 1672–1678.

Brown, W. H., Pfeiffer, K. A., McIver, K. L., Dowda, M., Almeida, M. J., & Pate, R. R. (2006). Assessing preschool children's physical activity: The observation system for recording physical activity in children—Preschool version. *Research Quarterly for Exercise and Sport, 77,* 167–176.

Brown, I., Sheeran, P., & Reuber, M. (2009). Enhancing antiepileptic drug adherence: A randomized controlled trial. *Epilepsy and Behavior, 16,* 634–639.

Burkhart, P. V., Rayens, M. K., Oakley, M. G., Abshire, D. A., & Zhang, M. (2007). Testing an intervention to promote children's adherence to asthma self-management. *Journal of Nursing Scholarship: An Official Publication of Sigma Theta Tau International Honor Society of Nursing/Sigma Theta Tau, 39,* 133–140. http://dx.doi.org/10.1111/j.1547-5069.2007.00158.x.

Carney, R. M., Schechter, K., Homa, M., Levandoski, L., White, N., & Santiago, J. (1983). The effects of blood glucose testing versus urine sugar testing on the metabolic control of insulin-dependent diabetic children. *Diabetes Care, 6,* 378–380.

Carr, K. A., & Epstein, L. H. (2011). Relationship between food habituation and reinforcing efficacy of food. *Learning and Motivation, 42,* 165–172.

Carroll, K. M., & Rounsaville, B. J. (2007). A vision of the next generation of behavioral therapies research in the addictions. *Addictions, 102,* 850–869. http://dx.doi.org/10.1111/j.1360-0443.2007.0.1798.x.

Centers for Disease Control and Prevention. (2011). How much physical activity do children need? Retrieved from: http://www.cdc.gov/physicalactivity/everyone/guidelines/children.html.

Charach, A., Gajaria, A., Skyba, A., & Chen, S. (2008). Documenting adherence to psychostimulants in children with ADHD. *Journal of the Canadian Academy of Child and Adolescent Psychiatry, 17,* 131–136.

Crawford, M. A. (2014). Diet and cancer and heart disease. *Nutrition and Health, 22,* 67–78. http://dx.doi.org/10.1177/0260106014523361.

Dallery, J., Kurti, A., & Erb, P. E. (2014). A new frontier: Integrating behavioral and digital technology to promote health behavior. *Behavior Analyst. 38*(1). http://dx.doi.org/10.1007/s40614-014-0017-y.

Dallery, J., Meredith, S., & Glenn, I. M. (2008). A deposit contract method to deliver abstinence reinforcement for cigarette smoking. *Journal of Applied Behavior Analysis, 41,* 609–615.

Dallery, J., & Raiff, B. R. (2011). Contingency management in the 21st century: Technological innovations to promote smoking cessation. *Substance Use and Misuse, 46,* 10–22. http://dx.doi.org/10.3109/10826084.2011.521067.

Daniels, S. R., Donna, K. A., Eckel, R. H., Gidding, S. S., Hayman, L. L., Kumanyika, S., et al. (2005). Overweight in children and adolescents: Pathophysiology, consequences, prevention, and treatment. *Circulation, 111,* 1999–2012. http://dx.doi.org/10.1161/01.CIR.0000161369.71722.10.

De Luca, R. V., & Holborn, S. W. (1985). Effects of a fixed-interval schedule of token reinforcement on exercise with obese and non-obese boys. *Psychological Record, 35,* 525–533.

De Luca, R. V., & Holborn, S. W. (1990). Effects of fixed-interval and fixed-ratio schedules of token reinforcement on exercise with obese and non-obese boys. *Psychological Record, 40,* 67–82.

De Luca, R. V., & Holborn, S. W. (1992). Effects of a variable-ratio reinforcement schedule with changing criteria on exercise in obese and non-obese boys. *Journal of Applied Behavior Analysis, 25,* 671–679.

DeMaio, J., Schwartz, L., Cooley, P., & Tice, A. (2001). The application of telemedicine technology to a directly observed therapy program for tuberculosis: A pilot project. *Clinical Infectious Diseases, 33,* 2082–2084.

Ding, D., Sallis, J. F., Kerr, J., Lee, S., & Rosenberg, D. E. (2011). Neighborhood environment and physical activity among youth: A review. *American Journal of Preventive Medicine, 41,* 442–455. http://dx.doi.org/10.1016/j.ampre.2011.06.036.

Donaldson, J. M., & Normand, M. P. (2009). Using goal setting, self-monitoring, and feedback to increase calorie expenditure in obese adults. *Behavioral Interventions*, *24*, 73–83. http://dx.doi.org/10.1002/bin.277.

Epstein, L. H. (1992). Role of behavior theory in behavioral medicine. *Journal of Consulting and Clinical Psychology*, *60*, 493–498.

Epstein, L. H. (1998). Integrating theoretical approaches to promote physical activity. *American Journal of Preventative Medicine*, *15*, 257–265.

Epstein, L. H., Jankowiak, N., Nederkoorn, C., Raynor, H. A., French, S. A., & Finkelstein, E. (2012). Experimental research on the relation between food price changes and food-purchasing patterns: A targeted review. *American Journal of Clinical Nutrition*, *95*, 789–809.

Epstein, L. H., Leddy, J. J., Temple, J. L., & Faith, M. S. (2007). Food reinforcement and eating: A multilevel analysis. *Psychological Bulletin*, *133*, 884–906.

Epstein, L. H., Lin, H., Carr, K. A., & Fletcher, K. D. (2011). Food reinforcement and obesity. Psychological moderators. *Appetite*, *58*, 157–162. http://dx.doi.org/10.1016/j.appet.2011.09.025.

Epstein, L. H., Myers, M. D., Raynor, H. A., & Saelens, B. E. (1998). Treatment of pediatric obesity. *Pediatrics*, *101*, 554–570.

Epstein, L. H., Salvy, S. J., Carr, K. A., Dearing, K. K., & Bickel, W. K. (2010). Food reinforcement, delay discounting and obesity. *Physiology and Behavior*, *100*, 438–445. http://dx.doi.org/10.1016/j.physbeh.2010.04.029.

Epstein, L. H., Temple, J. L., Neaderhiser, B. J., Salis, R. J., Erbe, R. W., & Leddy, J. J. (2007). Food reinforcement, the dopamine D2 receptor genotype, and energy intake in obese and nonobese humans. *Behavioral Neuroscience*, *121*, 877–886.

Epstein, L. H., Valoski, A., Wing, R. R., & McCurley, J. (1994). Ten-year outcomes of behavioral family-based treatment for childhood obesity. *Health Psychology*, *31*, 373–383.

Finkelstein, E. A., Khavjou, O. A., Thompson, H., Trogdon, J. G., Pan, L., Sherry, B., et al. (2012). Obesity and severe obesity forecasts through 2030. *American Journal of Preventive Medicine*, *42*, 563–570. http://dx.doi.org/10.1016/j.amepre.2011.10.026.

Flegal, K. M., Carroll, M. D., Ogden, C. L., & Curtin, L. R. (2010). Prevalence and trends in obesity among US adults, 1999-2008. *The Journal of the American Medical Association*, *303*, 235–241. http://dx.doi.org/10.1001/jama.288.14.1723.

Flegal, K. M., Carroll, M. D., Ogden, C. L., & Johnson, C. L. (2002). Prevalence and trends in obesity among US adults, 1999-2000. *The Journal of the American Medical Association*, *288*, 1723–1727. http://dx.doi.org/10.1001/jama.288.14.1723.

Fogel, V. A., Miltenberger, R. G., Graves, R., & Koehler, S. (2010). The effects of exergaming on physical activity among inactive children in a physical education classroom. *Journal of Applied Behavior Analysis*, *43*, 591–600.

Friman, P. C. (2010). Come on in, the water is fine: Achieving mainstream relevance through integration with primary medical care. *The Behavior Analyst*, *33*, 19–36.

Granger, B. B., & Bosworth, H. B. (2011). Medication adherence: Emerging use of technology. *Current Opinion in Cardiology*, *26*, 279–287. http://dx.doi.org/10.1097/HCO.0b013e328347c150.

Gulløv, A. L., Koefoed, B. G., Petersen, P., Pedersen, T. S., Andersen, E. D., Godtfredsen, J., et al. (1998). Fixed minidose warfarin and aspirin alone and in combination vs adjusted-dose warfarin for stroke prevention in atrial fibrillation: Second Copenhagen Atrial Fibrillation, Aspririn, and Anticoagulation Study. *Archives of Internal Medicine*, *158*, 1513–1521.

Hand, D. J., Heil, S., Sigmon, S. C., & Higgins, S. T. (2014). Improving Medicaid health incentives programs: Lessons from substance abuse treatment research. *Preventive Medicine*, *63*, 87–89.

Hanley, G. P., Iwata, B. A., & McCord, B. E. (2003). Functional analysis of problem behavior: A review. *Journal of Applied Behavior Analysis, 36,* 147–185. http://dx.doi.org/10.1901/jaba.2003.36-147.

Hardman, C. A., Horne, P. J., & Lowe, C. F. (2009). A home-based intervention to increase physical activity in girls: The Fit 'n' Fun Dudes program. *Journal of Exercise Science and Fitness,* 7(1), 1–8.

Hardman, C. A., Horne, P. J., & Lowe, C. F. (2011). Effects of rewards, peer-modelling and pedometer targets on children's physical activity: A school-based intervention study. *Psychology and Health, 26,* 3–21.

Harvard Heart Letter. (2012). Fun and exergames: Not just for kids anymore. Retrieved from: http://www.health.harvard.edu/newsletters/Harvard_Heart_Letter/2012/March/fun-and-exergames-not-just-for-kids-anymore.

Hastmann, T. J., Foster, K. E., Rosenkranz, R. R., Rosenkranz, S. K., & Dzewaltowski, D. A. (2013). Effect of adult leader participation on physical activity in children. *Open Journal of Preventive Medicine, 2,* 429–435.

Hill, R. J., & Davies, P. S. (2001). The validity of self-reported energy intake as determined using the doubly labelled water technique. *The British Journal of Nutrition, 85,* 415–430.

Hoffman, J. A., Cunningham, J. R., Suleh, A. J., Sundsmo, A., Dekker, D., Vago, F., et al. (2010). Mobile direct observation treatment for tuberculosis patients: A technical feasibility pilot using mobile phones in Nairobi, Kenya. *American Journal of Preventive Medicine, 39,* 78–80.

Horne, P. J., Greenhalgh, J., Erjavec, M., Lowe, C. F., Viktor, S., & Whitaker, C. J. (2011). Increasing pre-school children's consumption of fruit and vegetables. A modelling and rewards intervention. *Appetite, 56,* 375–385.

Horne, P. J., Hardman, C. A., Lowe, C. F., & Rowlands, A. V. (2009). Increasing children's physical activity: A peer modelling, rewards and pedometer-based intervention. *European Journal of Clinical Nutrition, 63,* 191–198.

Horne, P. J., Hardman, C. A., Lowe, C. F., Tapper, K., Le Noury, J., Madden, P., et al. (2009). Increasing parental provision and children's consumption of lunchbox fruit and vegetables in Ireland: The Food Dudes intervention. *European Journal of Clinical Nutrition, 63,* 613–618.

Horne, P. J., Lowe, C. F., Bowdery, M., & Egerton, C. (1998). The way to healthy eating for children. *British Food Journal, 100,* 133–140.

Hustyi, K. M., Normand, M. P., Larson, T. A., & Morley, A. J. (2012). The effect of outdoor activity context on physical activity in preschool children. *Journal of Applied Behavior Analysis, 45,* 401–405. http://dx.doi.org/10.1901/jaba.2012.45-401.

Hyers, T. M., Agnelli, G., Hull, R. D., Mirris, T. A., Samama, M., Tapson, V., et al. (2001). Antithrombotic therapy for venous thromboembolic disease. *Chest, 119,* 176–193.

Intille, S. S., Albinali, F., Mota, S., Kuris, B., Botana, P., & Haskell, W. L. (2011). Design of a wearable physical activity monitoring system using mobile phones and accelerometers. In: *Conference Proceedings: Annual International Conference of the IEEE Engineering in Medicine and Biology Society. IEEE Engineering in Medicine and Biology Society Conference,* pp. 3636–3639. http://dx.doi.org/10.1109/IEMBS.2011.6090611.

Iwata, B. A., Dorsey, M. F., Slifer, K. J., Bauman, K. E., & Richman, G. S. (1994). Toward a functional analysis of self-injury. *Journal of Applied Behavior Analysis, 27,* 197–209 (Reprinted from *Analysis and Intervention in Developmental Disabilities, 2,* 3-20, 1982).

Janssen, I., & LeBlanc, A. G. (2010). Systematic review of the health benefits of physical activity and fitness in school-aged children and youth. *International Journal of Behavioral Nutrition and Physical Activity, 7,* 40. http://dx.doi.org/10.1186/1479-5868-7-40.

Janz, K. F., Letuchy, E. M., Eichenberger Gilmore, J. M., Burns, T. L., Torner, J. C., Willing, M. C., et al. (2010). Early physical activity provides sustained bone health benefits later in childhood. *Medicine and Science in Sports and Exercise, 42*, 1072–1078. http://dx.doi.org/10.1249/MSS.0b013e3181c619b2.

Jeffery, R. W. (2012). Financial incentives and weight control. *Preventive Medicine: An International Journal Devoted to Practice and Theory, 55*(Suppl.), S61–S67.

Kamps, A., Roorda, R., & Brand, P. (2001). Peak flow diaries in childhood asthma are unreliable. *Thorax, 56*, 180–182.

Kaplan, R. M., & Stone, A. A. (2013). Bringing the laboratory and clinic to the community: Mobile technologies for health promotion and disease prevention. *Annual Review of Psychology, 64*, 471–498.

Kimmel, S. E., Chen, Z., Price, M., Parker, C. S., Metlay, J. P., Christie, J. D., et al. (2007). The influence of patient adherence on anticoagulation control with warfarin: Results from the international normalized ratio adherence and genetics (IN-RANGE) study. *Archives of Internal Medicine, 167*, 229–235. http://dx.doi.org/10.1001/archinte.167.3.229.

King, A. C., Hekler, E. B., Grieco, L. A., Winter, S. J., Sheats, J. L., Buman, M. P., et al. (2013). Harnessing different motivational frames via mobile phones to promote daily physical activity and reduce sedentary behavior in aging adults. *PLoS ONE, 8*, e62613.

Krummenacher, I., Cavassini, M., Bugnon, O., & Schneider, M. P. (2011). An interdisciplinary HIV-adherence program combining motivational interviewing and electronic antiretroviral drug monitoring. *AIDS Care, 23*, 550–561. http://dx.doi.org/10.1080/09540121.2010.525613.

Kumar, S., Nilsen, W., Pavel, M., & Srivastava, M. (2013). Mobile health: Revolutionizing healthcare through transdisciplinary research. *Computer, 46*, 28–35. http://dx.doi.org/10.1109/MC.2012.392.

Kurti, A. N., & Dallery, J. (2013). Internet-based contingency management increases walking in sedentary adults. *Journal of Applied Behavior Analysis, 46*, 568–581.

Larson, T. A., Normand, M. P., Morley, A. J., & Hustyi, K. M. (2014). The role of the physical environment in promoting physical activity in children across different group compositions. *Behavior Modification, 38*, 837–851. http://dx.doi.org/10.1177/0145445514543466.

Larson, T. A., Normand, M. P., Morley, A. J., & Miller, B. G. (2013). A functional analysis of moderate-to-vigorous physical activity in young children. *Journal of Applied Behavior Analysis, 46*, 199–207. http://dx.doi.org/10.1002/jaba.8.

Larson, T. A., Normand, M. P., Morley, A. J., & Miller, B. G. (2014). Further evaluation of a functional analysis of moderate-to-vigorous physical activity in young children. *Journal of Applied Behavior Analysis, 47*, 219–230. http://dx.doi.org/10.1002/jaba.127.

Lattal, K. A. (1969). Contingency management of toothbrushing behavior in a summer camp for children. *Journal of Applied Behavior Analysis, 2*, 195–198. http://dx.doi.org/10.1901/jaba.1969.2-195.

Lee, W. G., Kim, Y. G., Chung, B. G., Demirici, U., & Khademhosseini, A. (2010). Nano/microfluidics for diagnosis of infection diseases in developing countries. *Advanced Drug Delivery Reviews, 62*, 449–457. http://dx.doi.org/10.1016/j.addr.2009.11.016.

Legorreta, A. P., Christian-Herman, J., O'Connor, R. D., Hasan, M. M., Evans, R., & Leung, K. M. (1998). Compliance with national asthma management guidelines and specialty care: A health maintenance organization experience. *Archives of Internal Medicine, 158*, 457–464.

Lerman, D. C., & Iwata, B. A. (1993). Descriptive and experimental analyses of variables maintaining self-injurious behavior. *Journal of Applied Behavior Analysis, 26*, 293–319.

Li, X., Ballerini, D. R., & Shen, W. (2012). A perspective on paper-based microfluidics: Current status and future trends. *Biomicrofluidics, 6*, 011301.

Lieberman, D. A., Chamberlin, B., Medina, E., Jr., Franklin, B. A., Saner, B. M., & Vafiadis, D. K. (2011). The power of play: Innovations in getting active summit

2011: A science panel proceedings from the American Heart Association. *Circulation*, *123*, 2507–2516. http://dx.doi.org/10.1161/CIR.0b013e318219661d.

Loewenstein, G., Brennan, T., & Volpp, K. G. (2007). Asymmetric paternalism to improve health behaviors. *Journal of the American Medical Association*, *298*, 2415–2417.

Lopez-Meyer, P., Schuckers, S., Makeyev, O., Fontana, J. M., & Sazonov, E. (2012). Automatic identification of the number of food items in a meal using clustering techniques based on the monitoring of swallowing and chewing. *Biomedical Signal Processing and Control*, *7*, 474–480.

Lowe, C. F., Horne, P. J., Tapper, K., Bowdery, M., & Egerton, C. (2004). Effects of a peer modelling and rewards-based intervention to increase fruit and vegetable consumption in children. *European Journal of Clinical Nutrition*, *58*, 510–522.

Makeyev, O., Lopez-Meyer, P., Schuckers, S., Besio, W., & Sazonov, E. (2012). Automatic food intake detection based on swallowing sounds. *Biomedical Signal Processing and Control*, *7*, 649–656.

Mann, R. A. (1972). The behavior-therapeutic use of contingency contracting to control an adult behavior problem: Weight control. *Journal of Applied Behavior Analysis*, *5*, 99–109. http://dx.doi.org/10.1901/jaba.1972.5-99.

Mayer, J. A., Heins, J. M., Vogel, J. M., Morrison, D. C., Lankester, L. D., & Jacobes, A. L. (1986). Promoting low-fat entree choices in a public cafeteria. *Journal of Applied Behavior Analysis*, *19*, 397–402. http://dx.doi.org/10.1901/jaba.1986.19-397.

McIver, K. L., Brown, W. H., Pfeiffer, K. A., Dowda, M., & Pate, R. R. (2009). Assessing children's physical activity in their homes: The observational system for recording physical activity in children-home. *Journal of Applied Behavior Analysis*, *42*, 1–16. http://dx.doi.org/10.1901/jaba.2009.42-1.

McKenzie, T. L., Crespo, N. C., Baquero, B., & Elder, J. P. (2010). Leisure-time physical activity in elementary schools: Analysis of contextual conditions. *Journal of School Health*, *80*, 470–477. http://dx.doi.org/10.1111/j.1746-1561.2010.00530.x.

Morey, T. E., Booth, M., Wasdo, S., Wishin, J., Quinn, B., Gonzalez, D., et al. (2013). Oral adherence monitoring using a breath test to supplement highly active antiretroviral therapy. *AIDS and Behavior*, *17*, 298–306.

Morrissey, J. L., Wenthe, P. J., Letuchy, E. M., Levy, S. M., & Janz, K. F. (2012). Specific types of family support and adolescent non-school physical activity levels. *Pediactric Exercise Science*, *24*, 333–346.

Must, A., Spadano, J., Coakley, E. H., Field, A. E., Colditz, G., & Dietz, W. H. (1999). The disease burden associated with overweight and obesity. *The Journal of the American Medical Association*, *282*, 1523–1529.

Normand, M. P. (2008). Increasing physical activity through self-monitoring, goal setting, and feedback. *Behavioral Interventions*, *23*, 227–236.

Normand, M. P., & Kohn, C. S. (2013). Don't wag the dog: Extending the reach of applied behavior analysis. *The Behavior Analyst*, *36*, 109–122.

Normand, M. P., & Osborne, M. R. (2010). Promoting healthier food choices in college students using individualized dietary feedback. *Behavioral Interventions*, *25*, 183–190. http://dx.doi.org/10.1002/bin.311.

Ogden, C. L., Carroll, M. D., Curtin, L. R., Lamb, M. M., & Flegal, K. M. (2010). Prevalence of high body mass index in US children and adolescents, 2007-2008. *The Journal of the American Medical Association*, *303*, 242–249. http://dx.doi.org/10.1001/jama.288.14.1723.

Ogden, C. L., Carroll, M. D., Curtin, L. R., McDowell, M. A., Tabak, C. J., & Flegal, K. M. (2010). Prevalence of overweight and obesity in the United States, 1999-2004. *The Journal of the American Medical Association*, *295*, 1549–1555. http://dx.doi.org/10.1001/jama.288.14.1723.

Ogden, C. L., Flegal, K. M., Carroll, M. D., & Johnson, C. L. (2002). Prevalence and trends in overweight among US children and adolescents, 1999-2000. *The Journal of the American Medical Association, 288*, 1728–1732. http://dx.doi.org/10.1001/jama.288.14.1723.

Oldenmenger, W. H., Echteld, M. A., de Wit, R., Smitt, P. A. E. S., Stronks, D. L., Stoter, G., et al. (2007). Analgesic adherence measurement in cancer patients: Comparison between electronic monitoring and diary. *Journal of Pain and Symptom Management, 34*, 639–647.

Pence, S. T., Roscoe, E. M., Bourret, J. C., & Ahearn, W. H. (2009). Relative contributions of three descriptive methods: Implications for behavioral assessment. *Journal of Applied Behavior Analysis, 42*, 425–446. http://dx.doi.org/10.1901/jaba.2009.42-425.

Petry, N. M., Barry, D., Pescatello, L., & White, W. B. (2011). A low-cost reinforcement procedure improves short-term weight loss outcomes. *The American Journal of Medicine, 124*, 1082–1085.

Petry, N. M., Cengiz, E., Wagner, J. A., Hood, K. K., Carria, L., & Tamborlane, W. V. (2013). Incentivizing behaviour change to improve diabetes care. *Diabetes, Obesity and Metabolism, 15*, 1071–1076.

Petry, N. M., Rash, C. J., Byrne, S., Ashraf, S., & White, W. B. (2012). Financial reinforcers for improving medication adherence: Findings from a meta-analysis. *American Journal of Medicine, 125*, 888–896.

Raiff, B. R., & Dallery, J. (2010). Internet-based contingency management to improve adherence with blood glucose testing recommendations for teens with type 1 diabetes. *Journal of Applied Behavior Analysis, 43*, 487–491.

Reiss, M. L., & Bailey, J. S. (1982). Visiting the dentist: A behavioral community analysis of participation in a dental health screening and referral program. *Journal of Applied Behavior Analysis, 15*, 353–362. http://dx.doi.org/10.1901/jaba.1982.15-353.

Remington, G., Teo, C., Mann, S., Hahn, M., Foussias, G., & Agid, O. (2013). Examining levels of antipsychotic adherence to better understand nonadherence. *Journal of Clinical Psychopharmacology, 33*, 261–263.

Rigsby, M. O., Rosen, M. I., Beauvais, J. E., Cramer, J. A., Rainey, P. M., O'Malley, S. S., et al. (2000). Cue-dose training with monetary reinforcement: Pilot study of an antiretroviral adherence intervention. *Journal of General Internal Medicine, 15*, 841–847.

Rosen, M. I., Dieckhaus, K., McMahon, T. J., Valdes, B., Petry, N. M., Cramer, J., et al. (2007). Improved adherence with contingency management. *AIDS Patient Care and STDs, 21*, 30–40. http://dx.doi.org/10.1089/apc.2006.0028.

Rothney, M. P., Schaefer, E. V., Neumann, M. M., Choi, L., & Chen, K. Y. (2008). Validity of physical activity intensity predictions by ActiGraph, Actical, and RT3 accelerometers. *Obesity, 16*, 1946–1952.

Salvy, S. J., Nitecki, L. A., & Epstein, L. H. (2009). Do social activities substitute for food in youth? *Annals of Behavioral Medicine, 38*, 205–212. http://dx.doi.org/10.1007/s12160-009-9145-0.

Schneider, P. L., Crouter, S., & Bassett, D. R. (2004). Pedometer measures of free-living physical activity: Comparison of 13 models. *Medicine and Science in Sports and Exercise, 36*, 331–335.

Schoeller, D. A. (1995). Limitations in the assessment of dietary energy intake by self-report. *Metabolism, 44*, 18–22.

Schroeder, S. A. (2007). Shattuck lecture. We can do better—Improving the health of the American people. *The New England Journal of Medicine, 357*, 1221–1228. http://dx.doi.org/10.1056/NEJMsa073350.

Shapiro, D., & Surwit, R. (1979). Biofeedback. In O. F. Pomerleau & J. P. Brady (Eds.), *Behavioral medicine: Theory and practice* (pp. 45–73). Baltimore: Williams & Wilkins.

Shayne, R. K., Fogel, V. A., Miltenberger, R. G., & Koehler, S. (2012). The effects of exergaming on physical activity in a third-grade physical education class. *Journal of Applied Behavior Analysis, 45,* 211–215.

Silverstein, J., Klingensmith, G., Copeland, K., Plotnick, L., Kaufman, F., Laffel, L., et al. (2005). Care of children and adolescents with type 1 diabetes: Statement of the American Diabetes Association. *Diabetes Care, 28*(1), 186–212.

Sorensen, J. L., Haug, N. A., Delucchi, K. L., Gruber, V., Kletter, E., Batki, S. L., et al. (2007). Voucher reinforcement improves medication adherence in HIV-positive methadone patients: A randomized trial. *Drug and Alcohol Dependence, 88*(1), 54–63. http://dx.doi.org/10.1016/j.drugalcdep.2006.09.019.

Stock, L. Z., & Milan, M. A. (1993). Improving dietary practices of elderly individuals: The power of prompting, feedback, and social reinforcement. *Journal of Applied Behavior Analysis, 26*(3), 379–387. http://dx.doi.org/10.1901/jaba.1993.26-387.

Strong, W. B., Malina, R. M., Blimkie, C. J., Daniels, S. R., Dishman, R. K., Gutin, B., et al. (2005). Evidence based physical activity for school-age youth. *The Journal of Pediatrics, 146*(6), 732–737.

Tapper, K., Horne, P. J., & Lowe, C. F. (2003). The food dudes to the rescue!. *The Psychologist, 16,* 18–21.

Thompson, R. H., & Iwata, B. A. (2007). A comparison of outcomes from descriptive and functional analyses of problem behavior. *Journal of Applied Behavior Analysis, 40,* 333–338. http://dx.doi.org/10.1901/jaba.2007.56-06.

Troiano, R. P., Berrigan, D., Dodd, K. W., Mâsse, L. C., Tilert, T., & McDowell, M. (2008). Physical activity in the United States measured by accelerometer. *Medicine and Science in Sports and Exercise, 40,* 181–188.

Tudor-Locke, C. (2002). Taking steps toward increased physical activity: Using pedometers to measure and motivate. *President's Council on Physical Fitness and Sports Research Digest, 3,* 3–10.

Turner, R. D., Pooly, S., & Sherman, A. R. (1976). A behavioral approach to individualized exercise programming. In J. D. Krumboltz & C. E. Thoreson (Eds.), *Counseling methods* (pp. 349–359). New York: Holt, Rinehart & Winston.

United States Department of Agriculture (USDA). (2005). Dietary guidelines for Americans 2005. Retrieved from: http://www.health.gov/dietaryguidelines/dga2005/document/html/chapter2.htm.

Van Camp, C. M., & Hayes, L. B. (2012). Assessing and increasing physical activity. *Journal of Applied Behavior Analysis, 45,* 871.

van Onzenoort, H. A., Neef, C., Verberk, W. W., van Iperen, H. P., de Leeuw, P. W., & van der Kuy, P. H. (2012). Determining the feasibility of objective adherence measurement with blister packaging smart technology. *American Journal of Health-System Pharmacy (AJHP): Official Journal of the American Society of Health-System Pharmacists, 69,* 872–879.

Vance, B. (1976). Using contracts to control weight and to improve cardiovascular physical fitness. In J. D. Krumboltz, & C. E. Thoreson (Eds.), *Counseling methods* (pp. 527–541). New York: Holt, Rinehart & Winston.

VanWormer, J. J. (2004). Pedometers and brief e-counseling: Increasing physical activity for overweight adults. *Journal of Applied Behavior Analysis, 37,* 421–425. http://dx.doi.org/10.1901/jaba.2004.37-421.

Volpp, K. G., Loewenstein, G., Troxel, A. B., Doshi, J., Price, M., Laskin, M., et al. (2008). A test of financial incentives to improve warfarin adherence. *BMC Health Services Research, 8,* 272. http://dx.doi.org/10.1186/1472-6963-8-272.

Wade, V. A., Karnon, J., Eliott, J. A., & Hiller, J. E. (2012). Home videophones improve direct observation in tuberculosis treatment: A mixed methods evaluation. *PLoS ONE, 7,* e50155. http://dx.doi.org/10.1371/journal.pone.0050155.

Wang, Y., Beydoun, M. A., Liang, L., Caballero, B., & Kumanyika, S. K. (2008). Will all Americans become overweight or obese? Estimating the progression and cost of the US obesity epidemic. *Obesity*, *16*, 2323–2330. http://dx.doi.org/10.1038/oby.2008.351.

Wengreen, H. J., Madden, G. J., Aguilar, S. S., Smits, R. R., & Jones, B. A. (2013). Incentivizing children's fruit and vegetable consumption: Results of a United States pilot study of the Food Dudes Program. *Journal of Nutrition Education and Behavior*, *45*, 54–59.

Willett, W. (2012). *Nutritional epidemiology* (3rd). New York, NY: Oxford University Press.

Winett, R. A., Kramer, K. D., Walker, W. B., Malone, S. W., & Lane, M. K. (1988). Modifying food purchases in supermarkets with modeling, feedback, and goal-setting procedures. *Journal of Applied Behavior Analysis*, *21*, 73–80. http://dx.doi.org/10.1901/jaba.1988.21-73.

Wysocki, T., Green, L., & Huxtable, K. (1989). Blood glucose monitoring by diabetic adolescents: Compliance and metabolic control. *Health Psychology: Official Journal of the Division of Health Psychology, American Psychological Association*, *8*, 267–284.

Wysocki, T., Hall, G., Iwata, B., & Riordan, M. (1979). Behavioral management of exercise: Contracting for aerobic points. *Journal of Applied Behavior Analysis*, *12*, 55–64. http://dx.doi.org/10.1901/jaba.1979.12-55.

Zeller, A., Schroeder, K., & Peters, T. J. (2007). Electronic pillboxes (MEMS) to assess the relationship between medication adherence and blood pressure control in primary care. *Scandinavian Journal of Primary Health Care*, *25*, 202–207.

Zullig, L. L., Shaw, R. J., & Bosworth, H. B. (2015). Applying technology to medication management and adherence. In L. Marsch, S. Lord, & J. Dallery (Eds.), *Transforming behavioral health care with technology: The state of the science*. Oxford University Press.

CHAPTER 23

Applications of Behavior Analysis to Improve Safety in Organizations and Community Settings

David A. Wilder, Sigurdur O. Sigurdsson
School of Behavior Analysis, Florida Institute of Technology, Melbourne, Florida, USA

Safety is large concern in the workplace. Nearly 3 million nonfatal workplace injuries and illness were reported by private employers in 2012 in the United States, the most recent year for which data are available (United States Bureau of Labor Statistics, 2013). Although this number reflects a general decline in injuries over the last decade, the number of more serious injuries resulting in days away from work, job transfer, or job restriction has remained steady for 4 years. In addition, the rate of workplace injuries and illnesses is higher among *public* employees than private employees; local government (as opposed to state or federal) employees have a particularly high rate of on-the-job injuries and illnesses (United States Bureau of Labor Statistics, 2013). The types of injuries sustained in the workplace vary by industry, but the most common injuries result from overexertion (i.e., lifting, carrying, pulling, pushing items), slipping or tripping, and falling from heights (United States Bureau of Labor Statistics, 2013).

The cost of injuries and illness in the workplace is staggering. Direct costs, which include medical costs and indemnity payments, are only a portion of the overall costs. Indirect costs, such as a replacement worker, accident investigation, and maintenance of insurance coverage, often run much higher than direct costs. The estimated average cost of a work-related, non-fatal injury in 2012 was over $50,000, and the estimated average cost of a work-related death was over $1,400,000 (National Safety Council, 2013). Work-related injuries and illness in the United States are estimated to cost more than $250 billion per year overall (i.e., direct and indirect costs), which is more than overall costs for diseases such as cancer, diabetes, and strokes

Clinical and Organizational Applications of Applied Behavior Analysis
http://dx.doi.org/10.1016/B978-0-12-420249-8.00023-X

(Leigh, 2011). Of course, these data represent the United States only; the costs of accidents and injuries in other parts of the world may be even higher.

The typical approach to enhancing on-the-job safety includes elimination of risk through engineering, safety training, and use of various types of personal protective equipment (PPE; National Safety Council, 2013). Although these methods can be effective, they lack an appreciation of the environmental contingencies that may be supporting safe or unsafe employee behavior. This is the main contribution of the behavior analytic approach to safety; it is described in more detail below.

BEHAVIOR ANALYSIS AND SAFETY: A LONG HISTORY

Behavior analytic applications to safety, or *behavioral safety*, as it is often called, have a surprisingly long history. In the early twentieth century, Heinrich (1931), who worked for Traveler's Insurance Company, Inc., espoused the notion that worker injuries were largely due to unsafe worker behavior. This ran counter to popular ideas that injuries were largely a result of unsafe environments. Heinrich advocated engineering-based interventions to improve safety, as well as interventions such as hiring safety-conscious personnel, safety training, disciplinary policies which emphasized safety, and termination of repeated safety violators (Heinrich, Petersen, & Roos, 1980).

One criticism of this focus on employee behavior has been that behavioral safety "blames the employee." While earlier applications of behavioral safety may have had this drawback, this is not true for modern applications of behavioral safety that are informed by behavioral science. State-of-the-art behavioral safety views the behavior of the employee as a function of his or her history of reinforcement and the current environmental contingencies. That is, if an employee performs unsafely, he does so because behaving in that manner has been effective and successful in the past (i.e., it resulted in a savings of time or effort, attention or praise from a supervisor, or money). In addition, behaving safely may have been punished in the past because it resulted in a loss of time or money, or required greater effort. In short, the behavior of the employee is a result of what has and has not worked in the past and the current contingencies operating in the environment. Because the employee's history is inaccessible, changing the current contingencies will be most effective to change the employee's behavior.

The influential psychologist B.F. Skinner popularized behavioral approaches to safety and other community concerns late in the twentieth century. Although Skinner himself did not directly conduct research on safety, his conceptual work (e.g., Skinner, 1953) set the stage for this research to be conducted. The field of applied behavior analysis formally began with the publication of the first issue of the *Journal of Applied Behavior Analysis* in 1968. Research on behavioral safety in this journal appears as early as 1978 (Yeaton & Bailey, 1978). One year earlier, in 1977, the *Journal of Organizational Behavior Management* (*JOBM*) was founded; publication of safety-related studies in this journal began almost immediately. Although not published in *JOBM*, Smith, Anger, and Uslan (1978) first described the utility of positive reinforcement to improve safety in organizations. That same year, Komaki, Barwick, and Scott (1978) studied and improved safe performance in a food-manufacturing plant.

Since the 1990s, specific approaches to behavioral safety have been developed (Agnew & Snyder, 2002; Geller, 2001; Krause, 1997; McSween, 2003). Although all of these approaches involve behavioral techniques such as operationally defining safe and unsafe performances, directly observing and collecting data on performance in the natural environment, and delivering precise feedback on safe performance, they differ in their emphasis on various steps and the specific processes within which these tasks are accomplished. A number of behavior analytic consulting firms provide safety services, including Aubrey Daniels International (aubreydaniels.com), the Continuous Learning Group (clg.com), and Quality Safety Edge (qualitysafetyedge.com).

BEHAVIORS TARGETED FOR IMPROVEMENT IN BEHAVIORAL SAFETY

Behavioral safety researchers and practitioners have targeted a wide range of behaviors for improvement. However, many applications of behavioral safety can be arranged into three broad categories: applications focusing on improving position or posture, applications focusing on wearing PPE, and applications focusing on the use of safety belts or other restraint systems.

Applications to Improve Position or Posture

Ergonomics is a scientific discipline which focuses on understanding the interaction among humans and other elements of a system. Proper ergonomic design is necessary to prevent muscle strain due to repetitive movements and musculoskeletal disorders, such as carpal tunnel syndrome (International Ergonomics Association, 2014). Behavioral safety has contributed to proper ergonomic design in a number of ways, one of which is by teaching employees to perform their jobs in a safe position. Sasson and Austin (2005) provided one-on-one training and feedback on safe ergonomic performance for 11 computer terminal operators. In addition, 6 of the 11 workers participated in observations of, and data collection on, the remaining five participants. The purpose of the observations was to determine if simply observing peers performing safely would increase safe ergonomic behavior on the part of the observers. The results showed that safe behavior increased during the intervention for all participants and maintained at high levels even at a 4-month follow-up. In addition, those participants who took part in observations of their peers performed more safely than those who did not.

Culig, Dickinson, Lindstrom-Hazel, and Austin (2008) evaluated two interventions to increase safe ergonomic behavior among seven office employees. The first intervention consisted of adjusting participant workstations. Specifically, the adjustments consisted of either moving the computer monitor, collapsing the keyboard legs, or adjusting the chair angle. The second intervention, which consisted of performance management, was only applied to postures that did not respond to the workstation adjustment intervention. Performance management consisted of ergonomic information, graphic feedback, and praise. The results showed that two of the seven participants increased five safe postures by at least 50% with the workstation adjustment intervention. All targeted postures by all participants increased between 50% and 80% when the performance management intervention was introduced. Results suggest that these two interventions, when implemented successively, can be effective in increasing safe ergonomic performance.

Fante, Gravina, and Austin (2007) conducted a preintervention assessment to determine variables that contributed to safe ergonomic postures in a pharmacy. The three pharmacy employees who participated had experienced over 30 lost days of work in the time period that preceded the intervention. The preintervention assessment determined that employees were most at-risk for poor ergonomic posture when they were on the telephone. The authors then implemented a behavioral safety package, which included training, feedback, and peer observations. The package was effective in that safe performance by all employees improved over baseline levels.

Similarly, Fante, Gravina, Betz, and Austin (2010) conducted a structural assessment on variables that contributed to wrist posture safety among three pharmacy technicians. Specifically, they collected data on employees' wrist posture in the presence and absence of a wrist support device. Safe wrist position was higher when the wrist support device was used. An intervention consisting of the addition of a keyboard tray was then evaluated. The intervention produced large increases in safe wrist posture for all three employees.

Yu, Moon, Oah, and Lee (2013) developed an automated system to collect data on safe sitting postures among office workers. They also measured the system's effectiveness to deliver two types of feedback to improve safe postures. The first type of feedback was delayed and infrequent. The second type was immediate and frequent. Both types of feedback improved postures, but the immediate and frequent feedback was more effective than the delayed and infrequent feedback.

Finally, in a follow-up study, Moon and Oah (2013) compared prompts to feedback to increase safe sitting postures among three office workers. They found that feedback was very effective in increasing safe sitting. However, prompts alone were ineffective. The authors suggest that a combination of antecedent- and consequence-based interventions are likely to be most effective.

Applications to Increase Wearing of PPE

Another focus of behavioral safety has been increasing the use of PPE by employees. PPE is a general term that describes clothes and equipment that protect against workplace hazards. Although governments regulate the use of PPE, employees in many settings do not wear the PPE as often as they should. Behavior analysts have increased the frequency with which employees wear various types of PPE.

Casella et al. (2010) evaluated an intervention to increase the use of gloves when delivering food to children with autism. Gloves are a form of PPE; they help prevent direct contact with blood, saliva, mucus, or other bodily fluid. The researchers manipulated the location of the gloves so that they were more convenient to the therapists working with the children. In the high-effort condition, the gloves were over 6 m away from the area in which therapists worked with the children. In the medium-effort condition, gloves were 3 m away from therapists. In the low-effort condition, gloves were less than 1 m away from therapists. The results indicated that therapist wore their gloves much more often in the low-effort condition relative to the medium- and high-effort conditions.

Abellon and Wilder (2014) examined the effects of PPE proximity on safe performance in a manufacturing setting. Three employees at a hydraulics supply company served as participants. These employees regularly used dangerous machinery; the company required them to wear safety glasses, but they did not always comply. After a baseline period in which the protective eyewear was kept 6 m from employee workstations, the conditions under which they were to wear the glasses were described. Next, the glasses remained 6 m from employee workstations. Next, the glasses were moved to within 1.5 m of employee workstations. The results showed that employees did not wear the glasses often when they were 6 m from workstations, even after the conditions under which they were required to wear the glasses had been described. In contrast, when the glasses were 1.5 m from workstations, employees wore the glasses more frequently. A social validity measure suggested that safe performance increased to levels comparable to those of an exemplary employee at the company. Together, data from these two studies suggest that use of PPE can be increased simply by making it easy for employees to access PPE when they need it.

Applications to Increase the Use of Safety Belts

One of the most dangerous things most of us do daily is drive or ride in a car. Behavior analysis has a long history of contributing to safe driving practices. Rudd and Geller (1985) evaluated an incentive program to increase safety belt use on a university campus. In this study, campus police officers observed faculty and students in cars. If they were wearing their seatbelt, the officers wrote down their license plate number and they were eligible for a raffle, which included gift certificates donated by local businesses. The program was effective in that safety belt use increased substantially among faculty members and increased some among students.

Sowers-Hoag, Thyer, and Bailey (1987) assessed the safety belt use of 16 children riding to and from school. Safety belt use was very low (0-6%) during baseline. The authors used training, rehearsal, and a lottery to increase safety belt use. Results showed that safety belt use increased to 75-100%, and a questionnaire suggested it was socially valid.

Engerman, Austin, and Bailey (1997) took a different approach. They assessed the effects of a prompt on wearing of safety belts by supermarket customers. They had grocery carriers tell customers to "have a nice day and don't forget to buckle up" when they left the supermarket. The prompt produced a 12% increase in the number of customers who wore their safety belt upon exiting the store. Austin, Alvero, and Olson (1998) replicated this finding at a restaurant. Later, Cox, Cox, and Cox (2000) used a sign to prompt wearing of safety belts in senior communities. They replicated and extended this finding a few years later (Cox, Cox, & Cox, 2005).

Van Houten, Malenfant, Austin, and Lebbon (2005) manipulated the gearshift system of a car to examine the effect of a delay to placing the vehicle in gear on safety belt use. They evaluated the system in five cars, and participant belt use increased for all participants. The delay that was most effective varied, but was between 5 and 20 s in duration. When the device was deactivated, safety belt use dropped. The authors proposed that a system similar to this might be effective to increase safety belt use in other cars. This finding was later replicated among 101 commercial drivers (Van Houten et al., 2010). These studies suggest that a number of behavioral procedures, from prompting to negative reinforcement, can be effective to increase safety belt use.

INDUSTRY-SPECIFIC APPLICATIONS OF BEHAVIORAL SAFETY

Behavioral safety techniques have been applied in a wide variety of industries. However, many applications of behavioral safety can be arranged into four industries: transportation, health care/human services, the food service industry, and manufacturing.

Applications in the Transportation Industry

In addition to the many behavioral applications involving wearing safety belts in cars, behavioral safety has contributed to transportation safety in other ways. Ludwig, Biggs, Wagner, and Geller (2002) examined the effects of feedback and coupons for free vehicle maintenance on the safe driving behavior of 82 pizza delivery drivers in two college towns. Each week, data collectors discretely collected data on use of turn signals, safety belts, and complete stopping at stop signs. During baseline, safe performance was poor. During intervention, safe performance increased by 17-22%, even among those drivers who did not win coupons for vehicle maintenance. Other studies (Ludwig & Geller, 1999) in which similar interventions were employed have shown effects such as these on these same dependent variables.

Austin, Hackett, Gravina, and Lebbon (2006) used sign prompts to increase complete stopping at stop signs on a university campus. These researchers held up signs that read "Please Stop—I Care" when motorists approached an intersection. If the motorist stopped, the researcher flipped the sign, which said "Thank you for Stopping" on the other side. The intervention increased stopping from 13% to 52%.

Olson and Austin (2001) taught four public bus drivers to self-monitor their complete stopping and safe performance when letting riders on and off of the bus. To do this, they simply noted it on a sheet of paper near the driver's seat. In addition to self-monitoring, individual and group feedback and supervisor prompts were used to increase safe performance. All four bus drivers increased their safe performance by 10-14% during the intervention phase.

Hickman and Geller (2003) assessed a self-management intervention with 33 truck drivers. They targeted speeding and extreme braking and used computers in the trucks to measure these variables. Drivers were required to complete self-monitoring forms; the accuracy of this information was verified via the computer. The intervention involved feedback delivered via a detailed graph each week. The results showed that both speeding and extreme braking decreased during the intervention.

Applications in the Health Care/Human Services Industry

Safety is always a concern in the health care and human service industry. In addition to the risk of infection from pathogens (addressed earlier under use of PPE), client lifting, waste disposal, and cleanliness/sterilization of patient or client service areas are often concerns. Stephens and Ludwig (2005) measured a number safe behaviors by nurses in a hospital setting. Among these behaviors was proper disposal of catheter needles after use. The intervention included goal setting and feedback; the results showed an increase in safe performance among all nurses. One nurse even acknowledged that he was more satisfied with his job as a result of the intervention.

Alavosius and Sulzer-Azaroff (1986) examined safe lifting of clients with physical disabilities. They used written and verbal performance feedback to increase safe lifting. The results showed that the feedback was effective; that is, safe client lifting increased across all participants. An informal cost-benefit analysis suggested that this procedure saved the organization a great deal of money.

Carr, Wilder, Majdalany, Mathisen, and Strain (2013) used a preintervention assessment tool, the performance diagnostic checklist-human services (PDC-HS), to determine the variables responsible for poor cleaning and sanitizing by therapists in a clinic for children with autism. The assessment revealed that a lack of training and a lack of appropriate feedback were responsible for the performance problem. The authors then implemented an intervention based on the PDC-HS and found that it was effective in increasing cleaning and sanitizing on the part of therapists. Interestingly, they also implemented a nonassessment-based intervention, and it was ineffective, suggesting that the PDC-HS is effective in identifying appropriate interventions.

Ditzian, Wilder, King, and Tanz (2015) also used the PDC-HS to identify the variables responsible for poor performance in a clinic for children with autism, but they evaluated closing therapy room doors by therapists. They targeted this because many of the children were running from the therapy rooms and attempting to leave the building, which was a safety hazard. The PDC-HS suggested that few consequences supported closing of doors, so they implemented an intervention in which the therapists received immediate feedback, and the intervention was effective. Like Carr et al. (2013), the authors evaluated a non-PDC-HS intervention, which was ineffective.

Applications in the Food Service Industry

The food service industry employs nearly 10 million people in the United States alone (United States Bureau of Labor Statistics, 2013). Safety is a major concern in this industry and behavioral safety has been applied to increase safe performance in restaurants, bars, and food distribution centers. Scherrer and Wilder (2008) evaluated safe tray carrying among servers at a busy bar. First, a physical therapist created a list of safe tray carrying practices. Baseline data were then collected on how safely three servers carried trays. Next, the servers were trained in safe tray carrying practices. Data continued to be collected on their safe performance. The training was effective; safe tray carrying increased to near 100% for all three servers.

Goomas (2012) implemented a behavioral safety procedure at a meat distribution center. He used wireless ring scanners, which produced immediate auditory and visual feedback, to increase the performance and accuracy of order selectors. The intervention also impacted food safety. During the intervention, meat distribution met the required time frames established by the US Food and Drug Administration.

Applications in Manufacturing

Manufacturing settings are among the most dangerous places to work. Behavioral safety has been applied in a variety of manufacturing settings, including metal fabrication (Zohar, Cohen, & Azar, 1980), communication product manufacturing (Sulzer-Azaroff, Loafman, Merante, & Hlavacek, 1990), and oil processing (Myers, McSween, Medina, Rost, & Alvero, 2010) to increase employee safety.

Zohar et al. (1980) evaluated hearing loss in a noisy metal fabrication plant. Before the study began, the authors measured hearing loss and earplug use among employees. Earplug use was low. The authors used the information regarding hearing loss to provide feedback to employees regarding how they could conserve their hearing over time. They attained 85-90% compliance with wearing earplugs after the intervention. Only 10% of employees in a control group that did not receive the feedback wore earplugs.

Sulzer-Azaroff et al. (1990) assessed a behavioral safety program among 225 employees in three departments at an industrial plant. Specific safety-related behaviors were determined for each department. The intervention consisted of feedback, reinforcement, and goal setting. More specifically, employees received weekly graphed feedback with praise. Major celebrations followed goal attainment. Safety scores gradually improved once the intervention was implemented and the organization saved over $50,000 in costs.

Myers et al. (2010) described a behavioral safety process spanning 20 years at an oil refinery. During this time, safety observation training, feedback, recognition, and celebration were continuously performed to reduce recordable incidents, lost-time cases, and injuries. The authors reported that the safety procedure was associated with an 81% decrease in recordable incidents, a 79% decrease in lost-time cases, and a 97% savings in annual workers compensation costs over a 20-year period. This is a great example of the long-term benefits that can result from the sustained use of behavioral safety process.

BEHAVIORAL SAFETY ASSESSMENT METHODS

Before a behavioral safety process can be developed, a comprehensive safety assessment needs to be conducted to develop behavioral pinpoints (Cunningham & Geller, 2012; McSween, 2003). Safety-related behaviors to be pinpointed may include behaviors that have been associated with injury in the past (e.g., not wearing PPE), the products of safety-related behaviors (e.g., a spill on the floor constituting a slip hazard), and behaviors that have the potential to support safety (e.g., managers visibly supporting safety over production and allocating resources to safety).

Injury Analysis

A key feature of most safety assessments is a retrospective analysis of past on-site safety incidents. Analyses can vary in terms of the time frame of the assessments. For example, Cunningham and Geller (2012) analyzed injury data for the previous year, Cooper (2006) analyzed 2 years of data, and Lee, Shon, and Oah (2014) analyzed 3 years of data. One exception to this method is Lingard and Rowlinson (1998), in which the safety assessment took the form of identifying common types of injuries in the industry to which the site belonged. Reported instances of critical incidents that may have led to injury (near misses) may also be analyzed retrospectively (Ray, Bishop, & Wang, 1997). Alternative safety assessment strategies include identification of job categories that are especially at risk for injury (Killimett, 1991), identification of behaviors in which the consequences of error can be fatal or catastrophic (Komaki et al., 1978), on-site observations (Lebbon, Sigurdsson, & Austin, 2012), interviews with employees or safety committee members (Harper et al., 1996; Lee et al., 2014), safety culture surveys (Cunningham & Geller, 2012), consultations with occupational therapists (Fante et al., 2007), and discussions with supervisors and union safety representatives (Ray et al., 1997).

Once a sample of safety-related incidents has been collected, an attempt is made to identify common features of incidents. Common features may include the cause of injury based on the Occupational Safety and Health Administration classifications, locations or units where injuries frequently occur, the type of process involved in incidents, and the time of day or shift when incidents occurred (Cunningham & Geller, 2012). Injuries may also be categorized by employee title (Cunningham & Geller, 2012), task (Harper et al., 1996), or body part injured. A common feature of incident analysis is some form of causal analysis, in which events leading up to the incident are identified and categorized (Cooper, 2006). Various tools, such as root cause analyses of injuries (ABS Consulting, 2005) and PIC/NIC (an interview to determine if the results of the behavior are positive, immediate, and certain) analysis of consequences (Agnew & Snyder, 2002; Daniels & Daniels, 2006), have been developed to aid in the identification of causes of at-risk behaviors leading to injury, such as conditions leading up to the event (e.g., production pressure at end of shift) or equipment variables (e.g., inappropriate or damaged tools).

Checklist Development

When common behaviors and conditions leading to an injury have been identified, a checklist is developed to track these events. Checklists may include as many as 50 general items under several categories (e.g., housekeeping, personal protection, procedures, and environment; Krause, 1997), whereas others may include as few as three items (Agnew & Snyder, 2002). The items on the checklist then become the focus of specific behavior-change interventions with the assumption that improvements in identified safety-related behaviors will lead to improved safety outcomes.

BEHAVIORAL SAFETY PROCESS COMPONENTS

Common features of behavioral safety processes include forming safety committees, delivering safety observer training, and conducting safety observations. Common behavior change strategies in behavioral safety processes include safety training, feedback, praise, rewards, recognition, and goal setting (Wirth & Sigurdsson, 2008).

Safety Committee

Committees with representation from safety personnel, management, supervisors, and employees can be formed to provide support for a behavioral safety process (Harper et al., 1996; Lebbon et al., 2012; McSween, 2003; Sulzer-Azaroff & De Santamaria, 1980). Safety committees can function to provide feedback on the process, provide input on safety-related policy changes, and prioritize purchases of safety equipment. Safety committees may also serve to analyze and discuss trends in injury, near misses, and observation data, and to troubleshoot safety challenges identified through these data inputs.

Safety Training

A safety training package was developed by Komaki et al. (1978), in which workers are shown pictures of safe and at-risk behaviors, followed by discussions of why, or why not, the pictures depict safe or at-risk behavior. This training has been replicated by a number of other researchers (Fante et al., 2007; Harper et al., 1996; Lebbon et al., 2012). While safety training is important to enable workers to discriminate between safe and at-risk behaviors, it is usually used as a part of an intervention package (e.g., Fante et al., 2007; Lebbon et al., 2012; Ray et al., 1997). For example, Ray et al. found that training alone was not effective in increasing safe behavior and that incorporating motivational strategies was necessary to improve safety behaviors.

Employee Observer Training and Safety Observations

A key part of a behavioral safety process is regular safety observations by on-site personnel (McSween, 2003). Observers may be safety staff (Hermann, Ibarra, & Hopkins, 2010), experimenters (Ray et al., 1997), employees

(Cooper, 2006; Lebbon et al., 2012), or both managers and employees (Harper et al., 1996). Some authors recommend that managers be involved in observations and verbal feedback, as managerial feedback may be more effective because they control valuable outcomes in organizations (e.g., Stajkovic & Luthans, 1997). There is some variability in published studies in terms of the percentage of trained observers across an organization. For example, Lebbon et al. trained employee observers across two phases, such that informal leaders were trained in each intervention site in the first phase to establish buy-in for the process, and the remaining employees were trained in the second phase. In contrast, Harper et al. trained only 10% of the workforce to conduct observations.

One possible benefit of training employees to conduct observations is that the observers themselves may behave more safely as a result of conducting peer observations (Alvero & Austin, 2004; Alvero, Struss, & Rappaport, 2007; Taylor & Alvero, 2012), a phenomenon which has been termed the *observer effect*. Nielsen, Sigurdsson, and Austin (2009) were also able to improve safe behavior by having employees score videos of models performing routine tasks and providing employees specific feedback on the accuracy of their safety observations.

As a part of the training, observers may also be trained in delivering immediate and specific verbal feedback to employees based on the checklist items scored during the observation (Cooper, 2006; Fante et al., 2007). Emphasis is placed on the delivering praise for items that are scored as safe (Komaki et al., 1978; Sulzer-Azaroff & De Santamaria, 1980), and corrective feedback may be delivered as needed (Hermann et al., 2010). Checklist data are then collected by a safety committee or safety representatives and form the basis of motivational interventions such as graphed feedback, goal setting, and celebrations.

Feedback

The two most common types of feedback delivered as a part of a behavioral safety process are immediate verbal feedback following a safety observation, and graphed feedback summarizing data from safety observations over a certain span of time (e.g., Fante et al., 2007; Fellner & Sulzer-Azaroff, 1984; Komaki et al., 1978; Lingard & Rowlinson, 1998; Zohar, 2002). The graphed feedback often serves as the basis for safety-related discussions (Cooper, 2006; Harper et al., 1996) at regular site safety meetings or at the start of a shift.

Other feedback interventions merit mention. For example, in Zohar (2002), feedback was provided to supervisors and managers on their safety-related interactions with their crewmembers, and Sulzer-Azaroff and De Santamaria (1980) provided supervisors with copies of observational data, a congratulatory message, and comments from a senior company executive. Lee et al. (2014) compared global safety feedback to behavior-specific safety feedback and found similar results for both types of feedback. The authors also noted that nontargeted safety behaviors increased more in the global feedback condition.

Social praise is often combined with feedback interventions. Immediate praise may be delivered immediately for safe behavior (e.g., Komaki et al., 1978; Lebbon et al., 2012) or for improving trends in feedback graphs (Cooper, 2006). Praise may also be delivered to managers for safety improvements (Sulzer-Azaroff & De Santamaria, 1980; Zohar, 2002).

Goal setting

Goal setting is commonly used in behavioral safety processes to establish desired outcomes for process measures (e.g., number of observations, number of environmental hazards identified and fixed, number of safety interactions by managers; Cooper, 2006; Komaki et al., 1978), or behavioral measures (e.g., percentage of observations scored as "safe"; Cooper, 2006; Fellner & Sulzer-Azaroff, 1986; Harper et al., 1996; Komaki et al., 1978; Lingard & Rowlinson, 1998). Fellner and Sulzer-Azaroff attempted to determine whether participative goal setting, in which employees as the targets of intervention are consulted in deciding on goal levels, was more effective than supervisor-assigned goals. Results of the Fellner and Sulzer-Azaroff investigation seemed to favor neither approach, but practitioners appear to prefer participative goal setting to assigned goal setting (e.g., Cooper, 2006; Harper et al., 1996; Komaki et al., 1978; Lingard & Rowlinson, 1998), which is consistent with the participative nature of behavioral safety processes advocated by experts (e.g., Agnew & Snyder, 2002; McSween, 2003).

Incentives

Incentives should be used with caution in behavioral safety, as financial incentives provided for the absence of recorded injuries have been historically criticized for motivating underreporting of injuries (Mathis, 2009; Wirth & Sigurdsson, 2008). A viable alternative strategy is to provide incentives for improvements in process measures, such as conducting observations (Lebbon et al., 2012) or acting on safety suggestions (Fox, Hopkins, & Anger, 1987), or to organize celebrations around achievements of safety milestones (Hermann et al., 2010).

Management-Level Interventions

A common criticism of behavioral safety has been that it places the blame for injury on the worker and absolves the organization's management structure of responsibility for safety (Mathis, 2009). As Mathis has pointed out, a behavioral safety process that does not involve management in design and implementation represents an implementation failure. Modern behavioral safety interventions involve tracking and accountability systems for management safety support behaviors. For example, Hermann et al. (2010) used behavioral principles to manage the behavioral safety process responsibilities and traditional safety responsibilities of managers, such as consistently conducting injury investigations, consistent identification and correction of hazardous conditions, and consistently chairing weekly safety talks. In other studies (Harper et al., 1996; Zohar, 2002), accountabilities were established for management so that safety would not be compromised because of production quotas.

EVALUATION OF BEHAVIORAL SAFETY PROCESS OUTCOMES

The outcomes of behavioral safety processes can be evaluated along a number of different dimensions. Most organizations implementing behavioral safety do so in the hopes of ultimately reducing injuries. However, injuries are generally low-frequency events (Komaki et al., 1978), and hence it may be difficult to observe improvements in safety if injuries are the sole outcome of interest. In that sense, injuries can also be conceptualized as a lagging measure (Killimett, 1991), in that improvements in safety behavior may not be realized until injury data have been collected over a considerable time span. As a result, behavioral safety processes can be evaluated both in terms of lagging indicators (e.g., injury rates over time), as well as leading indicators (e.g., behaviors, process measures, hazardous conditions).

Injury-Related Metrics

Krause, Seymour, and Sloat (1999) reviewed injury data from 73 companies that had implemented behavioral safety processes and found that companies could expect an average of 26% reduction in injuries in the first year of implementation and a 69% reduction after 5 years. For individual implementations, the data are often equally impressive. Hermann et al. (2010) reported reductions of 99% in lost-time case rates over the span of 7 years,

Fellner and Sulzer-Azaroff (1984) reported a 50% decrease in injuries over the span of 6 months, Cooper (2006) observed a 25% decrease in injuries in the first year of implementation and an additional 25% decrease in the second year, and Lebbon et al. (2012) reported an approximately 30% reduction in injuries over the span of 5 years.

Alternative injury-related metrics include severity of injury (Hermann et al., 2010; Lebbon et al., 2012). Hermann et al., for example, also analyzed first-time occupational injuries, to account for injuries not related to cumulative trauma. Finally, Alavosius, Getting, Dagen, Newsome, and Hopkins (2009) recorded impressive injury reductions over the span of 3 years and further demonstrated that the return on investment was between 1:4 and 1:5 when factoring the cost of the intervention and direct cost of injuries.

Safety Behavior

Direct observation of safety behavior in work areas has been used to demonstrate the impact of a behavioral safety process. For example, Cooper (2006), Cooper, Phillips, Sutherland, and Makin (1994), and Komaki et al. (1978) all observed approximately 25% increases in site safety behaviors following the introduction of a behavioral safety process, and Lee et al. (2014) reported slightly higher increases. Fante et al. (2007) demonstrated increases in safety behavior ranging from 40% to 55%, Harper et al. (1996) reported improvements ranging from 2% to 23%, and Fellner and Sulzer-Azaroff (1984) showed a mean improvement of 8% in safe practices following the implementation of a behavioral safety process.

Hazardous Conditions

The products of at-risk behaviors, such as hazardous conditions, can be tracked to demonstrate the effectiveness of a behavioral safety process. Fellner and Sulzer-Azaroff (1984) showed a mean improvement of 6% in safe conditions following the implementation of a behavioral safety process, Lingard and Rowlinson (1998) showed an improvement of up to 10%, and Harper et al. (1996) demonstrated improvements ranging from 2% to 28%.

Safety Process Measures

Safety-related activities, such as frequency of safety observations, hazardous conditions alleviated, and supervisory delivery of feedback, are all important metrics to track during the course of a behavioral safety process, as they are leading indicators of the fidelity of implementation. Cooper (2006) represents a systematic approach to tracking behavioral safety process measures. Over the course of an approximately year-long behavioral safety process, the author reported that over 200 hazardous conditions were identified and that 70% of those were addressed through administrative action. In the same study, observers conducted over 14,000 observations, and that 76-88% of planned observations actually occurred. Management support behaviors (e.g., holding weekly safety meetings, accompanying employee observers during observations) were tracked by employees and occurred as planned 25% of the time. Zohar (2002) increased safety-related interactions between managers and employees and observed simultaneous changes in minor-injury rate, earplug use, and safety climate scores. Finally, Lebbon et al. (2012) tracked number of observations across 5 years of implementation and found a negative correlation between observation frequency and injuries.

SPECIAL CONSIDERATIONS IN BEHAVIORAL SAFETY

Behavioral safety has historically received criticism for ignoring root causes of injuries, suppressing injury reporting, and setting up a system that promotes "spying" on employees (Mathis, 2009). Some unions have also voiced reservations about behavioral safety. Below, we cite studies that show that behavioral safety processes that are truly informed by behavioral science can address these issues as a part of implementation (Wirth & Sigurdsson, 2008) and that processes that led to these criticisms do not represent the core philosophies of behavioral safety (Mathis, 2009).

Addressing Root Causes of Injuries

A common argument against behavioral safety states that by focusing on behavior, the blame for injuries is put on the individual employee (Hermann et al., 2010; Mathis, 2009). From a behavioral perspective, the problem can be reconceptualized as to whether the environment supports safe behavior or not (see above). As mentioned earlier, Hermann et al. used behavioral principles to manage traditional safety responsibilities of managers, such as consistently conducting injury investigations, consistent identification and correction of hazardous conditions, and consistently chairing weekly safety talks. Cooper (2006) provided another excellent demonstration of how managerial and supervisory behaviors can be tracked and managed through behavioral procedures (see above). However, Harper et al. (1996) reported that situations may arise in which safety may suffer as a result of management and employees placing production priorities first, despite a stated commitment to safety at the outset of the process.

Suppression of Injury Reporting

Providing incentives for injury-free periods has been criticized for leading to nonreporting of injuries (Mathis, 2009). That is, group-based incentives for no injuries may lead to group pressure not to report an injury. Even though steps can be taken to reduce the likelihood that injuries are not reported (e.g., Alavosius et al., 2009; Fox et al., 1987; Hermann et al., 2010), we recommend extreme caution in using incentives for injury-free periods in a behavioral safety process and suggest that alternative behavior change strategies be used (e.g., reinforcement of safety milestone achievements).

Privacy of Data

Employees often voice concerns that data collected as a part of a behavioral safety process will be used to "write up" violators and that behavioral safety data will feed into progressive discipline systems for the purpose of ridding the organization of employees. To address these concerns, checklists may be designed so as not to include the name of the employee observed, employees may opt out of being observed, or managers may sign letters of support for the process that include a stipulation that any data gathered will not be used for disciplinary purposes or for employment decisions (Lebbon et al., 2012). Another example, provided by Harper et al. (1996), collected results of separate checklist items which were not presented to managers without the informed consent of employee representatives.

Union Involvement in the Process

To increase employee buy-in of a behavioral safety process, some researchers have included unions in development and implementation. For example, in Hermann et al. (2010), the site union stated that it would not support any workers who did not report injuries, and in Ray et al. (1997), union representatives conducted safety training, initiated the safety process, and developed goal levels.

SUMMARY

The application of behavior analysis to safety is an active field with a long history. Its future may be even more impressive; job opportunities for safety specialists, particularly those with advanced degrees, are expected to be good in the coming decade (United States Bureau of Labor Statistics, 2011). Behavioral safety provides an evidence-based method of managing safety concerns. In addition, the workforce in many developed countries is aging, and people are postponing retirement. This, along with an increase in compensation and insurance costs for many organizations, will create a number of new opportunities for those in the field of behavioral safety.

REFERENCES

Abellon, O. E., & Wilder, D. A. (2014). The effect of equipment proximity on safe performance in a manufacturing setting. *Journal of Applied Behavior Analysis*, *47*(3), 628–632.

ABS Consulting. (2005). *Root cause analysis handbook: A guide to effective incident investigation.* Brookfield, CT: Rothstein Associates.

Agnew, J. L., & Snyder, G. (2002). *Removing obstacles to safety.* Tucker, GA: Performance Management Publications.

Alavosius, M. P., Getting, J., Dagen, J., Newsome, W. D., & Hopkins, B. (2009). Use of a cooperative to interlock contingencies and balance the commonwealth. *Journal of Organizational Behavior Management*, *29*, 193–211.

Alavosius, M. P., & Sulzer-Azaroff, B. (1986). The effects of performance feedback on the safety of client lifting and transfer. *Journal of Applied Behavior Analysis*, *19*, 261–267.

Alvero, A. M., & Austin, J. (2004). The effects of conducting behavioral observations on the behavior of the observer. *Journal of Applied Behavior Analysis*, *37*(4), 457–468.

Alvero, A. M., Struss, K., & Rappaport, E. (2007). Measuring safety performance: A comparison of whole, partial, and momentary time-sampling recording methods. *Journal of Organizational Behavior Management*, *27*(4), 1–28.

Austin, J., Alvero, A. M., & Olson, R. (1998). Prompting patron safety belt use at a restaurant. *Journal of Applied Behavior Analysis*, *31*, 655–657.

Austin, J., Hackett, S., Gravina, N., & Lebbon, A. (2006). The effects of prompting and feedback on drivers stopping at stop signs. *Journal of Applied Behavior Analysis*, *39*, 117–121.

Carr, J. E., Wilder, D. A., Majdalany, L., Mathisen, D., & Strain, L. (2013). An assessment-based solution to a human-service employee performance problem: An initial evaluation of the performance diagnostic checklist-human services. *Behavior Analysis in Practice*, *6*, 16–32.

Casella, S., Wilder, D., Neidert, P., Rey, C., Compton, M., & Chong, I. (2010). The effects of response effort on safe performance by therapists at an autism treatment facility. *Journal of Applied Behavior Analysis*, *43*, 729–734.

Cooper, M. D. (2006). Exploratory analyses of the effects of managerial support and feedback consequences on behavioral safety maintenance. *Journal of Organizational Behavior Management*, *26*(3), 1–41.

Cooper, M. D., Phillips, R. A., Sutherland, V. J., & Makin, P. J. (1994). Reducing accidents using goal setting and feedback: A field study. *Journal of Occupational and Organizational Psychology*, *67*, 219–240.

Cox, B. S., Cox, A. B., & Cox, D. J. (2000). Motivating signage prompts safety belt use among drivers exiting senior communities. *Journal of Applied Behavior Analysis, 33,* 635–638.

Cox, C. D., Cox, B. S., & Cox, D. J. (2005). Long-term benefits of prompts to use safety belts among drivers exiting senior communities. *Journal of Applied Behavior Analysis, 38,* 533–536.

Culig, K. M., Dickinson, A. M., Lindstrom-Hazel, D., & Austin, J. (2008). Combining workstation design and performance management to increase ergonomically correct computer typing postures. *Journal of Organizational Behavior Management, 28*(3), 146–175.

Cunningham, T. R., & Geller, E. S. (2012). A comprehensive approach to identifying intervention targets for patient-safety improvement in a hospital setting. *Journal of Organizational Behavior Management, 32*(2), 194–220.

Daniels, A. C., & Daniels, J. E. (2006). *Performance management: Changing behavior that drives organizational effectiveness* (4th, revised). Atlanta, GA: Performance Management Publications.

Ditzian, K., Wilder, D., King, A., & Tanz, J. (2015). An evaluation of the performance diagnostic checklist-human services to assess an employee performance problem in a center-based autism treatment facility. *Journal of Applied Behavior Analysis, 48,* 199–203.

Engerman, J. A., Austin, J., & Bailey, J. S. (1997). Prompting patron safety belt use at a supermarket. *Journal of Applied Behavior Analysis, 30,* 577–579.

Fante, R., Gravina, N., & Austin, J. (2007). A brief pre-intervention analysis and demonstration of the effects of a behavioral safety package on postural behaviors of pharmacy employees. *Journal of Organizational Behavior Management, 27*(2), 15–25.

Fante, R., Gravina, N., Betz, A., & Austin, J. (2010). Structural and treatment analyses of safe and at-risk behaviors and postures performed by pharmacy employees. *Journal of Organizational Behavior Management, 30*(4), 325–338.

Fellner, D. J., & Sulzer-Azaroff, B. (1984). Increasing industrial safety practices and conditions through posted feedback. *Journal of Safety Research, 15*(1), 7–21.

Fellner, D. J., & Sulzer-Azaroff, B. (1986). Occupational safety: Assessing the impact of adding assigned or participative goal-setting. *Journal of Organizational Behavior Management, 7,* 3–24.

Fox, D. K., Hopkins, B. L., & Anger, W. K. (1987). The long-term effects of a token economy on safety performance in open-pit mining. *Journal of Applied Behavior Analysis, 20*(3), 215–224.

Geller, E. S. (2001). *The psychology of safety handbook.* Boca Raton, FL: CRC Press.

Goomas, D. (2012). Immediate feedback on accuracy and performance: The effects of wireless technology on food safety tracking at a distribution center. *Journal of Organizational Behavior Management, 32*(4), 320–328.

Harper, A. C., Gunson, C., Robinson, L., de Klerk, N. H., Osborn, D., Sevastos, P., et al. (1996). Curtin industrial safety trial: Methods and safe practice and housekeeping outcomes. *Safety Science, 24*(3), 159–172.

Heinrich, H. W. (1931). *Industrial accident prevention: A scientific approach.* New York: McGraw-Hill.

Heinrich, H. W., Petersen, D., & Roos, N. (1980). *Industrial accident prevention* (5th). New York, NY: McGraw-Hill.

Hermann, J. A., Ibarra, G. V., & Hopkins, B. L. (2010). A safety program that integrated behavior-based safety and traditional safety methods and its effects on injury rates of manufacturing workers. *Journal of Organizational Behavior Management, 30*(1), 6–25.

Hickman, J. S., & Geller, E. S. (2003). Self-management to increase safe driving. *Journal of Organizational Behavior Management, 23*(4), 1–20.

International Ergonomics Association. (2014). *What is ergonomics.* Website. Retrieved from: http://www.iea.cc/whats/index.html. 8 April.

Killimett, P. T. (1991). The identification of critical behaviors: The first step in a behavior-based safety process. *Tappi Journal, 74,* 251–253.

Komaki, J., Barwick, K. D., & Scott, L. R. (1978). A behavioral approach to occupational safety: Pinpointing and reinforcing safe performance in a food manufacturing plant. *Journal of Applied Psychology, 63*(4), 434–445.

Krause, T. R. (1997). *The behavior-based safety process* (2nd). New York, NY: John Wiley & Sons.

Krause, T. R., Seymour, K. J., & Sloat, K. C. M. (1999). Long-term evaluation of a behavior-based method for improving safety performance: A meta-analysis of 73 interrupted time-series replications. *Safety Science, 32,* 1–18.

Lebbon, A., Sigurdsson, S. O., & Austin, J. (2012). Behavioral safety in the food industry: Challenges and outcomes. *Journal of Organizational Behavior Management, 32,* 44–57.

Lee, K., Shon, D., & Oah, S. (2014). The relative effects of global and specific feedback on safety behaviors. *Journal of Organizational Behavior Management, 34*(1), 16–28.

Leigh, P. (2011). Economic burden of occupational injury and illness in the United States. *The Milbank Quarterly, 89,* 728–772.

Lingard, H., & Rowlinson, S. (1998). Behaviour-based safety management in Hong Kong's construction industry: The results of a field study. *Construction Management and Economics, 16*(4), 481–488.

Ludwig, T. D., Biggs, J., Wagner, S., & Geller, E. S. (2002). Using public feedback and competitive rewards to increase the safe driving of pizza deliverers. *Journal of Organizational Behavior Management, 21*(4), 75–104.

Ludwig, T. D., & Geller, E. S. (1999). Behavior change among agents of a community safety program. *Journal of Organizational Behavior Management, 19*(2), 3–24.

Mathis, T. L. (2009). Managing safety: Unions and behavior-based safety: The 7 deadly sins. *EHS Today.* Retrieved from, http://search.proquest.com/docview/224606531?accountid=27313.

McSween, T. E. (2003). *The values-based safety process.* Hoboken, NJ: John Wiley & Sons.

Moon, K., & Oah, S. (2013). A comparison of the effects of feedback and prompts on safe sitting posture: Utilizing an automated observation and feedback system. *Journal of Organizational Behavior Management, 33*(2), 152–162.

Myers, W. V., McSween, T. E., Medina, R. E., Rost, K., & Alvero, A. (2010). The implementation and maintenance of a behavioral safety process in a petroleum refinery. *Journal of Organizational Behavior Management, 30*(4), 285–307.

National Safety Council. (2013). http://www.mhi.org/downloads/industrygroups/ease/technicalpapers/2013-National-Safety-Council-Injury-Facts.pdf. Retrieved from July 21, 2014.

Nielsen, D., Sigurdsson, S. O., & Austin, J. (2009). Preventing back injuring in hospital settings: The effects of video modeling on safe patient lifting by nurses. *Journal of Applied Behavior Analysis, 42*(3), 551–561.

Olson, R., & Austin, J. (2001). Behavior-based safety and working alone: The effects of a self-monitoring package on the safe performance of bus operators. *Journal of Organizational Behavior Management, 21*(3), 5–43.

Ray, P. S., Bishop, P. A., & Wang, M. Q. (1997). Efficacy of the components of a behavioral safety program. *International Journal of Industrial Ergonomics, 19,* 19–29.

Rudd, J. R., & Geller, E. S. (1985). A university-based incentive program to increase safety belt use: Toward cost-effective institutionalization. *Journal of Applied Behavior Analysis, 18,* 215–226.

Sasson, J. R., & Austin, J. (2005). The effects of training, feedback, and participant involvement in behavioral safety observations on office ergonomic behavior. *Journal of Organizational Behavior Management, 24*(4), 1–30.

Scherrer, M., & Wilder, D. (2008). Training to increase safe tray carrying among cocktail servers. *Journal of Applied Behavior Analysis, 41*, 131–135.

Skinner, B. F. (1953). *Science and human behavior.* New York, NY: The Free Press/MacMillan Company.

Smith, M. J., Anger, W. K., & Uslan, S. S. (1978). Behavioral modification applied to occupational safety. *Journal of Safety Research, 10*, 87–88.

Sowers-Hoag, K. M., Thyer, B. A., & Bailey, J. S. (1987). Promoting automobile safety belt use by young children. *Journal of Applied Behavior Analysis, 20*, 133–138.

Stajkovic, A. D., & Luthans, F. (1997). A meta-analysis of the effects of organizational behavior modification on task performance, 1975-95. *Academy of Management Journal, 40*, 1122–1149.

Stephens, S., & Ludwig, T. (2005). Improving anesthesia nurse compliance with universal precautions using group goals and public feedback. *Journal of Organizational Behavior Management, 25*(2), 37–71.

Sulzer-Azaroff, B., & De Santamaria, M. C. (1980). Industrial safety hazard reduction through performance feedback. *Journal of Applied Behavior Analysis, 13*(2), 287–295.

Sulzer-Azaroff, B., Loafman, B., Merante, R. J., & Hlavacek, A. C. (1990). Improving occupational safety in a large industrial plant: A systematic replication. *Journal of Organizational Behavior Management, 11*(1), 99–120.

Taylor, M. A., & Alvero, A. M. (2012). The effects of safety discrimination training and frequent safety observations on safety-related behavior. *Journal of Organizational Behavior Management, 32*(3), 169–193.

United States Bureau of Labor Statistics. (2011). *Occupational outlook handbook.* Retrieved from, http://www.bls.gov/ooh/healthcare/occupational-health-and-safety-specialists.htm#tab-6.

United States Bureau of Labor Statistics, Occupational Employment. (2013). Survey, http://www.bls.gov/oes/tables.htm.

Van Houten, R., Malenfant, J. E. L., Austin, J., & Lebbon, A. (2005). The effects of a seatbelt gearshift delay prompt on the seatbelt use of motorists who do not regularly wear seatbelts. *Journal of Applied Behavior Analysis, 38*, 195–203.

Van Houten, R. V., Malenfant, J. E. L., Reagan, I., Sifrit, K., Compton, R., & Tenenbaum, J. (2010). Increasing seat belt use in service vehicles with a gearshift delay. *Journal of Applied Behavior Analysis, 43*, 369–380.

Wirth, O., & Sigurdsson, S. O. (2008). When workplace safety depends on behavior change: Topics for behavioral safety research. *Journal of Safety Research, 39*, 589–598.

Yeaton, W. H., & Bailey, J. S. (1978). Utilization analysis of a pedestrian safety program. *Journal of Applied Behavior Analysis, 16*, 203–216.

Yu, E., Moon, K., Oah, S., & Lee, Y. (2013). An evaluation of the effectiveness of an automated observation and feedback system on safe sitting postures. *Journal of Organizational Behavior Management, 33*(2), 104–127.

Zohar, D. (2002). Modifying supervisory practices to improve subunit safety: A leadership-based intervention model. *Journal of Applied Psychology, 87*(1), 156–163.

Zohar, D., Cohen, A., & Azar, N. (1980). Promoting increased use of ear protectors in noise through information feedback. *Human Factors, 22*(1), 69–79.

CHAPTER 24

Organizational Behavior Management: An Enabler of Applied Behavior Analysis[*]

Timothy D. Ludwig
Department of Psychology, Appalachian State University, Boone, North Carolina, USA

The growth in clinical behavior analysis has been encouraged by its successes in treating behaviors related to autism and other developmental disabilities. Sharing in this success has been the advance of behavior analysis in education where schools and academies offer accelerated learning paths to families who join waiting lists to receive this benefit. In both settings, the market of clients has grown to record levels. In response, clinics have expanded, staff have been hired and trained, and the business of behavior analysis (BA) has become an industry. Applied behavior analysis resides in an industry that relies unequivocally on the front-line provider of behavior analytic services. Such a service industry, like all others, finds itself challenged to maintain the level of performance in their employees required to realize the benefits of behavior analytic offerings.

Consider the employee who directly supplies behavioral analytic services to clients. This person sets the context for interactions, trains, delivers prompts and reinforcers on a planned schedule, graphs behaviors, and produces reports. If any of these are done poorly, then the efficacy of behavior analysis to achieve client goals is greatly diminished.

Let's consider a scenario in which an employee is sitting with a clinic supervisor during a regular performance appraisal. The supervisor is reviewing reports generated by the employee and notes that they were incomplete and not very well done and are thereby harming the clinic because accreditation and insurance audits may find fault with the incomplete records. The employee is sent away with an exhortation to "do better." The next quarter

[*] More information on Organizational Behavior Management can be found at OBMNetwork.com and at the website hosting the *Journal of Organizational Behavior Management*, www.tandfonline.com/toc/worg20/current.

Clinical and Organizational Applications of Applied Behavior Analysis
http://dx.doi.org/10.1016/B978-0-12-420249-8.00024-1

the supervisor and employee find themselves in the same situation, citing the same problems. However, this time both are more frustrated. The supervisor has begun to suspect that the employee is "lazy" or otherwise not able to perform to standard. The employee is seeking other employment, thus contributing to the continuing high turnover in the clinic. In fact, there may be a number of undesirable side effects whereby the employee may be decreasing performance in other areas or actively sabotaging the clinic's processes (Ludwig, 2002).

Our problem here is that, while experts in behavior analysis, these clinics are not applying behavior analysis to the management of their staff. Staff performance is maintained by the same behavior analytic principles that we apply to clients. Yet this simple fact escapes many who revert to traditional management techniques, such as the performance appraisal, which can be inadequate in managing contingencies (Daniels, 2009). However, behavior analysts need only to look to their own field for help.

The field of organizational behavior management (OBM) studies and applies behavior analytic techniques to assess and intervene in organizational problems (Frederiksen, 1982; Johnson, Mawhinney, & Redmon, 2001; Luthans & Kreitner, 1985; O'Brien, Dickinson, & Rosow, 1982). Indeed, OBM, for more than 30 years, has produced robust evidence (its flagship journal, the *Journal of Organizational Behavior Management*, is publishing its 30th volume) that behavior analytic principles can change human behavior in the workplace.

It is too easy to "blame the worker" and focus solely on the inadequacies of employee behavior as if the employee intended not to comply with the work process, as much of the literature in industrial/organizational psychology, the champion of performance appraisals, would have us believe (Brown, Cron, & Slocum, 1998; Cervone, Jiwani, & Wood, 1991; Tubbs, 1994). Thus, organizations expend too much effort to fix employees through selection and training in the absence of sound behavioral principles.

In OBM we do not blame the worker. We apply Skinner's rationale that the subject is always right. "I remember the rage I used to feel when predictions went awry. I could have shouted at the subjects of my experiments, 'Behave, damn you! Behave as you ought!' Eventually I realized that the subjects were always right. They always behaved as they should have behaved. It was I who was wrong" (Skinner, 1948, p. 240). The management "guru" Deming (1982) suggested that 94% of organizational problems are attributed to the inefficient systems in which employees operate. Managing the worker with exhortations to "do better" without fundamentally fixing the system is an ineffective way to manage an organization. Rummler and Branche (1995) stated that an organization is only as effective as its processes. Because of this, bad processes within the organization can limit strong employees. An employee cannot compensate for a flawed process. Rummler and Branche noted that most employees want to perform their job well but may be unable to due to systemic constraints. Thus, the quality of employee output is a function of the quality of the system components and the interlocking contingencies based on the interactions guided by the systems.

Behaviors enacted throughout the system, by managers, insurance contacts, clients, and other staff, influence the behavior of the service provider. In these metacontingencies, individual behaviors of one person in the organization (e.g., a manager) serve as antecedents and consequences for others' behavior (Clayton, Mawhinney, Luke, & Cook, 1997; Glenn, 1988, 1991; Mawhinney, 1992). To understand these often-complex metacontingencies, we need to define the interlocking behavioral contingencies, what they produce, and who receives these products of behavior (Glenn & Malott, 2004). Each member of a clinic, an outside agency, or other group influences the behaviors of behavior analytic service providers. Reciprocally, the service provider behaviors reinforce or punish the behaviors of these other members. Over time, these reciprocal social consequences will further adapt employee behaviors thereby creating group behavior that can be hard to change (Clayton et al., 1997). The interlocking behavioral contingencies continue to maintain individual and, as a composite, a clinic's ability to serve its clients.

To break through the complexity of organizational metacontingencies, Ludwig and Houmanfar (2010), Malott (2003), McGee and Diener (2010), McGee and Diener-Ludwig (2012), and Hyten (2009), among others, argue that an organization's internal system, processes, and business environment must be considered as the strongest context of behavioral contingencies and subsequent interlocking contingencies. By analyzing the system in this way, the analyst can then better understand the true contingencies governing employee behavior. Therefore, system assessment may be a first step in any organizational improvement initiative (Rummler & Branche, 1995), including those offered by OBM (Hyten, 2009; McGee & Diener-Ludwig, 2012).

BEHAVIORAL SYSTEMS ANALYSIS

System theory, with references as far back as 1931 (Baridon & Loomis, 1931), is interested in problems related to relationships, structure, and interdependence of organizational and human functions (Hall & Fagen, 1956; Katz & Kahn, 1966; Miller, 1971; Weiss, 1971). As behavior analysis began to consider human performer's behavior in the context of a system, Harshbarger and Maley (1974) and Malott (1974) began referring to this brand of systems theory as behavioral systems analysis (BSA). Ludwig and Houmanfar (2010) emphasized in their introduction to BSA in special issues of the *Journal of Organizational Behavior Management* that "systems are adaptive entities that survive by meeting environmental demands (consumers, competition, economy, governmental policies, etc.) through the development and maintenance of subsystems ultimately designed to manage behavior. Thus, organizations are behavioral systems that encompass complex patterns of behavioral interactions among its members and the environment" (p. 85). BSA seeks to understand these complex response patterns in the context of critical aspects of the organizational system. Through this process, we can better manipulate the relationships between the organization and behavioral contingencies.

To emphasize this parsimony, Brethower (1972, 1982, 2001) and Brethower and Dams (1999) developed a systems model called the total performance system (TPS) which represented a "map" of an organization defining how it received inputs, added value by processing these inputs to outputs, and how those outputs were received by the next system (e.g., another individual, business function, or, ultimately, consumers). The TPS interactions are regulated by feedback from the processing system as well as feedback from the receiving system. A similar systems model was created by Rummler (Rummler, 2004, 2001; Rummler & Branche, 1995) who described three levels within organizations where systemic relationships exist: an organizational level that incorporates the company goals or strategy; a process level such as workflow or information flow across functional departments that make up the organization; and a job/performer level focusing on the behavior of individual employees and managers.

The organizational level of performance emphasizes the organization's relationship with outside environments, internal structure, and distribution of resources. As a first step in assessing a behavior analysis service clinic, we would outline the inputs to the system that may include referring agencies, insurance companies, BCBA providers, behavior analytic researchers, curriculum providers, and the like. Next, environmental influences such as government regulations would be considered along with other entities that compete for resources such as other behavior analysis clinics, psychology service providers, and the medical community. The largest consideration is focused on the receiving system of clients, families, and communities that the clinic serves. We must assure that our contingency management schemes focus on delivering quality products and services to our customers/clients (Rummler & Branche, 1995). Any other contingencies in the organization would be nonvalue adding.

The processing system focuses on the internal design and structure of the organization that contribute to the throughput of the organization (Rummler & Branche, 1995). We seek to understand how departments interact to complete work and identify where these interactions may be flawed, thereby producing metacontingencies that create the context for suboptimal performance.

Let us consider our behavior analysis service provider whose performance appraisals set the stage for low performance and untimely turnover. We would diagnose the problem by first asking what components of the larger system might impact the context within which they behave (do their job). The behavior analysis service provider is attempting to serve their direct client, say a 5-year-old girl with autism by applying evidence-based behavioral tactics to build communication skills. Note that the employee's behavior is interlocked with her client because her behavior sets the contingencies for the client and the client's behaviors then dictate the employee's future behaviors. If the job were this well designed then the clinic would not have a problem with its service-level employees.

Instead, consider the demands on the behavior of this service-level employee made by the greater system. What do insurance companies require as they audit the services and outcomes of the clinic? These create contingencies for managers who must meet these requirements. The managers behave by building reporting processes to prove that required services were delivered. These reporting processes create contingencies for the service-level employees to engage in a set of behaviors that add content to these reports. We could ask the same set of questions (and we do) that track government regulations through the compliance contingencies on the managers that result in other types of rigid contingencies on the service provider who must also engage in a set of behaviors in this context. Referring agencies, BCBA supervision requirements, and other external system entities all come with their own sets of contingencies that are filtered down, adding to the complexity of the service provider's job.

Internal factors also create metacontingencies that have wide ranging impacts. Businesses attempt to make a profit and not-for-profit organizations must create resources to survive, especially in the context of competitors who are trying to pull clients and their best employees. Financial contingencies shape manager behaviors as they interlock with their service-level employees, thereby requiring the production of client billable hours and procedures. Financial considerations will dictate how much training or modern curricula will be available to employees. Other internal functions such as human resources (HR), information technology (IT), records, and physical plans interlock with these employees. One has to ask (and we do), "do these added contingencies add value by increasing the quality of the service provider's behaviors in their delivery of behavior analysis to the girl with autism?"

By the time we get to the performer, our service provider, you can see all of the systemic contingencies dictating her behavior. As you would a client, you can do an assessment of the behaviors with which the service provider engages. I think you will find that the system was perfectly designed to produce the low quality performance that was discussed in the performance appraisal.

Conducting behavioral observations on the service provider and timing engagement in different activities would reveal that their time is bifurcated across many different tasks, each with different contingent behaviors and schedules. Behaviors occur within time, and time is limited. In the case of our pretend service provider, we may find that, as her shift progressed she would fall behind in her different reporting responsibilities created by the system's metacontingencies. This process would be particularly true if the client or the client's family or representative wanted to speak with her about the client's progress or challenges—another contingency that may not be reinforced by the system and thereby not considered in the client production schedules.

So our service provider's behavior is negatively reinforced by the growing backlog of reporting to spend more time on this reporting to get it done. This, in turn, punishes the behavior of spending time with the client. Less time with the client translates into lower client outcomes that show up on the report. Alternatively, if our service provider spends more time with the client then her time to fill out all the reporting forms is truncated.

However, if the supervisor were managing without a behavioral approach, then he would only look at the limited outcomes, the artifacts of behavior, in an attempt to manage performance. In the end both would be frustrated.

Instead, Diener, McGee, and Miguel (2009) argue that the analysis of the organization outside the basic three-term contingency of antecedents, behaviors, and consequences helps to better identify the variables that can significantly impact individual and organizational performance. Thus, BSA is the first step in developing multilevel solutions that may include OBM interventions, but also process design, automation, changes in policy, changes in resource deployment, strategy development and/or realignment, development of incentive systems, organizational restructuring, and managing the manager initiatives, to name a few (McGee, 2007). As we consider the systemic changes needed to better manage the service provider, we would also begin to look closely at the proximal contingencies of our service provider to determine the best performer-level interventions to shape more desirable behaviors.

FUNCTIONAL ASSESSMENT

The use of a functional assessment for the selection of an intervention has become common practice within the field of OBM over the last couple decades (Austin, Carr, & Agnew, 1999) and has been shown to increase the effectiveness of an OBM intervention such as the one we would create for our service provider. Functional assessment is a method used to pinpoint problem behaviors using informant assessment, descriptive assessment, and experimental analysis (Austin et al., 1999).

Our first goal is to pinpoint the behaviors that are most likely to create outcomes that will benefit the organization. From our previous discussion, we would be most interested in the behaviors that relate directly to the quality of product to the receiving system. In other words, our priority would be targeting the service provider's behaviors that are most related to desirable client outcomes. Hopefully, by this point we have solved some of the system flaws that directed the service provider's behaviors elsewhere through differential reinforcement to minimize competing contingencies.

Austin (2000), Daniels and Bailey (2014), Diener et al. (2009), and Malott (2003) all offered OBM methodologies to "pinpoint" the behaviors and response classes that would be most associated with performance. All spoke of the need to make sure that the resulting behavior is actionable (e.g., passing the dead person test), observable, measurable, and under the control of the employee. Once pinpointed, regular behavioral observations would commence with the employee; you would not intervene on a client without establishing a baseline would you?

Once pinpointed, baseline observations serve as a pretreatment control to show subsequent change due to the intervention. However, more importantly for the functional assessment, baseline observations allow us to find sources of variance in the behavior and understand the potential covariates (Ludwig, 2002). For example, we may find that our service provider maintains desirable levels of pinpointed behaviors early in her shift. However, as the shift lengthens we see more variance in her behaviors where she may begin omitting some behaviors and adapting others. We can then seek to understand why this variance occurs by looking for covariates such as emerging contingencies (e.g., getting behind in completing paperwork), competing behaviors (e.g., talking with clients and their families), or interlocks (e.g., other staff wanting to socialize). Assessing the behavioral variance then leads to a further assessment of the contingencies creating this variance.

A popular assessment tool in OBM has been the performance diagnostic checklist (PDC: Austin, 2000). Using this tool, managers are asked to describe the employee's job, its inputs and desired outputs, and are asked to pinpoint behaviors by considering performance needs and other behaviors competing with the desired performance. Managers also answer questions about antecedents and information, knowledge and skills, equipment and processes, and consequences. Examples include antecedents such as the presence of supervisors or availability of written job descriptions and consequences such as feedback or rewards. The PDC has been used to address cash register shortages (Rohn, Austin, & Lutrey, 2002), promote employee marketing behaviors in restaurants (Rodriguez et al., 2005), establish setup of machines used in physical therapy (Gravina, VanWagner, & Austin, 2008), and assess behaviors involved in maintenance tasks (Pampino, Heering, Wilder, Barton, & Burson, 2003).

The functional analysis method most prominent in OBM has been the traditional antecedent-behavior-consequence (ABC) contingency analysis (Petrock, 1978), most often applied as the popular PIC/NIC analysis offered by Daniels and Bailey (2014). Such analyzes first pinpoint the behavior to be analyzed, and then analysts identify the antecedents that may prompt the behavior or act as discriminant stimuli for the full contingency. Finally, through the same methodology, the consequences of the behavior are listed and evaluated based on the fundamental behavioral principles such as reinforcing versus punishing, immediate versus delayed, and certain versus uncertain types of consequences. This process is repeated for each class of behaviors and would include existing systemic metacontingencies if still present.

A good ABC analysis will also analyze the three-term contingency for competing or alternative behaviors (those exhibited instead of the target behavior). Amigo, Smith, and Ludwig (2008), Doll, Livesey, McHaffie, and Ludwig (2007) and Rose and Ludwig (2009) used the PIC/NIC analysis to identify the contingencies dictating the lack of cleaning behaviors in various settings. For a more empirically based approach to the ABC analysis, the reader is referred to the structural assessment method demonstrated by Fante, Gravina, and Austin (2007) to assess and intervene upon ergonomic safety.

Too often, the OBM assessor will conduct the ABC or PDC without going to the trouble of a more systemic analysis. This behavior on the part of the OBM assessor is influenced by the fact that the BSA can take a lot more time and effort than the more proximal ABC assessments. The response cost of a full systemic assessment may be too great and the assessment therefore only includes the proximal ABC analysis.

Critics of the ABC and PDC conclude that these assessments rely on informant assessments relying heavily on manager, employee, and researcher perceptions of environmental variables instead of understanding the performance problem in the context of the organizational system that, ultimately, influences the target behaviors through its associated contingencies (Hyten, 2009). By ignoring the systemic context where the performance problem lies we would not concurrently manage the interlocking contingencies between parts of that system nor would we understand the leverage points to make changes to affect the system's performance (Hyten, 2009). Instead, by combining behavioral system analysis (BSA) with the proximal ABC contingency analyzes, we can better design interventions for lasting change while preventing unintended adverse effects (see Mihalic & Ludwig, 2009).

A BSA and ABC on our service provider may indeed pinpoint behaviors that reflect her use of time during daily shifts. There may be plenty of system-based antecedents that created variance in the schedule such as families wanting consults, and competing demands of other functions (insurance, HR, IT, agencies, government, etc.) such as those discussed earlier. Moreover, observational data showed that these demands appear randomly throughout the shift via e-mail, texts, and personal communication. Other more proximal antecedents may include other staff socializing, smart phone availability, and the like. Establishing operations (Laraway, Snycerski, Michael, & Poling, 2003; Olson, Laraway, & Austin, 2001) such as fatigue as the shift wears on, may also influence the behavior. The consequences of the current behavior (i.e., attending to all these demands) resulted in immediate reinforcers in the form of family interactions and the negative reinforcement effect of complying with the demands of other functions to "get them off her back."

The OBM assessments would then lead us to pinpoint the behavior(s) that would result in improved performance. The clinic supervisor wants the service provider to fully complete the clinical reports with client behavioral data. He wants important information documented for the clinical staff and, most importantly, he wants to see client data showing improvement in the skills being trained. We now know that the service providers' behaviors were being directed toward less client focused activities that would appear randomly throughout the shift.

To solve this behavioral problem, a new class of behaviors needs to be shaped. The pinpointed behavior may focus on the use of a daily scheduler to plan for client interaction sessions with some variance for client/family discussions. Then, directly after, the plan would call for a set period of the required reporting. Antecedents directing this type of planning were most likely nonexistent. The consequences of daily planning have never been experienced. Therefore, our next step is to intervene in this organizational system, within its work groups, and with its performers to build new behaviors and their maintaining contingencies.

The purpose of the functional assessments in OBM is to understand the contingencies maintaining current performance before designing and implementing an intervention aimed at adapting organizational contingencies to improve performance. OBM has a long scholarly history of demonstrating the efficacy of different intervention tactics that have been put to very effective use by OBM practitioners.

OBM INTERVENTIONS

Effective interventions based on these assessments leverage key contingencies that impact performance. These interventions can offer new processes across many subsystems that ultimately impact the antecedents and consequences of managerial, support staff, and employee behaviors contributing to performance improvement.

Process-Level Strategies

System process-level interventions create or adapt processes that still accomplish organizational goals while at the same time better manage the contingencies of the different performers who interact with that process and interlock with each other. Gravinese and Ludwig (2007) investigated the excessive latency of call bell response time of nursing home staff. Their assessment showed that other staff responsibilities, especially during feeding time, kept the staff engaged in behaviors that competed with responding to call bells, a response that, by law, must occur within 2 min. The solution was to adapt the staffing process so that one person would be assigned to call bell responses during high activity times such as during client feeding. Response time means fell below the 2-min goal, and prevalence of excessive latencies decreased substantially.

Blasingame, Hale, and Ludwig (2014) determined that welder non-productive time reduced the number of welded products they were able to complete in a shift. This lack of productivity on the part of the welders, created, in turn, idle time for the painters whose job it was to finish the products before shipping. OBM assessments showed that when welders did complete their tasks they would have to call a supervisor to retrieve their next product from the manufacturing part of the plant. It often took supervisors as much as 10 min to deliver products during which time problematic habits were shaped in the welders (e.g., taking extra breaks or socializing with colleagues) that, inevitably, resulted in additional delays and decreases in production. Blasingame et al. (2014) reported on the implementation of a new process whereby new behaviors were shaped in the welders to alert their managers 10 min before completion so that the next product could be retrieved just-in-time. Welder production increased, as did product cycle time.

One of the most successful process-based interventions documented in the OBM literature and marketed by OBM practitioners is what has come to be known as Behavior-Based Safety (Boyce & Geller, 2001; Hermann, Ibarra, & Hopkins, 2010; McSween, 1995; Myers, McSween, Medina, Rost, & Alvero, 2010). The behavioral safety process approach to decreasing occupational injury builds a process to encourage employee involvement, peer observations, and feedback (Gravina, Lindstrom-Hazel, & Austin, 2006). Most variations of behavioral safety consist of a process encouraging peer-to-peer observations and feedback. In this method, employees observe each other's behavior while on the job and record the results on a behavioral checklist. Observers then discuss the results with the employee and provide praise for safe behavior and corrective feedback for at-risk behaviors. Behavioral checklists are collected and analyzed to identify and intervene on the causes of the at-risk behaviors (Sulzer-Azaroff & Austin, 2000). The behavioral safety process has been shown to be effective within the human service industry across numerous studies (e.g., Alavosius & Sulzer-Azaroff, 1985, 1986, 1990; Babcock, Sulzer-Azaroff, Sanderson, & Scibek, 1992; DeVries, Burnette, & Redirion, 1991; Fleming & Sulzer-Azaroff, 1992; Stephens & Ludwig, 2005; Sulzer-Azaroff & Alavosius, 1988).

Alternatively, OBM interventions can directly target the performers themselves through targeted individual or group treatments or operations.

The "tool bag" of interventions contains numerous items. A taxonomy of behavior change techniques has been offered (Geller, Berry, et al., 1990; Geller, Ludwig, Gilmore, & Berry, 1990; Ludwig & Geller, 2000) and numerous reviews have documented the prevalence of these techniques in the research records (Nolan, Jarema, & Austin, 1999; VanStelle et al., 2012).

Antecedent-Based Strategies

Adapting or introducing new antecedents is often the cheapest intervention strategy because they can be implemented with large groups of people, typically during relatively short time frames. While moderately effective by themselves, they are most effective when paired with consequences. Therefore, many of the documented interventions using antecedent strategies also include consequence-based strategies.

Task clarification is a method that simply specifies the desirable behavior to the performer. It is often used with consequence-based strategies to improve behaviors (Anderson, Crowell, Hantula, & Siroky, 1988; Austin, Weatherly, & Gravina, 2005; Pampino et al., 2003). Similarly, a prompt is an antecedent to behavior and serves as a reminder that will initiate a desired behavior or chain of behaviors. Prompts have been used successfully to train successful software use (Karlsson & Chase, 1996), to increase sales (Martinko, White, & Hassell, 1989; Milligan & Hantula, 2005; Mueller, Moore, Tingstrom, & Doggett, 2001), and to improve cleanliness (Clayton & Blaskewicz, 2012) and safety (Clayton & Myers, 2008; Moon & Oah, 2013), to name just a few.

Goals often serve as the discriminative stimulus occasioning the behavior and specifying the consequence. Goal setting is an antecedent strategy that is often paired with consequence-based strategies such as feedback and/or incentives. Goal setting has been used with some efficacy in the human service industry (Calpin, Edelstein, & Redmon, 1988; Huberman & O'Brien, 1999; Johnson & Frederiksen, 1984; Langeland, Johnson, & Mawhinney, 1997).

Behavioral checklists have gotten much attention in the business world with the publication by a former surgeon (Gawande, 2010) of *The Checklist Manifesto*, which has its roots in OBM (Gravina & Cunningham, 2010; McSween, 2010; Smith, 2010). There are a number of examples from the human service industry where the use of checklists improved staff performance and safety, again, often paired with consequence strategies (Bacon, Fulton, & Malott, 1983; Gravina et al., 2008; Porterfield, Evans, & Blunden, 1985).

Perhaps the most pervasively misused antecedent strategy in the business world is training. Too often it focuses on building "competencies" without incorporating methods to build behavioral "skills" through guided practice and reinforcement. Brethower and Smalley (1998) documented effective behavioral methods of training in organizations in his book *Performance-Based Instruction* (1998). The effective use of training in human services setting has been demonstrated by Fleming, Oliver, and Bolton (1996), Haberlin, Beauchamp, Agnew, and O'Brien (2012), Miller and Lewin (1980), and Krumhus and Malott (1980). In these training methods, modeling, role playing practice, and feedback are prominent tactics used. For example, Catania, Almeida, Liu-Constant, and DiGennaro Reed (2009) used video modeling within training to improve human services staff discrete trial instruction behaviors.

There are certainly dozens more antecedent strategies that can be used to manage behavior in organizational settings. Supervisory statements prompt and set goals, industrial processes create work flow patterns that automatically direct future behaviors, and handheld "smart" technologies can be exploited in a number of ways to provide antecedents (Goomas & Ludwig, 2007; Ludwig & Goomas, 2007).

Consequence-Based Strategies

Consequence-based strategies are typically introduced with proper antecedents that provide discriminative stimuli to occasion the behavior and to facilitate the reinforcement of the behavior. While numerous, we will review the most prominently researched methods here.

The use of performance feedback is so widely accepted in the field of OBM that its prevalence and implementation has been the topic of a number of literature reviews (Alvero, Bucklin, & Austin, 2001; Balcazar, Shupert, Daniels, Mawhinney, & Hopkins, 1989; Nolan et al., 1999). In a study of research articles published in the *Journal of Organizational Behavior Management* over a 10-year period, Nolan et al. (1999) reported that in 71% of the articles performance feedback was used in some form, increasing 21% from a review performed 10 years prior (Balcazar et al., 1989). Performance feedback has, in fact, been successfully implemented through multiple mediums, using a variety of contingencies and across numerous organizational settings (Alvero et al., 2001).

In the review conducted by Balcazar et al. (1989), one of the most significant findings was that the addition of rewards and/or goal setting to performance feedback increased its effectiveness. In a more recent review, feedback plus goal setting was found to be the most consistently effective (Alvero et al., 2001). Furthermore, private feedback was shown to be more consistently effective than public feedback. The most commonly used frequency for feedback was weekly and was shown to be effective 52% of the time. The supervisor was identified as the most common source of performance feedback.

Williams, Di Vittorio, and Hausherr (2003) reported on the impact of service providers' self-recording of client outcome data and nonjudgmental feedback during meetings with supervisors. The results showed that correct documentation of scheduled program implementation increased substantially. They then evaluated a combination of this feedback with the introduction of a direct contact level decision making procedure and its effects on program implementation. One could assume that similar methods would be useful with our service provider who, instead of quitting, could demonstrate the same improvements in performance.

Reinforcement is certainly the key to behavior change. Reinforcement can be delivered through incentives, verbal praise, and other methods. When a bank employees' pay became contingent on performance, the performance increased, and there was also a significant decrease in turnover (Dierks & McNally, 1987). Haynes, Pine, and Fitch (1982) showed that the combination of feedback, team competition, and rewards decreased the rate, severity, and costs of accidents among urban transit drivers. Bateman and Ludwig (2003) used goal setting, feedback, and an adapted incentive program to improve performance in a food distribution company and found significant decreases in error-causing behaviors. In their adaptation, the disincentive levied for errors could be avoided if the goal was reached. Miller, Carlson, and Sigurdsson (2014) used a lottery-based incentive to increase the fidelity of discrete trial training procedures. Dickinson and her colleagues have conducted full reviews on the operations of incentives in OBM (Bucklin, McGee, & Dickinson, 2003; Frisch & Dickinson, 1990; Honeywell-Johnson & Dickinson, 1999).

Schedules of reinforcement have also been widely researched in OBM as they apply to the complex climate of concurrent schedules present in the real world (Latham & Huber, 1991). Behavioral economists have noted the strength of different schedules in consumer behavior (Nicholson & Xiao, 2010). When OBM seeks to help in homeland security, its researchers turn to reinforcement schedules (Hogan, Bell, & Olson, 2009). The reinforcement of alternate activities, specifically the differential reinforcement of other behaviors (DRO; Myerson & Hale, 1984), is particularly effective.

CONCLUSIONS

Our service provider would benefit from a new process with multiple components. Based on the assessments of her behavior, the behavioral systems that impact her behaviors, and the more proximal antecedents and consequences contingent on her behavior, we can use OBM to improve her service to her client and the stakeholders of the clinic. A scenario can be built where the clinic service hours could be adapted to systematically sequence the onset of client interaction and reporting. Prompts for other responsibilities dealing with other function demands could either be eliminated and dealt with elsewhere in the system, or they could be scheduled only for the last hour in the day when our service provider would have dedicated time scheduled. Note this arrangement would also help with fatigue by changing the task at the end of the day.

Our service provider would have to learn a new set of behaviors. We could pinpoint the correct use of a personal schedule, model and practice the use of the schedule, provide supervisory prompting, and, at least until fluency has been attained, monitor and provide feedback on planning performance. Other client and reporting behaviors that had been truncated by the existing system may need to be retrained and brought to fluency in the same way (see Williams et al., 2003). A particularly instructive intervention for our hypothetical situation was described by Fleming et al. (1996). Their strategy targeted supervisors in their OBM techniques to build their skills in training their service providers the client teaching skills that would result in the best outcomes. They used all manner of OBM interventions including antecedents such as task clarification, modeling, role-play, feedback, prompts, and goal setting as well as consequences such as praise, behavioral feedback, and outcome feedback. Supervisors were observed using greater amounts of antecedents and consequences in their own interactions with staff that, in turn, showed increases and maintenance in critical client training behaviors.

REFERENCES

Alavosius, M. P., & Sulzer-Azaroff, B. (1985). An on the job method to evaluate patient lifting technique. *Applied Ergonomics, 16*(4), 307–311.
Alavosius, M. P., & Sulzer-Azaroff, B. (1986). The effects of performance feedback on the safety of client lifting and transfer. *Journal of Applied Behavior Analysis, 19*, 261–267.
Alavosius, M. P., & Sulzer-Azaroff, B. (1990). Acquisition and maintenance of health-care routines as a function of feedback density. *Journal of Applied Behavior Analysis, 23*, 151–162.

Alvero, A. M., Bucklin, B. R., & Austin, J. (2001). An objective review of the effectiveness and essential characteristics of performance feedback in organizational settings. *Journal of Organizational Behavior Management, 21*(1), 3–30.

Amigo, S., Smith, A., & Ludwig, T. D. (2008). Using task clarification and feedback to decrease busing times in a franchise pizza restaurant. *Journal of Organizational Behavior Management, 28*(3), 176–187.

Anderson, D. C., Crowell, C. R., Hantula, D. A., & Siroky, L. M. (1988). Task clarification and individual performance posting for improving cleaning in a student-managed university bar. *Journal of Organizational Behavior Management, 9*(1), 73–90.

Austin, J. (2000). Performance analysis and performance diagnostics. In J. Austin, & J. Carr (Eds.), *Handbook of applied behavior analysis* (pp. 304–327). Reno, NV: Context Press.

Austin, J., Carr, J. E., & Agnew, J. A. (1999). The need for measures of maintaining variables in OBM. *Journal of Organizational Behavior Management, 19*(2), 73–90.

Austin, J., Weatherly, N., & Gravina, N. (2005). Using task clarification, graphic feedback, and verbal feedback to increase closing task completion in a privately owned restaurant. *Journal of Applied Behavior Analysis, 38*, 117–120.

Babcock, R., Sulzer-Azaroff, B., Sanderson, M., & Scibek, J. (1992). Increasing nurses' use of feedback to promote infection control practices in a head injury treatment center. *Journal of Applied Behavior Analysis, 25*, 621–627.

Bacon, D. L., Fulton, B. J., & Malott, R. W. (1983). Improving staff performance through the use of task checklists. *Journal of Organizational Behavior Management, 4*(3-4), 17–25.

Balcazar, F. E., Shupert, M. K., Daniels, A. C., Mawhinney, T. C., & Hopkins, B. L. (1989). An objective review and analysis of ten years of publication in the Journal of Organizational Behavior Management. *Journal of Organizational Behavior Management, 10*(1), 7–37.

Baridon, F. E., & Loomis, E. H. (1931). *Personnel problems.* New York: McGraw-Hill.

Bateman, M. J., & Ludwig, T. D. (2003). Managing distribution quality through an adapted incentive program with tiered goals and feedback. *Journal of Organizational Behavior Management, 23*(1), 33–55.

Blasingame, A., Hale, S., & Ludwig, T. D. (2014). The effects of employee-led process design on welder set-up intervals. *Journal of Organizational Behavior Management, 34*(3), 207–222.

Boyce, T. E., & Geller, E. S. (2001). Applied behavior analysis and occupational safety: The challenge of response maintenance. *Journal of Organizational Behavior Management, 21*, 31–60.

Brethower, D. M. (1972). *Behavioral analysis in business and industry: A total performance system.* Kalamazoo, MI: Behaviordelia Inc.

Brethower, D. M. (1982). The total performance system. In R. M. O'Brien, A. M. Dickinson, & M. P. Rosow (Eds.), *Industrial behavior modification: A management handbook* (pp. 350–369). New York: Pergamon Press.

Brethower, D. M. (2001). Managing a person as a system. In L. J. Hayes, J. Austin, R. Houmanfar, & M. C. Clayton (Eds.), *Organizational change* (pp. 89–105). Reno, NV: Context Press.

Brethower, D. M., & Dams, P. C. (1999). Systems thinking (and systems doing). *Performance Improvement, 38*(1), 37–52.

Brethower, D. M., & Smalley, K. (1998). *Performance based instruction: Linking training to business results.* San Francisco: Jossey-Bass.

Brown, S. P., Cron, W. L., & Slocum, J. W. (1998). Effects of trait competitiveness and perceived intra-organizational competition on salesperson goal setting and performance. *Journal of Marketing, 62*(4), 88–98.

Bucklin, B. R., McGee, H. M., & Dickinson, A. M. (2003). The effects of individual monetary incentives with and without feedback. *Journal of Organizational Behavior Management, 23*(2), 65–94.

Calpin, J. P., Edelstein, B., & Redmon, W. K. (1988). Performance feedback and goal setting to improve mental health center staff productivity. *Journal of Organizational Behavior Management*, *9*(2), 35–58.

Catania, C. N., Almeida, D., Liu-Constant, B., & DiGennaro Reed, F. D. (2009). Video modeling to train staff to implement discrete-trial instruction. *Journal of Applied Behavior Analysis*, *42*, 387–392.

Cervone, D., Jiwani, N., & Wood, R. (1991). Goal setting and the differential influence of self-regulatory processes on complex decision-making performance. *Journal of Personality and Social Psychology*, *61*(2), 257–266.

Clayton, M. C., & Blaskewicz, J. (2012). The use of visual prompts to increase the cleanliness of restrooms on a college campus. *Journal of Organizational Behavior Management*, *32*(4), 329–337.

Clayton, M. C., Mawhinney, T. C., Luke, D. E., & Cook, H. G. (1997). Improving the management of overtime costs through decentralized controls: Managing an organizational metacontingency. *Journal of Organizational Behavior Management*, *17*(3), 77–97.

Clayton, M. C., & Myers, E. (2008). Increasing turn signal use by drivers exiting a university parking garage: A comparison of passive and mediated prompting. *Journal of Organizational Behavior Management*, *27*, 53–61.

Daniels, A. (2009). *Oops! 13 management practices that waste time and money (and what to do instead)*. Atlanta, GA: Performance Management Publications.

Daniels, A., & Bailey, J. (2014). *Performance management: Changing behavior that drives organizational effectiveness* (5th). Atlanta: Performance Management.

Deming, W. E. (1982). *Quality, productivity, and competitive position*. Cambridge, MA: Center for Advanced Engineering Study, MIT.

DeVries, J. E., Burnette, M. M., & Redirion, W. K. (1991). AIDS: Improving nurses' compliance with glove wearing through performance feedback. *Journal of Applied Behavior Analysis*, *24*, 705–711.

Diener, L. H., McGee, H. M., & Miguel, C. (2009). An integrated approach to conducting a behavioral systems analysis. *Journal of Organizational Behavior Management*, *29*(2), 108–135.

Dierks, W., & McNally, K. (1987). Incentives you can bank on (Union National Bank applies B.F. Skinner's principles of behavior). *Personnel Administrator*, *32*, 60–65.

Doll, J., Livesey, J., McHaffie, E., & Ludwig, T. D. (2007). Keeping an uphill edge: Managing cleaning behaviors at a ski shop. *Journal of Organizational Behavior Management*, *27*(3), 41–60.

Fante, R., Gravina, N., & Austin, J. (2007). A brief pre-intervention analysis and demonstration of the effects of a behavioral safety package on postural behaviors of pharmacy employees. *Journal of Organizational Behavior Management*, *27*(2), 15–25.

Fleming, R. K., Oliver, J. R., & Bolton, D. M. (1996). Training supervisors to train staff. *Journal of Organizational Behavior Management*, *16*(1), 3–25.

Fleming, R., & Sulzer-Azaroff, B. (1992). Reciprocal peer management: Increasing and maintaining beneficial staff-client interactions. *Journal of Applied Behavior Analysis*, *25*, 611–620.

Frederiksen, L. W. (1982). On the prospects of a behavioral approach to managerial effectiveness. *Journal of Organizational Behavior Management*, *3*(3), 85–90.

Frisch, C. J., & Dickinson, A. M. (1990). Work productivity as a function of the percentage of monetary incentives to base pay. *Journal of Organizational Behavior Management*, *11*(1), 13–34.

Gawande, A. (2010). *The checklist manifesto*. New York: Metropolitan Books.

Geller, E. S., Berry, T. D., Ludwig, T. D., Evans, R. E., Gilmore, M. R., & Clarke, S. W. (1990). A conceptual framework for developing and evaluating behavior change interventions for injury control. *Health Education Research: Theory and Practice*, *5*(2), 125–137.

Geller, E. S., Ludwig, T. D., Gilmore, M. R., & Berry, T. D. (1990). A taxonomy of behavior change: Techniques for community intervention. *The Community Psychologist, 23*(2), 4–6.

Glenn, S. (1988). Contingencies and metacontingencies: Toward a synthesis of behavior analysis and cultural materialism. *The Behavior Analyst, 11*, 161–179.

Glenn, S. (1991). Contingencies and metacontingencies: Relations among behavioral, cultural, and biological evolution. In P. A. Lamal (Ed.), *Behavioral analysis of societies and cultural practices* (pp. 39–73). NY: Hemisphere Publishing Corporation.

Glenn, S. S., & Malott, M. E. (2004). Complexity and selection: Implications for organizational change. *Behavior and Social Issues, 13*, 89–106.

Goomas, D. T., & Ludwig, T. D. (2007). Enhancing incentive programs with proximal goals and immediate feedback: Engineered labor standards and technology enhancements in stocker replenishment. *Journal of Organizational Behavior Management, 27*(1), 33–68.

Gravina, N. E., & Cunningham, T. R. (2010). "Check" this out: A review of Gawande's The Checklist Manifesto. *Journal of Organizational Behavior Management, 30*(3), 271–277.

Gravina, N., Lindstrom-Hazel, D., & Austin, J. (2006). The effects of workstation changes and behavioral interventions on safe typing postures in an office. *IOS Press, 29*, 245–253.

Gravina, N., VanWagner, M., & Austin, J. (2008). Increasing physical therapy equipment preparation using task clarification, feedback and environmental manipulations. *Journal of Organizational Behavior Management, 28*(2), 110–122.

Gravinese, K., & Ludwig, T. D. (2007). Dirty laundry and dirty dishes: Reducing call bell response latency by altering contingencies through differential staffing reinforcement. In *Poster presented at the OBM conference*, Sarasota, FL.

Haberlin, A. T., Beauchamp, K., Agnew, J., & O'Brien, F. (2012). A comparison of pyramidal staff training and direct staff training in community-based day programs. *Journal of Organizational Behavior Management, 32*(1), 65–74.

Hall, A. D., & Fagen, R. E. (1956). Definition of a system. *General Systems: Yearbook of the Society for the Advancement of General Systems Theory, 1*, 18–28.

Harshbarger, D., & Maley, R. F. (1974). *Behavior analysis and systems analysis: An integrative approach to mental health programs.* Kalamazoo, MI: Behaviordelia, Inc.

Haynes, R. S., Pine, R. C., & Fitch, H. G. (1982). Reducing accident rates with organizational behavior modification. *Academy of Management Journal, 25*, 407–416.

Hermann, J. A., Ibarra, G. V., & Hopkins, B. L. (2010). A safety program that integrated behavior-based safety and traditional safety methods and its effects on injury rates of manufacturing workers. *Journal of Organizational Behavior Management, 30*, 6–25.

Hogan, L. C., Bell, M., & Olson, R. (2009). A preliminary investigation of the reinforcement function of signal detections in simulated baggage screening: Further support for the vigilance reinforcement hypothesis. *Journal of Organizational Behavior Management, 29*(1), 6–18.

Honeywell-Johnson, J. A., & Dickinson, A. (1999). Small group incentives. *Journal of Organizational Behavior Management, 19*(2), 89–121.

Huberman, W. L., & O'Brien, R. M. (1999). Improving therapist and patient performance in chronic psychiatric group homes through goal-setting, feedback, and positive reinforcement. *Journal of Organizational Behavior Management, 19*(1), 13–36.

Hyten, C. (2009). Strengthening the focus on business results: The need for systems approaches in OBM. *Journal of Organizational Behavior Management, 29*(2), 87–107.

Johnson, R. P., & Frederiksen, L. W. (1984). Process vs outcome feedback and goal setting in a human service organization. *Journal of Organizational Behavior Management, 5*(3-4), 37–56.

Johnson, C. M., Mawhinney, T. C., & Redmon, W. K. (2001). Introduction to organizational performance: Behavior analysis and management. In C. M. Johnson, W. K. Redmon, & T. C. Mawhinney (Eds.), *Handbook of organizational performance: Behavior analysis and management* (pp. 3–22). New York, NY: Haworth.

Karlsson, T., & Chase, P. N. (1996). A comparison of three prompting methods for training software use. *Journal of Organizational Behavior Management, 16*(1), 27–44.

Katz, D., & Kahn, R. L. (1966). *The social psychology of organizations* (2nd). New York: John Wiley & Sons.

Krumhus, K. M., & Malott, R. W. (1980). The effects of modeling and immediate and delayed feedback in staff training. *Journal of Organizational Behavior Management, 2*(4), 279–293.

Langeland, K. L., Johnson, C. M., & Mawhinney, T. C. (1997). Improving staff performance in a community mental health setting. *Journal of Organizational Behavior Management, 18*(1), 21–43.

Laraway, S., Snycerski, S., Michael, J., & Poling, A. (2003). Motivating operations and terms to describe them: Some further refinements. *Journal of Applied Behavior Analysis, 36*, 407–414.

Latham, G. P., & Huber, V. L. (1991). Schedules of reinforcement. *Journal of Organizational Behavior Management, 12*(1), 125–149.

Ludwig, T. D. (2002). On the necessity of structure in an arbitrary world: Using concurrent schedules of reinforcement to describe response generalization. *Journal of Organizational Behavior Management, 21*(4), 13–38.

Ludwig, T. D., & Geller, E. S. (2000). Intervening to improve the safety of delivery drivers: A systematic behavioral approach. Monograph. *Journal of Organizational Behavior Management, 19*(1), 1–124.

Ludwig, T. D., & Goomas, D. T. (2007). Performance, accuracy, data delivery, and feedback methods in order selection: A comparison of voice, handheld, and paper technologies. *Journal of Organizational Behavior Management, 27*(1), 69–107.

Ludwig, T. D., & Houmanfar, R. (Eds.), (2010). *Understanding complexity in organizations: Behavioral systems*. Philadelphia: Routledge.

Luthans, F., & Kreitner, R. (1985). *Organizational behaviour modification and beyond: An operant and social learning approach*. Glenview, IL: Scott Foresman.

Malott, R. W. (1974). A behavior systems approach to the design of human services. In D. Harshbarger, & R. F. Maley (Eds.), *Behavior analysis and systems analysis: An integrative approach to mental health programs* (pp. 318–343). Kalamazoo, MI: Behaviordelia.

Malott, M. E. (2003). *Paradox of organizational change*. Reno, NV: Context Press.

Martinko, M. J., White, J. D., & Hassell, B. (1989). An operant analysis of prompting in a sales environment. *Journal of Organizational Behavior Management, 10*(1), 93–107.

Mawhinney, T. C. (1992). Evolution of organizational cultures as selection by consequences: The Gaia hypothesis, metacontingencies, and organizational ecology. *Journal of Organizational Behavior Management, 12*(1), 1–26.

McGee, H. M. (2007). An introduction to behavioral systems analysis for OBMers and non-OBMers alike. *OBM Network Newsletter, 21*(2), 5–12.

McGee, H. M., & Diener, L. H. (2010). Behavioral systems analysis in health and human services. *Behavior Modification, 34*, 415–442.

McGee, H. M., & Diener-Ludwig, L. H. (2012). An introduction to behavioral systems analysis for rehabilitation agencies. *Journal of Rehabilitation Administration, 36*(2), 59–71.

McSween, T. E. (1995). *The values-based safety process: Improving your safety culture with a behavioral approach*. New York: Wiley.

McSween, T. E. (2010). The checklist manifesto: A practitioner's perspective. *Journal of Organizational Behavior Management, 30*(3), 278–279.

Mihalic, M. T., & Ludwig, T. D. (2009). Behavioral system feedback measurement failure: Sweeping quality under the rug. *Journal of Organizational Behavior Management, 29*(2), 155–174.

Miller, J. G. (1971). The nature of living systems. *Behavioral Science, 16*(4), 277–301.

Miller, M. V., Carlson, J., & Sigurdsson, S. O. (2014). Improving treatment integrity in a human service setting using lottery-based incentives. *Journal of Organizational Behavior Management, 34*(1), 29–38.

Miller, R., & Lewin, L. M. (1980). Training and management of the psychiatric aide. *Journal of Organizational Behavior Management, 2*(4), 295–315.

Milligan, J., & Hantula, D. A. (2005). A prompting procedure for increasing sales in a small pet store. *Journal of Organizational Behavior Management, 25*, 37–44.

Moon, K., & Oah, S. (2013). A comparison of the effects of feedback and prompts on safe sitting posture: Utilizing an automated observation and feedback system. *Journal of Organizational Behavior Management, 33*(2), 152–162.

Mueller, M. M., Moore, J. W., Tingstrom, D. H., & Doggett, R. A. (2001). Increasing seating opportunities using a behavioral prompt. *Journal of Organizational Behavior Management, 21*(2), 99–109.

Myers, W. V., McSween, T. E., Medina, R. E., Rost, K., & Alvero, A. M. (2010). The implementation and maintenance of a behavioral safety process in a petroleum refinery. *Journal of Organization Behavior Management, 30*, 285–307.

Myerson, J., & Hale, S. (1984). Practical implications of the matching law. *Journal of Applied Behavior Analysis, 17*, 367–380.

Nicholson, M., & Xiao, S. H. (2010). On the evolutionary bases of consumer reinforcement. *Journal of Organizational Behavior Management, 30*(2), 127–144.

Nolan, T. V., Jarema, K. A., & Austin, J. (1999). An objective review of the journal of organizational behavior management. *Journal of Organizational Behavior Management, 19*(3), 83–114.

O'Brien, R. M., Dickinson, A. M., & Rosow, M. (Eds.), (1982). *Industrial behavior modification: A management handbook.* New York: Pergamon Press.

Olson, R., Laraway, S., & Austin, J. (2001). Unconditioned and conditioned establishing operations in organizational behavior management. *Journal of Organizational Behavior Management, 21*(2), 7–35.

Pampino, R. N., Heering, P. W., Wilder, D. A., Barton, C. G., & Burson, L. M. (2003). The use of the performance diagnostic checklist to guide intervention selection in an independently owned coffee shop. *Journal of Organizational Behavior Management, 23*(2/3), 5–19.

Petrock, F. (1978). Analyzing the balance of consequences for performance improvement. *Journal of Organizational Behavior Management, 1*(3), 196–205.

Porterfield, J., Evans, G., & Blunden, R. (1985). Involving families and staff in service improvement. *Journal of Organizational Behavior Management, 7*(1-2), 117–134.

Rodriguez, M., Wilder, D. A., Therrien, K., Wine, B., Miranti, R., Daratany, K., et al. (2005). Use of the performance diagnostic checklist to select an intervention designed to increase the offering of promotional stamps at two sited of a restaurant franchise. *Journal of Organizational Behavior Management, 25*, 17–33.

Rohn, D., Austin, A., & Lutrey, S. M. (2002). Using feedback and performance accountability to decrease cash register shortages. *Journal of Organizational Behavior Management, 22*, 33–46.

Rose, H. M. S., & Ludwig, T. D. (2009). The effects of self-monitoring, task clarification, and performance feedback on lifeguard cleaning behaviors. *Journal of Organizational Behavior Management, 29*(1), 69–79.

Rummler, G. A. (2001). Performance logic: The organization performance rosetta stone. In L. J. Hayes, J. Austin, R. Houmanfar, & M. C. Clayton (Eds.), *Organizational change* (pp. 111–132). Reno, NV: Context Press.

Rummler, G. A. (2004). *Serious performance consulting according to Rummler.* Silver Spring, MD: International Society for Performance Improvement.

Rummler, G. A., & Branche, A. P. (1995). *Improving performance: How to manage the white space on the organizational chart* (2nd). San Francisco, CA: Jossey-Bass.

Skinner, B. F. (1948). *Walden two*. New York: MacMillian.

Smith, A. J. (2010). The checklist manifesto: Examples from the hotel industry. *Journal of Organizational Behavior Management, 30*(3), 280–282.

Stephens, S. D., & Ludwig, T. D. (2005). Improving anesthesia nurse compliance with Universal Precautions using group goals and public feedback. *Journal of Organizational Behavior Management, 25*(2), 37–71.

Sulzer-Azaroff, B., & Alavosius, M. C. (1988). Preventing back injuries at an institutional infirmary. *Performance Management Magazine, 6*(4), 14–16.

Sulzer-Azaroff, B., & Austin, J. (2000). Does BBS work? Behavior-based safety & injury reduction: A survey of the evidence. *Professional Safety, 45*, 19–24.

Tubbs, M. (1994). Commitment and the role of ability in motivation: Comment on Wright, O'Leary-Kelly, Cortina, Klein, and Hollenbeck (1994). *Journal of Applied Psychology, 79*(6), 804–811.

VanStelle, S. E., Vicars, S. M., Harr, V., Miguel, C. F., Koerber, J. L., Kazbour, R., et al. (2012). The publication history of the journal of organizational behavior management: An objective review and analysis: 1998-2009. *Journal of Organizational Behavior Management, 32*(2), 93–123.

Weiss, P. A. (1971). *Hierarchically organized systems in theory and practice*. New York: Hafner.

Williams, W. L., Di Vittorio, T., & Hausherr, L. (2003). A description and extension of a human services management model. *Journal of Organizational Behavior Management, 22*(1), 47–71.

CHAPTER 25

Organizational Behavior Management: Systems Analysis

Sigurdur O. Sigurdsson[1], Heather M. McGee[2]

[1]School of Behavior Analysis, Florida Institute of Technology, Melbourne, Florida, USA
[2]Western Michigan University, Kalamazoo Michigan, USA

INTRODUCTION TO BEHAVIORAL SYSTEMS ANALYSIS

There are two generally accepted approaches to performance improvement within the subfield of Organizational Behavior Management (OBM): Performance Management (PM) and Behavioral Systems Analysis (BSA). Also referred to as the performer or individual level approach to performance improvement, PM involves the analysis of the antecedents and consequences operating on the behaviors of employees and employers and the development of interventions designed to affect these variables to either decrease unproductive or increase productive performance (Austin, 2000; Daniels & Daniels, 2004). This approach to performance improvement involves the direct application of applied behavior analysis (ABA) concepts and principles. A variety of PM diagnostic models and algorithms have been developed over the years for the purpose of analyzing antecedents and consequences (e.g., ABC analysis, Mager & Pipe Flowchart, Behavior Engineering Model, Performance Diagnostic Checklist). The most common PM interventions are feedback, training, antecedent manipulations (e.g., task clarification, checklists), goal setting, incentives, and praise (VanStelle et al., 2012).

Sometimes referred to as the systems level approach to performance improvement, BSA involves analysis of the various components of the organizational system at the performer, process, and organization levels, as well as how those components interact with and affect each other. BSA blends ABA with General Systems Theory, an approach to understanding organizational systems by examining the relationships between parts of the system, as well as the relationships between the system and the external environment (Ackoff & Emery, 1972; Bertalanffy, 1950, 1968). As with PM, there are several BSA diagnostic models and algorithms (e.g., Total Performance System, Human Performance System, Relationship Map, process mapping, and the Behavioral Systems Analysis Questionnaire). The BSA approach to intervention

Clinical and Organizational Applications of Applied Behavior Analysis
http://dx.doi.org/10.1016/B978-0-12-420249-8.00025-3

development typically results in multilevel solutions that may include PM interventions, but also process design, automation, changes in policy, changes in resource deployment, strategy development and/or realignment, development of incentive systems, organizational restructuring, and managing the manager initiatives, to name a few (Diener, McGee, & Miguel, 2009; Malott, 2003; McGee, 2007).

HISTORY OF BSA

The roots of BSA (referred to as Human Performance Technology, or HPT, by performance improvement professionals affiliated with the International Society for Performance Improvement) can be traced back to the University of Michigan and the Training Systems Workshop that Drs. Dale M. Brethower and Geary A. Rummler developed in 1965 for the Center for Programmed Learning for Business (CPLB), which was founded by Rummler and George Odiorne in 1962 and housed in the university's Graduate School of Business (Dickinson, 2001; Rummler, 2007). The workshop was founded on the framework that would go on to define BSA: (a) Brethower's Total Performance System (TPS) and (b) Rummler's three levels of performance (organization, process, job/performer). Over the years, the systems approach to performance improvement continued to grow and spread with the addition of more CPLB workshop staff (e.g., Karen Brethower, David Markle) and guest speakers (e.g., Tom Gilbert, Joe Harless), as well as through dissemination by staff, speakers, and graduates (e.g., Ed Feeney) of the workshops at conferences and in books, journal articles, and other publication outlets. Additionally, collaborations with other systems thinkers (Brethower began collaborating with Richard "Dick" Malott of Western Michigan University in the mid-1960s, while Rummler formed the consulting firm Praxis with Tom Gilbert in 1969) resulted in more widespread education and adoption of systems concepts and principles. The term "Behavioral Systems Analysis" was first introduced to describe the subfield by Dick Malott and Dwight Harshbarger in 1973 (Brethower, 2002). By the end of the 1970s, the behavioral systems approach could be found in books, articles, among the services provided by consulting firms, and in graduate coursework. For more detailed historical accounts of BSA and its founders, readers are strongly encouraged to read Dickinson's, 2001 paper, *The Historical Roots of OBM in the Private Sector* (BSA history in the context of OBM) and Rummler's, 2007 paper, *The Past is Prologue: An Eyewitness Account of HPT* (BSA history in the context of HPT).

BSA PROCESS AND FRAMEWORK

At its core, BSA relies on the assumption that organizations are systems comprised of various interrelated components and that a change in one part of the system affects other parts of the system. Therefore, all analysis and improvement efforts should follow a clear process that promotes analysis before change and evaluation throughout. Malott (1974) introduced the ASDIER (Analyze, Specify, Design, Implement, Evaluate, and Recycle), process while Rummler (2007) proposed the four-phase Results Improvement Process (desired results determined and project defined; barriers determined and changes specified; changes designed, developed, and implemented; and results evaluated and maintained or improved).

It would not be difficult to quickly locate a number of other performance improvement process models with a search on the Internet. Most models include essentially the same fundamental requirements for effectively improving performance. Any of these processes could be applied to PM work as well, but BSA performance improvement efforts must follow a process to analyze and improve not only the behaviors of individuals, but also all components of the system that could impact performance (through TPS analysis), as well as the system as a whole (through a three-level approach; Brethower, 1982, 2000, 2001, 2002; Malott, 2003; Sulzer-Azaroff, 2001).

Total Performance System

Brethower's (1972) Total Performance System provides the framework for analyzing systems at all levels of performance. The TPS creates a shared language and tool for identifying business problems, designing performance improvement interventions, and delivering results. Each TPS component must be in place without deficiencies and without negatively impacting other system components. The TPS is composed of seven system components, each of which requires effective functioning for the system's survival: mission/goal, products/services, customers/stakeholders, external feedback (customer measures), processing system, inputs, and internal feedback (processing system measures). In their book *Improving Performance: How to Manage the White Space on the Organizational Chart*, Rummler and Brache (1995) described two additional components (environmental variables and competition) in their Super-System, a variant of the TPS. Table 25.1 provides a description of each TPS component, including environmental variables and competition along with a suggested order of analysis (Diener et al., 2009).

Table 25.1 The Total Performance System

TPS components	Description
1. Mission/goal	Begin by analyzing the mission of the organization. Why does this system exist? All other system components exist to support the achievement of the mission and, therefore, any changes to the system should be functionally consistent (or "aligned") with the mission/goal
2. Products/services	Next look at the products and services produced by the processing system. Focusing on these organizational outputs helps you to see how the mission is carried out. Additionally, it is the sale of products/services to customers that creates the revenue required for organizational success
3. Customers/stakeholders	Customers are those individuals who receive the product or service. Stakeholders are those who receive the financial outputs of the organization (e.g., parent company, stockholder, lending institution, employees). Without customers and stakeholders, the organization ceases to exist. Therefore, it is critical to assess this component early in your analysis
4. External feedback (customer measures)	Customer measures describe the impact/value the product or service has on its customers. If customers are not satisfied, products or services may not be consumed and the system will not thrive
5. Processing system	The processing system consists of the various activities that produce the products/services, which are then sold to customers, thereby creating value for the system. Effectiveness and efficiency of the processing system is paramount, because both the activities engaged in to convert inputs into outputs, as well as the inputs themselves, represent costs to the organization (e.g., inputs must be purchased, people must be paid to work), while the outputs (products/services) create value for the organization (are sold to customers)
6. Inputs	Inputs consist of resources needed for the system to operate and often include raw materials, capital, people, information, equipment, and technology. According to Brethower (2000), inputs are a costly, but necessary component of the TPS

Table 25.1 The Total Performance System—Cont'd

TPS components	Description
7. Internal feedback (processing system measures)	Processing system measures provide information about process performance and are a form of quality control. This feedback allows the organization to correct defective process steps before outputs reach the customers, thus increasing the probability that the system's products/services will be valued
8. Environment	Next we identify environmental factors that impact the system (e.g., economy, government, culture, natural environment, marketplace). These variables tend to be outside the control of the organization but can have a profound effect on organizational performance. This information should guide strategic and tactical decision making
9. Competition	Finally, we identify the system's competitors (i.e., those who are competing for inputs or customers). How does this system compare to competing systems? This information should also guide strategic and tactical decision making

Three Levels of Performance

Organizations are multifaceted, multilevel systems. The TPS allows practitioners to analyze the various facets of the system, while the three-level framework ensures that practitioners consider the various subsystems of the organization as well as the organization as a whole (Rummler & Brache, 1995). Said another way, the TPS allows practitioners to view individual systems or subsystems, while the three-level framework allows practitioners to assess the interrelatedness of those systems and subsystems (Figure 25.1).

At the organization level, practitioners are primarily concerned with understanding the environment in which the organization operates, determining the strategies that organizational leaders will employ to adapt to changes in that environment, and assessing whether the organization is structured in a way to support the strategies employed. At the process level, practitioners are concerned with understanding and improving how work gets done within the processing system of the organization, which includes assessing and developing the input/output relationships between the various departments/functions of the organization. Finally, at the performer level

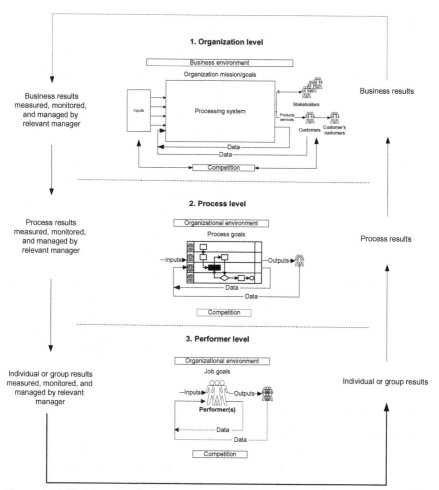

Figure 25.1 The three-level approach to performance improvement.

(where the PM work occurs), practitioners are targeting the job characteristics and antecedents, behaviors, and consequences of the individuals who work within the system.

Organizational performance is a function of those individuals working in it. However, performance is not a unidirectional relation. Employees are only as good as the systems they are a part of. As Rummler and Brache (1995) stated, "If you pit a good performer against a bad system, the system will win almost every time" (p. 13). Because behavior is a function of its environment, it will not be maintained unless there are organizational contingencies in place to support (i.e., reinforce) it. BSA typically focuses on the organizational and process levels first so specific contingency support can be put in place for individuals to excel. That said, it is only through the performance of individual employees that well-defined processes and organizational systems can be optimized. This combination of contingency (behavior analysis) and system (General Systems Theory) design is what makes BSA a holistic approach to organizational performance improvement.

BSA TOOLS

While the TPS and three-level approach provide the general frameworks for BSA, there are important additional tools that are specific to certain levels of analysis. Additionally, several modifications to the TPS and the three-level approach have been developed since these were first introduced. Often, students and colleagues of Brethower and Rummler developed these modifications. It is impossible to describe every tool and level approach available to BSA professionals, especially because the reach of systems analysis extends beyond BSA (e.g., HPT specific models and tools), so the present chapter will cover those most common within BSA (from a behavior analytic context). We begin this section with a description of level-specific tools, indicating those that could be considered modifications of other tools, and then move into variations on the three-level approach (including relevant tools when applicable).

Organization Level Tools

The TPS not only provides a framework for BSA, but also serves as a tool to be used at any level of performance. As previously stated, the TPS (Brethower, 1972) consists of seven components: mission/goal, products/services, customers/stakeholders, external feedback (customer measures), processing system, inputs, and internal feedback (processing system measures). Rummler and Brache (1995) introduced the Super-System (Figure 25.2), which added two additional external elements for consideration when analyzing the organization: external variables (e.g., government regulations, economy) and competition (for inputs and customers).

Rummler and Brache (1995) also introduced the Relationship Map (Figure 25.3), which illustrated the various functions of the organization, the input-output relationships between them (i.e., who produces what for whom?), and where goals, standards, and feedback loops should exist

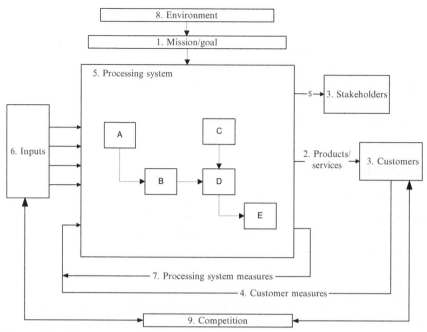

Figure 25.2 The super-system.

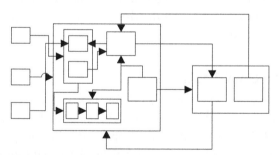

Figure 25.3 The Relationship Map.

between the suppliers and customers (internal or external). Once the various functions, suppliers, customers, and inputs/outputs are mapped, the Relationship Map is used to identify any missing, unnecessary, confusing, or misdirected inputs and outputs as well as develop cross-functional relationships that eliminate disconnects between functions and (a) external suppliers, (b) external customers, and (c) other functions, which can be viewed as internal suppliers and customers.

Process Level Tools

The cross–functional process map (Figure 25.4) is the primary tool used at the process level of analysis (Rummler & Brache, 1995). A process is a series of steps designed to produce a product or service. Processes typically involve more than one organizational function. Those processes that only involve one function are often considered to be subprocesses and should never be analyzed in isolation, because a change in one part of a system impacts other parts of the system. In other words, changing a process within one function will likely impact other functions upstream or downstream. The cross–functional process map provides a visual depiction of a process from beginning to end. The map helps the systems analyst identify the scope of process being analyzed (where it starts and stops); the performers/functions involved in the specified process; the steps or tasks involved; and the inputs, outputs, and standards of each step.

Once a map is created showing the process as it currently exists (called an "Is" or "Current State" map), it is analyzed (preferably by a cross–functional team) to identify disconnects with respect to missing, redundant, or convoluted steps, standards, time, and resources involved. Once the disconnects within the process are identified, a "Should" or "Future State" map is developed (either by the same team or by a new solutions design team), which represents what the process will look like once the disconnects have been addressed. Cross-functional process maps are often quite detailed (and large). Therefore, many systems experts recommend beginning process analysis with a high-level process map (referred to by Rummler as the Value Creation System; VCS) before analyzing process in detail (Ludwig & McGee, 2014; Malott, 2003; Rummler, Ramias, & Rummler, 2009). A high-level

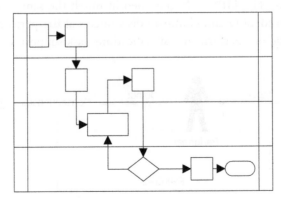

Figure 25.4 Cross-functional process map.

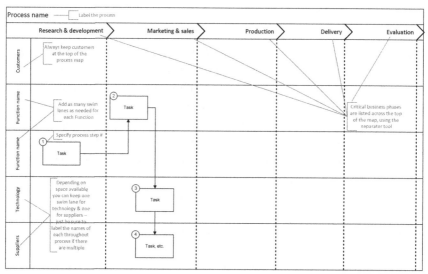

Figure 25.5 High-level process map.

map (Figure 25.5) is a variant of the cross-functional map described by Rummler and Brache (1995) and identifies the major phases of the process (usually three to five phases), along with the main steps of each phase (typically no more than five steps per phase).

Performer Level Tools

Several tools exist within BSA to analyze performance at the individual performer level; however, most of these tools are variants of Rummler's (1972) Human Performance System (HPS; Figure 25.6) with or without contingency analysis. The HPS is diagrammed in much the same way as a TPS and is used to identify and eliminate disconnects at the performer level by assessing six factors: performance specifications, task support, consequences,

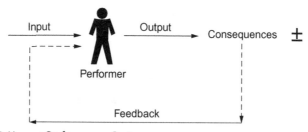

Figure 25.6 Human Performance System.

Table 25.2 The Human Performance System

HPS components	Description
1. Performance specifications	Are there performance standards? Do the performers know what the desired outputs and standards are? Do they find them acceptable?
2. Task support	Do performers know when to engage in the task? Are there any interfering tasks? Do they have appropriate resources to engage in the task? Are procedures and workflow logical?
3. Consequences	Do consequences support desired behaviors? Are consequences supporting undesired behaviors minimized? Are consequences timely and meaningful to the performers?
4. Feedback	Do performers receive timely, accurate, specific, relevant, and easily understood feedback about both desired and undesired performance?
5. Knowledge/skill	Do performers have the knowledge, skills, and abilities to perform successfully? Do they know why the performance is important?
6. Individual capacity	Are performers physically, mentally, and emotionally able to perform their job duties?

feedback, knowledge/skill, and individual capacity (see Table 25.2). Several variants of the HPS are available and widely used. Gilbert's (1978) Behavior Engineering Model (BEM) is essentially the HPS in a matrix format and organizes the six factors into two main categories (environmental supports and person's repertoire of behavior). More recently, Binder (1998) translated the BEM into a more user-friendly, diagnostic tool known as The Six Boxes[TM], and Austin (2000) condensed the six categories of the HPS, BEM, and Six Boxes[TM] into four (antecedents and information, equipment and processes, knowledge and skills, and consequences) in his Performance Diagnostic Checklist (PDC).

Variants of the Three-Level Approach

While the minimum number of levels considered to represent a complete systems analysis remains three, some BSA professionals have proposed as many as six levels of analysis (though whether this represents the addition of three distinct levels, the division of the three levels into sublevels, or a combination of these approaches is arguable). Gilbert (1978) introduced the Performance Matrix, a model for assessing performance at the philosophical, cultural, policy, strategic, tactical, and logistic levels. Malott (2003) introduced the Behavioral Systems Engineering Model: a drill-down approach to performance analysis that begins at the macrosystem (industry level analysis) and moves from there to the organization, process (high-level process and function analysis), task (detailed process analysis), behavior (contingency analysis), and management (analysis of management contingencies across all levels of performance). Rummler et al. (2009) expanded the traditional three-level approach into the Processing System Hierarchy, a five-level, process-based approach to performance analysis and improvement that begins with the enterprise/business level (super-system/organization level analysis), then moves to the VCS (high-level process), processing subsystems (analysis of processes that fall within the subsystems of products/services launched, sold, and delivered—still somewhat high-level), process (detailed process analysis), and finally subprocess/task/subtask (HPS/performer level analysis). Finally, Ludwig and McGee (2014) offer a series of seven BSA tools, each of which includes diagnostics, prioritization of opportunities, and action-planning solution development and implementation. These tools comprise strategic goal setting, organizational mapping (organization level—TPS/super-system), relationship mapping (organization level—Relationship Map), macro-level process mapping (high-level process analysis), detailed process mapping (detailed process analysis), job mapping (job level—HPS), and behavior mapping (job level—contingency analysis).

SYSTEMS INTERVENTIONS

Though there are several consulting firms dedicated to performance improvement through systems analysis and though there have been many articles and books written and talks and workshops given, about BSA, research that is explicitly informed by systems analyses is still somewhat scarce. The following section describes studies that incorporated systems interventions at the three levels of systems analysis (organizational, process, and/or individual performer) but may not have used systems tools explicitly to inform the intervention selection. This section concludes with two interesting studies that deserve special mention. In the first study, Alavosius, Getting, Dagen, Newsome, and Hopkins (2009) described a system design for multiple organizations that formed a co-operative to manage workers' compensation costs. In the second study, Sasson, Alvero, and Austin (2006) evaluated the independent and interactive effects of manipulating process-level variables and traditional PM variables at the individual performer level.

Organizational Level Systems Interventions

Frederisken, Riley, and Myers (1985) described a case study of an insurance company that experienced challenges associated with automating key business functions, and facing business challenges in terms of creating new products for an ever-changing marketplace. The authors discussed how a complementary change in organizational structure, in addition to the formation of self-managed work teams was necessary to address these challenges. The self-managed work teams, who were tasked, for example, with creating new products, were supported by corporate mandates that team members should receive "pay for learning," such that a pay increase was automatically awarded when an employee had learned a new skill. The self-managed teams did not have a typical supervisor but could turn to an advisory group composed of managers from different departments. Finally, all team members received training in decision making, how to work in a group, and how to cross-train others. To maintain these process changes, the organization also changed information flow throughout the organization through the VP of Human Resources, and team updates were continually fed to internal stakeholders. Results of the automation and organization level system changes suggested increased work volume on the order of 25–40% by the same number of people, with less overtime costs.

Strouse, Carroll-Hernandez, Sherman, and Sheldon (2004) describe the effects of a revised scheduling system for employees in a human service program. The existing scheduling system required employees to work the same 8–9 h on the same days of the week, and generally the same people were required to work nights, weekends, or both. An analysis of the existing system revealed that call-outs were frequent, and that part-time employees were used to cover those. In addition, weekend positions had much higher turnover than full-time, and those positions stayed vacant for longer. Finally, many resources were devoted to training staff (part and full-time) that left after a few months or worked infrequently. The revised schedule involved 12-h shifts for either three consecutive days or three and a half consecutive days. All employees were guaranteed to have either Saturday or Sunday off every week. Salary increases were introduced and were offset by the virtual elimination of part-time positions, which represented a considerable shift in organizational structure. The revised scheduling system resulted in 43% less turnover and vacancies over the course of the study without affecting staff-to-client ratios, which was the main goal of the study. In addition, significant savings were observed in terms of number of staff involved in the care of clients, and in payroll.

Process Level Systems Interventions

Berglund and Ludwig (2009) described a process change and feedback system on product preparation error rates in a retail furniture distribution warehouse. Before the intervention, employees worked independently to prepare a delivery, and hand-offs between employees followed a linear process. Following a systems analysis, employees started working together in teams to prepare products for shipment, and all team members were specifically cross-trained to perform another employee's function in the team. Customer service representatives also communicated more frequently with team members on different customer requirements and alerted team members of potential "problem" products before they were shipped. Multiple feedback loops were added to the process. If a delivery had zero errors, an air horn was sounded over the whole facility, with different sounds for each team. Daily feedback on delivery quality was posted publicly, and each team also received detailed written feedback on both individual and aggregate measures of the quality of order delivery. Results suggested that the intervention was highly effective for two out of three teams in terms of reducing errors and resulted in considerable savings for the organization.

Clayton, Mawhinney, Luke, and Cook (1997) attempted to reduce overtime costs in a residential organization for persons with developmental disabilities. During baseline analysis, overtime had to be approved through a central office. A process change was implemented so that middle management at the location was given budgets for overtime and was held responsible for staying within that budget. If budget was exceeded, cuts had to be made in other areas, or managers had to provide coverage. Any remaining funds from the budget could be transferred to the next year for special projects. In 1 year of implementation, overtime costs were reduced by approximately 50%. In another setting, however, the same intervention did not yield decreases in overtime costs.

Goomas (2010) described an automation process change implemented in two auto parts distribution centers. In the baseline condition, order selectors used a voice system to pick items for orders. If there was a discrepancy between the spoken tag number and the actual tag number on a tote used to fill the order, the tote was automatically routed to an area for misidentified order totes. A new process was implemented in which a stylus was used to scan tote tag numbers for accuracy before they even left the hands of the picker. The stylus also provided auditory feedback on the accuracy of the scan. Each incorrectly filled tote costs the organization an estimated $500, and up to 90 min to replace the items to their original slots. The intervention resulted in savings of $220,000 for the company in the first year alone.

In Goomas (2012a), a process change for loading palettes onto trucks going from an auto parts distribution center to individual stores was implemented. The presenting problem was that pallets were not loaded on the truck in the correct (reverse) order based on the delivery route. It was estimated that 3% of all trucks were incorrectly loaded, and that each loading mistake could add up to 18 min to the unload time at the stores. The process change involved the introduction of scanners connected to a central database via wireless technology. The scanner provided auditory feedback for successful scans, and on-screen error feedback if a pallet was scanned for loading out of order. The results suggested that the new process saved $10,000 annually, and that these savings would return the cost of the equipment after 2 years of use.

Goomas (2012b) described a process change for filling orders in a meat distribution center. Paper sheets were used to track key food safety and costing information for individual items that comprised orders. The presenting problem was the order selectors often failed to enter important date and weight information, and shipping clerks often manually entered incorrect values for these variables in the center's computer tracking system. The process change involved the introduction of a ring scanner that automatically captured date and weight information for all items picked for orders. The scanner also tracked if the item scanned was appropriate for a given order. The scanner provided auditory feedback for correct scans, and error feedback was provided on the device's screen if an error occurred. Prior to the intervention, the average time to complete daily store orders was approximately 500 min. Following the introduction of the new process, completion times decreased by approximately 60 min. The average number of errors per day also went from approximately 14 to 0.

Hybza, Stokes, Hayman, and Schatzberg (2013) implemented a district-wide process change for submission of Medicaid billing forms for services rendered by school psychologists. After a process analysis, it was determined that the psychologists did not receive prompts that performance goals were absent, and feedback was inconsistent and infrequent. An intervention was implemented that involved goal setting, weekly prompts, and feedback from supervisor on meeting billing deadlines. It took only 30 min every 2 weeks for an internal consultant to provide the supervisor with the data that formed the basis for goal setting and feedback, and it took the supervisor 15 min every 2 weeks to deliver the goals and feedback. The intervention resulted in the increases of approximately $3000 in billing per 2 weeks, which was an increase of almost 400% over baseline. Social validity data suggested that the school psychologists overall were happy with the intervention, although the lowest acceptability ratings were obtained for the acceptability of the goals and their attainability.

Finally, Mihalic and Ludwig (2009) conducted an analysis of how measurement of the performance of furniture delivery drivers failed as a result of attending to systemic variables. Although the authors did not implement any process changes, this study represents an interesting analysis of a failure to attend to process quality. A key variable the organization was interested in measuring was the number of pieces of furniture in need of return or repair that were left in the customer's home without getting clearance to do so. The organization had developed an elaborate database to keep track of this and a multitude of other important measures, and part of the employees' pay was contingent on the number of these errors. While the number of these errors had decreased historically in a dramatic fashion, a systems analysis revealed that the vague nature of the definitions of errors led to some manipulation of the system. That is, errors that should have been coded as left in home were not. As a result, the feedback that employees received was highly inaccurate, as they were indeed making errors, and they were not docked pay when they should have been. The authors then made recommendations for a system with fewer error codes, consistent and regular auditing of error coding, and accurate feedback.

Individual Performer Level Systems Interventions

Lafleur and Hyten (1995) described an intervention in which Gilbert's BEM was used as a need assessment to address poor hotel banquet table setup. The analysis revealed that formal training systems were absent, equipment was not optimally arranged, no checklists were available for staff to self-monitor their performance, no goals were set, and that no feedback or other consequences were provided. An intervention that addressed all these issues resulted in an increase from 69% to over 99% in a measure of accuracy and timeliness of banquet setup.

Rohn, Austin, and Lutrey (2002) used the PDC to determine the possible causes of cash shortages in a retail store. In terms of equipment and processes, the authors found that store workers were not assigned individual cash registers, making it impossible to determine accountability for shortages. In terms of consequences, no feedback was provided to workers. By assigning one worker to the same register for an entire shift and adding daily verbal and posted feedback, shortages decreased to near $0 values.

Pampino, Heering, Wilder, Barton, and Burson (2003) used the PDC to improve maintenance tasks in a coffee shop. The assessment revealed that improvements were needed in the area of antecedents and information, as well as the area of consequences. To address antecedents and information, training in and use of a 95-item checklist were implemented. To address consequences, a lottery incentive was arranged so that participants increased their chances of winning by scoring higher on the checklist, which was scored by peers. Following the implementation of the package intervention, performance of maintenance tasks increased by 42% and 45% points across two employee groups.

Finally, Miller, Carlson, and Sigurdsson (2014) conducted a PDC assessment of implementation of teachers' three-step prompting, record keeping, and presession preparation in a special education school. On the dimension for antecedents and information, employees reported that no updated or challenging goals were set for the employees. In terms of consequences, the majority of employees indicated that they received infrequent feedback and that they doubted the validity of feedback they received from peers. Intervention consisted of daily verbal and graphic feedback and a lottery-based incentive system in which staff had to perform at a set goal level for the week in order to be eligible for entry into a drawing. The intervention resulted in near 100% performance for two teachers (up from 72% and 44%) and 76% for a third (up from 54%).

System Design at the Level of Multiple Organizations

Alavosius et al. (2009) described a unique system design that involved multiple businesses in Rhode Island. Many businesses in the state were forced to form groups of self-insured employers after traditional insurers refused to write workers' compensation insurance in the state. A third-party administrator functioned to manage the groups and design system-wide contingencies for risk management, risk financing, injury claims management, and other aspects of safety management. The group members were offered education and consulting services related to safety management, and all member companies sent representatives to training in basic safety. Over the span of 7 years, members in the group went from spending 6% of their payroll for workers' compensation costs to 3%. Companies with a long history of high injury rates were exposed to intensive training and consultation, and subsequently were able to reduce injuries to below industry averages. Lottery-style monetary incentives were arranged system-wide so that individual employees could become eligible for monthly incentives if they worked without a work-related injury requiring more than 3 days away from work (the 3-day stipulation served to prevent possible underreporting of injuries). In addition, a member had to work in a company that met certain criteria related to safety management to be eligible for the incentive. Finally, companies that met criteria for excellence in their safety processes were eligible for monetary incentives as well. These criteria were based on the demonstrated excellence in areas such as safety innovations, safety committee operations, safety observations, and specialized safety training programs. The system was a resounding success in terms of injury reductions, and Return-on-Investment ratios of 1:4 and 1:5 were observed for the two groups within the system.

Examining the Interplay of Systems Factors and PM

Sasson et al. (2006) described a study that involved a two-level, two-factor group comparison of the individual and complementary effects of a process-level change and a performer-level ("behavioral intervention") change. The process change involved participants going from an in-person delivery of work products by hand to email delivery. The performer-level intervention involved incentives for quick handoff and disincentives for errors. Participants were undergraduate students that completed a simulated work task, and the dependent variables were the turnaround time of their work products and the number of errors in their work. The results indicated that both types of intervention were effective by themselves and that the most effective intervention was a combination of the two.

RECOMMENDATIONS FOR FUTURE RESEARCH IN BSA

BSA has a long history, and the language of BSA is often used to explain interventions and analyses in OBM, as is evident from the descriptions of the studies above. However, there are opportunities for research that would include more explicit descriptions of comprehensive systems analyses and how they explicitly informed the selection of one intervention or system change over another. Respected scholars and practitioners in OBM have repeatedly encouraged more attention to systems variables in OBM research (e.g., Diener et al., 2009; Hyten, 2009). For example, Diener et al. stated "It is important to note that although several studies have used a BSA approach similar to the one described in this article [...] it has never been clear how the use of BSA impacted the choice of intervention and the results obtained" (p. 133).

At the organization level, there are opportunities for studies that detail how organizational leaders make changes directly informed by the BSA approach to meet marketplace challenges. For example, the results of the BSA analyses could be reported in terms of TPS and Relationship Maps. Results postintervention could be reported in terms of insights gained (similar to Krapfl, Cooke, Sullivan, & Cogar, 2009), new customers, customers retained, revenue, and customer satisfaction, to name a few.

At the process level, studies could be conducted that describe process analysis from "is" to "should" maps and explicitly explain why specified process changes were made, and others were not. The impact of the process changes could then be reported in terms of their impact on one or more measures of process performance as listed by Rummler and Brache (1995): cost, timeliness, regulatory compliance, quality, or capability (throughput, resource consumption, etc.).

There are numerous published studies that address individual level systems variables, as is evident from the previous studies. In fact, many of the studies published in the *Journal of Organizational Behavior Management* can be conceptualized as individual performer interventions from a systems perspective (Sasson & Austin, 2003). However, there are opportunities for more studies that validate analysis tools, such as the BEM or PDC, for example, by comparing interventions informed by these tools to nonindicated interventions (as was done in Ditzian, Wilder, King, & Tanz, in press) or research that compares the effectiveness of one form of analysis to another.

REFERENCES

Ackoff, R. L., & Emery, F. E. (1972). *On purposeful systems*. Chicago, IL: Aldine-Atherton, Inc.

Alavosius, M. P., Getting, J., Dagen, J., Newsome, W. D., & Hopkins, B. (2009). Use of a cooperative to interlock contingencies and balance the commonwealth. *Journal of Organizational Behavior Management, 29*, 193–211.

Austin, J. (2000). Performance analysis and performance diagnostics. In J. Austin, & J. E. Carr (Eds.), *Handbook of applied behavior analysis* (pp. 321–349). Reno, NV: Context Press.

Berglund, K. M., & Ludwig, T. D. (2009). Approaching error-free customer satisfaction through process change and feedback systems. *Journal of Organizational Behavior Management, 29*, 19–46.

Bertalanffy, L. V. (1950). An outline of general system theory. *British Journal for the Philosophy of Science, 1*(2), 134–165.

Bertalanffy, L. V. (1968). *General systems theory.* New York, NY: Geroge Braziller, Inc.

Binder, C. (1998). The Six Boxes™: A descendent of Gilbert's behavior engineering model. *Performance Improvement, 37*(6), 48–52.

Brethower, D. M. (1972). *Behavioral analysis in business and industry: A total performance system.* Kalamazoo, MI: Behaviordelia, Inc.

Brethower, D. M. (1982). The total performance system. In R. M. O'Brien, A. M. Dickinson, & M. P. Rosow (Eds.), *Industrial behavior modification: A management handbook* (pp. 350–369). New York: Pergamon Press.

Brethower, D. M. (2000). A systematic view of enterprise: Adding value to performance. *Journal of Organizational Behavior Management, 20*(3/4), 165–190.

Brethower, D. M. (2001). Managing a person as a system. In L. J. Hayes, J. Austin, R. Houmanfar, & M. C. Clayton (Eds.), *Organizational change* (pp. 89–105). Reno, NV: Context Press.

Brethower, D. M. (2002). *Behavioral systems analysis: Fundamental concepts and cutting edge applications.* Retrieved February 28, 2003, from, http://www.behavior.org/performancemgmt.

Clayton, M. C., Mawhinney, T. C., Luke, D. E., & Cook, H. G. (1997). Improving the management of overtime costs through decentralized controls: Managing an organizational metacontingency. *Journal of Organizational Behavior Management, 17*(2), 77–98.

Daniels, A. C., & Daniels, J. E. (2004). *Performance management: Changing behavior that drives organizational effectiveness.* Atlanta, GA: Performance Management Publications.

Dickinson, A. M. (2001). The historical roots of organizational behavior management in the private sector: The 1950s-1980s. *Journal of Organizational Behavior Management, 20*(3–4), 9–58.

Diener, L. H., McGee, H. M., & Miguel, C. F. (2009). An integrated approach for conducting a behavioral systems analysis. *Journal of Organizational Behavior Management, 29*(2), 108–135.

Ditzian, K., Wilder, D., King, A., & Tanz, J. (in press). An evaluation of the performance diagnostic checklist-human services to assess an employee performance problem in a center-based autism treatment facility. *Journal of Applied Behavior Analysis.*

Frederisken, L. W., Riley, A. W., & Myers, J. B. (1985). Matching technology and organizational structure: A case study in white collar productivity improvement. *Journal of Organizational Behavior Management, 6*(3), 59–80.

Gilbert, T. F. (1978). *Human competence: Engineering worthy performance.* New York, NY: McGraw-Hill.

Goomas, D. T. (2010). Replacing voice input with technology that provided immediate visual and audio feedback to reduce employee errors. *Journal of Organizational Behavior Management, 30*(1), 26–37.

Goomas, D. T. (2012a). The impact of wireless technology on loading trucks at an auto parts distribution center. *Journal of Organizational Behavior Management, 32*(3), 242–252.

Goomas, D. T. (2012b). Immediate feedback on accuracy and performance: The effects of wireless technology on food safety tracking at a distribution center. *Journal of Organizational Behavior Management, 32*(4), 320–328.

Hybza, M. M., Stokes, T. F., Hayman, M., & Schatzberg, T. (2013). Increasing medicaid revenue generation for services by school psychologists. *Journal of Organizational Behavior Management, 33*(1), 55–67.

Hyten, C. (2009). Strengthening the focus on business results: The need for systems approaches in organizational behavior management. *Journal of Organizational Behavior Management, 29*(2), 87–107.

Krapfl, J. E., Cooke, J., Sullivan, T., & Cogar, W. (2009). Iterative processes and reciprocal controlling relationships in a systemic intervention. *Journal of Organizational Behavior Management, 29*(2), 136–154.

Lafleur, T., & Hyten, C. (1995). Improving the quality of hotel banquet staff performance. *Journal of Organizational Behavior Management, 15*(1/2), 69–93.

Ludwig, L. H., & McGee, H. M. (2014). *Performance Blueprints, Inc. Toolkit.* Retrieved from, http://performanceblueprints.com/.

Malott, R. W. (1974). A behavioral systems approach to the design of human services. In D. Harshbarger, & R. F. Maley (Eds.), *Behavior analysis and systems analysis: An integrative approach to mental health programs.* Kalamazoo, MI: Behaviordelia.

Malott, M. E. (2003). *Paradox of organizational change.* Reno, NV: Context Press.

McGee, H. M. (2007). An introduction to behavioral systems analysis for OBMers and non-OBMers alike. *Organizational Behavior Management Newsletter, 21*(2).

Mihalic, M. T., & Ludwig, T. D. (2009). Behavioral system feedback measurement failure: Sweeping quality under the rug. *Journal of Organizational Behavior Management, 29*(2), 155–174.

Miller, M. V., Carlson, J., & Sigurdsson, S. O. (2014). Improving treatment integrity in a human service setting using lottery-based incentives. *Journal of Organizational Behavior Management, 34*, 29–38.

Pampino, R. N., Heering, P. W., Wilder, D. A., Barton, C. G., & Burson, L. M. (2003). The use of the performance diagnostic checklist to guide intervention selection in an independently owned coffee shop. *Journal of Organizational Behavior Management, 23*(2/3), 5–20.

Rohn, D., Austin, J., & Lutrey, S. M. (2002). Using feedback and performance accountability to decrease cash register shortages. *Journal of Organizational Behavior Management, 22*(1), 33–46.

Rummler, G. A. (1972). Human performance problems and their solutions. *Human Resource Management, 11*(4), 1–10.

Rummler, G. A. (2007). The past is prologue: An eyewitness account of HPT. *Performance Improvement, 46*, 5–9.

Rummler, G. A., & Brache, A. P. (1995). *Improving performance: How to manage the white space on the organization chart* (2nd). San Francisco: Jossey-Bass.

Rummler, G. A., Ramias, A. J., & Rummler, R. A. (2009). *White space revisited: creating value through process.* San Francisco: Jossey-Bass.

Sasson, J. R., Alvero, A. M., & Austin, J. (2006). Effects of process and human performance improvement strategies. *Journal of Organizational Behavior Management, 26*(3), 43–78.

Sasson, J. R., & Austin, J. (2003). Performer-Level Systems Analysis: How systemic are behavioral interventions? A ten-year review of the Journal of Organizational Behavior Management. *Journal of Organizational Behavior Management, 22*(4), 27–58.

Strouse, M. C., Carroll-Hernandez, T. A., Sherman, J. A., & Sheldon, J. B. (2004). Turning over turnover: The evaluation of a staff scheduling system in a community-based program for adults with developmental disabilities. *Journal of Organizational Behavior Management, 23*(2/3), 45–63.

Sulzer-Azaroff, B. (2001). Of eagles and worms: Changing behavior in a complex world. *Journal of Organizational Behavior Management, 20*(3–4), 139–163.

VanStelle, S. E., Vicars, S. M., Harr, V., Miguel, C. F., Koerber, J. L., Kazbour, R., et al. (2012). The publication history of the Journal of Organizational Behavior Management: An objective review and analysis: 1998–2009. *Journal of Organizational Behavior Management, 32*(2), 93–123.

INDEX

Note: Page numbers followed by *f* indicate figures and *t* indicate tables.

CPSIA information can be obtained at www.ICGtesting.com
Printed in the USA
BVOW10*0628170715

409216BV00001B/2/P